Silverlight 4 in Action

SILVERLIGHT 4, MVVM, AND WCF RIA SERVICES

PETE BROWN

Revised Edition of *Silverlight 2 in Action*
by Chad Campbell and John Stockton

MANNING
Greenwich
(74° w. long.)

For online information and ordering of this and other Manning books, please visit
www.manning.com. The publisher offers discounts on this book when ordered in quantity.
For more information, please contact

> Special Sales Department
> Manning Publications Co.
> 180 Broad Street
> Suite 1323
> Stamford, CT 06901
> Email: orders@manning.com

Manning Publications Co.	Development editor:	Jeff Bleiel
180 Broad Street, Suite 1323	Copyeditor:	Benjamin Berg
Stamford, CT 06901	Cover designer:	Marija Tudor
	Typesetter:	Gordan Salinovic

ISBN 9781935182375
Printed in the United States of America
1 2 3 4 5 6 7 8 9 10 – MAL – 15 14 13 12 11 10

Silverlight 4 in Action

brief contents

contents

preface

My background is in client application development. I started on the Commodore 64 in seventh grade in the 1980s, later moved to DOS with dBase, QuickBasic, and C++, and eventually Windows programming using C++, Borland Delphi 1.0, PowerBuilder, Visual Basic 3-6, and .NET.

Though I've written plenty of pure HTML/JavaScript web applications, I've always preferred client programming over strict web programming because I felt HTML/JavaScript programming treated the immensely powerful PC as a dumb terminal, squandering its CPU cycles for applications that were almost entirely network bound in performance. Only recently is this changing.

Back when web applications started to become more popular, customers loved the flexibility of the blank canvas of HTML versus the old battleship gray look, as well as the ease of deployment of web applications. On the client development side, we had some things that came close (WPF for appearance, for one) but nothing that combined the ease of deployment with the modern look.

For a while, it looked like the world was going to move to relatively dumb web applications, treating the local PC as just a keyboard and display—a disappointing move to say the least.

Back in 2006, long before I took my job as a Silverlight and WPF Community PM with Microsoft, I attend the first Microsoft MIX conference in Las Vegas. On March 21, day two of the conference, I attended some sessions about WPF/E, the product that would later be named Silverlight. Even then, Microsoft had a strong vision for Silverlight, a vision that included desktops, mobile devices, and set-top boxes. It was planned to be a lightweight version of WPF optimized for cross-platform scenarios, which would both take advantage of client-side processing power (when the .NET CLR was incorporated) as well as provide the ease of deployment of a traditional web application. This was exactly what I was looking for!

I was pretty jazzed about WPF/E at the time. I was also a little concerned about making the case for adoption. I took a wait-and-see approach. When Silverlight 1.0 CTPs and betas hit the street, I was less than impressed, because they were JavaScript only. I wasn't a big fan of JavaScript at the time and felt WPF/E wouldn't make any meaningful impact until they delivered on the promise of the CLR inside the browser. Nevertheless, early in 2007 I took on a project to create a carbon offset calculator in WPF/E, to be hosted in SharePoint on a public internet site.

Then, we had MIX07 and the name *Silverlight* was given to WPF/E. Along with it, Microsoft introduced Silverlight 1.1 alpha—a version that worked with managed code and included a cross-platform version of the .NET CLR. Yay! No JavaScript! (Hey, this was before jQuery proved to me that JavaScript can also be awesome.) Right at that point, I lobbied the project sponsors to let us work in Silverlight 1.1a. I also spoke with some contacts at Microsoft and received permission to go live with the Silverlight 1.1a application, happily foisting alpha code on unsuspecting users.

Despite, or perhaps because of, having to code many primitives from scratch (we needed buttons and drop-down lists, none of which existed in Silverlight 1.1a), I was completely hooked. It felt like the old days of DOS programming when you had to spelunk without much support and make up your own tricks for how to best accomplish things. It was the Wild West of programming. (And, by that, I mean the Wild West with giant Steampunk spiders added into the mix.)

I still had (and have) a place in my heart for Silverlight's big brother WPF, but it was easy to see that Silverlight was going to take the world by storm. WPF is still an incredibly powerful technology, but it tends to appeal more to niche users and ISVs as opposed to the broad group building web-based applications for a living.

The two of us on the carbon calculator development team released the first Silverlight managed code application ever to go live. It included video, Windows Live Maps integration, web services integration with SharePoint, carbon offset calculations of course, and a completely data-driven, configurable UI with SharePoint as the back-end, supporting everything.

At the time, there was no real ecosystem around Silverlight, and the idea of using real designers on client applications in the Microsoft stack hadn't yet caught on. Despite the primitive UI we designed, I'm still impressed with what we put together. I was thrilled to be able to use .NET skills in something that was truly unique in the .NET space.

Later that year, Silverlight 1.1a would be updated to a stronger subset of WPF and rebranded as Silverlight 2, laying the groundwork required for Silverlight 4, a release that continues to impress and engage me every day I use it.

PETE BROWN

acknowledgments

A book like this is a team effort from start to finish. Though my name may be on the cover, there's no way I could've completed this without the support and hard work of many others. I'd like to thank:

- Chad Campbell and John Stockton for creating such an excellent first edition. Without their hard work covering Silverlight 2, I would never have thought to create a Silverlight 4 edition.

- Marshal Agnew, Brendan Clark, and Jordan Parker on the Silverlight product team for their help in digging into the darkest recesses of the rendering and layout system. If not for these folks, I wouldn't have been able to provide the level of detail chapter 6 includes.

- David Ferguson and Seema Ramchandani, both on the Silverlight product team, for help on performance questions around transformations.

- Tim Heuer on the Silverlight product team for help on the Silverlight installation experience covered in chapter 25.

- Jeff Handley on the WCF RIA Services product team for reviewing the RIA Services chapter on a really tight schedule.

- Ashish Shetty on the Silverlight product team for encouraging my Silverlight blogging very early on, including much of the app model and startup process content that ended up in this book.

- Tom McKearney, Tad Van Fleet, Al Pascual, and Ben Hayat for their excellent tech reviews. They caught a ton of mistakes, including differences between Silverlight 2, 3, and 4, and changes from the early builds through to the release of Silverlight 4.

- René Schulte for keeping my imaging and pixel shader sections honest and up to date. René is the go-to guy for working with bitmaps and shaders.
- Mike Street on the forums for his helpful and thorough review of many of the chapters on the forums. Mike was a great unofficial tech reviewer for this book.

In addition, there were numerous editors, proofreaders, and reviewers at Manning Publications who deserve thanks for their hard work. I dropped on them a book twice as large as they were expecting with a third of the production time they normally take. People like Benjamin Berg, Mary Piergies, Nermina Miller, Gordan Salinovic, and others worked tirelessly to get this book published in time. I thank them and the rest of the folks at Manning for not freaking out when the book missed two deadlines, came in three months late, and at twice the expected length.

Unique in this thanks is my editor, Jeff Bleiel. This was the first book I've written, so I wasn't sure what to expect. A good editor can make the difference between a horrible authoring experience and a good one. Jeff definitely made that difference, respected our different areas of expertise, and kept the book on track. He was my interface with Manning and my mentor as an author. Jeff made a positive contribution to this book and to my writing in general.

In addition to the individuals who helped me with the book itself, there are those who have made it possible through their presence or actions.

Most of all, I'd like to thank my wife Melissa for being a single mom for most of 2010 and my children Ben and Abby for understanding when mom told them "Papa's writing and can't play right now." Writing a book this size, for a product that revs every 10 to 12 months, is an undertaking that involves your whole family.

I'd like to thank my manager at Microsoft, Scott Hanselman, for making sure I had time to finish the book. This book took an incredible amount of time to write and, if not for Scott offering me some flexibility, it simply wouldn't have been completed.

Of course, I thank the Silverlight and WPF community, my Twitter followers, the Silverlight and WPF insiders, the MVPs, and all the people who've read and commented on my blog posts since Silverlight was first released. The community support for and excitement around these technologies kept me motivated to create the best book possible.

My gratitude also to my mum for encouraging me in my computer work and for helping me get that first job writing a database application from scratch in C++. I wouldn't be where I am today without her.

I'd like to thank my dad, who passed away during the writing of this book. He never quite understood what I was doing with the Commodore in my room, typing in all that hex code from the back of a magazine, but he supported me from the start and encouraged me to pursue a career doing what I love.

Finally, I'd like to thank you, my readers.

about this book

The overall goal of this book is to inform and educate you about the exciting and powerful Silverlight 4 platform. Think of it as a guided tour through the Silverlight 4 plug-in, runtime libraries, and SDK. After you've read this book, you should be able to confidently design, develop, and deliver your first rich interactive applications using Silverlight. To facilitate the learning process, I've structured the book to get you developing as soon as possible, while providing quality, in-depth content.

Within each chapter, I've included a collection of devices to help you build a firm understanding of Silverlight. The following list explains how each agent helps along the journey:

- *Figures*—Visual depictions that summarize data and help with the connection of complex concepts.
- *Listings*—Small, concise pieces of code primarily used for showing syntactical formats. These individual segments generally can't be run on their own.
- *Tables*—Easy-to-read summaries.

In addition to these learning devices, my personal site http://10rem.net contains links to the code samples used in this book. Additionally, http://silverlightinaction. com, the web site for the first edition, includes assets, images, and services used in this book.

Audience

This book is intended for developers who want to create nontrivial applications using Microsoft Silverlight 4. Though Silverlight provides numerous avenues for interactions with designers, this book primarily targets people who live and breathe inside Visual Studio. Team members in the integration role (those who take designs and implement in Silverlight) will also find the information valuable and useful.

This book assumes you have at least a passing familiarity with common web standards such as HTML, CSS, XML, and JavaScript. In addition, this book assumes you have a background using the .NET framework and Microsoft Visual Studio. Although we'll be using C# as the primary development language, we won't be reviewing the C# language or explaining basic programming constructs such as classes, methods, and variables.

Experience with previous versions of Silverlight isn't required for this book.

The bits: what you need

This book provides ample opportunity for hands-on learning. But, it also provides a great deal of flexibility by allowing you to learn the material without using the hands-on content or optional tools. If you want to get the greatest value out of this book and use the hands-on opportunities, the following tools are recommended:

- Visual Studio 2010 Pro or higher, or Visual Studio Web Developer 2010 (free)
- Silverlight 4 tools for Visual Studio 2010, including the Silverlight 4 SDK and WCF RIA Services 1.0
- The Silverlight toolkit
- Microsoft Expression Blend 4 (optional)
- Microsoft Expression Blend 4 SDK for Silverlight 4 (installed with Blend 4) for creating and using behaviors

You'll find links to all of these tools at http://silverlight.net/GetStarted.

Roadmap

This book is designed to give you a guided tour of Silverlight 4. This tour will focus on three main areas: introducing Silverlight, structuring your application, and completing the experience.

Part 1: Introducing Silverlight

Chapter 1 introduces Silverlight. The introduction shows you the advantages of Silverlight and explains its place in the desktop and web applications arenas. The chapter wraps up with a walkthrough of building your first Silverlight application.

Chapter 2 covers one of the most fundamental parts of Silverlight: XAML. Though most of the book covers XAML in one form or another, this chapter takes you from the fundamentals all the way through the visual and logical trees, the dependency property system, and XAML extensions.

Chapter 3 explains how the Silverlight plug-in and application startup process work. You'll learn about the application object, the .xap file, and caching assemblies. We'll also look at how to instantiate the plug-in and use it on a web page.

Chapter 4 builds on the browser integration introduced in chapter 3 and shows how to manipulate the HTML DOM from Silverlight, work with the browser window, and bridge the scripting and managed code worlds. This chapter also introduces the Silverlight WebBrowser control, used to display web content within Silverlight itself when running out of the browser.

Chapter 5 takes us out of the Web and onto the desktop. Silverlight supports creating both sandboxed and elevated trust desktop applications. This chapter covers out-of-browser applications, local file access, COM automation, custom window chrome, working full screen, and using isolated storage.

Chapter 6 covers the layout and rendering system and both 2D and 3D transformations. If you truly want to understand what's happening when you put pixels on the screen, knowledge of the layout and rendering system is a must. This is information that I personally found deeply interesting; I hope you do as well. This chapter also covers 2D transformations, such as skew and translate, as well as 3D plane and matrix projection.

Chapter 7 builds on the layout information from chapter 6 to show how to use the various types of layout panels in Silverlight including the Grid, StackPanel, and Canvas.

Chapter 8 brings us the human connection. Though everything so far has been about presenting, this is about gathering. We'll learn how to use the keyboard, mouse, ink, and touch interfaces to perform actions in our applications.

Chapter 9 covers text input and output. I start off with a discussion of the text stack, including information on antialiasing strategies and the common text properties of controls and the TextBlock element. From there, I look at text input controls such as the TextBox and RichTextBox, with a side journey into IME and international text.

Chapter 10 introduces several of the nontext controls including the Button, RadioButton, CheckBox, ComboBox, ListBox, and more. This chapter also covers the base control types common to the stock and custom controls, such as ContentControl and ItemsControl.

Part 2: Structuring your application

Chapter 11 covers binding. In Silverlight, if you find yourself assigning values directly to controls in the code-behind, as the meme goes, "you're doing it wrong." Binding is one of the most powerful features of Silverlight and is something we'll build upon in the chapters that follow.

Chapter 12 builds on what we learned in chapter 11 to make use of the DataGrid and DataForm controls. In this chapter, I also cover the use of data annotations to control display attributes for your entities.

Chapter 13 also builds on chapter 11 and 12 to provide validation capabilities to our applications. I cover exception-based validation, synchronous and asynchronous validation using interfaces, validation using attributes, and creating your own custom validators.

Chapter 14 helps our Silverlight applications break out of the client and communicate with servers on the Internet and intranet. In this chapter, we learn how to use

SOAP and REST web services, the underlying web stack, sockets, and even local connections between Silverlight applications.

Chapter 15 is a deep dive into using the Navigation Framework, windows, and dialogs in your application. We'll look at how to structure your application as a series of pages, handle URL addressing and mapping, and parameter passing. We'll also learn about the built-in dialogs and the ChildWindow class.

Chapter 16 covers the MVVM pattern and unit testing. Without picking any one specific MVVM (or ViewModel) framework, I show you the concepts behind the View-Model pattern and how to implement them in your own application. This chapter wraps up with information on testing Silverlight applications using the Silverlight Unit Testing Framework.

Chapter 17 covers one of the most exciting developments for business and other data-oriented applications: WCF RIA Services. We'll walk through creating a RIA Services application using the Business Application template and look at everything from query and update operations to business rules and validation to security.

Part 3: Completing the experience

Chapter 18 dives into vector graphics and brushes—key concepts for creating applications that move beyond the usual controls. This chapter also goes into depth on effects and pixel shaders, wrapping up with information on how to build your own custom shader in HLSL and C#.

Chapter 19 covers working with the printer from Silverlight. Silverlight 4 introduced the ability to print short documents or handle print-screen functionality. We go over the API and wrap up this chapter with an implementation of a custom reporting solution for short reports.

Chapter 20 is all about media: video and audio. In this chapter, I go over the various ways to present video and audio in your application, including IIS Smooth Streaming and custom managed code codecs using MediaStreamSource. I also dive into the webcam and microphone API covering basic use as well as creating your own Video-Sink to manipulate the returned data.

Chapter 21 is to still images as chapter 20 is to video and audio. In this chapter, we look at how to use bitmap images in your application, including approaches for generating images at runtime.

Chapter 22 covers animation and behaviors. You'll learn how to use storyboards to liven up your interface. After that, we take a look at using and creating behaviors to package up your own reusable functionality, often containing animations.

Chapter 23 covers styles, templates, and resources. We look at how to package up style information for controls and how to create completely new templates using the lookless control model.

Chapter 24 teaches us how to create layout panels and custom controls. Though you can do almost anything in Silverlight with a new control template, there are times when creating your own control or panel is the way to go.

Chapter 25 wraps up the book with information on creating the best possible install experience for the plug-in, as well as the best possible loading experience for your own applications.

Code conventions and downloads

All the code used in this book is presented in a monospace font like this. This code can be in one of a variety of languages; the language used is indicated at the beginning of the code block. For longer lines of code, a wrapping character may be used to be technically correct while forming to the limitations of a printed page. Annotations accompany many of the code listings and numbered cueballs are used when longer explanations are needed.

The source code for all of the examples in the book is available for download from the publisher's website at www.manning.com/Silverlight4inAction and from the author's website at http://10rem.net.

Author online

The purchase of *Silverlight 4 in Action* includes free access to a private forum run by Manning Publications where you can make comments about the book, ask technical questions, and receive help from the author and other users. You can access and subscribe to the forum at www.manning.com/Silverlight4inAction. This page provides information on how to get on the forum once you're registered, what kind of help is available, and the rules of conduct in the forum.

Manning's commitment to our readers is to provide a venue where a meaningful dialogue between individual readers and between readers and the author can take place. It isn't a commitment to any specific amount of participation on the part of the author, whose contributions to the book's forum remains voluntary (and unpaid). We suggest you try asking the author some challenging questions, lest his interest stray!

The Author Online forum and the archives of previous discussions will be accessible from the publisher's web site as long as the book is in print.

In addition to the Author Online forum available on Manning's website, you may also contact us regarding this book, or anything else, through one of the following avenues:

- *Pete's site and blog* http://10rem.net
- *Pete's Twitter account* http://twitter.com/pete_brown

About the author

Pete Brown is a Community Program Manager with Microsoft on the developer community team led by Scott Hanselman, as well as a former Microsoft Silverlight MVP, INETA speaker, and RIA Architect for Applied Information Sciences, where he worked for more than 13 years. Pete's focus at Microsoft is the community around client application development (WPF, Silverlight, Windows Phone, Surface, Windows Forms, C++, Native Windows API, and more).

From his first sprite graphics and custom character sets on the Commodore 64 to 3D modeling and design through to Silverlight, Surface, XNA, and WPF, Pete has always had a deep interest in programming, design, and user experience. His involvement in Silverlight goes back to the Silverlight 1.1 alpha application that he co-wrote and put into production in July 2007. Pete has been programming for fun since 1984 and professionally since 1992.

In his spare time, Pete enjoys programming, blogging, designing and building his own woodworking projects, and raising his two children with his wife in the suburbs of Maryland.

About the title

By combining introductions, overviews, and how-to examples, the *In Action* books are designed to help learning and remembering. According to research in cognitive science, the things people remember are things they discover during self-motivated exploration.

Although no one at Manning is a cognitive scientist, we are convinced that for learning to become permanent it must pass through stages of exploration, play, and, interestingly, retelling of what is being learned. People understand and remember new things, which is to say they master them, only after actively exploring them. Humans learn *in action*. An essential part of an *In Action* book is that it's example driven. It encourages the reader to try things out, to play with new code, and explore new ideas.

There is another, more mundane, reason for the title of this book: our readers are busy. They use books to do a job or solve a problem. They need books that allow them to jump in and jump out easily and learn just what they want just when they want it. They need books that aid them *in action*. The books in this series are designed for such readers.

about the cover illustration

The figure on the cover of *Silverlight 4 in Action* is a "Janissary in Dress of Ceremony." Janissaries were the personal troops and bodyguards of the Ottoman sultan. The illustration is taken from a collection of costumes of the Ottoman Empire published on January 1, 1802, by William Miller of Old Bond Street, London. The title page is missing from the collection and we have been unable to track it down to date. The book's table of contents identifies the figures in both English and French, and each illustration bears the names of two artists who worked on it, both of whom would no doubt be surprised to find their art gracing the front cover of a computer programming book...two hundred years later.

The collection was purchased by a Manning editor at an antiquarian flea market in the "Garage" on West 26th Street in Manhattan. The seller was an American based in Ankara, Turkey, and the transaction took place just as he was packing up his stand for the day. The Manning editor did not have on his person the substantial amount of cash that was required for the purchase and a credit card and check were both politely turned down. With the seller flying back to Ankara that evening the situation was getting hopeless. What was the solution? It turned out to be nothing more than an old-fashioned verbal agreement sealed with a handshake. The seller simply proposed that the money be transferred to him by wire and the editor walked out with the bank information on a piece of paper and the portfolio of images under his arm. Needless to say, we transferred the funds the next day, and we remain grateful and impressed by this unknown person's trust in one of us. It recalls something that might have happened a long time ago.

The pictures from the Ottoman collection, like the other illustrations that appear on our covers, bring to life the richness and variety of dress customs of two centuries ago. They recall the sense of isolation and distance of that period—and of every other historic period except our own hyperkinetic present. Dress codes have changed since then and the diversity by region, so rich at the time, has faded away. It is now often hard to tell the inhabitant of one continent from another. Perhaps, trying to view it optimistically, we have traded a cultural and visual diversity for a more varied personal life. Or a more varied and interesting intellectual and technical life.

We at Manning celebrate the inventiveness, the initiative, and, yes, the fun of the computer business with book covers based on the rich diversity of regional life of two centuries ago, brought back to life by the pictures from this collection.

Part 1

Introducing Silverlight

The first part of this book starts by building your first Silverlight application and then dives into what makes Silverlight tick. We'll cover the markup language used for creating the interface, drill into the application model, and look at integrating with both the browser and the desktop. You'll then learn about the layout system and panels—two concepts critical for an effective UI design. The part wraps up with mouse, touch, and keyboard input; display and input of text; and a discussion of the common types of controls you'll use in your projects.

Introducing Silverlight

This chapter covers

- Silverlight, the web, and WPF
- The best applications for Silverlight
- Getting started with Silverlight
- Changes in Silverlight since the first edition of this book
- Building your first Silverlight "Hello World!" application

First of all, let me thank you for starting at chapter 1. I'm one of those people who tend to read magazines backwards and skim technology books, so I appreciate it when someone reads a book's chapters in order. Then again, maybe you read this book backwards as well. In that case, you'll find the "Hello World!" walkthrough in this chapter to be a refreshingly simple take on building Silverlight applications unencumbered with patterns such as Model View ViewModel (MVVM), words such as `DependencyProperty`, and technologies such as Windows Communication Foundation (WCF) Rich Internet Application (RIA) Services. For the rest of you, don't worry—we'll cover each of those throughout the rest of the book, steadily building our Silverlight skills as we go.

Since you've picked up a Silverlight book, you would probably like to know what Silverlight is. Luckily, I'm horrible at marketing, so I'll put it simply: Silverlight is a cross-platform .NET runtime, cross-browser plug-in, and a set of Windows-based developer tools for building RIAs. At its heart, Silverlight is an implementation of the concepts and standards from Windows Presentation Foundation (WPF) such as binding, the property system, and Extensible Application Markup Language (XAML) in a cross-platform version of the .NET Common Language Runtime (CLR) and libraries.

There. I think that paragraph managed to get all of the acronyms defined for the rest of the book. Then again, this is a Microsoft technology, so expect more acronyms before we're through.

Silverlight runs on Windows and Mac as well as on Linux through the Moonlight project. It runs on Windows Phone 7 and Nokia Symbian S60 phones. We've seen demos of it running on set-top boxes connected to televisions and serving up ads and content on the Xbox. Put simply, short of ASP.NET, Silverlight is the broadest reaching technology ever produced by Microsoft.

Silverlight applications work on the web as well as on the client. You can create virtually any type of application in Silverlight, from web content, to widgets, to media players to full-blown client applications.

In this section, we'll introduce Silverlight, looking at how it fits into the developer stack both on the web and on the desktop. We'll then look at some of the different types of applications Silverlight is well suited for. Then, we'll check out the features and capabilities that have been added since the first edition of this book, before we wrap up with a walkthrough of creating your own first Silverlight application.

Silverlight got its start as a web page plug-in, so that's where we'll start as well.

1.1   *Silverlight and the web*

Silverlight sits in that interesting place between desktop applications and browser applications. In many ways, it's like a little traditional desktop application embedded in HTML. Of course, the same can be said of many JavaScript Ajax applications, themselves modeled on the code-on-the-client desktop application paradigm.

Great frameworks such as jQuery and the impending, somewhat nebulously defined HTML 5 further muddy the waters. Where's Silverlight's place on the web? Why should you use Silverlight instead of these other technologies?

I'll give you a few reasons:

- Silverlight is here, now.
- Silverlight works across platforms and browsers, now.
- Silverlight has top-tier media support, including digital rights management (DRM), far more advanced than the proposed HTML 5 standards.
- Silverlight is a no-brainer if you're already a .NET developer looking to expand to other platforms.

Don't get me wrong; I think HTML 5, when fully spec'd and adopted, will be a great thing for the web—both exciting and capable. Having said that, Silverlight has more advanced authoring tools, faster execution, and more capabilities than HTML 5 is expected to have. Rather than carrying out a zero-sum game, I believe HTML 5 will raise the floor, driving the quality and experience up across the spectra of platforms and developer tools.

I don't personally think that the code-on-the-client application development approach is going to disappear. Though doom has been forecast for many major development approaches over the years, few have actually declined when another rose in popularity. Silverlight and HTML 5 will just provide more options for how to implement the solution you need in the most optimal way, using the tools you're comfortable with and the skills you already have.

Also remember that HTML/JavaScript and Silverlight aren't mutually exclusive. Silverlight applications can happily coexist on a page with Ajax applications, each complementing the other with features that play to their strengths.

Silverlight is far more than a web technology. Though it can live on a web page, it's also common to have out-of-browser Silverlight applications, either connected to services or simply using resources on the client. In those instances, you may wonder when to use WPF and when to use Silverlight.

1.2 *Silverlight and WPF*

Silverlight and WPF were born of the same ideas. WPF came first and broke the ground required to make XAML a UI-friendly markup language. WPF also introduced us to dependency properties and binding, storyboard-based animation, and subpixel-rendered vector UI.

But WPF is large and complex. It's also deeply rooted in Windows, with no good way to substitute alternate stacks for those it relies on. WPF also relies on the rather outdated and web-unfriendly code access security model for application security. So, when Microsoft decided to enter the RIA space with a CLR based vector UI technology, they took the concepts and some of the code from WPF and reimplemented it in a smaller, tighter, and more platform-independent way.

Silverlight primarily is a subset of WPF with some additions. Some of the additions, such as the Visual State Manager, have been migrated back from Silverlight into WPF. Others, such as Deep Zoom, Media Stream Source, and the webcam and microphone APIs, are currently Silverlight-only features. Ignoring alternative solutions to the same problems, figure 1.1 shows this relationship using our friend, the Venn diagram.

I recommend that developers new to both technologies learn Silverlight before learning WPF. In general, you'll find it easier to learn Silverlight first and then scale up to WPF, should your needs dictate. Silverlight is smaller, typically having a single

Figure 1.1 Silverlight primarily is a subset of WPF with a few extras added. Ignoring alternative solutions to the same problems, the places where WPF differs most are in the integration with the Windows OS and the access to the full .NET framework.

approach to solving a given problem, whereas WPF may have several solutions for the same task. Though Silverlight doesn't have everything WPF has, Silverlight is an excellent, capable development platform and can cover many types of applications we would've previously written in Windows Forms, WPF, or even HTML.

1.3   Types of Silverlight applications

You can build just about anything you'd like using Silverlight. Of course, Silverlight is better suited for some types of applications over others. For example, though possible, you wouldn't necessarily want to build an entire website using Silverlight; there are better tools for the job.

Silverlight excels at media. When Silverlight 1.0 was first introduced, one of the few capabilities it had was an excellent media stack. Silverlight through version 4 has built upon that to include new media capabilities such as smooth streaming, pluggable codecs using the Media Stream Source API, and even the DRM technologies required for the large content producers to adopt Silverlight.

Silverlight's early focus on media was both helpful and hurtful. Video on the web is a great way to gain product adoption, especially when you have a capable high-def video technology. Early on, many potential Silverlight developers failed to see past the media roots and missed the rich business capabilities Silverlight provides.

Starting with versions 3 and 4, Silverlight gained serious business capabilities. From simple things such as sync and async validation, to patterns such as MVVM and Prism, and entire middle-tier frameworks such as WCF RIA Services, Silverlight showed itself to be a mature platform, able to absorb the best practices from other areas and build upon them.

Though business and media applications certainly are great staples, another fun application type is games. Silverlight has good support for casual games, including the ability to generate bitmaps on the fly, create sound from bits, loop audio in the background, and more. The community has successfully ported over physics and gaming engines to Silverlight, making it even easier to create complex casual games. Future versions of Silverlight are expected to be even more gaming friendly; we've just seen the tip of the iceberg so far.

There are many other types of Silverlight applications ranging from ads, to photo viewers, to social media clients, to analogs for virtually every type of major desktop and web application. Some of those, such as desktop applications, weren't possible with Silverlight 2, the version used in the first edition of this book. Let's take a high-level view of what has changed in that time.

1.4   What's new since the first edition

The first edition of this book was written for Silverlight 2. Silverlight 3 and 4 have added an amazing number of new capabilities to the platform in all areas, from core capabilities, to device access, to the introduction of both trusted and sandboxed out-of-browser client applications. The advancements in Silverlight can be loosely grouped into four main areas: business and client applications, media and graphics, user interaction, and text.

1.4.1 *Features for business and client applications*

When the first edition of this book was released, Silverlight 2 was just starting to gain adoption. It was a brand new technology from Microsoft (the managed code version was, anyway), one with strong competition. Though Silverlight 2 could have been used to build rich business applications, it didn't have the chops to be a strong contender in that space yet. Many of the features in this section are useful in applications of all sorts; I hate to classify them under the heading of "business," but that's the largest consumer of these features.

Validation, covered in chapter 13, was one of the biggest new features for business applications. Silverlight didn't add just validation but included support for validation through attributes, validation through exceptions, and even asynchronous validation, all of which work with the Silverlight controls. Silverlight even made it possible to completely customize the style of the validation information provided to the end-user.

One technology that builds heavily on the validation stack is WCF RIA Services (chapter 17). A good bit of the validation functionality rolled into the Silverlight runtime actually came from that project. WCF RIA Services provides a way to share validation and logic between the client and server as well as a framework for validation, data access, and security, shareable between Silverlight and other clients.

WCF RIA Services builds upon the WCF stack, but it's not the only enhancement there. The Silverlight networking stack, described in chapter 14, was greatly enhanced to support in-browser and out-of-browser operation, as well as SOAP 1.2 and a number of new protocol enhancements. These changes make it easier to use Silverlight behind a firewall where the services often have different requirements than those on the Internet.

Despite the promises of a paperless office, printing (covered in chapter 19) is still a staple of business applications everywhere. Printing in Silverlight is optimized for relatively short reports or documents, as well as for the equivalent of print-screen operations. It's super simple to use—as easy as working with XAML on the pages.

Finally, we come to a biggie: out-of-browser sandboxed and trusted applications. Covered in section 5.1, out-of-browser mode was one of the most significant enhancements made to how Silverlight operates. Silverlight 3 introduced the basic out-of-browser mode with a sandbox roughly equivalent to the one in browser. Silverlight 4 opened up whole new classes of applications by adding the trusted application mode with its reduction in prompts, increased file access, and (on Windows) access to IDispatch COM Automation servers. All of these features add up to a platform that's more than capable of being the client for our complex business applications.

One of the next major areas of enhancement for Silverlight is media.

1.4.2 *Media and graphics enhancements*

Silverlight was first and best known for its media capabilities. The Silverlight media team didn't rest on that, instead pumping out enormous advances in media in both Silverlight 3 and 4.

Silverlight 2 included a Media Stream Source API for pushing media through the pipeline. But that API required that the bits be preencoded into one of the formats natively understood at the time. Though useful, this could lead to double-encoding and made transcoding even more difficult.

Silverlight 3 added support for pushing raw video and audio out of custom Media Stream Source implementations, as covered in section 20.6. As a result, you can write a managed codec for any type of media or even do something crazy like I did and use it to generate audio and video in real time for an emulator. Another option for generating video or at least images in real-time is the new bitmap API covered in section 21.2.

Speaking of codecs, one of the new codecs added was H.264 for video. H.264 has emerged as one of the most popular codecs for TV and video for devices. It was a logical choice for an additional native Silverlight format because now content producers can use even more of their content without reencoding. To appeal to the same audience, Silverlight 3 and 4 also continued to improve DRM capabilities, including the addition of offline DRM.

A new and exciting feature for Silverlight 4 is built-in support for video and audio capture devices or, specifically, webcams and microphones. Though not yet quite at the level that would allow you to create a real-time video chat application, the support does open up a number of new possibilities for application development. Webcam and microphone support are both covered in section 20.7.

Under the covers, Silverlight now has support for all formats of portable network graphics (PNG), something that was only partially supported in previous versions. Silverlight 4 also has support for pixel shaders and a set of built-in performance-tuned effects such as drop-shadow and blur, covered in section 18.4.

With all of these advancements plus a number of performance optimizations and even additions such as the Silverlight Media Framework, Silverlight continues its leadership in the media space, offering everything you need to build rich media-centric applications.

Sometimes, what you want is more than just a media experience; you want an application that can be truly interactive. Silverlight has your back there, too.

1.4.3   *User interaction*

Since Silverlight 2, user interaction has received a number of important enhancements. Two of the most requested features, mouse scroll wheel and right-click mouse support (both covered in section 8.2), are now baked into the Silverlight core runtime.

One of the newer and hotter user interaction mechanisms is multi-touch, covered in section 8.3. The ability to support multipoint interaction with the user interface, especially in kiosk and handheld/tablet scenarios, is quickly becoming a requirement for many applications. Silverlight now includes core runtime support for multipoint touch interaction with Silverlight application.

Another user interaction piece missing from Silverlight 2 was the easy ability to show dialogs and pop-up windows (simulated) within your applications. Silverlight now not only has those (covered in chapter 15) but also notification toast, covered in chapter 5.

Finally, all the interaction in the world has no value if your user can't read the text on the screen. Happily, Silverlight includes plenty of improvements in text as well.

1.4.4 Text

By far, the biggest improvement to text since Silverlight 2 is proper ClearType font rendering. Silverlight 2 performed only grayscale rendering, giving text a fuzzy appearance unless you carefully picked your color schemes.

While ClearType may be important for font rendering in general, right-to-left or bidirectional (BiDi) text is something that's absolutely essential for the correct rendering of many non-European languages. Silverlight supports not only BiDi text but also input method editors (IMEs) for complex composite characters for many languages, especially eastern languages.

Finally, one great improvement to text rendering and entry is the inclusion of the new rich text box control. This control allows you to display or edit text that includes multiple fonts and styles. The control can even embed other elements that can be interactive when the control is in read-only mode.

ClearType, BiDi and IME text, and the rich text box are all covered in chapter 9, along with insight into the text rendering stack in general and how to apply these new features to text throughout Silverlight.

Those are the major items. Of course, there are many more improvements sprinkled throughout. In addition to capturing the major items in this book, I've also added information based on the experience gained from working with Silverlight since its inception as well as recent knowledge gained from working closely with the Silverlight product team. In important areas, such as layout and rendering, I've gone deeper than needed by the average developer to provide some insight into the inner workings of Silverlight.

That was a lot to cover. I hope you enjoy reading it as much as I enjoyed writing it. Before we start covering individual feature areas, we'll need to get our development environment set up and build a small "Hello World!" application.

1.5 Getting started with Silverlight development

If you're a .NET developer, you're already well on your way to becoming a Silverlight developer. Silverlight builds on the .NET framework and uses the same tools as other .NET framework applications. You'll use Visual Studio and, optionally, Expression Blend to build your applications. You'll be able to turn to CodePlex and other open-source sites for sample code to use. And, of course, you'll have a huge community of peers to lean on when trying to figure out those hard problems.

Before you can do any of that, though, you need to make sure your development environment is set up.

1.5.1 Setting up your development environment

Silverlight 4 requires Visual Studio 2010 to work with projects and build the solutions. The multitargeting support of Visual Studio 2010 means that your applications can target either Silverlight 3 or Silverlight 4, once you have the Silverlight 4 tools installed.

If you don't already have a version of Visual Studio 2010, you can get the free Visual Web Developer 2010 Express from Microsoft at www.microsoft.com/express/Web/. The free web developer tools will enable you to create Silverlight 4 applications as well as ASP.NET applications. If you want additional features and tools as well as the ability to create more than just web applications, upgrade to Visual Studio 2010 Pro or higher.

Once you have installed Visual Studio 2010, visit http://silverlight.net/getstarted/ and use the Web Platform Installer to install the Silverlight 4 tools and SDK as well as any optional components.

The Silverlight tools for Visual Studio 2010 and the SDK contain everything you need to develop Silverlight 4 applications, including WCF RIA Services 1.0.

Optionally, you may want to install Microsoft Expression Blend 4. The link for that is also available on the Get Started page on Silverlight.net. Expression Blend 4 provides a designer-friendly set of tooling that makes creating complex animations, behaviors, and layouts a snap.

Microsoft and the community have created a number of helpful sites that will make your learning process go smoothly.

1.5.2   *Helpful sites*

The official Microsoft Silverlight developer site is http://silverlight.net. There you'll find videos, sample applications, tutorials, add-ons and the community forums, all designed to help you be the best and most efficient Silverlight developer you can be.

In addition to Silverlight.net, http://channel9.msdn.com includes interviews with community and product team members, as well as tutorials. Silverlight.TV, located on Channel 9 at http://channel9.msdn.com/shows/SilverlightTV/, is a great resource for timely insight into the Silverlight products and releases.

The MSDN documentation for Silverlight 4 may be found at http://bit.ly/SL4MSDN.

Also, as a completely shameless plug, you may want to subscribe to my own blog at http://10rem.net. You can also follow me on twitter; my id is @pete_brown.

Finally, one other place you'll want to visit is Dave Campbell's Silverlight Cream: http://bit.ly/SilverlightCream. Dave has done a spectacular job, daily compiling the best Silverlight posts on the web. From Dave's link blog, you'll get an idea of what other community member blogs to subscribe to.

At this point, your developer machine is set up, you've subscribed to a few blogs, created an account at Silverlight.net, and maybe even poked around a little on the sites. Before we get into the features in detail in the rest of the book, I thought it would be good to see just how easy it is to build your first Silverlight "Hello World!" application.

1.6   *Building your first Silverlight web application*

Expectations have come a long way since the days of C, where just getting "Hello World!" to compile and output to the screen was considered a great accomplishment. Rather than rehash that tired example, I think it would be neat if our "Hello World!" example actually did something interesting-like hit a public service on the web. Twitter is the ubiquitous example, and far be it for me to buck a trend.

Using Twitter—Twitter search in this example—also allows us to explore a number of the features of Silverlight, including layout, network access, LINQ to XML, and more.

1.6.1 Project setup

Open Visual Studio 2010. Choose File > New Project and create a new Silverlight Application project. The name isn't important but I chose *FirstSilverlightApplication* for mine. Figure 1.2 shows the dialog with the correct project type selected and named.

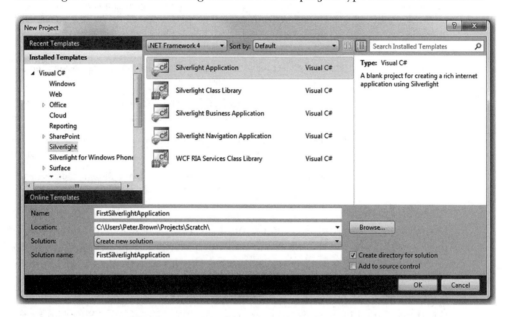

Figure 1.2 Visual Studio 2010 New Project dialog with the correct project type selected and named

Once you click OK, you'll be presented with another dialog. This dialog provides options specific to the Silverlight project. Figure 1.3 shows the dialog.

Figure 1.3 The New Silverlight Application options dialog

Typically, you'll leave the options at their default values and just click through this dialog. But it's important to understand what's available to you. Table 1.1 describes each of the options presented in this dialog.

Table 1.1   The New Silverlight Application dialog options

Option	Description
Host in a new website	Silverlight applications, even out-of-browser apps, are served from a website. You can also serve them from a static HTML page on the file system but this is a limiting option. You'll typically want to leave this checked, unless you have an existing website you want to use when building your application.
New Web Project Name	Provide a project name for the website. The default is usually sufficient.
New Web Project Type	If you're an ASP.NET programmer and have a preference as to the ASP.NET project type, set it here. Otherwise, leave at the default.
Silverlight Version	This allows you to select either Silverlight 3 or Silverlight 4. For this book, every example will assume Silverlight 4.
Enable WCF RIA Services	Check this if you want to link the web project to the Silverlight project as a WCF RIA Services endpoint. This enables additional compile-time tooling.

Once the new solution is created, you'll see two projects. The first one is the Silverlight application; the second is the website. The website project contains a folder ClientBin, which will contain the compiled output (.xap file) from your Silverlight application. It also contains two test pages that may be used to test your Silverlight application. By default, the .aspx page is set as the startup page but you may use the HTML page if you later plan to host on a non-.NET server. (Yes, Silverlight applications may be hosted by any HTTP server and not just Internet Information Services [IIS] running ASP.NET.)

With the project open and ready, it's time to turn to the user interface.

1.6.2   *User interface*

Open the MainPage.xaml file; it's usually open by default when you create a new Silverlight project. MainPage.xaml is the start page for your application, set as such by a single line of code inside App.xaml.cs.

Inside the opening and closing `Grid` tags, add the following XAML markup:

```
<Button Content="Get Tweets"
        Height="23"
        HorizontalAlignment="Left"
        Margin="12,12,0,0"
        x:Name="GetTweets"
        VerticalAlignment="Top"
        Width="75"/>
<ListBox x:Name="TweetList"
        Margin="12,41,12,12"/>
```

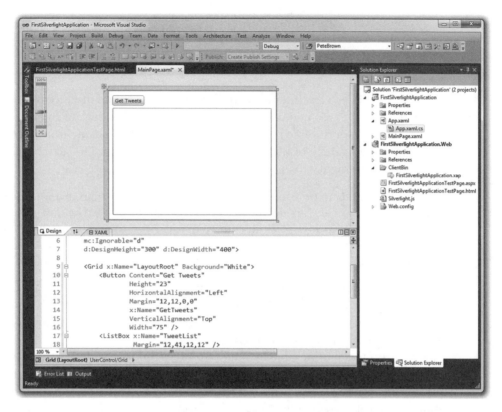

Figure 1.4 The Visual Studio 2010 IDE showing the markup correctly entered for MainPage.xaml

That markup creates two elements on the page: a `Button` and a `ListBox`. You could've dragged those controls from the toolbox onto the design view but that would be hard to describe in detail in this book. In the design view, you should end up with a form that looks like figure 1.4.

Next, double-click the Get Tweets button to create an event handler in the code-behind. Incidentally, this code, like all code in Silverlight, will run on the client inside the Silverlight plug-in. The event handler will be used in the next section, where we make a call to the Twitter search API.

1.6.3 *Calling Twitter search*

The next step is to call out to the Twitter search API. Fill out the event handler we just created in the code-behind to include this code:

```
private void GetTweets_Click(object sender, RoutedEventArgs e)
{
  WebClient client = new WebClient();

  client.DownloadStringCompleted += (s,ea) =>
    {
```

```
        System.Diagnostics.Debug.WriteLine(ea.Result);
    };

  client.DownloadStringAsync(
      new Uri("http://search.twitter.com/search.atom?q=silverlight"));
}
```

The code here does a few interesting things. First, it creates an instance of `WebClient`, one of the easiest to use network clients in Silverlight. It then sets up an event handler using a lambda expression to respond to the results. Finally, it asynchronously calls the method to download the result string from search.twitter.com. The search is for tweets mentioning "silverlight".

> **TIP**   The lambda expression approach here simply uses an anonymous delegate (an unnamed function) as the event handler. The beauty of this approach is that it doesn't clutter up your code with tons of event handlers that are really part of discrete processes. You can learn more about lambda expressions in the C# language on MSDN at http://bit.ly/CSharpLambda.

The network call is asynchronous because all network calls in Silverlight are asynchronous. This can take a little getting used to at first but is easy to deal with once you've done it a few times. Chapter 14 goes into detail on how to use the asynchronous methods as well as the reasons behind them.

If you run the application, click the Get Tweets button, and view the output window, you'll see that you've already built enough to call Twitter and pull back the results in XML format. Not bad for a few lines of code! Our next step is to parse the results and display them in the `ListBox` control.

1.6.4   *Parsing the results and binding the ListBox*

If you look in the output window from your last run, you'll see that the result format is an AtomPub document with an `entry` node for each of the results. In Silverlight, you can parse Atom a couple ways: you can use the built-in parsing of the `Syndication-Feed` class or you can use LINQ to XML to parse the results.

LINQ to XML is a great technology and has many uses above and beyond AtomPub document parsing, so I'm going to go that route. We'll end up with a little more code than the alternative approach, but I think it's worth it.

TWEET CLASS

Before we do the actual parsing, we'll need to create a simple class to hold the content we're interested in. In Visual Studio, right-click the Silverlight project and choose Add > Class. Name the class Tweet.cs and fill it out so it looks like this:

```
public class Tweet
{
    public string Message { get; set; }
    public Uri Image { get; set; }
}
```

Save that class and move back to MainPage.xaml.cs. Somewhere inside the Main-Page class, add the following collection variable. Above the `GetTweets_Click` method would be a perfect location:

```
private ObservableCollection<Tweet> _tweets =
   new ObservableCollection<Tweet>();
```

Be sure to right-click the `ObservableCollection` type name and choose Resolve to add the appropriate `using` statement to your code. This collection will be the location where we place all of the parsed tweets. It's also what we'll bind the `ListBox` to. We'll use the `ObservableCollection` class in chapter 11 when we cover binding.

PARSING WITH LINQ TO XML

LINQ is something you may have used on other .NET projects. If so, you'll feel right at home because it's supported in Silverlight as well. If not, it's pretty easy to pick up. Think of it almost like SQL but in code and working on objects and written backwards, with no database in sight. Okay, it's not exactly like SQL, but it's a great query language that lets you perform iterations and filters in a single line of code. In any case, you won't need to be a LINQ expert for this example.

Right-click the project and choose Add Reference; add a reference to `System.Xml.Linq`. Figure 1.5 shows the dialog with the correct reference selected.

Once the reference is added, replace the `Debug.WriteLine` statement and the event handler declaration in the code-behind with the code from listing 1.1. This code performs the actual parsing of the XML document returned by Twitter search and loads the `tweets` collection with the processed results.

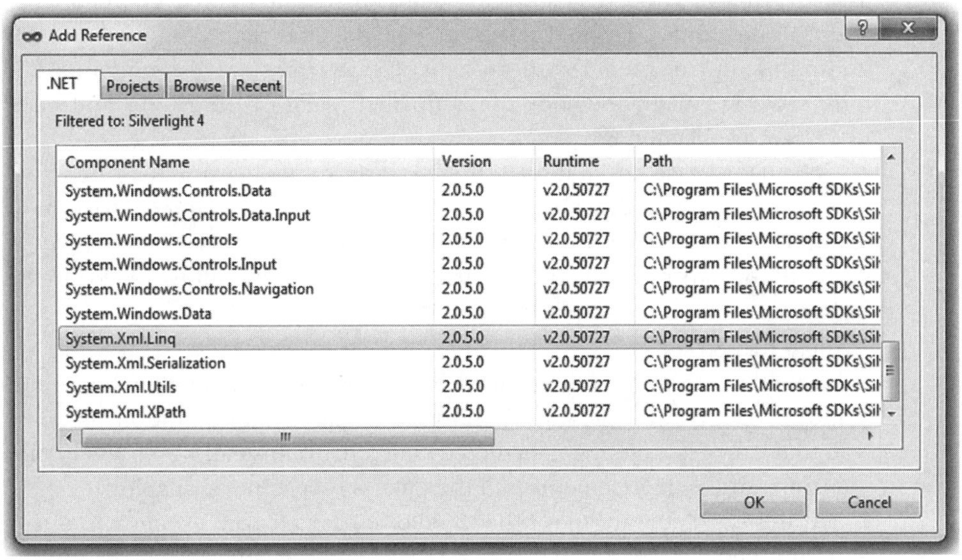

Figure 1.5   The Add Reference dialog with System.Xml.Linq selected for LINQ to XML functionality

Listing 1.1 Processing the Twitter search results using LINQ to XML

```
client.DownloadStringCompleted += (s, ea) =>
{
  XDocument doc = XDocument.Parse(ea.Result);          ❶        Atom
  XNamespace ns = "http://www.w3.org/2005/Atom";    ⟵──        namespace

  var items = from item in doc.Descendants(ns + "entry")    ❷
    select new Tweet()                                   ❸
    {
      Message = item.Element(ns + "title").Value,

      Image = new Uri((                                  ❹
          from XElement xe in item.Descendants(ns + "link")
          where xe.Attribute("type").Value == "image/png"
          select xe.Attribute("href").Value
          ).First<string>()),
    };

  foreach (Tweet t in items)          ❺
  {
    _tweets.Add(t);
  }
};
```

Be sure to right-click and resolve the XDocument class in order to add the correct
using statement to the top of your code.

The code does some interesting processing. It first loads the results into an XDocument ❶ so that it may be processed using LINQ statements. It then goes through
the document selecting each entry element ❷ and creating a new Tweet object
from each ❸. The Tweet object itself is filled out by first grabbing the title element's value and assigning that to the Message and then doing another LINQ query
to find the link element that has a type of image/png and assigning that to the Image
property ❹. Finally, the code loops through each of the results and adds them to
the tweets collection ❺.

The namespace declaration at the top is necessary because the Atom namespace is
the default xmlns in the document. When parsing XML, you need to have the default
namespace declared or the results will be empty.

With the parsing out of the way, the next step is to bind the ListBox to the _tweets
collection so that it has a place to pull the data from.

BINDING THE LISTBOX

Silverlight is all about binding data. Chapter 11 goes into detail on how binding works
and how to use it. For now, it's important to understand that rarely in Silverlight will
you find yourself assigning data directly to controls. Instead, you'll set up binding relationships and let the elements pull the data as it becomes available.

In this case, we want to set the ListBox's ItemsSource property to our collection,
so that it knows to load its individual items from the collection when the collection is
updated. Since we're using an ObservableCollection, the ListBox will be alerted
whenever an item is added to or removed from that collection.

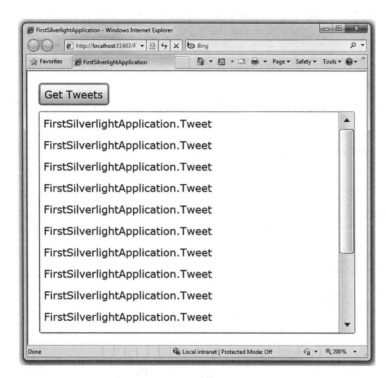

Figure 1.6   **The default presentation for the `ListBox` items leaves something to be desired. It looks like WinForms or something! I demand more from our first Silverlight example.**

Add the following line of code to the `MainPage` constructor, under the `Initialize-Component` call:

```
TweetList.ItemsSource = _tweets;
```

That's all you need to do to set up the binding relationship for the `ListBox`. Run the application and retrieve the tweets. You should end up with something that looks like figure 1.6.

That's not really what we want, though. All we see are a bunch of type names. We want to display images and text. The reason you see the type name is because this is the default item template behavior. By default, the individual items are presented as their `ToString` call. This works fine for a string or numbers or similar, but with complex types? Not so much.

Our final step in this walkthrough is to pretty up the `ListBox` results so we can see something more meaningful.

1.6.5 *Making the ListBox contents more meaningful*

To make the `ListBox` present items using a format of our own choosing, we need to use a `DataTemplate`. `DataTemplates` are covered in detail in section 11.4. For now, understand that they're a chunk of XAML that'll be used to format each item in the list.

The DataTemplate for this ListBox will contain two columns for each row. The first column will contain the picture of the tweeter; the second will contain the body of the tweet.

Open MainPage.xaml and replace the entire ListBox declaration with the XAML from listing 1.2.

Listing 1.2 DataTemplate to format the tweets

```
<ListBox x:Name="TweetList"
         HorizontalContentAlignment="Stretch"                          ❶
         ScrollViewer.HorizontalScrollBarVisibility="Disabled"
         Margin="12,41,12,12">
  <ListBox.ItemTemplate>
    <DataTemplate>                        ◁──  DataTemplate applied
      <Grid Margin="10">                        to each Tweet entity
        <Grid.ColumnDefinitions>
          <ColumnDefinition Width="Auto" />
          <ColumnDefinition Width="*" />                 ❷
        </Grid.ColumnDefinitions>

        <Image Source="{Binding Image}"          ❸
               Grid.Column="0"
               Margin="3"
               Width="50"
               Height="50"
               Stretch="UniformToFill"/>

        <TextBlock Text="{Binding Message}"          ❹
                   FontSize="14"
                   Margin="3"
                   Grid.Column="1"
                   TextWrapping="Wrap" />
      </Grid>
    </DataTemplate>
  </ListBox.ItemTemplate>
</ListBox>
```

In this markup, we first tell the ListBox that we want its content to take up the full width of the ListBox, without any horizontal scrolling ❶. The next bit of markup defines the grid, with an autosized first column and a full-width second column ❷. Then, we bind an Image to the Image property ❸ of the Tweet class and a TextBlock to the Message property ❹.

The end result of the work we've done, including this fine ListBox DataTemplate, is shown in figure 1.7.

I've been working with Silverlight and WPF for a number of years now, but it never fails to impress me just how easy it is to have complete control over what your application displays. I remember the days when you had to purchase specialty controls to do something as simple as display an image inside a ListBox. Now, all you need to do is a little XAML. And, if you don't feel like typing in XAML, you can crack open Expression Blend and use it to design the DataTemplate interactively on the design surface. As a famous dark lord of the Sith once said, "Impressive…most impressive."

Figure 1.7 **The end result of the Twitter search "Hello World!" example looks good!**

1.7 *Summary*

Silverlight is one of the most promising development platforms to come from Microsoft since the original release of .NET a decade ago. Silverlight fills a niche that sits solidly between traditional desktop applications and web applications, while offering capabilities that both lack. It does all this via a small plug-in that takes only minutes to install and runs on different browsers and different operating systems.

The code your write and the skills you gain are portable between the desktop and the web, devices in your pocket, game consoles in your living room, and the set-top box on your TV. That's a pretty good return on your investment.

Silverlight has come a long way since the Silverlight 2 version covered in the original edition of this book. It's amazing just how much the product teams have been able to pack into the product in those two years. Before I joined Microsoft, I heard rumors about people with sleeping bags in their offices and coffee delivered by the gallon. I suspect I now know which team they work for, and I have to say that I'm "super" impressed with the results.

Your environment is all set up, and you've whetted your appetite by building a simple "Hello World!" application in Silverlight 4. In the next chapter, we'll dive right into the meat of what makes Silverlight UI work: XAML. From there, we'll take a tour of all the features this platform has to offer.

Core XAML

This chapter covers

- The basics of XAML, including how to represent objects, properties, events, commands, and behaviors
- The structures Silverlight uses when working with XAML
- Using and creating XAML extensions
- Creating XAML at runtime
- Tooling choices for working with XAML

Before the sibling inventions of WPF and Silverlight, individual programming languages and platforms had a variety of ways of specifying the *user interface (UI)*. Most of them touted the concept of separating the UI from the implementation code. In some cases, such as on the web with HTML and CSS, the representation of the UI was theoretically separated from its underlying implementation but not truly so until tried and true patterns, such as Model-View-Controller (MVC), were applied. In others, such as Windows Forms, the separation was due only to hidden autogenerated, uneditable files that contained the language-specific code necessary to create the UI.

With WPF, Microsoft introduced XAML to provide a cleaner separation of concerns between the definition of the user interface and the code that makes it work.

This not only allows for some sleek design patterns such as the MVVM or ViewModel pattern (discussed in chapter 16 and here referred to simply as the ViewModel pattern) but also makes it easier to create tooling.

Consider Windows Forms for a moment. The definition of the interface was so tied to the compiler and the existing tooling that it was extremely difficult for a third party to create a tool that designed (or assisted in the design) of the UI. The files were hidden, made in multiple implementation languages, and had that "don't even think of editing this file" comment at the top of the generated code. It was good at the time but the world has moved on.

XAML helps fix those problems—it lets you, not the tools, own your UI. XAML files are editable individually and in relative isolation from the rest of the project. You can edit XAML in Expression Blend, Visual Studio, Notepad, Kaxaml, and other tools listed at the end of this chapter, thereby making it easier to incorporate into your own specific workflow. Even hand-edited XAML is round-trippable with tooling because the XAML rules are well-defined and consistent internally and across implementation languages.

XAML is so fundamental to Silverlight that this entire chapter is devoted to introducing you to it. Though XAML appears in just about every chapter in this book, we'll cover the core concepts here and ensure sufficient understanding so that, when you open an XAML file in Visual Studio or Notepad, you can read and understand what it's doing, even as you're still learning Silverlight. For those of you interested in the guts of XAML processing and use, I've included information on using tree structures, creating your own converters, and working with the property system.

2.1 XAML basics

XAML is a declarative language that enables you to create and initialize .NET objects in XML. Everything you can do in XAML you can do in code. But to make the most of the platform and its tooling, you'll want to embrace the code-plus-markup philosophy rather than go with a 100 percent code solution.

The XAML format enables you to easily visualize a hierarchy of elements while separating presentation from code. This separation is possible because each XAML element maps to a .NET type. Each attribute within an element corresponds to a property within a .NET type. This concept is illustrated in figure 2.1.

Figure 2.1 shows three code equivalents of an XAML segment. Note that the `TextBlock` element in the XAML code corresponds to an initialization statement within the code segments. This initialization occurs because, each time an element is created in XAML, the corresponding .NET type's default constructor is called behind the scenes.

To understand the structure of an XAML file, it's important to understand the representation and use of objects, namespaces, properties, and events.

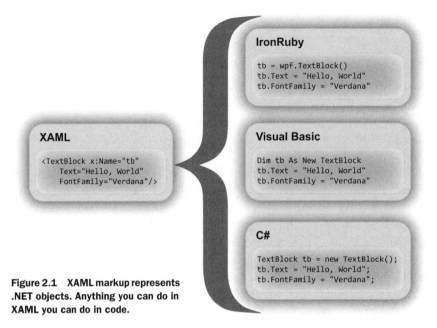

Figure 2.1   XAML markup represents .NET objects. Anything you can do in XAML you can do in code.

2.1.1   *Objects*

Objects (or instances of types) are represented in XAML using XML elements. The elements have the same name as the associated class and are considered instantiated upon declaration in the markup.

> **NOTE** Any type you use in XAML must have a default (parameterless) constructor. Silverlight XAML currently has no provision for passing arguments into a constructor or an initialization function, so you'll need to make sure your types can be initialized using defaults and properties alone.

Certain types of objects may contain one or more of other nested objects. For example, a button may contain a single content object, which itself may contain one or more other objects. In listing 2.1, the UserControl contains the Grid, the Grid contains the Button, and the Button contains a StackPanel, which is a panel that by default lays its children out in a vertical list. The StackPanel itself contains three TextBlock elements.

Listing 2.1   XAML showing a hierarchy of nested objects

Result:

First Line
Second Line
Third Line

XAML:

```
<UserControl x:Class="XamlElements.MainPage"          ⟵⌐  Outermost UserControl
  xmlns="http://schemas.microsoft.com/winfx/2006/xaml/presentation"
  xmlns:x="http://schemas.microsoft.com/winfx/2006/xaml">
  <Grid x:Name="LayoutRoot">                          ⟵⌐  Nested Grid
    <Button Height="100" Width="150">     ⟵  Button nested in Grid
      <StackPanel>                                          ⟵
        <TextBlock Text="First Line" />    | Three        | StackPanel
        <TextBlock Text="Second Line" />   | TextBlocks in | inside Button
        <TextBlock Text="Third Line" />    | StackPanel    |
      </StackPanel>
    </Button>
  </Grid>
</UserControl>
```

The UserControl and Button are both content controls, a concept we'll discuss in greater detail in chapter 10. For now, it's important to understand that a content control may only have one direct child element, typically a panel that holds other elements. The x:Name and x:Class properties are part of the namespace specified by the xmlns:x statement. More on that in a moment... The Grid and StackPanel are both Panels, which is a type that has a Children collection to allow multiple contained elements. We'll discuss panels in chapter 7.

The ability to flexibly nest objects permits a composition approach to UI design. Rather than having to purchase or custom-code a button control that allows, say, three lines of text and an image, you can simply compose those into an appropriate layout panel and make that panel the content of the button control.

The nesting of objects is part of what gives us an object tree. We'll cover that in more detail shortly.

Now that we've covered the basic structure of an XAML file, let's talk about how you differentiate your SuperButton control from my SuperButton control, even though we used the same control name: namespaces.

2.1.2 Namespaces

A *namespace* provides a way of organizing related objects within a common grouping. These groupings, or namespaces, give you a way to define where the compiler should look for a type. Namespaces in XAML are similar to namespaces in other languages such as C# and Java. To specify where to look, you reference a namespace within an element of an XAML file, typically the root or outermost element. Listing 2.2 illustrates the use of the two default namespaces.

Listing 2.2 A basic XAML file referencing the two default namespaces

```
<UserControl x:Class="Xaml01.MainPage"
  xmlns="http://schemas.microsoft.com/winfx/2006/xaml/presentation"
  xmlns:x="http://schemas.microsoft.com/winfx/2006/xaml"
  Width="400" Height="300">
  <Grid x:Name="LayoutRoot" Background="White">
    <TextBlock x:Name="myTextBlock" Text="Hello" />
  </Grid>
</UserControl>
```

NOTE WPF supports the Name property in both the namespace prefixed with x: and the default namespace, allowing them to be specified as x:Name or just Name. Silverlight supports only x:Name. For compatibility with Silverlight markup, the recommended approach for WPF is to use x:Name.

As listing 2.2 illustrates, you're permitted to reference multiple namespaces within a single XAML file. When you reference multiple namespaces, each namespace must be uniquely prefixed. For instance, the x prefix in this example is used in association with the http://schemas.microsoft.com/winfx/2006/xaml namespace. At the same time, the http://schemas.microsoft.com/winfx/2006/xaml/presentation namespace doesn't use a prefix.

STANDARD XAML NAMESPACES

The two namespaces we just mentioned will be used in almost every Silverlight application you work with or see. These namespaces are generally defined in the following manner:

- xmlns="http://schemas.microsoft.com/winfx/2006/xaml/presentation"— This is the default Silverlight namespace. It provides your applications with core Silverlight elements. For that reason, this namespace generally omits a prefix, making it the default namespace within the page. Such approach enables you to reference elements within this specific namespace without having to include the prefix.

- xmlns:x="http://schemas.microsoft.com/winfx/2006/xaml"—This is the common XAML namespace. It provides functionality that's common across XAML. It's important to remember that XAML is used by other technologies such as WPF, Oslo, and Windows Workflow Foundation (WF), all of which need access to common features such as Name, Key, and Class properties.

NOTE In addition to the standard namespaces, the Silverlight runtime supports the Silverlight-specific http://schemas.microsoft.com/client/2007 namespace as a default namespace. But, you should use the previously mentioned http://schemas.microsoft.com/winfx/2006/xaml/presentation namespace as the default because Expression Blend, Visual Studio, and other tools are all configured to recognize that namespace. The use of standard namespaces also makes it easier to share your markup with WPF applications.

REFERENCING OTHER LIBRARIES

When another assembly is referenced, it gets copied into the configuration-specific Bin folder of your Silverlight application. In fact, when you compile your Silverlight application, it gets compiled into an assembly that's placed in this directory. We'll discuss the application model later; for now, in order to reference these assemblies, you need to define a new XAML namespace, which includes a prefix, CLR namespace, and assembly. Listing 2.3 illustrates this concept.

Listing 2.3 Using a control from an external assembly

```
<UserControl x:Class="Xaml02.MainPage"
  xmlns="http://schemas.microsoft.com/winfx/2006/xaml/presentation"
  xmlns:x="http://schemas.microsoft.com/winfx/2006/xaml"
  xmlns:my="clr-namespace:MyNamespace;assembly=MyAssembly"     ◁──┐ External
  Width="400" Height="300">                                        │ assembly
  <Grid x:Name="LayoutRoot">                                       │ reference
    <my:MyControl x:Name="myControl1" />    ◁──┐ Use
  </Grid>                                       │ assembly
</UserControl>
```

As listing 2.3 illustrates, referencing other elements, including custom elements, only requires you to provide the namespace and assembly name of the external element. Of course, you'll still need to reference the external assembly so that its types are accessible to code and to the XAML parser/compiler. The name my was used as a convenience here; you can use any identifier that makes sense to you.

If the referenced type is defined in the same assembly as the markup, you'll still need to create an XAML namespace reference for it. But the ;assembly= clause of the namespace definition may optionally be left out, as illustrated in listing 2.4.

Listing 2.4 Using a control from a different namespace in the same assembly

```
<UserControl x:Class="Xaml03.MainPage"
  xmlns="http://schemas.microsoft.com/winfx/2006/xaml/presentation"
  xmlns:x="http://schemas.microsoft.com/winfx/2006/xaml"
  xmlns:controls="clr-namespace:Xaml03.Controls"     ◁──┐ Namespace
  Width="400" Height="300">                               │ reference
  <Grid x:Name="LayoutRoot">
    <controls:MyControl x:Name="myControl1" />    ◁──┐ Use
  </Grid>                                              │ namespace
</UserControl>
```

Namespaces are typically declared within the outermost element of an XAML file, as in listing 2.4, but that doesn't always need to be the case. When using XAML generated by tools, you'll sometimes find namespaces defined at lower levels, particularly within control templates (covered in chapter 23). In those cases, the namespace only applies to the elements within the enclosing type (and the enclosing element itself) rather than to the XAML document as a whole.

Listing 2.5 shows the definition of a namespace at the Grid level rather than at the UserControl level. The namespace could also have been defined at the MyControl level, but then we'd need to do it for each instance of MyControl. This approach is sometimes taken when using control templates and other situations where you want to minimize possible namespace prefix collisions, while still preserving the ability to reference external code.

Listing 2.5 Namespace declaration at a level lower than the root

```
<UserControl x:Class="Xaml04.MainPage"
  xmlns="http://schemas.microsoft.com/winfx/2006/xaml/presentation"
```

```
    xmlns:x="http://schemas.microsoft.com/winfx/2006/xaml"
    Width="400" Height="300">
    <Grid x:Name="LayoutRoot"
          xmlns:controls="clr-namespace:Xaml03.Controls">
      <controls:MyControl x:Name="myControl1" />
      <controls:MyControl x:Name="myControl2" />
      <controls:MyControl x:Name="myControl3" />
    </Grid>
</UserControl>
```

<--- **Namespace declaration**

The namespace shown in listing 2.5 will only apply to the grid LayoutRoot and its children. Controls outside of that hierarchy won't have access to the controls namespace or prefix. You'll typically find this inside complex styles in resource dictionaries. The same approaches to referencing namespaces and assemblies apply to resource dictionaries, pages, and other types commonly associated with XAML. Though it's important to understand the rules for referencing namespaces, in practice, the tooling will create the namespaces for you either by IntelliSense or when you drag and drop items into the markup editor or onto the design surface.

2.1.3   *Properties*

There are two ways to reference properties in XAML: in line with the element as you would any XML attribute and as a nested subelement. Which you should choose depends on what you need to represent. Simple values are typically represented with inline properties, whereas complex values are typically represented with element properties.

INLINE PROPERTIES

The use of an inline property requires a type converter that will convert the string representation—for example, the "Black" in Background="Black"—into a correct underlying .NET type (in this case, a SolidColorBrush). We'll cover type converters later in this chapter. The example in listing 2.6 shows a built-in type converter in use to convert the string "Black" for the inline property Background.

Listing 2.6   Specifying a property value in line using an XML attribute

```
<UserControl x:Class="Xaml05.MainPage"
  xmlns="http://schemas.microsoft.com/winfx/2006/xaml/presentation"
  xmlns:x="http://schemas.microsoft.com/winfx/2006/xaml"
  Width="400" Height="300">
  <Grid x:Name="LayoutRoot" Background="Black" />
</UserControl>
```

<--- **Inline property**

ELEMENT PROPERTIES

Another way to specify properties is to use the expanded property element syntax. While this can generally be used for any property, it's typically required only when you need to specify something more complex than the inline syntax will easily allow. The syntax for element properties is *<Type.PropertyName>value</Type.PropertyName>*, as seen in listing 2.7.

Listing 2.7 Specifying a property value using property element syntax

```
<UserControl x:Class="Xaml06.MainPage"
  xmlns="http://schemas.microsoft.com/winfx/2006/xaml/presentation"
  xmlns:x="http://schemas.microsoft.com/winfx/2006/xaml"
  Width="400" Height="300">
  <Grid x:Name="LayoutRoot">
    <Grid.Background>
      Black                         Property
    </Grid.Background>              element syntax
  </Grid>
</UserControl>
```

The use of the string to invoke the type converter is, in its end result, identical to using `<SolidColorBrush Color="Black" />` in place of `"Black"`. Though these examples are rarely seen in practice, the more complex example of setting the background to a `LinearGradientBrush` is common, so we'll cover that next.

Rather than have the value represented as a simple string such as `"Black"`, the value can be an element containing a complex set of elements and properties such as the `<LinearGradientBrush>` seen in listing 2.8.

Listing 2.8 A more complex example of the property element syntax

```
<UserControl x:Class="Xaml07.MainPage"
  xmlns="http://schemas.microsoft.com/winfx/2006/xaml/presentation"
  xmlns:x="http://schemas.microsoft.com/winfx/2006/xaml"
  Width="400" Height="300">
  <Grid x:Name="LayoutRoot">          Background property
    <Grid.Background>
      <LinearGradientBrush>                    Type of brush
        <LinearGradientBrush.GradientStops>
          <GradientStop Offset="0.0" Color="Black" />      More property
          <GradientStop Offset="0.5" Color="LightGray" />  elements
          <GradientStop Offset="0.5" Color="DarkGray" />
          <GradientStop Offset="1.0" Color="White" />
        </LinearGradientBrush.GradientStops>
      </LinearGradientBrush>
    </Grid.Background>
  </Grid>
</UserControl>
```

Now that we know how to specify properties in markup, let's dive deeper into how those properties work.

2.1.4 Dependency properties

Dependency properties are part of the property system introduced with WPF and used in Silverlight. In markup and in consuming code, they're indistinguishable from standard .NET CLR properties, except that they can be data bound, serve as the target of an animation, or set by a style.

> **TIP** A property can't be the target of an animation or obtain its value through binding unless it's a dependency property. We'll cover binding in detail in chapter 11.

To have dependency properties in a class, the class must derive from `DependencyObject` or one of its subclasses. Typically, you'll do this only for visuals and other elements that you'll use within XAML and not in classes defined outside of the user interface.

In regular .NET code, when you create a property, you typically back it by a private field in the containing class. Storing a dependency property differs in that the location of its backing value depends upon its current state. The way that location is determined is called *value precedence.*

VALUE PRECEDENCE

Dependency properties obtain their value from a variety of inputs. What follows is the order the Silverlight property system uses when assigning the runtime values of dependency properties, with the highest precedence listed first:

- *Active or hold animations*—Animations will operate on the base value for the dependency property, determined by evaluating the precedence for other inputs. In order for an animation to have any effect, it must be highest in precedence. Animations may operate on a single dependency property from multiple levels of precedence (for example, an animation defined in the control template and an animation defined locally). The value typically results from the composite of all animations, depending on the type being animated.

- *Local value*—Local values are specified directly in the markup and are accessed via the CLR property wrappers for the dependency property. Because local values are higher in precedence than styles and templates, they're capable of overriding values such as the font style or foreground color defined in the default style for a control.

- *Templated properties*—Used specifically for elements created within a control or data template, their value is taken from the template itself.

- *Style setters*—These are values set in a style in your application via resources defined in or merged into the `UserControl` or application resource dictionaries. We'll explore styles in chapter 23.

- *Default value*—This is the value provided or assigned when the dependency property was first created. If no default value was provided, normal CLR defaults typically apply.

The strict precedence rules allow you to depend on behaviors within Silverlight, such as being able to override elements of a style by setting them as local values from within the element itself. In listing 2.9, the foreground of the button will be red as set in the local value and not black as set in the style. The local value has a higher precedence than the applied style.

Listing 2.9   Dependency property precedence rules in practice

```
<UserControl x:Class="Xaml08.MainPage"
  xmlns="http://schemas.microsoft.com/winfx/2006/xaml/presentation"
  xmlns:x="http://schemas.microsoft.com/winfx/2006/xaml"
  Width="400" Height="300">
```

```
<UserControl.Resources>
  <Style x:Key="ButtonStyle" TargetType="Button">
    <Setter Property="Foreground" Value="Black" />
    <Setter Property="FontSize" Value="24" />
  </Style>
</UserControl.Resources>
<Grid x:Name="LayoutRoot">
  <Button Content="Local Values at Work"
          Style="{StaticResource ButtonStyle}"
          Foreground="Red" />
</Grid>
</UserControl>
```

The Style tag in `UserControl.Resources` is a reusable asset that sets some key properties for our button.

We'll cover creating dependency properties in chapter 24 when we create our own controls. For the purposes of this chapter, it's sufficient to understand that the majority of the properties you'll refer to in XAML are dependency properties. One type of dependency property that has a slightly odd appearance is an attached property.

2.1.5 *Attached properties*

Attached properties are a specialized type of dependency property that is immediately recognizable in markup due to the *TypeName.AttachedPropertyName* syntax. For example, `Canvas.Left` is an attached property defined by the `Canvas` type. What makes attached properties interesting is that they're not defined by the type you use them with; instead, they're defined by another type in a potentially different class hierarchy.

Attached properties allow flexibility when defining classes because the classes don't need to take into account every possible scenario in which they'll be used and define properties for those scenarios. Layout is a great example of this. The flexibility of the Silverlight layout system allows you to create new panels that may never have been implemented in other technologies—for example, a panel that lays elements out by degrees and levels in a circular or radial fashion versus something like the built-in `Canvas` that lays elements out by `Left` and `Top` positions.

Rather than have all elements define `Left`, `Top`, `Level`, and `Degrees` properties (as well as `GridRow` and `GridColumn` properties for grids), we can use attached properties. The buttons in listing 2.10, for example, are contained in panels that have greatly differing layout algorithms, requiring different positioning information. In this case, we'll show a fictional `RadialPanel` in use.

> **Listing 2.10 Attached properties in use**

```
<UserControl x:Class="Xaml09.MainPage"
  xmlns="http://schemas.microsoft.com/winfx/2006/xaml/presentation"
  xmlns:x="http://schemas.microsoft.com/winfx/2006/xaml"
  xmlns:panels="clr-namespace:Xaml09.Panels"
  Width="400" Height="600">
  <StackPanel x:Name="LayoutRoot">
    <Canvas Width="400" Height="200">
```

```
    <Button Canvas.Left="10"          #A
            Canvas.Top="50"           #A
            Width="200" Height="100"
            Content="Button in Canvas" />
  </Canvas>

  <panels:RadialPanel Width="400" Height="400">
    <Button panels:RadialPanel.Degrees="25"
            panels:RadialPanel.Level="3"
            Width="200" Height="100"
            Content="Button in Radial Panel" />
  </panels:RadialPanel>
 </StackPanel>
</UserControl>
```

Attached properties

Attached properties aren't limited to layout. You'll find them in the animation engine for things such as `Storyboard.TargetProperty` as well as in other places of the framework.

PROPERTY PATHS

Before we wrap up our discussion of properties, there's one concept left to understand: *property paths*. Property paths provide a way to reference properties of objects in XAML both when you have a name for an element and when you need to indirectly refer to an element by its position in the tree.

Property paths can take several forms, and may dot-down into properties of an object. They can also use parentheticals for indirect property targeting as well as for specifying attached properties. Here are some examples of property paths for the `Storyboard` target property:

```
<DoubleAnimation Storyboard.TargetName="MyButton"
                 Storyboard.TargetProperty="(Canvas.Left)" ... />

<DoubleAnimation Storyboard.TargetName="MyButton"
                 Storyboard.TargetProperty="Width" ... />

...
<Button x:Name="MyButton"
        Canvas.Top="50" Canvas.Left="100" />
```

We'll cover property paths in detail in chapter 11 when we discuss binding.

Properties are one of the pieces that define an object's interface. Because XAML doesn't allow us to do anything specifically with methods, the only other part of the interface left is the definition of events.

2.1.6   *Events*

Events in Silverlight are used much like events in any other .NET technology. The sender of the event wants to notify zero or more receivers of something that happened. Silverlight enhances that, though, in that it may want events to work their way up the object tree, from the event source to the root element.

Silverlight and WPF introduce the concepts of *routed events* and event bubbling. These allow events to be generated at one level of the tree, and then provide an opportunity to be handled by each level above, until reaching the root of the tree—an effect known as *bubbling*.

The main difference between routed events and standard CLR events, to the handler of the event, is that the event sender isn't necessarily the original source of the event. In order to get the original source of the event, you need to check the `Originalsource` property of the `RoutedEventArgs` supplied to the handler.

User-created events, such as the ones you might create in your own code, can't bubble. Instead, bubbling is reserved only for built-in core events such as `MouseLeftButtonDown`. Bubbled events include a `Handled` property in the event arguments, as well as the standard `RoutedEventArgs` information.

> ### WPF routed events
>
> If you're familiar with the eventing system in WPF, you may wonder what happened to the `Tunneling` and `Direct` types of routed events. Silverlight doesn't currently implement these. In fact, Silverlight doesn't include the `EventManager` available in WPF, so routed events can't be created in user code. Some clever folks at control vendors have implemented their own analogue that allows for user-created routed events but isn't built into the core Silverlight runtime.

EVENTS REFERENCED IN XAML

In XAML, referencing an event handler defined in code-behind is simple. In fact, if you use Visual Studio when doing so, the event handler in the code-behind can be created for you automatically.

For example, if we have a button in XAML:

```
<Button Click="MyButton_Click" />
```

We can wire it up to an appropriate event handler in the code-behind:

```
private void MyButton_Click(object sender, RoutedEventArgs e)
{
  MessageBox.Show("Click event");
}
```

The approach is a good shortcut for hooking up events. When working in XAML, the tooling in Visual Studio will even let you define a new event handler or use an existing one. One slight advantage of this approach is that you don't necessarily need to define a name for your button.

EVENTS REFERENCED IN CODE

To attach an event handler from code, you follow the same approach you would for any normal CLR event: create a new event handler and add it to the event using the += syntax. So, if we have the same button as earlier and give it a name that can be referenced from the code-behind:

```
<Button x:Name="MyButton" />
```

We can then wire up the event handler in the constructor. Do this after the `Initial-izeComponent` call so that `MyButton` is valid:

```
public MainPage()
{
    InitializeComponent();

    MyButton.Click += new RoutedEventHandler(MyButton_Click);

}
private void MyButton_Click(object sender, RoutedEventArgs e)
{
  MessageBox.Show("Click event");
}
```

Both approaches are equally valid. The approach you use will depend primarily on your personal style. My preferred approach when not using commands is to wire up events in the code-behind, in the constructor as shown.

Silverlight 4 added the ability to use commands as a way to clean up event handling and wire-up code. Rather than specify an event handler, you can specify one or more command properties in XAML.

2.1.7   *Commands*

One of the more architecturally significant additions to Silverlight 4 was the addition of WPF-style commands. Commands allow you to remove the event handler middle-man from your code-behind when you want something other than the code-behind to handle the action. For example, if you follow the ViewModel pattern, you probably want the button clicks to be handled by the view model and not the code-behind. Typical event handler code to forward the event might look like this:

```
private void Save_Click(object sender, RoutedEventArgs e)
{
  _viewModel.Save();
}
```

That's extra goo that you don't necessarily want in your view. It complicates unit testing and makes the code-behind an essential ingredient. It also requires separate view-model properties to set the `IsEnabled` property on the Save button. It's not terrible, but it's not great. The command code that eliminates the code-behind goo might look like this:

```
 // no code in code-behind required :)
```

I love the code I don't have to write. It's all handled in the markup and the view model, so you don't need any forwarding code at all. The controls in the view bind to a command that exists somewhere in the binding path. Assuming you have the page's data context set to the view model, the markup to bind to the exposed view-model command looks like this:

```
<Button x:Name="SaveButton"
        Height="25"
```

```
Width="75"
Content="Save"
Command="{Binding SaveCommand}" />
```

The related bits of the view model might look something like this, assuming you've implemented an `EmployeeSaveCommand` that implements `ICommand`:

```
private EmployeeSaveCommand _saveCommand;
public ICommand SaveCommand
{
    get { return _saveCommand; }
}
```

In this way, you avoid having your code-behind stand in the way of separating your view from your view model. Commands also provide other capabilities such as automatically disabling the associated controls if the command can't be run at that time via an implicit binding of the `ICommand.CanExecute` method with `IsEnabled` property of the Button.

Commands are supported on any control that inherits from `ButtonBase` as well as on the `Hyperlink` control (not to be confused with `HyperlinkButton`, which inherits from `ButtonBase`).

We'll create our own commands in chapter 16 when we discuss how to build applications using the ViewModel pattern. Another interesting bit of attached functionality you may see in the markup is a behavior.

2.1.8 Behaviors

Behaviors are bits of designer-friendly packaged interactivity introduced in Silverlight 3, originally tied to Expression Blend to make it easy to drag functionality directly onto the design surface and associate it with controls. Behaviors included capabilities such as physics, sound, automatic shadows, drag and drop, and even nonvisual behaviors such as one that's used to wire up the window-close events to a view model in WPF. The appeal was much broader than just Blend users, though, so the functionality was released for all Silverlight and WPF developers to enjoy.

The SDK includes a number of default behaviors as well as a ton of community-created behaviors for both Silverlight and WPF on the Expression community site. Figure 2.2 shows the Behaviors section of the Assets panel in Expression Blend, listing the eight included behaviors.

Figure 2.2 The default behaviors in Expression Blend include items from utilitarian, to sound playing, to complex interactions such as mouse drag and drop. Additional behaviors may be found on the Microsoft Expression Community Gallery at http://gallery.expression.microsoft.com.

Behaviors typically don't require using any code because they're wired up using XAML. For example, listing 2.11 shows the markup required to use the `MouseDragElementBehavior`, one of the stock behaviors, with a `Border` element.

Listing 2.11   A MouseDragElementBehavior attached to a Border element

```
<UserControl
  xmlns="http://schemas.microsoft.com/winfx/2006/xaml/presentation"
  xmlns:x="http://schemas.microsoft.com/winfx/2006/xaml"
  xmlns:i="clr-namespace:System.Windows.Interactivity;
    assembly=System.Windows.Interactivity"
  xmlns:il="clr-namespace:Microsoft.Expression.Interactivity.Layout;
    assembly=Microsoft.Expression.Interactions"
  x:Class="SilverlightApplicationBehavior.MainPage"
  Width="640" Height="480">

  <Grid x:Name="LayoutRoot" Background="White">

    <Border Width="100" Height="100"
            BorderBrush="Black" Background="Orange"
            BorderThickness="2">

      <i:Interaction.Behaviors>
        <il:MouseDragElementBehavior/>
      </i:Interaction.Behaviors>

      <TextBlock Text="Drag Me"
              HorizontalAlignment="Center"
              VerticalAlignment="Center" />
    </Border>
  </Grid>
</UserControl>
```

Required behavior namespaces ◁

Attached behavior ◁

All of the code required to implement the dragging of the border is encapsulated within the behavior. Behaviors are a great way to package up common UI functionality that would augment other UI elements.

We'll discuss behaviors in more detail in chapter 22, where we'll also create our own custom behavior.

Objects, properties, events, commands, and behaviors make up the majority of what you'll see when you look at an XAML file. At this point, you should be able to read XAML and have a general understanding of what you're looking at. Another thing you may see in XAML is object and property names inside curly braces. We'll cover that later in this chapter, but first we'll go through what Silverlight sees when it looks at XAML source and builds out the in-memory representation of the elements.

2.2   *Object trees and namescope*

In the previous sections, I mentioned the concept of an object tree. In order to understand the object tree, you need to understand the layout and contents of XAML files. Once you do, it's easier to conceptualize the object tree and its related concept, *namescope.*

A common misconception is that Silverlight creates XAML for any objects you create in code. In fact, the opposite is what happens: Silverlight creates objects from XAML.

Objects you create in code go right into the trees as their native .NET object form. Elements in XAML are processed and turned into objects that go into the same tree.

2.2.1 Object trees

Now that we've covered the structure of an XAML file, you can look at one and quickly realize it represents a hierarchical tree of objects starting from the root (typically a `UserControl` or `Page`) and going all the way down to the various shapes, panels, and other elements that make up the control templates in use. That hierarchical structure is known as an *object tree*. Figure 2.3 shows a hypothetical object tree.

Each element has the concept of a parent (the containing element) and may have a child or children in panel-type collection properties, content properties, or other general-purpose properties.

> **NOTE** Unlike WPF, Silverlight doesn't expose the concept of a logical tree. Operations that, in WPF, might return logical tree information will, in Silverlight, return visual tree information. This distinction is really only important if you're coming from the WPF world or porting code from WPF that happened to use tree traversal functions.

The *visual tree* is a filtered view of the object tree. While the object tree contains all types regardless of whether they participate in rendering (collections, for example), the visual tree contains only those objects with a visual representation. Figure 2.4 shows the visual tree; note the lack of nonvisual objects such as collections.

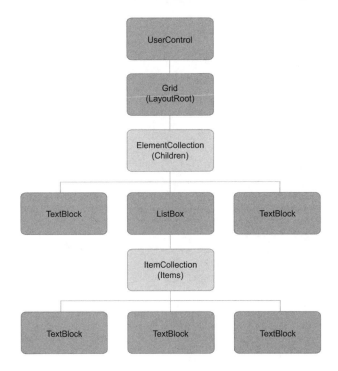

Figure 2.3 **A hypothetical object tree showing not only the visual elements such as** `TextBlocks` **and** `ListBoxes`, **but also the internal collections used to contain child elements.**

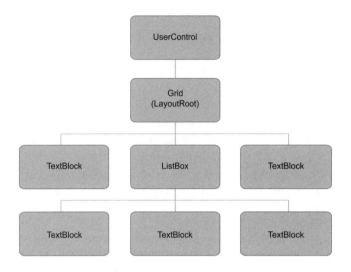

Figure 2.4   The visual tree representation of the object tree from figure 2.3. Note that only visual elements, not collections, are represented.

WALKING THE VISUAL TREE

Silverlight includes the `VisualTreeHelper` static class to assist in examining the visual tree. Using the `GetChild` and `GetChildrenCount` methods, you can recursively walk the tree from any element down as deeply as you want. The `GetParent` method allows you to trace the tree from a given element up to the visual tree root, as seen in listing 2.12.

Listing 2.12   Using the VisualTreeHelper to walk the tree from an element to the root

---

Result:
```
System.Windows.Controls.StackPanel
System.Windows.Controls.Border
System.Windows.Controls.Grid
System.Windows.Controls.Grid
VisualTree.MainPage
```

XAML:
```xml
<UserControl x:Class="VisualTree.MainPage"
  xmlns="http://schemas.microsoft.com/winfx/2006/xaml/presentation"
  xmlns:x="http://schemas.microsoft.com/winfx/2006/xaml"
  Width="400" Height="300">
  <Grid x:Name="LayoutRoot" Background="White">
    <Grid>
      <Border BorderThickness="1" BorderBrush="Black"
            Margin="10">
        <StackPanel Margin="10">                        Start
          <TextBlock x:Name="MyTextBlock"          ◁──┘  element
                  Text="Hello!" />
          <TextBlock Text="Lorem ipsum" />         ◁──┐  Sibling
        </StackPanel>                                   │  element
      </Border>
    </Grid>
  </Grid>
</UserControl>
```

C#:
```
public MainPage()
{
    InitializeComponent();

    Loaded += new RoutedEventHandler(MainPage_Loaded);
}
void MainPage_Loaded(object sender, RoutedEventArgs e)        ◁──┐ Start in
{                                                                 loaded event

    DependencyObject o = MyTextBlock;

    while((o = VisualTreeHelper.GetParent(o)) != null)       ◁──┐ Stop when
    {                                                             at root
        Debug.WriteLine(o.GetType().ToString());
    }
}
```

We start the tree walk in the `Loaded` event handler because the tree isn't valid until the `UserControl` has been loaded. We know the walk is complete when we hit an element with a null parent—the root of the tree.

You'll notice that, when you generate an object tree for an entire application, you'll have multiple instances of controls, each of which contains elements with the same name. Namescope, the next topic, is how Silverlight ensures that the names remain uniquely addressable across the breadth of the object tree.

2.2.2 *Namescope*

Earlier in this chapter we saw that you can define an `x:Name` for elements in XAML. This provides a way to find the control via code and perform operations on it, or handle its events.

Consider for a moment the idea of having multiple controls on the same page, each of which contains named elements. To handle this situation, XAML introduces the concept of a *namescope*. A namescope simply ensures that the names across instances of controls don't collide. This is similar in concept to the approach taken by ASP.NET to mangle control names to ensure they remain unique. Listing 2.13 shows an example where namescope is required to prevent duplicate control names.

> **Listing 2.13   Without namescope, the name MyButton would be duplicated in the tree**

XAML:
```
<UserControl x:Class="NamescopeExample.MyNestedControl"
    xmlns="http://schemas.microsoft.com/winfx/2006/xaml/presentation"
    xmlns:x="http://schemas.microsoft.com/winfx/2006/xaml"
    Width="200" Height="150">
    <Grid x:Name="LayoutRoot" Background="White">
        <Button x:Name="MyButton" />                        ◁──┐ MyButton in
    </Grid>                                                       UserControl
</UserControl>
```

XAML:
```
<UserControl x:Class="NamescopeExample.MainPage"
    xmlns="http://schemas.microsoft.com/winfx/2006/xaml/presentation"
```

```
         xmlns:x="http://schemas.microsoft.com/winfx/2006/xaml"
               xmlns:local="clr-namespace:NamescopeExample"
         Width="400" Height="300">
         <StackPanel x:Name="LayoutRoot" Background="White">
             <local:MyNestedControl x:Name="Control1" />
             <local:MyNestedControl x:Name="Control2" />
             <local:MyNestedControl x:Name="Control3" />
         </StackPanel>
     </UserControl>
```

**Multiple
Instances**

With three instances of the user control in listing 2.13, how does the XAML parser prevent naming collisions between all the `MyButtons` in the object tree but still allow you to uniquely reference each one? Namescope. As you'd expect, using the same name twice within the same XAML namescope will result in a parsing error. This is similar to the compile-time error you'd receive if you gave two variables the same name within the same scope level in a C# application.

> **NOTE** Silverlight 2 had a namescope bug that manifested itself when you named an element inside a tooltip (or pop up) attached to items in an `ItemsControl` such as a `ListBox`. The resulting error indicated that there were duplicate names in the object tree. This was fixed in Silverlight 3.

In practice, you typically don't need to worry about namescopes unless you're loading and parsing XAML at runtime using the `createFromXaml` JavaScript API or `XamlReader.Load` managed API. The namescopes are created for you automatically at runtime when you instantiate your controls.

Now that we understand namescope, let's go back to one of the other things you'll run into in XAML: the curly brace syntax for markup extensions.

2.3   *XAML extensions and type converters*

Now that we know the structure and rules for XAML files, let's look at a something that allows us to bend those rules a little: *extensions.*

XAML allows you to represent almost anything using the object element and property attribute syntaxes. But some things can get cumbersome to do that way. For that reason, XAML includes the concept of extensions in the form of markup extensions and type converters. Silverlight also includes the concept of a value converter but, because that's used almost exclusively with binding, we'll cover it in chapter 11.

You'll want to internalize both concepts to understand what's happening when XAML is parsed or what those curly braces mean. Though you can't currently create your own markup extensions, type converters will give you a powerful way to extend XAML using your own code. We'll start with markup extensions and then move into using existing type converters and, later, creating our own type converters.

2.3.1   *Markup extensions*

When viewing XAML of any complexity, you're going to come across things such as `Style="{StaticResource MyStyle}"` or `Text="{Binding LastName}"`. The curly braces indicate that you're looking at a markup extension. Markup extensions are code that can provide a value to a dependency property. In the case of the `Style` example, the markup extension provides a full style object to the `Style` property.

You can't create new markup extensions but you can use the built-in set, which currently consists of `StaticResource`, `Binding`, and `TemplateBinding`. Listing 2.14 illustrates the use of `StaticResource` and `Binding`.

Listing 2.14   The Binding and StaticResource markup extensions in XAML

```
<UserControl x:Class="MarkupExtensionExample.MainPage"
  xmlns="http://schemas.microsoft.com/winfx/2006/xaml/presentation"
  xmlns:x="http://schemas.microsoft.com/winfx/2006/xaml"
  Width="400" Height="300">
  <UserControl.Resources>
    <Style x:Key="TextBlockStyle"              ◁──┐ Style
           TargetType="TextBlock">                 │ resource
      <Setter Property="FontSize"
             Value="25" />
      <Setter Property="Foreground"
             Value="DarkGray" />
    </Style>
  </UserControl.Resources>

  <StackPanel x:Name="LayoutRoot">                    ┌ Binding
    <TextBlock Text="{Binding LastName}"         ◁──┘ extension
            Style="{StaticResource TextBlockStyle}" />     ◁──
    <TextBlock Text="{Binding FirstName}"
            Style="{StaticResource TextBlockStyle}" />     ◁──  Reused
    <TextBlock Text="{Binding MiddleInitial}"                    style
            Style="{StaticResource TextBlockStyle}" />     ◁──
  </StackPanel>
</UserControl>
```

In the case of the `Text` example in listing 2.14, the markup extension is providing a value from the data binding engine. We'll cover data binding in chapter 11.

Markup extensions are a great way to get some additional functionality out of XAML, without needing to use a verbose object syntax. One downside is that you can't create them yourself. The two extensions you can create yourself are type converters and value converters.

2.3.2   Type converters

Type converters are used throughout the .NET framework to handle translation of one CLR type to another. Specifically in the context of XAML, type converters are used to convert string representations such as "Black" into their equivalent .NET CLR objects. In the case of the example in listing 2.14, a `SolidColorBrush` with `Color` set to `Black` is converted to a string that resolves to the color Red=0, Green=0, Blue=0, Alpha=255. This is shown in listing 2.15.

Listing 2.15   A type converter in action

```
<UserControl x:Class="TypeConverterExample.MainPage"
    xmlns="http://schemas.microsoft.com/winfx/2006/xaml/presentation"
    xmlns:x="http://schemas.microsoft.com/winfx/2006/xaml">
```

```
<Grid x:Name="LayoutRoot"
      Background="Black">
</Grid>
```
◁——┐ **Brush type**
       converter

```
</UserControl>
```

There are enough built-in type converters that you may never have to write a new one yourself. But they're an extensibility point in XAML and, therefore, provide you with flexibility to do some things that XAML may not handle natively.

CREATING CUSTOM TYPE CONVERTERS

First, since you need to decorate your type with a type converter attribute, you'll need access to the source. If you don't have access to the type source and can specify the converter just for a single property of your own class, that'll work too. The difference is that a converter specified at the property level will only work for that one property in that one class and not in all instances of that type in all properties and in all classes.

Next, you'll need to decide on a string format. The options are wide open, with the exception that you can't use the curly braces {} because they initialize the processing of markup extensions (discussed earlier in this chapter). Listing 2.16 shows a sample type converter that converts a string into a Border object. The format for the border is *<color> <thickness>*, where *color* is a named color or an eight-digit hex color and *thickness* is a number greater than or equal to zero.

Listing 2.16   A custom type converter that converts from a string to a border (C#)

```
public class BorderTypeConverter : TypeConverter          ◁——┐ TypeConverter
{                                                              base class
  public override bool CanConvertFrom(
    ITypeDescriptorContext context,
    Type sourceType)
  {
    return sourceType == typeof(string);          ◁——┐ XAML only
  }                                                    requires strings
  public override object ConvertFrom(
    ITypeDescriptorContext context,
    CultureInfo culture,
    object value)
  {
    string val = value as string;

    if (val == null) return null;
                                                │ Delimit
    string[] parts = val.Split(' ');     ◁——────┘ on space

    if (parts.Length < 2)         ◁——┐ Guard against        XamlReader.Load
      return null;                     malformed strings     to parse color

    SolidColorBrush brush = (SolidColorBrush)XamlReader.Load(
      "<SolidColorBrush " + "xmlns=" +
        "'http://schemas.microsoft.com/winfx/2006/xaml/presentation'"
    + " Color='" + parts[0] + "' />");          ◁──────

    double d;
    double.TryParse(parts[1], out d);     ◁—— Parse thickness
```

```
    Thickness thick = new Thickness(d);

    Border border = new Border();
    border.BorderThickness = thick;
    border.BorderBrush = brush;

    return border;
  }
}
```

Create
Border

Resulting
Border object

Note that this example, in order to be production ready, would require additional guard conditions and the ability to delimit on commas as well as spaces.

To create a custom type converter, you must first inherit from the `TypeConverter` base class. For the type converter to be used in XAML, you only need to support converting from the string type. More general-purpose converters will support additional types.

Note the hack I use to get the color information—it allows us to use any color representation that the XAML parser can parse. `XamlReader.Load` is a nifty function that has lots of uses, not only for its intended purpose of creating branches of the object tree at runtime but also for simply invoking the parser as we did here. Some things in Silverlight are simply easier to parse in XAML than they are in code—color is one of them.

NOTE The Silverlight color enumeration understands only a few of the many named colors, and the Silverlight `Color` class has no parse method to get the remaining colors or the hex representation. Using the XAML parser via `XamlReader.Load()` in listing 2.16, you reduce hundreds of lines of parsing code down to a single line. We'll cover more on the `XamlReader` class in the next section.

Listing 2.17 illustrates a simple example of our custom type converter. Note that this example also shows how to declare a dependency property—something we'll cover in more detail in chapter 24.

Listing 2.17 A simple class that uses our custom type converter

```
public class TestClass : Control
{

    [TypeConverter(typeof(BorderTypeConverter))]        ⟵── TypeConverterAttribute
    public Border Border
    {
        get { return (Border)GetValue(BorderProperty); }
        set { SetValue(BorderProperty, value); }
    }

    public static readonly DependencyProperty BorderProperty =
        DependencyProperty.Register("Border", typeof(Border),
        typeof(TestClass), null);

}
```

The `TypeConverterAttribute` that specifies the type converter to use for this specific property in this class is shown in listing 2.17. The attribute is applied to the public property because that's what's used by XAML. The converter is declared on the single property so it'll apply only there and not to all instances of the `Border` type. It's also important to note that the border isn't actually used for anything other than illustrating how to use a type converter.

Finally, listing 2.18 shows the type converter implicitly in use in XAML.

```
<UserControl x:Class="TypeConverterExample.MainPage"
  xmlns="http://schemas.microsoft.com/winfx/2006/xaml/presentation"
  xmlns:x="http://schemas.microsoft.com/winfx/2006/xaml"
  xmlns:local="clr-namespace:TypeConverterExample">

  <Grid x:Name="LayoutRoot">                          Type converter
    <local:TestClass Border="Red 5" />         ◁────┘  in use
  </Grid>
</UserControl>
```

Because we used the `XamlReader.Load` method, we could easily use any valid color string such as `"LemonCream"` or `"#C830019F"`. Bonus points if you caught the *Star Wars* reference in listing 2.18.

Colors in XAML

You may have given the color string #C830019F a double-take if you're used to six-digit HTML hex colors. Colors in Silverlight are typically expressed as eight-digit hex numbers, the first pair representing the alpha component and the remaining three pairs the red, green, and blue components in that order. In the color #C830019F, the values are Alpha: 0xC8, Red: 0x30, Green: 0x01, and Blue: 0x9F. The alpha component is optional, so you may use an HTML-style hex color if you wish. For consistency across the application, I recommend you specify the alpha value and use all eight digits without any shortcuts.

Type converters are a great way to extend the flexibility of XAML to include types you create yourself or new representations of existing types. We've used them in projects to provide serialization support for legacy format strings stored in databases and to extend the known representations of existing types.

Now that we understand the basics of XAML and have seen a simple example of dynamically loading XAML to parse a color string, let's take that a bit further and look at runtime loading or more complex content.

2.4   *Loading XAML at runtime*

In listing 2.16, we saw a brief example of loading XAML at runtime using `XamlReader.Load`. Let's expand on that to do more than just some basic color conversion.

You can use dynamically loaded XAML to create entire sections of the object tree at runtime. This could be useful for rendering user-generated content such as shapes drawn on a screen and saved in a database or for creating highly dynamic controls.

The process of loading XAML at runtime is incredibly easy. You only need to rely on the XamlReader class, which belongs to the System.Windows.Markup namespace. This class empowers you to parse XAML and convert it into an in-memory object. This object can be created by a statically visible method called Load. This method takes a string of XAML and converts it to the appropriate object. Then you can insert this object into another UIElement. Listing 2.19 shows this entire process in action.

Listing 2.19   Loading and parsing XAML at runtime

Result:

XAML:

```
<UserControl x:Class="XamlReaderExample.MainPage"
xmlns="http://schemas.microsoft.com/winfx/2006/xaml/presentation"
  xmlns:x="http://schemas.microsoft.com/winfx/2006/xaml"
  Width="400" Height="300">
  <Grid x:Name="LayoutRoot">

  </Grid>
</UserControl>
```

C#:

```
public MainPage()
{
  InitializeComponent();
  Loaded += new RoutedEventHandler(MainPage_Loaded);
}

void MainPage_Loaded(object sender, RoutedEventArgs e)
{
  var element = CreateRectangle();             // Add to
  LayoutRoot.Children.Add(element);            // tree
}

private Rectangle CreateRectangle()
{
  StringBuilder xaml = new StringBuilder();

  string ns =
"http://schemas.microsoft.com/winfx/2006/xaml/presentation";

  xaml.Append("<Rectangle ");                          // Namespace
  xaml.Append(string.Format("xmlns='{0}'", ns));       // declaration
  xaml.Append(" Margin='5 10 5 15'");
```

```
xaml.Append(" Fill='Orange'");
xaml.Append(" Stroke='Black' />");

var rectangle = (Rectangle)
    XamlReader.Load(xaml.ToString());      ⟵—— XamlReader.Load

return rectangle;
}
```

This example dynamically creates a rectangle and adds it to the object tree. The code in `CreateRectangle` simply builds up a string with XAML similar to what we'd have inside a regular .xaml file. Note that we need to specify the namespaces used for any segment of XAML we'll pass into `XamlReader.Load`. The code that adds the generated XAML to the object tree can be seen inside the loaded event.

You can of course do more with the element than just add it to the `LayoutRoot`. Listing 2.20 illustrates how we can take the XAML and integrate it with the managed code representations of XAML constructs to create multiple instances of the rectangle.

> **Listing 2.20   Mixing dynamic XAML with code**

Result:

XAML:

```
<UserControl x:Class="XamlReaderExample2.MainPage"
  xmlns="http://schemas.microsoft.com/winfx/2006/xaml/presentation"
  xmlns:x="http://schemas.microsoft.com/winfx/2006/xaml"
  Width="400" Height="300">
  <Grid x:Name="LayoutRoot">

  </Grid>
</UserControl>
```

C#:

```
public MainPage()
{
...
}

void MainPage_Loaded(object sender, RoutedEventArgs e)
{
  for (int i = 0; i < 4; i++)                          ⟵—┘ Loop to create
  {                                                         four instances
    RowDefinition def = new RowDefinition();
    LayoutRoot.RowDefinitions.Add(def);

    Rectangle rect = CreateRectangle();              ⟵—┘ Set grid
    Grid.SetRow(rect, i);                                 row
```

```
    LayoutRoot.Children.Add(rect);
  }
}

private Rectangle CreateRectangle()
{
...
}
```

In this example, we loop to create four instances of the rectangle object. We then dynamically create grid row definitions (see chapter 6) in code rather than in parsed XAML and assign them via attached properties to our rectangle object.

This shows a mix of the CLR representations of elements such as the grid row and the XAML representations of elements such as the rectangle. In practice, you'll rarely create visual elements in code except for specific circumstances, but the power and flexibility to do so is available to you.

That covers the core concepts for XAML. Next, we'll look at some of the tools you can use to make working in XAML more efficient.

2.5 *Tools for working in XAML*

So far we've looked at a lot of raw XAML files. When working on Silverlight applications, you'll find yourself bouncing back and forth between raw XAML and some sort of visual editor or design surface. Here are some of the tools available for working with Silverlight XAML files:

- *Visual Studio 2010*—Visual Studio 2008 provides a great XAML editor but a fairly useless Silverlight design surface, and it is limited to Silverlight 2 and 3. Visual Studio 2010 includes a fully capable Silverlight design surface that'll handle most of a developer's needs and includes full support for Silverlight 3 and 4. If you want to do more design-type work, including finer-grained control over the UI, animations, states, behaviors, and transitions, you'll want to use Expression Blend.

- *Expression Blend*—Expression Blend's sole reason for existence is to edit XAML. This is the primary XAML editor for both design professionals and creative developers. While someone used to typing markup may bounce back and forth between the XAML editor and the design surface, there's little in Blend that you can't accomplish with the designer alone.

- *Kaxaml*—Sometimes you don't want an editor as heavy as Visual Studio or Expression Blend. Kaxaml is a lightweight XAML editor created by Robby Ingebretsen. You can download Kaxaml for free from www.kaxaml.com.

- *Eclipse*—If you want some freedom on other platforms such as the Mac, you can use the Silverlight tools for Eclipse found at www.eclipse4sl.org to edit XAML files.

Hundreds of other tools have support for exporting or importing XAML. Typically these are graphics tools, add-ins to existing graphics tools such as Adobe Illustrator, or 3D tools with XAML add-ins. Many of them are primarily targeted at WPF, but work at least partially with Silverlight.

2.6   *Summary*

Silverlight development is all about code plus markup. To make the most of the platform, you'll want to learn how to leverage the capabilities that XAML provides, while keeping a balance between what you write in code and what you put in the markup. Learning the markup language will allow you to use tooling to quickly create great user interfaces, work on a team including designers and developers without friction, and help enforce the separation of the view from the rest of the application architecture.

A basic understanding of XAML is fundamental to getting the most from the rest of this book and from Silverlight itself. In later chapters, we'll expand on what we did here to encompass topics such as brushes, shapes, controls, animation, and all of the other things that make Silverlight such a great presentation platform.

In the next chapter, we'll cover the Silverlight plug-in and how to use it to create applications that run inside and outside the browser.

The application
model and the plug-in

Application is an overloaded term that means different things to different people. Some may question what level of footprint, functionality, or other metrics you need to meet before something can be called an application. For example, is the weather tracker sidebar gadget in Windows an application? What about Notepad? The code for the sidebar gadget is almost certainly more complex than Notepad, but most people would see Notepad as an application and the sidebar gadget as, well, a gadget.

In my participation in the Silverlight community, I've been asked on a number of occasions what to call the Silverlight "thing" that the plug-in loads in the browser. How I answer that depends on the context of the question and the nature of the Silverlight thing. In this chapter we're going to talk about Silverlight applications. In the context of this chapter, we'll use the term *application* in the technical sense of the word: a compiled runnable Silverlight project. The application can be as small as a tiny menu widget or a "punch the monkey" ad on a web page or as complex as some of the Microsoft and Adobe tools I've used to write this book. We'll leave the other question of when something can be called an application open so we have something interesting to debate at code camp.

Regardless of our own individual definitions of application, a Silverlight application consists of a .xap file with our compiled code, entry-point information, potentially some resources, and a host for the Silverlight plug-in.

As we saw in chapter 1, you can get up and running with Silverlight with little understanding of these concepts, thanks to the great templates provided by Microsoft. But as a developer, you have a natural curiosity to dig deeper and learn more about what's going on when the magic happens and the Silverlight content lights up on the web page, both because you'll need the knowledge once your applications reach more than "Hello World!" complexity, and also because it's neat stuff. The core information upon which we'll build in the rest of this book is the Silverlight application model and the Silverlight plug-in.

3.1   The Silverlight application model

Silverlight applications consist of at least one or more compiled .NET dynamic-link libraries (DLLs) and a manifest file, all compressed into a file known as *XAP* (pronounced "zap"). This is all loaded into the plug-in at runtime and then executed at a specific entry point to start your application.

The .xap file is the key deployment mechanism for all Silverlight managed code applications. When we talk about deploying a Silverlight application, we're really talking about two things:

- Surfacing the .xap to the client via some URI
- Instantiating the Silverlight plug-in on the web page or within a hosting out-of-browser process

That's it. There's no additional installation, no .msi to install, no registry entries, no elevation prompts (unless you request elevated rights). It's all about getting content down to the end user and instantiated in the plug-in with as little friction as possible. The subtleties of how that process works are what I find particularly interesting.

When I first learned ASP.NET—back when a 17-inch display would take up your whole desk, contain more glass than your car, and weigh about 200 lb—one of the things I was most curious about was the startup cycle and the order of events when a request was made. If you want to understand how to target a particular application platform, you really need to know how it's going to run your application, when things get loaded, when they're rendered, and how key decisions are made—the application startup process.

3.1.1   Application startup process

What happens when you enter a web page that contains a Silverlight application? The application startup process is shown in figure 3.1. The flowchart includes the details for Silverlight 1 through 4 but doesn't address dynamic languages. The "XAML or

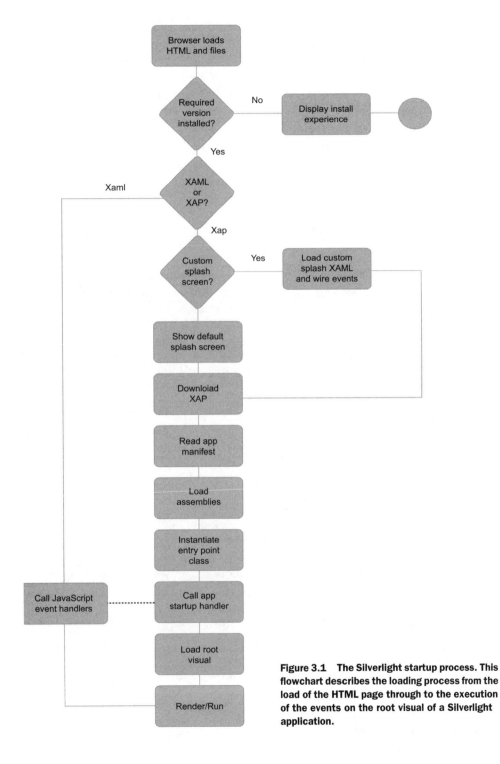

Figure 3.1 The Silverlight startup process. This flowchart describes the loading process from the load of the HTML page through to the execution of the events on the root visual of a Silverlight application.

XAP" step is what makes the decision between the old Silverlight 1.0 model and the current Silverlight 2+ model. That decision is based on a combination of the source (a .xaml or .xap file) and the specified type property of the plug-in.

The dotted line between the JavaScript and the managed code event handlers is there because, though you typically wouldn't do it, you can have both JavaScript and managed handlers active for the load event of the application. The order in which they fire in relation to each other isn't guaranteed.

Some additional parts of the process aren't displayed in figure 3.1 but are interesting nonetheless. For example, when the Silverlight plug-in determines it'll have a managed code .xap file to work with, it loads the Silverlight .NET CLR (CoreCLR) into the memory space of the browser.

CoreCLR

Silverlight 2+ uses a version of the Common Language Runtime (CLR) known as *CoreCLR*. This is a version of the .NET CLR that has been optimized for size and use for client-side rich Internet applications (RIAs). The CoreCLR shares code with the full .NET CLR for core bits such as the type system, the workstation-optimized garbage collector, and the just-in-time (JIT) compiler. These size optimizations and intelligent decisions on what is and isn't necessary for a client-side RIA allow the Silverlight plug-in, including the CoreCLR, to come in at around 5 MB total size. For more details on CoreCLR, see Andrew Pardoe's CoreCLR MSDN article at http://msdn.microsoft.com/en-us/magazine/cc721609.aspx.

Apparent in all this is that the most important artifact in the process is the Silverlight application itself: the .xap file.

3.1.2   *XAP*

A managed code Silverlight application is packaged into a .xap when built. A .xap is simply a ZIP file and may be inspected by renaming it to .zip and opening it with any zip-compatible archiver. The contents of a typical .xap file are shown in figure 3.2.

This compressed file will always contain a manifest file named AppManifest.xaml. In addition, there will always be a .dll file that serves as the entry point into the Silverlight application. This application may require other Silverlight libraries, service connection information, or other types of content. Content items and additional libraries may be in the application .xap file or downloaded at runtime; either way, they represent the dependencies of the application.

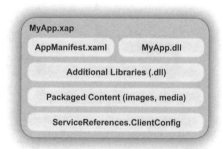

Figure 3.2 Structure of a typical .xap file showing the types of files that are normally included

Because the .xap file is a ZIP-compatible compressed archive, you may alter its contents and rezip it after compilation. Reasons for doing this include updating the service references to move from (for example) a test environment to a production environment or altering other environment or customer-specific XML configuration files, branding assets, or other content.

You can also slightly decrease a .xap file's size by rezipping it with an efficient ZIP tool such as 7-Zip, at the expense of a slightly slower decompression and application startup time on older machines. This may be important in situations where bandwidth is at an extreme premium.

The .xap contains a number of different files. One of which is the file that tells Silverlight what other files the .xap contains and where to find the application entry point—the application manifest file.

3.1.3   The application manifest file

The manifest file is responsible for describing the Silverlight application to the Silverlight runtime. This file is created at build time by Visual Studio and is typically not hand edited.

The Silverlight runtime reads the AppManifest.xaml file beginning with the root-most element, `Deployment`. This element exposes two attributes that tell the Silverlight runtime how to start the Silverlight application, as shown here:

```
<Deployment
  xmlns="http://schemas.microsoft.com/client/2007/deployment"
  xmlns:x="http://schemas.microsoft.com/winfx/2006/xaml"
  EntryPointAssembly="MyApp" EntryPointType="MyApp.App"
  RuntimeVersion="4.0.50401.0">
  <Deployment.Parts>
    <AssemblyPart x:Name="MyApp" Source="MyApp.dll" />
  </Deployment.Parts>
</Deployment>
```

This example shows a basic manifest file, which uses the `EntryPointAssembly` and `EntryPointType` attributes to launch the Silverlight application. The first attribute, `EntryPointAssembly`, will always reference one of the `AssemblyPart` elements in the `Deployment.Parts` section. The second attribute, `EntryPointType`, explains which class should be used to start the Silverlight application. The third attribute, called `RuntimeVersion`, broadcasts the version of the Silverlight runtime that the Silverlight application was built with.

> **NOTE** AppManifest.xaml is generated during project compilation based on the settings found in the project's property pages. If you change the name and/or namespace of the startup application class (`App`), then you must adjust the Startup object setting in the Silverlight property page. If you forget to make these changes, you'll get a runtime error mentioning an invalid or missing Silverlight application.

The `Deployment` section of the manifest contains two sections:

- `Deployment.Parts`
- `Deployment.ExternalParts`

We'll cover `Deployment.ExternalParts` in section 3.1.6 when we discuss assembly caching because it's only used in caching situations. `Deployment.Parts` is used regardless of the caching strategy used.

DEPLOYMENT.PARTS

The `Deployment.Parts` section includes a collection of `AssemblyPart` entries, each of which corresponds to a DLL in our application. In a complete application, at least one of the DLLs will be the entry point assembly.

As we saw here, the application manifest contains a reference to the startup object type and assembly. The startup object is always the Silverlight application object.

3.1.4 *The Silverlight application object*

The entry point into the Silverlight application is the `App` object. This object is defined in the App.xaml and App.xaml.cs files and derives from the `System.Windows.Application` type. This type allows you to interact with the three events affecting the application's lifecycle—the start of the application, the unhandled errors in the application, and the exit of the application. In addition to these events, you can also read the settings of the hosting plug-in.

MANAGING THE START OF A SILVERLIGHT APPLICATION

Once the `App` object has been created, the `Startup` event fires. By default, this event loads the default XAML page into view. You can also use this event to perform any other type of application initialization task. For instance, you may want to use this event to set application-wide resources or properties. Or, you may want to use this event to load the `initParams` that were passed into the application (see section 3.3.4). Either way, this type of task can be accomplished by using the `Startup` event:

```
private void Application_Startup(object sender, StartupEventArgs e)
{
  foreach (string key in e.InitParams.Keys)
  {
    // Process the initParam from the createObjectEx function
  }

  this.RootVisual = new MainPage();
}
```

This particular event handler shows how to parse the `initParams` that may have been passed into the application. The `Startup` event creates a `StartupEventArgs` variable that assists in the initialization tasks. The first iterates through the initialization parameters. You could access the individual dictionary entries by a string key. The second task in this listing displays the first page of the application. Both of these tasks introduce important facts about the Silverlight application lifecycle.

The first important fact is that the `StartupEventArgs` type is created only by the `Startup` event. No other event in Silverlight will create a `StartupEventArgs` object. Because of this, it's logical to deduce that the `InitParams` used in the preceding code are only available during application startup. If you're going to use initialization parameters, the `Startup` event is your only chance to use them. If you need to access them throughout the application, you'll want to store them in the singleton application settings or the data class of your own creation. In addition to the initialization parameters, you should consider the RootVisual.

The RootVisual is the content that Silverlight will load into the root of the object tree. (For more on object trees, see chapter 2.) Typically, this is a master-page style application page. In the default Silverlight templates, it's MainPage.

Once set, the RootVisual of the application can't be changed for the lifetime of the application. This may cause confusion because you may wonder how to switch pages in a Silverlight application. Think of the root visual in a complex multipage application more as a container for other content pages. We'll get to that when we discuss navigation in chapter 15. For now, know that when the Startup event has completed, the RootVisual will be loaded and rendered. At this point, a Silverlight application will be visible to your users, so let's begin discussing how to guard against unforeseen errors.

HANDLING UNFORESEEN ERRORS

The Application.UnhandledException event enables you to handle uncaught exceptions. Any Exception that hasn't been caught by a try-catch block in the application will be sent here. This is the last chance to gracefully deal with an unknown problem by displaying a message or perhaps logging to a service or isolated storage:

```
private void Application_UnhandledException(object sender,
  ApplicationUnhandledExceptionEventArgs e)
{
  LogError(e.ExceptionObject);
  e.Handled = true;
}
```

This shows a basic UnhandledException event handler. The event handler uses an argument to assist in properly handling an unhandled exception. This argument is of the ApplicationUnhandledExceptionEventArgs type, which gives you access to the Exception that caused the event through the ExceptionObject property. Once this Exception has been dealt with, you need to signal that you've found an acceptable solution. You can accomplish this by setting the ApplicationUnhandledException-EventArgs object's Handled property.

The Handled property is a bool value that signals whether an exception has been addressed. By default, this property value is set to false but you have the opportunity to set it to true within your code. By setting this property to true, you signal that your Silverlight application should continue to run. If this property remains false, the Silverlight plug-in will unload the application, causing the plug-in's onError event to be fired. We'll discuss this event in section 3.3.3. Note that this unnatural way of ending an application won't trigger the Application.Exit event.

EXITING THE SILVERLIGHT APPLICATION

The Application.Exit event is the last thing that occurs before an application is shut down and provides one last opportunity to wrap things up. This event can be useful for logging information or performing last-minute saves. The Application.Exit event is fired when one of the following happens:

- The user closes the browser window.
- The user closes the browser tab that the Silverlight application is running in.
- The user navigates away from the Silverlight application (such as going from www.mySilverlightApplication.com to www.silverlightinaction.com).
- The HTML element associated with the Silverlight plug-in is removed from the HTML Document Object Model (DOM).

This event doesn't have any special event handling parameters like the `Startup` and `UnhandledException` events, but it can still read settings associated with the plug-in, if needed. Note that, when this event is fired, the browser has already been closed (if closing was the cause) and the Silverlight application has already disappeared. Therefore, displaying XAML UI or attempting to prevent the browser page from closing isn't supported. You may display an HTML message box if you absolutely must get some UI in front of the user:

```
private void Application_Exit(object sender, EventArgs e)
{
    MessageBox.Show("Daisy, daisy...");
}
```

But you can still obtain information about the HTML page that's hosting the application. For example, this displays a message box containing the URL of the page hosting the Silverlight application, even though that page is no longer visible:

```
private void Application_Exit(object sender, EventArgs e)
{
    HtmlDocument doc = System.Windows.Browser.HtmlPage.Document;
    MessageBox.Show(doc.DocumentUri.ToString());
}
```

Keep in mind that other dynamic elements on the HTML page may have their own shutdown handling, so be careful of how much you access from this event. A best practice is to do as little as possible in this event, keeping in mind that you no longer have the Silverlight UI displayed to the user.

One thing you can do in this event (and the others) is read plug-in settings.

READING PLUG-IN SETTINGS

Once the Silverlight application has been loaded, you can retrieve information about the hosting plug-in. This plug-in exposes information set during the creation of the plug-in (`createObjectEx`; see section 3.2.3). This information is useful throughout the entire life of the application and can be accessed through the `Host` property of the `Application`:

```
Application.Current.Host;
```

The Host property on the `Application` object is a `SilverlightHost`, which gives you access to information about the plug-in. The information is listed and described in table 3.1.

This table shows the properties available through the `SilverlightHost` object. These properties give you access to most of the information discussed in this chapter,

Table 3.1   The properties of the SilverlightHost object

Property	Description
Background	Retrieves the background `Color` of the plug-in.
Content	The `content` subobject of the `createObjectEx` function call. This includes the height and width of the plug-in.
IsLoaded	Returns whether the hosting plug-in has completed loading.
Settings	The `settings` subobject of the `createObjectEx` function call. This subobject relays information about the Silverlight application's instantiation settings. In addition, this subobject provides values associated with the HTML DOM.
Source	The `Uri` of the currently loaded XAML content.

which enables you to dynamically create a truly integrated experience. This experience will have a beginning, which can be managed through the `Startup` event. In addition, this experience will have an ending, which can be handled through the `Exit` event. These are the main events affecting the life of an `Application`. In addition, this `Application` may have other types of content that it depends upon. This content makes up what are known as the application dependencies.

3.1.5   Application dependencies

Application dependencies are items that your application needs to run correctly. These items include assemblies, images, audio or video files, fonts, XAML files, configuration files, or any other type of file. Each file that'll be used by the Silverlight application can be included in the .xap file. This approach can ensure a faster access time, but it can also cause a slower initial download of your application.

To help you overcome long load times, Silverlight allows you to divide your application into smaller chunks that can be downloaded as they're needed. This approach can ensure a faster initial application download, but it doesn't happen automatically. Instead, you must rely on a class called `WebClient`, which is discussed in chapter 14, or use the built-in partitioning functionality from the Managed Extensibility Framework (MEF). For now, just know that you have a way of including application dependencies.

Application dependencies belong to just one set of the items you may find in a .xap file. This file also includes a DLL, which contains an `Application`. This `Application` is described by the AppManifest.xaml file, which is used by the Silverlight runtime to start the application.

Other DLLs required on initial load of the application must either be included in the .xap file or found through the assembly cache.

3.1.6   Assembly caching

Assembly caching was introduced with Silverlight 3 to provide a way to avoid packaging common DLLs into every application .xap. Since the DLLs are usually hosted on your own server, you may include both third-party DLLs as well as DLLs common across your own applications. This can reduce initial application load time and make subsequent upgrades to your application easy to deploy and superfast to download.

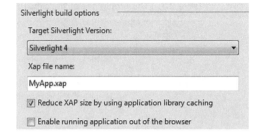

To use assembly caching, select the Reduce XAP Size by Using Application Library Caching option on the project Silverlight property page, as shown in figure 3.3.

Figure 3.3 Setting the assembly caching option via the project property pages for the Silverlight project

Note that assembly caching is available only for browser-hosted applications—it doesn't currently work for out-of-browser applications.

HOW IT WORKS

Here's the `Deployment.Parts` section of the application manifest for a simple application that uses one Microsoft assembly not included in the core runtime:

```
<Deployment.Parts>
   <AssemblyPart x:Name="AssemblyCaching"
                 Source="AssemblyCaching.dll" />
   <AssemblyPart x:Name="System.ComponentModel.DataAnnotations"
                 Source="System.ComponentModel.DataAnnotations.dll" />
</Deployment.Parts>
```

Note that we have our application assembly AssemblyCaching.dll and the Microsoft assembly all packaged in the same .xap file. The resulting file size is 29 KB. Hardly large by web standards, but we know it could be even smaller.

Once we select the option to use cached framework extension assemblies, the manifest changes to include a new section named `Deployment.ExternalParts`:

```
<Deployment.Parts>
   <AssemblyPart x:Name="AssemblyCaching" Source="AssemblyCaching.dll" />
</Deployment.Parts>
<Deployment.ExternalParts>
   <ExtensionPart Source="System.ComponentModel.DataAnnotations.zip" />
</Deployment.ExternalParts>
```

The `ExtensionPart` entries in the `Deployment.ExternalParts` section correspond to the Microsoft DLL that was originally packaged in our application. Now, instead of including them in the application package, they'll be downloaded from your server on first access and then cached locally for future use. Upon compiling your application, you'll see that the ClientBin folder on the website will have one ZIP file added for each `ExtensionPart` included in the manifest. Each ZIP file contains just the compressed DLL—no additional baggage.

TIP If you want to reduce per-application load time on a site that uses Silverlight on various pages, you could preload the cache by creating a small headless Silverlight application on a landing page and ensuring that it references all of the required assemblies and has assembly caching turned on. Your decision depends on the nature of the site and the landing page and whether you consider it okay to download several KB of binaries that may not be used.

Assembly caching is available for any assembly you use. The core Microsoft DLLs have a built-in support because they include *<dllname>*.extmap.xml files for each DLL in the software development kit (SDK). If you want to add support for your own (or a third party) DLLs, you'll need to create an .extmap.xml file for each DLL. The .extmap.xml file looks like this:

```
<?xml version="1.0"?>
<manifest xmlns:xsi="http://www.w3.org/2001/XMLSchema-instance"
          xmlns:xsd="http://www.w3.org/2001/XMLSchema">
  <assembly>
    <name>System.ComponentModel.DataAnnotations</name>
    <version>2.0.5.0</version>
    <publickeytoken>31bf3856ad364e35</publickeytoken>
    <relpath>System.ComponentModel.DataAnnotations.dll</relpath>
    <extension downloadUri="System.ComponentModel.DataAnnotations.zip" />
  </assembly>
</manifest>
```

If you provide an absolute URI, the assembly will be served up by that URI. This is useful for third parties or independent software vendors (ISVs) who may want to offer hosting of their DLLs or for organizations that want to have a centralized location for common application DLLs. Note that the server hosting the DLL will need to adhere to cross-domain restrictions by providing a ClientAccessPolicy.xml file to support clients calling it from other servers.

The files are cached in the default browser cache for the current browser so they can be used by any other Silverlight application that has enabled assembly caching. If you use multiple browsers, you'll need to download and cache for each browser just like any other web content. Similarly, the content can be cleared from the cache like any other browser content.

The end result is a .xap that weighs in at all of 4 KB, much smaller than most on-page icons and an almost instantaneous download for your users. Assembly caching can really make a difference in the load time of your applications.

At this point, we've covered all the core bits of a Silverlight application, including the startup process, key events, packaging applications, and sharing assemblies between applications. Next we'll discuss how to surface those applications on a web page using the Silverlight plug-in.

3.2   *Creating the Silverlight plug-in*

The Silverlight plug-in is a lightweight cross-platform browser plug-in responsible for rendering Silverlight content. To ensure cross-platform and cross-browser support, the Silverlight plug-in must take advantage of each browser's plug-in technology. This requirement forces the plug-in to be packaged differently across platforms. For instance, when Silverlight runs within Microsoft's Internet Explorer browser, the ActiveX model is used. Alternatively, if Safari or Chrome is used, the WebKit model is used. When any other browser is used, the plug-in uses the Netscape Server API (NSAPI) plug-in approach. Regardless of the combination of browsers a user chooses, Silverlight only needs to be installed one time on a workstation to work across all supported browsers.

The Silverlight installation is extremely compact, weighing in at around 5 to 6 MB on Windows. This installation requires that users have administrative privileges on their machines. If they don't have these privileges, an administrator will need to assist them. Once the Silverlight plug-in is installed on their machines, users are free to enjoy rich Silverlight content in the browser of their choice without additional installation requirements.

Installation rights

Silverlight requires administrative rights to install the plug-in on Windows operating systems. This was a conscious decision by the Silverlight team to allow Silverlight to be installed once per machine rather than require managing installations per user, per machine. In centrally managed environments, where administrative rights aren't typically given to users, Silverlight may be installed via tools such as Windows Server Update Services (WSUS). Once the plug-in is installed, individual applications don't require admin rights because they're treated as content by the browser.

The goal of creating a Silverlight plug-in is to host a Silverlight application. This plug-in can be created in at least three different ways. One approach is to use the HTML object tag directly. Another is to use the deprecated Silverlight server control that's part of the Silverlight 2 SDK, but is no longer included with Silverlight 3+.

Another approach for creating a Silverlight plug-in enables you to easily deliver Silverlight content through any server technology while ensuring maximum flexibility on the client. You can use Silverlight along with a variety of technologies including PHP, JSP, ASP, and ASP.NET. To get Silverlight to work with these technologies, you use the two steps covered in this section. The first step is to reference the required Silverlight JavaScript utility file. The second step involves writing the JavaScript that'll create an instance of the Silverlight plug-in.

The pros and cons of the three approaches are covered in table 3.2.

Table 3.2   Pros and cons of the three plug-in creation approaches

Approach	Pros	Cons
ASP.NET Silverlight control	Simple to use Server-side access to plug-in properties, including initialization parameters	Deprecated in Silverlight 3+ but still available as part of the Silverlight 2 SDK. No longer recommended for new projects.
HTML object tag	No additional libraries No server dependency	Basic installation experience Older versions of Internet Explorer displayed a warning dialog
Silverlight.js utility functions	Complete control over the installation experience for various client configurations No server dependency	Additional effort Requires keeping the Silverlight.js file up to date

What happened to the ASP.NET Silverlight control?

The ASP.NET Silverlight control is still available as part of the Silverlight 2 SDK and on the MSDN Code Gallery (http://go.microsoft.com/fwlink/?LinkId=156721), but it is no longer maintained as part of the Silverlight tools. The object tag and Silverlight.js approaches provide more flexibility. When porting your Silverlight 2 projects to Silverlight 4, you may continue to use the ASP.NET Silverlight control as long as you update the minimum version number and add the required iframe if using navigation. But it's recommended that you port to one of the other two approaches.

Since the ASP.NET approach is no longer supported, we'll skip that and instead cover the object tag approach. After that, we'll dig right into using the Silverlight.js utility functions.

3.2.1   Using the object tag

You may choose to explicitly create the object tag that hosts your Silverlight application. This approach is used in the "Instantiating a Silverlight Plug-In" section of the Silverlight SDK. The reason I use the Silverlight.js approach in this book is because there are additional methods, such as buildPromptInstall and isInstalled, in the Silverlight.js file. If you want to explicitly create an object tag, you can do so by embedding the code similar to the following:

```
<div id="mySilverlightHost" style="height:100%;">
  <object
    id="SilverlightPlugInID"
    data="data:application/x-silverlight-2,"
    type="application/x-silverlight-2"
    width="100%" height="100%">
    <param name="source" value="ClientBin/MySilverlightApp.xap" />
  </object>
  </div>
```

Note that the data and type are both `x-silverlight-2`. The `-2` in this case doesn't mean Silverlight 2; it means version 2 of the Silverlight MIME type. If, in the future, Microsoft decides to change the object tag signature in some way, they may introduce an `x-silverlight-3` for MIME type version 3 even though the related version of Silverlight may be something like Silverlight 8. That's not expected at this time.

In general, the properties specific to the Silverlight plug-in can be set through the `param` elements. There are some exceptions to this. If you decide to explicitly create the object tag, we recommend referring to the documentation in the Silverlight SDK.

Getting just a blank page?

There are many reasons why you might get the Silverlight White Screen of Death (WSOD), such as bad XAML, incorrect .xap file location, errors in startup code, and so forth. The WSOD appears when the Silverlight plug-in is present and instantiated (verified by right-clicking) but devoid of content.

One of the most common WSOD causes for first-time users is a missing MIME type on the web server. If you're using Windows Server 2003 or older, ensure the MIME type `x-silverlight-app` is registered. This MIME type is present on Server 2008 R1 and newer. Many other web servers, such as some versions of Apache, will serve the content up without any MIME type registration.

3.2.2   *Using the Silverlight.js utility file*

The Silverlight.js utility file is part of the free Silverlight SDK and also part of the Visual Studio Silverlight project templates. The Silverlight SDK is available through the Silverlight web site at http://silverlight.net/getstarted, and installed as part of the Silverlight tools installation package. Once you've downloaded the SDK, you can find the Silverlight.js file in the installation's Tools directory. This file is an integral part of every Silverlight application, so you should know where to find it. Then, you can distribute and reference this file within your applications. Once it's referenced, you can use any number of the valuable features exposed by this file.

> **NOTE** Microsoft periodically releases new versions of the Silverlight.js file, related files such as Silverlight.supportedUserAgent.js, and associated documentation. To facilitate distribution to developers, Microsoft created a Code Gallery project for Silverlight.js. You can download the latest version of Silverlight.js from http://code.msdn.microsoft.com/silverlightjs.

REFERENCING THE SILVERLIGHT.JS FILE

The Silverlight.js file is licensed under the Microsoft Public License (Ms-PL), which allows you to modify the file to suit your own needs if necessary. Referencing the Silverlight.js file is as easy as referencing any other script file: you set the `src` property of an HTML `script` tag:

```
<html xmlns="http://www.w3.org/1999/xhtml" >
<head>
  <title>My Silverlight Project</title>
  <script type="text/javascript" src="Silverlight.js">
```

```
➡    </script>
   <!-- Other Script and Style References -->
</head>
<body>
   <!-- We will create a Silverlight plug-in here -->
</body>
</html>
```

You gain the ability to create a Silverlight plug-in by adding a reference to the Silverlight.js JavaScript file. Let's look at what's inside.

THE FUNCTIONS OF THE SILVERLIGHT.JS FILE

The Silverlight.js file exposes a number of valuable functions. These functions give you the flexibility to tailor a custom experience within a web application. Table 3.3 describes the primary utility functions in alphabetical order.

Table 3.3   The primary utility functions exposed through the Silverlight.js utility file

Function name	Function description
`buildPromptHTML`	Returns the HTML that creates the Silverlight installation prompt. Takes a Silverlight object in order to determine the prompt to build.
`createObject`	Initializes and creates a Silverlight plug-in. The details and a sample of this method are posted in the next section.
`createObjectEx`	Initializes and creates a Silverlight plug-in. The details and a sample of this method are posted in the next section. In addition, the next section will explain the difference between the `createObjectEx` and `createObject` functions.
`HtmlAttributeEncode`	Performs some basic operations to encode a string into an HTML-encoded string. This internal function was primarily designed to be used only within the realm of the Silverlight.js file, so use caution. Here's an example: `var result = Silverlight.HtmlAttributeEncode('"Hello"');`
`isInstalled`	Returns whether a specific version of the Silverlight runtime is available. This method takes one parameter, a string that represents a version number. Here's an example: `var result = Silverlight.isInstalled("3.0");`

These methods provide a powerful arsenal of options to help deliver the appropriate experience to your users. But two options encapsulate most of the other functions under one roof—the `createObject` and `createObjectEx` functions. These two utility functions shoulder the responsibility of creating an instance of the Silverlight plug-in.

3.2.3   *Creating an instance of the Silverlight plug-in*

To initialize and create a Silverlight plug-in, you use one of two utility functions: `createObject` or `createObjectEx`. These methods do the same thing; in fact, `createObjectEx` calls `createObject`. But the `createObjectEx` function uses the more verbose JavaScript Object Notation (JSON) approach to pass in the necessary parameters. For this reason, we'll use `createObjectEx` in this book.

The createObjectEx function requires an HTML element as a parameter. This element ultimately serves as the host for the Silverlight plug-in. Because of this, you must first either identify or create the HTML element to serve as the host. Then within that element, you call the createObjectEx method to add a Silverlight control as a child to the hosting HTML element. The creation process is shown in listing 3.1.

Listing 3.1   Instantiating the Silverlight control (HTML)

```
<html xmlns="http://www.w3.org/1999/xhtml" >
<head>                                                    Silverlight.js
  <title>My Silverlight Project</title>                     reference
  <script type="text/javascript" src="Silverlight.js"></script>
</head>
<body style="height:100%">                               Hosting
  <div id="mySilverlightHost" style="height:100%;">      DIV
    <script type="text/javascript">
                                                          Create Silverlight
      Silverlight.createObjectEx({ #C                     object
        source: "ClientBin/MySilverlightApp.xap",
        parentElement: document.getElementById("mySilverlightHost"),
       id: "mySilverlightControl",
        properties: {
          width: "100%",
          height: "100%",
          version: "3.0"
        },
        events: {}
      });
    </script>
  </div>
</body>
</html>
```

This listing demonstrates the two main steps of creating a Silverlight plug-in. The first step is to reference the Silverlight.js utility file. Once this file is referenced, you create an instance of the Silverlight plug-in, in a specific HTML <div> tag, using the createObjectEx function.

This function accepts a wide range of parameters, which are responsible for specifying which Silverlight application to run and how it should be integrated within a web page. Because a Silverlight application will ultimately be integrated within a web page, even if only as the installation source for an out-of-browser application, we need to discuss how to integrate a Silverlight control with the surrounding page.

3.3   *Integrating the Silverlight plug-in*

Once you've decided to create a Silverlight plug-in, you must ensure that it integrates nicely within your web page. This integration must not only look right but it must also behave properly. So, let's study the items you can control. At a high level, these items give you the ability to:

- Relate your Silverlight application to the HTML DOM.
- Clarify the initial experience.
- Handle plug-in events.
- Send initialization parameters.

These general tasks cover a lot of ground, but we're going to dive into the details that make each task possible.

3.3.1 *Relating the Silverlight application to the HTML DOM*

The first three parameters of `createObjectEx` function build the relationship between a Silverlight application and the HTML DOM. These parameters are called `source`, `parentElement`, and `id`.

SOURCE

The `source` parameter specifies the URI of the Silverlight content that should be loaded. In a managed code application, this content is bundled up as a .xap file, as discussed earlier in this chapter. The `source` property can reference a .xap file on the hosting server or on a remote server. This gives you the ability to easily share your Silverlight applications and improve server performance through load balancing. This isn't as easy with Silverlight 1.0.

Silverlight 1.0 didn't have support for .xap files. Instead, Silverlight 1.0 relied on setting the source of a plug-in through one of two approaches. The first approach involves referencing a .xaml file that exists on the hosting server. The other approach is to reference XAML content defined in the hosting web page. This type of XAML content is known as *inline XAML*. Either way, both of these approaches are dependent upon the JavaScript programming model. Silverlight 2+ still supports these approaches so that the `source` property in Silverlight 4 can be used in three different ways, all of which are shown in table 3.4.

Table 3.4 The three approaches for referencing a Silverlight application

Approach	File extension	Example[a]
Packaged	.xap	`source: "http://www.myserver.com/myApp.xap"`
Loose	.xaml	`source: "/relativePath/page.xaml"`
Inline	[none]	`source: "#myXamlID"`

a. Assuming this is part of a `createObjectEx` call

We won't be discussing the loose and inline approaches in detail because the packaged approach is the most widely used and is the only option that supports the managed code Silverlight 2+ APIs. It's recommended because of its flexible, compact, and portable nature. Regardless of the approach you choose, the Silverlight plug-in is always placed inside the `parentElement`.

PARENTELEMENT

The parentElement parameter specifies the HTML object that hosts the Silverlight plug-in. It's important to recognize that this property requires an object and not just the ID of the parent. You may need to use the HTML DOM approach of retrieving an object using document.getElementById. Once the object is retrieved, a new HTML element will be appended to it when the Silverlight plug-in is created.

The specific type of object that is created is based on the user's browser. If the user is using Internet Explorer or Firefox, an HTML OBJECT element is created. Alternatively, if the user is using Safari, an HTML EMBED element is created. Regardless of the type of object, it gets appended to the element you defined as the parentElement.

This newly created HTML object is given the unique identifier you set in the id parameter.

ID

The unique identifier of the Silverlight plug-in is specified by the third parameter of the createObjectEx method, id. The value you must supply to this parameter is the id attribute of the OBJECT or EMBED element mentioned in the previous section. This parameter is the primary hook from the HTML DOM to the Silverlight plug-in. You can easily access a Silverlight plug-in using the document.getElementById function. This function is available within the HTML DOM Document object, and you can use it from a scripting environment such as JavaScript. This fact will come into play at the end of this chapter. But we should first discuss how to clarify a user's default experience.

3.3.2   *Clarifying the initial experience*

While a Silverlight plug-in is being initialized, a number of properties clarify how that plug-in will initially render. These properties are demonstrated here:

```
Silverlight.createObjectEx({
  source: "ClientBin/MySilverlightApp.xap",
  parentElement: document.getElementById("mySilverlightHost"),
  id: "mySilverlightControl",
  properties: {
    height: "100%",
    width: "100%",
    background: "blue",
    isWindowless: "true",
    frameRate: "30",
    inplaceInstallPrompt: true,
    version: "4.0",
    ignoreBrowserVer: "true",
    enableHtmlAccess: "true"
  },
  events: {}
});
```

These properties can be used to define an initial experience. (All the properties listed here use pretend values to show the syntax.) We'll explain the details of each of these properties in the order they're shown. In addition, these properties will be logically grouped together when possible, such as height and width.

HEIGHT AND WIDTH+

The `height` and `width` properties specify the boundaries of the rectangular region that the Silverlight application will be presented within. By default, these property values represent a rectangle with no `height` and no `width`. You can change this by providing either a pixel or percentage value, as you can with other HTML elements to provide either absolute or relative sizing.

Relative sizing is a widely used technique within the HTML world, so it's nice to see that the Silverlight plug-in provides this option to simplify integration efforts. To further integrate your Silverlight content within the HTML page, you need to use the `background` and `isWindowless` properties.

BACKGROUND AND ISWINDOWLESS

The `background` property allows you to specify the color of the rectangular region where the Silverlight plug-in will appear. By default, this property is set to `null`, which is the same as white. There are two techniques for setting this property value. The first is to use a hexadecimal color value. The second is to use a color name recognized by the user's browser, such as `Silver`. Perhaps the most interesting option, though, enables you to hide the background entirely.

By setting the `background` property to `transparent`, you can make the background of the plug-in region invisible. At the same time, your Silverlight application is still completely visible. Before you get too excited, we strongly recommend searching for alternatives before using this option. When the `background` property is set to `transparent`, your Silverlight applications will incur a significant performance hit, which may detract from a user's experience, especially when playing media or doing heavy animation. In addition, if you choose to use the `transparent` option, it's important to take the `isWindowless` property into consideration.

The `isWindowless` property lets you determine whether the plug-in allows any underlying HTML content to display through any transparent areas. By default, this property is set to `false`, meaning that your Silverlight plug-in will appear on top of any underlying HTML content. The reason why this property defaults to `false` is because, once again, when this value is set to `true`, your Silverlight application will take a significant performance hit.

Setting the `isWindowless` property to `true` does have an advantage. When this property is `true`, any underlying HTML content will show through the transparent areas of the Silverlight plug-in. This option is most useful when you want seamless integration with an HTML page such as flyovers and overlays. As figure 3.4 shows, the `background` and `isWindowless` properties are somewhat reliant upon each other.

It's critical to your integration efforts to understand how the `background` and `isWindowless` properties cooperate. As the third image in figure 3.4 shows, setting the `background` property to `transparent` is only half the battle. The fourth image shows that you truly have the ability to seamlessly integrate Silverlight content within your web assets by setting both the `background` and `isWindowless` properties. The process of integration will become clearer once we begin discussing the actual Silverlight content in the next chapter.

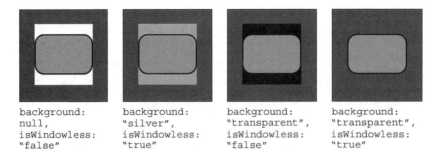

| background:
null,
isWindowless:
"false" | background:
"silver",
isWindowless:
"true" | background:
"transparent",
isWindowless:
"false" | background:
"transparent",
isWindowless:
"true" |

Figure 3.4   The consequences of various background **and** isWindowless
**property combinations. The outermost rectangle represents a section of HTML within
a web page. The inner rectangle represents the region occupied by a Silverlight plug-
in. The rounded rectangle is the pure Silverlight content that will be explained later.**

FRAMERATE

The frameRate property (object tag and ASP.NET property name: MaxFrameRate)
enables you to determine the maximum number of frames you want to render per second. This built-in throttling mechanism ensures that your Silverlight plug-in doesn't
hog the system resources. By default, this property is set to render 60, which is more
than most non-media applications need, so feel free to
experiment. Ultimately, the frame rate is based on the
available system resources. For more on frame rate and
the rendering process, see section 6.2.

To view the actual frame rate, set the EnableFrameRate-
Counter plug-in property (enableFrameRateCounter in
JavaScript) to true. This will show the actual and max frame
rates in the browser status bar as seen in figure 3.5. Note that
this feature only works in Internet Explorer on Windows.

**Figure 3.5   The browser
window displaying the current
and maximum frame rates in
a CPU-intensive application**

VERSION

When instantiating a Silverlight plug-in, you
need to set the version property in the createObjectEx function. This property represents the minimum runtime version required
by your Silverlight application. If users don't
have at least this version of the Silverlight runtime installed, they'll be greeted by a default
installation prompt. This installation prompt
looks like figure 3.6.

You can override this default image and
show something that may be branded or more
appropriate for your specific application. We'll
cover that in chapter 25 when we discuss optimizing the install experience. This figure shows

**Figure 3.6   The default Silverlight
installation badge displayed when
the user doesn't have the required
Silverlight version installed.**

the default visual prompt users will see if they don't have the necessary version of Silverlight installed.

Once Silverlight is installed, it'll automatically install future versions of Silverlight if configured to do so. These updates will continue to be installed as long as the users don't disable this feature in the Silverlight Configuration dialog box. Figure 3.7 shows the Silverlight Configuration dialog box, which can be accessed by right-clicking any Silverlight application in the browser.

> **NOTE** Windows 7 and Windows Vista users with User Account Control (UAC) enabled will not have the option to install updates automatically. In those instances, Silverlight will require permission to download and install updates when new updates are found. Windows Vista and Windows 7 users are encouraged to choose the second option shown in figure 3.7 to check for updates and be prompted to install new versions when available.

As you can see, this dialog box gives you the option of turning off automatic updates of Silverlight. But, by default, users' machines will typically have the latest and greatest version of Silverlight.

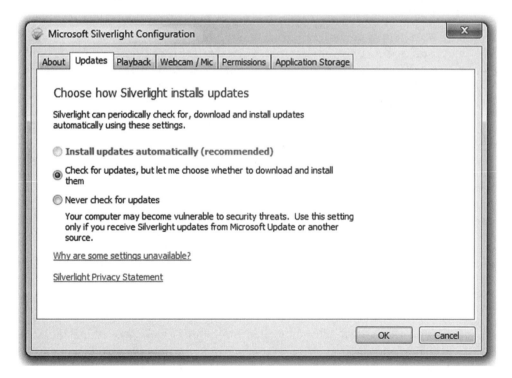

Figure 3.7   The Silverlight Configuration dialog box (Silverlight 4 adds a Webcam/Mic tab). This dialog box is accessible by right-clicking Silverlight content within a web browser. Administrators may configure the Silverlight auto-updater for all users, thereby disabling the ability to change options on this screen.

IGNOREBROWSERVER

The `ignoreBrowserVer` option empowers you to specify whether you should check to see if Silverlight can run within the browser environment. By default, this parameter is set to `false`, which ensures that only supported browsers will run a Silverlight application. You can set this property value to `true` to bypass this safety check. This brute-force approach can slightly speed up the plug-in initialization process but can lead to undesired effects. If you want to support browsers that mostly work but aren't officially supported, update the user agent file (available on http://code.msdn.microsoft.com/SLsupportedUA) instead, so you still maintain control over the spectrum of browsers that'll access your application.

ENABLEHTMLACCESS

The final Boolean property in the Silverlight plug-in initialization provides an extra layer of security. This property, called `enableHtmlAccess`, specifies whether the managed code running within a plug-in instance can access the HTML DOM. By default, this property is set to `true` for the same domain applications and `false` for cross-domain applications. This ensures a safe-by-default development experience. You can set this property value to `true` for cross-domain applications, but you should first consider the ramifications.

> **NOTE** Cross-domain applications are applications that run on one domain but are sourced from another. For example, if you host a web page at http://www.mycoolsite.com and the .xap file used by the Silverlight plug-in on that page is served up from http://PetesHouseOfXap.org, which would be a cross-domain application.

Let's pretend for a second that a political candidate, we'll call him Gill Thrives, has created a Silverlight application that everybody wants. This application is so amazing that even the competing political candidate, named Loth Slivering, wants it. Gill makes this control available for free download via a third-party control site. Gill has deceptively added code that will edit the hosting web page's DOM to say Vote for Gill on a future date before the election. Unfortunately for Loth, Loth added this application to his web site, and now his campaign site has been trashed with "Vote for Gill" all over it. What an embarrassment!

Loth could've easily avoided this time-bomb embarrassment by explicitly setting the `enableHtmlAccess` property value to `false`. When this property value is `false`, any managed code associated with the plug-in instance that attempts to access the HTML DOM will trigger an error. And, fortunately, an error is just a type of event, which Silverlight enables you to elegantly handle (more on that in a moment).

The `enableHtmlAccess` property is but one of the many configuration options you have. The others include `ignoreBrowserVer`, `inplaceInstallPrompt`, `version`, `isWindowless`, `background`, `height`, and `width`. Collectively, these options are all set through the `properties` nested object within `createObjectEx`. This nested object syntax may seem awkward at first but it's just a part of JSON syntax. This syntax gives you a way to logically group together items, making it easy to separate the items that define the look of a Silverlight plug-in instance from its behavior. The behavioral items are part of the events nested object.

3.3.3 Handling plug-in events

At this point, we've covered all of the items required to create an instance of the Silverlight plug-in. Remember that this plug-in has events that affect it and, in turn, your application. These events are onLoad and onError. We'll discuss each in detail in a moment. But, first, let's look at how to wire these event handlers up with a plug-in instance. This can be done in the createObjectEx function in the events subobject, as shown here:

```
Silverlight.createObjectEx({
...
  properties: {
...
  },
  events: {
    onLoad:plugin_Load,
    onError:plugin_Error
  }
});
```

This shows how to wire up the two events associated with a Silverlight plug-in. In reality, neither of these has to be set. But, by setting them, you can create a more tailored experience when loading or handling an unexpected error. Either way, you can accomplish what you need to by responding to the onLoad and onError events.

ONLOAD

The onLoad event occurs immediately after your Silverlight application has been loaded. By default, nothing special will happen when this event occurs. You do have the option of creating an event handler for when this event fires. Regardless of how you intend to use it, you can create an event handler by using JavaScript like this:

```
function plugin_Load(sender, context, source)
{
  alert("loaded");
}
```

This shows an extremely basic onLoad event handler with the three parameters that are passed with the onLoad event. These three parameters are sender, context, and source. The purpose of these parameters is described in table 3.5.

Table 3.5   The parameters of the onLoad event handler

Parameter	Description
sender	A handle to the Silverlight plug-in itself
context	A value specified to distinguish the plug-in instance; this value is provided by a developer
source	The root element of the content loaded into the plug-in

In addition to the parameters of this event, you should know that there are times when this event won't fire. This event won't be triggered if you attempt to reference a Silverlight application that doesn't exist. Along the same lines, the onLoad event won't fire if there's an error in your createObjectEx function call. You may think that an error will fire the onError event; in reality, the onError event will fire only after the Silverlight application has loaded.

ONERROR

The onError event is triggered when an exception hasn't been handled by managed code in your application. But, some errors, such as image and media errors, can't be handled with a managed code unhandled exception handler (they must be handled in specific events or the onError handler in JavaScript). Because of this, you may want to create an error handler at the plug-in level. This can be accomplished by using an onError event handler such as the following:

```
function plugin_Error(sender, errorArgs)
{
  errorType = errorArgs.ErrorType;

  if (errorType == "ImageError" || errorType == "MediaError")
    return;

  alert("An unexpected error has occurred.");
}
```

This all-purpose onError event handler can be used to gracefully handle errors that haven't been caught elsewhere. When called, the value in the sender parameter represents the plug-in where the error occurred. The second parameter, errorArgs, describes the error. This description is accessible through a variety of publicly visible properties. These properties are listed and described in table 3.6.

Table 3.6 The properties associated with the errorArgs parameter

Property	Description
ErrorCode	A numeric code associated with the error; this property can't be set
ErrorMessage	A read-only description of the error
ErrorType	The category of the error
Name	The name of the object that caused the error

You can learn a lot about an error through the errorArgs parameter. This parameter is a valuable part of the onError event handler. As hinted at earlier, this event handler is useful for some situations that can't be covered by application-level error handling. Examples of such an error would be a stack-overflow exception or the media errors shown earlier. Regardless of the error, it's nice to know that there's a way to handle those errors that can't be handled elsewhere. It's also nice to know how to pass some initialization information to a Silverlight application when it starts.

3.3.4 *Sending initialization parameters*

A Silverlight application is a lot like any other .NET application. As an example, imagine a basic command-line program. This program allows you to pass parameters to it before it starts. Then, when the application does start, it's responsible for parsing the parameters. Once parsed, the application decides what to do with these parameters. This is exactly how Silverlight uses initialization parameters as well.

The initialization parameters in Silverlight are sent through a parameter named `initParams`. `initParams` is another parameter in the `createObjectEx` function. Likewise, there's a parameter called `context`. This parameter allows you to uniquely tag a Silverlight plug-in instance. Both parameters are shown here:

```
Silverlight.createObjectEx({
...
  properties: {
...
  },
  events: { },
  initParams: "key1=value1, key2=123, keyX=valueY",
  context: "27d3b786-4e0c-4ae2-97a3-cee8921c7d3d"
});
```

This code demonstrates the basic usage of the `initParams` and `context` parameters. Each of these parameters serves its own special purpose. In reality, you'll probably only use the `initParams` parameter because the `context` parameter doesn't have as much value in the Silverlight 4 world. The reason is because each Silverlight application runs within its own domain and code sharing isn't necessary like it is in the scripting world of Silverlight 1.0. Regardless, we'll cover them both in detail for the sake of completeness.

INITPARAMS

The `initParams` parameter enables you to send any number of user-defined, key-value pairs to a Silverlight application. The application is then responsible for reading and interpreting the key-value pairs when it starts as shown in section 3.1.4. But first, let's build an understanding of how these key-value pairs are created.

The key-value pairs are represented in typical dictionary *[key]=[value]* form, separated by commas. Naturally, the entire `string` of `initParams` represents a collection of key-value pairs. This is different from `initParams` in Silverlight 1.0.

In Silverlight 1.0, the `initParams` parameter took a list of comma-delimited values. This is important to recognize if you're promoting your Silverlight 1.0 application to Silverlight 4 because this approach isn't valid in 4. If you are, in fact, doing this kind of migration, you may want to consider how the `context` parameter is used as well.

CONTEXT

The `context` parameter gives you a way to uniquely identify a Silverlight plug-in. This plug-in passes the value of the `context` parameter to the `onLoad` event associated with the plug-in. The event then uses this `string` value to distinguish the plug-in from others without having to check the HTML DOM. This empowers you to share scripted code across multiple Silverlight plug-ins that exist on the same web page.

The `context` and `initParams` serve as valuable initializers in the plug-in creation process, which involves deciding how to handle the `onError` and `onLoad` events impacting the plug-in. The initial look of this plug-in is set up through a variety of property settings declared within the `properties` sub-object.

Initialization parameters and context are great ways to get simple values to Silverlight applications running in the browser. But, keep in mind that those values don't currently carry over to applications running out of the browser—something we'll cover in chapter 5.

3.4   Summary

One of the most important things you can learn about any given platform or technology is how it handles the concept of an application, including the packaging of that application and the startup process. Back when I used to write straight C code, and everything started at `int main(int argc, char **argv)` with statically linked libraries into a single .exe or .com file, this was trivial to understand. In more complex technologies such as Silverlight, both the packaging and the startup processes are significantly more involved, but the benefits are great. Because of that, we get great things like Internet deployment, browser integration, hands-off memory management, an event-driven input model, full media, and rich graphics. Who could've foreseen that back when code editors only handled a line at a time, compiles were initiated from the command prompt, ASCII graphics were popular, and the presence of a working TCP/IP stack wasn't a given?

Once the plug-in is installed on the end-user machines and the hosting page set up, deploying the application can be as simple as those C programs of yore: just copy the deployment file (the .xap) to a known location and have at it. The various options available for creating the plug-in allow us to support just about any server environment and installation experience we'd like. In fact, we'll talk more about custom installation experiences in chapter 25.

In this chapter we covered HTML page integration primarily from a plug-in-centric view. In the next chapter we'll talk more about how to integrate Silverlight with a web page, including interacting with JavaScript and the DOM.

Integrating with the browser

4

This chapter covers
- Interacting with the HTML Document Object Model (DOM)
- Hosting HTML in Silverlight

Silverlight has always been a web technology, integrated into the web page. Even when a Silverlight application took over the entire browser client area, it was still contained within several layers of HTML tags. Given the history, it makes sense that a Silverlight plug-in would have complete access to the Document Object Model (DOM) on the page in which it resides. In fact, the access is so complete that a Silverlight application could take over all of the functionality normally provided by JavaScript if you wanted to go that route.

Despite the out-of-browser capability introduced with Silverlight 3, as a RIA technology, Silverlight is and will remain for the foreseeable future most popular as a browser plug-in. There's just too much synergy between the nature of a HTML application and the power of a .NET-based RIA plug-in like Silverlight to completely abandon that approach.

Silverlight 4 added the ability for Silverlight to host HTML within itself. Though currently restricted to out-of-browser applications (the topic of the next chapter), the integration is provided by the default browsing engine in the operating system and supports some script integration.

We'll start where Silverlight started, in the browser, where it can take advantage of the DOM. From there, we'll drill deeper into the HTML DOM and discuss the embedded Silverlight control. This control, which is also known as the Silverlight plug-in, ultimately hosts your Silverlight content. Finally, we'll move on to hosting HTML within our Silverlight application.

4.1   *Silverlight and the HTML DOM*

As mentioned in chapter 1, Silverlight is a browser-based plug-in. This plug-in was designed to be consistent with the well-established web architecture. This design decision ensures that you can integrate Silverlight content within any new or existing web property. The web property could be anything from a web page to a blog, intranet portal, or desktop gadget. As shown in figure 4.1, this decision gives you the flexibility to use as little or as much Silverlight as you want.

My Page Title

Thank you for visiting my home page. Take a look at how easily two different Silverlight controls were added to this page. These controls can interact with each other via the HTML DOM.

Integrating Silverlight within a web page

Using Silverlight to fill the entire web page

Figure 4.1   Two theoretical in-browser uses of Silverlight. The shaded areas represent Silverlight applications on web pages.

Figure 4.1 shows the amount of flexibility you have when it comes to using Silverlight. In reality, you can place Silverlight anywhere you want within a web property. This is accomplished through Silverlight's harmonious relationship with the well-known HTML DOM. The DOM allows you to embed a Silverlight plug-in within it. Once embedded, the overall application tree expands to something similar to that shown in figure 4.2.

The HTML DOM enables you to easily access and manage content in a web page. As illustrated in figure 4.2, this content is represented as a structured tree of elements. These elements represent children and contain attributes and text that give them definition. Each child of the tree can be accessed through the HTML DOM. This gives you the ability to add, edit, or remove content as needed. Unfortunately, as the tree has grown, it has become somewhat unwieldy.

In 1998, the World Wide Web Consortium (W3C) published the first version of the HTML DOM specification. Since then, this specification has been implemented, at least in some form, by every web browser. Over time, developers of some web browsers have decided to augment the original specification to provide additional functionality, causing a number of inconsistencies that can make it difficult to deliver platform-neutral content.

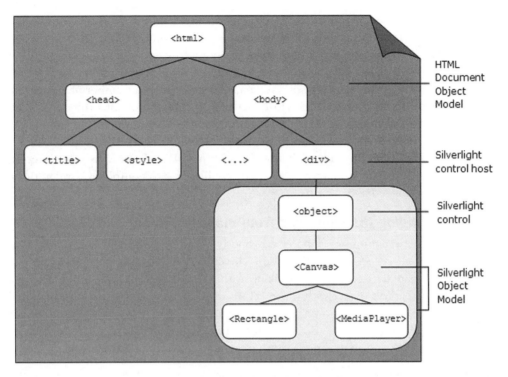

Figure 4.2   The darkly shaded area represents the HTML DOM. The lightly shaded area represents the Silverlight control. This control hosts the Silverlight Object Model.

To ensure that Silverlight could deliver platform-neutral content, the browsers supported by Silverlight had to be identified. Each of these browsers uses one of the Silverlight-supported DOM variants. These DOM variants and their descriptions are shown in table 4.1.

Table 4.1   The DOM variants officially supported by Silverlight

Specification	Browser(s)	Description
DHTML Object Model	Internet Explorer	The DHTML Object Model gives developers programmatic access to the individual elements within a web property.
Gecko DOM	Firefox Mozilla Netscape Safari Chrome	The Gecko DOM approach parses and renders HTML content and utilizes the HTML DOM.

Most web browsers implement one of the DOM variants supported by Silverlight. Regardless, these DOM variants enable you to programmatically access and manipulate the HTML DOM. Because of this, you can easily add an instance of the Silverlight plug-in to a new or existing web page.

At this point, you should have a basic understanding of what a Silverlight application is. If you don't, that's okay because it'll become clearer throughout this book. When a Silverlight application resides on a web page, you can use it to interact with the HTML DOM. To do this, you use the `System.Windows.Browser` namespace.

The `System.Windows.Browser` namespace exposes a number of classes that encapsulate the features of the HTML DOM. The entry point into this DOM is accessible through the `HtmlPage` class. This statically visible class gives you the ability to manage a web page from managed code. In addition, you can use the `HtmlPage` class to interact with users through their browser windows. What's perhaps most interesting, the `System.Windows.Browser` namespace enables you to completely bridge the scripting and managed code worlds.

4.2   Managing the web page from managed code

The `HtmlPage` object exposes a property called `Document`. This property is an `HtmlDocument` object that embodies the currently loaded HTML page and gives you admission to all OF the elements available within the page. This may sound familiar because the `Document` object within the HTML DOM exposes the same kind of functionality. The Silverlight version gives you the ability to do all OF this from managed code. This enables you to navigate the contents of a web page, work with individual element properties and styles, and retrieve information from the query string.

4.2.1   Navigating web page contents

The `HtmlDocument` gives you two entry points into the currently loaded document. These entry points are represented as properties and are shown in table 4.2.

Table 4.2   The entry points into the `HtmlDocument`

Property	Description
DocumentElement	This property represents the root element of the HTML DOM. It always represents the HTML element of a web page.
Body	This property gives you immediate access to the contents of the BODY element of a web page.

These properties represent great ways to enter into an `HtmlDocument`. More specifically, these items are geared toward navigating an `HtmlDocument` using a top-down approach. For situations where you need to dive into the middle of the action and find a nested element, you have two other options. These are shown in table 4.3.

This table introduces the powerful and often-used `GetElementById` and `GetElementsByTagName` methods. Note that these method names match their HTML DOM equivalents, so you have a familiar approach for retrieving elements from managed code:

```
HtmlDocument document = HtmlPage.Document;
HtmlElement element = document.GetElementById("myDiv");
```

Table 4.3 The navigation methods of an `HtmlDocument`

Method	Description
`GetElementById`	It empowers you to find any element within an `HtmlDocument` by referencing its unique identifier. If the element is found, an object-oriented version of the element, known as an `HtmlElement`, is returned. If the element isn't found, `null` will be returned.
`GetElementsByTagName`	It finds all of the elements with a specified tag name. The results are returned as a collection of browser elements.

This example shows how to access an HTML element, in this case `myDiv`, via managed code. Note that the `myDiv` element is simply an HTML `DIV` element within the HTML page hosting the Silverlight plug-in. The example also introduces the important `Html-Element` class. This class represents a strongly typed wrapper for any element in the HTML DOM. This wrapper exposes properties, listed in table 4.4, that enable you to interact with an HTML element from managed code.

Table 4.4 The navigation properties of an `HtmlElement`

Property	Description
`Children`	A collection of items hosted by the current `HtmlElement`
`CssClass`	The name of the Cascading Style Sheet (CSS) class in use by the `HtmlElement`
`Id`	The unique identifier of the `HtmlElement`
`Parent`	The `HtmlElement` that hosts the calling item; if the calling item is the `DocumentElement`, this value will be `null`
`TagName`	The name of the tag used by the `HtmlElement`

This table shows the properties that define an `HtmlElement`. The `Children` and `Parent` properties give you the ability to navigate a web page from a specific element. Each element will have a specific tag associated with it, which can be viewed through the `TagName` property. If this tag is an input tag, you can give it the focus by calling a method that's appropriately named `Focus()`. Beyond the `Focus` method and the properties listed in table 4.4, each HTML tag may contain several unique properties. Let's look at how to work with these element-specific properties.

4.2.2 Working with element properties

Each element in the HTML DOM exposes a number of descriptive properties. Some of these properties are shared with all other elements in the HTML DOM (such as `Tag-Name`). At the same time, some properties are only relevant to some HTML elements—for example, the `value` property of an HTML `input` tag. Because this property is only relevant to one kind of element, you may be wondering how `HtmlElement` works in these situations.

`HtmlElement` exposes two utility methods designed to interact with the properties of an HTML element. The first method, `GetProperty`, retrieves the value assigned to a property. The other method, `SetProperty`, can be used to assign a value to a property. These general methods give you the flexibility to work with any kind of `HtmlElement`:

```
HtmlDocument document = HtmlPage.Document;
HtmlElement myTextField = document.GetElementById("myTextField");
int value = Convert.ToInt32(myTextField.GetProperty("value"));
value = value + 1;
myTextField.SetProperty("value", Convert.ToString(value));
```

This code demonstrates how the `GetProperty` and `SetProperty` methods can be used. Note that this sample retrieves the value associated with the `value` attribute of an *HTML* Input field. This value is incremented by one and assigned back to the field. The `GetProperty` method takes a `string` that represents the name of the property value to retrieve. This value is then returned as a `string`. In a similar fashion, the `Set-Property` method takes a `string` that represents the value to set to a property. This property is identified by the first parameter in the `SetProperty` method. From this, you can see that it's pretty easy to work with property values programmatically. Thankfully, it's just as easy to work with an element's CSS information.

4.2.3 *Handling CSS information*

Elements within the HTML DOM are designed to separate content from presentation. The presentation information is stored in a variety of styles that describe how the element should be shown, which are set through a number of attributes that belong to the CSS recommendation. These attributes have values that can be accessed or assigned from managed code, similar to the following:

```
HtmlDocument document = HtmlPage.Document;
HtmlElement myDiv = document.GetElementById("myDiv");
myDiv.SetStyleAttribute("backgroundColor", "gray");
```

The first step in accessing a style attribute from managed code is to retrieve the `Htm-lElement` whose style needs to be used. Then, the style can be set using the `SetStyle-Attribute` method. Alternatively, you can retrieve the current style of an `HtmlElement` by using the `GetStyleAttribute` method. Both of these methods require you to reference a style using the scripting naming approach.

The scripting naming approach is used to interact with styles from JavaScript. This approach uses CamelCase for style names. This is slightly different than the HTML approach, which uses dashes to separate words. This means that the HTML name for the `backgroundColor` property used in the previous example is `background-color`. If you're an experienced web developer, you've probably run into this discrepancy before. Note that Silverlight requires the scripting approach. If you try to reference a style using the HTML approach, an exception won't be thrown but the style value also won't be set or retrieved. Either way, it's nice to know there are ways to get and set style attributes. It's also nice to know how to retrieve values from the query string.

4.2.4   *Accessing the query string*

One common approach for managing state in a web application involves using the query string. The query string empowers you to store small amounts of data relevant to a user's session. In addition, the query string can be used as a sort of a bookmark to allow a user to come back to a specific location at a later point in time. As an example, let's pretend we want to send you the search results for a query on Silverlight; we could email you the following web address:

```
http://search.msn.com/results.aspx?q=Silverlight&mkt=en-us&FORM=LVCP
```

This web address enables you to see the search results we're referring to. This is more convenient than telling someone to go to a search engine, enter "Silverlight" into the query box, and wait for the results. This simpler approach is made possible through the values that are stored after the ? (question mark)—values that represent the QueryString of the Uri for an HtmlDocument.

The QueryString is readable through a collection of key/value pairs. This collection is part of a larger entity known as the DocumentUri. The DocumentUri represents the Uri of the current page, allowing you to always gain your current bearings within an application. Figure 4.3 shows how the parts of the DocumentUri are related.

This figure shows the breakdown of a web address. Note that, significantly, the QueryString starts after the ? in a web address. In addition, each key/value pair is separated by an & (ampersand). The QueryString in figure 4.3 has two key/value pairs, which could be read using this code:

Figure 4.3   The elements of a web address

```
HtmlWindow window = HtmlPage.Window;
HtmlDocument document = HtmlPage.Document;
foreach (string key in document.QueryString.Keys)
{
   window.Alert("Key: " + key + "; Value: " + document.QueryString[key]);
}
```

Note that you can't set the key/value pairs of this collection from code. Instead, if you need to set the QueryString values, you'll need to use the navigation techniques shown table 4.6. This will reset the values associated with the QueryString, as well as the contents of the page. Once the contents of the page are loaded, you can use the HtmlDocument to navigate the page.

4.3   *Working with the user's browser window*

The hosting browser window is represented as an HtmlWindow object. This object can't be instantiated from code, but you can get the current instance of the hosting browser's HtmlWindow through the HtmlPage class's Window property. This can be accomplished by using the following code:

```
HtmlWindow window = HtmlPage.Window;
```

Once you have a handle to it, you can use the `HtmlWindow` to display prompts to a user. Alternatively, you can use this object to navigate the browser to a different location using the `Navigate` method. Either way, this browser window stores valuable information that can be discovered and used to enhance the user's experience.

4.3.1   *Prompting the user*

The `HtmlWindow` class enables you to deliver HTML prompts to your users. It's important to note that these prompts aren't Silverlight items. Instead, these prompts are constructed entirely by the user's browser window, so you have a limited ability to customize how these prompts are displayed. The good news is that these prompts provide a quick way to show or collect information from your users. The three prompt options available through the `HtmlWindow` class are listed in table 4.5.

Table 4.5   The prompt options available through the `HtmlWindow` class

Method	Description
`Alert(…)`	It shows a single message in an HTML alert window.
`Confirm(…)`	It prompts the user to agree or disagree with a statement or question. This prompt displays two buttons: OK and Cancel. The text of these buttons can't be customized. If a user selects OK, this method will return `true`; if a user selects Cancel, this method will return `false`.
`Prompt(…)`	It creates a dialog window that displays a single message. In addition, this dialog displays a single text box that the user can enter information into. If the user selects the OK button from this dialog window, the value of that text box will be returned as a `string`. Otherwise, if a user selects Cancel or exits the window, `null` will be returned.

These prompt options mimic the prompt choices available through the HTML DOM `Window` object. Using Silverlight, you can launch these prompts from managed code. This example shows one way to display an alert to a user using C#:

```
HtmlWindow window = HtmlPage.Window;
window.Alert("Welcome!");
```

Note how easy it is to deliver an HTML prompt to a user. It's also important to note that these prompts prevent the execution of succeeding code until the user responds to the prompt—they're blocking operations. Either way, you can use this approach to use the other prompt types shown in table 4.5.

Silverlight 3 introduced another easy way to alert the user. The `MessageBox.Show` method encapsulates the `HtmlWindow.Alert` functionality to provide a more discoverable way to display alerts. More importantly, the `MessageBox.Show` method also works for out-of-browser applications where there's no valid `HtmlPage` and has no dependence on the underlying JavaScript capabilities.

Most .NET Windows developers are used to `MessageBox.Show` and will find it just as intuitive in Silverlight:

```
MessageBox.Show("Welcome!");
```

The Show method also takes some additional parameters to allow you to set the window caption and display either the OK button or both the OK and the Cancel buttons:

```
MessageBox.Show("Format your C drive?",
            "Windows Caption",
            MessageBoxButton.OKCancel);
```

Just as in the case with Alert and the other methods, this is a blocking operation and will suspend your application until the user closes the window.

The MessageBox class and the HtmlWindow methods make it easy to display confirmation messages to the user via the browser. Luckily, it's just as easy to perform navigation tasks through the browser window.

4.3.2 Navigating the browser window

Navigation is an important part of any web application. There may be times when you want to redirect a user to another web page or perhaps you want to launch another browser window and load a web page into it. Either way, the HtmlWindow class provides two methods you can use to get the job done. These are shown in table 4.6.

Table 4.6 The navigation options available through the HtmlWindow class

Method	Description
Navigate(…)	This method will redirect the browser window to the provided URI. This URI can be loaded in an optional target window. The specifications of this target window can be set via an optional third parameter. The name and specification of the target window parameters match those used by the HTML DOM window.open function.
NavigateToBookmark(…)	This method is used to navigate to a location within the current HTML page.

It's important to recognize that these navigation methods can have undesired effects on your Silverlight application. For instance, if you redirect the hosting browser window away from the hosting web page, your Silverlight application will be unloaded. You should strongly consider loading a different web page into a new browser window, as shown here:

```
Uri uri = new Uri("http://10rem.net");
HtmlWindow window = HtmlPage.Window;
window.Navigate(uri, "_blank");
```

One of the key items to notice from this code is the fact that you must always use a Uri for a web address. In addition, you can still use a target with an address, just like in HTML, making it easy to fully control the experience.

In addition to the properties of the windows or elements in the DOM, you may also want to obtain information about the browser itself.

4.3.3   *Discovering the browser properties*

The statically visible `BrowserInformation` property exposes detailed information about a user's browser. This information is stored within a `System.Windows.Browser.BrowserInformation` object that corresponds nicely to the `Navigator` object available within the HTML DOM. Table 4.7 shows the properties exposed by the `BrowserInformation` object and the equivalent `Navigator` property.

Table 4.7   **Descriptions of the `BrowserInformation` properties and their corresponding `Navigator` properties**

BrowserInformation	Navigator	Description
BrowserVersion	appVersion	Represents the platform and version associated with the browser
CookiesEnabled	cookieEnabled	Specifies whether cookies are enabled within the browser
Name	appName	The name of the browser
Platform	Platform	The operating system
UserAgent	userAgent	The value of the user-agent header that will be sent from the browser to a server

Based on these options, you can see that you have access to a lot of information. This information can be useful for creating a statistical analysis of your application's users. To accomplish this, you must first get to the `BrowserInformation` by using code similar to this:

```
BrowserInformation browserInfo = HtmlPage.BrowserInformation;
HtmlWindow window = HtmlPage.Window;
window.Alert(browserInfo.Name);
```

This information can be useful if you're modifying the HTML DOM from managed code because of the rendering differences between different browsers. With the `BrowserInformation` class, you can easily code against these inconsistencies.

The `BrowserInformation` class provides a way to learn about the user's browser window, which is represented by the `HtmlWindow` class. With this class, you can navigate to locations within a web page or on the Internet. In addition, you can reach out to users and communicate with them through HTML prompts, if needed. These prompts are something you're probably familiar with if you've developed web applications using JavaScript. If you've used JavaScript in the past, you'll probably be excited to know that there are ways to bridge the scripting world with the managed code world.

4.4   *Bridging the scripting and managed code worlds*

Silverlight allows you to create a bridge between the scripting and managed code worlds to allow you to leverage each platform for the area in which it excels. For example, you can use Silverlight purely for its rich and powerful .NET features; Silverlight can provide value even if you don't need a rich vivid user interface. To take advantage of these features, you need to learn to call managed code from JavaScript. In addition, you'll also learn how to use JavaScript from managed code.

4.4.1   *Calling managed code from JavaScript*

Calling managed code from JavaScript is a fairly simple process—it consists of three basic steps intended to expose managed code elements to the scripting world. Once these tasks have been performed, you're free to reference the managed elements from JavaScript. To demonstrate this, let's pretend you want to use a method from managed code to call a web service.

The first step in calling managed code from JavaScript involves using the `Script-ableType` attribute. This attribute, which is part of the `System.Windows.Browser` namespace, makes a class accessible to the JavaScript world. This attribute doesn't expose any special properties, so you can apply it to any class using the following approach:

```
[ScriptableType]
public partial class MainPage : UserControl
```

This C# code shows how to make a type accessible to JavaScript by exposing the default Silverlight page to JavaScript. In reality, you can make any class accessible to the scripting world and will typically create a dedicated class or classes just for that interface. Once a class has been marked as a `ScriptableType`, all public properties, methods, and events are available to JavaScript. Alternatively, you can decide to only expose select member items. Fortunately, this is also an easy process.

To expose member items, you use a similar but different attribute—`ScriptableMember`. The `ScriptableMember` attribute may be applied to the events, methods, and properties that can be used with script. You add the attribute as shown in this C# code:

```
[ScriptableMember]
public void ExecuteWebService()
{
  // Make a call to a web service
}
```

This attribute gives you the ability to set a scripting alias if you so desire, which you can accomplish by setting the `string`-typed `ScriptAlias` property. This may be useful if you want to prevent naming conflicts within script. Everything you've seen up to this point is pretty basic, but we haven't created the bridge to JavaScript yet.

To create the bridge to the scripting world, you must register an instance of the class to be exposed by using the statically visible `RegisterScriptableObject` method. This method, which belongs to the `HtmlPage` class, empowers you to give a class instance an alias. This alias can then be used from script. You can accomplish this using the `RegisterScriptableObject` method shown in the following C# code:

```
public MainPage()
{
  InitializeComponent();
  HtmlPage.RegisterScriptableObject("bridge", this);
}
```

This method accepts an instance of a class described as being a ScriptableType. The object is registered with the scripting engine by passing it as the second parameter to the RegisterScriptableObject method, which then uses the first parameter to create an alias for the class instance. This alias is appended to the content property of the hosting Silverlight plug-in.

The Silverlight plug-in exposes a subobject called content, which exposes the content of a Silverlight plug-in; this is the scripting version of the Content property of the SilverlightHost class previously discussed. You can access your scriptable object by first retrieving the plug-in instance and then referencing the ScriptableMember you want, as demonstrated in listing 4.1.

Listing 4.1   Referencing a managed item from script on the HTML page

```
<!DOCTYPE html PUBLIC "-//W3C//DTD XHTML 1.0 Transitional//EN"
"http://www.w3.org/TR/xhtml1/DTD/xhtml1-transitional.dtd">
<html xmlns="http://www.w3.org/1999/xhtml" >
<head>
  <title>Silverlight Project Test Page </title>
  <script type="text/javascript" src="Silverlight.js"></script>
  <script type="text/javascript">
    function buttonClick()
    {
      var plugin = document.getElementById("mySilverlightControl");
      plugin.content.bridge.ExecuteWebService();          ◁──┐ Scriptable object
    }                                                          │ and method
  </script>
</head>
<body style="height:100%;">
  <div id="mySilverlightHost" style="height:100%;">
    <script type="text/javascript">
      var host = document.getElementById("mySilverlightHost");
      Silverlight.createObjectEx({
        source: "ClientBin/MySilverlightApp.xap",
        parentElement: host,
        id: "mySilverlightControl",
        properties: {
          height: "100%",
          width: "100%",
          version: "2.0"
        },
        events: { }
      });
    </script>
  </div>
  <input type="button" onclick="buttonClick();"
    value="Execute Web Service" />
</body>
</html>
```

This listing demonstrates how a scriptable object can be accessed from a plug-in instance. This plug-in gives you the ability to use managed code from JavaScript. This can be valuable in situations where you don't need the rich visual features of

Silverlight. For instance, you may decide to create something known as a *headless Silverlight application.*

A headless Silverlight application is an application that doesn't have a UI. Instead, it uses objects registered as `ScriptableType` elements as the brains for a traditional web page. This approach allows you to write nonvisual components using the .NET Framework and integrate existing code libraries. This type of application is valuable because you can use it to perform tasks that the browser's JavaScript engine can't do. For instance, you may choose to use a headless Silverlight application to make cross-domain requests or listen to a socket (both items discussed in chapter 14). Regardless, you may still need to rely on the features of a preexisting JavaScript library. For these situations, you can use Silverlight to call JavaScript from managed code.

4.4.2 *Using JavaScript from managed code*

Silverlight gives you the flexibility to call JavaScript from managed code and, in turn, the ability to call any method on an HTML or JavaScript object. This can be useful if you're integrating Silverlight with a preexisting web application. There's one spot in particular where this feature is especially valuable: printing.

Silverlight has basic printing capabilities (see chapter 19), but the `Window` object in the HTML DOM also exposes a `print` method. You can use Silverlight's ability to call a function on a JavaScript object to deliver this functionality. To accomplish this, you use a method called `Invoke`. This method can be used to execute a JavaScript function from managed code, as demonstrated in the following C# code:

```
HtmlWindow window = HtmlPage.Window;
window.Invoke("print", new object[]{});
```

This code can be used to print the current web page, including your Silverlight application. The `Invoke` method can be applied to any `HtmlDocument`, `HtmlElement`, or `HtmlWindow` object. The first parameter of this method represents the name of the function to be invoked. The second parameter represents the arguments that will be passed to this function when it's called. As you can see, this parameter is an array of objects, so you have the flexibility to pass anything you need to a JavaScript function.

Silverlight gives you the ability to execute JavaScript code from managed code. In addition, you can go the other way and call managed code from JavaScript. These two features show how you can use Silverlight to bridge the scripting and managed code worlds. This is important because you need to use this approach if you want to communicate between two different types of plug-ins, such as Flash and Silverlight, or between technologies such as AJAX and Silverlight.

Silverlight gives you the ability to bridge scripting and managed code running inside the browser. In addition, you can use Silverlight to learn about the user's browser window. What's perhaps even more interesting, you can use managed code to interact with the HTML DOM. All this is made possible by the rich HTML DOM API that's an integral part of Silverlight.

Running Silverlight in the browser is the primary use case for the technology. But Silverlight 3 introduced a new way of running your applications: out of the browser, on the user's desktop.

4.5   *Hosting HTML in Silverlight*

Silverlight 4 added the ability to host arbitrary HTML content on the Silverlight plug-in surface. This feature was added primarily to support advertising scenarios such as Flash and animated GIF banner ads, but can be used to display anything the web browser can display, including instances of other Silverlight applications.

> **NOTE**   Internally, this feature was implemented by hosting an instance of the system browser within Silverlight. On the Mac, this is the WebKit-based Safari; on Windows, it's Internet Explorer. This is an operating system setting independent from what browser you set as the default to open web content. Because you've now brought back the variability in rendering that's inherent across the spectrum of web browsers, I recommend you use this feature sparingly.

HTML hosting in Silverlight currently works only in out-of-browser applications (covered in chapter 5). When displayed in an in-browser application, you'll simply get a gray or otherwise boring-looking rectangle on the screen, as seen in figure 4.4. If your application supports running both in and out of the browser, you'll want to dynamically add or enable the control based on a runtime check to see which mode you're running in.

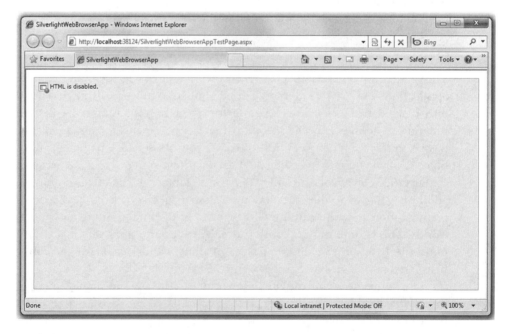

Figure 4.4   When running in the browser, HTML hosting features are disabled. This example shows the `WebBrowser` **control.**

There are two ways to host HTML content in your Silverlight application: you can host the WebBrowser control or you can use the WebBrowserBrush to paint HTML over other elements.

4.5.1 *Hosting the WebBrowser control*

The WebBrowser control allows you to display a rectangular region on the screen containing a functional and interactive web browser. There are three ways you can load content into the control: the Source property and the Navigate and NavigateToString methods.

SOURCE PROPERTY

The Source property is the XAML-friendly way to host content for the control. Simply set the Source to a valid URI on the same domain that originally served the Silverlight application:

```
<Grid x:Name="LayoutRoot" Background="White">
  <WebBrowser Source="http://www.mydomain.com" Margin="15" />
</Grid>
```

In the case of a cross-domain error, you'll simply get a blank control for the display and an XamlParseException (attribute out of range), which may be trapped in the application-level exception handler. If you want to host cross-domain content, you'll need to use the NavigateToString method and host an iframe.

Because Source isn't a dependency property and, therefore, doesn't support binding, its utility in real-world applications is pretty low. Instead, you'll want to use the Navigate method.

NAVIGATE METHOD

The Navigate method is the counterpart to the Source property. Though it doesn't support binding like the Source property, you have more control over exception handling when the page is cross-domain. Listing 4.2 shows how to load a local page using the Navigate method.

Listing 4.2 Loading a page using the Navigate method

HTML (example-page.aspx):

```
<html xmlns="http://www.w3.org/1999/xhtml">
<head runat="server">
  <title>Demo Page</title>
</head>
<body>
  <div style="margin:20px;font-family:Arial;font-size:20pt">
  This is HTML from the same domain as this out-of-browser
  application. If this were a cross-domain page, you
  wouldn't be able to see it here.
  </div>

  <div style="margin:20px">
    <img src="pete_headshot.jpg" />
  </div>
</body>
</html>
```

XAML:

```xaml
<Grid x:Name="LayoutRoot">
  <Grid.Background>
    <LinearGradientBrush StartPoint="0,0"
                         EndPoint="0,1">
      <GradientStop Color="#FF0055DD"
                    Offset="0" />
      <GradientStop Color="#FF00DDFF"
                    Offset="1" />
    </LinearGradientBrush>
  </Grid.Background>

  <WebBrowser x:Name="b"                    <⎯ WebBrowserControl
              Margin="15" />
</Grid>
```

C#:

```csharp
public partial class MainPage : UserControl
{
  public MainPage()
  {
    InitializeComponent();

    Loaded += new RoutedEventHandler(MainPage_Loaded);
  }

  void MainPage_Loaded(object sender, RoutedEventArgs e)
  {
    b.Navigate(new Uri("/example-page.aspx",           <⎯ Navigate Method
                       UriKind.Relative));
  }
}
```

Note that the URI is relative to the position of the .xap so, in this case, example-page.aspx is sitting in the ClientBin folder on the project. When you run this app, you get the result shown in figure 4.5, assuming you happen to have a gigantic photo of me hanging around for just such the occasion.

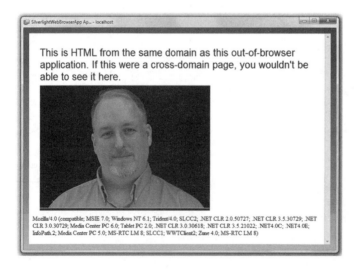

Figure 4.5   The WebBrowser control with a page loaded via the Navigate method

Like the Source property, we still have the cross-domain restrictions that make this method less than useful for the majority of circumstances. The most flexible approach for loading content into the WebBrowser control is to use the NavigateToString method.

NAVIGATETOSTRING METHOD

NavigateToString allows you to build and display arbitrary HTML in the control. This can be useful if, say, you're building an RSS reader or similar application where the source isn't exactly an HTML page but has HTML content you want to display. To use this method, simply provide a string containing the HTML source, as shown in listing 4.3. (Use the same XAML as in listing 4.2.)

Listing 4.3 Loading an HTML string via NavigateToString

```
void MainPage_Loaded(object sender, RoutedEventArgs e)
{
  StringBuilder html = new StringBuilder();
  html.Append("<html><head></head>");
  html.Append("<html><head></head>");
  html.Append("<body style='font-family:Arial;font-size:20pt'>");
  html.Append("<div style='color:blue'>");
  html.Append("This is the first div");
  html.Append("</div>");
  html.Append("<div style='color:orange'>");
  html.Append("This is the second div");
  html.Append("</div>");
  html.Append("<html><head></head><body>");
  html.Append("</body></html>");

  b.NavigateToString(html.ToString());          ⟵ NavigateToString
}                                                    method
```

When run, the resulting application looks like figure 4.6. Note that the styles all came through just as you'd expect it from any other browser page.

NavigateToString will allow you to host an iframe to enable loading content from another web domain. In this way, you can get around the same-domain limitations

Figure 4.6 Runtime-generated HTML loaded into the Silverlight Web- Browser control via the NavigateToString method

imposed by the Navigate method and Source properties. Simply change the HTML-generating code in listing 4.3 to this:

```
html.Append("<html><head></head><body>");
html.Append("<iframe width='100%' height='100%'");
html.Append("src='http://windowsclient.net/learn/video.aspx?v=289850'/>");
html.Append("<html><head></head><body>");
html.Append("</body></html>");
```

The resulting page will look like figure 4.7. Note that, on this page, we have a Silverlight media player with a loaded video and several animated GIF ads. This provides all the flexibility you'd need to be able to create your own Silverlight web browser or to incorporate browsing capabilities into your own application.

Figure 4.7 We're loading http://windowsclient.net in an iframe using the NavigateToString method. Note the embedded Silverlight player and animated gif ads, all hosted in the control inside our Silverlight out-of-browser application.

You can use normal HTML attributes and techniques to avoid the scrollbars and deal with overflow content just as you would on any other web page. Remember, though, the more HTML you put in your string, the more you'll have to test across the browsers. One of the biggest benefits of Silverlight is that it looks and behaves the same across different browsers. Relying too much on HTML content largely negates this benefit.

Though having an interactive web browser control may be enough for most cases, sometimes you may want to run scripts on the page or save the content off to a file.

INVOKING SCRIPTS

Up until now, the web page loaded in the WebBrowser control has been a black box. The user can type into it, but the application can't do anything other than load the content and let it fly. Sometimes you need to invoke behavior on the web page. The WebBrowser control includes two overloads of the InvokeScript method just for that.

Listing 4.4 shows how to invoke a script both with a parameter and without.

Listing 4.4 Invoking scripts on a loaded web page

HTML:
```html
<html xmlns="http://www.w3.org/1999/xhtml">
<head>
  <title></title>
  <script language="JavaScript">          ← JavaScript function
    function GreetMe(name) {                 expecting parameters
      div1.innerHTML += "<p>Hello " + name + "</p>";
    }

    function SayHello() {          ← Basic JavaScript
      div1.innerHTML += "<p>Hello</p>";   function
    }
  </script>
</head>
<body>
  Hello world!<br />

  <div id="div1">
  </div>
</body>

</html>
```

XAML:
```xml
...
<WebBrowser x:Name="b"
            Source="/script-page.htm" />
```

C#:
```csharp
public MainPage()
{
  InitializeComponent();

  b.LoadCompleted +=                              ← LoadCompleted
    new LoadCompletedEventHandler(b_LoadCompleted);    wire-up
}
```

```
void b_LoadCompleted(object sender, NavigationEventArgs e)
{
  b.InvokeScript("SayHello");
  b.InvokeScript("GreetMe","'Pete'");
}
```

Invoking without parameters ⟵

Invoking with parameters ⟵

You must ensure you wait for the LoadCompleted event before you attempt to call any scripts. Otherwise, there's no guarantee that the script functions are available. The resulting application looks like figure 4.8.

Another task you may want to perform with the web page is to render its content to a string for use elsewhere in the application. Though this could be done via a separate WebRequest, the information is already here and there's a handy function to expose the content to your application code.

Figure 4.8 **InvokeScript used to manipulate the contents of the web page in the WebBrowser control**

SAVING THE CONTENT

The WebBrowser control includes the SaveToString method, which takes the currently loaded HTML and, well, saves it to a string. From there you can upload it to a service, save it locally, display it to the user or do pretty much anything else you'd like with it:

```
string html = BrowserControlInstance.SaveToString();
```

But if the content is from a cross-domain location, you'll receive a SecurityException. This restricts the use of the control to saving the HTML generated by your local server.

The WebBrowser control forms the core of the embedded HTML in Silverlight applications. Building upon that and providing flexibility that's both useful and fun is the WebBrowserBrush.

4.5.2 *Using the WebBrowserBrush*

If you play with the WebBrowser control, you'll eventually notice that you can't overlay other Silverlight content on top of it. On Windows, the WebBrowser control has a separate *hWnd* or handle to a window in Windows (the equivalent thing happens on the Mac) and, therefore, has what we call airspace issues, in that it'll be on top of anything else you draw. If you want to have the content behave like normal Silverlight content, allowing transforms and otherwise respecting z-order, you'll need to use the WebBrowserBrush but at the cost of interactivity.

The WebBrowserBrush takes a WebBrowser control as its source and is then used to paint on any arbitrary path or shape. It doesn't allow the user to interact with the web page. During PDC09, Scott Guthrie demonstrated an application that puzzlefied a YouTube page with a Rick Astley video playing in a Flash player. This was accomplished using the Web Browser brush on the individual puzzle shapes.

Listing 4.5 shows how to use the `WebBrowserBrush` to show the contents of a web page within an ellipse. The HTML used is the same as that from listing 4.2.

> **Listing 4.5 Using the `WebBrowserBrush` to paint an ellipse with a web page**

XAML:
```
<Grid x:Name="LayoutRoot">
  <Grid.Background>
    <LinearGradientBrush StartPoint="0,0"
                         EndPoint="0,1">
      <GradientStop Color="#FF0055DD"
                    Offset="0" />
      <GradientStop Color="#FF00DDFF"
                    Offset="1" />
    </LinearGradientBrush>
  </Grid.Background>

  <WebBrowser x:Name="b"
              Height="1000"                  ⟵ Ensure that
              Width="1000"                      browser has size
              Visibility="Collapsed"
                Source="/example-page.aspx" />

  <Ellipse Margin="25"
           Stroke="Black"
           StrokeThickness="2">
    <Ellipse.Fill>                               Source for
      <WebBrowserBrush SourceName="b"     ⟵     brush
                       x:Name="EllipseBrush" />  ⟵  Name for
    </Ellipse.Fill>                                 use in code
  </Ellipse>

</Grid>
```

C#:
```
void MainPage_Loaded(object sender, RoutedEventArgs e)
{                                                      Wire up event
  CompositionTarget.Rendering += (s, ev) =>       ⟵   handler
    {                                        Redraw
      EllipseBrush.Redraw();            ⟵   on every frame
    };
}
```

The resulting application looks like figure 4.9.

In listing 4.5, the code is redrawing the control during the `CompositionTarget.Rendering` event. That event typically fires once for every frame being drawn. For a static web page, this is overkill, and you can simply use the `LoadCompleted` event of the `WebBrowser` control. But, if you have video content or a web page that otherwise constantly changes its appearance, you'll need to wire up to this event or to a timer to update the display.

Another point to note is that the `WebBrowser` control must have a size. What's rendered by the `WebBrowserBrush` is the same as what would be rendered by the `Web-Browser` if it were visible. If the `WebBrowser` was sized to 10×10, the `WebBrowserBrush`

Figure 4.9
`WebBrowserBrush`
used to paint web
content onto an
`Ellipse` **element**

would show that 10×10 content, scaled up to the size specified by the brush's stretch setting.

That's everything you need to be able to paint HTML all over your out-of-browser application whether running in a window or full screen.

4.6   Summary

Silverlight has always been, first and foremost, a web technology. As such, it has excellent integration with the hosting browser. Anything you can do from JavaScript can be done from within Silverlight.

When running in the browser, Silverlight provides you with enough control that you could automate the entire page without any JavaScript, if you desired, while benefitting from the capabilities and development model offered by managed code languages. The other end of the spectrum is a full-page Silverlight application hosted in a thin HTML shell. For many applications, a middle ground using the in-browser experience integrated with an existing web property or into a system such as SharePoint will be the way to go.

In the next chapter, we'll look at how Silverlight reaches beyond the browser both to interact with the local operating system while running in the browser and how to run Silverlight applications out of the browser, a capability first introduced in Silverlight 3.

Integrating with the desktop 5

This chapter covers

- Running Silverlight applications out of the browser
- Using the elevated trust mode
- Lighting up on Windows with COM automation
- Displaying the notification toast
- Controlling the out-of-browser window
- Running in full screen
- Storing and retrieving local information using isolated storage

Silverlight started as an in-browser technology, primarily used for media and simple games. It later evolved into a more capable business technology and added some useful but basic desktop integration with additions such as isolated storage and the `OpenFileDialog`. With version 3, Silverlight gained the ability to run outside of the browser as a sandboxed desktop application. Starting with Silverlight 4, the sandbox has been expanded and a whole new wave of desktop-integration capabilities included.

Elevated trust mode is one of the most exciting things to happen to out-of-browser applications. Now we have access to more local files and resources, fewer confirmation prompts, and a better integrated experience. On Windows, we also have all the power provided by COM automation. We get all this as the result of a single setting and a user confirmation dialog; no messing around with browser settings or code access security.

Elevated trust mode even lets you control the out-of-browser window, from simple sizing and location all the way through to creating your own custom window *chrome*— the borders, title bars, buttons, and other elements that decorate a typical window on a given operating system.

Sometimes what you want isn't a separate window but rather to take your in-browser or out-of-browser application and make it run in full screen. Silverlight supports that as well, a killer feature for media players and kiosk applications. When run in the elevated trust mode, full-screen applications have even more capabilities.

Even in the default partial-trust mode, Silverlight 4 gains new out-of-browser capabilities including the new notification API, or *toast*, as it's commonly called.

Applications both in and out of the browser need to integrate with the local OS at varying levels. In this chapter, we'll look at some of those local desktop integration features and dive deeply into out-of-browser capabilities using both the default partial trust mode introduced with Silverlight 3 and the elevated trust mode introduced with Silverlight 4. From there we'll look at the full-screen mode and isolated storage. Before we get into some of the deeper topics, it's fundamental to understand the out-of-browser mode.

5.1   Silverlight out of the browser

One of the most exciting new features introduced with Silverlight 3 and enhanced in Silverlight 4 is support for out-of-browser (OOB) applications. OOB applications give us the best of Silverlight's cross-platform support along with a locally installed and offline-enabled experience.

Out-of-browser Silverlight applications aren't hosted in a real browser instance—at least not in the way we'd typically think of a browser—and, therefore, don't have access to the HTML DOM described in the previous chapter. Instead, the applications must be full-page, self-contained applications, without reliance on HTML, JavaScript, or other in-page assets.

Out-of-browser Silverlight applications are already seeing significant uptake within corporations, behind the firewall, due to their simple installation and update models and their presentation and data manipulation capabilities.

Out-of-browser Silverlight applications look just like their full-page in-browser equivalents but without all of the extra browser chrome. A sample OOB Silverlight application may be seen in figure 5.1 and its in-browser version in figure 5.2.

Between the two screenshots, you can see that the Silverlight portion of the experience remains identical (with the exception of the frame rate display I've turned on when in the browser). The code and the .xap file are the same in both instances. What

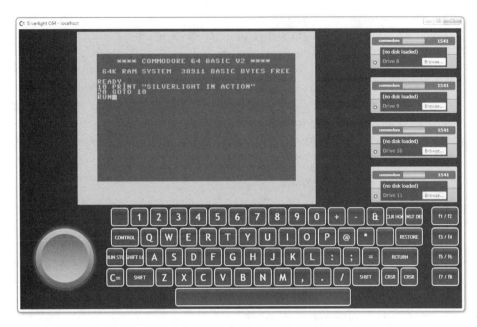

Figure 5.1 My first out-of-browser Silverlight application—a Commodore 64 emulator using the updated MediaStreamSource API described in chapter 20

Figure 5.2 The same Silverlight application running in the browser

changes is how much chrome surrounds the application and how much real estate is made available to Silverlight rather than to browser functionality.

Silverlight provides APIs for detecting and responding to changes in network connectivity as well as an API for indentifying whether the application is running in or out of the browser and if there are any updates available. All of these, combined with the already rich set of capabilities offered by Silverlight, make for a compelling out-of-browser application platform.

Before deciding on creating an out-of-browser application, it's important to understand both the capabilities and restrictions.

5.1.1 Capabilities and restrictions

Out-of-browser Silverlight applications work just like in-browser Silverlight applications with some minor differences:

- Isolated storage quota for out-of-browser applications is 25 MB by default as opposed to 1 MB for in-browser applications. In both cases, this can be extended by prompting the user.
- Out-of-browser applications provide access to keys that the browser normally captures, such as function keys.
- Out-of-browser applications can be pinned to the Start menu or taskbar on Windows systems and display custom icons but otherwise can't integrate with the Windows 7 taskbar without using COM automation in the elevated trust mode.
- Out-of-browser applications require an explicit check for a new version, whereas in-browser versions automatically update.
- Out-of-browser applications support the elevated trust mode, discussed in section 5.3.1.
- Out-of-browser applications can't receive initialization parameters or take advantage of any of the plug-in parameters while running out of the browser.
- Out-of-browser applications can't interact with the HTML DOM—there's no DOM to work with.

If you want those capabilities and can live with those restrictions, then an out-of-browser application may be for you. If you need more power and fewer restrictions, consider creating a click-once WPF application.

The end-user experience for installing Silverlight applications is slightly more complex than just hitting a web page and running Silverlight content but not nearly as involved as a regular platform application (.exe) install.

5.1.2 The end-user experience

An end-user visiting your site will see a typical Silverlight application. If the application is out-of-browser enabled, he or she will be able to right-click on the surface to install it locally, assuming you've left that capability intact. In addition, you may provide a onscreen button to perform the installation without requiring the right click. The default experience is shown in figure 5.3.

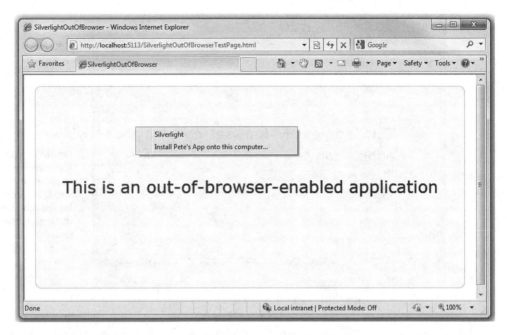

Figure 5.3 The install menu for an out-of-browser-enabled application is accessed by right-clicking on the Silverlight surface.

The installation process is painless, being simply a copy of files to an obfuscated location on the local machine. There are no registry entries required, no additional platform DLLs, and no admin rights—nothing extra. As seen in figure 5.4, there's only a choice of where to put shortcuts (Start menu and/or desktop) and whether to approve or cancel the install—a very low-friction experience compared to a typical platform application install.

Once the user takes the application out of the browser, the .xap will be rerequested from the server and stored in a low-trust location on the local machine along with the information about the original URI of the .xap and the download timestamp. It'll then appear in the places the user selected (Start menu and/or desktop) via the dialog shown in figure 5.4 and also on the taskbar. The user may, as with any other application, pin the shortcut to the Start menu or (in Windows 7) to the taskbar for convenience.

Figure 5.4 The install dialog gives the user the option to place shortcuts on the Start menu and on the desktop. The install icon on the left is customizable, as is the application name.

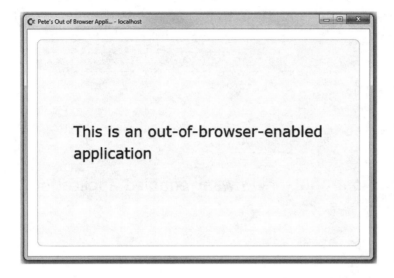

Figure 5.5   The application is running in the out-of-browser mode. Note that both the application window title and source domain (localhost in this case) are displayed in the title bar.

The application will also immediately launch in the out-of-browser mode, as seen in figure 5.5. At this point, the user may close the browser window if she wishes to do so.

Figures 5.6 and 5.7 show a Silverlight application (the Commodore 64 emulator) pinned to the Start menu and the task-bar on a Windows 7 machine. Note the use of custom icons and information about the name of the application.

To uninstall the application, the user may right-click the Silverlight application and select the menu option Remove This Application or use the control panel's Add/Remove Programs applet. Again, no special rights are required and the process is painless.

As you can see, out-of-browser Silver-light applications look and act much like any other desktop application while providing a simple installation experience for the end user. You get the local experience of a desktop applica-tion with the ease of deployment of a web application. Next, we'll look at how to configure and code your applica-tions for out-of-browser support.

Figure 5.6   An out-of-browser Silverlight application with custom icons pinned to the Start menu in Windows 7. The application below it, TweetDeck, is an Adobe AIR application, another competing out-of-browser RIA technology.

Figure 5.7   The same Silverlight out-of-browser application pinned to the taskbar in Windows 7

5.2   *Creating out-of-browser applications*

An out-of-browser application may be as simple as an existing Silverlight application enabled to be run outside the browser chrome or something more complex that uses the Silverlight APIs to check the network state and support offline scenarios. Perhaps it even has a very different user interface when running out of the browser, building upon those APIs and those for runtime mode detection. Before covering the more advanced scenarios, let's start with the minimal changes needed common for all three cases—the settings file.

5.2.1   *The out-of-browser settings file*

As we saw in chapter 3, the application manifest file tells the Silverlight plug-in all about the components of your Silverlight application. What it doesn't include is information about the out-of-browser configuration. That information is included in the out-of-browser configuration file OutOfBrowserSettings.xml (see listing 5.1).

Listing 5.1   A basic out-of-browser application configuration file

```
<OutOfBrowserSettings ShortName="Pete's App"           ◁──── Shown in
                      EnableGPUAcceleration="True"            Start menu
                      ShowInstallMenuItem="True">
  <OutOfBrowserSettings.Blurb>                          ◁──── Shortcut
     Pete's Application on your desktop; at home, at work      comment
     or on the go.
  </OutOfBrowserSettings.Blurb>
  <OutOfBrowserSettings.WindowSettings>
    <WindowSettings Title="Pete's Out-of-Browser Application"  ◁── Window title
                Top="100" Left="100"                   ◁─┐
                WindowStartupLocation="Manual"           │  Window
                Height="450" Width="700" />    ◁──┐       │  startup
  </OutOfBrowserSettings.WindowSettings>            Window │  position
  <OutOfBrowserSettings.Icons>          ◁──┐        startup
    <Icon Size="16,16">AppIcon016.png</Icon>        dimensions
    <Icon Size="32,32">AppIcon032.png</Icon>   Custom
    <Icon Size="48,48">AppIcon048.png</Icon>   icons
    <Icon Size="128,128">AppIcon128.png</Icon>
  </OutOfBrowserSettings.Icons>
</OutOfBrowserSettings>
```

The short name of the application is what's displayed in the right-click Silverlight menu, the installation dialog, and the created shortcuts. The title, when combined with the domain name, is shown in the title bar of the window hosting your application.

Typically, you won't edit the settings file directly. Instead, you'll use the Out-of-Browser Settings dialog from the project properties, as seen in figure 5.8.

This dialog is displayed when you click the Out-of-Browser Settings button on the Silverlight tab of the project properties. One of the options is Show Install Menu, which allows you to toggle whether the default right-click install experience is displayed. If you uncheck that option, you must provide another way for users to install your application out of the browser.

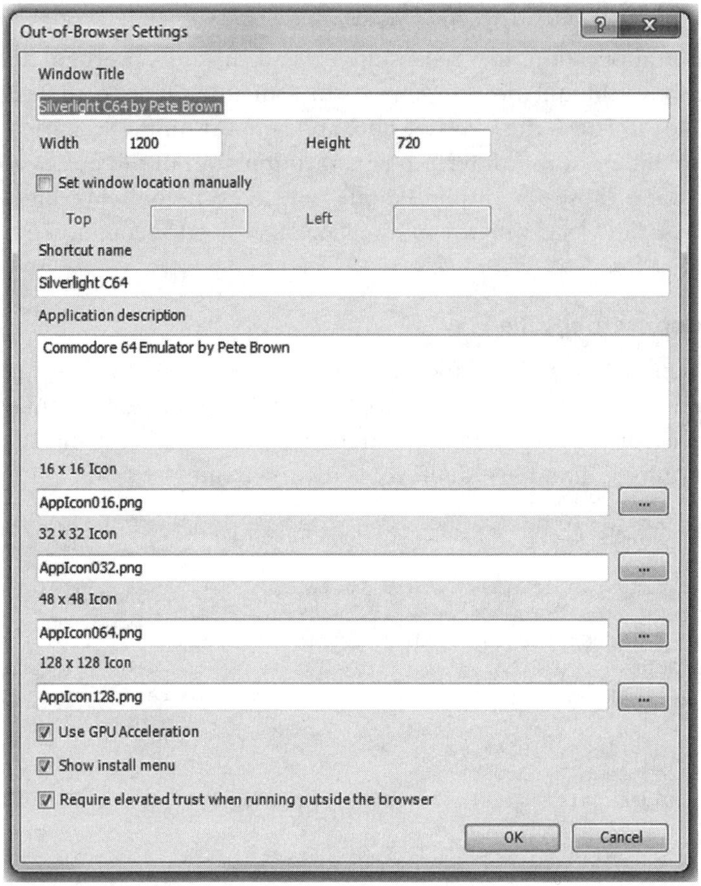

Figure 5.8   The Out-of-Browser Settings dialog

The default right-click installation experience is adequate, but there may be times when you want to provide a more controlled experience both with custom icons and with a more obvious way to take the application out of the browser. We'll cover that next.

5.2.2 *Controlling the experience*

Silverlight provides several useful APIs for both detaching your application from the browser and for checking the current state of your application. The first is the `Application.Current.InstallState` value. The values for `InstallState` are shown in table 5.1.

When the installation state is changed, the `Application` object will raise an `InstallStateChanged` event that informs you to look at `InstallState` for the latest state.

You can extend this concept to force an out-of-browser-only mode in your application simply by refusing to display the application UI unless running outside of the browser. In that case, your in-browser application would simply be an install-me-locally splash screen. Listing 5.2 shows how to set up your application so that it provides a meaningful experience only when run out of the browser.

Table 5.1 The various values of `InstallState`

State	Meaning
Installed	The application has been installed by the user. Note that the current instance of the application may still be running in the browser. This value only tells you it's available in the locally installed mode for the current user/machine.
InstallFailed	The application tried to install, but failed.
Installing	The application is currently installing. This is a good place to download the required assets if you intend to allow the application to run offline as well as out of the browser.
NotInstalled	This value indicates that the application hasn't been locally installed.

Listing 5.2 Forcing out-of-browser mode

XAML:

```
...
<Grid x:Name="IBNotInstalledExperience">
    <Button x:Name="InstallButton"
            Height="100"
            Width="400"
            FontSize="30"
            HorizontalAlignment="Center"
            VerticalAlignment="Center"
            Content="Take Out of Browser" />
</Grid>

<Grid x:Name="IBInstalledExperience">
    <Rectangle Fill="Azure"
               Stroke="LightBlue"
               RadiusX="10"
               RadiusY="10"
               Margin="20" />

    <TextBlock Text="This application is installed locally.
    Please run from the shortcut."
               FontSize="30"
               Margin="30"
               TextWrapping="Wrap"
               HorizontalAlignment="Center"
               VerticalAlignment="Center" />
</Grid>

<Grid x:Name="OobExperience"
      Visibility="Collapsed">

    <Rectangle Fill="Azure"
               Stroke="LightBlue"
               RadiusX="10"
               RadiusY="10"
               Margin="20" />

    <TextBlock Text="Running out of browser"
               FontSize="30"
```

```
                    Margin="30"
                    TextWrapping="Wrap"
                    HorizontalAlignment="Center"
                    VerticalAlignment="Center" />
</Grid>
```

C# code:

```
public MainPage()
{
  InitializeComponent();

  Loaded += new RoutedEventHandler(MainPage_Loaded);
  InstallButton.Click += new RoutedEventHandler(InstClick);
  Application.Current.InstallStateChanged +=
      new EventHandler(OnInstallStateChanged);
}
private void UpdateUserInterface()
{
  if (Application.Current.IsRunningOutOfBrowser)
  {
    OobExperience.Visibility = Visibility.Visible;
  }
  else
  {
    if (Application.Current.InstallState == InstallState.Installed)
    {
      IBInstalledExperience.Visibility = Visibility.Visible;
      IBNotInstalledExperience.Visibility = Visibility.Collapsed;
      OobExperience.Visibility = Visibility.Collapsed;
    }
    else
    {
      IBInstalledExperience.Visibility = Visibility.Collapsed;
      IBNotInstalledExperience.Visibility = Visibility.Visible;
      OobExperience.Visibility = Visibility.Collapsed;
    }
  }
}
void OnInstallStateChanged(object sender, EventArgs e)
{
  UpdateUserInterface();
}

void MainPage_Loaded(object sender, RoutedEventArgs e)
{
  UpdateUserInterface();
}

void InstClick(object sender, RoutedEventArgs e)
{
  Application.Current.Install();
}
```

Installation and execution state check ← (annotation pointing to `private void UpdateUserInterface()`)

Fired when Installed or uninstalled ← (annotation pointing to `void OnInstallStateChanged`)

Install button click handler ← (annotation pointing to `void InstClick`)

The experiences resulting from the code in listing 5.2 are shown in figures 5.9 and 5.10. Note that the `Install` method may only be called from a user-generated

Figure 5.9 The experience a user will see if he hasn't installed this application. Clicking the button calls `Application.Current.Install()`.

Figure 5.10 The same application after it's detected that it was installed and is running outside of the browser. Note that the browser-hosted version responded to the `InstallStateChanged` event by changing its own UI.

UI event, such as a button click. This is to prevent applications from self-installing without explicit user intervention.

So though you can't exactly *force* an application to install locally, you can design it to show different interfaces depending upon its installation state and current mode of operation. Think carefully before you use this type of code in your own applications; if there's no compelling reason to force an application to run out of the browser only, don't force the user.

The next step in customizing the experience is to change the icons displayed in the install dialog, the application window, the Start menu, and the taskbar.

5.2.3   *Customizing icons*

The next step in creating a customized out-of-browser experience is changing the icons used in the application. The icons, which must be .png files, are typically provided in four sizes from 128×128 to 16×16. The 128×128 size is used in the installation dialog. The other sizes are used in the Start menu, the window icon, shortcuts, and in the Apple OS X application list. Though you don't need to provide every size, I highly recommend that you do because they may not scale at runtime in quite the way you want them to. The approach is similar to exploding a typical Windows .ico file into four .png files.

To include icons, the `OutOfBrowserSettings.Icons` section is added to the Out-OfBrowserSettings.xml inside the `OutOfBrowserSettings` section, as shown:

```
<OutOfBrowserSettings ...>
...
  <OutOfBrowserSettings.Icons>
    <Icon Size="16,16">AppIcon016.png</Icon>
    <Icon Size="32,32">AppIcon032.png</Icon>
    <Icon Size="48,48">AppIcon048.png</Icon>
    <Icon Size="128,128">AppIcon128.png</Icon>
  </OutOfBrowserSettings.Icons>
</OutOfBrowserSettings>
```

The icons themselves are included in your project as `Content` and copied into the .xap file at compile time. In the preceding example, they're in the project root but you certainly may include them in a subfolder. The filenames can be anything you want as long as the actual resolution of the file matches up with the known resolution assigned to it in the `Size` property.

That's it for customizing the install experience. Next, we'll look at how to handle two common scenarios for out-of-browser applications: changing the network state and updating the application.

5.2.4   *Checking the network state*

You'll use two mechanisms to check the network state in your Silverlight application: the `GetIsNetworkAvailable` method and the `NetworkAddressChanged` event. Both are available in an out of the browser but are more commonly used in out-of-browser scenarios.

The `NetworkInterface` and `NetworkChange` classes included in the `System.Net.NetworkInformation` namespace provide access to the network state information. Typically, you'll use them together like this:

```
NetworkChange.NetworkAddressChanged += new
   NetworkAddressChangedEventHandler(OnNetworkAddressChanged);

...

void OnNetworkAddressChanged(object sender, EventArgs e)
{
  if (NetworkInterface.GetIsNetworkAvailable())
  {
    // Connected to some network
  }
  else
  {
    // Not connected to any network
  }
}
```

The call to `GetIsNetworkAvailable` will tell us only that there's some sort of network connection. It doesn't guarantee that we can access required services or even the Internet in general. On machines with network connections between the host and a virtual PC (VPC), which is typical in development environments, this may even detect the VPC connection as a valid network connection and return true.

Rather than rely just on this call, it's a good practice to first check to see whether any network is available and, if so, ping or call a known service on the server you plan to reach before assuming you're connected. Since the network state can change during the application runtime, you may want to call these methods on a timer or in the exception handlers in your network service interface layer.

One thing that can only happen when you're connected to the network is updating the application.

UPDATING

A real benefit of browser-based applications is the ability to automatically update the application without requiring any sort of explicit installation or push to the client machine. Out-of-browser Silverlight applications aren't very different in that regard, except that the developer controls the update process.

The Silverlight `Application` object includes a `CheckAndDownloadUpdateAsync` method that, as its name indicates, will check for any available .xap updates and download, if present. When the method completes, it fires the `CheckAndDownloadUpdate-Completed` event.

The code is fairly simple and, if you use a little lambda expression sugar to create the delegate, you can even fit it all into a single short function:

```
private void CheckForUpdates()
{
  Application.Current.CheckAndDownloadUpdateCompleted +=
    (s, e) =>
    {
```

```
      if (e.UpdateAvailable)
      {
        MessageBox.Show("A new version was downloaded.");
      }
    };

  Application.Current.CheckAndDownloadUpdateAsync();
}
```

When the `CheckForUpdates` call is made, Silverlight looks at the stored origin URI of the .xap file and makes a normal background HTTP request to that location to verify that the latest version is installed. If a new version is available, Silverlight will receive that in the background and programmatically indicate that a new version is available by setting the `UpdateAvailable` property to `true` in the returned event arguments class. Unless you prompt the user to shut down and relaunch the application, he'll still be running the old version. It's not until the next run that he'll execute the newly downloaded version.

But, when you detect that a new version is available, you can display a dialog to the user and request a restart. If the nature of the application allows it, you can also be more draconian and completely block all of the UI functionality until the user restarts the application. What you can't do is force an application to restart programmatically. A best practice is to gently inform your user (perhaps soothing music and pastel colors will help) that a new version is available and let him restart at his convenience. At the worst, he'll get the new version during the next session.

Once you've decided to take your application out of the browser, one of the capabilities you'll enable is the notification API, introduced in Silverlight 4.

5.2.5   *Alerting the user with Notification toast*

Windows notifications have been nicknamed *toast* due to their way of popping up from the bottom right of the desktop, like a piece of toast in an old toaster. Notification is used for everything from displaying new email messages in Outlook, to new tweets in the popular Twitter programs, to new items in the queue of a business application. Notifications are an essential tool for alerting the user when the application is sitting in the background or on another screen.

Creating a simple notification window is easy. All you need to do is create an instance of `NotificationWindow`, set the size, and set the content. The result will be less than stellar, though; it'll be a simple opaque white rectangle with your text overlaid:

```
if (Application.Current.IsRunningOutOfBrowser)
{
  NotificationWindow notify = new NotificationWindow();
  notify.Height = 75;
  notify.Width = 300;

  TextBlock text = new TextBlock();
  text.Text = "Basic Notification";

  notify.Content = text;

  notify.Show(5000);
}
```

The Show method takes a number of milliseconds representing how long to show the window. The value of 5000 milliseconds used in this example is 5 seconds.

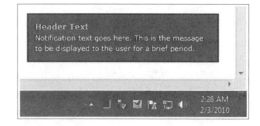

To really use NotificationWindow, you'll need to fill it up with something more meaningful. Typically you'll create a user control to represent the content and assign that rather than a simple

Figure 5.11 A customized notification window

TextBlock. Figure 5.11 shows an example of a user control with a red and black border, gray header text, and white body text.

On Windows, the notification windows will always display on the bottom-right corner on the screen. On Mac OS X, they display at the top-right corner.

The window may be closed by simply timing out or by calling the Notification-Window.Close method. In either case, the NotificationWindow.Closed event is fired, allowing you to take action as necessary.

Notifications are one of many capabilities enabled when you run your application out-of-browser. Before we delve more deeply into other capabilities, let's take a detour into the implementation specifics of out-of-browser applications.

5.2.6 *Implementation specifics*

When developing and debugging out-of-browser applications, it can be essential to understand how Silverlight implements them under the covers. This is especially important when you're developing a true cross-platform application and need to ensure consistent behavior.

On Windows, out-of-browser Silverlight applications run in a process named sllauncher.exe. That process hosts the IE rendering surface mshtml.dll hosted in shdocvw. The rendering surface is where your Silverlight application exists, visually. Similarly, on Apple OS X, the process hosts the Safari/WebKit rendering surface and related libraries. In both cases, Silverlight doesn't rely on the entire browser stack, just the core functionality required to host Silverlight content inside the native operating system window chrome.

Though the Silverlight team has gone through great pains to ensure performance is similar on all supported operating systems, understanding the limitations of Safari/ WebKit and Internet Explorer can really help with diagnosing performance issues. For example, current implementations of Safari use a plug-in compositing mode that's not as efficient as Internet Explorer. If your application has lots of animation and internal compositing going on, it's a good idea to test performance on OS X before the release.

As in the case with process-isolated tabs in the browser, each out-of-browser Silverlight application will have its own process, app domain, and instance of the CoreCLR.

Out-of-browser Silverlight support now enables us to create a new class of applications that combine the best of Silverlight web development with the great experience of a desktop application. If you want to enable out-of-browser and offline scenarios, need access to keys normally swallowed by the browser, or just want more screen real estate, you take advantage of the new OOB features. Best of all, the partial-trust applications are just as safe and secure as their browser-hosted versions and easier to install than typical desktop applications.

As compelling as that is, sometimes you need a bit more power. Silverlight 4 adds even more desktop-like functionality in the form of the new elevated trust mode.

5.3   *Escaping the sandbox—elevated trust*

Silverlight 4 introduces the concept of elevated-trust applications. Elevated-trust applications are out-of-browser applications that have access to additional capabilities on the machine on to which they're installed. For all intents and purposes, elevated-trust applications are actually full-trust applications. For example, elevated-trust applications can use the new COM automation capabilities discussed in section 5.2.2, as well as make web network requests without first checking for a client access policy. The full list of capabilities enabled by elevated trust includes:

- Using COM for native Windows integration.
- Calling web services and making network requests without requiring a client access policy check and without any cross-domain or cross-scheme restrictions.
- Relaxed user consent for clipboard, webcam, and microphone access.
- Relaxed user initiation requirements. For example, you can enter the full-screen mode in an `Application.Startup` event handler rather than requiring a button click or other user-initiated event.
- Reading and writing files in user document folders.
- Using the full-screen mode without keyboard restrictions and without the Press ESC to exit overlay and staying in full-screen mode even if the user switches focus to another window or display.
- Controlling the size, position, and ordering of the host window.

That's a pretty powerful list; it addresses most of the restrictions developers have been bothered by since the initial release of Silverlight 2. In particular, the ability to make network calls without worrying about cross-domain, and the new COM automation capability, both open up entirely new areas for Silverlight development.

We'll first cover how to create elevated trust applications and the important step of how to sign them and then follow that up with sections covering specific elevated trust features you'll use in your own applications—including enhancements to local file access and the COM automation support introduced in Silverlight 4.

5.3.1   *Creating elevated-trust applications*

To mark your application as requiring elevated trust, first you must make the application support the out-of-browser mode. Then, it's as simple as a check box on the Out-of-Browser Settings page, shown in figure 5.8 earlier in this chapter.

Figure 5.12   Normal out-of-browser installation prompt

It may seem simple to just mark all out-of-browser applications as requiring elevated trust, but the end-user install prompt is slightly scarier when elevated trust is used. Figure 5.12 shows the normal out-of-browser installation prompt. It's pretty tame, since the application is still running in a pretty tight sandbox.

Once you move into the elevated trust mode, the dialogs rightfully get scarier to encourage the user to install applications only from the sources they trust.

UNSIGNED APPLICATIONS

Figure 5.13 shows the elevated trust install dialog, in the case of an unsigned application. It's a pretty scary dialog that'll give most users pause. For that reason alone, it's good to be judicious about which applications really require elevated trust or perhaps even offer alternative versions of your application (perhaps the in-browser version) that don't require additional permissions.

If you want to have a friendly elevated trust installation dialog, you'll need to sign the application (sign the .xap) using a certificate from a trusted certificate authority.

SIGNED APPLICATIONS

The only way to have an elevated trust application without a scary dialog is to sign the .xap using a certificate from a trusted authority such as VeriSign, Thawte, GoDaddy,

Figure 5.13   Unsigned out-of-browser elevated trust install prompt

Figure 5.14   Signed out-of-browser elevated trust install prompt

or Comodo. Once you sign the .xap, you'll get a much friendlier dialog, as seen in figure 5.14.

Users are much more likely to install an application with the friendlier dialog and your publisher information than with the yellow-bannered "unverified source" shown in figure 5.13.

For testing purposes, you can self-sign your .xap using a test certificate. Visual Studio, via the options on the Signing tab for the Silverlight project, will generate the test cert for you. You'll then need to add the certificate to your own store in the Trusted Certificate Root. Anyone else who's going to test the application will also need to install the certificate. The fewer people with your test cert, the better, so be sure to get a real certificate early in the process.

Once you have a certificate, you can use it in Visual Studio 2010 to sign your .xap. This is accomplished via the Signing tab in the project properties window for the Silverlight application. Figure 5.15 shows a .xap file signed by my own test certificate.

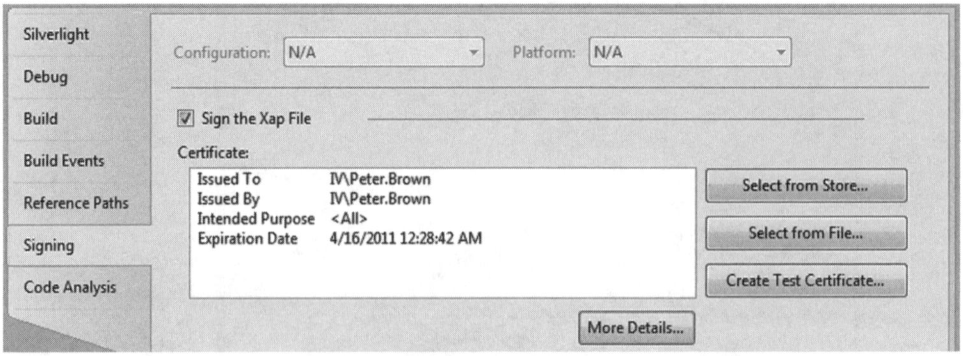

Figure 5.15   Signing options in Visual Studio 2010

Once you have the certificate installed and it's recognized by your target machines, you're good to test and deploy. Make sure you get the certificate early in the process because it typically is not a simple, quick, or completely online process. Nevertheless, this is the same process you'll go through for certificates for any use, including application signing and secure sockets.

> **TIP** Jeff Wilcox from the Silverlight team at Microsoft put together a great walk-through of purchasing and installing a certificate for personal use. You can find it on his blog here: http://www.jeff.wilcox.name/2010/02/codesigning101/.

Trusted applications have a lot going for them, but users can still reject elevated permissions. If you're going to build elevated trust applications and potentially share any code with a normal trust application, one thing you'll need to do is check to see whether the user has actually granted you elevated permissions.

5.3.2 Detecting elevated trust mode

Before enabling certain features in your application, it's a good practice to check to see if you're running in elevated trust mode. The `Application` object exposes the `HasElevatedPermissions` property, which allows you to do just that:

```
if (Application.Current.HasElevatedPermissions)
{
    /* Light up the awesomeness */
}
```

Checking for elevated permissions allows you to take alternative approaches in cases where the permissions weren't granted. Graceful downgrading of functionality is always a good idea when it comes to web applications. You can provide the users with the level of features they're comfortable with while maximizing the number of people you serve.

We've now turned on the elevated trust mode and considered what it takes to detect it. One of the areas that's available in Silverlight by default but is enhanced by elevated trust mode is local file access.

5.4 Local file access

Since version 2, Silverlight has offered the ability to load data from local files but it was restricted to isolated storage and to streams loaded via the `OpenFileDialog`. Starting with Silverlight 4 and the new elevated trust mode, you now have the ability to open any file in the My Documents folder (and the equivalent folder on the Mac) without injecting additional user interface in the process.

5.4.1 Accessing special folders

The paths to the special folders are accessed using `Environment.GetFolderPath` and passing it a value in the `Environment.SpecialFolder` enumeration. An example of enumerating all of the files in the My Music folder would look like this:

```
var music = Directory.EnumerateFiles(
  Environment.GetFolderPath(Environment.SpecialFolder.MyMusic));
```

The result would be an `IEnumerable<string>` containing all of the files in the
C:\Users\Pete.Brown\Music folder on my machine.

The full list of special folders currently supported in Silverlight is shown in table 5.2.
The enumeration itself has quite a few other values, but those are for compatibility with
the full framework. Using them in Silverlight will throw an exception.

Table 5.2   **The values of `SpecialFolder` currently supported in Silverlight**

Enum value	Description
`MyComputer`	The My Computer folder Note: The `MyComputer` constant always contains the empty string (`" "`) because no path is defined for the My Computer folder. Example: `" "`
`MyMusic`	The My Music folder Example: C:\Users\Pete.Brown\Music
`MyPictures`	The My Pictures folder Example: C:\Users\Pete.Brown\Pictures
`MyVideos`	The My Videos folder Example: C:\Users\Pete.Brown\Videos
`Personal`	The directory that serves as a common repository for documents This is the same as `MyDocuments`.
`MyDocuments`	The My Documents folder Example: C:\Users\Pete.Brown\Documents

In addition to enumerating files, you'd expect to be able to read from and write to the
files in those directories, and you'd be correct.

5.4.2   *Reading from a file*

You may read from a file rooted in one of the allowed directories using the `File`
object and opening a stream:

```
if (Application.Current.HasElevatedPermissions)
{
  string path = Environment.GetFolderPath(
                    Environment.SpecialFolder.MyDocuments);
  string fileName = System.IO.Path.Combine(path, "sltest.txt");

  if (File.Exists(fileName))
  {
    using (StreamReader reader = File.OpenText(fileName))
    {
      string contents = reader.ReadToEnd();

      // do something with contents

      reader.Close();
    }
  }
}
```

If you try to open from an unsupported location, Silverlight will throw an exception and you'll be unable to open the file.

In addition to reading files from the supported locations, you'll probably want to write files.

5.4.3 Writing to a file

Writing to a file works just as you'd expect it to, using the `File` object and a `Stream-Writer`, as long as you root your file in one of the allowed folders. Again, it's a good idea to check for elevated permissions before taking any action:

```
if (Application.Current.HasElevatedPermissions)
{
  string path = GetFolderPath(Environment.SpecialFolder.MyDocuments);
  string fileName = System.IO.Path.Combine(path, "sltest.txt");

  using (StreamWriter writer = File.CreateText(fileName))
  {
    writer.WriteLine("Test from Silverlight.");
    writer.Close();
  }
}
```

Reading and writing to files in the My Documents folder is great but still falls short of what full-fledged desktop applications enable. Should you desire to do so, COM automation will allow you to gain access to any folder the user would normally have access to. It also provides a lot of great new capabilities such as calling Windows APIs and automating programs like Excel.

5.5 COM automation

One of the more interesting capabilities introduced in Silverlight 4 in the `System.Windows.Interop` namespace is the ability to use COM automation to integrate with native code and applications on the desktop. The primary intent of this feature is to allow automation of other applications, including Microsoft Office. Secondarily, this feature may be used to gain access to a subset of the Windows APIs, specifically those that support `IDispatch`. Although there are hacks to make it work, it was not a goal of this feature to allow access to custom COM DLLs you may write or the third parties provide and which you package and install along with your Silverlight application or to allow access to the full desktop CLR.

With that disclaimer out of the way, the COM automation feature of Silverlight is an incredibly powerful way to extend the sandbox, both for good and for evil. Once you have access to an `IDispatch`-compatible API, you can do anything you want with it. It doesn't respect the sandbox otherwise enforced by Silverlight; the only security that comes into play is operating system-level security.

5.5.1 Detecting COM automation availability

COM automation may not be available in any particular running instance of your application. Reasons for this may be that it's running in the browser, the user has declined the elevation request, or the application is running on a platform other than Windows. In those cases, you want to nicely degrade the functionality in a way that both respects the user and still provides a good experience.

In addition to checking for elevated permissions as described in section 5.2.1, Silverlight provides some calls you may use to detect the presence of COM automation. The first is the call to check that you're running on Windows. The primary reason to get used to coding this check is that the future versions of Silverlight may include automation of scripting capabilities on other platforms and you'd want to branch to them here.

```
switch (System.Environment.OSVersion.Platform)
{
    // Mac
    case PlatformID.MacOSX:
        break;

    // Unix/Linux
    case PlatformID.Unix:
        break;

    // Windows
    case PlatformID.Win32NT:
        break;
}
```

I recommend using the OS check sparingly. You never know if capabilities available only on one platform may show up in another in the future. Rather than drive that based on the OS, drive it based on feature availability. The exception to this is COM automation, which is a Windows-only feature. We may have an approach to accomplish the same thing on Mac OS X in the future, but the implementation will differ substantially.

Once you check for the OS, the next logical check is to see that you're running out of the browser. While this isn't strictly necessary, you may want to do this to provide a different downgrade experience than the in-browser version:

```
if (Application.Current.IsRunningOutOfBrowser)
{
    /* Out-of-browser coolness goes here */
}
```

The final check is to see if COM automation is available. Technically, this is the only call you're required to make but, if I kept this book just to the required bits, it'd be a rehash of our documentation on msdn.microsoft.com and would seem too much like work:

```
if (AutomationFactory.IsAvailable)
{
    /* do awesome stuff */
}
```

Once you ensure automation is available, you can start using it to interact with other applications or operating system APIs. It truly is a powerful level of integration with the native code bits of the system. Let's look at some cool things you can do with it.

> **IDispatch**
>
> IDispatch is COM's standard interface that supports late binding using the OLE Automation protocol interface. IDispatch provides methods to allow a client to query the component to find out what properties and methods it supports as well as a method to invoke any one of those methods.
>
> Each method supported by the COM component is assigned an ID. When the `IDispatch` interface's `GetIDsOfNames` function is passed a string name of a function, it returns the ID. The calling code then uses the `Invoke` function to invoke that function.
>
> Due to the late binding nature of `IDispatch`, it supports scripting as well as clients using the dynamic functionality in .NET 4, along with older clients such as Visual Basic (pre-.NET)
>
> The method-ID table approach of IDispatch isn't as performant as the early bound references using custom interfaces. For that reason, consider alternative approaches when looking at calling many `IDispatch` methods in a large loop in an application.

5.5.2 Using COM automation to make Silverlight talk

As an example of one of the neat OS-level things you can do with the API, let's look at speech. `System.Speech`, available as part of the full .NET framework, makes speech easily accessible to any desktop or server application. But `System.Speech` simply wraps and makes .NET-friendly the Speech API (SAPI) native to Windows. As luck would have it, SAPI supports a script- and Silverlight-friendly `IDispatch` interface. The code here shows a simple "Hello World!" speech application using the C# dynamic keyword and Silverlight 4's new COM automation feature:

```
if (AutomationFactory.IsAvailable)
{
    using (dynamic voice =
    AutomationFactory.CreateObject("Sapi.SpVoice"))
    {
        voice.Speak("I'm better than any in-page midi file!");
    }
}
```

In order to use the C# dynamic keyword, you need to have a reference to Microsoft.CSharp.dll. The DLL is delivered with the Silverlight SDK.

Another interesting use of COM automation is access to the Windows 7 Sensor and Location API.

5.5.3 Accessing GPS data using COM automation

I'm writing this part of the chapter on the return trip from speaking at an event in Iceland (in-flight power and limitless coffee are a real win, in spite of how hot my US power supply is from the 240V power). Right above my multi-touch tablet screen is a small seat-back console that displays the graphical representation of our geographical position on the world map. (For reference, we're above Canada between the amusingly named Goose Bay and Gander.)

Watching that reminded me that all the nifty GPS work I've done with WPF on Windows 7 is also available in Silverlight because the native API supports `IDispatch`. Location-aware Silverlight applications? Awesome.

Access to location information was first offered as part of the full .NET 4 framework in the `System.Device.Location` namespace. Much like `System.Speech`, `System.Device.Location` simply (or not so simply if you're the one who had to write it) wraps and makes .NET-friendly the Windows 7 Location API. Though you do lose some convenience such as the `INotifyPropertyChanged` implementation (see chapter 9) by going directly against the native COM API, it's still pretty usable.

The following example shows how to access location information, specifically the latitude and longitude reported by a GPS receiver such as the u-blox device included with Microsoft Streets and Trips 2010. Note that this example requires a version of Windows 7 that supports the Sensor and Location API (all versions except the Starter edition):

```
if (AutomationFactory.IsAvailable)
{
  using (dynamic factory =
    AutomationFactory.CreateObject("LocationDisp.LatLongReportFactory"))
  {
    AutomationEvent newReportEvent =
      AutomationFactory.GetEvent(factory, "NewLatLongReport");

    newReportEvent.EventRaised += (s, ev) =>
    {
      using (dynamic report = factory.LatLongReport)
      {
        LatitudeDisplay.Text = factory.Latitude.ToString();
        LongitudeDisplay.Text = factory.Longitude.ToString();
      }
    };

    factory.ListenForReports(1000);

  }
}
```

In addition to working only on a Windows 7 PC (I don't check for that in this example, but you should), this code will only work if you have a GPS attached to your PC and you're in a spot where you can get a satellite signal. If you don't have a different Location API-compatible receiver, I recommend getting the inexpensive u-blox one and downloading the Location API drivers from www.ublox.com/en/usb-drivers/windows-7-driver.html. The device itself is fairly simple, reporting only latitude and longitude (no altitude, speed, or heading) but is otherwise quite capable.

Speech and location are fun and likely to be used by lots of applications, but the one example requested more than any else and the one feature many people have requested of Silverlight is the automation of Microsoft Office applications such as Outlook and Excel.

5.5.4 Automating Excel

Finally, the canonical example of using COM automation in Silverlight is to automate Excel to populate data. Listing 5.3 shows an example of creating a worksheet with data and a chart.

Listing 5.3 Automating Excel to create data and a chart

```
if (AutomationFactory.IsAvailable)
{
  dynamic excel =
    AutomationFactory.CreateObject("Excel.Application");
  excel.Visible = true;

  dynamic workbook = excel.workbooks;      | Create
  workbook.Add();                        <—| worksheet

  dynamic sheet = excel.ActiveSheet;

  int i = 1;

  double[] data = new double[] { 1.0, 5.0, 9.5, 2.7, 3.2, 0.6 };

  foreach (double d in data)                         <—| Iterate
  {                                                     | dummy data
    dynamic cell = sheet.Cells[i, 1];
    cell.Value = "Row " + i;        <—| Label
    cell.ColumnWidth = 10;            | cell

    cell = sheet.Cells[i, 2];
    cell.Value = d;          <—| Value
    i++;                       | cell
  }
  dynamic shapes = sheet.Shapes;           | Add 3d rotated
                                           | chart (type –4I00)
  shapes.AddChart(-4100, 120, 2, 300, 200);  <—|
}
```

The resulting worksheet with data and chart looks like figure 5.16. Note that the communication need not be one way as shown in this example. You can also wire up Excel data change events to update the data back in your own Silverlight application.

That's pretty impressive from what's otherwise thought of as a web application technology. Though you can't actually embed Office UI (such an Excel worksheet) into your application, the ability to automate Excel and other Office applications really helps to make Silverlight ready for business.

You can do quite a bit with elevated trust mode applications in Silverlight 4 and above. The local file access capability makes for an even richer cross-platform experience and enables scenarios previously restricted to platform-specific desktop applications.

Special among the elevated trust features, the COM capabilities are almost endless but should be used with discretion and caution. This feature provides yet another option for creating Windows client applications.

COM automation is exciting, powerful, and a little scary. The sky is the limit with what you can do. Coming back down to Earth on the elevated trust capabilities, we'll next cover the control you have over the window hosting the out-of-browser application.

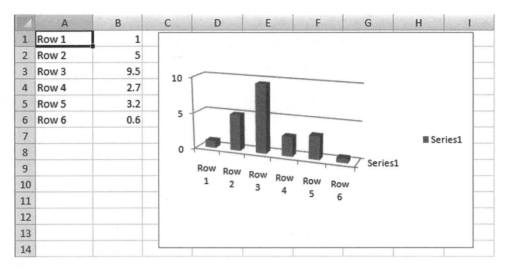

Figure 5.16   An Excel worksheet and chart generated through COM Interop using the Silverlight elevated trust mode

What about other platforms?

Silverlight is a cross-platform product so it's reasonable to ask what the strategy is for the Mac and Linux. Though nothing is official at this point, the Silverlight team is looking into providing access to similar or equivalent technologies on other supported platforms. One example of that may be AppleScript on the Mac. Though that means we'd have to write different code for different platforms, I think the nature of this feature makes that a necessary evil, should you desire deep integration with the operating system features.

5.6   *Controlling the host window*

To create a truly differentiated out-of-browser experience, you'll probably want to have complete control over the title bar, resize bar, window buttons, and other elements that make up the window chrome. You may want to just change the color or you may want to provide a completely different look and feel that blends seamlessly with the application, without any jarring window borders.

Silverlight supports several levels of customization to the out-of-browser window. The simplest is setting the size and position of the window. From there, you can also set it to be a topmost window—one that floats above all others. You can also programmatically activate it.

Those are all easy controls, but often you need to go a step further. Silverlight supports customizing the out-of-browser window chrome. It even includes functions and properties that make it possible for you to easily replicate the normal window behavior, including minimizing, maximizing/restoring, closing, moving, and resizing the window.

In this section we'll start with the basic properties, but as they're simple and pretty self-explanatory, we won't linger there. Instead, we'll hop right into the meatier topics of changing the window chrome, modifying the window state, and moving and resizing the window.

5.6.1 *Basic window properties*

Elevated trust applications can change the properties of the host window at runtime, including size, location, and even the chrome. The `Window` class used is similar to the one used by WPF, so many of the properties and methods may be familiar to you. The list of important properties and functions is shown in table 5.3.

Table 5.3 Runtime-controllable properties of the out-of-browser host window

Member	Description
`Top, Left`	Gets or sets the position of the window
`Height, Width`	Gets of sets the size of the window
`TopMost`	Set to `true` to make the Silverlight application float above all other windows Useful for certain types of utility applications, but don't abuse
`WindowState`	Get or set the state of the window Possible values are `Normal`, `Minimized`, and `Maximized`
`IsActive`	Read-only Returns a Boolean indicating whether the window is currently active
`Activate`	Attempts to activate the application window by bringing it to the foreground and setting focus to it

The following example uses all of these properties and functions to size and position the window, set its state, ensure it's topmost, and then activate if it's not already activated. We'll cover the window state changes after we cover customizing the window chrome because that's where the window state typically comes into play:

```
if (Application.Current.HasElevatedPermissions)
{
  Window win = Application.Current.MainWindow;

  win.TopMost = true;
  win.Height = 200;
  win.Width = 200;

  win.Left = 150;
  win.Top = 150;

  if (!win.IsActive)
    win.Activate();
}
```

Setting the size and state of the window is important, but that's not changing the look of the window chrome itself. To do that, you'll need to use a few more features introduced with Silverlight 4.

5.6.2   *Changing window chrome*

Silverlight applications tend to be highly visual and highly branded experiences. When an out-of-browser application with a custom look gets wrapped in the standard OS window chrome, it can really ruin the experience. What you really want is edge-to-edge control over the look of your application, including the borders, buttons, and title bar.

Elevated trust out-of-browser applications enable you to control the window chrome. You can choose to have the default OS chrome, no border, or borderless rounded corners. At this point, you can't have irregularly shaped windows or windows with transparency, but that may show up in a future version. Figure 5.17 shows the various options inside the out-of-browser configuration dialog in Visual Studio 2010.

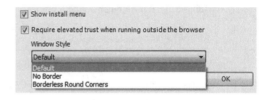

The setting here adds an attribute to the `Window` element in the OutOfBrowserSettings.xml file. The possible values for the style are shown in table 5.4.

Figure 5.17   Custom chrome settings for elevated trust out-of-browser applications

Table 5.4   Window styles for out-of-browser applications

Value	Description
(unspecified element)	The default window chrome is based on the operating system in use.
`BorderlessRoundCornersWindow`	The window is drawn with a 5-pixel corner radius on all four corners.
None	The window is a rectangular shape with no border.

Figure 5.18 shows a close-up of the corner of the window when using the `BorderlessRoundCornersWindow` as the window style. The result is a rectangle with a 5 px corner radius on all four corners, with no anti-aliasing or operating system drop shadow. This is a clipping function in Silverlight; you don't need to make any changes to your layout to accommodate the rounded corner, unless you want to.

Figure 5.18   A close-up view of the top-left corner of a black window using the round-corners setting. The radius is fixed by Silverlight itself.

When you create custom chrome for your windows, you're suddenly responsible for the full behavior of the window, including creating a title bar (should you want one), adding your own minimize, maximize, and close buttons, and handling moving and resizing. Luckily, Silverlight provides several functions and events to help you do this.

5.6.3 *Minimizing, maximizing, restoring, and closing*

Most chrome implementations will have at least three buttons on the upper right of
the window: Minimize, Maximize/Restore, and Close. When you use the normal OS
chrome, those buttons are provided for you. When using custom chrome, you'll need
to set the window state or call the `Close` method on the `Application.Current.Main-`
`Window` object. Listing 5.4 shows how to handle these functions in an application with
custom chrome. The `Grid` is assumed to be the main layout root in MainPage.xaml.

Listing 5.4 Handling window state with custom chrome

XAML:
```
<Grid x:Name="LayoutRoot" Background="Orange">
  <StackPanel Orientation="Horizontal" HorizontalAlignment="Right"
              VerticalAlignment="Top" Margin="8">
    <Button x:Name="MinimizeButton" Width="15" Height="15" />
    <Button x:Name="MaximizeButton" Width="15" Height="15" />
    <Button x:Name="CloseButton"    Width="15" Height="15" />
  </StackPanel>
</Grid>
```

C#:
```
public MainPage()
{
  InitializeComponent();

  MaximizeButton.Click +=
        new RoutedEventHandler(MaximizeButton_Click);
  MinimizeButton.Click +=
        new RoutedEventHandler(MinimizeButton_Click);
  CloseButton.Click +=
        new RoutedEventHandler(CloseButton_Click);
}

void CloseButton_Click(object sender, RoutedEventArgs e)
{
  Application.Current.MainWindow.Close();            <─── Close
}

void MinimizeButton_Click(object sender, RoutedEventArgs e)
{
  Application.Current.MainWindow.WindowState =
      WindowState.Minimized;                        <─── Minimize
}

void MaximizeButton_Click(object sender, RoutedEventArgs e)
{
  if (Application.Current.MainWindow.WindowState ==
      WindowState.Maximized)
  {
    Application.Current.MainWindow.WindowState =
        WindowState.Normal;                         <─── Restore
  }
  else
  {
```

```
      Application.Current.MainWindow.WindowState =
          WindowState.Maximized;                    ◁— Maximize
  }
}
```

In this example, you can see how easy it is to add your own window state management buttons to the elevated trust out-of-browser application. That gets you half way there. The other half of the required functionality is the ability to move your window by dragging it with the mouse.

5.6.4   *Moving*

There are three approaches to moving your window in Silverlight: making the whole window draggable, making an element (such as the title bar) draggable, or not bothering. The last option isn't going to make you any friends unless you're writing some sort of a docking tool that can only sit on certain positions on the screen, so that leaves the first two.

   Silverlight includes the DragMove method on the MainWindow object we used in the previous examples. DragMove can be called from anything but is typically called from the MouseLeftButtonDown event of a title bar, or of the window itself. Listing 5.5 builds on the previous example by adding a grid to represent the title bar and one event handler.

Listing 5.5   Code to implement dragging a window

XAML:
```
<Grid x:Name="LayoutRoot" Background="Orange">     ┐ Stand-in
  <Grid x:Name="TitleBar"                        ◁─┘ title bar
        Background="Blue" Height="30"
        VerticalAlignment="Top" />

  <StackPanel Orientation="Horizontal" ...
```
C#:
```
public MainPage()
{
  InitializeComponent();

  ...

  TitleBar.MouseLeftButtonDown +=
    new MouseButtonEventHandler(TitleBar_MouseLeftButtonDown);
}

void TitleBar_MouseLeftButtonDown(object sender,
                                  MouseButtonEventArgs e)
{                                                      ┐ Dragging
  Application.Current.MainWindow.DragMove();         ◁─┘ to move
}
```

The DragMove method is interesting because it takes over the mouse management until the mouse is released. For that reason, you don't need to wire up any mouse movement events, or worry about the mouse getting outside the bounds of the window, or any of the other cruft you may have thought would be required.

Silverlight provides one more method for window management, this one to allow the user to resize the window when using custom chrome.

5.6.5 Resizing

While all of the other functions are considered pretty essential to window management, resizing is completely optional. Some applications don't allow resizing by the end user. But, since Silverlight makes it so simple to rescale or resize elements when the window is resized, this decision should be made only for aesthetic reasons and not for lack of time to implement.

To support resizing, DragMove has a sister function named DragResize. The DragResize move works much like DragMove, except it takes in a parameter that allows you to specify exactly where in the window the user is resizing. Listing 5.6 builds on the previous examples and shows how to use DragResize with a typical corner resize. Keep in mind that you can specify any edge by using multiple resize elements and calling DragResize with the appropriate parameter.

Listing 5.6   Implementing resize using an element in the bottom right corner

XAML:
```
<Grid x:Name="ResizeArea"                                        ◁─┐ Stand-in resize
  Background="Blue" Height="30" Width="30"                          │ corner
  VerticalAlignment="Bottom" HorizontalAlignment="Right" />

<StackPanel Orientation="Horizontal" ...
```

C#:
```
public MainPage()
{
  InitializeComponent();
  ...

  ResizeArea.MouseLeftButtonDown +=
      new MouseButtonEventHandler(ResizeArea_MouseLeftButtonDown);
}

void ResizeArea_MouseLeftButtonDown(object sender,
                               MouseButtonEventArgs e)
{                                                                ┐ Dragging to
    Application.Current.MainWindow.DragResize(            ◁──┘ resize
                        WindowResizeEdge.BottomRight);
}
```

Controlling the main window when running in the out-of-browser mode is an essential addition to the Silverlight platform. It enables you to write applications that really look and feel like native operating system apps—if you want them to. It also enables you to create truly branded experiences that extend all the way to the edges of the window.

Silverlight provides a number of ways you can control the window, from simply setting its size and position, to floating it above other windows, all the way to using custom chrome. Silverlight also provides functions and properties to make window manipulation easier when you implement your own chrome.

Sometimes what you want isn't actually a host window in an out-of-browser application but rather just the ability to take your in- or out-of-browser application to full screen, overlaying even the operating system shell UI elements. Yes, Silverlight can do that too.

5.7   *Running in full screen*

Most browsers support the ability to run in the full-screen mode, typically by pressing F11 or selecting the Full Screen option from the Tools menu equivalent. Though this mode is nice, the amount of real estate given over to the application isn't consistent between browser versions. For example, the older versions of Internet Explorer kept the status bar and some other elements on the screen. Internet Explorer 8+ and Google Chrome both allow the browser to take over the entire screen, without any additional, ahem, chrome visible. Firefox (as of this writing) shows a small gray bar at the top used as a hotspot for the toolbar. All of these also require the user to navigate a browser-specific menu or press a browser-specific (but currently identical) hotkey. The other problem is that there is no way to handle this when running in the out-of-browser mode.

Silverlight also supports its own full-screen mode, available both in and out of the browser. The experience is the same across browsers and the mode may be invoked via a button you provide in the Silverlight application. This allows you to keep the user's focus inside the application (no "Best viewed in full-screen mode, accessed by F11" prompts) and enable the functionality in a way that's consistent with your application's experience.

In a sandboxed application in the browser or a non-elevated application out of the browser, Silverlight's full-screen support limits the types of keyboard entry just to those typically used in media players and games (arrow keys, page navigation keys, and so on). The reason for this is to prevent taking over the entire screen and spoofing an operating system login experience, thereby capturing the user's password and perhaps sending it off to some scary site to be used to gain access to your private information, like your tax returns for the past five years and that passwords.txt file you thought no one would notice.

There are some significant differences between the capabilities enabled by full screen in the partial-trust mode and full screen in the elevated-trust mode. Let's tackle them separately.

5.7.1   *Normal full-screen mode*

In keeping with the promise of delivering rich interactive experiences, Silverlight goes far beyond the standard web capabilities by providing a full-screen mode. This mode enables a user to enjoy immersive visual experiences and interactive media outside the bounds of the web browser. This full-screen experience comes with some limitations that you'll see in a bit. Because of these limitations, the full-screen mode is generally used strictly with media. This section will show you the differences between the full-screen and the normal screen modes. Then, you'll learn how to programmatically toggle between the screen modes.

If a Silverlight application is put in the full-screen mode, the user will be greeted with a brief overlay message that looks like figure 5.19.

Figure 5.19   The prompt displayed to users when they enter the full-screen mode

Note that full-screen mode doesn't support the `OpenFileDialog` and `SaveFileDialog` classes nor does it support multi-touch input (covered in chapter 8). But full-screen mode is supported whether running in-browser or out.

Figure 5.19 shows the prompt shown to users when they enter the full-screen mode. This message will overlay the Silverlight content for approximately 3.5 seconds. After that time, the prompt will gracefully fade out of view. This prompt can't be customized and, in the normal partial trust mode, it can't be turned off because this prompt is designed to prevent spoofing.

Spoofing is a security attack used by malicious developers who try to deceptively mask their application as another or as Windows itself. The purpose of this malicious attempt is to collect otherwise sensitive information such as bank account numbers and passwords.

Because of the severity of this type of attack, Silverlight imposes two safeguards when running in the partial trust mode. The first safeguard limits user input to the arrow, Tab, Enter, Home, page up, page down, and space keys, as well as mouse events. Additional information entered through the keyboard won't be passed to the Silverlight application. The second safeguard ensures that the full-screen mode can only be entered through a user-initiated event such as a button click. Once this happens, you can switch the Silverlight plug-in into the full-screen mode through the host.

TOGGLING BETWEEN SCREEN MODES

The `SilverlightHost` class gives you access to the information associated with a plug-in instance. The switch to the full-screen mode is made using the `Content` property, which exposes a `bool` property of its own called `IsFullScreen`. As you might expect, this property can be used to toggle between the full-screen and the embedded modes:

```
private void GoFullScreen_Click(object sender, RoutedEventArgs e)
{
  Application.Current.Host.Content.IsFullScreen = true;
}
```

This example shows how to switch a plug-in into the full-screen mode. As you probably already guessed, you can set the `IsFullScreen` property to `false` to go back to the embedded mode. Regardless of which direction you're going, a change in the screen mode will cause the `FullScreenChanged` event to be triggered. This event is useful for resizing the content so that it scales to an appropriate size based on the screen mode.

If you want to avoid the onscreen message, keyboard restrictions, and the requirement for user initiation, you'll need to run in the elevated trust mode.

5.7.2   *Elevated trust full-screen mode*

Out-of-browser applications can go full screen whether they're running in the normal partial trust mode or in the elevated trust mode. The mechanisms for going full screen and detecting the mode are the same. But the elevated trust mode provides some real benefits to applications that require it.

First of all, elevated-trust applications allow you to enter the full-screen mode from any branch of code and not just something that's user-initiated. For example, you can go full screen from the Loaded event of the main page:

```
private void MainPage_Loaded(object sender, RoutedEventArgs e)
{
   if (Application.Current.HasElevatedPermissions)
   {
       Application.Current.Host.Content.IsFullScreen = true;
   }
}
```

Elevated trust also eliminates the "Press ESC to exit full-screen mode" prompt that's displayed when the full-screen mode is first entered. At the same time, it eliminates the use of the Escape key for this purpose altogether. You'll need to provide the user with another way to exit the full-screen mode either by capturing the Escape key and/ or providing a button to drop out of full screen.

The keyboard restrictions on the partial-trust full-screen mode make it suitable for only a small class of applications. The full-screen mode in the elevated trust also provides access to all the keys you get in the normal out-of-browser mode. This is a huge boon that makes the mode acceptable for kiosks, full-screen games, interactive media players with chat, and many other application types.

The full-screen mode works whether running in or out of the browser, in partial trust or elevated trust. Once in the full-screen mode, you can simulate an entire desktop, provide your own window management, and so forth. It effectively gives you a work space that's larger than what we'd traditionally consider a window.

So far, we've covered a number of different ways Silverlight can integrate with the local machine. One final area of local machine integration, available both in and out of the browser, is isolated storage.

5.8   *Storing data in isolated storage*

Even in the out-of-browser mode, Silverlight is a browser-based plug-in so, by default, it has the lowest of security privileges to ensure a safe browsing experience for your users. This safety restriction introduces a number of development challenges, such as working with data across browser sessions. Although working with data across browser sessions may not be a problem if the data is stored on a web server, it can be a problem if the data needs to be stored locally.

Isolated storage is a mechanism that allows you to preserve data across browser sessions on a user's machine. This storage area is tied to an individual user and helps you overcome the 4 KB limitation of a cookie. Unlike a cookie, isolated storage lies outside of the browser cache—if a user clears the browser history, the items within isolated storage will remain in place. In order to access this storage area, you use the `System.IO.IsolatedStorage` namespace.

The `System.IO.IsolatedStorage` namespace provides the functionality to work with a user's isolated storage area. This area can be accessed through the `IsolatedStorageFile` class, which exposes two statically visible methods that retrieve an `IsolatedStorageFile`. These methods are `GetUserStoreForApplication` and `GetUserStoreForSite`. The `GetUserStoreForApplication` can be used to retrieve a user's isolated storage for a specific Silverlight application, defined by the full URL to the .xap. The `GetUserStoreForSite` method gets a user's isolated storage for an entire domain. As you may have guessed, this method gives you the ability to share information across multiple Silverlight applications.

> **NOTE** The `GetUserStoreForSite` method doesn't exist in the full .NET framework. You should consider this fact if you want to promote your Silverlight application to WPF down the road.

Either way, an example of retrieving an `IsolatedStorageFile` is shown here:

```
IsolatedStorageFile isoFile =
  IsolatedStorageFile.GetUserStoreForApplication();
```

This code gives you access to a user's isolated storage area. Once you've retrieved an `IsolatedStorageFile`, you can use it to manage a virtual filesystem, which gives you the ability to read and write files and directories. This information can be leveraged through the `IsolatedStorageFile` and `IsolatedStorageFileStream` classes.

5.8.1 *IsolatedStorageFile: the virtual filesystem*

The `IsolatedStorageFile` class represents a virtual filesystem that a Silverlight application can manage. Note the word *virtual*; outside of the elevated security mode, you can't directly access the user's local filesystem due to security constraints. As the previous example showed, you can still access data related to the requesting Silverlight application but, in reality, the term *filesystem* is a probably a stretch.

The `IsolatedStorageFile` object represents a specific partition within the isolated storage area. This partition is tied to both the user and the application. It's easiest to think of this partition as a specific folder or directory. And, like a regular directory, the isolated storage area enables you to perform several operations, including the ability to list the contents of a directory. This directory can have other files or directories added to or removed from it, so you should probably keep track of the isolated storage usage statistics to ensure you don't run out of space. Fortunately, the `IsolatedStorageFile` allows you to check these statistics and request more space if you need it.

LISTING THE CONTENTS OF THE VIRTUAL FILESYSTEM

The `IsolatedStorageFile` class provides two methods that enable you to retrieve the items within a storage area. The first method, `GetDirectoryNames`, enables you to

retrieve the names of the directories that match a certain
pattern; the GetFileNames method allows you to search
for files that match a particular filter. To gain a solid
understanding of how these filters work, look at the sample isolated storage area structure in figure 5.20.

The isolated storage area depicted in figure 5.20 contains a number of common filesystem items. For instance,
there are three text files, one XAML file, and one subdirectory. With this hierarchical structure in mind, let's turn our

**Figure 5.20   An illustration
of a potential isolated storage
area**

focus to mastering the filtering string syntax used for searching the isolated storage area.

The first and most verbose approach involves searching for a specifically named
item. This approach works with both the GetDirectoryNames and GetFileNames methods. To perform the search, you simply provide the exact path to the file or directory.
If the filename or directory is found, a string array with one element will be returned.
Otherwise, an empty result set will be returned. Both approaches are shown here:

```
string[] directory1 = isoFile.GetDirectoryNames("Directory1");
string[] noDirFound = isoFile.GetDirectoryNames("Directory2");
string[] testfile1 = isoFile.GetFileNames("testfile1.txt");
string[] noFileFound = isoFile.GetFileNames("testfile2.txt");
string[] nestedFile = isoFile.GetFileNames("Directory1/file1.txt");
```

Similarly, wildcard characters may be used to pattern-match file names. Following normal Windows operating system rules, the * character matches any number of characters, and the ? character matches any single character:

```
string[] results1 = isoFile.GetFileNames("*");
string[] results2 = isoFile.GetFileNames("Directory1/*");
string[] results3 = isoFile.GetFileNames("textfile*");
string[] results4 = isoFile.GetFileNames("*.txt");
```

The * and ? wildcard characters are applicable within the GetDirectoryNames
method as well. Once you have the file you're looking for, you can open it and work
on it just like you would any other file, including deleting it.

REMOVING ITEMS FROM ISOLATED STORAGE

The IsolatedStorageFile class exposes two utility methods that enable you to
remove items from the storage area. The first method, DeleteDirectory, is used to
remove a directory from the isolated storage area. The second method, DeleteFile,
similarly allows you to remove a file. The usage of the DeleteFile method is illustrated here:

```
soFile.DeleteFile("testfile1.txt");
isoFile.DeleteFile("Directory1/file1.txt");
```

As this example shows, you must explicitly provide the absolute path to the file
you want to delete. If you provide an invalid path, an IsolatedStorageException
will be thrown. In addition, this same exception will be thrown if you attempt to
remove a directory that isn't empty. Other than that, the syntax is the same when

using the `DeleteDirectory` method. But, before you can delete a directory, it needs to be created.

CREATING DIRECTORIES WITHIN ISOLATED STORAGE

The `IsolatedStorageFile` class exposes a method called `CreateDirectory` that enables you to create a directory within the isolated storage space. There isn't anything too shocking about the syntax associated with this method—to create a directory, you state the name of the folder:

```
isoFile.CreateDirectory("Directory1");
```

In addition to creating directories at the root of the isolated storage area, the `Create-Directory` method enables you to create subdirectories. To do this, you use a URL-style syntax that uses forward slashes as separators:

```
isoFile.CreateDirectory("Directory1/SubDirectory1");
isoFile.CreateDirectory("Directory1/Sub2/Leaf");
```

The first line of code is pretty simple; it creates a subdirectory under an existing directory. The second line of code shows an additional feature. If you provide an absolute path to a subdirectory further down the line, all missing directories along the way will automatically be added. Once a directory exists, you can add files to it. We'll discuss adding files later in this section. But first, let's make sure there's space for a new file.

CHECKING THE AVAILABLE SPACE

The `IsolatedStorageFile` class exposes two read-only properties that inform you of an isolated storage area's memory situation. The first property, `Quota`, holds the total number of bytes allocated to the storage area. The other property, `Available-FreeSpace`, represents the number of bytes remaining in the storage area. You can use these properties together to create a cool little memory quota bar (see listing 5.7). Note that this sample will only show the green bar if you pair it with other code that actually uses some space in isolated storage; otherwise the bar will be white, showing zero quota usage.

> **Listing 5.7 Creating a file quota bar associated with the user's isolated storage area**

Result:

XAML:

```xml
<UserControl x:Class="IsolatedStorgageExample.QuotaBar"
  xmlns="http://schemas.microsoft.com/winfx/2006/xaml/presentation"
  xmlns:x="http://schemas.microsoft.com/winfx/2006/xaml"
  Width="400" Height="300">
  <Canvas x:Name="LayoutRoot" Background="White">
    <Rectangle x:Name="maximumRectangle" Width="1" Height="20"
      Fill="#FFFFFFFF" Stroke="#FF000000"
      Canvas.Left="1" Canvas.Top="5" RadiusX="5" RadiusY="5"/>
    <Rectangle x:Name="currentRectangle" Width="1" Height="20"
```

```
        Stroke="#FF000000" Canvas.Left="1" Canvas.Top="5"
        RadiusX="5" RadiusY="5" StrokeThickness="0">
        <Rectangle.Fill>
          <LinearGradientBrush EndPoint="0.5,1.35" StartPoint="0.5,-0.3">
            <GradientStop Color="#FF54CDEA" Offset="0"/>
            <GradientStop Color="#FF017328" Offset="0.5"/>
            <GradientStop Color="#FF54CDEA" Offset="1"/>
          </LinearGradientBrush>
        </Rectangle.Fill>
      </Rectangle>
    </Canvas>
  </UserControl>
```

C#:

```
...
public MainPage()
{
  InitializeComponent();
  // Set the rectangle sizes accordingly
  using (IsolatedStorageFile isoFile =
    IsolatedStorageFile.GetUserStoreForApplication())
  {
    double usedSpace = isoFile.Quota - isoFile.AvailableFreeSpace;
    maximumRectangle.Width = (isoFile.Quota / 10024) * 2;
    currentRectangle.Width = (usedSpace / 10024) * 2;
  }
}
...
```

Listing 5.7 shows one way you can put the AvailableFreeSpace and Quota properties to use. These properties are used to set the widths of the Rectangle elements based on the available and used space. In this example, we divided these values by 10024 (a convenient number for sizing the control) and then multiplied them by 2 to create a reasonably sized quota bar.

By default, the Quota property value is set to 1,048,576. The reason why is because, by default, each isolated storage area is given 1 MB of space. If you remember that the Quota property represents the number of bytes allocated to an isolated storage area, you can see how 1,048,576 bytes equals 1024 KB, which equals 1 MB. Significantly though, you have the option to ask the user for more space should your application need it.

REQUESTING MORE SPACE

The IsolatedStorageFile class enables the application to ask the user for more storage space. This request can be made by calling the IncreaseQuotaTo method, which accepts a long parameter that represents the new quota size you want. This size signals the total number of bytes you want to allocate to the isolated storage area; it doesn't represent the number of bytes by which you want to increase the storage. When the IncreaseQuotaTo method is called, the user will be shown a dialog box, as shown in listing 5.8.

> **Listing 5.8   Requesting more isolated storage space**

Result:

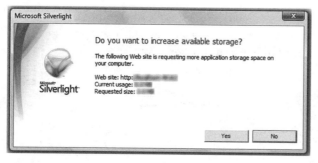

C#:
```
IsolatedStorageFile isoFile =
   IsolatedStorageFile.GetUserStoreForApplication();
long newQuotaSize = isoFile.Quota * 2;
bool requestAccepted = isoFile.IncreaseQuotaTo(newQuotaSize);
```

This listing shows how to request more space for an application from a user. You also have the option of asking for more storage for a domain if you retrieve the Isolated-StorageFile through the GetUserStoreForSite method. Either way, the Increase-QuotaTo method can only be called from a user-initiated event such as a button click. Once this request is made, the dialog box shown in listing 5.8 will be displayed to the user. This dialog box displays the name of the website requesting the new quota. This value is automatically set behind the scenes to prevent malicious coding. In addition, this dialog box shows how much space is currently being used and the quota size being requested. The user's accept or deny decision will be returned from the IncreaseQuotaTo method in the form of a bool.

The IsolatedStorageFile represents a virtual filesystem. This file system gives you the flexibility to create, navigate, and remove items from within it. To make sure that you have space to create items, you may need to check the Available-FreeSpace property, which represents the number of bytes available within the allocated storage Quota. If you need more space, you can request it using the IncreaseQuotaTo method. Requesting more space can come in handy as you read and write files.

5.8.2   Reading and writing files: the isolated storage way

Files stored within the isolated storage area can be created and retrieved through a file stream. This file I/O task is like any other in the .NET framework but, because you're working within a special area that provides additional security features, you must use a specific type of file stream. This particular type of file stream is appropriately named IsolatedStorageFileStream.

The IsolatedStorageFileStream object provides in-memory access to a file stored within the isolated storage area. With this object, you can create, update, and read a file from the isolated storage area. Because a file must exist before you can read it, it makes sense to first discuss how to create and update files within isolated storage.

ISOLATED FILE CREATION

Creating a file within a user's isolated storage area is a simple process. This process hinges on the System.IO.StreamWriter object. You can use a StreamWriter to write content into a file stored within isolated storage. Listing 5.9 shows the process of writing a text file to the user's isolated storage area.

Listing 5.9 Creating a text file within a user's isolated storage area

```
using (IsolatedStorageFile isoFile =
  IsolatedStorageFile.GetUserStoreForApplication())
{
  using (IsolatedStorageFileStream stream =
        new IsolatedStorageFileStream(
            "file1.txt", FileMode.Create, isoFile))
  {
    using (StreamWriter writer = new StreamWriter(stream))
    {
      writer.Write("Hello, from the isolated storage area!");
    }
    stream.Close();
  }
}
```

Listing 5.9 shows how easily you can write a text file into the isolated storage area. The first step is to retrieve a user's isolated storage area. Then, you create an Isolated-StorageFileStream that represents a file within isolated storage. The contents of this file are created using a StreamWriter. This StreamWriter gives you the flexibility to write either binary data or plain text. This is important to recognize because the contents of an isolated storage area aren't encrypted automatically. Because of this, you may want to manually encrypt your data when writing it to a file.

You may have noticed the use of the FileMode enumeration. This value determines how the file will be opened. In all, there are six different ways to open a file. All six options are explained in table 5.5.

Table 5.5 The FileMode enumeration

FileMode	Description
Append	Opens an existing file and prepares to add content onto the end
Create	A brute-force approach to creating a new file If a file of the same name exists, it'll be overwritten. Either way, a new, empty file with the specified name will be created.
CreateNew	Attempts to create a new file If a file of the same name exists, an IsolatedStorageException will be thrown. If there isn't a preexisting file with the same name, a new, empty file will be created.

Table 5.5 The `FileMode` enumeration *(continued)*

FileMode	Description
Open	Attempts to open a file with the given name If the file exists, the `IsolatedStorageFileStream` will have access to the file. If the file doesn't exist, an `IsolatedStorageException` will be thrown.
OpenOrCreate	Opens a file if it exists. If the file doesn't exist, a new one will be created with the given name.
Truncate	Open an existing file and removes all its contents. This `FileMode` doesn't allow read operations.

The `FileMode` options shown in this table cover a wide variety of file operations. These values are useful when you're creating files or attempting to read a file from isolated storage.

READING AN ISOLATED FILE

The process of reading a file from a user's isolated storage area is similar to writing to a file. Instead of taking advantage of a `StreamWriter`, you use of a `StreamReader`. The process of using a `StreamReader` to read a file is shown in listing 5.10.

Listing 5.10   Reading a file from the user's isolated storage area

```
using (IsolatedStorageFile isoFile =
  IsolatedStorageFile.GetUserStoreForApplication())
{
  using (IsolatedStorageFileStream stream =
    new IsolatedStorageFileStream("file1.txt", FileMode.Open, isoFile))
  {
    using (StreamReader writer = new StreamReader(stream))
    {
      myTextBlock.Text = writer.ReadToEnd();
    }
    stream.Close();
  }
}
```

As this example shows, reading a file is almost identical to creating a file. The first step involves retrieving the user's isolated storage area. Then, you create an `Isolated-StorageFileStream` object—this time using the `FileMode.Open` option. Once the file is opened, you can read through it using a `StreamReader`.

Both the `StreamReader` and `StreamWriter` classes provide a lot of features for working with character-based and binary input and output. These I/O features provide a lot of flexibility in regard to the client-side storage within the isolated storage area. Once an isolated storage area is created, you may need to remove it for testing during development. For this reason, it's beneficial to know how to administer it.

5.8.3   *Administering isolated storage*

Administering an isolated storage area involves interacting with the physical filesystem. The reason you'd want to do this is to test a user's initial interaction with a Silverlight application. During development, it can be easy to get lost in the action and forget a user's initial experience with an application. Because the isolated storage area is separate from the browser's cache, you need an easy way to remove information from the isolated storage area, so you should know where the isolated storage area is located on the physical filesystem.

The isolated storage area is located in different locations based on the user's operating system. The specific location for each operating system is shown in table 5.6.

Table 5.6   The base location of the isolated storage area on each operating system supported in Silverlight

Operating system	Location
Mac OS X	AppData/Local
Windows XP	C:\Documents and Settings\[UserName]\Application Data\Microsoft\Silverlight\is
Windows Vista and Windows 7	C:\Users\[UserName]\AppData\LocalLow\Microsoft\Silverlight\is

This table shows the base location for the isolated storage area. Each unique Silverlight application that uses isolated storage will create a new directory under this location. This new directory will be given a name that appears encrypted, but don't let this fool you. The data stored in the isolated storage area isn't encrypted so you shouldn't store sensitive information, such as passwords, in the isolated storage.

Isolated storage is a great way to store nonpermanent data on the end user's local machine. It's flexible in that it works in all modes of Silverlight operation (in-browser, out-of-browser, elevated out-of-browser) and works as a virtual filesystem. When combined with the other features described in this chapter, it really helps round out a feature set that makes for extremely capable connected and disconnected rich Internet applications.

5.9   *Summary*

For a web technology, Silverlight provides an unprecedented level of desktop integration. With Silverlight 4, we now have the ability to run in and out of the browser in the partial trust mode or out of the browser in the elevated trust mode.

When running out of the browser in partial trust, you gain additional storage capacity without prompting, additional keyboard information, and a reduction in host chrome that allows you to take a greater advantage of screen real estate and provide a truly custom experience. For many behind-the-firewall business applications, and both custom experiences and self-contained Internet-delivered applications, this is a compelling option with no real downside.

When running in the elevated trust mode, your Silverlight applications gain a level of desktop integration rivaled only by the native applications. You can access the local files on all supported operating systems, eliminate many of the user confirmation prompts, have a truly usable full-screen mode, have almost complete control over the window chrome, and even automate installed applications and call native APIs when running on Windows.

In either out-of-browser mode, you have access to the notification APIs to provide a richer desktop experience as well as access to the virtual file system in the isolated storage.

With both in-browser and out-of-browser support, you get access to the new network connectivity detection APIs to allow you to create an even more robust application that can work online or offline, in the browser or on the desktop. You get the ability to run full screen to provide a truly differentiated experience. You also get the simplicity of web-based deployment combined with the confidence that the application is secure and sandboxed.

With both approaches, you get the full Silverlight application model discussed in chapter 3 as well as support for great user experience capabilities, including the layout and transformation capabilities we'll discuss in the next chapter. It's hard not to get excited about something so compelling.

Rendering, layout, and transforming

This chapter covers

- UI elements and framework elements
- The layout system
- The rendering pipeline
- Using 2D and 3D transformations

Over the past few chapters, we covered some fairly big-picture topics, such as how to have Silverlight work in and out of the browser and how to use XAML. Those are all important to understand in order to create Silverlight applications that work in or out of the browser. XAML and the property system are also important, and we build upon that knowledge in every subsequent chapter, including this one.

In this chapter, we're going to dig back down under the covers and look at some fundamentals of the core user interface base classes and the rendering and layout systems that make everything fit on the screen and render to the user.

Silverlight's rendering process involves a number of steps, and has provisions for several developer-provided optimizations to the process. Silverlight also has a far more advanced layout system than simple left/top positioning of elements on

138

the screen. The multipass layout system handles measuring and arranging elements across the entire visual tree.

Once the rendering, layout, and core object fundamentals are down, we'll have some fun with performing 2D transformations on our objects. If you've ever wanted to rotate or scale an object on the screen, you'll find the section on render transformations to your liking.

Of course, if you have 2D, you always want one more, so we also have 3D transformations. You can do some wild things with the power of the `PlaneProjection` and the `Matrix3dProjection` classes. The former is great for most use cases, including the ubiquitous CoverFlow scenario. The latter is one of the most powerful transformations in Silverlight. If you've ever wanted to do something akin to a 3D-rotated, sparsely populated, and z-layered deep zoom, you'll definitely get a kick out of the power of the 3D matrix.

We've covered the fundamentals of XAML already, so let's start with the base classes that underlie all those angle-bracketed elements that make up the user interface: the `UIElement` and `FrameworkElement` classes.

6.1 The UIElement and FrameworkElement

In previous chapters, we saw examples of `TextBlocks`, `TextBoxes`, and other controls and elements. All of the UI elements in XAML are `FrameworkElement` items, so they're also inherently `UIElement` items because `FrameworkElement` inherits from `UIElement`.

A `UIElement` is an object that represents a visual component. These types of elements have built-in support for layout, event handling, and rendering. Although this extremely generic description may seem pointless, it isn't. In fact, by deriving from this type, a large majority of the elements within Silverlight share the same types of features. These features are exposed through a number of extremely valuable methods and properties.

Throughout this section, we'll cover the methods and properties that you'll probably use most often. It's important to recognize that some of these belong to the `FrameworkElement` class, while others belong to the `UIElement` class. We'll point this out as we go along but, for now, let's begin by addressing some of the common properties.

6.1.1 Properties

The `UIElement` and `FrameworkElement` classes expose a number of properties common to all of the visual elements in your application. Because of the abstract nature of the `UIElement` and `FrameworkElement` classes, these properties may be set on any control in a variety of scenarios.

In this section, we'll start with a look at cursors and then look at how to make your entire element partially or completely transparent. Sometimes, transparent isn't good enough and what you really want is to have the control logically removed from the visual tree, so we'll look at the `Visibility` property. From there, we'll look at how to align an element in the horizontal and vertical spaces. Finally, we'll cover how to set margins to give your elements a little breathing room and how to snap the layout to whole pixels so your lines look crisp and fully rendered.

CURSOR

When a user navigates the mouse cursor over a `FrameworkElement`, the cursor will change to indicate the type of action the user can take. For instance, when you hover around a `Canvas`, you'll see a basic arrow. Alternatively, if you move your mouse over a `HyperLinkButton`, you'll see a cursor that looks like a hand. But, you can use whatever cursor you want by setting the `Cursor` property; for example, using the `Stylus` cursor with a `TextBlock`:

```
<Canvas Cursor="Hand" Background="Green" Height="60" Width="180">
  <TextBox Cursor="Stylus" Height="20" Width="60" />
</Canvas>
```

This example uses two nondefault cursor options: `Stylus` and `Hand`. These options represent `Cursor` items, each of which is accessible through the `System.Windows.Input.Cursors` class. This class exposes nine statically visible `Cursor` properties:

- Arrow
- IBeam
- SizeWE
- Eraser
- None
- Stylus
- Hand
- SizeNS
- Wait

This shows the values you can use in a `FrameworkElement`'s `Cursor` property. These cursor options provide an excellent way to communicate with your users. Most of these options reflect the cursor options found in Cascading Style Sheets (CSS). But, short of newer advances in the proposed HTML 5 spec, it'd be a challenge to find a W3C CSS equivalent for our next property: `Opacity`.

> ### Web cursor standards
>
> The ubiquity of browser applications has altered some of the user interface standards we've traditionally followed on the desktop. For example, a common standard to apply in your web application is to use the `Hand` cursor for many things a user can click and not just hyperlinks. This standard is slowly finding its way to traditional desktop applications, where it's helpful to differentiate "dead space" from active areas such as buttons. In the end, anything that helps the users explore your application and quickly identify actions they can take is a good thing.

OPACITY

The `Opacity` property represents an element's transparency. By default, this double-precision value is set to 1.0, which means the element is completely visible. You have the flexibility to set this value as low as 0.0, making it completely transparent. To get a feel for how the `Opacity` property renders content, look at figure 6.1, which shows a `TextBlock` with varying `Opacity` values.

The `Opacity` values ensure that a `UIElement` is visible. If you set the `Opacity` value to 0.0, the element wouldn't be visible. But, just because a `UIElement`

Opacity = 1.0   Opacity=0.5   Opacity=.25

Figure 6.1   An example of the `Opacity` property

can't be seen, it doesn't mean it's not there. Instead, even if a UIElement has an Opacity of 0.0, it'll still behave as though it can be seen. For instance, a transparent element will still respond to mouse events. If you want to completely hide an element, you must change the Visibility property.

VISIBILITY

The Visibility property gives you the ability to toggle whether a UIElement can be seen and whether it participates in layout. By default, all UIElement objects have a Visibility of Visible. This ensures that a UIElement can be seen and occupies its allotted layout area. If you set the Visibility of a UIElement to Collapsed, no layout area is reserved for the UIElement. Consider the StackPanel in listing 6.1.

Listing 6.1   Three visible elements in a StackPanel

Result:

```
<StackPanel x:Name="myStackPanel" Background="Orange" Width="90">
  <TextBox x:Name="tb1" Width="60" Background="LightGray" />
  <TextBox x:Name="tb2" Width="60" Background="DarkGray" />
  <TextBox x:Name="tb3" Width="60" Background="Gray"  />
</StackPanel>
```

Listing 6.1 shows three TextBox elements. By default, each of these elements has a Visibility of Visible. Watch what happens when the Visibility of the middle TextBox is set to Collapsed, as in listing 6.2.

Listing 6.2   Two visible elements and one collapsed element in a StackPanel

```
<StackPanel x:Name="myStackPanel" Background="Orange" Width="90">
  <TextBox x:Name="tb1" Width="60" Background="LightGray" />
  <TextBox x:Name="tb2" Width="60" Background="DarkGray"
    Visibility="Collapsed" />
  <TextBox x:Name="tb3" Width="60" Background="Gray"  />
</StackPanel>
```

Listing 6.2 highlights the effects of Collapsed. The TextBox with the name tb2 isn't shown. You could just set the Opacity to 0.0, but the layout space wouldn't be freed. In addition, using the Opacity property to hide an element can be wasteful; an element with an Opacity of 0.0 still participates in the layout and rendering. Elements with a Visibility of Collapsed skip the rendering stem and report no size in the layout steps.

Cursor, Visibility, and Opacity all affect visible portions of the UIElement, but not the layout. The alignment properties typically have a great impact on the layout of an element, depending upon the panel in which the element is hosted.

What about `Visibility.Hidden`?

In WPF, the `Visibility` enumeration contains `Hidden` in addition to the `Collapsed` and `Visible` values supported by Silverlight. `Hidden` hides an element but reserves a space for it during layout. Originally, Silverlight 1.0 supported the `Hidden` value, but it actually acted like `Collapsed`, so they decided to change it to `Collapsed` during the 1.0 beta cycle. To get the same effective behavior as `Hidden`, set the `Opacity` to 0.0 and `IsHitTestVisibile` to `False`. The end result will be an element that takes up space on the screen but is both invisible to the eye and to the mouse. But unlike `Visibility.Hidden`, the control will still participate in the layout and rendering—a potential performance concern if you use this often or in animation-heavy scenarios.

HORIZONTALALIGNMENT AND VERTICALALIGNMENT

Every `FrameworkElement` gives you the opportunity to specify how it should be aligned within its parent. This alignment setting will trickle down through the object tree and affect the alignment of all child elements—well, at least until another `FrameworkElement` sets its alignment. You have two ways to align visual elements.

Visual elements can be aligned both vertically and horizontally by setting the `VerticalAlignment` and `HorizontalAlignment` property values to one of the acceptable values. These values belong to two separate enumerators, aptly called `VerticalAlignment` and `HorizontalAlignment`.

Listing 6.3 Horizontal and vertical alignment

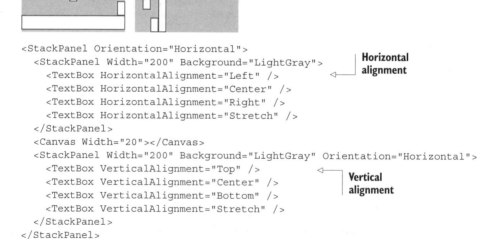

```
<StackPanel Orientation="Horizontal">
  <StackPanel Width="200" Background="LightGray">          Horizontal
    <TextBox HorizontalAlignment="Left" />                 alignment
    <TextBox HorizontalAlignment="Center" />
    <TextBox HorizontalAlignment="Right" />
    <TextBox HorizontalAlignment="Stretch" />
  </StackPanel>
  <Canvas Width="20"></Canvas>
  <StackPanel Width="200" Background="LightGray" Orientation="Horizontal">
    <TextBox VerticalAlignment="Top" />
    <TextBox VerticalAlignment="Center" />               Vertical
    <TextBox VerticalAlignment="Bottom" />               alignment
    <TextBox VerticalAlignment="Stretch" />
  </StackPanel>
</StackPanel>
```

Listing 6.3 shows the effects of all four `HorizontalAlignment` options and all four `VerticalAlignment` options. The `HorizontalAlignment` property accepts the `Left`, `Center`, `Right`, and `Stretch` values, whereas the `VerticalAlignment` property accepts the Top, Center, Bottom, and Stretch values. The alignment properties behave differently depending upon the container in which the UIElement resides. For example, they have no effect when put into a Canvas due to the Canvas panel's lack of layout functionality.

Both properties default to their Stretch values. Because the Stretch options alter the rendered height or width of an element to take up the maximum amount of space available, you may want to consider giving the element some breathing room with the Margin property.

MARGIN

Similar in nature to the Padding property, the Margin property enables you to specify a cushion, but this specific cushion works outside the bounds of a FrameworkElement. This cushion can be set using a single value or a space-delimited or comma-delimited list of four values just like the Padding property, as shown in listing 6.4.

Listing 6.4   Margin and padding

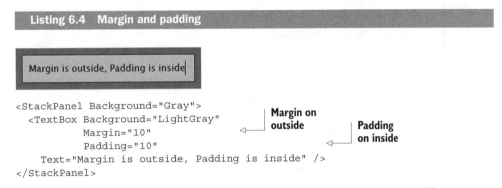

```
<StackPanel Background="Gray">
  <TextBox Background="LightGray"
           Margin="10"                     ← Margin on outside
           Padding="10"                    ← Padding on inside
      Text="Margin is outside, Padding is inside" />
</StackPanel>
```

Listing 6.4 shows the Margin and Padding properties working together. The Padding property is valid in this code because this property is exposed by the System.Windows.Controls.Control class. This is explained further in the next chapter. For now, it's important to recognize that the Padding property isn't accessible to all FrameworkElement items, but the Margin property is.

Margins and padding can alter the location of contained elements, sometimes pushing them to subpixel locations and making them look fuzzy. Luckily, Silverlight has the UseLayoutRounding property to help us avoid that.

USELAYOUTROUNDING

Silverlight supports aligning elements on subpixel boundaries. An unfortunate side effect of this is the loss of crisp lines. Sometimes, you really want that 1 px line to be just 1 px thick and not antialiased to 2 px in thickness.

One simple way to avoid this problem is to place your elements on whole pixel locations. But when your element is nested inside a panel, which is inside a control, which is in a stack panel located in another grid—all of which can have margins, padding, and other properties affecting layout—you can't easily calculate exactly where your element will appear.

Silverlight supports a property of the UIElement called UseLayoutRounding. When UseLayoutRounding is set to true, the layout system (see section 6.3) will round the points of your element to the nearest whole pixel. When false, Silverlight will respect the subpixel location of the points and won't attempt to move them. Listing 6.5 shows the impact of layout rounding on two rectangles. The first rectangle has layout rounding turned on; the second has it turned off.

Listing 6.5 Layout rounding in action with two rectangles

Result:

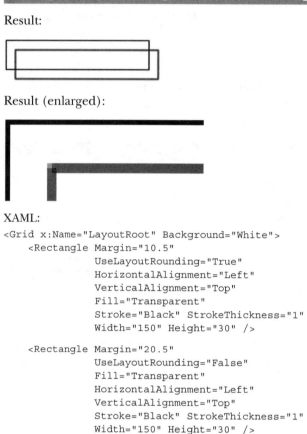

Result (enlarged):

XAML:
```
<Grid x:Name="LayoutRoot" Background="White">
    <Rectangle Margin="10.5"
               UseLayoutRounding="True"
               HorizontalAlignment="Left"
               VerticalAlignment="Top"
               Fill="Transparent"
               Stroke="Black" StrokeThickness="1"
               Width="150" Height="30" />

    <Rectangle Margin="20.5"
               UseLayoutRounding="False"
               Fill="Transparent"
               HorizontalAlignment="Left"
               VerticalAlignment="Top"
               Stroke="Black" StrokeThickness="1"
               Width="150" Height="30" />
</Grid>
```

In listing 6.5, you can see that the rectangle that isn't rounded to the nearest pixel has lines that are two pixels thick and light gray. When viewed in its native resolution, it looks fuzzy. When layout rounding is turned on, the result is a crisp line with sharp corners and no fuzz.

UseLayoutRounding is respected by almost every element in Silverlight. The Polygon class exposes this property but ignores it. Polygons are expected to be complex shapes where layout rounding wouldn't really make sense, so layout rounding is a no-op.

NOTE When sharing code with WPF, it's important to note that layout rounding is turned on by default in Silverlight. This is in contrast to WPF, where it's turned off by default.

We covered the Margin property as well as the useful HorizontalAlignment and VerticalAlignment properties. In addition, we also highlighted the value of the Visibility, Opacity, and Cursor properties. Finally, we looked at how to scare away the fuzzies with UseLayoutRounding. Collectively, these represent some of the more widely used properties of the FrameworkElement and UIElement classes. But these properties only serve to describe an element. There are times when you need to perform an action on them; in these scenarios, you need to rely on their methods.

6.1.2 Methods

Two common tasks are often performed during runtime. The first task involves managing attached properties. The second involves finding an element within the element tree. We'll cover each of these in detail.

MANAGING ATTACHED PROPERTIES

Every UIElement is a DependencyObject. A DependencyObject gives you the ability to retrieve and change attached property values. Consider the process of altering the position of an element within a Canvas. Although you might initially think to set the Canvas.Left and Canvas.Top properties, you'll quickly run into a wall. Instead, you must take advantage of the SetValue method as shown in listing 6.6.

Listing 6.6 Moving a TextBlock five pixels with GetValue and SetValue

XAML:
```xml
<Canvas x:Name="parentCanvas"
  Width="400" Height="400" Background="LightGray">
  <TextBlock x:Name="myTextBlock"
    Text="Click Me"
    Cursor="Hand"
    MouseLeftButtonUp="MyTextBlock_Click"
    FontFamily="Verdana" />
</Canvas>
```

C#:
```csharp
private void MyTextBlock_Click(object sender, MouseButtonEventArgs e)
{
  double top =
    (double)(myTextBlock.GetValue(Canvas.TopProperty));    // GetValue
  double left =                                            // method
    (double)(myTextBlock.GetValue(Canvas.LeftProperty));

  myTextBlock.SetValue(Canvas.TopProperty, (top+5));       // SetValue
  myTextBlock.SetValue(Canvas.LeftProperty, (left+5));     // method
}
```

When a TextBlock is clicked and the click event raised, it'll move five pixels down and to the right. This is made possible by retrieving the current Left and Top positions of the TextBlock within the Canvas through the GetValue methods. Then, the TextBlock is moved within the Canvas using the SetValue methods. But where do the TopProperty and LeftProperty values come from?

These properties are `DependencyProperty` elements—a special type of property designed to depend on information from multiple sources, covered in chapter 2. For instance, as shown in listing 6.6, you use two `DependencyProperty` (specifically attached properties) attributes—`Canvas.Left` and `Canvas.Top`—to position the `TextBlock`. At the same time, there could be an animation affecting the `TextBlock`, so the position of the `TextBlock` would be dependent upon both the layout panel (the `Canvas`) and the animation. (Animations are discussed in chapter 22.)

Thanks to the `DependencyProperty`, it's incredibly easy to manage or retrieve the value associated with an attached property. Dependency properties also provide several other advantages discussed in more detail in section 2.1.4. For now, let's look at how to find elements within the element tree.

FINDING ELEMENTS

As described in chapter 2, the Silverlight Object Model is represented as a hierarchical tree of elements. Considering that each element in this visual tree is, at its core, a `FrameworkElement`, you have the flexibility to navigate this tree. With this element, you have the ability to go either up or down the tree.

To go down the tree, you must call the `FindName` method. This method takes the name of an element and retrieves it. It doesn't matter if the element is a child, grandchild, or located even further down the tree. The `FindName` method will retrieve it as long as it's a descendent. If it isn't found, the method will return `null`.

Alternatively, if you need to find an element up the tree, you use the `Parent` property to recursively navigate up the tree and search the sibling nodes, as described in chapter 2.

Finding elements is a task that you may need to perform in certain circumstances, such as when you dynamically load XAML. Once these elements are found, you can readily get or set the attached property values of a `UIElement` using the `GetValue` and `SetValue` methods. These methods aren't difficult to understand, but the process of using a `DependencyProperty` to set the value of an attached property may seem strange at first. As you grow more familiar with it, it's easier to see the power of this approach, which can lead to new ways of delivering a rich and interactive user experience.

The `UIElement` and `FrameworkElement` classes form the base of everything that's rendered in Silverlight. We've seen that they offer a number of useful properties and methods to control everything from their alignment, to visibility, to how opaque they should appear. Now that we understand the capabilities they offer, it's time to take a step back and look at the rendering process as a whole, in which the `UIElement` and `FrameworkElement` play a core role.

6.2 *The rendering process*

User interfaces in Silverlight are complex. They often have multiple layers of semi-transparent or overlapping content, animation, video, and more. The level of problems the runtime must solve is more akin to that of a gaming platform than, say, something like Windows Forms.

The problem is made even more complex by the restrictions and capabilities of the various browser platforms. Most browsers have a simple threading model, varying sandboxed capabilities, and what can only be described as personality.

It's important to understand the rendering process, especially as it relates to performance. In this section, we'll cover some of the highlights of the process, including browser threading, drawing, performance optimizations, and how you can plug into the process using the callback function.

The rendering process can be broken down into the steps described in table 6.1.

Table 6.1 The steps of the render process

Step	Description
Update hosted HTML	Get updated visuals for the hosted `WebBrowser` control, if used—for example, a hosted web page playing a video.
Clock tick	Increment the animation and video clock.
Event handlers	Run the user code in event handlers, except for the per-frame render callback.
Layout	Measure and arrange elements for display. Because this is one of the most important steps in this process, we'll cover this in more detail in section 6.3.
Per-frame render callback	Run the per-frame callback `CompositionTarget.Rendering`.
Rasterize	Rasterize the vector content, media, images, and more onto their intermediate render surfaces. Then composite to the back buffer.
Show Frame	Show the frame in the browser. *Blit* (direct memory chunk copy; short for *bit block transfer*) the back buffer to video memory or to the software rendering surface.

More than just that happens, of course. There's user code, media decoding, network access, and so on, but this table captures the essence of the rendering process. Though it can help to conceptualize this as an ongoing loop, the individual steps trigger off timers and window messages and not off a single cycle timer, it'd be slightly inaccurate to do so. Nevertheless, just as we still refer to the various timer- and event-driven processes in game development as the game loop, it's a reasonable abstraction.

This process is continually optimized from release to release and even across devices. For example, the Windows Phone 7 process, though similar to what I've just described, actually runs the animations on a separate thread.

One of the most significant limitations of the rendering process for any browser plug-in is the UI thread. Each browser offers up one UI thread per process, shared across all plug-ins in that process. For some browsers, the scope of a process is a single tab; for others, it's the entire browser.

Of the preceding steps, a few demand additional explanation. Specifically, the clock tick, the per-frame render callback, rasterization, and layout all require more detail. We'll start with an explanation of rasterization and the various steps involved in it and then look at how we can plug into the process via the render callback. Finally, since it's a much larger topic and arguably is the most important one to understand, we'll cover layout in section 6.3. Before that, let's look at a few of the other steps, starting with the clock tick.

6.2.1   *Clock tick*

Animation and video in Silverlight are governed by clock time and not by frame rate. Because of this, Silverlight can skip frames on the machines that can't keep up while still maintaining the correct real time of the media or the animation frames shown. In other words, an animation that lasts two seconds will last two seconds on a slow machine and on a fast machine.

The clock tick on Windows happens at 60 frames per second at the most (it happens to be capped at 30 frames per second on the Windows Phone 7). If you set the Silverlight MaxFrameRate to a value lower than that or the system can't keep up, the tick will happen at a lower rate but will ensure the time remains correct. Figure 6.2 shows an example of the dropped frame approach.

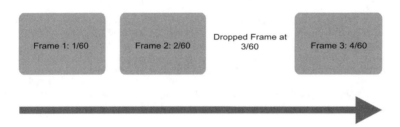

Figure 6.2   If the machine can't keep up with the workload, Silverlight will drop frames but will ensure that the displayed frames are correctly synchronized with the clock tick.

Figure 6.2 shows a theoretical dropped frame. Both frames 1 and 2 are at their correct times. What would've been frame 3 (timed at 3/60 of a second) was dropped, so the next presented frame, the new frame 3, picks up at the correct time. This prevents the undesired effect of slow-running animations or movies.

After the clock has ticked and all the animations and media elements incremented, the next step is to call an optional per-frame rendering callback function.

6.2.2   *Per-frame rendering callback*

There may be times when you want to perform an action during every frame that's rendered on the screen. That may be a simple as keeping a count of frames, swapping a back buffer to simulate an immediate-mode rendering system, or performing game loop-style operations.

Silverlight includes the Rendering event on the CompositionTarget class, which is suitable for these tasks. CompositionTarget.Rendering is an event that fires once per frame, allowing you to synchronize code with the rendering system.

There's no guarantee that the callback will happen at the max frame rate. Though it often does work out this way, many factors, including the amount of work being done inside the callback and the overall speed of the system, contribute to how often this runs. You can generally expect the callback to happen once per frame, assuming your code is well-behaved.

Listing 6.7 shows how to wire up the `Rendering` event and show the current timestamp.

Listing 6.7   Using the per-frame rendering callback

```
public MainPage()
{
  InitializeComponent();

  CompositionTarget.Rendering += new EventHandler(OnRendering);
}
void OnRendering(object sender, EventArgs e)
{                                                           Cast to
  RenderingEventArgs args = e as RenderingEventArgs;   ◀── RenderingEventArgs

  Debug.WriteLine(args.RenderingTime.ToString());
}
```

Note the cast to `RenderingEventArgs` in listing 6.7. This is pretty unusual and not something you'd intuit without knowing something about the underlying code. The underlying code is actually sending an instance of `RenderingEventArgs`, but the event signature is just regular `EventArgs`. By casting to `RenderingEventArgs`, we gain access to the `RenderingTime` property, which we can use to synchronize our logic to Silverlight's own rendering process.

> **NOTE** `CompositionTarget.Rendering` may not have a 1:1 correspondence with the actual rendering frame rate. For example, a static scene with no changes may require no actual render, but `CompositionTarget.Rendering` will still fire at the expected frame rate.

The event signature uses `EventArgs` simply for historical reasons. The additional property was added late during the WPF v1 development cycle, and it was considered too late to introduce a new event signature—a breaking change. Silverlight strives to maintain WPF compatibility whenever possible, so the same signature was carried over to Silverlight.

You can modify layout inside this callback, but that'll cause another layout pass to happen. For that reason, you may want to consider other approaches to avoid the double layout tax on each frame. We'll cover layout in detail in section 6.3. Before we do that, let's look at another processing-intense operation in this cycle: rasterization.

6.2.3   *Rasterization*

Rasterization is the process of turning the vectors in the vector cache into their bitmap representation. Though not exactly rasterization by that definition, we'll also include video and image blitting in this process.

In this section, we'll cover the basics of how rasterization works, including the order of the steps. Then, we'll look at some optimizations in the process and, finally, dive into the use of caching and hardware acceleration to improve performance.

The most fundamental aspect of rasterization that you'll need to understand is the order in which elements are rasterized.

ORDER OF RENDERING

As you recall from chapter 2, elements in Silverlight are organized into the visual tree. This tree has a single root and it branches off into hundreds or thousands of nodes depending upon the complexity of what's on the screen.

The structure of that tree is key to the rendering process. For any branch of the tree, Silverlight rasterizes elements in the visual tree in the following order:

1	Children	2	Cache
3	Opacity mask	4	Opacity
5	Effects (intermediate surface)	6	Clip
7	Projection (intermediate surface)	8	Render transform
9	Layout offset (internal layout transform)	10	Parent node

This is a recursive process; it starts at leaf nodes (the furthest children) and works its way back to the root.

Note that the clipping happens after the opacity calculations. One performance consideration is that a large shape that has opacity other than 1.0 and has only a small portion shown due to clipping (manual or via a panel) can waste a fair number of CPU cycles due to the opacity calculation. Similarly, effects are also calculated prior to the clip and have even more impact on performance.

The intermediate surfaces mentioned are all bitmap caches that are later composited together. Note that the `Writeable` bitmap is a special case because it essentially is an intermediate surface of its own.

The rendering process involves a recursive traversal of the visual tree, with optimizations to eliminate branches of the tree that have been already cached and haven't changed. Another optimization is the handling of occluded pixels.

OCCLUSION

I used to play around with 3D rendering. One of the most basic performance optimizations you'd make is the culling of occluded triangles. When 3D objects are rendered in 2D, the surface is typically broken down into many planar triangles. You'd check to see whether the *normals* (the direction the surface faces) for the triangles are pointing away from you and you are, therefore, looking at the back side of a triangle. If so, you'd remove the triangle from the pipeline. You'd also then check to see if there are any triangles that are completely covered by other triangles.

Though a simplification, consider a complex scene where there's an opaque wall in front of you (the camera) and a bunch of complex shapes on the other side of the wall, as shown in figure 6.3. In such a scene, the shapes would be occluded by the wall; it'd be wasteful to include them in the rendering process.

Occlusion culling in a 3D system can be expensive to calculate. The least performant but most accurate approach would be to shoot an imaginary ray from the camera to each and every point in the geometry making up the shapes, and see if the ray must cross through any other geometry before hitting the target. If it does, then that point is occluded.

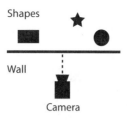

Surprisingly, in a 2D system such as Silverlight, where you can have transforms and effects that play into both the size and shape of elements and as varying degrees of opacity, occlusion culling is more complicated.

Figure 6.3 An overhead view of occlusion in a 3D system. The shapes are occluded by the wall; the camera can't see them. It'd be wasteful to include their geometry in the rendering process. Silverlight does occlusion culling at the pixel level rather than the shape level.

Silverlight doesn't handle occlusion culling at the shape level. Instead, it handles it at the brush pixel level. If you consider that performing blends between multiple pixels can be an expensive operation, it makes sense that Silverlight would optimize that process out of the loop for any pixels that wouldn't be visible in a frame.

This optimization does speed up rendering in most cases. But, if you know an element won't be visible on the screen and you either have many elements or that specific element is expensive to render, you'll want to set its Visibility property to Collapsed so that Silverlight doesn't spend any time on its rendering or layout. Similarly, you need to take into consideration the complexity of any alpha blending you perform, especially when there could be several layers of pixels in play.

One way to cut down on the number of layers and also avoid several other rendering and layout steps, is to cache segments of the visual tree into their own bitmaps.

CACHED COMPOSITION

Cached composition enables branches of the visual tree to be stored in bitmap form after the first rendering. (For the web programmers reading this, understand that the cache is a local in-memory cache on the client.) This bitmap is then used on subsequent frames until the elements change. For complex subtrees, cached composition can realize huge performance benefits. Figure 6.4 helps visualize how cached composition works.

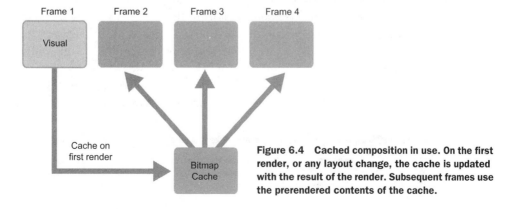

Figure 6.4 Cached composition in use. On the first render, or any layout change, the cache is updated with the result of the render. Subsequent frames use the prerendered contents of the cache.

On first render, any elements that have been marked to be cached are rendered as usual and then the output of that render is stored in the bitmap cache. Listing 6.8 shows how to enable caching for a group of elements in a `Grid`.

Listing 6.8   Caching a group of elements in a `StackPanel`

Result:

XAML:

```
<Grid x:Name="LayoutRoot" Background="White"
      CacheMode="BitmapCache">           ⟵—┐ Cachemode
  <Rectangle Height="60" Width="50"           directive
          Fill="Green" />
  <Ellipse Height="30" Width="200" Opacity="0.75"
          Fill="Blue" />
  <Path Stroke="Orange"
        StrokeThickness="10"
        Height="200" Width="200"
        Data="M 10,80 C 150,5 100,0 200,50 H 100" />
  <Path Stroke="Purple"
        Height="100" Width="300"
        StrokeThickness="10"
        Data="M 80,10 C 350,5 100,0 100,55" />
</Grid>
```

Listing 6.8 shows some Silverlight artwork (suitable for submission to the Freer and Sackler Galleries, no doubt!) composed of a number of shapes and paths. The paths here are relatively simple, but more complex artwork may be made of hundreds or thousands of points. The process of rasterizing complex artwork has a real CPU cost but, when cached, that cost is one time rather than per frame.

In section 6.4 we discuss render transforms. Render transforms can affect size and orientation of a group of elements. If you apply a render transform to a subtree that has been cached—for example, to increase its size to 200 percent—you may end up losing the benefit of the cache because Silverlight has to render at the larger size. Luckily, there's another form of the `CacheMode` property that enables you to cache the render at a different size. Listing 6.9 shows how to cache elements at four times their natural size.

Listing 6.9   Caching at a size larger than the default (XAML)

```
<Grid x:Name="LayoutRoot" Background="White">
  <Path Stroke="Orange" StrokeThickness="10"
        Height="200" Width="200"
```

```
       Data="M 10,80 C 150,5 100,0 200,50 H 100" />
  <Path Stroke="Purple" Height="100" Width="300"
        StrokeThickness="10"
        Data="M 80,10 C 350,5 100,0 100,55" />              2× Scale
  <Grid.RenderTransform>                                     transform
    <ScaleTransform ScaleX="2" ScaleY="2" />      ◁──────┘
  </Grid.RenderTransform>
  <Grid.CacheMode>
    <BitmapCache RenderAtScale="4" />        ◁───  4× Caching
  </Grid.CacheMode>
</Grid>
```

Note that the bitmap cache is set to a 4× render whereas I'm only using a 2× transform. That's a bit wasteful but certainly is allowed and useful, and you can always scale down without losing quality. If the `RenderAtScale` option hadn't been used, caching wouldn't have worked for this subtree of elements.

Caching the elements as bitmaps allows Silverlight to use hardware acceleration by keeping those surfaces as textures cached on the video card—assuming sufficient texture memory and assuming hardware acceleration has been enabled at the plug-in level.

ENABLING HARDWARE ACCELERATION FOR THE CACHE

Once a tree of visual elements has been cached, you can take advantage of hardware acceleration for compositing those elements with other layers in the application. In addition, hardware acceleration can benefit transforms, such as stretching and rotation.

In order to use hardware acceleration, you must set the `EnableGPUAcceleration` plug-in parameter to true. In chapter 4, we covered how to build up the object tag. Here's the line for enabling acceleration:

```
<param name="EnableGPUAcceleration" value="true" />
```

If your application is an out-of-browser application (chapter 5), you can set this via the `OutOfBrowserSettings.EnableGPUAccelerationProperty`, typically handled through the out-of-browser settings dialog.

Hardware (GPU) acceleration can help you realize real performance gains. But there can also be times when it's a net performance drain in your application. The main reason for this is the number of surfaces that must be created when hardware caching is used.

For each bitmap of cached content, Silverlight must then create two additional surfaces in video RAM: a surface to hold all content above the cached bitmap and one to hold the content below it. In an application with a large height/width on a machine with relatively low video memory (especially all those integrated graphics chips), you can quickly run out of memory should you try to cache too many separate subtrees.

When caching, especially when using hardware acceleration, you should endeavor to create as few bitmap caches as possible. When using acceleration, you may want to debug how the process is working. For that, you can use the cache visualization debug settings.

VISUALIZING THE CACHE AND REDRAW REGIONS

When performance is important, one thing that can really help is visualizing the bitmap caches in use in your application. Silverlight provides a setting that draws colored overlays on different regions in your UI, indicating which content is or isn't cached. Cached content shows up normally; uncached content shows up with a colored overlay.

Cache visualization is another parameter on the plug-in object described in chapter 4. The parameter is named `enableCacheVisualization`:

```
<param name="enableCacheVisualization" value="true"/>
```

You can also set this value via code, which is essential for debugging out-of-browser applications. The setting is the `EnableCacheVisualization` property of the `Settings` object:

```
Application.Current.Host.Settings.EnableCacheVisualization = true;
```

In both cases, this is a debug setting, so be sure to turn it off when you move your application to testing or production environments. The in-code approach allows you to turn the property on and off via a menu setting or similar approach.

Similarly, you can visualize redraw regions to see exactly what content Silverlight must redraw for each frame. Like cache visualization, this is an object tag setting:

```
<param name="enableRedrawRegions" value="true" />
```

When you enable this visualization, Silverlight will display redraw regions in a different color for each frame, making it obvious what elements are causing which parts of the interface to be redrawn at runtime. Just as with the other setting, this isn't something you want to leave enabled in production. Also with the other settings, this has a runtime-settable version especially useful for out-of-browser applications:

```
Application.Current.Host.Settings.EnableRedrawRegions = true;
```

Between the redraw visualization and the cache visualization, you should have a good start on debugging any rendering performance issues in your application.

Rasterization is an important process to understand in Silverlight, especially if you're creating an application, such as a game or media player, which is performance sensitive. Consider using cached composition and hardware acceleration to help you out but understand the limitations and where the point of diminishing returns lies for your application.

The rendering process as a whole has a number of important steps. Of those, the key steps to understand are the clock tick, which increments all the animation and media counters; the per-frame rendering callback, which is useful for game loops and similar operations; and the rasterization process.

One other important step we haven't yet covered is layout. Layout is important enough to require a more in-depth look than some of the other steps. In fact, of all of them, I'd consider layout the most important step for the majority of Silverlight developers.

6.3 *The layout system*

Layout systems across different technologies vary greatly in complexity. Take, for example, the Windows Forms layout system. Fundamentally, that layout system involves absolute x and y coordinate pairs and an explicit or implicit z-order. Controls can overlap each other, get clipped on the edge of the window, or even get obscured completely. The algorithm is pretty simple—sort by z order (distance from the viewer) and then blit the bits to the screen.

For another example, look to HTML and CSS. HTML and CSS support elements that must size to content and page constraints (tables, divs), as well as support absolute positioning, overlapping, and so forth. It's more of a fluid approach, where the size and position of one element can affect the size and position of another. Therefore, the layout system for HTML and CSS is significantly more complex than that for something like Windows Forms.

Silverlight and WPF support both types of layout: content that self-sizes based on constraints, and content that's simply positioned by way of an x and y coordinate pair. Depending on the container in use, it can even handle laying elements out on curves or radially from a central point. The complexity that makes that possible deserves a deeper look.

6.3.1 *Multipass layout—measuring and arranging*

Layout in Silverlight and WPF involves two primary passes: the *measure pass* and the *arrange pass*. In the measure pass, the layout system asks each element to provide its dimensions given a provided available size. In the arrange step, the layout system tells each element its final size and requests that it lay itself out and also lay out its child elements. A full run of measuring and arranging is called a *layout pass*.

In this section, we'll go through the layout system in more detail, especially these two key steps and their implications for performance and design. If you're curious about layout or you've ever been confused by something like `Height` and `Width` versus `ActualHeight` and `ActualWidth`, read on.

THE MEASURE PASS

Whenever elements need to be rendered to screen due to having just been added, made visible, or changed in size, the layout system is invoked for an asynchronous layout pass. The first step in layout is to measure the elements. On a `FrameworkElement`, the measure pass is implemented inside the virtual `MeasureOverride` function, called recursively on the visual tree:

```
protected virtual Size MeasureOverride(Size availableSize)
```

The `availableSize` parameter contains the amount of space available for this object to give to itself and child objects. If the `FrameworkElement` is to size to whatever content it has, the `availableSize` will be `double.PositiveInfinity`.

The function returns the size the element requires based on any constraints or sizes of child objects.

Note that MeasureOverride isn't called directly from the layout system: it's a protected function. Instead, this function is called from the UIElement's Measure function, which, in turn, is called by the layout system.

Height and Width versus ActualHeight and ActualWidth

If you don't explicitly set the height and width properties of a control, the ActualHeight and ActualWidth properties may be zero or not a number (NaN). Why is that? Due to the asynchronous nature of the layout pass, ActualHeight and ActualWidth might not be set at any specific point in time from run to run or, more importantly, might actually change their values over time as the result of layout operations.

ActualHeight and ActualWidth are set after the rendering pass and may also be affected by layout rounding settings or content.

In short, check them and, if they're zero, they haven't been set. If you want a single place where you can guarantee they'll have a value, subscribe to the LayoutUpdated event on the element and check them there.

THE ARRANGE PASS

The second pass of layout is to arrange the elements given their final sizes. On a FrameworkElement, the Arrange is implemented inside the virtual ArrangeOverride function, also called recursively:

```
protected virtual Size ArrangeOverride(Size finalSize)
```

The finalSize parameter contains the size (the area within the parent) this object should use to arrange itself and child objects. The returned size must be the size actually used by the element and smaller than the finalSize passed in; larger sizes typically result in clipping by the parent.

Similar to the relationship between the measure pass and MeasureOverride, ArrangeOverride isn't called directly by the layout system. Instead, the Arrange method on UIElement is called, which then calls the protected ArrangeOverride function.

At the end of the arrange pass, Silverlight has everything it needs to properly position and size each element in the tree. But it doesn't have everything it needs to actually display the element because its render position or size could be affected by a render transform, as covered in the previous section.

LAYOUT COMPLETED

Despite the name, the LayoutCompleted event isn't technically part of the layout pass. Instead, it's fired as the last event before an element is ready to accept input. Layout-Completed is the safe location for inspecting the actual size and position of the element or otherwise responding to changes in same.

Don't do anything in LayoutCompleted that would cause another layout pass. For example, don't change the size or position of an element, modify its contents, change its layout rounding, or otherwise manipulate properties that could change the size of the element's bounding box. If you have multiple nested layout passes and they take longer than the time allowed for that frame, the Silverlight runtime may skip frames or throw a layout exception.

6.3.2 *The LayoutInformation class*

The `LayoutInfomation` class in `System.Windows.Controls.Primitives` contains a few methods that are useful to folks implementing their own `MeasureOverride` and `ArrangeOverride` code. Specifically, `GetLayoutSlot` and `GetLayoutClip` are helpful when hosting child elements in a custom panel.

GETLAYOUTSLOT

Regardless of its actual shape, each visual element in Silverlight can be represented by a bounding box or *layout slot*. This is a rectangular shape that takes into account the element's size and any margins, padding, or constraints in effect. Figure 6.5 shows the relationship between a layout slot and the child element hosted in a panel.

The layout slot is the maximum size to be used when displaying an element. Portions of the element that fall outside the slot will be clipped. To see the layout slot for an element, you can call the static function `GetLayoutSlot`:

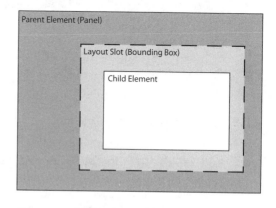

Figure 6.5   The relationship between the layout slot and the child element for an element smaller than the slot

```
public static Rect GetlayoutSlot(FrameworkElement element)
```

The returned `Rect` will contain the bounding box or layout slot for that element. This return value can be useful when creating a custom panel or when debugging layout issues.

GETLAYOUTCLIP

Sometimes elements may be larger than their layout slots, even after measuring and arranging have attempted to fit them. When that happens, you have a layout clip that represents the intersection of the child element's size and the layout slot.

Figure 6.6 shows the relationship between the layout slot, the child element, and the layout clip for that child element in an instance where the child element is too large for its slot.

The function `GetLayoutClip` returns the intersection that represents the layout clip. In this case, the function returns an actual geometry object, useful for setting the clip geometry for an element should you need to:

```
public static Geometry GetLayoutClip(FrameworkElement element)
```

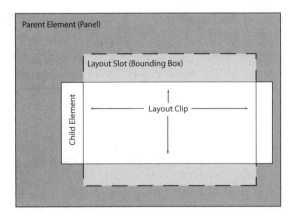

Figure 6.6 The relationship between the layout clip and the layout slot for a child element too large for its slot

The returned `Geometry` contains the intersection or null, if the element wasn't clipped. It should be noted that, in WPF, the `GetLayoutClip` method has a counterpart by the same name that actually resides on the `UIElement` and takes in the slot size and returns clip geometry.

6.3.3 *Performance considerations*

Layout is a recursive process; triggering layout on an element will trigger layout for all the children of that element, and their children, and so on. For that reason, you should try to avoid triggering layout for large visual trees as much as possible. In addition, when implementing your own `MeasureOverride` or `ArrangeOverride` code, make sure it's as efficient as possible.

VIRTUALIZATION

An example of this has to do with large collections of children in controls such as lists and grids. Drawing the elements takes a certain amount of time but that only happens for elements that are onscreen. Creation of the CLR objects representing the items also takes a certain amount of time. Most importantly for us, the measure and layout passes happen for all children, regardless of their potential position on screen or off. Therefore, if you have a thousand elements in a `ListBox`, `MeasureOverride` and `ArrangeOverride` will be called for each of them. More importantly, if those elements contain children (as often is the case with item templates), you'll have even more calls in the layout passes.

One solution to this is virtualization. A subset of the built-in controls (such as the `DataGrid`) support UI virtualization. For those, precreated elements are reused with new data. The end result is a reduction in the number of in-memory elements, as well as a reduction of `MeasureOverride` and `ArrangeOverride` calls.

SIZING AND POSITIONING

Another performance consideration has to do with sizing and positioning elements. For example, if you change the margin of an element or modify its width or height, you'll trigger a layout pass. But, if you instead call a render transform to either move or resize that element, you won't trigger a pass. We'll cover render transforms in the next section.

Understanding the layout system helps take some of the mystery out of what happens when you size elements in Silverlight, and they don't quite do what you might've expected them to do. It's also a key concept to understand if you plan to implement your own panels/container controls.

WPF has the concept of a layout transform. This type of transform is parallel to a render transform but triggers a layout pass. As we've seen here, triggering a layout pass can be an expensive operation, especially if done inside an animation. For performance considerations and due to their relatively low adoption, layout transforms were omitted from Silverlight.

The render transforms provided by Silverlight are almost always adequate to solve problems we used to solve with layout transforms—and often superior. Let's look at them next.

6.4   *Render transforms*

The `Transform` element gives you the flexibility to alter the appearance of any `UIElement` within Silverlight. Transforms give you the flexibility to change the size, location, gyration, and angling apart from the other related properties that have been defined up to this point. The real value of transforms will become apparent when you learn about animations in the next chapter. But first, table 6.2 lists the ways `UIElement` objects can be altered.

Table 6.2   A list of the available transformation options

Transform	Description
RotateTransform	Rotates an object by a specific `Angle`.
ScaleTransform	Provides a zoom in or out effect by specified amounts
SkewTransform	Tilts an element by defined amounts
TranslateTransform	Moves an element by specified amounts
TransformGroup	Not a type of transform; rather, a container that groups multiple transforms to be applied
CompositeTransform	Provides an easy way to combine the other four transforms
MatrixTransform	Provides a way to use a low-level matrix to perform multiple simultaneous transforms

As table 6.2 describes, each `Transform` has its own special purpose. As you'll see within the next few sections, applying a transformation generally involves altering one or two basic properties.

6.4.1   *RotateTransform*

The `RotateTransform` is responsible for rotating an object clockwise around a specified point by a specified angle. This rotation affects the local coordinate system of the rotated object. If you need to rotate an object in place, you need to specify the center point as the center of the object being rotated. Listing 6.10 shows a basic square rotated clockwise by 30 degrees. The dashed version represents the original square before the transform was applied.

Listing 6.10   A square that has been rotated by 30 degrees

Result:

XAML:
```
<Rectangle Width="50" Height="50" Fill="Green" Stroke="Black">
  <Rectangle.RenderTransform>
    <TransformGroup>
      <RotateTransform Angle="30"/>
    </TransformGroup>
  </Rectangle.RenderTransform>
</Rectangle>
```

The `Angle` property specifies to rotate clockwise around the optional `CenterX` and `CenterY` properties, which default to 0. Because these values are initially set to 0, an element will rotate around the upper-left corner. If you set these values to the center of the object you're rotating, it'll give the element the appearance of rotating in place.

When rotating elements, sometimes it becomes necessary to rotate them counter-clockwise. As you may have already guessed, you perform this task by providing a negative value within the `Angle` property. Note that an element will complete one full rotation if the `Angle` is set to 360 or –360.

6.4.2   *ScaleTransform*

The `ScaleTransform` enables you to expand or contract an object horizontally or vertically, empowering you to create the effect of zooming in or out. Listing 6.11 shows how a basic square was zoomed in on via a `ScaleTransform`.

Listing 6.11   A square that has been scaled by a magnitude of 2.5

Result:

XAML:

```
<Rectangle Width="30" Height="30" Fill="Green"
  Stroke="Black" Canvas.Left="35" Canvas.Top="35">
  <Rectangle.RenderTransform>
    <TransformGroup>
      <ScaleTransform ScaleX="2.5" ScaleY="2.5"/>
    </TransformGroup>
  </Rectangle.RenderTransform>
</Rectangle>
```

The ScaleX and ScaleY properties determine the magnitude by which to zoom in or out. As you may expect, the ScaleX property stretches or shrinks the element along the x-axis. The ScaleY property stretches or shrinks the element along the y-axis. If you provide the same value in both properties, the object will expand or contract proportionally.

You may have also noticed that the Rectangle expands from the upper-left corner. This is because the CenterX and CenterY properties determine the point from where the scale operation should take place. By default, these values are set to 0.

6.4.3   *SkewTransform*

A SkewTransform warps the coordinate space in a divergent manner. By *skewing* or *shearing* an element, you basically slant the element in a direction. Listing 6.12 illustrates a basic square skewed by 18 degrees on both the x and y-axes.

Listing 6.12   A Rectangle that's been skewed by 18 degrees

Result:

XAML:

```
<Rectangle Width="75" Height="75" Fill="Green"
  Stroke="Black" Canvas.Left="12" Canvas.Top="12">
  <Rectangle.RenderTransform>
    <TransformGroup>
      <SkewTransform AngleX="18" AngleY="18"/>
    </TransformGroup>
  </Rectangle.RenderTransform>
</Rectangle>
```

The AngleX and AngleY properties specify the amount to shear the rectangle horizontally and vertically. Much like the other transforms we've reviewed, the SkewTransform also exposes CenterX and CenterY properties to specify the horizontal and vertical origin of the skew rendering.

6.4.4   *TranslateTransform*

The TranslateTransform element allows you to define how to transfer an element from one location to another. Listing 6.13 shows a square translated by 25 pixels vertically and horizontally.

> **Listing 6.13   A basic translation in action**

Result:

XAML:
```
<Rectangle Width="50" Height="50" Fill="Green" Stroke="Black">
  <Rectangle.RenderTransform>
    <TransformGroup>
      <TranslateTransform X="25" Y="25"/>
    </TransformGroup>
  </Rectangle.RenderTransform>
</Rectangle>
```

As this listing demonstrates, by specifying a double-precision floating-point value within the X and Y properties of a TranslateTransform, you can move a visual element horizontally or vertically. As you can imagine, the TranslateTransform and the other transforms mentioned give you a lot of flexibility with your visual elements. These transforms can be used to provide even more radical changes when you group them.

6.4.5   *TransformGroup*

In the previous transform-related examples, you may have noticed the TransformGroup element. This element wasn't required when there was only one applied transform. However, it's usually a good idea to include it if there's any chance you'll be adding additional transformations and you aren't using the new CompositeTransform described in the next session. The TransformGroup element makes it possible to simultaneously define multiple transformations on a visual element in any arbitrary order.

Up to this point, we've primarily used a Rectangle as the visual element for transformations but you can also apply these interesting renderings to any UIElement. You can apply these transformations to items such as TextBox elements, Buttons, the MediaElement, and so many more that you'll need to refer to the Silverlight SDK to see. For the sake of illustration, all the primary transforms that have been discussed are applied to the TextBox shown in listing 6.14.

> **Listing 6.14   Four transforms on a TextBox-note how the TextBox is still active**

Result:

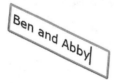

XAML:

```
<TextBox x:Name="myTextBox"
        Text="Ben and Abby"
        Height="25" Width="100">
    <TextBox.RenderTransform>
        <TransformGroup>
            <ScaleTransform ScaleX="2" ScaleY="2" />
            <SkewTransform AngleX="10" AngleY="10" />
            <RotateTransform Angle="15" />
            <TranslateTransform X="10" Y="10" />
        </TransformGroup>
    </TextBox.RenderTransform>
</TextBox>
```

Although the use of transforms in this example is a bit over the top, it does accurately display the true flexibility provided by the transform elements.

6.4.6 *CompositeTransform*

Introduced in Silverlight 4, the `CompositeTransform` applies the four built-in render transforms using a single statement. Though a `TransformGroup` with all four transforms is still supported, you'll find this approach generally easier to use. The `CompositeTransform` applies the transforms in the following order:

1 Scale
2 Skew
3 Rotate
4 Translate

That's the order generally recommended for transformation. If you play with transforms much, you'll quickly find out that the order has a real impact on the final result. The transforms themselves are equivalent to the same individual transforms applied using a `TransformGroup`. Listing 6.15 shows the same example from listing 6.14 but now implemented via a `CompositeTransform`.

> **Listing 6.15 The same four transforms on a `TextBox` using a `CompositeTransform`**

Result:

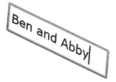

XAML:

```
<TextBox x:Name="myTextBox"
        Text="Ben and Abby"
        Height="25" Width="100">
    <TextBox.RenderTransform>
        <CompositeTransform ScaleX="2" ScaleY="2"
```

```
                                SkewX="10" SkewY="10"
                                TranslateX="10" TranslateY="10"
                                Rotation="15" />
        </TextBox.RenderTransform>
    </TextBox>
```

As you'd expect, the result is the same as the previous listing. But now the code is arguably easier to read, contains four fewer elements (three fewer transforms and no transform group), and is slightly more efficient due to the use of a single set of transformation matrices multiplied together in a single function.

Once all the tooling switches over to using this approach, it'll be much simpler to animate transforms without having to remember lengthy and error-prone property paths for the nested transform elements.

Having said that, we actually had the ability to do all of this in previous versions of Silverlight using the `MatrixTransform`.

6.4.7 *MatrixTransform*

`MatrixTransform` is a powerful class that's rarely used in Silverlight applications. Why? Because the idea of matrix math is, to many, something new. But all of the other transforms use matrix math behind the covers; it's just nicely shielded behind friendly property names.

The Silverlight transformation matrix is a 3×3 affine transformation row-major matrix. The size is three rows by three columns. *Affine* means that the edges all need to stay the same length (proportionally) as they originally were. All points on a single line in the original shape will remain in a single line in the resulting transformed shape. You can't do a true perspective transform in an affine matrix or other transform that would violate this. *Row major* means the vectors are expressed as rows and not columns.

As a result of the affine nature and row-major approach, the last column of the matrix will always contain the rows "0,0,1." Here's what the structure looks like, including the default values:

	1	2	3
1	M11 (1.0)	M12 (0.0)	0
2	M21 (0.0)	M22 (1.0)	0
3	OffsetX (0.0)	OffsetY (0.0)	1

To perform a translate transform that moves the shape 10 pixels in the positive x-axis and 20 pixels in the positive y-axis, you'd supply 10 for `OffsetX` and 20 for `OffsetY`.

To increase the x scale of the target, provide a value larger than 1.0 to the M11 property. Similarly, to increase the y scale, provide a value larger than 1.0 to the M22 property. Values smaller than 1.0 will shrink the size.

You can skew the target in the x direction using M21. A value of 1.0 will skew it 100 percent. Similarly, you can skew the target in the y direction using M12.

To rotate, you'd need to plug in the sine and cosine values into M11, M12, M21, and M22. For example, to rotate by 15 degrees, the matrix would look like this:

	1	**2**	**3**
1	M11 (Cos(15))	M12 (Sin(15))	0
2	M21 (-Sin(15))	M22 (Cos(15))	0
3	OffsetX (0.0)	OffsetY (0.0)	1

Listing 6.16 shows the hard-coded values for a rotation of 15 degrees plus an offset of 100 pixels in the x-axis and 20 pixels on the y-axis.

Listing 6.16 Rotation and translation using a `Matrix`

Result:

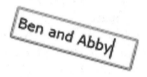

XAML:

```
<TextBox x:Name="myTextBox"
         Text="Ben and Abby"
         Height="25" Width="100">
    <TextBox.RenderTransform>
        <MatrixTransform>
            <MatrixTransform.Matrix>
                <Matrix M11="0.96592583"     ⟵        Cos(15)
                        M12="0.25881905"                      Sin(15)
                        M21="-0.25881905"     ⟵   -Sin(15)
                        M22="0.96592583"      ⟵
                        OffsetX="100"                  Cos(15)
                        OffsetY="20" />
            </MatrixTransform.Matrix>
        </MatrixTransform>
    </TextBox.RenderTransform>
</TextBox>
```

One nice thing you can do with `MatrixTransform` is perform multiple transformations in a single step. Prior to the introduction of `CompositeTransform`, this was the only way to achieve that operation. If you need to control the order of those transformations, you can multiply together two or more matrices.

Render transforms are a powerful way to manipulate the display of your elements. You'll find transforms essential in animation, both to provide gross-level movement and to provide more subtle effects such as a pop when you click a button. They're also helpful in that they don't force a layout pass to happen, as would be the case if you animated something like the actual `Width` and `Height` of the element.

One thing none of the transformations can do, though, is a nonaffine transform such as a perspective effect. For that, you need to turn to 3D projection.

6.5   *3D projection transforms*

3D projection transforms, introduced in Silverlight 3, provide a way to do nonaffine (perspective and distortion) transforms on an object. The UI elements to which the transforms are applied remain active and available, just as with render transforms.

Like render transforms, projections don't affect layout; they're a render-time transformation that exists outside the layout pass.

We'll start with the `PlaneProjection`, the easiest and most popular of the two types of projections, and then look at the somewhat more obscure, but extremely powerful, `Matrix3dProjection`.

6.5.1   *PlaneProjection*

Plane projection (`System.Windows.Media.PlaneProjection`), introduced in Silverlight 3, was one of the most anticipated features to make it into the product. At the time of Silverlight 3, the CoverFlow effect from iTunes was all the rage. You could simulate it using skew transforms and stitching of images but the result was never quite right.

`PlaneProjection` has several key properties, as described in table 6.3. You may wonder why it exposes denormalized properties instead of three 3D point structures. The reason is binding and animation: by providing the individual properties as `DependencyProperty` properties, they can be used in binding and animation.

Table 6.3 `PlaneProjection` properties

Property	Description
`RotationX`, `RotationY`, `RotationZ`	These represent the overall rotation of the object, in degrees for each axis.
`CenterOfRotationX`, `CenterOfRotationY`, `CenterOfRotationZ`	These represent the object-oriented center of rotation. 0.5, 0.5 is the center of the plane on that axis and is the default value.
`GlobalOffsetX`, `GlobalOffsetY`, `GlobalOffsetZ`	These values translate the object along the specified axis, providing for motion in 3D space. The values are relative to the screen. So the y-axis will always be vertical and point up, and the x-axis will always be horizontal and point to the right.
`LocalOffsetX`, `LocalOffsetY`, `LocalOffsetZ`	Unlike the `GlobalOffset` values, these values translate on an object-relative axis. So, if the object was already rotated 20 degrees to the left, the positive y-axis would point 20 degrees to the left and the positive x-axis would point 70 degrees to the right. The values of `RotationX`, `RotationY`, and `RotationZ` directly impact how `LocalOffsetX`, `LocalOffsetY`, and `LocalOffsetZ`, respectively, are interpreted.

For each of the properties, the screen axes are defined as shown in figure 6.7. Positive y is vertical top, positive x is horizontal right. Silverlight, at least in the case of the `PlaneProjection`, follows a right-hand coordinate system, so positive z is closer to you, and negative z is further "into" the screen.

Both the `PlaneProjection` and its related `Matrix3dProjection` are assigned to an object via its `Projection` property.

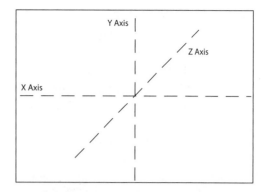

Figure 6.7 The x, y, and z-axes as recognized by the `PlaneProjection` element

Listing 6.17 shows a simple `PlaneProjection` applied to a set of UI elements. In this case, the projection is on the y-axis, giving you that classic CoverFlow look but applied to live input controls.

Listing 6.17 Simple perspective effect on a `Grid` containing multiple elements

Result:

XAML:

```
<Grid Width="200"
      Height="175">
  <Rectangle Fill="#FFe0e0c0"
             Stroke="#FF000000"
             StrokeThickness="3"
             RadiusY="10"
             RadiusX="10" />
  <StackPanel Margin="10">
    <TextBlock Text="Pete, Melissa, Ben, Abby" Margin="5" />
    <TextBox Text="Silverlight" Margin="5" />
    <TextBox Text="In Action" Margin="5" />
    <Button Content="I'm a Button!" Margin="5" />
  </StackPanel>

  <Grid.Projection>
    <PlaneProjection RotationY="-45" />     ⟵—— PlaneProjection
  </Grid.Projection>

</Grid>
```

6.5.2 *Matrix3dProjection*

As with 2D affine transforms, Silverlight also supports a lower-level Matrix transform for 3D. The class is named `System.Windows.Media.Matrix3dProjection`.

Due to the complexity of explaining 4×4 nonaffine matrices, and the relatively small subset of readers who'll be interested in that, we'll leave the fine details of 3D matrix projections out. But let's look at a simple code example to get you started.

Listing 6.18 shows how to do something that isn't provided just by 3D rotation on an axis. This combines skew effects with rotation to come up with something that can only be described as interesting.

> **Listing 6.18 Mangling elements using a `Matrix3dProjection`**

Result:

XAML:

```
<Grid Width="200"
      Height="175">
  <Rectangle Fill="#FFe0e0c0"
             Stroke="#FF000000"
             StrokeThickness="3"
             RadiusY="10"
             RadiusX="10" />
  <StackPanel Margin="10">
    <TextBlock Text="Pete, Melissa, Ben, Abby" Margin="5" />
    <TextBox Text="Silverlight" Margin="5" />
    <TextBox Text="In Action" Margin="5" />
    <Button Content="I'm a Button!" Margin="5" />
  </StackPanel>

  <Grid.Projection>
    <Matrix3DProjection>                         <--- Matrix3dProjection
      <Matrix3DProjection.ProjectionMatrix>
        <Matrix3D M11="0.4269" M12="0.0592"  M13="0.0" M14="-0.0012"
                  M21="-0.3600" M22="1.0548" M23="0.0" M24="-0.0028"
                  M31="0.0" M32="0.0" M33="1.0" M34="0.0"
                  OffsetX="9.0" OffsetY="-117.0" OffsetZ="0"
                  M44="1.0" />
      </Matrix3DProjection.ProjectionMatrix>
    </Matrix3DProjection>
  </Grid.Projection>

</Grid>
```

`Matrix3dProjection` is something you may only ever use once but, for that one time, it'll be exactly what you need to solve a specific problem. The sky's the limit when it comes to 3D transformations (actually 2.5D because Silverlight doesn't yet have a true 3D engine) for your Silverlight applications.

One thing you may have noticed with the projection transforms is that they add some fuzziness to the elements when they render. That's because the render transforms operate on frame-by-frame bitmap representations of the objects. That makes them extremely performant, but also causes them to have a slight degradation in quality, especially when you do something such as an extreme z scale, as in the `Matrix3dProjection` example.

Silverlight provides two easy-to-use but powerful ways to transform objects in 3D space: `PlaneProjection` and `Matrix3dProjection`. `PlaneProjection`, in particular, will find its way into a lot of your applications. In fact, if you develop for Silverlight for the Windows Phone, you'll find the `PlaneProjection` indispensible for providing the expected page flip UI transitions.

In the last two examples, I used a combination of `Grids` and `StackPanels` to hold the elements I was transforming. Both of these are types of `Panels` and will be something you use over and over again in your own applications.

6.6   Summary

The basis for all onscreen elements is the `FrameworkElement` and `UIElement` pair. The two of them define the majority of the commonly used properties and methods for other elements. In addition, they define the abstract methods for measuring and layout, the core of the layout system.

Framework elements, UI elements, and panels are the fundamental players in the layout system. Layout in Silverlight is so flexible because so much of the measurement and layout are delegated to the elements themselves. An understanding of the layout system is important for both performance and flexibility reasons and is a must should you wish to create your own panels.

The layout system is a major part of a much larger rendering system. The rendering system in Silverlight does a good job at optimizing the elements onscreen for efficient rendering, but also provides appropriate places where you can tune that process to fit your own applications. Silverlight enables you to cache elements, for example, and even to control whether cached elements are cached to hardware surfaces on a compatible video card.

Render transformations allow us to transform the location, rotation, skew, or size of any visible element without incurring the performance hit of a layout system pass. For that reason, they're perfectly suited to animation and more performance-hungry uses. What render transformations lack is support for nonaffine or perspective transforms.

The two types of 3D projections pick up where render transforms leave off, and provide support for nonaffine, perspective, and distorting 3D transformations. The `PlaneProjection` is the easiest to use and suitable for most types of basic projection work. The `Matrix3dProjection` is a little harder to use but is extremely powerful. If you want to do basic CoverFlow-style work, `PlaneProjection` is for you. If you want to do a more immersive 3D experience with floating panels zipping past you and appearing off in the distance, you're probably looking at the `Matrix3dProjection` class and some of its helper libraries on www.codeplex.com.

With framework and UI elements, the rendering and layout system, transformations, and projections under our belt, we're ready to move on to the fundamentals of working with layout panels. Panels form the root elements for most of our interfaces and are the main elements responsible for layout in Silverlight.

Panels

This chapter covers

- Absolute layout with the `Canvas`
- Stacking items with the `StackPanel`
- Cell-based layout with the `Grid`

Panels in Silverlight provide a way to host multiple elements and provide unique layout logic. For example, you may want a panel that lays out elements so they appear to radiate out of a central point (think of the wheel on *Wheel of Fortune*). Rather than provide each and every control with the knowledge required to perform that layout, Silverlight leaves it to the panel.

This delegation to panels and the layout system is why you won't see `Left` and `Top` properties on UI elements—those properties are provided by the panels in the form of attached properties (see section 2.1.5 for more information on attached properties).

In typical use, any control you place in the UI in Silverlight is going to be hosted in a panel at some level. Understanding how the different panels work is essential to making the most of Silverlight's UI capabilities.

Though there are numerous types of panels available, the three most important and widely used are the `Canvas`, the `StackPanel`, and the `Grid`.

We'll start with the simplest panel, the Canvas, and from there move on to panels that provide more layout functionality. The StackPanel forms the basis of most list and menu implementations but is still relatively simple in its layout and functionality. The Grid, the final panel in this section, is typically the root of our interfaces and is one of the most powerful, flexible, and complex panels available.

7.1   *Canvas*

Envision a painter inspired to recreate a mountainous landscape. As you can imagine, a tremendous amount of artistic freedom is required to adequately mimic this majestic view. Painters have the luxury of a conventional canvas, which gives them free rein over their illustrations. Unfortunately, traditional web technologies can occasionally be overly rigid, imprisoning you and making it difficult to deliver awe-inspiring content over the Internet.

Thankfully, in addition to being the highest-performing and lightest-weight layout panel, the Canvas element gives you the same type of freedom that painters have long taken for granted. This Panel allows you to say, "I want this element at this exact location," and accomplish that. Before we discuss the details of Canvas, we should look at the basic syntax of a Canvas, as shown here:

```
<Canvas Height="200" Width="300" Background="White">
</Canvas>
```

This bit of XAML shows an empty Canvas with a white background. To show something contained within the canvas, you need to add some content, such as a basic block of text, as seen here:

```
<Canvas>
  <TextBlock Text="Hello, Silverlight" />
</Canvas>
```

This shows a basic Canvas with a small amount of content: a single TextBlock. The content of a Canvas consists of elements inside the Canvas. These child elements are added to a collection, called Children, which is accessible from code. Each item in this collection derives from the UIElement type described in section 6.1. We'll use a UIElement called TextBlock to show you how to arrange content within a Canvas.

> ### Canvas performance
> As described in section 6.3 on the layout system, the process of determining where elements are positioned can be quite involved. As each element is added to its container, Silverlight must perform layout calculations. The number of calculations is usually based on the requirements placed on an element by its ancestors and by siblings in the same container. In general, as the number of relative elements grows, so does the number of necessary calculations.

(continued)

Because of its explicit nature and minimal layout requirements, Canvas can minimize the number of necessary calculations, providing a potentially important performance boost for applications with many onscreen elements. To realize this performance gain, though, you'd need to have thousands or tens of thousands of visible elements on the screen.

7.1.1 Arranging content of a Canvas

You can arrange the content within a Canvas by using at least one of two approaches. The first approach involves setting the vertical and/or horizontal offsets of an element within a Canvas. The other method revolves around setting the stack order of an element within a Canvas. These methods can be used in combination for full control over how each piece of content is shown. Let's take it one step at a time and investigate how to set an element's offsets.

SETTING THE OFFSETS

By default, the content within a Canvas is automatically arranged at 0,0. This approach places all of the content in the upper-left corner of a Canvas. To move content out of this corner, you must take advantage of two attached properties—Left and Top—which are shown here:

```
<TextBlock x:Name="tb" Text="Hello" Canvas.Left="20" Canvas.Top="30" />
```

This TextBlock uses the Left and Top attached properties to set its position within an imaginary Canvas. The Left property specifies the distance, in pixels, from the left edge of the TextBlock element to the left edge of the parent Canvas. Likewise, the Top property sets the number of pixels between the top edge of the parent Canvas and the top edge of the TextBlock. This specific sample places the TextBlock 20 pixels from the left and 30 pixels from the top of a parent Canvas. Alternatively, you may need to set these values at runtime.

To set the position of an element within a Canvas at runtime, you must do so programmatically. The Canvas element exposes two statically visible methods that enable you to set an element's position at runtime. There are also two other methods—illustrated here using the TextBlock from the previous example—that enable you to retrieve an element's position at runtime:

```
double newLeft = Canvas.GetLeft(tb) + 15.0;
Canvas.SetLeft(tb, newLeft);

double newTop = Canvas.GetTop(tb) + 30.5;
Canvas.SetTop(tb, newTop);
```

This example shows how the GetLeft and SetLeft methods are used to move a Text-Block 15 pixels to the right. Alternatively, you could've subtracted a value to move the TextBlock to the left. This example also moves a TextBlock down by 30.5 pixels using the GetTop and SetTop methods. In a similar approach, you could've subtracted a value to move the TextBlock up. Either way, it's important to note that you could've passed any UIElement to this method in place of the TextBlock.

Wait... 30.5 pixels?

Silverlight's rendering and layout system support subpixel layout and rendering. This allows you to specify fractions of pixels and allow Silverlight to create the appropriate display. For example, if you have a white canvas with a black vertical line located halfway between two pixels—a width of one pixel at position 30.5, for example—Silverlight will show two gray lines side by side (the average of white and black) in order to produce the illusion of a line at the fractional offset. The end result can be described as fuzzy or blurry and is often something you want to avoid. To have exact pixel snapping and crisp lines, set the UseLayoutRounding property of the panel or control you want snapped.

Any time you set the location of an element, you must use a double value. This double-precision value represents a specific number of pixels. If you aren't careful, you may inadvertently overlap the content within a Canvas. Although this overlapping effect can occasionally be desirable, it's still useful to know how to set the stacking order.

SETTING THE STACK ORDER

By default, when content is rendered within a layout panel, each element is rendered on its own imaginary layer. This ensures that the last element in a layout panel is shown on top of all the others. The other elements are still present; they're just over-drawn by the overlapping content, as shown in listing 7.1.

Listing 7.1   Natural stacking order

Result:

XAML:

```
<Canvas Width="180" Height="180" >          Background
  <Canvas Width="60"                  ⊲——┘ canvas
          Height="60"
          Background="LightGray"/>          Middle
  <Canvas Width="60"                  ⊲——┘ canvas
          Height="60"
          Canvas.Left="20"
          Canvas.Top="20"
          Background="Gray" />              Foreground
  <Canvas Width="60"                  ⊲——┘ canvas
          Height="60"
          Canvas.Left="40"
```

```
         Canvas.Top="40"
         Background="Black"/>
</Canvas>
```

Listing 7.1 shows the natural stacking approach used when rendering overlapping content. The content overlaps in this orderly fashion because, by default, its ZIndex (or stacking position) is set to 0.

> **TIP** Even though `Canvas.ZIndex` is an attached property on the `Canvas` type, it works within other panels such as the grid, even if there's no canvas present anywhere in the visual tree. Note that `ZIndex` is relative only to the panel and not to the application as a whole.

You can change the ZIndex value to a value greater than 0 to move the Canvas farther into the foreground, as shown in listing 7.2. The element will be placed on top of the elements that have a smaller ZIndex within the same panel.

Listing 7.2   Changing the stacking order using ZIndex

Result:

XAML:

```
<Canvas x:Name="myCanvas">
  <Canvas Canvas.ZIndex="2"              Foreground
          Width="60" Height="60"         canvas
          Background="LightGray"/>
  <Canvas Canvas.ZIndex="1"              Middle
          Width="60" Height="60"         canvas
          Canvas.Left="20" Canvas.Top="20"
          Background="Gray" />
  <Canvas Width="60" Height="60"         Background
          Canvas.Left="40" Canvas.Top="40"   canvas
          Background="Black"/>
</Canvas>
```

This short example shows how to move an element further into the foreground of a Canvas. You add a value to the integer value represented by the ZIndex. Alternatively, you could've moved the element somewhere into the background by subtracting a value. Either way, the Canvas gives you the ability to set the stack order and offsets to your liking. In addition, the Canvas provides some performance features that really pack a punch.

> **TIP** Playing around with ZIndex can get frustrating and difficult to track once you have several overlapping panels, each with elements with specific ZIndex values. Whenever possible, arrange your elements so they make sense in the natural order. In addition, try not to animate ZIndex because the Silverlight runtime rearranges the visual tree to get the required z positioning. This can be a real performance drain.

7.2   *The StackPanel*

Once in a while, I'll peel my eyes away from my computer and pick up a newspaper. One thing (other than the funnies) that catches my eye in the paper is the crossword puzzle. The layout of a typical puzzle looks like that shown in figure 7.1.

If you look at the overall structure of this crossword puzzle, you can derive that each word consists of either a horizontal or vertical stack of letters. Each of these stacks represents a small segment of the overall puzzle. This representation is used to position each letter successively to create a recognizable word within a smaller context.

Figure 7.1   A sample crossword puzzle that could be built using stack panels

Much like a word is a grouping of letters in a crossword puzzle, a StackPanel is a grouping of visual elements. Each successive visual element is positioned vertically or horizontally within a single row or column, as seen in listing 7.3.

Listing 7.3   The StackPanel in vertical mode

Result:

XAML:

```
<StackPanel>
  <Canvas Width="90" Height="30" Background="Red"/>
  <Canvas Width="90" Height="30" Background="Green"/>
  <Canvas Width="90" Height="30" Background="Blue"/>
</StackPanel>
```

As shown in the listing, elements within a StackPanel are rendered one after another from top to bottom. The StackPanel exposes an Orientation property, which allows you to specify whether child elements are stacked in a Vertical or a Horizontal manner, as shown in listing 7.4.

Listing 7.4   The StackPanel in horizontal mode

Result:

XAML:

```
<StackPanel Orientation="Horizontal">
  <Canvas Width="90" Height="30" Background="Red"/>
  <Canvas Width="90" Height="30" Background="Green"/>
  <Canvas Width="90" Height="30" Background="Blue"/>
</StackPanel>
```

Purchase Order				
Item #	**Description**	**Price**	**Quantity**	**Total**
1	Lollipops	$0.25	5	$1.25
2	Gum	$1.00	4	$4.00
3	Jelly Beans, bagged, assorted	$2.95	2	$5.90
4	Toothbrushes	$3.50	5	$17.50
5	Pliers	$10.00	1	$10.00
6	Topical anesthetic	$7.95	1	$7.95
7	Gauze	$1.75	3	$5.25
			Total	$51.85

Figure 7.2 A basic purchase order, using tabular layout. This would be perfect for a Grid.

As you can see in listing 7.4, shifting the layout from a vertical to horizontal orientation is as simple as including a single property. In addition, layout panels of any type can be nested within one another to fully dictate an application's arrangement.

Nesting layout panels is incredibly important when you begin to consider the entire scope of an application. Although the StackPanel is great for one-dimensional (vertical or horizontal) content, it's not suited for organizing large amounts of elements. Consider the illustration in figure 7.2.

Imagine attempting to recreate the purchase order shown in figure 7.2 using a series of StackPanel elements. Up front, you'd have to decide if you want to create vertical or horizontal elements. Then, you'd have to specify the Width of each Stack-Panel because StackPanel elements are arranged and sized independently of each other. There has to be a better way to organize tabular data. Thankfully, Silverlight provides the powerful Grid panel to do just that.

7.3   *The Grid*

Of all the layout panels, the Grid is the one you're likely to use the most. It's the default root layout element for all the UserControl and Page templates, and is the one control that allows you to easily resize (not rescale) content to take up the space available to the plug-in.

Though the Grid is similar to an HTML table element, it expands on a number of features, such as proportional and absolute row and column sizing, the ability to have any row or column be the one that takes up all the available space, gracefully handling of column and row spanning, and an easily consumed API for manipulating rows and columns at runtime.

Throughout the remaining sections, we'll take a deep look at the Grid, starting with the basics of how to position content in rows and columns. From there, we'll work on cell spanning and sizing of Grid cells. Up until that point, we'll primarily be working with XAML. For that reason, we'll look at what's required to build and manipulate the Grid from code. Finally, we'll cover using the splitter to allow the end user to resize Grid columns and rows.

The Grid panel gives you the ability to easily lay out content in a tabular format. This tabular format is similar to the table element in HTML, but the table element can occasionally be difficult to work with during development. For instance, it can be challenging to determine how many rows or columns exist in a table while coding. To help overcome this challenge, the Grid in Silverlight defines its rows and columns in two distinct collections. Appropriately, these collections are called ColumnDefinitions and RowDefinitions.

7.3.1   *Arranging Grid content*

The RowDefinitions collection stores the definitions of the rows of a Grid. Each row is set through an element called RowDefinition. This element is primarily responsible for defining the dimensions of a single horizontal row. Similarly, the Grid also enables you to create a ColumnDefinition element. This element must be defined within the ColumnDefinitions collection. As you'd expect, this element generally sets the dimensions of a vertical column within a Grid. By default, you don't have to set these dimensions, as shown in listing 7.5.

Listing 7.5   Grid with uniformly sized cells

Result:

XAML:

```
<Grid x:Name="myGrid" ShowGridLines="True"
  Height="120" Width="120" Background="LightGray">
  <Grid.ColumnDefinitions>
    <ColumnDefinition />                    Column
    <ColumnDefinition />                    definitions
    <ColumnDefinition />
  </Grid.ColumnDefinitions>

  <Grid.RowDefinitions>
    <RowDefinition />                       Row
    <RowDefinition />                       definitions
    <RowDefinition />
  </Grid.RowDefinitions>
</Grid>
```

This listing defines a Grid with three columns and three rows. The rows and columns of this Grid are defined within the Grid.RowDefinitions and Grid.ColumnDefinitions elements. These elements represent strongly typed collections that serve as containers for the row and column definitions. The individual row and column definitions are shown by the RowDefinition and ColumnDefinition elements. These elements intersect at different points across the Grid, creating a total of nine cells.

Each cell represents the area allocated to a specific region within a Grid. This region is created by the intersection of a row and a column within a Grid. The easiest way to see the boundaries of each cell is to use the Grid element's ShowGridLines property. Although this property defaults to a value of False, you can set it to True to see the area reserved for each cell. Because these particular grid lines aren't customizable, they're generally only used during development. As you'll see in section 7.3.6, you can add several GridSplitter elements to customize the cell boundaries while giving the user control of cell sizing. Nevertheless, the ShowGridLines property and the GridSplitter element are both useful when sizing a Grid's rows and columns or arranging its content.

The content of a Grid consists of the elements that you want to arrange in a tabular fashion. These elements could be controls such as TextBox and TextBlock. TextBlock will be covered at the end of this chapter, but TextBox won't be covered until the next chapter when we cover collecting user input. For now, we'll use these basic controls to show how to arrange content in a Grid to create an input form, as shown in listing 7.6.

Listing 7.6   Grid Row, Column, and ColumnSpan properties on a simple form

Result:

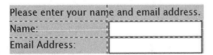

XAML:
```
<Grid x:Name="myGrid" ShowGridLines="True"
  Background="LightGray" Width="310" Height="75">
  <Grid.ColumnDefinitions>
    <ColumnDefinition />
    <ColumnDefinition />
  </Grid.ColumnDefinitions>
  <Grid.RowDefinitions>
    <RowDefinition />
    <RowDefinition />
    <RowDefinition />
  </Grid.RowDefinitions>

  <TextBlock Text="Please enter your name and email address."
    Grid.ColumnSpan="2" />
  <TextBlock Text="Name: " Grid.Row="1" />
  <TextBlock Text="Email Address: " Grid.Row="2" />
```

ColumnSpan
property

```
<TextBox Width="150" Grid.Column="1" Grid.Row="1" />
<TextBox Width="150" Grid.Column="1" Grid.Row="2" />
</Grid>
```

**Grid.Row, Grid.Column
properties**

Listing 7.6 shows a basic input form that uses a Grid to arrange its content. This content is arranged using a number of the Grid's attached properties. The first attached property is ColumnSpan. This property gives you the ability to span an element across multiple cells. We'll discuss this feature in greater detail in a moment. But first, we'll cover the Grid.Row and Grid.Column attached properties. These properties are used more often and enable you to position content within a Grid.

7.3.2   *Positioning Grid content*

Positioning content within a Grid is handled mainly by two attached properties—Column and Row–which store integer values. These values specify the row and/or column in which to place the content. To illustrate the syntax of these attached properties, we'll use the TextBlock:

```
<TextBlock Text="Rock On!" Grid.Row="3" Grid.Column="2" />
```

The properties in this example are assigned explicit integer values. If values aren't assigned, they default to 0. Alternatively, if you provide a value outside the available row or column range, they're simply capped at the end of that range, and the element will be displayed as though you specified the max row or max column for your grid, possibly overlapping other elements.

Although overlapping can be an unwanted side effect, *clipped content* is also undesirable. Clipped content can happen when a row or column is too small for its content. One way to overcome this problem is to size your row or column using one of the techniques discussed in section 7.3.1. Another option is to let your content span multiple cells.

7.3.3   *Spanning cells*

Occasionally, you run into situations where you need to allow content to span multiple cells. You saw this in section 7.3.1, where we had a heading that demanded this functionality. As you saw then—to accomplish this, you need to use the ColumnSpan attached property.

The ColumnSpan attached property empowers you to spread content across several cells horizontally. By default, this integer value is set to 1, meaning that the content can occupy a single column. If this value is larger than the number of columns available in the row, the content extends to the end of the row but not beyond it. In addition to the ability to span horizontally, you can span vertically with RowSpan, which works just like ColumnSpan:

```
<TextBox Grid.Row="1" Grid.RowSpan="3"
         Grid.Column="1" Grid.ColumnSpan="2" />
```

The ColumnSpan and RowSpan properties are easy to add to any piece of content in a Grid. Occasionally, though, allowing content to span multiple cells isn't desirable, but you may need more space for content. Let's look at the Grid's sizing options.

7.3.4 Sizing it up

The overall dimensions of a Grid can be set to a specific number of pixels using the Height and Width properties. These dimensions are set like almost every other element in Silverlight. Defining the dimensions of a row or column within a Grid is an entirely different story because the Height of a RowDefinition and Width of a ColumnDefinition are represented as GridLength values.

The System.Windows.GridLength type provides three different ways to specify how to allocate space. We'll discuss each of these options throughout this section. It's important to understand how each approach works because these options can be intertwined within the same Grid. Based on this fact, we'll naturally cover the typical pixel approach to sizing. In addition, we'll also cover the more dynamic auto-sizing approach. But first, we'll cover the default option used for sizing rows and columns: *star sizing*.

STAR SIZING

Star sizing enables you to equally distribute the available area of a Grid across its rows and columns. This is the default approach used within a Grid. But, if any row or column in a grid uses some other form of sizing, the other approach will take precedence. (It may be more appropriate to say that star sizing is used by the remaining available area.) Listing 7.7 illustrates this concept.

Listing 7.7 Absolute and star sizing

Result:

XAML:
```
<Grid x:Name="myGrid" ShowGridLines="True"
   Background="LightGray" Width="200" Height="200">
   <Grid.RowDefinitions>
     <RowDefinition Height="50" />          Absolute sizing
     <RowDefinition Height="2*" />     Star
     <RowDefinition Height="3*" />     sizing
   </Grid.RowDefinitions>

   <Grid.ColumnDefinitions>
     <ColumnDefinition Width="50" />
     <ColumnDefinition Width="2*" />
     <ColumnDefinition Width="3*" />
   </Grid.ColumnDefinitions>
</Grid>
```

Listing 7.7 shows a Grid using star sizing in addition to absolute sizing. *Absolute sizing* will be discussed in just a moment; for now, observe the values with the *n** in them, for example the Height and Width values for the second and third rows and columns. This asterisk signals that the element will use star sizing with a multiplier. Although this example only uses integer values, you can use any positive double-precision value. This value specifies the proportion of the remaining space to allocate to the element.

Star sizing works by determining how much space is available after the other sizing schemes have rendered. These calculations will return a remaining amount of available space. This space is divided proportionally across all the items using star sizing. As you can see, this approach provides an easy way to provide a proportionate-looking interface. Occasionally, you may want the size of the cells to be automatically determined based on their content. For these situations, it's appropriate to use the Auto GridLength option.

AUTO SIZING

The Auto GridLength option automatically determines how large or small to make an element, as shown in listing 7.8. With this option, the element's size is based primarily on the content that occupies it, but other factors can also dictate the size of an element using the Auto approach.

Listing 7.8   Auto sizing

Result:

XAML:

```
<Grid x:Name="myGrid" Height="100" Width="300"
  ShowGridLines="True" Background="LightGray">
  <Grid.ColumnDefinitions>
    <ColumnDefinition Width="Auto" />            ⟵ Auto
    <ColumnDefinition Width="Auto" />                sizing
  </Grid.ColumnDefinitions>
  <Grid.RowDefinitions>
    <RowDefinition Height="Auto" />
    <RowDefinition Height="Auto" />
  </Grid.RowDefinitions>
  <TextBlock Text="Hello there, how are you?" />
  <TextBlock Text="I'm fine thanks!" Grid.Column="1" />
  <TextBlock Text="That's Great" Grid.Row="1" />
</Grid>
```

Listing 7.8 uses the Auto sizing approach for the Grid's columns and rows. The result produced from this XAML shows two key aspects of Auto sizing. First, if a row or column uses Auto sizing, the size of the largest element in the row or column determines the size of the others. Second, any remaining space is allocated to the last row or column—this is why the cells in the last row look so bloated. If you want to have complete control over the size of your cells, you need to use a more exact approach.

ABSOLUTE

The final approach for allocating the available area to a row or column involves using a double. This double-precision floating-point value represents a number of pixels.

These pixels single-handedly dictate the area reserved for a row or column. If this space is larger than the content, there's no problem. If the amount of space is smaller than the content, you may get some undesired results because the overlapping content is clipped, as shown in listing 7.9.

Listing 7.9   Absolute sizing

Result:

XAML:

```xaml
<Grid x:Name="myGrid" Height="100" Width="300"
  ShowGridLines="True" Background="LightGray">
  <Grid.ColumnDefinitions>
    <ColumnDefinition></ColumnDefinition>
  </Grid.ColumnDefinitions>
 <Grid.RowDefinitions>
    <RowDefinition Height="68.5" />
    <RowDefinition Height="12" />
    <RowDefinition Height="19.5" />
  </Grid.RowDefinitions>
  <TextBlock Text="This row is too tall" />
  <TextBlock Text="This row is too small" Grid.Row="1" />
  <TextBlock Text="This row is just right!" Grid.Row="2" />
</Grid>
```

Listing 7.9 shows the absolute sizing approach in action. The rows use a double-precision value to specify their `Height`. The third row displays the text: "This row is just right!" Although you could use the `Auto` sizing approach for this row, we chose the absolute approach, primarily for illustration. It's important to know that the absolute approach takes precedence over all other sizing options, giving you some flexibility to get a `Grid` to look exactly how you want.

As you've seen, the `Grid` provides three valuable sizing options. These options give you the flexibility to create a great-looking layout at design time. Occasionally, you may need to set the sizing options at runtime. Alternatively, you may need to add or remove rows and columns at runtime. For both these reasons, it's important to understand how to work with the `Grid` programmatically.

7.3.5   *Working with the grid programmatically*

Usually, the rows and columns of a `Grid` are created at design time using XAML. This approach ensures that you can easily arrange the content of a `Grid` before an application is up and running. Once the application is running, there may be situations where you need to dynamically add or remove rows or columns from a `Grid`. In times like these, it's nice to know how to both add and remove these items at runtime.

ADDING ROWS AND COLUMNS AT RUNTIME

Adding rows or columns programmatically at runtime is as simple as writing two lines of code. The first line of code is responsible for creating either a `RowDefinition` or `ColumnDefinition` object. The other line of code is then responsible for adding the newly created object to the appropriate collection. Significantly, there are two different ways to add the object to the collection. First, here's how to programmatically add a row:

```
RowDefinition myRow = new RowDefinition();
myGrid.RowDefinitions.Add(myRow);
```

The preceding adds a row to the grid created in the previous example. Similarly, this code adds a column to the same grid but uses the `Insert` method to insert the column definition at the far left of the grid:

```
ColumnDefinition myColumn = new ColumnDefinition();
myGrid.ColumnDefinitions.Insert(0, myColumn);
```

The first approach adds a single row to the bottom of the `Grid` because the `Add` method always appends an object to the end of a collection. In situations where you need to have more control over where a column or row is added to a `Grid`, you may consider using the `Insert` method. Either way, you can see how easy it is to add rows and columns on the fly. And, fortunately, it's just as easy to remove them.

REMOVING ROWS AND COLUMNS AT RUNTIME

To remove either a row or a column from a `Grid`, you must use one of two approaches. The first approach uses the `Remove` method, which attempts to remove the first occurrence of the object provided. If the row or column is successfully removed, this method returns `true`. Otherwise, if something unexpected has occurred, this method returns `false`:

```
RowDefinition myRow = myGrid.RowDefinitions[0];
myGrid.RowDefinitions.Remove(myRow);
```

Occasionally, you may want to explicitly state which row or column to remove based on an index. For these situations, you should consider using the `RemoveAt` method:

```
int lastColumnIndex = myGrid.ColumnDefinitions.Count - 1;
myGrid.ColumnDefinitions.RemoveAt(lastColumnIndex);
```

The `RemoveAt` method enables you to specify which row or column to remove by using a specific index. This index is based on the zero-based indexing scheme used by the `RowDefinitions` and `ColumnDefinitions` collections. Once the row or column is removed, the remaining rows or columns will simply move up in the collection. This process occurs completely at runtime and demonstrates how powerful the `Grid` can be. Another feature that shows the power of the `Grid` is the ability to customize the cell boundaries.

7.3.6   *Customizing cell boundaries*

Silverlight provides a way to customize the cell boundaries of a `Grid` that's similar to the border property in CSS. But, Silverlight goes one step further and gives the *user* the ability to use this boundary to dynamically resize the cells of a `Grid`. This user-controlled sizing feature enables a user to reallocate space from one cell to another. During this process, as one cell increases in size, other cells in the `Grid` may decrease in size. Significantly, this resizing process doesn't change the dimensions of the overall `Grid`. To take advantage of this powerful feature, you use a `GridSplitter`.

A `GridSplitter` is an element in the `System.Windows.Controls` namespace. But, this item isn't part of the core Silverlight runtime. Instead, this element is known as an *extended control*. These types of controls must be accessed slightly differently than a standard element such as a `Grid`. Over the course of this section, you'll learn how to access the library of extended controls. Then you'll learn how to use the `GridSplitter` within a `Grid`.

ACCESSING EXTENDED CONTROLS

The extended controls, including the `GridSplitter`, are part of an assembly called `System.Windows.Controls`, which is included in the Silverlight SDK, itself part of the developer tools download. This assembly includes a number of controls designed to complement the core Silverlight controls. You'll learn about the core Silverlight controls in chapter 10 and the other extended controls throughout this book. For now, it's important to recognize that this assembly is *not* part of the core Silverlight runtime; if you want to use any of the extended controls, you must reference the `System.Windows.Controls` assembly. You can do so by adding a reference to the assembly in Visual Studio and then referencing the namespace through a prefix:

```
<UserControl x:Class="ExtendedControls.Page"
  xmlns="http://schemas.microsoft.com/winfx/2006/xaml/presentation"
  xmlns:x="http://schemas.microsoft.com/winfx/2006/xaml"
  xmlns:ext="clr-namespace:System.Windows.Controls;
 [CA]assembly=System.Windows.Controls"
  Width="400" Height="300">
  <Grid x:Name="LayoutRoot" Background="White" />
</UserControl>
```

This code shows how to reference the extended controls assembly to pull in a control not included in the core Silverlight runtime.

> **WARNING** Referencing the `System.Windows.Controls` assembly will cause it to be bundled with your application's .xap, increasing the size of the .xap file by about 427 KB before compression (as of the time of writing). This can cause your application to take slightly longer to download unless you take advantage of assembly caching described in chapter 3.

We've given this assembly the friendly prefix *ext* to reference the extended controls. The *sdk* prefix will also be used in relation to our current discussion involving the `GridSplitter`.

USING THE GRIDSPLITTER

The `GridSplitter` defines a divider within a `Grid`. This divider can be used to style the boundaries of the cells in the `Grid`. Alternatively, a `GridSplitter` can be moved by a user with the mouse or keyboard. To get a feel for how this works and the basic syntax of a `GridSplitter`, take a look at listing 7.10.

Listing 7.10 `GridSplitter`

Result:

XAML:

```
<Grid x:Name="LayoutRoot" Background="White">
  <Grid.RowDefinitions>
    <RowDefinition />
    <RowDefinition />
    <RowDefinition />
  </Grid.RowDefinitions>
  <Grid.ColumnDefinitions>
    <ColumnDefinition />
    <ColumnDefinition />
    <ColumnDefinition />
  </Grid.ColumnDefinitions>
  <Canvas Background="Silver" Margin="10" />
  <Canvas Background="Gray"
        Margin="10" Grid.Column="1" />
  <Canvas Background="Silver"
        Margin="10" Grid.Column="2" />
  <sdk:GridSplitter Width="2" />
  <Canvas Background="Gray"
        Margin="10" Grid.Row="1" />
  <Canvas Background="Silver" Margin="10"
        Grid.Column="1" Grid.Row="1" />
  <Canvas Background="Gray" Margin="10"
        Grid.Column="2" Grid.Row="1" />
  <sdk:GridSplitter Background="Black" Width="2"
                Grid.Column="1" Grid.RowSpan="2" />
  <Canvas Background="Silver" Margin="10" Grid.Row="2" />
  <Canvas Background="Gray"
        Margin="10" Grid.Column="1" Grid.Row="2" />
  <Canvas Background="Silver"
        Margin="10" Grid.Column="2" Grid.Row="2" />
</Grid>
```

Basic GridSplitter control ← (annotation pointing to `<sdk:GridSplitter Width="2" />`)

GridSplitter with appearance (annotation pointing to `<sdk:GridSplitter Background="Black" Width="2" Grid.Column="1" Grid.RowSpan="2" />`)

Listing 7.10 shows a 3×3 `Grid` that has two `GridSplitter` elements. The first `GridSplitter` shows the most basic implementation of a `GridSplitter`. At the same time, the second `GridSplitter` goes a step further and shows how to control the appearance. The appearance of a `GridSplitter` is based on a variety of properties, including `Width` and `Background`.

The `Width` property is a double-precision value that defines the thickness of a `GridSplitter`. By default, this property is *not* set to a value so the `GridSplitter` takes on a default appearance of a bar with a handle the user can grab. When the `Width` is set to a value greater than 0, the `GridSplitter` takes the shape of a basic line. This line will be visible as long as the `Background` isn't `Transparent`.

The `Background` property defines how a `GridSplitter` is painted. We use the term *painted* because the `Background` property is defined as a `Brush`. We'll cover brushes in chapter 18. For now, just know that the `Background` defaults to being transparent. Also know that you have the `GridSplitter` to empower a user to resize the columns of a `Grid` at runtime.

In general, the `Grid` is the most powerful layout panel in Silverlight because it can do almost everything that the other layout panels can do. There may be times when you don't want the additional bulk of the `Grid`. For these situations, it's nice to know you have the `StackPanel` and `Canvas` layout options. For other situations, you may want to tap into the new layout panels included in the Silverlight SDK or Silverlight Toolkit: `DockPanel` and `WrapPanel`.

7.4 Summary

A rich and interactive user experience is primarily about presenting information. The users' acceptance and adoption of your application can hinge on how that information is presented to them, so it's important to understand how to show this information in a pleasing way. To help accomplish an orderly UI, Silverlight provides the `Canvas`, `StackPanel`, and `Grid` layout options, as well as the other brand new panels such as the `DockPanel` and `WrapPanel`.

The `Canvas` is the panel to use if you want to have the lightest layout possible and simply position elements using `Left` and `Top` properties. Canvas offers no scaling and no other layout.

When you want to build a list of items, such as you'd see in a `ListBox` or a `Menu`, the `StackPanel` is the panel to use. Like the `Canvas`, it offers no scaling but it does offer automatic placement of elements in a vertical or horizontal list.

Finally, if you want to lay out elements using a grid or tabular format and take advantage of automatic scaling, the `Grid` is the panel for you. By far, the `Grid` is the most commonly used layout panel in Silverlight.

With the layout and rendering background from the previous chapter and the information about panels from this chapter under our belt, we're ready to move on to the fundamentals of working with human input such as mouse, keyboard, and touch.

Human input

This chapter covers

- Capturing keystrokes
- Responding to mouse clicks, movement, and the wheel
- Handling multi-touch input
- Working with pen ink input

Real-world applications need a way to accept input from users. This process of collecting input is managed by a wide range of input devices including the mouse, touch, stylus, and keyboard. Silverlight provides direct support for these devices through the System.Windows.Input namespace.

Whether you're implementing drag and drop or mouse-wheel zoom or creating your own right-click context menus, you'll almost certainly end up handling mouse input in your applications. Silverlight has great support for mouse states as well as for handling both left and right mouse buttons and allowing you to respond to the mouse wheel.

Multi-touch is now coming of age due to the proliferation of multi-touch devices, PC displays, and notebooks available to us. Silverlight can now accept single and multi-touch input to allow you to write next-generation touch-enabled applications.

If you have a tablet PC, an external drawing pad, or perhaps one of the newer tablet form factors that we're just dreaming about as I write this, then ink input using a stylus is a must. Ink is also a nice way to capture drawings done with the mouse.

Most keyboard input will be handled by the TextBox and similar controls. But what happens when you want to implement custom accelerators or write a game that responds to keystrokes? In those instances, you'll need to access the lower-level keyboard events like I did in the Commodore 64 emulator shown in chapter 5.

The keyboard has been our input of choice since the dawn of terminal-based computing (no, Silverlight doesn't have a paper tape input API, but you could probably write one) and is used by virtually all applications, so we'll start there.

8.1 Capturing the keyboard

Have you ever considered how an application determines how to handle your keystrokes? Often, we click and clack our way through our days and take for granted how our information gets where we intend it to go. But if we'd slow down for a second, we'd notice that there's an intermediary step.

Before typing any information, you must target an element and give it the focus. This section will provide an explanation of the concept of focus. Once an item has focus, it can begin receiving keyboard events—the topic of our second subsection. Finally, for the special situations where you want to handle key combinations, you must learn to deal with modifier keys—our final keyboard topic.

8.1.1 Understanding focus

When an element has *focus*, it becomes the primary target for any information entered through the keyboard. This target element must be a System.Windows.Controls. Control element because only Control elements can be given focus in Silverlight. You can give these elements focus by selecting them with the mouse, by tabbing to them through the keyboard, or via the Focus method. Regardless of your approach, the concept of focus is especially important within the realm of the World Wide Web.

Web pages pose a unique challenge with focus because Silverlight plug-in instances are part of a larger ecosystem. In chapter 2, this ecosystem was shown to begin with an HTML document. This document may have multiple Silverlight controls or a mix of Silverlight controls and other control types such as Flash. In order for a Silverlight control to accept input from the keyboard on an HTML page with additional content, the Silverlight control itself must first have the focus. To accomplish this, you can use the following JavaScript:

```
var silverlightControl = document.getElementById('SilverlightControl');
if (silverlightControl)
  silverlightControl.focus();
```

This example uses the HTML DOM to manually give the focus to an instance of the Silverlight plug-in. This approach can be useful if you want to give your Silverlight application the focus when a web page is loaded. If you don't do this, a user will either have to click or tab to your Silverlight plug-in instance. Once that's done, you'll be able to set focus to individual controls.

ELEMENT FOCUS

Individual elements on the Silverlight page receive focus by click or tab. But you can manually set focus to an element by calling the Focus method of the UIElement:

```
myTextBox.Focus();
```

You may want to do that in response to a special accelerator key, or to automatically set focus to a field with a validation error, or perhaps to allow for skipping fields based on prefilled data.

Once the plug-in instance has focus and one of the input controls on your page has focus, you can begin handling keyboard events within your Silverlight application.

8.1.2 *Handling keyboard events*

Silverlight provides two events directly related to the keyboard. These events, KeyDown and KeyUp, are available through the UIElement class. The KeyDown event happens when a user presses a key. Once that key is released, the KeyUp event will fire. When either event is triggered, its event handler will receive a KeyEventArgs parameter. This parameter and the KeyDown and KeyUp events are shown in listing 8.1.

Listing 8.1 A page in Silverlight that responds to the KeyDown and KeyUp events

XAML:
```
<UserControl x:Class="Keyboard01.MainPage"
  xmlns="http://schemas.microsoft.com/winfx/2006/xaml/presentation"
  xmlns:x="http://schemas.microsoft.com/winfx/2006/xaml"
  Width="400" Height="300"                        ⟵  Handler wired
  KeyDown="MainPage_KeyDown">                          up in XAML
  <Canvas x:Name="LayoutRoot" Background="Black">
    <TextBlock x:Name="myTextBlock" Foreground="White" Text="Waiting..." />
  </Canvas>
</UserControl>
```

C#:
```
public partial class MainPage : UserControl
{
  public MainPage()
  {
    InitializeComponent();
    this.KeyUp += new KeyEventHandler(MainPage_KeyUp);    ⟵  Handler wired
  }                                                          up in code
  private void MainPage_KeyUp(object sender, KeyEventArgs e)
  {
    myTextBlock.Text = "Key (" + e.Key + ") was released.";
  }
  private void MainPage_KeyDown(object sender, KeyEventArgs e)
  {
    myTextBlock.Text = "Key (" + e.Key + ") is down.";
  }
}
```

This listing shows a page in Silverlight that responds to the KeyDown and KeyUp events. The event handlers associated with these events update the TextBlock to show the key that was used. These events are watched through the UserControl element, which is inherently a UIElement. We'll discuss this element further in section 10.5 but, for now, note how the keyboard events are attached in two different ways. In one, the KeyDown event is attached through the XAML declarative approach. The other approach uses traditional procedural code. Regardless of the method, the appropriate keyboard event handler will receive a KeyEventArgs parameter.

> **NOTE** If the user holds the key down, and his system is set up to allow key repeating (the default), multiple KeyDown events will be fired and KeyUp will only be fired when the key is released. If you want to process typing, you should process KeyDown (to capture each character) but, if you want to process keystrokes for hotkeys or similar functionality, KeyUp may be a better event to use.

The KeyEventArgs class enables you to fetch data relayed from a user's keyboard. Once a user begins typing, you can use this object to interpret the user's keystrokes and act accordingly. The KeyEventArgs class provides the properties shown in table 8.1.

Table 8.1 The properties of the KeyEventArgs class

Property	Description
Handled	A bool that signals whether the key event has been handled.
OriginalSource	A reference to the element that originally raised this event. Since the keyboard events are bubbling routed events, you need this to identify the source of the event as opposed to the sender of the event.
Key	This value identifies which key has been pressed. Unlike the PlatformKey-Code property, this value is consistent across all operating systems.
PlatformKeyCode	An integer value that provides the key code of a pressed key. This value is specifically tied to the operating system the user is using.

After reviewing this table, you may be scratching your head and thinking, "Why would I ever use the PlatformKeyCode property when Silverlight is cross-platform?" When I ported the C64 emulator to Silverlight, I had to use the PlatformKeyCode to gain access to a number of keys Silverlight didn't surface through the Key enumeration—for example, the bracket and pipe keys. The key codes for those keys will be different on each supported platform and each type of keyboard, such as Qwerty in the US and Azerty in France.

> ### If it's not Windows, don't assume it's a Mac
> One thing that got me into trouble with my friends on the Moonlight team was my assumption in code that, if the keystroke wasn't from Windows, it was from a Mac. Remember, there are other platforms that support Silverlight without a recompile: Linux, Moblin, Nokia Symbian OS, and more.

Another reason is because some keys are irrelevant on other operating systems. For instance, checking for a Windows Logo keystroke on OS X makes as much sense as checking for a Command key press on Windows. If handling other OS-specific keystrokes is necessary, you can use the PlatformKeyCode. Otherwise, we recommend sticking with the Key property.

In addition to straight key presses, you may need to capture key combinations such as Ctrl-C.

8.1.3 *Dealing with modifier keys*

Modifier keys are specific keys used in combination with other keys. Modifier keys are necessary because the KeyEventArgs class only exposes information about the currently pressed key. If you press something like the Shift key or Ctrl key and then another key, the initially selected key data will be lost. You can overcome this problem with the help of the statically visible Keyboard class.

The Keyboard class, in the System.Windows.Input namespace, exposes information directly related to the selected modifier keys. This information is available through the Modifiers property, which is a bit field enumeration that represents the set of ModifierKeys that are pressed. These ModifierKeys represent options of an enumeration.

Table 8.2 shows the options available in the ModifierKeys enumeration. Notably, the Apple key is equal to the Windows key in value, as they serve conceptually similar roles on the two platforms. The reason for this enumeration is to allow for bitwise operations.

Table 8.2   The ModifierKeys available within Silverlight

Key	Description
None	No modifier keys are pressed.
Alt	The Alt key is pressed. This key is available on all supported platforms. On an Apple keyboard, this key is also referred to as the Option key.
Apple	The Command key is pressed on an Apple system. These keys used to have open apples on them.
Control	The Ctrl key is pressed. This key is available on all supported platforms, despite usage differences between Windows and Mac.
Shift	The Shift key is pressed. This key is available on all supported platforms.
Windows	The Windows Logo key is pressed on a Windows-enabled keyboard.

The modifiers are important because they allow you to check whether multiple keys are selected at the same time. For instance, if you want to change the KeyDown event used in listing 8.1 to listen for Shift-B, you could use this code:

```
private void MainPage_KeyDown(object sender, KeyEventArgs e)
{
  if (e.Key == Key.B)
  {
```

```
    if (Keyboard.Modifiers.HasFlag(ModifierKeys.Shift))
      myTextBlock.Text = "You pressed SHIFT+B";
  }
}
```

This shows how you can go beyond individual key events in Silverlight. By appropriately listening to and responding to these events, you can extend the input and navigation of your application beyond just the mouse alone. Though that's compelling, especially for those of us who grew up with 40- or 80-character displays and a fondness for the command prompt, the mouse is the primary input device for most web applications today.

8.2 *Mouse input*

The mouse requires very different input processing compared with the keyboard. In addition to responding to button-related events, the mouse can also respond to movement. It's also common for the mouse to be moving with one or more buttons depressed. Another input vector on the mouse, one that's relatively new compared to the mouse itself, is the scroll wheel or mouse wheel. Though implementations vary from traditional wheels to capacitive touch pads, it's rare to find a modern mouse that omits this handy feature, so it's important that Silverlight developers be able to gather meaningful input from it.

We'll start with mouse button and movement events. The two are often used together to handle dragging and resizing operations. Even when used separately, they're often thought of together due to their ubiquity from the first days of mouse-based user interfaces.

From there, we'll look at the mouse wheel support added with Silverlight 3 and refined in Silverlight 4. The mouse wheel isn't necessarily an essential input like the mouse button and mouse movement, but it can make the difference between a mediocre user experience and an awesome one.

8.2.1 *Mouse button and movement events*

Silverlight supports a range of movement and click-related events emitted from the mouse. These events can be handled by any UIElement. The most familiar of these events are probably the click-handling events because they behave similarly to the keyboard events. Table 8.3 shows these click-related actions along with their descriptions.

Table 8.3   The click-related events associated with the mouse

Event	Description
MouseLeftButtonDown	Responds to the user depressing the left mouse button
MouseLeftButtonUp	Reacts to the user releasing the left mouse button
MouseRightButtonDown	Responds to the user depressing the right mouse button
MouseRightButtonUp	Fired when the user releases the right mouse button

This table shows two pairs of events tied to the mouse buttons. When a mouse button is selected, the corresponding event handlers will receive a `MouseButtonEventArgs` object. This object derives from the `MouseEventArgs` class, which describes the mouse state at the time the event was raised.

You can receive the location of the mouse cursor in relation to a specific `UIElement` through the `GetPosition` method. This method is part of the `MouseEventArgs` class and will be discussed more in a moment. For now, please look at the properties available in the `MouseEventArgs` class (shown in table 8.4).

Table 8.4   The properties exposed by the `MouseEventArgs`

Property	Description
Handled	A `bool` that flags whether the mouse event has been dealt with Set to true on a `RightMouseButtonDown` event to avoid showing the default Silverlight configuration menu
OriginalSource	A reference to the element that originally raised this event Since the mouse events are bubbling routed events, you need this to identify the source of the event as opposed to the sender of the event.
StylusDevice	Includes information associated with a tablet pen

Table 8.4 lists the properties available through the `MouseEventArgs` class. As this table shows, Silverlight has built-in support for working with a stylus, which we'll discuss in a bit. One method in the `MouseEventArgs` class demands more immediate attention—`GetPosition`.

The `GetPosition` method gives you immediate access to the current location of the mouse. This location is returned from the `GetPosition` method as a `Point` in relation to any `UIElement`. This `UIElement` is determined by passing it as the sole parameter to the method. Optionally, you can pass `null` as the parameter to the `GetPosition` method to get the location of the mouse in relation to the Silverlight plug-in instance. Regardless of how you use it, this method is useful when handling both click and movement events. The `UIElement` class exposes the mouse-movement events shown in table 8.5.

Table 8.5   The mouse-movement-related event handlers

Event	Description
MouseEnter	Triggers when the user enters the boundary of a `UIElement`
MouseMove	Reacts to mouse movement within the boundary of a `UIElement`
MouseLeave	Fires when the move leaves the boundary of a `UIElement`

The events in table 8.5 are passed a `MouseEventArgs` parameter so you can be readily informed of a mouse's position as it moves around a surface. This feature can especially be useful if you want to implement drag-and-drop features in Silverlight or track the mouse for drawing.

> ### Implementing a custom click event
>
> Implementing a custom click event (rather than using a click-enabled base class such as `ButtonBase`) is more involved than simply handling the `MouseLeftButtonUp` event. Back in Silverlight 1.1a, when we had to create buttons from scratch, we all learned that a click event requires the following steps:
>
> 1 On `MouseLeftButtonDown` on your control, capture the mouse using `UIElement.CaptureMouse`.
>
> 2 On `MouseEnter`, update an internal flag that indicates that the mouse is currently over your control. On `MouseLeave`, set that flag to false.
>
> 3 On `MouseLeftButtonUp`, verify that the mouse is still over your control, using the flag you set in step 2. If it is, raise your own custom click event. If isn't, do nothing. In either case, release the mouse capture using `UIElement.ReleaseMouseCapture`.
>
> You may never need to implement your own click event but, if you do, ensure that you follow these steps rather than simply responding to `MouseLeftButtonUp`.

Besides buttons and pointer movement, modern mice offer one more form of input: the mouse wheel.

8.2.2 *Using the mouse wheel*

Silverlight 3 added built-in support for the mouse wheel, in the form of the `UIElement.MouseWheel` event. It was possible to wire up a mouse wheel handler in Silverlight 2, but you had to resort to JavaScript to do it—something that won't work out of browser, always seemed a bit of a hack, and is difficult to support cross-browser and cross-platform. Silverlight 4 expanded that by adding in support in the controls themselves.

> **NOTE** In the initial Silverlight 4 release, the `MouseWheel` event only worked in specific situations: windowed controls on IE and Firefox for Windows, as well as windowless controls for IE. The approach used with the Netscape Plug-in API (NPAPI) didn't provide the plug-in with mouse wheel information, so Silverlight didn't support the mouse wheel in Safari or Firefox on the Mac. Support is planned, though, and will be in place by the time you read this book. On Windows, when using windowed mode on those browsers, the Silverlight runtime bypasses the plug-in API and grabs the underlying window handle (hWND) for the control as a workaround.

Silverlight includes first-class mouse wheel support in the form of the `MouseWheel` event on the `UIElement` class. When the user scrolls the mouse wheel, this event is raised with an instance of the MouseWheelEventArgs class. The properties available in the MouseWheelEventArgs class are detailed in table 8.6.

Table 8.6   The properties exposed by MouseWheelEventArgs

Property	Description
Delta	An integer representing the relative change since the last time the event was raised
	A positive value indicates that the mouse wheel was scrolled up or away from the user. A negative value means the mouse wheel was scrolled down or toward the user. The higher the absolute value of the number, the faster the mouse wheel was scrolled.
Handled	A bool that flags whether the mouse event has been dealt with
OriginalSource	A reference to the element that originally raised this event
	Since the mouse events are bubbling routed events, you need this to identify the source of the event as opposed to the sender of the event.
StylusDevice	Includes information associated with a tablet pen

Listing 8.2 shows the mouse wheel properties in action.

Listing 8.2   Responding to the mouse wheel

XAML:

```
<UserControl x:Class="SilverlightApplication17.MainPage"
  xmlns="http://schemas.microsoft.com/winfx/2006/xaml/presentation"
  xmlns:x="http://schemas.microsoft.com/winfx/2006/xaml"
  Width="400" Height="300">
  <Grid x:Name="LayoutRoot" Background="White">
    <TextBlock x:Name="Info" />
  </Grid>
</UserControl>
```

C#:

```
public MainPage()
{
  InitializeComponent();
  MouseWheel += new MouseWheelEventHandler(OnMouseWheel);   ← Wiring up event
}

void OnMouseWheel(object sender, MouseWheelEventArgs e)
{
  if (e.Delta > 0)
    Info.Text = string.Format("Up {0}", e.Delta);           Responding to scroll
  else
    Info.Text = string.Format("Down {0}", Math.Abs(e.Delta));
}
```

Listing 8.2 shows how to obtain the Delta value from the MouseWheel event in order to determine both direction and speed. Negative values mean the wheel was scrolled down or toward the user; positive values mean the wheel was scrolled up or away from the user.

The `ScrollViewer` control automatically handles the `MouseWheel` event, so the `ListBox`, `ComboBox`, `TextBox`, and other `ScrollViewers` will automatically scroll using the wheel. If you want to support the mouse wheel on other controls, simply handle the `MouseWheel` event as shown in listing 8.2. As another example, here's the mouse wheel integrated with a `Slider`:

```
private void OnMouseWheel(object sender, MouseWheelEventArgs e)
{
  if (e.Delta > 0)
    slider_X.Value += slider_X.LargeChange;
  else
    slider_X.Value -= slider_X.LargeChange;
}
```

First-class support for the mouse wheel event isn't the only advanced input supported by Silverlight. Silverlight also has a great feature for Windows 7 systems and beyond: multi-touch support.

8.3   *Using multi-touch*

Microsoft Windows 7 is the first Microsoft OS to have official built-in support for multi-touch-enabled hardware. For a platform to be touch enabled, it simply needs to recognize a single finger on the screen. Many tablets and portable devices support this, as do touch screens going all the way back to the 80s. Multi-touch is a pretty new ground. A multi-touch-enabled display will recognize more than one finger on the screen, allowing you to do things such as resize and rotate images by touching both corners or make complex multifinger gestures to perform specific functions, such as sweeping a screen to the side.

It's hard to predict how popular multi-touch will be on the desktop, but it's already finding use in new classes of portable hardware as well as in kiosk and kitchen-PC scenarios (as long as you have a cake-batter-and-grease-proof screen).

The static `Touch.FrameReported` event is the primary entry point into the touch API in Silverlight. This event fires on a regular interval, the timing and triggering of which depends on the touch-enabled hardware and drivers in use. As soon as you wire up the event handler, you'll begin receiving notifications.

The `FrameReported` event includes an instance of the `TouchFrameEventArgs` class with members as described in table 8.7.

Table 8.7   The properties and methods exposed by the `TouchFrameEventArgs` class

Property or method	Description
`Timestamp`	An integer representing the time for this specific frame You can use this to facilitate time-sensitive gestures.
`SuspendMousePromotionUntilTouchUp`	Use this method when the primary touch point is down in order to suspend promoting that point to a mouse gesture until all the touch points are up.

Table 8.7   The properties and methods exposed by the `TouchFrameEventArgs` class *(continued)*

Property or method	Description
GetPrimaryTouchPoint	Returns the first touch made since the last time all touches were lifted from the screen
	This is the touch point that'll be promoted to a mouse event.
GetTouchPoints	Use this method to return a collection of `TouchPoint` values for the frame.

The `GetPrimaryTouchPoint` function returns a single instance of the `TouchPoint` class. The `GetTouchPoints` collection returns a collection of `TouchPoints`, including the primary touch point. The `TouchPoint` class includes the members listed in table 8.8.

Table 8.8   The properties and methods exposed by the `TouchPoint` class

Property	Description
Action	The user activity associated with this touch
	Possible values are `Down`, for finger down on the screen, `Move` for finger moved/dragged on the screen, and `Up` for finger up from the screen.
Position	The x,y coordinates of the touch. This is relative to the application's `RootVisual`.
Size	A rectangle describing the size of the touch point. You can use this to differentiate between, say, a light tap and a full press.
TouchDevice	Information about the device that provided the touch information.
TouchDevice.DirectlyOver	This property is located on the `TouchDevice` for WPF compatibility reasons. It'll return the topmost `UIElement` over which the touch occurred.

Listing 8.3 shows how to listen for the `FrameReported` event, enumerate the TouchPoint objects, and display their positions to the debug window.

Listing 8.3   Responding to the `FrameReported` event and reporting touch points

```
public MainPage()
{
  InitializeComponent();
  Touch.FrameReported += new TouchFrameEventHandler(OnTouchFrameReported);
}

void OnTouchFrameReported(object sender, TouchFrameEventArgs e)
{
  foreach (TouchPoint tp in e.GetTouchPoints(this))
  {
    Debug.WriteLine(tp.Position);
  }
}
```

One final method of interaction with your application is ink input. Though ink is typically used with tablet-style PCs, it can be used with mice as well. With new pen-enabled devices such as multi-touch tablet PCs, there's renewed interest in ink collection in Silverlight applications.

8.4 *Collecting ink drawings*

Silverlight provides an intuitive way to collect hand-written information through an element known as the InkPresenter. This element empowers you to collect and display a kind of content known as *ink*, a term that refers to a series of points related to the movement of a device. These points can be collected from a mouse, stylus, or touch screen and are stored as a Stroke. The process of collecting Stroke elements is handled through the InkPresenter.

Over the course of this section, you'll learn how to gather and display ink with the InkPresenter. This process involves three simple but important steps. The first step involves creating a canvas to collect the ink. After that, you must wire up the canvas to collect ink-related information. Finally, once the ink has been collected, you can decide how to style the content.

8.4.1 *Creating the InkPresenter*

To create a place to capture and display the ink, you must define an InkPresenter object. This object can be thought of as a Canvas because the InkPresenter class derives from that type. And like the Canvas, you can create an InkPresenter in XAML, as shown here:

```
<Grid x:Name="LayoutRoot" Background="White">
  <InkPresenter x:Name="myInkPresenter" Background="Silver"/>
</Grid>
```

This example creates a basic InkPresenter within a Grid. If you were to create a Silverlight application using this XAML, it'd look like the InkPresenter doesn't do anything.

The InkPresenter is designed to dynamically render ink as it's drawn, so let's look at how to dynamically collect ink content.

8.4.2 *Collecting ink*

The first step in collecting ink involves listening for the mouse button or stylus to be depressed. When this event occurs, the MouseLeftButtonDown will fire and you can signal that the input device is depressed. At that point, you can begin to construct a Stroke object that can be added to an InkPresenter.

The Stroke object represents a continuous series of points. As a user moves a device around an InkPresenter, you build on that Stroke until the user releases the device. It's a general practice to define a Stroke object as a member variable of your Silverlight page, so you can interact with the same instance within the MouseLeftButtonDown, MouseMove, and MouseLeftButtonUp events. The MouseLeftButtonDown event is generally responsible for instantiating or resetting the Stroke, as shown in listing 8.4.

Listing 8.4   Receiving mouse events and creating ink strokes

```
private Stroke _stroke;                            ← Ink stroke
public MainPage()
{
  InitializeComponent();

  myInkPresenter.MouseLeftButtonDown +=            ← Mouse capture
    new MouseButtonEventHandler(ipMouseLeftButtonDown);   event handler

  myInkPresenter.MouseMove +=                      ←
    new MouseEventHandler(ipMouseMove);

  myInkPresenter.MouseLeftButtonUp +=              ← Handlers for
    new MouseButtonEventHandler(ipMouseLeftButtonUp);     upcoming listings

  myInkPresenter.MouseLeave +=                     ←
    new MouseEventHandler(ipMouseLeave);
}
public void ipMouseLeftButtonDown(object sender, MouseButtonEventArgs e)
{
  myInkPresenter.CaptureMouse();                   ← Capture
                                                      mouse
  _stroke = new
    Stroke(e.StylusDevice.GetStylusPoints(myInkPresenter));

  _stroke.DrawingAttributes.Color = Colors.Blue;
  _stroke.DrawingAttributes.OutlineColor = Colors.White;   ← Add ink
                                                              stroke
  myInkPresenter.Strokes.Add(_stroke);
}
```

This example shows the member variable stroke used on these listings as well as the event handler wire-up required for listings 8.4 through 8.6. Importantly, it also shows the initial mouse capture established when the mouse left button is pressed.

The member variable _stroke is reset each time the user depresses the input device. This reset process involves retrieving the styles points that have been collected. This task is handled by the GetStylusPoints method of the StylusDevice object. Because of the reset, you must also reapply the styling settings, which we'll discuss shortly. With the styled Stroke in hand, you can add it to the InkPresenter, which will be immediately rendered. You can even do this as the move moves around an InkPresenter, as shown in listing 8.5.

Listing 8.5   Adding points to the InkPresenter

```
public void ipMouseMove(object sender, MouseEventArgs e)
{
  if (_stroke != null)
  {                                                ← Add points
    _stroke.StylusPoints.Add(                         to stroke
```

```
              e.StylusDevice.GetStylusPoints(myInkPresenter));
    }
}
```

This adds to the `Stroke` initialized in the previous example. You'll notice that this task is wrapped in a `null` check statement. The reason for this will become apparent as you complete the final step of drawing ink.

The final step involves completing the `Stroke`. The `Stroke` needs to be completed when the user releases the input device or leaves the `InkPresenter`. For this reason, you need to handle two events: `MouseLeave` and `MouseLeftButtonUp`. These two events perform the tasks of nullifying the `Stroke` and releasing the input device, as shown in listing 8.6.

Listing 8.6   Completing the stroke

```
public void ipMouseLeftButtonUp(object sender, MouseButtonEventArgs e)
{
  myInkPresenter.ReleaseMouseCapture();          ◁──┐  Release on
  _stroke = null;                                    │  mouse up
}

public void ipMouseLeave(object sender, MouseEventArgs e)
{                                                     ┌─ Release on
  myInkPresenter.ReleaseMouseCapture();          ◁──┘   mouse leave
  _stroke = null;
}
```

This completes the process of drawing a `Stroke` on an `InkPresenter`. By setting the `Stroke` to null, you can determine whether you should build on it when the `Mouse-Move` event occurs.

In the event that you do draw a `Stroke`, you should know how to stylize it.

8.4.3   *Styling the ink*

The `Stroke` element provides a property called `DrawingAttributes` that may be used to alter its appearance. This utility class is defined within the `System.Windows.Ink` namespace. It provides four properties that allow you to specify a `Stroke` element's `Color`, `Height`, `OutlineColor`, and `Width`. Collectively, you can use these values to deliver truly expressive web content.

The `Color` property represents the `System.Windows.Media.Color` used to paint the interior of a `Stroke`. By default, this value is set to `Colors.Black`. This default value is different than the default `OutlineColor` property, which defaults to `Trans-parent`. This property must be set if you wish to specify the `Color` surrounding a `Stroke`. If it's set, a two-pixel boundary of the given `Color` will be added around the `Stroke`. The dimensions of the `Stroke` are just as important as colors.

The dimensions of a `Stroke` are defined through the `Height` and `Width` properties of the `DrawingAttributes`. These two double-precision values do exactly what you'd expect them to do. These properties can be used to help create `Stroke` elements that represent different drawing tools. Here's some code so you can get a feel for all these `DrawingAttributes`:

```
<InkPresenter x:Name="ip" Background="Silver"
              Height="300" Width="300">
  <InkPresenter.Strokes>
    <Stroke>
      <Stroke.DrawingAttributes>
        <DrawingAttributes Color="Blue" OutlineColor="Black"
                           Height="4" Width="6" />
      </Stroke.DrawingAttributes>
      <Stroke.StylusPoints>
        <StylusPoint X="10" Y="10" />
        <StylusPoint X="10" Y="50" />
      </Stroke.StylusPoints>
    </Stroke>
  </InkPresenter.Strokes>
</InkPresenter>
```

As this shows, you can define the DrawingAttributes of a Stroke within XAML. It also shows the one property that the InkPresenter exposes that the Canvas doesn't: the Strokes property. As these two properties remain consistent with the relationship between XAML and code, so too does the StylusPoints collection. This collection defines the continuous line of a Stroke, which is composed of a series of Stylus-Point elements.

A StylusPoint, which is found in the System.Windows.Input namespace, represents an individual point within a Stroke. This point is positioned based on the values of two properties called X and Y. These values are double-precision values that represent a coordinate. This coordinate is relative to the containing InkPresenter.

Like multi-touch, ink may not be common in many desktop applications. But as devices continue to add support for the stylus, supporting ink in your own applications will become increasingly important.

8.5   *Summary*

Without input, an application would just be an automated slide show. Though controls will get you most of the way there, sometimes you just need lower-level access to the input devices. Luckily, Silverlight doesn't disappoint.

Silverlight provides complete access to the keyboard information as the user presses and releases keys. Constants are provided for the most common and cross-platform keys, and you can always get to the low-level keycode information should you need to.

The most common interaction device for many Silverlight applications is the mouse. Silverlight now provides access to the left and right mouse buttons as well as normal mouse movement and the scroll wheel.

Two other modes of interaction are gaining in popularity. Pen-and-ink input has been around for a while but hasn't seen serious interest until new waves of devices started becoming popular. Multi-touch, on the other hand, is both new and popular, especially in the device space.

Now that you know how input works behind-the scenes, including keyboard input, we're ready to discuss how to work with text.

This chapter covers

- An overview of the text system
- Displaying text
- Working with fonts
- Understanding input method editors
- Moving text to and from the clipboard
- Entering and editing plain and rich text

Most applications you write will display or manipulate text at some point. Even many games have text input requirements for signup, registration, or to log a high score. Media players often have rolling commentary by other viewers and the ability to add to the social aspects of what you're watching. In short, working with text is important.

For as long as computers have been around and attached to video displays or teletypes, the display of text has been an important aspect of user interaction. Silverlight includes great support for displaying text, with a number of options that control formatting and other aspects of the display.

Of course, if all that the platform supported were the display of text, we'd be pretty limited in the types of applications we build. In addition to its display capabilities, Silverlight includes first-class support for editing text, both plain and rich text formats.

If you can enter and edit text, you may find yourself wanting to copy and paste it between various applications. Silverlight also includes facilities to enable programmatic manipulation of the clipboard to share data within the same application and across applications.

What do you do if you want to show text using a font the user doesn't necessarily have? You embed the font. Silverlight supports font embedding to ensure that your users have the exact experience you'd intended. We'll cover that and the support for international text using input method editors before we get into rich text.

Plain text is useful in many scenarios but, for others, you may want richer text with embedded formatting, images, and even UI elements. Silverlight 4 introduced the `RichTextBox` control, which can be used for both the display and editing of rich text.

We'll start this chapter with the coverage of the text stack and then move on to the basics of text, under the task of displaying text. Along the way, we'll look at font embedding, displaying international text, and integrating with the clipboard. The information learned when formatting the text for display will be used later when we work on entering and editing plain and rich text.

9.1   *The text system*

You'd be forgiven if you looked at the title of this section and thought, "System? Really? It's just text." Getting the text from the Unicode string and presenting it on displays of varying resolutions using different fonts on different systems is actually fairly complex. It's also a task we only notice when done poorly.

In reality, a text stack needs to:

- Read in the source text string.
- Lay out an overall block of text.
- Lay out individual lines within that block.
- Obtain the font information for each character, including combining characters for certain languages.
- Figure out how to display bold and italics (and other styles/weights). There may be a font for it or it may need to generate pseudo-italic and pseudo-bold text.
- Deal with any text expansion for fonts that support it.
- Lay out individual characters within that line, including subpixel font rendering.
- Render it all out to a rendering surface in software or hardware.

Any one of those individual steps is a pretty serious programming effort. Though all interesting, the internals of the text stack are pretty well abstracted away from the work we'll normally need to do. There are some places where the team has provided options we can set, though.

Before we get on to the high-level controls and elements that allow us to put text on the screen, let's take a look at how Silverlight handles character rendering using ClearType.

9.1.1 Subpixel text rendering

In chapters 6 and 7 we learned about the layout system and subpixel layout and rendering. Silverlight can handle elements aligned on subpixel boundaries, such as having a `Left` of 15.76 rather than just 16. This makes layout easier for design professionals and is also essential for smooth animation.

Subpixel layout and rendering applies to text as well. On Windows machines, Silverlight uses the ClearType algorithm, provided by DirectWrite, to render text using the best quality for a given resolution. An example of ClearType rendering is shown in figure 9.1.

**Figure 9.1
ClearType subpixel font
rendering in Silverlight**

Silverlight supports subpixel rendering and layout of anything, so the text itself may already start on a partial pixel boundary (for example, a `Left` of 10.32). For that reason and others, the Silverlight ClearType algorithm will produce results slightly different from the base Windows platform. The end result will still be text that's more readable and more pleasing to the eye than no antialiasing or the grayscale used in Silverlight 2.

The ClearType text rendering algorithm is a relatively expensive subpixel antialiasing algorithm that you wouldn't necessarily want to recalculate 60 times per second. Also, as a side effect of the antialiasing, you may also see text that jumps around a bit when you animate it (you'd have to look closely). For those reasons, and to support other optimizations, Silverlight includes a `TextOptions.TextHinting-Mode` attached property.

9.1.2 Text hinting

ClearType is an excellent text rendering algorithm, but it's not something you want to be calling thousands of times because it's a complex algorithm with performance implications. In addition, there are other visual optimizations applied to text that would be unnecessary if the text were animated.

Silverlight offers the `TextOptions.TextHintingMode` attached property to control how hard Silverlight tries to make the text look great. When set to `Fixed`, it uses the quality ClearType rendering and performs the calculations that make static text look great. When set to `Animated`, it optimizes for text that's going to change size, rotation, or angle, probably multiple times per second. Listing 9.1 shows the setting in action.

Listing 9.1   `TextOptions.TextHintingMode`

Results:

Lorem ipsum (Fixed)
Lorem ipsum (Animated)
Lorem ipsum (Fixed)
Lorem ipsum (Animated)

XAML:

```
<StackPanel Width="150" Height="100">
  <StackPanel Background="White">
    <TextBlock Text="Lorem ipsum (Fixed)"
               Foreground="Black"
               TextOptions.TextHintingMode="Fixed" />       <-
    <TextBlock Text="Lorem ipsum (Animated)"
               Foreground="Black"
               TextOptions.TextHintingMode="Animated" />     <-
  </StackPanel>
  <StackPanel Background="Black">
    <TextBlock Text="Lorem ipsum (Fixed)"
               Foreground="White"
               TextOptions.TextHintingMode="Fixed" />        <-
    <TextBlock Text="Lorem ipsum (Animated)"
               Foreground="White"
               TextOptions.TextHintingMode="Animated" />     <-
  </StackPanel>
</StackPanel>
```

Fixed text rendering

Animated text rendering

It'll be hard to tell in a printed book (one benefit of the electronic copy), but the `Animated` text hinting renders the text using grayscale antialiasing, whereas the `Fixed` text hinting (the default) renders using ClearType rendering. Figure 9.2 shows a close-up of the first word from each line on a white background as well as black.

The rendering optimized for animation avoids both the costly ClearType calculations as well as the jumping/jittering effect. If you use the animation-optimized text in small font sizes for regular text in your application, you'll see it's noticeably fuzzier than ClearType. In fact, this was an issue with Silverlight adoption for line-of-business applications in the Silverlight 2 timeframe, before ClearType was integrated into the stack.

As of this writing, ClearType isn't supported on the Mac, so it always uses some form of grayscale rendering. Also, an interesting limitation of ClearType is that it's

Figure 9.2   The first line uses `Fixed` text hinting and, therefore, ClearType rendering. The second line uses `Animated` text hinting and is, therefore, grayscale.

sensitive to the orientation of the display. Since the modern ClearType implementation is meant only for LCD displays (if you have an old tube monitor hanging around, don't enable ClearType on it or the world will end in an explosion of subpixels), it takes into account the position of the actual elements (red, green, blue) and uses them to make the text more readable. If you tilt the monitor 90 degrees, those positions are out of whack, and ClearType won't work correctly.

Now that we know a little about what's going on behind the scenes and how to optimize text rendering for different situations, let's look at what's available to us to actually push characters onto our display and how we can set the higher-level properties like what font to use and what size to use when rendering the text.

9.2 *Displaying text*

Displaying text is primarily addressed by an element called `TextBlock`. This element, which belongs to the `System.Windows.Controls` namespace, but which itself doesn't derive from `Control`, is designed to flexibly display text within a variety of scenarios. The following example shows one such scenario, as well as the basic syntax of a `TextBlock`:

```
<TextBlock x:Name="myTextBlock"
  Text="Eating a lot of fruit can help you live to a ripe old age."/>
```

This shows a basic way to include text within your Silverlight applications. The `TextBlock` can be hosted in any of the panels discussed in chapter 7.

As you've probably guessed, the `Text` property of a `TextBlock` is used to set the text to display. The text direction (right to left or left to right) is controlled via the `FlowDirection` property. The `TextBlock` provides a rich set of other styling options that mimic or exceed those found in CSS. We'll cover all of these styling options, including setting the font properties, controlling the flow of text, setting the text-related properties, and specifying the spacing options.

9.2.1 *Font properties*

The `TextBlock` has five properties related to the styling of a selected font. These properties replace a lot of the familiar friends from CSS. Table 9.1 shows a font-related CSS property and its equivalent Silverlight `TextBlock` property.

Table 9.1 The font-related properties available in Silverlight and their CSS equivalents

CSS property name	TextBlock property name	Summary
font-family	FontFamily	A list of font names for an element
font-size	FontSize	The size of the font
font-weight	FontWeight	The weight of the font
font-stretch	FontStretch	Expands or compresses the font
font-style	FontStyle	The style of the font (for example, italics)

These items are related specifically to the font capabilities of Silverlight. We'll now cover each of these items in detail, in the order they appear in the table.

FONTFAMILY

By default, the `TextBlock` displays text using the Lucida Sans Unicode font on Windows machines. On Apple Macintosh computers, an almost identical font known as Lucida Grande is used. Alternatively, you can specify a different font.

The `FontFamily` property enables you to specify the font. More specifically, this property represents the name of the top-level font family. This is important to recognize because some fonts share a common family name; the differences between them lie in their individual features—things such as bold and italic options. Silverlight has built-in support for the font families shown in figure 9.3.

Arial	Lucida Grande / Lucida Sans Unicode
Arial Black	Times New Roman
Comic Sans MS	Trebuchet MS
Courier New	Verdana
Georgia	

Figure 9.3 A sampling of the font families supported within Silverlight

Figure 9.3 shows the nine TrueType fonts supported within Silverlight. In addition to these fonts, Silverlight has support for Eastern Asian fonts. Collectively, the nine TrueType and Eastern Asian fonts are guaranteed to look almost identical on all platforms supported by Silverlight as long as someone hasn't uninstalled the core fonts for those platforms. If you need to use a custom font, you can do so using font embedding or by referring to a local font on the machine. Previous versions of Silverlight restricted you to embedding or a white list of fonts, with no support for local fonts.

Once the `FontFamily` has been set, this will be the font used within the `TextBlock`. If your users don't have the font on their machines, the `TextBlock` will fall back to the default font. You can set fallback priority by providing a comma-delimited list of font family names.

`FontFamily` is one of the more widely used font options. Another widely used option is the `FontSize` property.

FONTSIZE

The `FontSize` property allows you to set the size of a `TextBlock` using a double-precision value. This value is set by default to 14.66 pixels, which is roughly an 11 pt font. This fact is significant because the `FontSize` property always represents a specific number of device-independent pixels. This can have undesired effects, because fonts are generally discussed in terms of points (pt). Thankfully, you can easily convert points to pixels using the formula found in figure 9.4.

This formula is based on the fact that Silverlight uses 96 pixels per inch and a point is defined as 72 points per inch. If you want to use a 24 pt font in a `TextBlock`, you need to set the `FontSize` property to 32 (24 * 96 / 72 = 32):

$$\frac{points \times 96}{72} = pixels$$

Figure 9.4 The formula to convert font points to pixels in Silverlight

```
<TextBlock Text="I'm a Big Boy Now." FontSize="32" />
```

This basic line of XAML sets the FontSize to a 24 pt font. In addition to setting the FontSize, there are also times where you may need to work with the weight of a font.

FONTWEIGHT

The FontWeight property represents the heaviness, or *weight*, of the displayed text. This weight is often depicted as a bolding effect, but you can also go the other way and make text appear lighter or thinner. This is made possible by the fact that the Font-Weight property accepts any numeric value between 1 and 999. Alternatively, you can use one of the friendly constants available in the FontWeights class:

- Thin
- Light
- Medium
- Bold
- Black
- ExtraLight
- Normal
- SemiBold
- ExtraBold
- ExtraBlack

These values are shown in the order of increasing weight. Note that not all fonts support varying weights. In fact, most fonts support only two font weights: Normal and Bold. If the font specified within the FontFamily property doesn't support a specific weight, it falls back to the closest weight supported by the font. The fallback support for this property is also shared by another property called FontStretch.

FONTSTRETCH

The FontStretch property gives you the ability to either condense or expand the font associated with a TextBlock. The CSS equivalent of this property is defined within the third version of CSS (CSS3), but few browsers currently implement it. For this reason, this property is one text-related feature not usually seen within a traditional web application. But, with Silverlight, you can stylize your text with this feature using one of the FontStretches values shown in table 9.2.

Name	Stretch percentage
UltraCondensed	50.0%
ExtraCondensed	62.5%
Condensed	75.0%
SemiCondensed	87.5%
Normal	100.0%
Medium	100.0%
SemiExpanded	112.5%
Expanded	125.0%
ExtraExpanded	150.0%
UltraExpanded	200.0%

Table 9.2
Acceptable values for the FontStretch property

These values represent the acceptable values for the FontStretch property. The percentages represent the proportion by which the normal font size is stretched. Any value less than 100 percent will condense a font and any percentage greater than 100 percent will expand a font. Either way, the percentage is only taken into consideration if the selected FontFamily has support for font stretching. Even if a font does have support for stretching, it may not have support for all stretch values. If the font doesn't support the stretch value you've selected, the FontStretch resorts to using an algorithm that searches the available fonts for one that matches the properties as closely as possible.

FONTSTYLE

The FontStyle property gives you the ability to switch the text of a TextBlock into italic mode. As you've probably guessed, this property is set to a value of Normal by default. You can easily change this to Italic to give your text an italic effect:

```
<TextBlock x:Name="myText" Text="Going Italic" FontStyle="Italic" />
```

The code shows how to set the FontStyle at design time. Setting the FontStyle during runtime involves using a slightly different approach. To set a TextBlock to italic during runtime, you use the FontStyles class:

```
myTextBlock.FontStyle = FontStyles.Italic;
```

Note how this uses a FontStyles static property called Italic. This static property represents a FontStyle definition. This fact is significant because, even though you can only set a FontStyle to italic in Silverlight, WPF is a different story. WPF, which is Silverlight's parent technology, provides additional FontStyle options.

The FontStyle is but one of the five font styling options available within a TextBlock. The other four are the FontStretch, FontWeight, FontSize, and FontFamily. Collectively, these give you a significant amount of control over the font styling of a TextBlock. In addition to basic font styling, Silverlight gives you the ability to control the overall flow of text.

9.2.2   *Flow control*

The TextBlock enables you to control the overall flow of text through two nested elements. These elements, called Run and LineBreak, belong to the System.Windows.Documents namespace. Both elements derive from the Inline class and have built-in support for the font features we discussed in section 9.1.1. Listing 9.2 shows how these elements can be used.

Listing 9.2   TextBlock Run and LineBreak Inlines

Result:

Scene 1: The Greeting
Actor 1: Hello, how are you?
Actor 2: I am fine, thank you!

XAML:

```
<TextBlock Text="Scene 1: The Greeting"
        FontWeight="Bold" FontSize="17">
  <LineBreak />
    <Run FontWeight="Bold" FontSize="14"
        Text="Actor 1:" />
    <Run FontWeight="Normal" FontSize="14"
        Text="Hello, how are you?" />
  <LineBreak />
  <Run FontWeight="Bold" FontSize="14"
      Text="Actor 2:" />
  <Run FontWeight="Normal" FontSize="14"
      Text="I am fine, thank you!" />
</TextBlock>
```

Line break

Formatted Run

The conversation in this listing shows one way to use the Run and LineBreak Inline elements. These elements get appended in succession to the text defined in the Text property of the hosting TextBlock. In fact, the value inside the Text property itself gets converted to a Run element at runtime. This element and all the other Run and LineBreak items get stored in a collection called Inlines.

The Inlines collection stores the Inline elements of a TextBlock. By default, all the items in this collection use the styling options set by the parent TextBlock. You can override these settings by specifying new values for them within the Inline item itself. This is the approach used in listing 9.2. But, to fully demonstrate how the LineBreak and Run items can be customized, we should jog through several text properties.

9.2.3 *Text properties*

Silverlight gives you the ability to further customize your text through four useful properties. These properties focus on rendering text in combination with the font properties we discussed in 9.2.1. To further control how the text is rendered, you can use the Foreground, TextDecorations, TextWrapping, TextTrimming, and TextAlignment properties.

FOREGROUND

The Foreground property allows you to set the color of a block of text. More specifically, this property represents a Brush, which allows you to do a lot more than just apply solid colors. The various Brush options aren't covered until chapter 18. For now, just know that you can use the name of a color, as shown here, in an example that changes a TextBlock from the default black SolidColorBrush to blue:

```
<TextBlock Text="I'm feeling blue." Foreground="Blue" />
```

Significantly, you can use the Foreground property with the Inline elements we discussed in 9.2.2. These Inline elements also have baked-in support for the TextDecorations property.

TEXTDECORATIONS

The TextDecorations property gives you the ability to underline text. This can be accomplished using the Underline TextDecorations property as shown here:

```
<TextBlock Text="I'm Serious" TextDecorations="Underline" />
```

Much like the `FontStyle` property, the `TextDecorations` property has more options in WPF—the reason why it has such an abstract name.

The next property is more line or paragraph-oriented: `TextWrapping`.

TEXTWRAPPING

The `TextWrapping` property enables you to specify how text should wrap across multiple lines within a `TextBlock`. By default, Silverlight doesn't wrap text within a `Text-Block`. You can set the `TextWrapping` attribute to `Wrap`, and the text will break and resume on the next line if the `Width` of the `TextBlock` is exceeded. This wrapping effect is shown in listing 9.3.

Listing 9.3   Text wrapping

Result:

Eating a lot of fruit
can help you live to
a ripe old age.

XAML:

```
<Canvas Width="200" Height="140">
  <TextBlock Text="Eating a lot of fruit can help you live to
[CA]ripe old age."
            Width="150"
            TextWrapping="Wrap" />        ◁— ⎤ TextWrapping
</Canvas>                                         ⎦ property
```

Listing 9.3 shows how to change the `TextWrapping` property from its default value of `NoWrap`. The value and its destination value of `Wrap` belong to the `TextWrapping` enumeration. This type is only available to `TextBlock` elements—you can't use it in `Inline` elements such as `Run`. The `Run` element also lacks the ability to specify its own `TextTrimming` or `TextAlignment`, separate from the `TextBlock`.

TEXTTRIMMING

There are often cases when you want to show only as much text as will fit into a predefined rectangle on the screen. The remaining text should be clipped off. In those cases, it's common to provide the user with a visual cue that the text's been trimmed.

Rather than have you calculate the trimming manually, Silverlight supports the `TextTrimming` property. As shown in listing 9.4, Silverlight supports the `WordEllipsis` style of text trimming, where the ellipsis is shown after the last whole word that will fit in the rectangle.

Listing 9.4   Text trimming with a small font

Result:

Well, hello there! I'm...

XAML:

```
<Grid x:Name="LayoutRoot" Background="White">
    <TextBlock Width="150"
```

```
          Height="30"                     ┌─ Font Size          ┌─ Text Trimming
          FontSize="12"            ◄──────┘                ◄────┘  Option
          TextTrimming="WordEllipsis"
          Text="Well, hello there! I'm Pete" />
</Grid>
```

Listing 9.4 shows the `TextTrimming` option in place with a regular sized font. If you increase the font size, less text will fit in the space. Listing 9.5 shows what happens when you leave everything else the same, but increase the font size.

Listing 9.5   Text trimming with a larger font

Result:

Well, hello...

XAML:
```
<Grid x:Name="LayoutRoot" Background="White">
    <TextBlock Width="150"
          Height="30"                     ┌─ Font Size          ┌─ Text Trimming
          FontSize="20"            ◄──────┘                ◄────┘  Option
          TextTrimming="WordEllipsis"
          Text="Well, hello there! I'm Pete" />
</Grid>
```

Note how the text is still broken at the word boundary. That's one of the nice things about `WordEllipsis` trimming. Breaking at a character boundary just looks unprofessional in many cases and can lead to unexpected and inappropriate final words in the worst cases.

Another way to control the layout of text is to use the `TextAlignment` property. Though text trimming is typically used with left-justified text, it can also be used with any of the other alignments available to the `TextBlock`.

TEXTALIGNMENT

The `TextAlignment` property gives you the ability to align the text within a `TextBlock`. You can specify whether information should be aligned to the `Left`, `Center`, or `Right` of the rectangular region defined by the `Height` and `Width` properties of a `TextBlock`, as shown in listing 9.6.

Listing 9.6   Text alignment property values

Result:

Everybody	Everybody	Everybody
to the Left	to the	to the
side of	Center of	Right side
the	the	of the
Canvas.	Canvas.	Canvas.

XAML:
```
<Canvas Width="640" Height="480" Background="White">
  <TextBlock Text="Everybody to the Left side of the Canvas."
```

```
      TextWrapping="Wrap"
      Width="75"
      Canvas.Left="5" Canvas.Top="5" />
   <TextBlock Text="Everybody to the Center of the Canvas."
      TextAlignment="Center"
      TextWrapping="Wrap"
      Width="75"
      Canvas.Left="100" Canvas.Top="5" />
   <TextBlock Text="Everybody to the Right side of the Canvas."
      TextAlignment="Right"
      TextWrapping="Wrap"
      Width="75"
      Canvas.Left="195" Canvas.Top="5" />
</Canvas>
```

Centered text

Right-aligned text

Listing 9.6 demonstrates the TextAlignment options. These options provide one way to stylize your text. The TextWrapping, TextDecorations, TextTrimming, and Foreground properties enable you to further format this text. In addition, there's one more important feature that shouldn't be overlooked: the ability to control text spacing.

9.2.4   *Spacing*

Spacing is effective for making text easier to read. This can help individuals with diminished eyesight or just make an application look better. To control the spacing of text, the TextBlock exposes two properties: LineHeight and Padding.

LINEHEIGHT

The LineHeight property determines the height of the bounding box that a single line of your text will be contained within. This height is represented as the number of pixels and specified as a double-precision value. Listing 9.7 demonstrates this property as well as its relationship to FontSize.

| Listing 9.7   Line height for vertical spacing |

Result:

Just testing	Just testing	Just testing
some line	some line	
height related	height related	some line
stuff. This	stuff. This	
could actually	could actually	height related
be pretty	be pretty	
interesting.	interesting.	stuff. This
		could actually
		be pretty
		interesting.

XAML:

```
<Canvas Height="450" Width="485">
   <TextBlock Width="110" LineHeight="1"
```

Ignored LineHeight

```
                    FontSize="14" TextWrapping="Wrap">
   Just testing some line height related
   stuff.  This could actually
   be pretty interesting.
 </TextBlock>
 <TextBlock Width="110" LineHeight="24"
            FontSize="14"
            TextWrapping="Wrap" Canvas.Left="125">
   Just testing some line height related
   stuff.  This could actually
   be pretty interesting.
 </TextBlock>
 <TextBlock Width="110" LineHeight="44"
            FontSize="14"
            TextWrapping="Wrap" Canvas.Left="250">
   Just testing some line height related
   stuff.  This could actually
   be pretty interesting.
 </TextBlock>
</Canvas>
```

As listing 9.7 illustrates, the LineHeight property often alters the layout of wrapped text. Notably, if the LineHeight is smaller than the FontSize, the LineHeight value is ignored. If the LineHeight is larger than the FontSize, some extra padding is generated around the text. The LineHeight doesn't affect the FontSize.

While LineHeight works on individual lines in the TextBlock and only controls vertical spacing, Padding controls the overall spacing within the outside border of a TextBlock.

PADDING

The Padding property represents the amount of cushion to use within a TextBlock. This space represents the area between the border of the TextBlock and the text of the element. By default, this property doesn't specify any spacing. Using a double-precision value, you can provide a consistent buffer between the text and the virtual borders of a TextBlock, as shown in listing 9.8.

> **Listing 9.8   Uniform padding in a TextBlock**

Result:

Give Me Some Space!

   I've got your space right here!

XAML:
```
<StackPanel x:Name="myStackPanel" Background="LightGray">
  <TextBlock Text="Give Me Some Space!" />
  <TextBlock Text="I've got your space right here!"
             Padding="20.2" />                        Padding
</StackPanel>
```

Listing 9.8 shows how a `Padding` of 20.2 pixels creates a nice bubble around some text. You'll probably notice that the size of this buffer is the same on each side of the content. The `Padding` property also enables you to use a more granular approach when defining the buffer, as shown in listing 9.9.

Listing 9.9   Per-side padding in a `TextBlock`

Result:

XAML:

```
<StackPanel x:Name="LayoutRoot"
            Background="White"
            Margin="10">
    <Border Background="LightGray"
            BorderBrush="Black"
            HorizontalAlignment="Left"
            VerticalAlignment="Top">
        <TextBlock Text="HELLO"
                   Padding="3.5 6 9.7 12" />    <--- Padding
    </Border>

</StackPanel>
```

Listing 9.9 shows the `Padding` property using a space-delimited list of values. The values can also be comma-delimited. This list of values represents the amount of spacing to use on each side of the text, within the outer limits of the `TextBlock` element. The first value in the list represents the thickness of the spacing on the left side of the text. The subsequent values represent the top, right, and bottom thicknesses of the buffer. As you can see, these values specify the thicknesses in a clockwise order. This granular approach gives the `Padding` property a significant amount of flexibility.

The `Padding` property represents one of the more basic features of the `TextBlock`, which is one of the more basic elements in Silverlight. This element will be used in most Silverlight applications you write.

The `TextBlock` always renders text using the specified font or a default fallback if unspecified or if the font is unavailable. If the font you're using in your `TextBlock` or other control isn't a standard font, you may want to consider embedding it with your application.

9.3   *Embedding fonts*

Sometimes you want to use a special font in your application. Maybe it's the typeface in use in your company logo. Sometimes it's a slick headline font. Or perhaps it's just a sharp and readable font you want to use in your news reading application. I had this issue when I built the trivia application that ran on the screens at Microsoft PDC 2009. I had to use the PDC font but couldn't guarantee it would be on the machines.

What do you do when you can't guarantee that end users will have that font on their machines? One way to tackle this problem is to embed the font into the application.

I'm not a lawyer

But that's not going to stop me from giving pseudo-legal advice. Before you go and embed that font, check its license. Most fonts don't legally allow embedding in applications. In fact, most fonts haven't even caught up with the idea that fonts can be used outside of documents.

Once the font foundries get out of the '80s and start allowing more font embedding in applications, user interfaces will really start to shine.

In the mean time, I suggest you consult someone with a real legal background before embedding that font in your application.

Silverlight supports embedded fonts—whole fonts and subsets—in applications. When not using font subsetting, you simply add the font to your project and mark it as a resource. You can then refer to it by name using the format *FileName*#*FontName*:

```
<TextBlock FontFamily="Fonts/MSPDC.TTF#Microsoft PDC Squared" … />
```

The folder name *Fonts* is the location where the original TTF file is placed in the project. The name *MSPDC.TTF* is the name of the font file on disk, and *Microsoft PDC Squared* is the name of the actual font.

Packaging with font subsetting requires Expression Blend. Even if you use Visual Studio, the required build action is supplied by Expression Blend and can be compiled in Visual Studio, but must be created the first time in Blend. This makes sense, as font subsetting and font embedding are very designer-oriented tasks; most of us programming grunts just default to Comic Sans MS and call it a day.

To support *subsetting*—reducing the number of glyphs to only those used in the application—the font is packaged up into a zip file and later referred to by its embedded location. For example:

```
<TextBlock FontFamily="Fonts/Fonts.zip#Microsoft PDC Squared" … />
```

The folder name *Fonts* is the location where the original TTF file is placed in the project. The zip name is the name Expression Blend generated for the archive, and the name after the hash tag is the name after the font. Note that this can be different from the TTF filename itself.

The issue isn't really the technical aspect of embedding itself (it's just a zip file embedded into the DLL as a resource); it's the act of subsetting the font that makes embedding legal for those fonts that support it. Expression Blend actually creates a subset font that has only the glyphs (characters) you use in your application.

In short, though you may find a way to manually embed the fonts, you're better off trusting Expression Blend to do it for you.

Once you have fonts embedded in your application, they can be used anywhere you'd use a regular typeface. For example, they may be used in text boxes for gathering text, which is the subject of the next section.

9.4   *Entering and editing text*

Collecting and displaying text is a vital part of almost every web application. Silverlight provides several controls designed to make this important task easy. Silverlight supports standard keyboard text input as well as input from *input method editors* (IMEs). (If you don't know what those are, don't worry; we'll get to that in a minute.) In this section, we'll cover the core of text input, including the two main controls used for gathering plain text from the user.

The most basic text input control is the TextBox. For most forms and other simple data, this is the control you'll use to capture input. TextBox supports all the usual text entry functions, as well as multiline input.

Similar to the TextBox but optimized for sensitive data, we have the PasswordBox. The PasswordBox is what you should use when collecting passwords or other data you want masked from view.

Over the course of this section, you'll learn how to handle basic text entry with the TextBox. In addition, you'll see how to collect sensitive information, such as passwords, with the PasswordBox. Finally, we'll look at the ways to collect and format text simultaneously using the RichTextBox.

9.4.1   *Handling basic text input*

The TextBox control enables your users to edit and view text. As basic as this may sound, it'd be difficult to consider a UI technology that didn't include this type of functionality. When a user enters text into a TextBox, it gets stored as a string in the Text property. This property can be programmatically set at runtime, giving you the ability to prepopulate a form. Optionally, this property value can be set at design time if you have a more static value.

XAML:
```
<TextBox x:Name="NameField" Text="Pete Brown" />
```

C#:
```
TextBox nameField = new TextBox();
nameField.Text = "Pete Brown";
```

This example shows the XAML and C# definitions for a TextBox with a preset Text value. This value will change if a user decides to change the contents of a TextBox. This change will cause the TextChanged event to fire asynchronously, which gives you the opportunity to respond to characters after they're entered. You can also limit how many characters a user can enter by setting the MaxLength property. Limiting the number of characters can be useful for ensuring that data isn't truncated when it's sent back to a data source. In addition, some of the values from a data source should only be seen, not edited. In these cases, you can change the IsReadOnly property to true to prevent a user from editing a `TextBox`. These basic members of a `TextBox` are useful, but the multiline and text selection features are perhaps even more interesting.

ENABLING MULTILINE TEXT SUPPORT

The `TextBox` has built-in support for handling multiline text input. By default, this feature is turned off. You can turn it on by toggling two of the properties of a `TextBox` control. These two properties, `AcceptsReturn` and `TextWrapping`, are shown in listing 9.10.

> **Listing 9.10   Multiline `TextBox`**

Result:

Description:

> Here is an example of some basic text wrapping automatically.
>
> You will also notice I can press the "Enter" key in this area. In a sense, when AcceptsReturn and TextWrapping are enabled, the TextBox will behave like the TextArea control in HTML.

XAML:

```
<Grid>
  <Grid.RowDefinitions>
    <RowDefinition Height="Auto" />
    <RowDefinition />
  </Grid.RowDefinitions>
  <TextBlock Text="Description:" FontFamily="Verdana" FontSize="14" />
  <TextBox x:Name="myTextBox" AcceptsReturn="True" TextWrapping="Wrap"
    FontFamily="Verdana" FontSize="14"
    Grid.Row="1" Height="150" Width="450" />
</Grid>
```

The listing shows a multiline `TextBox` enabled through the `AcceptsReturn` and `Text-Wrapping` properties. The `AcceptsReturn` property is a `bool` that tells the `TextBox` whether to show and permit newline characters. This property is important because it is what enables a user to press the Enter key and go to a new line within a `TextBox`. A true multiline `TextBox` isn't complete until the `TextWrapping` property is set to `Wrap`. We discussed this property in relation to the `TextBlock` element in section 9.2.3; those same rules apply with the `TextBox`. With this property and the `AcceptsReturn` property, you can easily implement a multiline `TextBox`.

Implementing a multiline `TextBox` in Silverlight is simple. This approach is slightly different than the approach used in HTML, which requires a separate element altogether (the `TextArea`). The Silverlight approach simplifies the overall API and provides exciting text selection features not found in HTML.

MASTERING TEXT SELECTION

The `TextBox` has built-in support for selecting portions of text within a `TextBox`. A user can highlight information and you can programmatically retrieve it through three properties, appropriately named `SelectedText`, `SelectionStart`, and `SelectionLength`. These properties can also be programmatically set, which is especially useful when implementing incremental search and auto-complete functionality in a `TextBox`. Each is shown in figure 9.5.

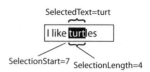

Figure 9.5   The text selection parts: `SelectedText`, `SelectionStart`, **and** `SelectionLength`

This figure shows the three properties associated with text selection. The first property is a `string` called `SelectedText` that represents the content currently selected within a `TextBox`. This content has a specific length, which is available through the `SelectionLength` property. This `int` gives you the number of characters currently selected within a `TextBox`. These characters begin at a specific index, which is accessible through the `SelectionStart` property. When text isn't selected, the `SelectionStart` property will return the index of the carat. The selection properties are read/write and allow you to programmatically change their values.

The HTML text box doesn't provide a way to select only portions of text. As shown here, the `TextBox` in Silverlight does enable you to select text at a more granular level. At the same time, Silverlight still has support for both single and multiline text boxes.

Not all applications are written for the en-US market. If you're writing applications for other markets, especially where the languages have different characters, you'll want to understand input method editors and how they work with Silverlight.

9.4.2   *Understanding input method editors*

IMEs are operating system components or added programs that allow, among other things, multiple keystrokes to be composited into a single character. This supports languages where there are more possible characters than keys on the keyboard or where the keyboard doesn't have the required character.

IME text is important for handling text from most Eastern languages. Figure 9.6 shows an example of a typical Japanese Romaji-based IME in operation.

In this section, we'll look at what IMEs are and how to use them in Silverlight. We'll even take a look at how to change your Windows keyboard settings to allow you to test the functions that support IME in Silverlight.

In Silverlight, the `TextBox` and other controls handle IME-entered text through events defined at the `UIElement`-level. In particular, if you want your application to work in IME situations, don't respond to `KeyDown`/`KeyUp` events of the `TextBox`. Instead, if you do use editing based on keystrokes, use the `TextInput` `TextInputStart` and `TextInputUpdated` events.

Figure 9.6   Operation of a typical Japanese Romaji-based IME (source: Wikimedia Commons)

Note that, depending on the IME mode in use and the control you're interacting with, some of these events may be handled by the control and not otherwise bubbled up.

> **TIP** In Windows 7, to change your keyboard layout to US International (if you're in the US) to test basic IME, use Start > Control Panel > Region and Language. Then select the Keyboards and Languages tab and click Change Keyboards.
>
> If you already have the United States - International keyboard listed, select it. Otherwise click Add… to add it, and then select it from the list.
>
> From there, you can type diacritic characters. For example, to type the é in Claudé you'd select the US International keyboard from your system tray, then type the single quote followed by the letter *e*.

In addition, if you want finer control over IME in your application, use the `Input-Method` class and the attached properties it exposes. For space reasons and to stay on topic, we won't cover those numerous options, but we'll look at an example of the differences between the keyboard and text input events.

To do that, you may want to set the `InputMethod.IsInputMethodEnabled` to true on your `TextBox`. While the underlying value of the `IsInputMethodEnabled` property is True, its actual value is influenced by the state of available input methods at runtime. Setting it to true isn't essential but helps convey your intent, especially if you'll be handling IME events in code.

Listing 9.11 shows the difference between the keyboard events and the text input events. For example, to type the accented e in the first word, I must hit Shift-6 and then the letter *e*.

Listing 9.11 Wiring up the TextInputStart event

Result:

```
arrêtez Claudé|
```

Debug window output:
```
Down:A, TextInputStart:a, Up:A
Down:R, TextInputStart:r, Up:R
Down:R, TextInputStart:r, Up:R
Down:Shift, Down:D6, Up:D6, Up:Shift, Down:E, InputStart:ê, Up:E
Down:T, TextInputStart:t, Up:T,
Down:E, TextInputStart:e, Up:E,
Down:Z, TextInputStart:z, Up:Z
```

XAML:
```xml
<Grid x:Name="LayoutRoot" Background="White">
  <TextBox x:Name="FirstName"
           InputMethod.IsInputMethodEnabled="True"          Optional IME
           Width="150"                                  ◁──┘ enable
           Height="24" />
</Grid>
```

C#:
```csharp
public MainPage()
{
    InitializeComponent();

    FirstName.KeyDown += new KeyEventHandler(FirstName_KeyDown);
    FirstName.KeyUp += new KeyEventHandler(FirstName_KeyUp);
    FirstName.TextInputStart +=
        new TextCompositionEventHandler(FirstName_TextInputStart);
}

void FirstName_TextInputStart(                                         ◁─┐ IME
        object sender, TextCompositionEventArgs e)                        │ event
{
    Debug.WriteLine("InputStart:" + e.Text);
}

void FirstName_KeyUp(object sender, KeyEventArgs e)                    ◁──┐
{                                                                        │ Standard key
    Debug.WriteLine("Up:" + e.Key.ToString());                           │ events
}
                                                                         │
void FirstName_KeyDown(object sender, KeyEventArgs e)                  ◁──┘
{
    Debug.WriteLine("Down:" + e.Key.ToString());
}
```

If you have an IME installed on your system or have changed your keyboard layout to do so, you'll be able to type diacritic characters using an IME.

If you live and work in the United States, it can be tempting to create applications that work only with US keyboards. But if you want to move your product to an international market or at least understand what's necessary to support those markets, you'll want to read up on internationalization, including input method editing on Windows and the Mac.

Input method editing is something not every application needs. However, it's a staple of Windows development. Another staple of modern application development is the clipboard. Think about how isolated our applications would be if we didn't have a way to get data from one to another! Luckily, Silverlight allows you to programmatically access the clipboard to move text between applications.

9.4.3   *Copying text with the Clipboard API*

Silverlight 4 added a new API for use with transferring text via the clipboard. Though currently limited to just Unicode strings, the clipboard is an excellent way to enable your Silverlight application to integrate with the rest of the applications on the hosting system.

The Clipboard object is your Silverlight application's interface to the system clipboard. In this section, we'll take a quick look at the clipboard API and its capabilities, starting with the three member functions of the Clipboard class. Table 9.3 shows the static member functions exposed by this object.

Table 9.3 The `Clipboard` type's static member functions

Member	Description
ContainsText	Queries the clipboard and returns true if the clipboard contains compatible text
GetText	Returns the Unicode text from the clipboard
SetText	Places Unicode text on the clipboard

`Clipboard` exposes static members, so you don't need to instantiate it to use it. For example, to place text on the clipboard, simply call `Clipboard.SetText`:

```
Clipboard.SetText("This text will be on the clipboard.");
```

Similarly, to retrieve text this or another application placed on the clipboard, call the `GetText` method:

```
string text = Clipboard.GetText();
```

Note that, in both cases, you'll receive a security exception if you're running in the standard (not elevated) permissions mode and either didn't initiate the action from a user event or the user didn't allow access to the clipboard when prompted to do so. Figure 9.7 shows the prompt the user receives when you initiate a clipboard operation.

The prompt helps to protect the user from potentially malicious applications that may try to steal data from the clipboard or fill the clipboard with garbage.

One thing you probably won't want to allow on the clipboard is a user's password. For that and for masking reasons, Silverlight includes a specialized `PasswordBox`.

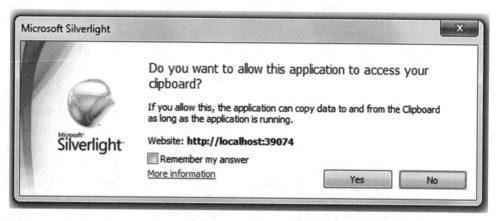

Figure 9.7 The clipboard access prompt. When running in standard permissions (sandboxed) mode, Silverlight displays this when you attempt to access the clipboard from the application.

9.4.4 *Collecting sensitive data*

Silverlight provides a special control called `PasswordBox`. This element is designed to hide information from someone who may be lurking behind a user. This is accomplished by hiding the contents of a `PasswordBox` behind asterisks (*), which serve as familiar reminders to end users that they're entering a password. But, if you'd like to use something other than an asterisk, you're free to use any character you like by setting the `PasswordChar` property. This property, as well as the syntax of a `PasswordBox`, is shown in listing 9.12.

Listing 9.12 The syntax for the `PasswordBox`—note the mask used in each field

Result:

Password: [   ]

Confirm: [   ]

XAML:
```
<Grid>
  <Grid.RowDefinitions>
    <RowDefinition Height="Auto" />
    <RowDefinition Height="Auto" />
  </Grid.RowDefinitions>

  <Grid.ColumnDefinitions>
    <ColumnDefinition Width="Auto" />
    <ColumnDefinition Width="Auto" />
  </Grid.ColumnDefinitions>

  <TextBlock Text="Password: " FontFamily="Verdana" />
  <PasswordBox Width="200" Grid.Column="1" />

  <TextBlock Text="Confirm: " FontFamily="Verdana" Grid.Row="1" />
  <PasswordBox PasswordChar="#" Width="200"
    Grid.Column="1" Grid.Row="1" />
</Grid>
```

Default mask character

Custom mask character

This example shows a default `PasswordBox` and a custom `PasswordChar` to show how Silverlight takes a small step beyond the masking approach used in HTML. Still, once a user enters information into these fields, you'll probably need to retrieve it. This is possible thanks to the `Password` property.

The `Password` property is a `string` that represents the value in a `PasswordBox`. This property can be programmatically set and retrieved. Interestingly, this value can't be copied or cut at runtime by a user. This restriction is designed to ensure a user's password remains protected, short of hacker heroics such as wiring a debugger to the code and inspecting values. To provide this feature, along with the general input control features, the `PasswordBox` needs to derive from the `Control` class instead of the `TextBox` class.

The `PasswordBox` and `TextBox` are two controls used for capturing user input. However, they are limited in how the text can be formatted. Unlike the `TextBox`, the

`RichTextBox` allows the user to have a true document experience with multiple fonts and styles.

9.5 Entering and displaying rich text

From email composition to document creation, we've gotten so used to the simplicity of creating text with multiple fonts, colors, and font styles that, when we see a multi-line text box with no formatting control, it simply looks strange. Prior to the introduction of the `RichTextBox` in Silverlight 4, Silverlight had no way of allowing the user to enter formatted text.

The `RichTextBox` follows many of the same patterns as the regular `TextBox` but enhances it with the ability to store the formatting information such as fonts and colors. The `RichTextBox` also takes it one step further by allowing the embedding of images and other UI elements, even controls, into the text.

In our tour of the `RichTextBox` control, we'll look at how to format text using different fonts and colors, how to embed hyperlinks in rich text, and even how to embed other controls such as the `Button` and `ComboBox`. As you'll want your users to actually work with your text, we'll then look into what it takes to work with the text the user has selected or text you select from code and then change its attributes.

As the main reason the `RichTextBox` exists is to enable the display and editing of text with multiple fonts, colors, and other visual attributes, we'll start there.

9.5.1 Formatting and inline elements

The `RichTextBox` enables you to format text and add elements inline. This includes formatting tags, text spans, other controls, and—perhaps the most important and most basic of these elements—the `Paragraph`.

PARAGRAPHS

The `Paragraph` element enables you to break the text in the `RichTextBox` into one or more separate paragraphs. Each paragraph can have its own formatting independent of the overall control.

Listing 9.13 shows three different paragraphs, each with separate formatting independent of the overall control's formatting.

> **Listing 9.13** `RichTextBox` showing paragraphs with different formatting and alignment

Result:

This is the first paragraph of the text I'm going to place in this RichTextBox. It has two sentences. Actually, it has three sentences.

This is the second paragraph, and its text is set to justify, as you can tell from the pretty screen shot. Please note that the last sentence in the paragraph is not justified.

One ring to rule them all, one ring to bind them. One ring to bring them all, and in the darkness bind them, in the land of Mordor where the Shadows lie.

XAML:

```
<RichTextBox x:Name="RichText"
             Width="350"
             Height="200">
  <Paragraph>
    This is the first paragraph of the text I'm going to place
    in this RichTextBox. It has two sentences. Actually, it has
    three sentences.
  </Paragraph>
  <Paragraph TextAlignment="Justify"
             FontWeight="Bold">
    This is the second paragraph, and its text is set to
    justify, as you can tell from the pretty screen shot.
    Please note that the last sentence in the paragraph is not
    justified.
  </Paragraph>
  <Paragraph TextAlignment="Right">
    One ring to rule them all, one ring to bind them. One ring
    to bring them all, and in the darkness bind them, in the
    land of Mordor where the Shadows lie.
  </Paragraph>
</RichTextBox>
```

Listing 9.13 shows several interesting features. First, the text in a `RichTextBox` can be easily broken apart into separate paragraphs. The second feature is that each of those paragraphs can have formatting separate from the others. In this case, I used different text alignment on each of them and also set the middle paragraph to be bold.

In addition to setting the styles at a paragraph level, you can surround blocks of text with formatting markup, called *inline styles*.

INLINE STYLES AND SPANS

If formatting could be applied only at the paragraph level, the `RichTextBox` wouldn't be all that useful. Luckily, formatting can be applied at a much finer-grained level using inline formatting elements such as `Bold`, `Italic`, and the versatile `Span`. Listing 9.14 shows several formatting approaches in a single paragraph.

Listing 9.14   Inline styles and spans in the paragraph text

Result:

One **ring** to rule them all , one ring to find them. *One* ring to
bring them all, and in the darkness bind them, in the
land of Mordor where the Shadows
lie.

XAML:

```
<RichTextBox x:Name="RichText"
             Width="350"
```

```
          Height="125">
    <Paragraph TextAlignment="Left">
      One <Bold>ring</Bold> to <Span Foreground="Red">rule them all</Span>,
      one ring to find them. <Italic>One</Italic> ring to bring them all,
      and in the darkness bind them, <Span FontSize="18">in the land of
      Mordor where the Shadows lie.</Span>
    </Paragraph>
</RichTextBox>
```

Listing 9.14 shows the use of the Bold and Italic inline styles, as well as Span. Bold and Italic are handy shortcuts, but Span is the most flexible of the three, supporting myriad formatting options. Span itself inherits from Inline and from that gets a number of useful properties. Section 9.2.1 goes into detail about the commonly used properties shared by the Span, TextBlock, and Run elements.

In addition to these inline styles, the RichTextBox also supports LineBreaks via the LineBreak element:

```
One ring to rule them all,<LineBreak />
one ring to find them.<LineBreak />
```

As expected, the LineBreak element causes the text following it to start on a new line. You can think of the paragraph tag like the HTML <p></p> pair, and the LineBreak element much like the HTML <br /> tag.

One thing that the other text-display controls can't include is a hyperlink. The RichTextBox is currently unique in its ability to display active Hyperlink controls.

INLINE HYPERLINKS

The RichTextBox has the ability to host any UIElement, but it has first-class support for hosting Hyperlinks without requiring any special containers or other work on your part, while keeping them active even for editable text. This makes it easy to display HTML-like text with embedded links.

For example, listing 9.15 shows two Hyperlink elements embedded in the Rich-TextBox control.

Listing 9.15   Hyperlink support in the RichTextBox

Result:

One ring to rule them all, one ring to find them. *One* ring to bring them all, and in the darkness bind them, in the land of Mordor where the Shadows lie.

XAML:

```
<RichTextBox x:Name="RichText"
            Width="350"
            Height="125">
```

```
  <Paragraph TextAlignment="Left">
    One ring to <Hyperlink NavigateUri="http://manning.com">rule
    them all, one ring to find</Hyperlink> them. <Italic>One
    </Italic> ring to bring them all, and in the darkness bind them,
    <Hyperlink NavigateUri="http://10rem.net"><Span FontSize="18">in
    the land of Mordor where the Shadows lie.</Span></Hyperlink>
  </Paragraph>
</RichTextBox>
```

Listing 9.15 shows the use of two hyperlinks embedded in the paragraph text. Note how the hyperlinks also have support for cleanly nesting `Spans` and other formatting elements.

The `Hyperlink` control in the `RichTextBox` is a fully functional Silverlight `Hyperlink` control, but it's not the same as the one you'd place in regular XAML. Instead, it derives from `Span`. You can still wire up `Click` events, supply a `NavigateUri` as I did here, and otherwise do everything you'd expect to be able to do with a `Hyperlink`. The `Hyperlink` control itself is covered in more detail later in this chapter.

In addition to the `Hyperlink` control, `RichTextBox` includes support for hosting any other `UIElement` through the use of `InlineUIContainer`.

INLINE IMAGES AND ELEMENTS

The `RichTextBox` control allows you to embed any `UIElement` inline into the text, as long as you contain it in an `InlineUIContainer`. The catch is that the elements won't be active; they'll only show their disabled representation unless the `RichTextBox` is set to read-only mode via the `IsReadOnly` property as shown in listing 9.16.

> **Listing 9.16   A mad-lib of a `RichTextBox` showing embedded controls**

Result

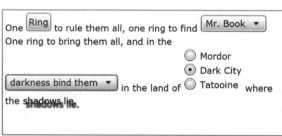

XAML:
```
<RichTextBox x:Name="RichText" IsReadOnly="True"
             Width="350" Height="150">
  <Paragraph TextAlignment="Left">
    One
    <InlineUIContainer>
      <Button Content="Ring" />
    </InlineUIContainer>
    to rule them all, one ring to find
    <InlineUIContainer>                        #A
      <ComboBox SelectedIndex="0">
        <ComboBox.Items>
          <ComboBoxItem Content="Mr. Book" />
```

```
            <ComboBoxItem Content="Mr. Hand" />
            <ComboBoxItem Content="Deckard" />
        </ComboBox.Items>
    </ComboBox>
</InlineUIContainer>
One ring to bring them all, and in the
<InlineUIContainer> #A
    <ComboBox SelectedIndex="0">
        <ComboBox.Items>
            <ComboBoxItem Content="darkness bind them" />
            <ComboBoxItem Content="darkness find them" />
            <ComboBoxItem Content="snarkiness unwind them" />
        </ComboBox.Items>
    </ComboBox>
</InlineUIContainer>
in the land of
<InlineUIContainer> #A
    <StackPanel>
        <RadioButton Content="Mordor" />
        <RadioButton Content="Dark City" />
        <RadioButton Content="Tatooine" />
    </StackPanel>
</InlineUIContainer>
where the
<InlineUIContainer>                        <─── InlineUIContainer
    <TextBlock Text="shadows lie.">
        <TextBlock.Effect>
            <DropShadowEffect BlurRadius="2" />
        </TextBlock.Effect>
    </TextBlock>
</InlineUIContainer>
        </Paragraph>
</RichTextBox>
```

As listing 9.16 shows, you can do some pretty neat things with the inline UIElements, including add items with effects such as drop shadows. The example shown may be a real dog's breakfast of a UI, but the ability to embed controls of any sort into a rich text interface really opens up the options for creating your own UI, especially for scripted questionnaires and similar free-flowing interfaces.

Getting back to basic text manipulation, one thing you may need to do is programmatically select text or work with a selection a user has made. The nature of rich text makes this slightly more complex than plain text, as we'll see in the next section.

9.5.2 *Working with selected text*

Programmatic manipulation of the RichTextBox beyond simply reading or writing the entire contents requires that you work with selections. The selections may be set in code or you may be taking an action based upon a selection the user has made. Either way, the methods are consistent.

SELECTION

There may be times when you need to programmatically select content in the RichTextBox. For example, if you're doing a search and replace, the Find Next function should search the content for the next occurrence of the search term and then automatically select it. The RichTextBox exposes the Selection property, which has a Select function to support programmatic selection.

The Select method takes two parameters, both of type TextPointer: the anchor-Position and the movingPosition. If you think about how you select text with a mouse, you start with one point that stays fixed in place, and you move the mouse cursor, changing the selection relative to that point. Similarly, the anchorPosition remains fixed and the movingPosition is the second or movable point.

Figure 9.8 shows the three main data points of interest. The first, the Selection.Text property, is a public read/write property that enables us to read or modify the text inside the two points.

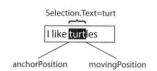

The anchorPosition is the place where you or the user (or your code) started the selection. The movingPosition is the end of the selection.

Note that, unlike the case with the TextBox, we're not dealing with numeric values for the start

Figure 9.8 RichTextBox selection information, assuming the user selected left to right, starting with the first T in "turtles"

and end points. Instead, we have pointers to the text. Though this can make it slightly more complex to work with, it both supports the addition of nonvisible markup and makes it more flexible when adding text between the points and the substitution character count isn't 1:1 with the original.

Listing 9.17 shows how to use the anchorPosition and movingPosition Text-Pointer objects to programmatically select text in the control.

Listing 9.17 Programmatically selecting text in the RichTextBox

Results:

> **We're off to outer space**
> We're leaving Mother Earth
> To save the human race
> *Our Star Blazers*
> **Searching for a distant star**
> Heading off to Iscandar
> Leaving all we love behind
> Who knows what danger we'll find?

> Select Next 10

XAML:

```
<StackPanel>
  <RichTextBox x:Name="RichText" Margin="10"
               Width="350" Height="150">
    <Paragraph TextAlignment="Left">
      <Bold>We're off to outer space</Bold><LineBreak />
      We're leaving Mother Earth<LineBreak />
```

```
      To save the human race<LineBreak />
      <Italic>Our Star Blazers</Italic>
    </Paragraph>
    <Paragraph TextAlignment="Left">
      <Bold>Searching for a distant star</Bold><LineBreak />
      Heading off to Iscandar<LineBreak />
      Leaving all we love behind<LineBreak />
      Who knows what danger we'll find?
    </Paragraph>
  </RichTextBox>

  <Button Content="Select Next 10" Click="SelectNext_Click"
          Width="150" Margin="10" />
</StackPanel>
```

C#:

```
private void SelectNext_Click(object sender, RoutedEventArgs e)
{
  TextPointer start = RichText.Selection.Start;          ◄─┐ Start is
  TextPointer end = start;                                  │ current
                                                          ◄─┘ position
  end = start.GetPositionAtOffset(10, LogicalDirection.Forward);   End adds 10
                                                          ◄─┘

  RichText.Selection.Select(start, end);   ◄─┐ Perform
                                              │ selection
  RichText.Focus();
}
```

The code in listing 9.17 takes the Selection.Start, which by default is where the caret is currently positioned, and adds 10 characters to it and ends the selection. The end result is the visible text selection.

Selecting text itself is interesting, but it's more interesting to actually manipulate the contents of the selection.

CHANGING SELECTION PROPERTIES

Once either the user or code has made a selection, you can alter the properties of that selection via code. For example, you can change the font face, the weight, the foreground, and other properties for the selection.

If you want to set the foreground color of the 10 characters to Red, simply alter the code in listing 9.17 to add the following ApplyPropertyValue call, passing the Foreground dependency property and a brush with the color red:

```
RichText.Selection.Select(start, end);
RichText.Selection.ApplyPropertyValue(
    TextElement.ForegroundProperty, new SolidColorBrush(Colors.Red));

RichText.Focus();
```

Similarly, you can call GetPropertyValue to get the value of a dependency property for the selected text.

REPLACING TEXT

Once you have a valid selection, you can also replace the text with your own plain text. The Selection.Text property is a two-way street: you can read the text that's in the selection and you can also assign new text to it. Again modifying listing 9.17, this will replace the 10 characters with *haha!!*:

```
RichText.Selection.Select(start, end);
RichText.Selection.Text = "haha!!";

RichText.Focus();
```

Replacing text is a good common operation, but what about inserting new text without overwriting something else? For that, you'll want to use the `Selection.Insert` method.

INSERTING NEW TEXT

In addition to replacing the selected text, you can insert new text anywhere you create a selection start point. In this example, we'll modify listing 9.17 and insert text wherever the caret happens to be positioned:

```
private void SelectNext_Click(object sender, RoutedEventArgs e)
{
  Run run = new Run();
  run.Text = "This is some text we're going to insert";
  RichText.Selection.Insert(run);

  RichText.Focus();
}
```

While `Run`s can be implicit in the XAML, the `Insert` method requires a `Run` element, or something that derives from `Run`. You can click the button as many times as you'd like and it'll happily insert new text wherever the caret is positioned.

RETRIEVING RICH TEXT AS XAML

This being Silverlight, you'd expect there to be some way to get the XAML representation of the selected text—and you'd be right. The `Selection` type exposes a `Xaml` property that returns the XAML for the selection. Modify listing 9.17 to include the following code to see the XAML representation of the text:

```
RichText.Selection.Select(start, end);
Debug.WriteLine(RichText.Selection.Xaml);

RichText.Focus();
```

If you wish to get the XAML for the entire control, first call the `SelectAll` method and then retrieve the XAML.

The `RichTextBox` control is a powerful control that allows you to create applications with serious text editing requirements. It builds upon the concepts from the `TextBlock` and `TextBox`, and combines them with inline formatting, `Hyperlinks`, and `UIElements` to create a versatile Silverlight control for both the display and editing of rich text.

9.6   *Summary*

Text handling is one of the most basic and important functions of any presentation layer. Silverlight has a complete text stack, including support for subpixel rendering and ClearType and grayscale font smoothing. Silverlight also includes the `TextBlock` element, which may be used to display read-only text.

Though typically used for things such as field labels and description paragraphs, the `TextBlock` supports multiple `Run`s of text, each with their own distinct attributes.

Any text element in Silverlight can take advantage of embedded fonts. Embedded fonts are useful for situations where you have a custom font or one that's unlikely to be on end-user machines. Rather than compromise and use a different font, you can embed the font or a subset of the glyphs in the font directly into your application.

Silverlight has several ways for entering and displaying text. There's significant overlap between them, but each has its own niche where it performs best. Table 9.4, adapted from information from MSDN, shows how you should think of each control or element when trying to decide between them.

Table 9.4 Recommended uses for the various text display and editing elements

Scenario	Recommended element
Display unformatted text in a single font	`TextBlock`
Display formatted text including paragraphs, hyperlinks, images, multiple fonts and styles	`RichTextBox`
Enter or edit plain text, such as would be used for data entry of a single field like a person's name	`TextBox`
Enter or edit formatted text including paragraphs, hyperlinks, images, multiple fonts and styles	`RichTextBox`
Enter sensitive information, such as a password, which must be masked for display	`PasswordBox`

Choosing the correct one for any given situation means balancing the runtime resources required with the features desired. In general, the elements from lightest to heaviest in terms of runtime resource requirements are:

1 `TextBlock`
2 `TextBox`
3 `RichTextBox`

So, although replacing all the `TextBlock` elements in your application with read-only `RichTextBox` controls in order to allow for selectable formatted text may seem appealing, you need to test it in your specific scenario and see if the runtime trade-off is worth the additional functionality. All three controls can display multibyte and right-to-left text and support the use of input method editors (IMEs).

The `TextBlock` lives in the `System.Windows.Controls` namespace but, unlike `TextBox` and `RichTextBox`, it's not actually a `Control`. This keeps it lightweight but means that some properties have to be duplicated between `TextBlock` and `System.Windows.Control.Control`. In the next chapter, we'll look at the various types of controls in the Silverlight runtime and how they all fit together.

Controls and UserControls

This chapter covers

- Understanding the control base types
- Working with button controls
- Working with items controls
- Creating your own UserControls
- Implementing dependency properties

In the previous chapter, we covered the basics of text, including how to display and edit it. Two of the items discussed—the TextBox and RichTextBox—are both actually controls. The TextBlock isn't.

If you're coming from another technology, you may assume that anything you can see or interact with is a control, and you'd be partially right. Interaction generally requires a Control but, to see something such as a TextBlock, it requires only that it be a UIElement (covered in chapter 6).

In this and the following sections, we'll look at the base control types Control and ContentControl and then dive into the various types of controls, including Button controls and ItemsControls. In your Silverlight travels, you'll find that understanding these categories of controls will be pretty much all you need to make sense of any new control you run across.

Toward the end of this chapter, we'll also take our first trip into creating controls of our own. In this case, we'll follow the simple reuse model: the `UserControl`. In chapter 24—once we've covered binding, resources, styles, and templates—we'll again revisit creating controls, but with a more robust custom control model.

We've already covered the `UIElement` and `FrameworkElement` in chapter 6, so let's continue our walk up the stack and take a look at the base `Control` type.

10.1 Control

Almost every element you'll deal with that accepts input in some form derives from `Control`. Even the pages and user controls you create in your application ultimately end up deriving from this type. It's also the lowest-level type you can typically get away with when trying to share styles (see chapter 23) between different elements.

The `System.Windows.Controls.Control` abstract class derives from `FrameworkElement`. In addition to a number of protected methods that the derived controls can override to provide additional functionality, `Control` adds a number of new public properties and methods. We'll break these up into several logical groups and cover them separately, starting with appearance, then navigation and state, and finally the support for control templating.

10.1.1 Appearance

Controls are visual by definition. For that reason, several properties can be shared as a baseline implementation for anything visual and potentially interactive. The appearance-related properties for control are shown in table 10.1.

Table 10.1 Visual style properties for the `Control` abstract type

Member	Description
Background	The brush used to paint the background
BorderBrush	The brush used to paint the border
BorderThickness	The thickness of the border line
Foreground	The color used for foreground elements
Padding	The amount of space to reserve between the control's exterior and interior
HorizontalContentAlignment	Controls how the internal control content is aligned
VerticalContentAlignment	Controls how the internal control content is aligned

The `Background` property is used to hold the background brush of the control. This can be a simple color or a complex gradient. Similarly, the `BorderBrush` property does the same for the brush used to paint the border. The `BorderThickness` is a size to be used to control the pen weight or thickness of the border for the control. The Foreground brush should be used when displaying text or other content for which the user hasn't provided a specific color. The last three—Padding, HorizontalContentAlignment, and VerticalContentAlignment–all control how the content will be displayed.

It's important to know that no specific user interface is implied by these properties. The control author (or person creating the style/template) is required to apply these properties to specific elements in the template. Common sense would say that a BorderBrush should control the color of the outline of the control, but nothing enforces that.

Two other common traits that controls share is the ability to be navigated to via mouse and keyboard and set as either enabled or disabled.

10.1.2 *Navigation and state*

Silverlight controls also support Tab-key navigation as well as manual focusing via the mouse or API. The properties and methods that support that are shown in table 10.2.

Table 10.2   Navigation and state members for the Control abstract type

Member	Description
IsEnabled	Set to True if this control is in a state where it can accept user interaction
IsTabStop	True if the user can tab into this control
TabIndex	The tabbing position of this control, relative to its peers in the same panel
TabNavigation	Controls how the Tab key navigates in this control. It can either cycle, be local, or be a one-stop navigation. More on this shortly.
Focus method	Calling this method attempts to set focus to the control.

IsEnabled controls the enabled state for the control. The expected behavior is that, if IsEnabled is false, the control won't accept any keyboard, mouse, or other human input and isn't considered a tab stop. It should also display itself using a faded or grayed-out look to convey this state.

The Focus method may be used to attempt to manually set focus to a control via code. If the control can't receive focus (for example, IsEnabled is False), the method will return false.

Three properties control tab navigation for the control. The first—IsTabStop—controls whether the Tab key can be used to access the control. The TabIndex controls the order within the container that the Tab key will navigate between controls. Lower-numbered controls come earlier in the tabbing sequence. Finally, the TabNavigation property controls how tabbing works for elements hosted inside this control. The possible values and their meanings are listed in table 10.3.

If you were to create a composite control, such as the LockableListBox at the end of this chapter, Local tab navigation would be the expected behavior. But, if you

Table 10.3   Possible values for the `TabNavigation` property

Member	Description
Local	Your control is tabbed into. The next tab starts going through the child elements. Once the last child element is focused and the user hits Tab, the next element outside of your main control receives focus.
Cycle	Once this control is tabbed into, individual controls inside this control may be navigated to using Tab. When the last child control has been reached and the user hits Tab, the first one will receive focus again. Doing this effectively traps the user inside your control until he clicks elsewhere.
Once	Individual child elements other than the first one don't receive focus via the tab control.

created a `ListBox`-like control, you'd expect the `Once` behavior because you'd use the arrow keys to navigate between the individual items.

The next key area of support in the `Control` type is templating. Templates give Silverlight controls their appearance and user experience.

10.1.3   Templating

One key feature that the controls add over the base type is the ability to template the control. As we'll learn in section 23.3, a *template* is a definition for the visual representation of the control. By default, controls in Silverlight are defined by their model and functionality. The user interface elements can be completely replaced; they're considered *lookless* controls. Table 10.4 shows the properties and methods that support templating.

Table 10.4   Styling and templating properties for the `Control` abstract type

Member	Description
DefaultStyleKey	This is the key of the style to be used when no other style is assigned. Typically, it's set to the type of the class and, therefore, uses an implicit style.
Template	Reference to the template that makes up the control's visuals
ApplyTemplate method	It attempts to rebuild the visual tree from the template. It returns `true` if succeeded.

The `Template` property enables this flexible control templating. The `Default-StyleKey` property is used by control authors to wire up the control to a default style and template, something which may be overridden by consumers of the control. The `ApplyTemplate` method is used to rebuild the visual tree for the control, using the supplied template.

Control also supports the `FontFamily`, `FontSize`, `FontStretch`, `FontStyle`, and `FontWeight` properties we covered in the chapter on text. For more detail, please refer back to section 9.2.

It's rare that you'll create new controls that derive directly from `UIElement` or `FrameworkElement`. Instead, you'll usually derive from `Control` or one of its descendents such as `ContentControl`. `ContentControl` provides functionality above and beyond `Control` by enabling the containment and templating of arbitrary content.

10.2 ContentControl

In older technologies, the content of a control was usually very specific: a button could hold a text string in a caption property; an `ImageButton` could hold an image and text split across two properties; and so forth. Silverlight and WPF demanded a more flexible content model where a control could indicate that it supports the inclusion of arbitrary content rather than a specific atomic item of known type. From this requirement, the `ContentControl` was born.

`ContentControl` is a descendent of `Control`. As such, it inherits all of the properties, methods, and behaviors `Control` provides. It also adds the key concept of `Content`. Table 10.5 shows the two content-related properties that `ContentControl` adds to the `Control` type.

Table 10.5 Properties for the `ContentControl` abstract type

Member	Description
Content	Assign the content (anything that can be rendered) to this property. If the content isn't a `UIElement` and there's no `ContentTemplate`, Silverlight will call the object's `ToString` method to display it.
ContentTemplate	This is a data template used to display the content assigned via the `Content` property. We'll cover more on data templates in chapter 11 when we discuss binding.

The `Content` for a `ContentControl` can be any arbitrary object. But, if the type isn't something that can be natively added to the visual tree (a `UIElement`), Silverlight will call the object's `ToString` method to display it. This allows you to add any other Silverlight visual elements or a string value without having to do any additional work. If you've wondered why a button can have a simple string or a complex tree of elements as the content property, this is why.

The `ContentTemplate` is a data template that can be used to format the content. Consider that you may assign a complex object, such as a Person, to the content property. The `ToString` approach will leave you with something like `MyLib.MyNamespace.Person` as the actual text—probably not what you want. The `ContentTemplate` uses binding to format the object for display. We'll cover data templates in detail in chapter 11.

Table 10.6 shows the flexibility of the content control even without relying on a content template. Note how you can have anything inside the button, including a `TextBox` and a video. You can even type in the `TextBox` and watch the video because they're real, live elements.

Table 10.6 The flexibility of a `ContentControl` as displayed by three buttons

Button	XAML
Hello!	`<Button Width="150" Height="75"` `            Content="Hello!" />`

TextBox	`<Button Width="150" Height="75">`
	`    <Button.Content>`
	`        <TextBox Height="24" Text="TextBox"`
	`                Width="100" />`
	`    </Button.Content>`
	`</Button>`

Playing	`<Button Width="200"  Height="100">`
	`    <StackPanel>`
	`        <TextBlock Text="Playing"`
	`                   HorizontalAlignment="Center" />`
	`        <MediaElement Height="75" Width="125"`
	`                Stretch="Uniform"`
	`                Source="PeteAtMIX10ch9.wmv" />`
	`    </StackPanel>`
	`</Button>`

This table begins to show the flexibility provided with a ContentControl, in this case a Button. The first example shows a simple string for content. The second shows the explicit setting of the content property. This is optional, as we see in example three, where the Content property is omitted but the StackPanel is still assigned to it.

As you progress through this book, you'll learn how to make the contents of a ContentControl look exactly how you want. For now, note how the innards of a ContentControl are specified through the Content property.

Most controls that inherit from ContentControl use a ContentPresenter to do that actual display work in their control template. We'll cover more about templates in section 23.3 but, for now, a brief introduction to the ContentPresenter is in order.

10.2.1 The ContentPresenter

The ContentPresenter is a descendent FrameworkElement that exists primarily to support the display of content in a ContentControl. Rather than require you to put a TextBlock, Image, or other strongly typed content presentation element into your control template, you can use a ContentPresenter to bind to and display the content from the Content property.

Table 10.7 shows the properties of the ContentPresenter element.

Without the ContentPresenter, the ContentControl can't do much of anything exciting. The ContentPresenter holds the logic to try and render the object passed

Table 10.7   Properties for the `ContentPresenter` element

Member	Description
Content	The value assigned from the same property of a `ContentControl`
ContentTemplate	The template value assigned from the same property of a `ContentControl`

into it. In fact, in a typical control template, the `ContentPresenter` simply is assigned values from the `ContentControl` via template binding, as seen here:

```
<ContentPresenter
  Content="{TemplateBinding Content}"
  Margin="{TemplateBinding Padding}"
  HorizontalAlignment="{TemplateBinding HorizontalContentAlignment}"
  VerticalAlignment="{TemplateBinding VerticalContentAlignment}" />
```

We'll cover `TemplateBinding` in chapter 23 when we work with control templates. For now, understand that `TemplateBinding` is used to bind an element in XAML to a dependency property in the control's implementation. For example, the `Content` property of the `ContentPresenter` in the preceding code is bound to the `Content` property of the containing `ContentControl`.

Together, `Controls`, `ContentControls`, and the associated `ContentPresenter` make up the core of the control tree in Silverlight. One other type of control, the `ItemsControl`, is equally as important. But before we look at the various types of `ItemsControls`, let's look at some concrete implementations of `ContentControls`—specifically, those based on `Button`.

10.3   *Button controls*

A *button* is a type of control that responds to a single-click event. This event can be triggered by either a mouse or a keyboard. With a mouse, a user can click a button by pressing and releasing the left mouse button while hovering over it. With the keyboard, a button can be clicked by pressing Enter or the spacebar when the button has the focus. Either way, the general implementation of a button is spread across two classes, `ButtonBase` and `ContentControl`.

`ButtonBase` is an abstract base class used by all buttons in Silverlight. This class provides three members that are directly related to a user's interaction with a button: `IsPressed`, `Click`, and `ClickMode`. `IsPressed` returns whether a button is currently depressed. By default, this `bool` property is set to `false`. If a user clicks and holds a button, this property will change to `true`. But, once a user releases the mouse button, the `IsPressed` property will change back to `false`. At that point, the `Click` event will fire, assuming the default `ClickMode` is used.

The `ClickMode` property specifies when the `Click` event will fire. Setting this property can be useful if you want to fully customize a user's experience with your buttons. This experience can be set to any of the options available within the `ClickMode` enumeration. These options are shown and described in table 10.8.

Table 10.8   The options available within the `ClickMode` enumeration

Option	Description
Hover	Fires the `Click` event when the user moves the mouse pointer over a button
Press	Causes the `Click` event to execute when the user depresses a button
Release	Triggers the `Click` event when the user releases the left mouse button within the bounds of the button This is the default `ClickMode` used for a button.

The `ClickMode` enumeration can be used to define a small part of the behavior of a button. The rest of the behavior is defined in the `ButtonBase` class itself.

As the default property for the content control, you can omit the explicit `<Button.Content>` reference and simply nest the content as shown in the third example in the table. This property is available on all `ContentControl` elements, a category that naturally includes all `ButtonBase` elements such as the `Button`, `HyperlinkButton`, `RadioButton`, and `CheckBox` elements.

10.3.1 *The Button*

The traditional `Button` is a simple `ContentControl` that a user can click to perform an action. This control is defined by the `Button` class, which derives directly from the `ButtonBase` class. The `Button` automatically exposes the `Click` event. The thing that makes the `Button` class special is the default appearance it creates around the `Content`. This appearance and the syntax of a `Button` are shown in listing 10.1.

Listing 10.1   The syntax for a button

Result:

XAML:
```
<Button x:Name="myButton" Content="Save" Height="30" Width="90" />
```

As you can see, the buttons in table 10.6 are slightly more complex than the one shown in this example, but it's intended to show only the basic syntax and look of a `Button`. This appearance includes a small container that makes a Silverlight `Button` look similar to the buttons seen in other technologies. This container is designed to hold a `Button` element's `Content`. Occasionally, you may want this `Content` to behave more like a hyperlink. For these situations, you should look to the `HyperlinkButton`.

10.3.2 *The HyperlinkButton*

The `HyperlinkButton` control is designed to create a button that looks and behaves like a hyperlink. This behavior is provided through two publicly visible properties called `NavigateUri` and `TargetName`, which are shown here:

```
<HyperlinkButton x:Name="myHyperlinkButton"
  Content="Search in a New Window"
  NavigateUri="http://www.live.com"
  TargetName="_blank" />
```

The `HyperlinkButton` control uses the `NavigateUri` property to determine which page to load. By default, this `Uri` will be loaded in the current window, forcing your Silverlight application to unload. As you can imagine, this side effect may not be desirable. But, you can take control of this behavior with the `TargetName` property.

The `TargetName` property is a `string` that represents the name of the frame or window to load the `NavigateUri` within. By default, the `TargetName` value will be an empty `string`. You can use any of the values in table 10.9 to create the intended experience.

Table 10.9   The acceptable options for the `TargetName` property

Target Value	Description
`_blank`, `_media`, or `search`	Launches the URL specified in the `NavigateUri` property in a new browser window
`_parent`, `_self`, or `top`	Loads the URL specified in the `NavigateUri` property in the current browser window

This table describes the values that can be assigned to the `TargetName` property. If you happen to assign an unrecognized value to the `TargetName` property, one of two things will happen. If the value has one or more whitespace characters, an `InvalidOperationException` will be thrown. Alternatively, if the `TargetName` doesn't have any whitespace characters, the `NavigateUri` will load in a new window. It's important to remember that, despite its behavior as a hyperlink, the `HyperlinkButton` is still a type of button.

The `HyperlinkButton` class derives from the `ButtonBase` class; it still acts like a button and supports the `Click` event. In the case of a `HyperlinkButton`, the `Click` event will fire before the `NavigateUri` is evaluated so you can dynamically change the location of the `NavigateUri` just before it gets loaded. In addition, this event can be useful for performing cleanup operations if you're redirecting the user away from your Silverlight application.

10.3.3 *The RadioButton*

A `RadioButton` represents a choice within a group of options. For instance, imagine having to choose your favorite pizza topping or flavor of ice cream. Each of these situations requires one and only one choice to be selected. To properly deliver this kind of functionality, you need to familiarize yourself with the selection and grouping behaviors of the `RadioButton`.

RADIOBUTTON SELECTION

A `RadioButton` is a kind of `ToggleButton`. A `ToggleButton` represents a button that can change states. For a `RadioButton`, this state can change between a checked state and the default unchecked state. The state can be set at design time through the Boolean-based `IsChecked` property, the value of which affects both behavior and appearance, as shown in listing 10.2.

Listing 10.2 The default appearances of a checked and unchecked `RadioButton`

Result:

What is your favorite flavor of ice cream?
- ⊙ Chocolate
- ○ Vanilla
- ○ Chocolate Chocolate
- ○ More Chocolate

XAML:

```xaml
<StackPanel>
    <TextBlock Text="What is your favorite flavor of ice cream?" />
    <RadioButton Content="Chocolate"
                 IsChecked="true" />
    <RadioButton Content="Vanilla"
                 IsEnabled="False"/>
    <RadioButton Content="Chocolate Chocolate" />
    <RadioButton Content="More Chocolate" />
</StackPanel>
```

This example shows four answers for a single question, one of which is disabled. You can see that the first option is selected by default when the application starts. Note also that it's chocolate. If it's not chocolate, it's not a dessert.

Once a `RadioButton` has been selected, it can't be unselected by clicking it again. A `RadioButton` can only be unselected by using one of two approaches: set the `IsChecked` property to `false` at runtime using code or selecting a different `RadioButton` within the same group.

RADIOBUTTON GROUPING

A grouping of `RadioButton` items represents the choices available for a single situation. In the previous listing, you saw a `StackPanel` that grouped together a couple of ice cream flavor choices. These choices were grouped because the `StackPanel` was the immediate parent of both of the `RadioButton` items. A problem begins to emerge if you add unrelated `RadioButton` items to the scenario. For these situations, you use the `GroupName` property.

The `GroupName` property allows you to control how `RadioButton` elements are grouped together. By default, this string-typed property is set as an empty string, indicating there's no group. Because of this, all `RadioButton` elements with a direct parent will belong to the same group. By explicitly setting this property, you can control the groupings. You can even do this for `RadioButton` elements that share the same parent, as shown in listing 10.3.

Listing 10.3 Manually controlling RadioButton grouping

Result:

What is your favorite flavor of ice cream?
◉ Chocolate
◯ Vanilla

What is your favorite pizza topping?
◯ Green Peppers
◯ Onions
◉ Pepperoni

XAML:

```
<StackPanel>
  <TextBlock Text="What is your favorite flavor of ice cream?" />
  <RadioButton Content="Chocolate" IsChecked="true" />
  <RadioButton Content="Vanilla" />

  <TextBlock Padding="0,15,0,0"
    Text="What is your favorite pizza topping?" />
  <RadioButton Content="Green Peppers" GroupName="pizza" />
  <RadioButton Content="Onions" GroupName="pizza" />
  <RadioButton Content="Pepperoni" IsChecked="true"
               GroupName="pizza" />
</StackPanel>
```

The listing shows how the GroupName property can be used to force RadioButtons to work together. A close relative of the radio button, but one that doesn't handle mutually exclusive choices and, therefore, needs no grouping, is the CheckBox.

10.3.4 *The CheckBox*

The CheckBox control enables a user to select whether an option is chosen. Unlike the RadioButton, the CheckBox control allows you to select multiple elements that belong to the same grouping so you could do something like select multiple pizza toppings (see listing 10.4).

Listing 10.4 A basic CheckBox setup

Result:

Please select your favorite pizza toppings:
☑ Green Peppers
☐ Onions
☑ Pepperoni

XAML:

```
<StackPanel>
  <TextBlock Text="Please select your favorite pizza toppings:" />
  <CheckBox Content="Green Peppers" IsChecked="true" />
  <CheckBox Content="Onions" />
  <CheckBox Content="Pepperoni" IsChecked="true" />
</StackPanel>
```

Selecting multiple CheckBox elements at the same time is possible because the Check-Box isn't bound to a specific group. In fact, the CheckBox does little more than extend the ToggleButton class. Because the CheckBox does extend the ToggleButton class, you can use three-state checkboxes by switching the IsThreeState bool property to true. What happens to the IsChecked property? Well, this property is actually a nullable type so it also supports three states. These states and the look of a three-state CheckBox are shown in listing 10.5.

Listing 10.5   Using three-state mode with the CheckBox control

---

Result:

☐ Unchecked
☑ Checked
⊟ Indeterminate

XAML:

```
<StackPanel>
  <CheckBox IsThreeState="True" IsChecked="False" Content="Unchecked" />
  <CheckBox IsThreeState="True" IsChecked="True" Content="Checked" />
  <CheckBox IsThreeState="True" IsChecked="" Content="Indeterminate" />
</StackPanel>
```

Listing 10.5 shows the look and syntax of a three-state CheckBox. The fact that the CheckBox can support three different states demonstrates one way in which Silverlight is an improvement over HTML. Another improvement is found in the flexibility of the ContentControl class in general. This class was discussed at the beginning of section 10.2 and can be used in the CheckBox, RadioButton, HyperlinkButton, and Button controls. In addition, the flexibility of the ContentControl can be used with Silverlight's item controls.

In this section, we discussed the controls derived from the ButtonBase class that represent buttons available within Silverlight. Often, these controls are used to trigger an action. Occasionally, you may need to provide to present a list of items rather than a single item. This type of functionality can be delivered through an ItemsControl.

10.4   ItemsControls

An ItemsControl is a type of control designed to show a collection of items. This control exposes the collection of items through a publicly visible property called Items. This property represents an ItemsCollection where each element in the collection is some kind of object. This object can be added at design time through XAML or at runtime through code. Three controls in the Silverlight API are descendents of the ItemsControl class: the ListBox, the ComboBox, and the TabControl.

Though you'll most often use one of its derived classes, the base ItemsControl can be used whenever you want to present a list of items and don't need any selected item tracking. You'll get similar results from using a StackPanel but, if you need to bind items, the ItemsControl is the way to go.

The ItemsControl adds a few properties above and beyond what you would get from a regular Control. These properties are shown in table 10.10.

Table 10.10   Key ItemsControl members

Member name	Description
Items	The collection of items to be displayed in the control
ItemsPanel	The panel to be used to display the items
	By default, this is a StackPanel, but you could change it to a WrapPanel or anything else you'd like.
ItemsSource	Used in binding, this is the source of the items, typically a collection.
ItemTemplate	The data template used to display a single item

We'll show these properties in use with the ListBox, ComboBox, and TabControl. But they could be just as easily used with a plain old ItemsControl.

10.4.1 The ListBox

The ListBox is one of the most commonly used items controls. Though much of its functionality is directly inherited from ItemsControl, it adds the important distinctions of exposing a selected item and including scrolling in its default template. This control enables you to show multiple items from a collection of items at the same time. If there are more items than the space allowed for the control, the ListBox will display scrollbars to allow scrolling through the content. An example of this scrolling feature as well as the syntax of a ListBox is shown in listing 10.6.

Listing 10.6   A ListBox that displays the days of the week

Result:

Sunday, June 1
Monday, June 2
Tuesday, June 3
Wednesday, June 4
Thursday, June 5

XAML:
```
<ListBox x:Name="myListBox">
  <ListBox.Items>
    <ListBoxItem><TextBlock Text="Sunday, June 1"/></ListBoxItem>
    <ListBoxItem><TextBlock Text="Monday, June 2"/></ListBoxItem>
    <ListBoxItem><TextBlock Text="Tuesday, June 3"/></ListBoxItem>
    <ListBoxItem><TextBlock Text="Wednesday, June 4"/></ListBoxItem>
    <ListBoxItem><TextBlock Text="Thursday, June 5"/></ListBoxItem>
  </ListBox.Items>
</ListBox>
```

This `ListBox` uses the `Items` property to load options at design time. You also have the option of binding to a data source to make this list of items more dynamic. Binding to a data source will be covered in the next chapter. Regardless of whether you're binding to a data source or defining items at design time, each item in the control is a `ListBoxItem`. A `ListBoxItem` is a type of `ContentControl` so you can use any visual tree you want for an item, as shown in listing 10.7.

Listing 10.7 Using a `ListBoxItem` as a `ContentControl`

Result:

XAML:

```
<ListBox x:Name="myListBox">
  <ListBox.Items>
    <ListBoxItem>  #A
      <StackPanel Height="80" Orientation="Horizontal">
        <Canvas Width="87" Height="77">
          <Image Source="http://www.silverlightinaction.com/month.png" />
          <TextBlock Width="77" TextAlignment="Center" FontFamily="Arial"
            FontWeight="Bold" FontSize="32" Padding="30" Text="1" />
        </Canvas>
        <TextBlock FontFamily="Arial" FontWeight="Bold" FontSize="44"
          Padding="20">Sunday</TextBlock>
      </StackPanel>
    </ListBoxItem>
    <ListBoxItem>  #A
      <StackPanel Height="80" Orientation="Horizontal">
        <Canvas Width="87" Height="77">
          <Image Source="http://www.silverlightinaction.com/month.png" />
          <TextBlock Width="77" TextAlignment="Center" FontFamily="Arial"
            FontWeight="Bold" FontSize="32" Padding="30" Text="2" />
        </Canvas>
        <TextBlock FontFamily="Arial" FontWeight="Bold" FontSize="44"
          Padding="20">Monday</TextBlock>
      </StackPanel>
    </ListBoxItem>
    <ListBoxItem> #A
      <StackPanel Height="80" Orientation="Horizontal">
        <Canvas Width="87" Height="77">
          <Image Source="http://www.silverlightinaction.com/month.png" />
          <TextBlock Width="77" TextAlignment="Center" FontFamily="Arial"
            FontWeight="Bold" FontSize="32" Padding="30" Text="3" />
        </Canvas>
        <TextBlock FontFamily="Arial" FontWeight="Bold" FontSize="44"
          Padding="20">Tuesday</TextBlock>
      </StackPanel>
    </ListBoxItem>
```

```
<ListBoxItem>                                        ◁—— ListBoxItem
  <StackPanel Height="80" Orientation="Horizontal">
    <Canvas Width="87" Height="77">
      <Image Source="http://www.silverlightinaction.com/month.png" />
      <TextBlock Width="77" TextAlignment="Center" FontFamily="Arial"
        FontWeight="Bold" FontSize="32" Padding="30" Text="4" />
    </Canvas>
    <TextBlock FontFamily="Arial" FontWeight="Bold" FontSize="44"
      Padding="20">Wednesday</TextBlock>
  </StackPanel>
</ListBoxItem>
</ListBox.Items>
</ListBox>
```

This listing shows a `ListBox` control with much richer `ListBoxItem` elements than those shown in listing 10.6. Ultimately, one of the main reasons for using a `ListBox` is to enable your users to select an item from it. Luckily, the `ListBox` exposes some properties for this.

Selector controls

The `ListBox` and `ComboBox` are two controls that inherit from `Selector`. `Selector` enhances `ItemsControl` by adding the `SelectedIndex` and `SelectedItems` properties, as well as the underlying infrastructure to manage them. If you want to create your own `ListBox`-like class, such as a dedicated carousel control or perhaps a simple menu, you should probably inherit from `Selector` as your starting point.

The `ItemsControl` by itself can be useful to show a list of elements on a page as long as you don't need to support the selection of one of those items. Note that, unlike `ListBox`, it doesn't include scrolling in its presentation.

The `ListBox` exposes two properties and an event—`SelectedIndex`, `SelectedItem`, and `SelectionChanged`, respectively—all of which help you handle item selection. The `SelectedIndex` is a zero-based `int` that reflects the index of the currently selected item in the `ListBox`. If no item is selected, this property will return –1. Even more informative is the `SelectedItem` property, which returns the current selection in `object` form. This property type is a powerful improvement over the value/text property of items in HTML. Regardless, whenever an item is selected, whether by the user or programmatically, the `SelectionChanged` event will fire. This event, as well as the `SelectedItem` and `SelectedIndex` properties, is also available on the `ComboBox`.

10.4.2 *The ComboBox*

The `ComboBox` gives users the ability to select a single option from a list of choices. These choices are visible to a user as long as the `ComboBox` is in an open state, which is set when a user interacts with a `ComboBox`. Alternatively, this state can be set programmatically through the `IsDropDownOpen` property. This `bool` property is by default set to `false` so a `ComboBox` starts in a compacted, closed state, as shown in listing 10.8.

> **Listing 10.8 A `ComboBox` that has been used to select an item**

Result:

> Monday, June 2

XAML:

```
<ComboBox x:Name="myComboBox" Height="28" Width="180">
  <ComboBox.Items>
    <ComboBoxItem><TextBlock Text="Sunday, June 1"/></ComboBoxItem>
    <ComboBoxItem><TextBlock Text="Monday, June 2"/></ComboBoxItem>
    <ComboBoxItem><TextBlock Text="Tuesday, June 3"/></ComboBoxItem>
    <ComboBoxItem><TextBlock Text="Wednesday, June 4"/></ComboBoxItem>
    <ComboBoxItem><TextBlock Text="Thursday, June 5"/></ComboBoxItem>
  </ComboBox.Items>
</ComboBox>
```

Listing 10.8 shows the appearance of a closed `ComboBox`. As you can see, this control delivers a compact approach for displaying a list of items. In fact, this control resembles the `DropDownList` found in ASP.NET and the `select` element used in HTML. But, unlike those controls, each item in the `ComboBox` can have a fully customized appearance; each item is a `ComboBoxItem`, which happens to be a kind of `ContentControl`. This fact enables you to recreate the list shown in listing 10.7 in the more compact form of a `ComboBox`.

The `ComboBox` also provides three members that make it unique from the other list controls. The first member is a `double` property called `MaxDropDownHeight` that allows you to customize the maximum height of the drop-down list. The second member is an event named `DropDownOpened` that fires when the drop-down list is shown. The third member is an event that triggers when the drop-down list closes. This event is called `DropDownClosed`. Collectively, these three members make the `ComboBox` special—they won't be found on the third and final type of `ItemsControl`, the `TabControl`.

10.4.3 The TabControl

The `TabControl` is another `ItemsControl` available within Silverlight. This `ItemsControl` is designed to show multiple content items in the same physical space on the screen using a tab metaphor to switch between them. Each of these pieces of content is defined within a `TabItem`, which happens to be a `ContentControl`. Because of this, you can define the complete visual tree for each `TabItem`. Before you can do this, you must reference the `System.Windows.Controls` assembly. The tab-related controls are extended controls like the `GridSplitter` mentioned in chapter 7, so the `sdk` prefix will be used once again throughout this section, as shown in listing 10.9.

Listing 10.9   The basic syntax of a `TabControl`

Result:

My Grocery List

Apples

Bananas

Grapes

XAML:

```
<UserControl x:Class="Listing10_9.Page"
  xmlns="http://schemas.microsoft.com/winfx/2006/xaml/presentation"
  xmlns:x="http://schemas.microsoft.com/winfx/2006/xaml"
  xmlns:sdk="http://schemas.microsoft.com/winfx/2006/xaml/presentation/sdk"
  Width="400" Height="300">
  <StackPanel x:Name="LayoutRoot" Background="White"
    HorizontalAlignment="Left">
    <TextBlock Text="My Grocery List" />
      <sdk:TabControl x:Name="myTabControl" Height="200" Width="240">
        <sdk:TabItem>
          <ListBox>
            <ListBoxItem Content="Apples" />
            <ListBoxItem Content="Bananas" />
            <ListBoxItem Content="Grapes" />
          </ListBox>
        </sdk:TabItem>
        <sdk:TabItem>
          <StackPanel Orientation="Vertical">
            <ListBox>
              <ListBoxItem Content="Beef" />
              <ListBoxItem Content="Pork" />
              <ListBoxItem Content="Chicken" />
            </ListBox>
            <TextBlock TextWrapping="Wrap" Width="200"
              Text="NOTE: You may want to pick up some barbeque sauce." />
          </StackPanel>
        </sdk:TabItem>
      </sdk:TabControl>
    </StackPanel>
</UserControl>
```

This listing shows an entire page, which includes a basic `TabControl`. Because `TabControl` is an extended control and is part of the `System.Windows.Controls.dll`, we've shown the entire page's XAML to demonstrate the use of the `ext` namespace. Now that you can use a `TabControl`, it's important to understand the behavior of the headers.

Each of the tab headers in listing 10.9 is hardly visible because each header is set by a `TabItem` property called `Header`. This property represents the `object` used when rendering the `Header`, so you should consider using some `UIElement` such as a `Panel` for the Header. Listing 10.10 shows a TextBlock used for one Header and a Stack-Panel for the other.

Listing 10.10 Customizing the header of a TabItem

Result:

My Grocery List

XAML:
```
<StackPanel x:Name="LayoutRoot" Background="White"
            HorizontalAlignment="Left">
  <TextBlock Text="My Grocery List" />
  <sdk:TabControl x:Name="myTabControl" Height="200" Width="240">
    <sdk:TabItem Header="Fruits">
      <ListBox>
        <ListBoxItem Content="Apples" />
        <ListBoxItem Content="Bananas" />
        <ListBoxItem Content="Grapes" />
      </ListBox>
    </sdk:TabItem>
    <sdk:TabItem>
      <sdk:TabItem.Header>
        <StackPanel Orientation="Horizontal">
          <Image Source="http://www.silverlightinaction.com/meat.png" />
          <TextBlock Text="Meats" />
        </StackPanel>
      </sdk:TabItem.Header>
      <StackPanel Orientation="Vertical">
        <ListBox>
          <ListBoxItem Content="Beef" />
          <ListBoxItem Content="Pork" />
          <ListBoxItem Content="Chicken" />
        </ListBox>
        <TextBlock TextWrapping="Wrap" Width="200"
          Text="NOTE: You may want to pick up some barbeque sauce." />
      </StackPanel>
    </sdk:TabItem>
  </sdk:TabControl>
</StackPanel>
```

This shows a TabControl with two TabItem elements. Each element has a Header. Note that, if a TabItem has its Header property set, the HasHeader property of the TabItem will change to true. This bool property defaults to false and is useful in the event you need to check whether a TabItem has a header at runtime. For situations where you want to change the location of the tabs, there's another property.

The TabStripPlacement property determines how the tabs align in relation to the tab content area. This property represents an enumeration that can be set to Bottom, Left, Right, or Top. By default, this property value is set to Top on a TabControl.

The TabControl, ComboBox, and ListBox represent three ItemsControl elements available in Silverlight. ItemsControl elements give you the flexibility to allow a user to select from any kind of content. ItemsControls are the key type of control to use whenever you need to display lists of content: menus, list boxes, tab strips, carousels, and more.

Together with the content controls such as Buttons, the ItemsControls help make up the majority of the user interface elements you'll use in Silverlight. Chances are, if you create your own custom control, it'll derive from one of those core types.

Creating your own custom controls is a deep topic, and one that will need to wait for the discussion of styling, templating, binding, and the Visual State Manager—all covered in later chapters. But there's one type of control you can create that doesn't require all this additional complexity. In fact, it was designed for simple reuse and UI composition of existing controls such as those we've discussed in this chapter. That type of control is the UserControl.

10.5   *Creating UserControls*

There may be times when none of the controls provided within Silverlight contain the functionality you need. For these situations, you may want to consider creating a *reusable control*. A reusable control can be useful when you want something more than UI enhancements. After all, these types of enhancements can be provided with the style and template features discussed in chapter 23. A reusable control allows you to reuse functionality not found in a preexisting control. For instance, imagine wanting to create a TextBox that can be locked by a user and looks like figure 10.1.

Figure 10.1   A TextBox that can be locked

This figure shows a control that provides functionality beyond a basic TextBox. This control adds an image that projects whether the TextBox can be edited. Although the desired functionality is easy to implement, you may not want to recreate it every time; this provides an excellent opportunity to create a reusable control. Now, imagine wanting to name this control LockableTextBox to use it in other projects. To do this, you must create an instance of the UserControl class.

UserControls are intended for simple reuse. You want to be able to compose a control in the designer but not to worry about enabling templating or other advanced control functionality. We'll discuss templating in greater detail in section 23.3 but, for now, understand that the template for a UserControl is the XAML file you create with it.

The UserControl type itself is similar to ContentControl. Like ContentControl, it can have only a single item of content in the Content property. In the default item template in Visual Studio, that content is a grid, as shown in listing 10.11.

Listing 10.11   The default UserControl template

```
<UserControl x:Class="SilverlightApplication36.LockableTextBox"
  xmlns="http://schemas.microsoft.com/winfx/2006/xaml/presentation"
  xmlns:x="http://schemas.microsoft.com/winfx/2006/xaml"
```

```
xmlns:d="http://schemas.microsoft.com/expression/blend/2008"
xmlns:mc="http://schemas.openxmlformats.org/markup-compatibility/2006"
mc:Ignorable="d"
d:DesignHeight="300" d:DesignWidth="400">

<Grid x:Name="LayoutRoot" Background="White">        <---- Content

</Grid>
</UserControl>
```

If they're so similar, why doesn't the UserControl derive directly from ContentControl? The ContentControl type allows you to provide a custom template for the Content. In a UserControl, that would be redundant because the content template is the XAML file created when you created the UserControl.

The UserControl also provides compile-time code generation for all the named (using x:Name) elements in the XAML file. The InitializeComponent function, called from the constructor, handles associating the elements in the XAML file with the generated properties. There's no magic; the code is simply loading the associated XAML using the equivalent of XamlReader.Load, then calling FindName for each expected element, and assigning the result to the named property.

You could do this in your own code if you preferred to. If you create the more flexible but marginally more difficult custom controls, you'll perform many of these steps.

The UserControl class is designed to represent a new control or extend an existing one. This class gives you the ability to organize small portions of a UI into more manageable components, which can then be used in your application or shared with other applications. The process to provide this kind of functionality involves:

1 Defining the appearance of the control.
2 Defining the behavior of the control.
3 Calling the control.

This three-step process forms the ABCs of user-control development (Appearance, Behavior, and Call). Over the course of this section, as you create a LockableTextBox, you'll see how these three steps relate to one another.

10.5.1 *Defining the appearance*

Defining the appearance of a UserControl involves creating the XAML for the user interface. This process is the same as defining the UI for a page in Silverlight because every page in Silverlight is a UserControl. The XAML for the UserControl (LockableTextBox) is shown in listing 10.12.

Listing 10.12 The user interface for the LockableTextBox UserControl

```
<UserControl x:Class="MyClassLibrary.LockableTextBox"
  xmlns="http://schemas.microsoft.com/winfx/2006/xaml/presentation"
  xmlns:x="http://schemas.microsoft.com/winfx/2006/xaml"
  Width="400" Height="300">
  <StackPanel x:Name="LayoutRoot" Orientation="Horizontal">
    <TextBox x:Name="myTextBox" Height="24" Width="120" />
    <Image x:Name="myImage" Height="24"  Margin="5,0,0,0"
```

```
          Cursor="Hand" MouseLeftButtonUp="myImage_MouseLeftButtonUp"
       Source="http://www.silverlightinaction.com/unlocked.png" />
   </StackPanel>
</UserControl>
```

This listing shows the XAML that makes up the default appearance of the Lockable-
TextBox. This UI defines a TextBox and an Image within a StackPanel. The Stack-
Panel is important because, as we discussed, each UserControl can have only one
UIElement as a child, so you'll almost always use one of the Panel elements discussed
in chapter 7 as the content of a UserControl.

   Also note that, in order to make the control truly reusable, we've put it into a separate Silverlight class library project named MyClassLibrary. This project is referenced
from our main Silverlight application.

   Setting the Content of a UserControl is an important first step in creating a reusable control. This step defines the static parts of the UI, but the real value in creating a
reusable control is to provide some kind of new functionality. This functionality is generally delivered when you define the behavior of a control.

10.5.2 *Defining the behavior*

The functionality of a reusable control is also known as the control's *behavior*. This
behavior is defined in the code-behind file of the XAML file, which will contain a class
that derives from the UserControl class. It's your responsibility to make sure this class
provides the events, methods, and properties that detail the behavior of the control.
Look at the code for the LockableTextBox control shown in listing 10.13. This listing
uses a DependencyProperty, which was covered in chapter 2.

> **Listing 10.13 The LockableTextBox class definition (C#)**

```
public partial class LockableTextBox : UserControl
{
  public LockableTextBox()
  {
    InitializeComponent();          ◁─── InitializeComponent
  }

  private void myImage_MouseLeftButtonUp(object sender,
    MouseButtonEventArgs e)
  {                                       │ Toggle on
    IsLocked = !this.IsLocked;    ◁───────┘ mouse click
  }

    public void UpdateUI()         ◁───┐ Worker
  {                                    │ function
    if (IsLocked)
    {
      myImage.Source = new BitmapImage(
        new Uri("http://www.silverlightinaction.com/locked.png",
        UriKind.Absolute));
    }
    else
```

```
    {
      myImage.Source = new BitmapImage(
        new Uri("http://www.silverlightinaction.com/unlocked.png",
        UriKind.Absolute));
    }
    myTextBox.IsReadOnly = IsLocked;
}
public bool IsLocked                          ◄─── CLR property wrapper
{
    get { return (bool)(GetValue(IsLockedProperty)); }
    set { SetValue(IsLockedProperty, value); }          Dependency
}                                                          property

public static readonly DependencyProperty IsLockedProperty =   ◄───
    DependencyProperty.Register(
      "IsLocked",
      typeof(bool),
      typeof(LockableTextBox),
      new PropertyMetadata(new PropertyChangedCallback(OnIsLockedChanged))
      );

private static void OnIsLockedChanged(DependencyObject o,    ◄─── Changed
    DependencyPropertyChangedEventArgs e)                          handler
{
    LockableTextBox textBox = (LockableTextBox)(o);
    textBox.UpdateUI();
}
}
```

This class includes the call to `InitializeComponent` inside the constructor. If left out, our control references (to the textbox and the image, for example) would be null at runtime.

The class also includes the creation of a `DependencyProperty` for `IsLocked`. We introduced dependency properties in chapter 2, but let's dive a bit deeper into what's required to create them in your own class.

REGISTERING DEPENDENCY PROPERTIES

To register a property as a `DependencyProperty`, you must call the statically visible `DependencyProperty.Register` method. This method requires the name of the CLR wrapper, the type of the property value, and the type of the object that owns the property. Listing 10.14 shows how to register the `IsLocked` property.

Listing 10.14 Registering a `DependencyProperty` with the property system

C#:
```
public static readonly DependencyProperty IsLockedProperty =    ◄─
    DependencyProperty.Register(
      "IsLocked",              ◄─── Property        DependencyProperty
      typeof(bool),                  name
      typeof(LockableTextBox),
      new PropertyMetadata(                    ◄─── On change
          new PropertyChangedCallback(OnIsLockedChanged))   callback
    )
```

```
public bool IsLocked                                    CLR property
{                                                       wrapper
  get { return (bool)(GetValue(IsLockedProperty)); }
  set { SetValue(IsLockedProperty, value); }
}
```

This listing shows how to register a property as a DependencyProperty. Note the name of the DependencyProperty itself. This name can be anything, but it generally follows a naming template of *[CLR Wrapper Name]Property*. This DependencyProperty serves as a key in the property dictionary used by the GetValue and SetValue methods of a CLR property wrapper. Also note the fourth parameter, which allows you to define behavioral aspects and automatically respond to property value changes.

While the rest of the runtime uses the dependency properties directly, the CLR property wrapper is required because it's used by direct property assignments in XAML or from your own code. Note that, unlike a normal CLR property, you'll assign the value to and read it from the dependency property system. In addition, you won't perform any other logic in the setter; you'll do that inside the changed callback instead.

RESPONDING TO PROPERTY VALUE CHANGES

Dependency properties have the ability to automatically respond to property value changes in a way that you determine. To stay connected with a value change, the PropertyChangedCallback passes along a DependencyPropertyChangedEventArgs instance, which gives you three properties to help you react to a change as necessary. These three properties are described in table 10.11.

Table 10.11   The properties of the DependencyPropertyChangedEventArgs structure

Property	Description
NewValue	The value of the property after the change has completed
OldValue	The value of the property before the change has completed
Property	The DependencyProperty that triggered the change

This table shows the properties of the DependencyPropertyChangedEventArgs structure. This structure is associated with the dependency property that was changed. To get the object that this property is associated with, you must rely on the first parameter passed from the PropertyChangedCallback. This parameter represents the DependencyObject whose property value was changed, so you'll most likely need to perform a conversion, as shown here:

```
private static void OnIsLockedChanged(DependencyObject o,
    DependencyPropertyChangedEventArgs e)
{
    LockableTextBox textBox = (LockableTextBox)(o);
    textBox.UpdateUI();
}
```

This example shows the event handler for the `PropertyChangedCallback` delegate specified earlier. As you can see, this is an event handler that updates the user interface of the `UserControl`. This optional event handler completes the implementation for the `IsLocked` dependency property.

At first glance, it seems that a lot of additional coding is associated with creating a dependency property. But, considering the fact that only dependency properties can be animated or used in styling, it's clear that understanding dependency properties is an important part of `UserControl` development. Once the behavior of a `UserControl` is completed, you can use the control by calling it.

10.5.3 *Calling the control*

To include a `UserControl` in your application, you must do two things. First, you must add an XML namespace that references the location of the `UserControl`. Then, you must add an instance of that control within your XAML. These two steps are the same for any `UserControl`. Listing 10.15 shows how to reference the `LockableTextBox` control built over the past two sections.

Listing 10.15 Using the `LockableTextBox`

```
<UserControl x:Class="MySilverlightApp.Page"
  xmlns="http://schemas.microsoft.com/winfx/2006/xaml/presentation"
  xmlns:x="http://schemas.microsoft.com/winfx/2006/xaml"
  xmlns:my="clr-namespace:MyClassLibrary;assembly=MyClassLibrary"      ◁──┐
  Width="400" Height="300">                              Namespace definition │
  <StackPanel x:Name="LayoutRoot" Margin="10">
    <my:LockableTextBox x:Name="myLockableTextBox" />       ◁─── LockableTextBox
  </StackPanel>
</UserControl>
```

This snippet shows how to add the `LockableTextBox` to a basic Silverlight page. The `my` namespace is used to tell Silverlight where to look for the `LockableTextBox` definition. This definition is used to build the control, which is referenced later. That's all there is to it.

Creating a reusable control in Silverlight is as simple as defining a `UserControl` that consists of an appearance and a behavior. These two items generally represent a small component within a Silverlight application. Alternatively, a `UserControl` can represent a component as large as an entire page. This fact is important because it can affect how you decide to share your content.

`UserControls` are intended for simple reuse. They're great for those times when you need to compose a number of existing elements and reuse them within your application. But they're generally not the best approach for creating controls for broader reuse, which often require binding support and styling flexibility. In those instances, you need to create a custom control, which we'll cover in chapter 24—once we get binding, styling, and visual state management under our belts.

10.6 Summary

The `Control`, `ContentControl`, and `ItemsControl` types form the base for almost everything you'll interact with on a page in Silverlight.

The `Control` is a basic type, providing core interaction logic for controls. The `ContentControl` expands upon that base to provide a type of control that can hold a single item of content. The Button-based controls derive from `ContentControl`.

`ItemsControls` are the place to turn to should you ever need to create or use a control that shows a list of items. Remember, it doesn't need to be a traditional list; it could be something like a tab strip, or a carousel, or even a menu. In all of those cases, the `ItemsControl` base type provides the binding and templating support you need to work with lists of items.

The intent behind the first part of this chapter was to provide enough background so that you can both understand how existing controls function and apply that knowledge to new controls as they appear. New Silverlight controls appear almost daily, but they're almost always variations on one of the control models shown here.

In the last part of this chapter, we introduced the concept of a `UserControl`. `UserControls` are great for your own simple reuse scenarios, but you'll also find them handy for creating pages and encapsulating data templates. Though you may never create your own `LockableTextBox` control, you certainly will work with `Pages` and the other Silverlight items based on the humble `UserControl`.

Several times in this chapter, I mentioned the concept of binding. Binding is one of the most important concepts in Silverlight, especially when you start working with controls and templates; we'll cover it next.

Part 2

Structuring your application

Once you move beyond the basics, it's important to consider how you architect applications. Effective use of binding and patterns such as MVVM (or ViewModel) is key for ensuring that your application can be both designed and tested. Along with the binding system, features such as annotations and validation help to reduce the code burden while maximizing reuse. Controls such as the DataGrid and DataForm build upon binding, annotations, and validation to make UI work a breeze.

Networking is a key component of a structured Silverlight application. If you want to access data on a server, you'll need to use a service. We'll discuss how to use the underlying networking stacks, traditional web services, sockets, and advanced services.

A key component of structure is the organization of the pages as seen by the user. The Navigation Framework enables you to integrate with browser navigation to properly handle deep linking and browser history. We wrap up this part with an extensive look at WCF RIA Services using a business application template that builds on the navigation template. RIA Services pulls together the rest of the section including networking, navigation, binding, validation, and many of the other topics.

Binding

11

This chapter covers

- Mastering binding with a binding source
- Binding UI elements together
- Using value converters
- Creating data templates

If I included a top-three list of the most important features to learn in-depth in Silverlight or WPF, binding would be on that list. Binding—specifically, data binding—tends to conjure up images of the old Visual Basic VCR control bound directly to tables in an Access database, mishandled lost-focus events, and circular validation problems. In more recent times, binding tends to be associated with specialized data controls on web forms. In both cases, binding is associated with traditional business or application data on its way to or from a persistent data store.

Though binding is most commonly thought of in relation to persistent application or business data, it's used for much more than that in Silverlight and WPF.

In Silverlight and WPF, you can bind properties such as IsEnabled to bool values hanging off any arbitrary object. You can also bind controls to each other so that, for example, a slider controls the z-axis rotation of an object in 3D space. Neither of those properties (IsEnabled or z rotation) would normally be thought of as "data" in a data binding sense but, in the strictest sense of the term, they are.

Want to show the number of characters entered in a TextBox? You guessed it: binding will help you do that with no code required.

What if you want to set up a ListBox so each item displays a photo on the left along with a name and description stacked on the right? Binding and data templates are essential for that type of user interface customization.

In chapter 16, when we cover the ViewModel pattern, you'll see just how essential binding can be for good application architecture. Throughout this chapter, we'll prepare the foundation by covering the mechanics of binding the input controls we discussed in chapter 10 with in-memory objects, as well as how to bind controls to each other. Then, because data may come in any format, you'll learn how to format and convert it using value converters and binding expressions. Finally, we'll end the chapter with a discussion about data templates.

11.1 *Binding with your data*

Binding is a powerful way to create a connection between your UI and a source of data. This simple technique can be used to create a clean separation between your user interface and its underlying data and is essential for good application architecture, as we'll see in chapter 16. Regardless of the reason, you can use data binding in your application by creating an instance of the Binding class.

The Binding class is used to define a connection between a CLR object and a UI component. This connection is defined by three essential elements: the source of the data (the CLR object), the binding mode, and the target for the data (the dependency property; see section 2.1.4 for more information). These three items are part of a conceptual model that explains binding, which is shown in figure 11.1.

This illustration uses the situation of binding the current time of day to a TextBox to give a high-level overview of what data binding looks like. This conceptual binding sets the Text property of a TextBox to the current TimeOfDay. To create a binding like this, you must use one of the two available binding syntaxes. These syntaxes require you to define both the source and the target of a binding. Each approach is appropriate at a different time, so we'll cover each in its own right in section 11.1.1. Once you've decided which syntax is appropriate for your situation, you must decide how data can pass between the source and the target. This is the responsibility of the BindingMode, which will be covered in section 11.1.2.

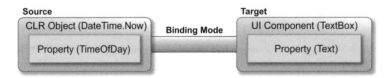

Figure 11.1 A conceptual view of data binding. The source owns the data; the target operates on (displays, edits, and so forth) the data.

11.1.1 *Mastering the binding syntax*

Silverlight gives you the ability to create a `Binding` using two different approaches. The first approach allows you to dynamically create a binding at runtime. The second gives you the opportunity to specify a binding at design time. Either way, the scenario from figure 11.1 will be used to show both approaches.

BINDING AT RUNTIME

Binding to a data source at runtime is a common approach used in event-driven application development. For instance, you may decide to display a list of basketball games based on a date selected by a user. Or, you may decide to show the current time when an application is loaded. Either way, creating a `Binding` at runtime follows a common pattern, which is shown here. First, the XAML in the page:

```
<TextBox x:Name="myTextBox" />
```

Next the code to create the binding source and the binding itself:

```
DateTime currentTime = DateTime.Now;
Binding binding = new Binding("TimeOfDay");
binding.Source = currentTime;
binding.Mode = BindingMode.OneWay;
myTextBox.SetBinding(TextBox.TextProperty, binding);
```

This shows how to bind the value of a CLR property to a UI element at runtime. The preceding code binds the current time of day to the `TextBox` created in XAML. You first retrieve the `DateTime` object that represents the current moment in time. This object is then bound to the UI element (the `TextBox`) in just four lines of code. These four lines of code specify the source, the binding mode, and the target of a binding.

The source of a binding is made up of two codependent items that specify which property of a CLR object to bind to. The name of the property to bind to is set when you create a `Binding` instance through the constructor. This constructor takes a single `string` parameter, which represents the name of the property to bind to. This property belongs to a CLR object that must be associated with a `Binding` through the `Source` property. Once this happens, the source of the binding is officially set. You can then choose a `BindingMode`, which we'll cover in section 11.1.2 (in this case, `OneWay`). Once the source and binding mode have been set, you need to turn your focus to the target.

The target element of a binding will always derive from the `DependencyObject` class. Virtually every visual element in Silverlight can be a target because the `DependencyObject` class exposes a method called `SetBinding`. This method associates a target property, which must be a dependency property, with a `Binding` instance. After this method is called, the source will be bound to the target.

Occasionally, you may want to unbind a data source. Fortunately, data binding can be halted by manually setting the target property of a binding. For example:

```
myTextBox.Text = "Binding Removed";
```

This feature is only available at runtime because that's the only time it makes sense. Using a `Binding` at runtime is a powerful option. Equally as powerful and more often used is the ability to create a `Binding` at design time in XAML.

BINDING AT DESIGN TIME

Binding to a data source at design time is a common feature in declarative markup languages such as XAML. You've probably seen the power of this data-binding approach if you've used ASP.NET or WPF. If you haven't, don't worry. In essence, this approach allows you to keep your code separate from its presentation so that you can take advantage of the developer/designer workflow available within Silverlight. It also helps to keep your code clean and maintainable, as seen in this markup:

```
<TextBox x:Name="myTextBox" Text="{Binding TimeOfDay, Mode=OneWay}" />
```

This shows how to create a binding at design time in XAML. The binding is associated with a target through the use of the XAML markup extension syntax, which uses curly braces ({}). These braces, along with the use of the Binding extension name, inform a property that a data source will be bound to it. This data source will be a CLR object that has a TimeOfDay property, which may provide or receive a value, depending on the binding mode. The other properties associated with the binding are set using a *propertyName=propertyValue* syntax (Mode=OneWay).

The curly brace syntax is helpful, but it's simply shorthand. We'll use the shorthand syntax throughout XAML in the rest of this book, but it can be helpful to understand the fuller version of the syntax. For example, the longer form (using property element syntax) of the earlier TextBox binding is this:

```
<TextBox x:Name="myTextBox">
  <TextBox.Text>
    <Binding Path="TimeOfDay" Mode="OneWay" />
  </TextBox.Text>
</TextBox>
```

The markup in this example does exactly the same thing as the previous but doesn't invoke the markup extension triggered by the curly brace. Obviously, the syntax is much more verbose and would be cumbersome to use for all values. If Silverlight ever gets MultiBinding (a concept currently in use in WPF), understanding the full binding syntax will be essential to its use.

> **NOTE** All parameters in a binding expression may be set using name=value syntax. The binding expression {Binding TimeOfDay} is just shorthand for {Binding Path=TimeOfDay}. Though you'll find that certain tools, such as Expression Blend and Visual Studio 2010, prefer one syntax over the other, both may be used interchangeably and are equally valid.

When creating a binding in XAML, the source may be set in procedural code. This code is responsible for setting the context in which a data source can be used via the appropriately named DataContext property. This property will be explained in further detail in section 11.2.2. For now, know that this is how a CLR object can be bound to a DependencyObject. In this case, the code-behind would have the following code to set the DataContext for the TextBox:

```
DateTime currentTime = DateTime.Now;
myTextBox.DataContext = currentTime;
```

The DataContext may also be set in markup using a StaticResource, if the type being used supports it. This approach is sometimes used for binding to a view model, which we'll see in chapter 16.

Binding at design time is a valuable option when it comes to working with data. It empowers you to separate UI from code. This functionality allows a designer to enhance a UI without worrying about where the data is actually coming from. In a similar light, binding at runtime enables you to create a more dynamic form of data binding. Regardless of where you define the binding, both approaches define a bridge between a source and a target. Data can flow in multiple directions across this bridge. To control the direction of that flow, you must learn about the various binding modes.

11.1.2 Choosing a binding mode

The Binding class gives you the ability to determine how data can flow between the source and the target. This flow can be controlled by setting the Binding instance's Mode property. This property represents one of the three options available in the BindingMode enumerator—OneTime, OneWay, and TwoWay.

ONETIME

The OneTime option sets the target property to the source property when a binding is initially made. When this BindingMode is used, any changes to the data source won't be automatically sent to the target. Instead, the target will be set only when the source is initialized, as shown in figure 11.2.

This figure shows the simplistic nature of the OneTime BindingMode. As you can imagine, this BindingMode is appropriate in situations where you only care about the initial value of a property. For instance, you may want to display the creation date of a database record. Because this value shouldn't change, the OneTime BindingMode is a great choice. For property values that will change such as the date/time when a database record was last modified, you may want to use the OneWay binding option.

ONEWAY

The OneWay BindingMode is the default when you create a Binding. This option gives you the ability to automatically receive changes from a source property. Whenever the binding source property changes, the target property will automatically change, but the source property won't change if the target is altered. This process is shown in figure 11.3.

This figure shows how the OneWay BindingMode works at a high level. Think of the speedometer in your car as a OneWay binding from your gas pedal. When you press or release the gas pedal, the speedometer changes; but, if you somehow changed the value of the speedometer itself, your gas pedal wouldn't change. This inability to send

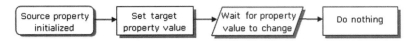

Figure 11.2 A conceptual view of OneTime binding to a data source. The value is initially read from the source and is never updated again.

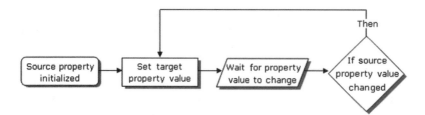

Figure 11.3   A conceptual view of OneWay **binding to a data source. The value is updated each time the source changes, but changes to the value in the target control don't make it back to the source.**

a change from the target back to the source shows how OneWay binding works. For situations where you do want to send changes in the target back to the source, you use the TwoWay option.

TWOWAY

TwoWay binding enables two properties that are bound to change each other. This may sound recursive, but it's not. A TwoWay binding changes the target when the source changes. If the target changes, the source is updated. This process can be seen in figure 11.4.

This figure shows a conceptual view of the TwoWay binding. This binding approach is useful for data entry forms using Silverlight because forms generally allow users to add as well as edit data. This process of editing the preexisting data practically begs for TwoWay binding.

The TwoWay BindingMode is one of the options available to control the flow of your data. The other alternatives are available through the OneWay and OneTime options. Collectively, these options are an important part of setting up a binding.

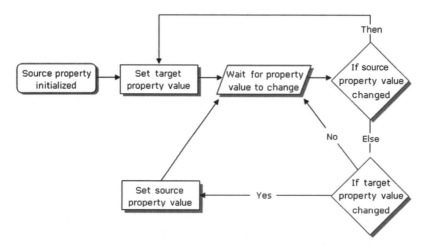

Figure 11.4   A conceptual view of TwoWay **binding to a data source. The target control reflects changes to the source, and the source is updated with any changes made in the target.**

After the target and binding mode have been selected, you need to choose an appropriate source.

11.2 Understanding your binding source

In section 11.1, we looked at the general concept of binding. We discussed this concept in the limited scope of binding to an individual property. This approach can be valuable in certain situations but, to truly harness the power of data binding, we must build a better understanding of data sources, which we'll do over the course of this section.

We'll discuss what it takes to bind to a property of a CLR object, but we won't cover just any property. We've already done that. Instead, we'll discuss what it takes to bind to properties in your CLR objects and how to bind to entire CLR objects. We'll cover how to bind UI elements to each other and how to bind a UI element to itself. We'll close out the section by talking about binding to entire collections of objects. Collectively, these items will help you to wield the power of binding.

11.2.1 Binding to a property

Silverlight gives you the flexibility to bind to any CLR property you want. You saw this with the examples using the `TimeOfDay` property in section 11.1. Significantly, if you visited http://www.silverlightinaction.com and ran the application, you saw that, once the time was displayed, it just sat there. It didn't automatically update with each passing second because, by default, CLR properties don't broadcast their changes—that and because the `TimeOfDay` property doesn't automatically continue ticking. To update the target with a change in the CLR property, you must create a *change-notification handler.*

A change-notification handler notifies a binding target that a change has been made. This enables a target to automatically respond to changes. Dependency properties already have this feature built in, but CLR properties don't. If you want your CLR properties to broadcast their changes, you must implement the `INotifyProperty-Changed` interface, which is demonstrated in listing 11.1.

Listing 11.1 Implementing the `INotifyPropertyChanged` interface (C#)

```
public class Emoticon : INotifyPropertyChanged
{
  public event PropertyChangedEventHandler PropertyChanged;

  private string _name;
  public string Name
  {
    get { return _name; }
    set
    {
      _name = value;
      NotifyPropertyChanged("Name");
    }
  }

  private ImageSource _icon = null;
  public ImageSource Icon
```

PropertyChanged event

INotifyPropertyChanged interface

```
  {
    get { return _icon; }
    set
    {
      _icon = value;
      NotifyPropertyChanged ("Icon");
    }
  }

  public Emoticon(string name, string imageUrl)
  {
    _name = name;
    _icon = new BitmapImage(new Uri(imageUrl));
  }

  public void NotifyPropertyChanged(string propertyName)
  {
    if (PropertyChanged != null)
    {
      PropertyChanged(this,
        new PropertyChangedEventArgs(propertyName));      <--- Notification
    }
  }
}
```

Listing 11.1 shows how to implement the System.ComponentModel namespace's INotifyPropertyChanged interface on a class. This class represents an emoticon (such as a smiley face) that uses the INotifyPropertyChanged interface as a guide for broadcasting changes in property values. The interface can be used to ensure that your UI component and desired CLR property are in sync during OneWay and TwoWay binding. This synchronization effort will take effect as long as you've implemented the PropertyChanged event.

The PropertyChanged event is what keeps things in sync, so you must make sure this event is triggered whenever a property value has changed. You can accomplish this by firing the event in a property's setter. Alternatively, if you plan on keeping multiple properties in sync, you may want to refactor the PropertyChanged event to a common method—as shown in listing 11.1. Either way, the binding system's PropertyChanged event handler uses reflection to examine the value of a property and pass it on to the binding target. This is why the PropertyChangedEventArgs type takes a string parameter that represents the name of the CLR property that changed.

Binding to a CLR property is a powerful way to work with your objects. These objects generally represent real-world entities that may also need to be bound to. Fortunately, Silverlight also provides an elegant way to bind to a CLR object.

11.2.2 *Binding to an object*

Up to this point, we've primarily focused on binding individual properties to UI components. This technique is pretty simple, but it can also be somewhat tedious if you need to bind multiple properties of an object to a UI. You can make this task less tiresome by using the DataContext property.

The `DataContext` property allows you to share a data source throughout a DependencyObject. This data source can be used by all the child elements of a `Dependency-Object` that define a `Binding`. `Binding` uses the most immediate ancestor's `DataContext` unless another data source is set to it. If another data source is set, that source is used for the `Binding`. Either way, by relying on the `DataContext` of an ancestor, you can easily bind several properties of an object to a UI. This approach is shown in listing 11.2.

Listing 11.2 Binding an `Emoticon` object to a `Grid`

XAML:

```xaml
<UserControl x:Class="Chapter011.MainPage"
  xmlns="http://schemas.microsoft.com/winfx/2006/xaml/presentation"
  xmlns:x="http://schemas.microsoft.com/winfx/2006/xaml">

  <Grid x:Name="LayoutRoot" Background="White">        ⟵── LayoutRoot
    <Grid.RowDefinitions>
      <RowDefinition Height="Auto" />
      <RowDefinition Height="Auto" />
    </Grid.RowDefinitions>
    <Grid.ColumnDefinitions>
      <ColumnDefinition />
      <ColumnDefinition />
    </Grid.ColumnDefinitions>
    <TextBlock Text="Name:" />
    <TextBlock Text="Image:" Grid.Column="1" />
    <TextBox Text="{Binding Name, Mode=TwoWay}" Grid.Row="1" />
    <Image Source="{Binding Icon}" Grid.Row="1" Grid.Column="1" />
  </Grid>
</UserControl>
```
Binding statements

C#:

```csharp
Emoticon emoticon =
  new Emoticon("Smiley Face",
    "http://www.silverlightinaction.com/smiley.png");
LayoutRoot.DataContext = emoticon;
```
LayoutRoot's DataContext

Listing 11.2 shows how an object can be bound to elements within a DependencyObject. The `TextBox` and `Image` elements in this example show their intent to bind to two different properties of an object. These elements don't have their `DataContext` property set in the code behind, so the elements look to their immediate parent, `myGrid`, and try to use its `DataContext`. This `DataContext` has been set in the codebehind. The object assigned to the `DataContext` serves as the data source for the `Grid` and its children. If the `DataContext` of the `Grid` hadn't been set, the elements would've continued up the tree and checked the `UserControl` element's `DataContext`. If that `DataContext` were set, it would've been used. Either way, this example shows how much more succinct and maintainable the `DataContext` approach can be.

So far, our examples have fallen squarely in the zone we tend to think of as traditional data binding. But, Silverlight also supports the ability to bind controls to each other simply as a way to reduce plumbing code.

Setting the DataContext in XAML

In the previous section, I mentioned that you can set the data context using a static resource, all from within XAML. Though the `DateTime` example didn't fit that model, the `Emoticon` example can.

Recall from chapter 2 that XAML is, in essence, a way to represent and initialize CLR objects in markup. To support binding this way, we'll add in a resources section (covered in chapter 23), which holds a reference to a single `Emoticon` object in the `local` namespace:

```
<UserControl x:Class="Chapter011.MainPage"
  xmlns="http://schemas.microsoft.com/winfx/2006/xaml
 /presentation"
  xmlns:x="http://schemas.microsoft.com/winfx/2006/xaml"
  xmlns:local="clr-namespace:Chapter11">
  <UserControl.Resources>
    <local:Emoticon x:Key="emoticon"
      Name="SmileyFace"
      Icon="http://www.silverlightinaction.com/smiley.png"/>
  </UserControl.Resources>
```

The `Emoticon` in the resources section is initialized directly on the page when the rest of the elements are constructed. But as written, the `Emoticon` class requires parameters in its constructor, something that isn't supported in the .NET 4 version of XAML used by Silverlight 4. This is remedied by adding a default (parameterless) constructor to the class:

```
public Emoticon() {}
```

Finally, we set up the relationship via the `DataContext` using the `StaticResource` markup extension and referring to the `x:Key` of the resource that corresponds to our emoticon:

```
<Grid x:Name="LayoutRoot"
      DataContext="{StaticResource emoticon}" …
```

The end result is a binding relationship set entirely from within XAML in a tool and designer-friendly way. We'll see more examples of this when we look at .WCF RIA Services in chapter 17, and some of the optional XAML data source controls it provides.

11.2.3 *Binding to a UI element*

Binding one or more properties of a UI element to the values on an entity, view model, or business object is a compelling use of binding. Sometimes, though, you want to use binding for things we wouldn't traditionally consider "data"—things within the user interface. You may want to bind the height of two controls together so that they resize equally or perhaps you want to bind three sliders to the x, y, and z-axis rotations of a plane (see section 6.5 for more information on 3D rotation in Silverlight). Rather than binding to gather input or display data to the user, you're binding to avoid writing extra plumbing code.

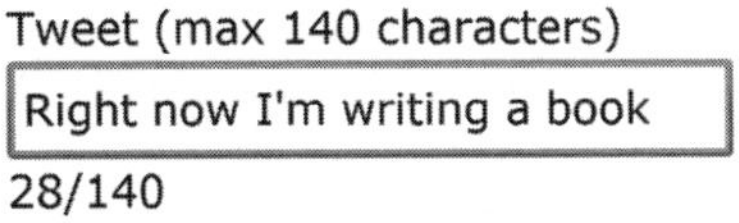

Let's say that you want to display a count of characters entered into a `TextBox` in real time, something like figure 11.5.

You could do that in code, but that would be fairly uninteresting code to write. It would need to refer to XAML elements by name or have event handlers wired in XAML, introducing a

Tweet (max 140 characters)

Right now I'm writing a book

28/140

Figure 11.5   Using element binding to count characters as you type into a `TextBox`

dependency on the specific page's code-behind and making it less portable and potentially more brittle. In addition, you'd find yourself doing it enough that you'd either wrap the `TextBox` in your own `CountingCharsTextBox` control or add a helper buddy class or something.

Or, if you prefer a XAML approach, which I hope I've sold you on by now, you would use *element binding* introduced in Silverlight 3. Element binding allows you to bind the properties of one `FrameworkElement` to another `FrameworkElement`. The usual restrictions apply (the target must be a `DependencyProperty`; the source must notify of changes), so you can't use element binding quite everywhere.

To produce the `TextBox` shown in figure 11.5 with the automatic count of characters using element binding, the markup is pretty straightforward and entirely self-contained:

```
<StackPanel Orientation="Vertical" Margin="50">
  <TextBlock Text="Tweet (max 140 characters)" />
  <TextBox x:Name="tweetText"
           MaxLength="140"
           Text="Right now I'm writing a book" />
  <StackPanel Orientation="Horizontal">
    <TextBlock Text="{Binding Text.Length, ElementName=tweetText}" />
    <TextBlock Text="/" />
    <TextBlock Text="{Binding MaxLength, ElementName=tweetText}" />
  </StackPanel>
</StackPanel>
```

This XAML will show a `TextBox` with a count of characters underneath it. The character count will update in real time to show the number of characters typed into the `TextBox`. Note also that the `MaxLength` displayed under the text box is actually coming from the `TextBox` itself (the 140 in the label is not, though). The key item that makes this happen is the `ElementName` parameter in the binding expression. `ElementName` is, as it suggests, the name of another element on the XAML page.

Sometimes, you'll want to bind two elements together, as we've done here. Other times, you may want to bind an element to a value on itself using something called *relative source binding*.

USING A RELATIVE SOURCE

WPF supports a number of different types of relative source bindings. In Silverlight, it's used for one thing: binding an element to itself. Let's assume for a moment that we have a simple property in our user control's code-behind. It could (and should) be a `DependencyProperty` but, to keep it short, we're going to declare a good old CLR property and assume it's set only in the constructor. We could then refer to that property in

XAML but, without somehow telling the binding system that the source of the data is the control hosting the XAML, we'd be stuck.

> **WARNING** Here be dragons. Relative source binding can not only encourage bad application practices, such as binding to things defined in code-behind instead of following a pattern such as ViewModel, but also be hard to debug, especially when you get into changes to DataContext set by external consumers of your user control. Use RelativeSource Self binding, but understand that your debugging workload will probably go up for the choice. Don't use RelativeSource Self binding just to avoid creating an appropriate container or abstraction for your data.

This is where RelativeSource Self binding comes in. RelativeSource can be set anyplace you'd normally have a binding statement, including the DataContext. Listing 11.3 shows how to bind a TextBlock in the UI to a simple CLR property in the code-behind.

Listing 11.3 Binding elements in XAML to properties in the code-behind

C# code-behind:
```
private string _pageTitle = "Page Title";
public string PageTitle
{
  get { return _pageTitle; }
  set { _pageTitle = value; }
}
```

XAML:
```
<UserControl x:Class="Chapter011.RelativeSource"
  xmlns="http://schemas.microsoft.com/winfx/2006/xaml/presentation"
  xmlns:x="http://schemas.microsoft.com/winfx/2006/xaml"
  DataContext="{Binding RelativeSource={RelativeSource Self}}">     ⟵  RelativeSource Self
  <Grid x:Name="LayoutRoot" Background="White">
    <TextBlock Text="{Binding PageTitle}" />     ⟵  Binding to property
  </Grid>
</UserControl>
```

RelativeSource Self binding is useful for those occasions when you really do need to bind to a property of the control or need to bind a property of a control to itself. Use it sparingly and not as a part of the overall application architecture and you'll find it helps enable those few scenarios where other solutions are just too cumbersome.

Another quiet addition to Silverlight binding is the ability to bind to a specific element in an array or list.

11.2.4 *Binding to an indexed element*

Silverlight 3 introduced the ability to bind to a numerically-indexed element in a collection. This can be useful in instances where you may have an indexed property bag hanging off a class or you really do want to get just a specific element out of a larger collection without prefiltering it in code.

Let's assume for a moment that we have a class `Repository` that exposes a collection of `Emoticon` objects through a property named `Emoticons`. We could then set up a static resource for pure XAML binding or set the `DataContext` from the page or within the code-behind, as shown in the previous examples. Once that's set up, we'd be able to refer to individual elements in the collection using the index syntax within the binding statement, as shown in listing 11.4.

Listing 11.4 Binding to a specific element in a collection, using a numeric index

C#:
```csharp
public class Repository
{
...
  private ObservableCollection<Emoticon> _emoticons;          Collection
  public ObservableCollection<Emoticon> Emoticons            to bind to
  {
    get { return _emoticons; }
  }
}
```

XAML:
```xaml
<UserControl.Resources>
  <local:Repository x:Key="repository" />
</UserControl.Resources>

<Grid x:Name="LayoutRoot"
  DataContext="{StaticResource repository}">             Indexed
                                                         binding
  <TextBlock Text="{Binding Emoticons[2].Name}" />
</Grid>
```

In listing 11.4, the `TextBlock` will resolve its text property to be the value in `repository.Emoticons[2].Name` and display that on the screen. The syntax is consistent with C# indexing conventions.

Binding to a single element in a collection using a numeric index in a binding expression is useful, but often we want to bind using a string key instead.

11.2.5 *Binding to a keyed (string indexed) element*

Property bags and datasets are commonplace in the desktop application world. Silverlight 4 introduced the ability to bind to these types of structures by introducing keyed or string-indexed binding expressions.

Listing 11.5 shows the same example as 11.4 but now the collection is being accessed via a string key.

Listing 11.5 Binding to a specific element in a collection, using a numeric index

C#:
```csharp
public class Repository
{
...
```

```
    private Dictionary<string, Emoticon> _emoticons;
    public Dictionary<string, Emoticon> Emoticons
    {
      get { return _emoticons; }
    }
}
```

⟵┐ **Collection
    to bind to**

XAML:

```
<UserControl.Resources>
  <local:Repository x:Key="repository" />
</UserControl.Resources>

<Grid x:Name="LayoutRoot"
  DataContext="{StaticResource repository}">

  <TextBlock Text="{Binding Emoticons[Smiley].Name}" />
</Grid>
```

┐ **Keyed/string-
⟵┘ indexed binding**

Listing 11.5 works assuming your `Emoticons` dictionary has an element with the key `Smiley`. This feature enables a ton of must-have scenarios in Silverlight, specifically around binding to the data of a shape unknown at design time.

Binding to a single element in a collection using a numeric index or string key in a binding expression is useful, but it's more common to bind to an entire collection rather than a single element within that collection. That's the situation you'll run into when you want to populate a `ListBox` or other `ItemsControl`.

11.2.6 *Binding to an entire collection*

Binding to a collection is an important task in a lot of applications. There are numerous times when you need to show a list of the items in a collection. You may want to display a collection of emoticons or you may want to show a list of the days of the week. Either way, these lists are made up of individual items, so it's only natural to use a control derived from `ItemsControl`.

An `ItemsControl` is a basic control used to show a collection of items. We discussed this control in chapter 10, but we didn't talk about the process of binding data to the control. Instead, you saw the manual approach of adding items one by one to the `Items` collection. Although this technique is useful in some situations, the `ItemsControl` provides a more elegant approach through the `ItemsSource` property (see listing 11.6).

Listing 11.6 Binding a collection of `Emoticon` objects to a `ListBox`

Result:

XAML:

```
<ListBox x:Name="myListBox" Height="100" />
```

C#:
```
List<Emoticon> emoticons = GetEmoticons();
myListBox.ItemsSource = emoticons;
```

This listing shows how to bind a collection of objects to an `ItemsControl`—in this case, a `ListBox` control (which derives from `ItemsControl`). Using the `ItemsSource` property, this `ListBox` loads a collection of `Emoticon` objects from our earlier examples using a function we'll assume exists in our code: `GetEmoticons`.

The `ItemsSource` property is used solely for the sake of data binding. This property can be used to bind to any collection that implements `IEnumerable`. This property is necessary because the `Items` collection of the `ItemsControl` class isn't a `DependencyProperty`, and only `DependencyProperty`-typed members have support for data binding.

The `ItemsSource` property can only be used if the `Items` collection of an `Items-Control` is empty. If the `Items` collection isn't empty, your application will throw an `InvalidOperationException` when you try to set the `ItemsSource` property. If you intend to use this property, you should also consider using the `DisplayMemberPath` property.

The `DisplayMemberPath` property determines which CLR property value to use for the text of a list item. By default, each list item will use the `ToString` method of the object it's bound to for the display text—the reason each of the items in listing 11.5 is shown as `MyLibrary.Emoticon`. You can override the `ToString` method to fully customize the text shown for an item. If you want to go a step further, you can customize the entire look of an item using the data template information discussed in section 11.3.2. But, for the quickest approach, you can use the `DisplayMemberPath` as shown in listing 11.7.

Listing 11.7 Using the `DisplayMemberPath` to improve the display of a list of items

Result:

XAML:
```
<ListBox x:Name="myListBox" DisplayMemberPath="Name" Height="100" />
```

C#:
```
List<Emoticon> emoticons = GetEmoticons();
myListBox.ItemsSource = emoticons;
```

This shows the impact of the `DisplayMemberPath` property on binding items. As you can see, this property makes the items in a list much more meaningful. This approach allows you to easily display information from a CLR property, an object, or a collection.

The approaches we've talked about so far work well when you need to bind a single value to a single property without modifying the display format of the values in any way. We covered how to bind to simple values, how to get individual values by index or key, and how to set the display member when it's different from the data member.

In the next two sections, we'll cover how to build upon what we learned in this section to customize the display of single values and aggregate several values up into a single data template to be repeated for each entry in a collection.

11.3 *Customizing the display*

As you saw throughout section 11.2, data binding is a powerful way to show data. Occasionally, this information may be stored in a format not suitable to display in a UI. For instance, imagine asking your user, "Does two plus two equal four?" This question clearly demands a yes or no response. The problem begins to arise when the response is saved to a more persistent data source.

A lot of times, a piece of data such as a property will be saved one way but need to be presented in another. In the case of a yes-or-no question, the answer may be stored in a `bool` CLR property. This property may run under the assumption that "yes" is equivalent to `true` and "no" is the same as `false`. This assumption can become a problem if you need to bind to that data because, by default, data binding calls a type's `ToString` method. Your users could see a statement that looks like "Does two plus two equal four? True." when, in reality, it'd be better to show "Does two plus two equal four? Yes." This small but common problem demands a better approach.

If Silverlight couldn't handle the simple task of formatting values for display, binding wouldn't be particularly useful. Luckily, Silverlight has everything you need to format display values, convert both inbound and outbound values, provide special handling for null values and even provide fallbacks for cases when binding fails. Throughout this section, you'll see how to customize the visual representation of your data using these powerful features, several of which are new to Silverlight 4.

11.3.1 *Formatting values*

When writing code, you can format values using the `string.Format` function. But until Silverlight 4, there was no good way to do the equivalent during a binding operation. You could write a custom value converter, but that gets old quickly, and becomes another testing and maintenance point.

Silverlight 4 introduced the ability to use string formatting when binding. The syntax is essentially the same as the `string.Format` function. For example, this will set the value of the `TextBlock` to be "DOB: May 19, 2007" assuming the `DateOfBirth` property on your binding source contains the value 5/19/2007:

```
<TextBlock Text="{Binding DateOfBirth, StringFormat=DOB:\{0:D\}}" />
```

Similarly, this binding expression will set the value of the `TextBlock` to be $1,024.10 assuming the `decimal BilledAmount` field contains the value `1024.10m`:

```
<TextBlock Text="{Binding BilledAmount, StringFormat=\{0:C\}}" />
```

Sometimes, simply formatting the value isn't enough. In those cases, you may need to perform a real data conversion and write your own custom value converter.

11.3.2 *Converting values during binding*

Silverlight allows you to dynamically convert values during data binding. You can accomplish this by first creating a custom class that implements a value converter. This value converter can then be referenced directly in XAML. This approach is recommended over custom setter/getter code because it helps keep the design separate from the code. Let's begin by discussing how to create a value converter.

CREATING A VALUE CONVERTER

To create a value converter, you must create a class that implements the `IValueConverter` interface, which enables you to create some custom logic that transforms a value. This transformation may take place in one of two methods depending on the flow of your data. The first method, `Convert`, is used when the data is moving from the source to the target—for example, from your object to a `TextBox`. If the data is flowing from the target back to the source, such as when the value entered in a `TextBox` goes back to your object, a method called `ConvertBack` is used. Both methods are members of the `IValueConverter` interface. This interface and its methods are demonstrated in listing 11.8.

Listing 11.8 A value converter that converts a Boolean to "`Yes`" or "`No`" (C#)

```
public class YesNoValueConverter : IValueConverter
{
  public object Convert(object value, Type targetType,          Convert
    object parameter, System.Globalization.CultureInfo culture)  function
  {
    bool isYes = bool.Parse(value.ToString());
    if (isYes)
      return "Yes";
    else
      return "No";
  }
  public object ConvertBack(object value, Type targetType,       ConvertBack
    object parameter, System.Globalization.CultureInfo culture)   function
  {
    string boolText = value.ToString().ToLower();

    if (boolText == "yes")
      return true;
    else if (boolText == "no")
      return false;
    else
      throw new InvalidOperationException("Please enter 'yes' or 'no'.");
  }
}
```

This listing shows a value converter that converts between a `bool` and Yes or No. This converter uses the `Convert` method when data is being bound to your UI. It's this method that converts a `bool` to Yes or No. When the UI is passing data back to its source (`TwoWay` binding), the `ConvertBack` method is used. This method converts Yes to `true` and No to `false`. These methods control the conversion process. To assist in this process, both these methods give you the opportunity to provide custom information.

Both the Convert and ConvertBack methods allow you to use two optional pieces of information. The first is an arbitrary object called parameter that can be used by your conversion logic. By default, this object will be null, but you can set it to any value that you find useful. The other piece of information specifies the CultureInfo object to use when converting the values. We'll discuss both parameters in a moment. But, to set the CultureInfo or pass along a custom parameter, you first must know how to use a value converter from markup.

USING A VALUE CONVERTER

Using a value converter involves setting the Converter property of a Binding object. This property determines which IValueConverter to use when transforming data. By default, this property isn't set to anything (null), but you can set it to reference an IValueConverter you've created. Before you can reference an IValueConverter, you must add it as a resource. Resources will be discussed in chapter 23. For now, just know that you can reference an IValueConverter by first adding it to the Resources collection, as shown here:

```
<UserControl x:Class="Chapter11_9.MainPage"
  xmlns="http://schemas.microsoft.com/winfx/2006/xaml/presentation"
  xmlns:x="http://schemas.microsoft.com/winfx/2006/xaml"
  xmlns:local="clr-namespace:Chapter11_9"
  Width="400" Height="300">

  <UserControl.Resources>
    <local:YesNoValueConverter x:Key="myConverter" />
  </UserControl.Resources>

  <Grid x:Name="LayoutRoot" Background="White" />
</UserControl>
```

This shows how to introduce a custom value converter to the XAML world. The local prefix is assumed to be defined as a namespace (see chapter 2). The key myConverter is used to reference the YesNoValueConverter in XAML. The following is an example of referencing a value converter:

```
<TextBlock x:Name="myTextBlock"
  Text="{Binding IsCorrect, Converter={StaticResource myConverter}}" />
```

This example shows a basic Binding that uses a custom converter. This converter alters the displayed text of a bool property called IsCorrect. The example shows that the custom converter is referenced through the Converter property. This property uses the curly-brace markup extension syntax just like the Binding syntax because it's the syntax used to reference a resource. You can also pass a custom parameter or the culture information if you need to.

> **TIP** A statement such as the binding statement shown in the previous example can seem to be a jumble of curly braces. Think of each matched set of braces as a separate statement, substituted in when parsed and evaluated. For example, the {StaticResource myConverter} statement is a complete StaticResource markup extension statement itself, the result of which, after evaluation, is passed in to the Converter parameter of the Binding statement.

The `Binding` class exposes an `object` property called `ConverterParameter`, which can be used to pass an arbitrary value to an `IValueConverter`. The value converter uses the value of the `ConverterParameter` in the `Convert` and `ConvertBack` methods. By default, this value is `null` but you can use it to pass along any data you want, such as a format string or an index. If you need to pass along culture-related data, we recommend using the `ConverterCulture` property.

The `ConverterCulture` property of the `Binding` class allows you to set the culture. This culture is passed along as a `CultureInfo` object that can be used by the `Convert` and `ConvertBack` methods. By default, the `CultureInfo` object reflects the value of the `Language` attribute of the calling `FrameworkElement`. The `Language` attribute is used for localization and globalization. This value uses a `string` that defaults to `en-US`, which represents U.S. English.

Value converter tricks

Value converters are powerful and allow you to extend binding to support scenarios not natively supported in Silverlight or let you manipulate object data for objects that may otherwise have schemas you can't touch.

For example, a colleague created a value converter that has a field name as a parameter and then implements binding to a dictionary of fields, much like a `DataSet`. At the time, Silverlight had no support for binding to indexed values, so this was a huge time-saver and allowed us to use existing business objects (which included a dictionary of additional values) in case we couldn't alter the implementation of the existing objects.

Since `MultiBinding` (the ability to bind two fields to a single control) isn't supported in Silverlight, in another instance we used a purpose-built value converter to combine all the address fields in an object into a single string to be displayed in a grid column. In that case, the binding source was the entire object and the value converter looked for specific fields in that object. The `ConvertBack` method was left empty in that case, since it supported only `OneWay` binding.

Though you don't want value converters to be the solution to all your binding woes (in many cases, an alternate design may serve you better), they're powerful enough to provide lots of options in situations where you may be otherwise tempted to write a bunch of code in your code-behind.

Creating and using a value converter can be valuable when working with data, as shown with our basic yes/no example. Value converters can be useful in even more complex scenarios. For instance, Silverlight doesn't have support for HTML tags in regular text controls, so you may consider using a value converter to scrub the HTML tags from a string before binding it to your UI.

Value converters were often used to format values for binding. We've already seen a way to format strings for display. Let's now look at how to handle fallback values and null value display.

11.3.3 *Providing default fallback values*

Things can go wrong during binding. The property path may be unable to be resolved or an exception may be thrown when getting the value. Perhaps the index or key doesn't exist. In those cases, it can be helpful to have a fallback value defined in your binding expression. These values are provided using the `FallbackValue` property.

In this example, assuming you have an `ApprovalCode` field in your object, but it throws an exception in the getter (odd, I know) or is otherwise unavailable, the `Text-Block` will display the value "Unavailable".

```
<TextBlock Text="{Binding ApprovalCode, FallbackValue=Unavailable}" />
```

In many cases, I think it's preferable to have default values and fallbacks defined in your model or view model, especially because that'll make it easier to test. But fallback values in binding can help in a pinch or in cases where you need to handle an exception condition happening between your view model and view.

More common than fallback values is custom null value handling.

11.3.4 *Handling null values*

Similar to fallback values but more useful, in my opinion, is the `TargetNullValue` property of the binding expression. `TargetNullValue` allows you to display a custom value when the value you've bound to is `null`.

In many applications, a value of `null` truly means something different than the value of empty or zero. In the former, it means that no value has been entered. The latter indicates that a value has been entered but it's blank or zero. To make it easier to work with, many applications disregard the `null` value and simply replace it with the default value for the type. This makes it easier to display in the UI, but at the cost of losing the distinction.

Starting with Silverlight 4, you can preserve the `null` value and still have a friendly UI. Simply provide a `TargetNullValue` in your binding expression:

```
<TextBlock Text="{Binding ApprovalCode, TargetNullValue=(missing)}" />
```

In this example, when the `ApprovalCode` returns null, the `TextBlock` will display the text "(missing)".

These techniques all handle the formatting and display of a single bound value. Though powerful on their own, often you'll want to display something more complex, perhaps containing multiple bound values in a list. That's where a data template comes into play. Happily, data templates build upon everything we've covered so far, so you'll find their implementation easy to understand.

11.4 *Creating data templates*

In section 11.2, we learned how to bind individual properties and entire collections. In section 11.3, we covered how to provide formatting and conversion for single-bound values. What about those cases when you need to have even more control over the presentation of your list-based data? What about something like a `ListBox` item that contains three or four pieces of data in each row? That's where data templates come in.

A data template is a way to define how a piece of information will be shown. Imagine looking at a baseball player's statistics. Although these statistics can be easily viewed in tabular format, it's much more interesting to look at them on a baseball card. For an example, see table 11.1.

Raw data (statistics)	Presentation via data template
Player: Scarpacci Position: Pitcher (P) Team: J-Force Picture: [A URL]	

Table 11.1 One example of a data template

This table demonstrates the general idea of a data template: it gives your data a face. The value in this approach is that it allows you to quickly change the way your data looks without changing your code—the main raison d'être for XAML. Just as baseball card designs change each year, your data may change its look based on its context. Data templates allow you to make this change easily, without affecting the underlying model. To take advantage of this feature, you must create a DataTemplate object.

A DataTemplate object describes the visual representation of a piece of information. This object can be used with two types of controls within the Silverlight class library. The first is a ContentControl. More interesting and probably more commonly used is the ItemsControl. Within this section, you'll see how to create a data template with each of these control types.

11.4.1 Using a DataTemplate with a ContentControl

A ContentControl is a type of control defined by a single piece of content, which we discussed in chapter 10. Every ContentControl exposes a property called Content-Template, which specifies the DataTemplate to use when displaying the content of a ContentControl. This content can be styled with a DataTemplate using an approach similar to that shown in listing 11.9.

Listing 11.9 A DataTemplate used with a ContentControl

Result:

XAML:

```
<Button x:Name="myButton" Height="70" Width="210">
  <Button.ContentTemplate>
    <DataTemplate>
      <StackPanel Orientation="Horizontal">
        <Image Source="{Binding Icon}" Height="40" Margin="10" />
        <TextBlock Text="{Binding Name}" FontSize="20"
          VerticalAlignment="Center" />
      </StackPanel>
    </DataTemplate>
  </Button.ContentTemplate>
</Button>
```

C#:

```
Emoticon emoticon = new Emoticon("Smiley Face",
  "http://www.silverlightinaction.com/smiley.png");
myButton.Content = emoticon;
```

This shows a DataTemplate applied to a Button. This DataTemplate is applied to an assumed Emoticon (from the previous examples in this chapter) assigned to the Button object's Content property. This property must be set at runtime when using a DataTemplate. If the Content property is set at design time, it'll be trumped by the DataTemplate, resulting in no data being shown in your UI. In addition, if you set the DataContext property at runtime instead of the Content property, your data won't be shown. When you're binding data to a ContentControl, you may want to remember the following:

- When assigning your data source to the DataContext property, use the binding syntax within the control's Content.

- When assigning your data source to the Content property, use a DataTemplate instead.

These two points make it seem like you're running in circles. You may be wondering why you should use a DataTemplate. Well, a DataTemplate can be defined as a resource (discussed in chapter 23), which makes it usable across multiple ContentControl elements simultaneously. The DataTemplate approach is much more flexible. In reality, you probably won't use a DataTemplate with a ContentControl often, but you should expect to use data templates frequently with ItemsControl elements.

11.4.2 *Rendering an ItemsControl with a DataTemplate*

The ItemsControl element is designed to display a collection of items, which are bound to a control through the ItemsSource property. By default, each item is displayed by using an object's ToString method. By setting the DisplayMemberPath property, you can use a specific CLR property for the text of an item, but you can go one step further using the ItemTemplate property.

The ItemTemplate property of the ItemsControl class allows you to fully control how each item will be displayed. This property uses a DataTemplate to determine how to show each item in an `ItemsControl`. A basic `ItemTemplate` for a collection of Emoticon objects is shown in listing 11.10.

This shows a basic `DataTemplate` associated with an `ItemTemplate`. There's nothing complex about this example—the main thing is to understand that this `DataTemplate` is used with the items bound through the `ItemsSource` property. In addition, this begins to show the power of using data templates.

> **Listing 11.10   An `ItemTemplate` used in an `ItemsControl`**

Result:

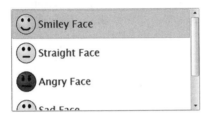

XAML:
```xaml
<ListBox x:Name="myListBox" Height="200">
  <ListBox.ItemTemplate>
    <DataTemplate>                              <----  DataTemplate
      <StackPanel Orientation="Horizontal">     <----  Child
        <Image Source="{Binding Icon}" Height="40" Margin="5" />
        <TextBlock Text="{Binding Name}" FontSize="20"
          VerticalAlignment="Center" />
      </StackPanel>
    </DataTemplate>
  </ListBox.ItemTemplate>
</ListBox>
```

C#:
```csharp
List<Emoticon> emoticons = GetEmoticons();
myListBox.ItemsSource = emoticons;
```

This example shows the `DataTemplate` assigned to the `ItemTemplate` property of the `ListBox` control. Note that a `DataTemplate` must have only one child, typically a panel. Within that panel you may have any number of other controls.

Data templates are a powerful way to use everything you've learned about binding to provide a top-notch customized display for your list-based data. In technologies before WPF and Silverlight, the idea of having complete control over what's displayed in a `ListBox` was a dream at best. Now, using binding and templates, it's an easy reality.

11.5   Summary

Throughout this chapter, you've seen the power of the `Binding` object and the vast tree of functionality that grows from it. This object gives you the flexibility to bind to individual entities, to collection of entities, to indexed entries in a collection, and even to other UI elements. If you need to massage the data either coming or going,

Silverlight provides a way for you to create your own value converters to do that. If you simply need to format the display, Silverlight provides a way for that too.

Throughout this chapter, you've seen how to fully customize the look of your data with data templates. Data templates are an amazingly powerful way to control the presentation of your list-based data.

Most importantly, you've seen binding in action. Binding rises to the near top of the most important topics to understand when getting into Silverlight. Once you master binding, you may find that you never again will write another line of `control.property = value` code.

Silverlight includes two complex and useful controls that were designed to work well with binding: the `DataGrid` and the `DataForm`. We'll discuss those in the next chapter.

Data controls:
DataGrid and DataForm

This chapter covers

- Learning about the `DataGrid`
- Turning the grid on its side with the `DataForm`
- Controlling binding display through attributes

In chapter 11, we covered binding. I believe binding to be one of the most important topics for Silverlight developers. One reason behind that is because the `DataGrid` and `DataForm`, as well as data annotations for display, all require binding in order to be useful.

Silverlight 2 included the `DataGrid`, and Silverlight 3 added the `DataForm` to the mix of data-centric controls. The `DataGrid` provides tabular Excel-like data view and editing. The `DataForm` is like a `DataGrid` rotated 90 degrees. Where the `DataGrid` is all about rows and columns for multiple visible entries, the `DataForm` is about fields and labels for a single visible entry.

Once we cover the `DataGrid` and `DataForm`, we'll see how to annotate properties with simple attributes to control display within the `DataGrid` and `DataForm`. We'll cover the related validation attributes in chapter 13.

When used together, the `DataForm`, `DataGrid`, and data annotations can form the heart of the user interface for any forms-over-data or business application and can save you a ton of implementation time. Of the three, the `DataGrid` is the most often used, so we'll start there.

12.1   The DataGrid

The `DataGrid` is a list-style control that belongs to the `System.Windows.Controls` namespace. This control provides capabilities for displaying a collection of entities in a tabular format. In addition, it enables users to add, edit, delete, select, and sort items from a binding data source. This data source is bound to a `DataGrid` through the `ItemsSource` property just like an `ItemsControl`, so the data binding features you've seen so far are applicable within the realm of the `DataGrid`. Before you can bind data to a `DataGrid`, you must first reference the correct assembly.

The `DataGrid` control is defined in its own assembly called `System.Windows.Controls.Data.dll`. This assembly can be found within the Silverlight SDK, which is available at www.silverlight.net. Note that the `DataGrid` control's assembly isn't part of the default Silverlight runtime installation; it's an extended control, so you must reference the `System.Windows.Controls.Data` assembly within your Silverlight application. The process of referencing an assembly like this was discussed in section 2.1.2. Part of this process involves choosing a prefix in order to use the control at design time.

Throughout this section, we'll use a prefix called `data`. Referencing the `DataGrid` control's assembly will package it up with your application, ensuring that your users can enjoy the power of the `DataGrid`.

Throughout this section, you'll experience the power of the `DataGrid`. You'll first see how easy it is to use the `DataGrid` to display data. From there, you'll learn how to leverage the built-in features to enable a user to edit the data within a `DataGrid`. Finally, you'll see how to empower your users to sort the data in a `DataGrid`.

12.1.1   Displaying your data

The `DataGrid` was designed to make displaying data easy. The easiest way to display data from an `ItemsSource` is to use the `AutoGenerateColumns` property. This Boolean property defaults to `true`, causing the content within the `ItemsSource` to be rendered in tabular format. This ability is demonstrated in listing 12.1.

Listing 12.1   The `DataGrid`—assume the `ItemsSource` property is set in code

Result:

Name	Icon
Smiley Face	System.Windows.Media.Imaging.BitmapImage
Straight Face	System.Windows.Media.Imaging.BitmapImage
Angry Face	System.Windows.Media.Imaging.BitmapImage
Sad Face	System.Windows.Media.Imaging.BitmapImage
Sick	System.Windows.Media.Imaging.BitmapImage

XAML:

```
<UserControl x:Class="Chapter12.MainPage"
  xmlns="http://schemas.microsoft.com/winfx/2006/xaml/presentation"
  xmlns:x="http://schemas.microsoft.com/winfx/2006/xaml"
  xmlns:data="clr-namespace:System.Windows.Controls;
      assembly=System.Windows.Controls.Data">

  <Grid x:Name="LayoutRoot" Background="White">
    <data:DataGrid x:Name="myDataGrid" />                    ◀──── DataGrid
  </Grid>
</UserControl>
```

C#:

```
List<Emoticon> emoticons = GetEmoticons();
myDataGrid.ItemsSource = emoticons;
```

Voilà! This example relies on the `System.Windows.Controls.Data` assembly to deliver the `DataGrid`. This `Control` instance relies on its default behavior to automatically create columns based on the data that it's bound to. This approach is the fastest way to show the data bound to a `DataGrid`, and it also has some details that are worth examining.

The `DataGrid` isn't an `ItemsControl`

The `DataGrid` takes advantage of a feature known as *UI virtualization*. UI virtualization means that only the items that are visible to the user are created in memory. This performance enhancement ensures that the `DataGrid` can support millions of rows of data. In Silverlight 2, the `ItemsControl` elements mentioned in chapter 10 didn't have support for UI virtualization. But, in Silverlight 3 and beyond, virtualization is built into some controls such as the `ListBox`.

Let's look at what makes a bound column tick. From there, you'll learn how to customize the columns, rows, and headers of a `DataGrid`.

EXPLORING BOUND COLUMNS

When the `AutoGenerateColumns` property is set to `true`, the columns in a `DataGrid` are automatically ordered and rendered based on the type of the underlying data. Regardless of the type of data, the column type will always derive from the abstract base class `DataGridBoundColumn`, which serves as the base for the two types shown in table 12.1.

This table shows the kinds of columns that can be automatically generated within a `DataGrid`. If you want to manually create a column, you can also use these types. But, when you're manually defining your columns, you must set the `Binding` property, which represents the `Binding` associated with a column (the property name and the type name are, in fact, the same). Because of this, you can use the `Binding` syntax explained in chapter 11. This `Binding` declaration may be necessary because by default, when you use a `DataGridBoundColumn`, a `TwoWay` binding is used.

The `DataGridBoundColumn` is one of the main types of `DataGrid` columns. The other main type is a `DataGridTemplateColumn`, which uses a `DataTemplate` to determine how

Table 12.1   The types of columns that can be automatically generated within a `DataGrid`

Type	Description
`DataGridTextColumn`	This type of column is used to display textual data. Most of the data from a binding source will be rendered in a `DataGridTextColumn` through calling the binding property's `ToString` method. This column type won't show the default Silverlight `TextBox`, but the rendered content can be edited as if it were in a visible `TextBox`.
`DataGridCheckBoxColumn`	This column type generates a `CheckBox` within a cell. When the `AutoGenerateColumns` property is `true`, any `bool` will be rendered using this column type.

to render the binding source. Note that every type of column that can be added to a `DataGrid` derives from the `DataGridColumn` class, which is used to represent the column of a `DataGrid`. Objects of this type can be manually added to a `DataGrid` at design time and managed at runtime.

MANUALLY WORKING WITH COLUMNS

The `DataGrid` can use any column that derives from `DataGridColumn`. These columns can be added to a `DataGrid` at design time through the `Columns` property. This approach is demonstrated in listing 12.2.

Listing 12.2   Manually adding columns to a `DataGrid`

Result:

XAML:

```
<data:DataGrid x:Name="myDataGrid" AutoGenerateColumns="False">
  <data:DataGrid.Columns>                                         ← Columns property
    <data:DataGridTextColumn Binding="{Binding Name, Mode=OneWay}" />
    <data:DataGridTemplateColumn>
      <data:DataGridTemplateColumn.CellTemplate>
        <DataTemplate>
          <Image Source="{Binding Icon}" />
        </DataTemplate>
      </data:DataGridTemplateColumn.CellTemplate>
    </data:DataGridTemplateColumn>
  </data:DataGrid.Columns>
</data:DataGrid>
```

This example shows how to add columns manually to a `DataGrid` at design time. These columns are added to the `Columns` property. The items of this read-only collection will be displayed in the order they appear in XAML, but you can change this through the `DisplayIndex` property.

The `DisplayIndex` property represents the position of a `DataGridColumn` in a `DataGrid`. This zero-based integer can be set at design time to override the default ordering approach. Alternatively, the `DisplayIndex` property can be set at runtime. This property makes it possible to create a truly dynamic `DataGrid`, but the dynamic features don't stop there. They also continue at the row level.

CUSTOMIZING THE ROWS

A row within a `DataGrid` will most likely represent a summarized view of an item. In these situations, it's not unusual to redirect the user to another page to get the details associated with the item, but the `DataGrid` provides the ability to display these details within the row itself. This approach can reduce the strain of waiting for another page to load for the user. To make this happen, you define the `RowDetailsTemplate`.

The `RowDetailsTemplate` is a `DataTemplate` that can be used to show the finer points of a specific row. This information may be shown if the `RowDetailsVisibilityMode` property is set accordingly. You'll learn more about that in a moment. For now, just assume that a row will show its details when a user selects it. When this occurs, the `DataGrid` will reveal the details using a smooth sliding animation. The details can take up as much or as little space as needed. To demonstrate how this works, imagine adding a `string` property called `Keys` to the `Emoticon` class defined earlier in this chapter. This property represents the keyboard shortcut to use for an emoticon. The `DataTemplate` for revealing this information is shown in listing 12.3.

Listing 12.3 Using the `RowDetailsTemplate` to show the per-item keyboard shortcut

Result:

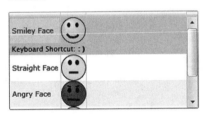

XAML:
```xml
<data:DataGrid x:Name="myDataGrid" AutoGenerateColumns="False"
  RowDetailsVisibilityMode="VisibleWhenSelected">      <⎯ RowDetailsVisibilityMode
  <data:DataGrid.Columns>
    <data:DataGridTextColumn Binding="{Binding Name, Mode=OneWay}" />
    <data:DataGridTemplateColumn>
      <data:DataGridTemplateColumn.CellTemplate>
        <DataTemplate>
          <Image Source="{Binding Icon}" />
        </DataTemplate>
      </data:DataGridTemplateColumn.CellTemplate>
    </data:DataGridTemplateColumn>
  </data:DataGrid.Columns>
```

```
      <data:DataGrid.RowDetailsTemplate>
        <DataTemplate>
          <StackPanel Orientation="Horizontal">
            <TextBlock Text=" Keyboard Shortcut: " FontSize="11" />
            <TextBlock Text="{Binding Keys}" FontSize="11" />
          </StackPanel>
        </DataTemplate>
      </data:DataGrid.RowDetailsTemplate>
    </data:DataGrid>
```
RowDetails Template

This shows how to use the RowDetailsTemplate property. This property uses a DataTemplate to display additional details about a row in a way dependent upon the value of the RowDetailsVisibilityMode property.

The RowDetailsVisibilityMode property determines when the details associated with a row are shown. By default, this property is set to Collapsed, but you can change this value to any option available within the DataGridRowDetailsVisibilityMode enumeration. This enumeration provides three options. All are shown in relation to the DataGrid with the emoticons (table 12.2).

This table shows the options available within the DataGridRowDetailsVisibilityMode enumeration. These options, coupled with the RowDetailsTemplate property,

Table 12.2   The options available within the DataGridRowDetailsVisibilityMode enumeration

Option	Example	Description
Collapsed		When this option is used, the content in the RowDetailsTemplate won't be shown.
Visible		This option forces the content in the RowDetailsTemplate to be shown for every row. The content will be shown regardless of user interaction.
VisibleWhenSelected		This option will show the content in the RowDetailsTemplate for each selected row.

give you the ability to customize the experience with item-level details. The `DataGrid` extends the same type of power to the column headers.

CUSTOMIZING THE HEADERS

The `DataGrid` gives you the ability to customize every part of it, including the headers. The headers of a `DataGrid` are split across two separate categories: row and column. By default, your `DataGrid` will show both, but you can control this by changing the `HeadersVisibility` property. This property uses one of the options available in the `DataGridHeadersVisibility` enumeration, which are shown in table 12.3.

Table 12.3   The options available through the `DataGridHeadersVisibility` enumeration

Option	Example	Description
All		This option displays both row and column headers. This is the default value.
Column		This option displays only the column headers.
None		This option displays neither the row nor column headers.
Row		This option displays only the row header.

The `DataGridHeadersVisibility` enumeration is used to set whether a header type is visible. You can also customize what the header looks like and how it behaves through the `DataGridColumn` class's `Header` property. This property simply represents the column header content, so it uses the same content-related information you've already learned about.

As you've seen, the DataGrid empowers you to fully customize how your data is presented. These customizations can be applied at the header, row, and column levels. Note that you don't have to make any of these adjustments. If you're looking for a quick way to show your data in a tabular format, you can rely on the fact that the AutoGenerateColumns property defaults to true. Either way, once your data is loaded, you can enable your users to edit the data directly within the grid.

12.1.2 *Editing grid data*

In addition to presenting data, the DataGrid has the ability to edit data. Users will be able to edit the contents of a DataGrid as long as the IsReadOnly property is set to false. By default it is, so your users have the flexibility to interact with their data in a familiar interface. As they do so, you can watch for the beginning of the editing process through two events. These events are triggered by the DataGrid and are called BeginningEdit and PreparingCellForEdit.

The BeginningEdit event gives you the opportunity to make last-minute adjustments just before users do their thing. In some situations, you may want to prevent a user from editing a cell due to previous inputs. For these occasions, the Beginning-CellEdit event exposes a bool Cancel property within its DataGridBeginningEdit-EventArgs parameter. By setting this property to true, the event will stop running. If the event does complete in its entirety, the PreparingCellForEdit event will also be fired.

The PreparingCellForEdit is fired when the content of a DataGridTemplateColumn enters the editing mode. This event exists to give you the opportunity to override any changes that may have been made in the BeginningEdit event. Once this event and/or the BeginningEdit event have completed without cancellation, users will be given the reins. After they're done editing the data in the DataGrid, they may decide they want to re-sort the data.

12.1.3 *Sorting items*

The DataGrid has built-in support for sorting collections that implement the IList interface. This interface is a part of the System.Collections namespace and is heavily used throughout the Silverlight .NET framework so you can readily sort almost any collection of objects. If you don't like the way that the DataGrid sorts your collection, you're free to customize the sorting by binding to a collection that implements the ICollectionView interface. Either way, the DataGrid can be used to sort these collections via the SortMemberPath property.

The SortMemberPath property is a string available on the DataGridColumn class, so this property can be used by any of the options shown in table 12.3. Regardless of which option you use, the user will be empowered to sort the column in either ascending or descending order, as demonstrated in listing 12.4.

Listing 12.4 Built-in `DataGrid` sorting

Result:

XAML:

```
<data:DataGrid x:Name="myDataGrid" AutoGenerateColumns="False">
  <data:DataGrid.Columns>
    <data:DataGridTextColumn Binding="{Binding Name}"
      Header="Name" SortMemberPath="Name" />
    <data:DataGridTextColumn Binding="{Binding Keys}"
      Header="Shortcut" SortMemberPath="Keys" />
    <data:DataGridTemplateColumn>
      <data:DataGridTemplateColumn.CellTemplate>
        <DataTemplate>
          <Image Source="{Binding Icon}" />
        </DataTemplate>
      </data:DataGridTemplateColumn.CellTemplate>
    </data:DataGridTemplateColumn>
  </data:DataGrid.Columns>
</data:DataGrid>
```

SortMemberPath

This snippet shows two `DataGridColumn` instances enabling the user to sort the underlying `ItemsSource`. The first `DataGridColumn` enables the user to sort the `Emoticon` objects by their `Name` property. The other `DataGridColumn` lets the user sort by the `Keys` property. If the user were to select a column header, it would first be sorted in ascending order. Then, if the column header were to be selected again, it would be sorted in descending order. The `SortMemberPath` property is what makes this feature of the `DataGrid` possible.

As you've just seen, the `DataGrid` has an incredibly rich development model. This model is important because it can help you assist your users in their data entry tasks, which may include editing data or simply viewing it. Either way, the `DataGrid` provides the ability to efficiently deliver items from a data source in a tabular format.

The `DataGrid` is great for tabular data, but what do you do when you want similar functionality in a form-based layout model? New in Silverlight 3 and originally considered part of WCF RIA Services (covered in chapter 17), the `DataForm` is the `DataGrid`'s form-based counterpart.

12.2   The DataForm

Silverlight 3 introduced a control that does for forms what the `DataGrid` does for lists: the `DataForm`. The `DataForm` can be thought of as a single-row `DataGrid` turned on its side. It shares similar capabilities in that it can be read-only or editable and can infer column names and edit controls based on the types bound to it. Like the `DataGrid`, it also provides full customization of the representation of each of the bound fields.

Like the `DataGrid`, the `DataForm` can work with multiple rows of data. The presentation differs in that you'll see only one row at a time, as is typical in a details form. In fact, the `DataGrid` and `DataForm` are sometimes used together to show a master-detail relationship where the `DataGrid` contains all the records and the `DataForm` is used to show an editable form for the `DataGrid` row.

The `DataForm` was originally developed for Silverlight by the same team that brought us WCF RIA Services. In order to support continued iteration on the control, it was moved from the SDK, where the now-mature `DataGrid` resides, and placed in the Silverlight Toolkit in the `System.Windows.Controls.Data.DataForm.Toolkit` assembly. The Silverlight Toolkit can be thought of as an agile extension of the Silverlight SDK, with the bonus that you have access to the source code for the controls and tests it contains.

Though not all applications will use the `DataForm`, it's much richer and more customizable than it initially appears. Virtually any forms-over-data application can use this control to show a UI that can be as simple as a list of fields or as complex as a customized layout with specific field styles, sizes, and positioning. How it looks is up to you.

In this section, we'll take a tour through the capabilities of the `DataForm`, starting with a simple binding to a single object and then to a collection of objects. Next, we'll work with the command buttons for canceling updates and submitting data. Once we have the functional mechanics down, we'll customize the display of fields using properties and then using richer data templates for the edit, add, and display modes. The section will wrap up with a discussion of `IEditableObject` and how that interface can make working with the `DataForm` even easier.

12.2.1 *Displaying your data*

The easiest thing to do with the `DataForm` is to bind it to an object and watch it generate all the fields you need. We'll step away from the `Emoticon` class for the remaining examples here to show the breadth of controls the `DataForm` understands. Let's create a new simple `Person` class, as shown in listing 12.5. (The `Required` attribute, used in this class, will be covered in chapter 13, which focuses on validation.)

Listing 12.5 The `Person` class

```
public enum MaritalStatus
{
    Unknown,
    Married,
    Single,
    Divorced
}

public class Person
{
    [Required]
```

```
        public string LastName { get; set; }
        [Required]
        public string FirstName { get; set; }
        public bool IsRegistered { get; set; }
        public MaritalStatus MaritalStatus { get; set; }
        public DateTime DateOfBirth { get; set; }
        [Required]
        public string EmailAddress { get; set; }
        [Required]
        public int NumberOfChildren { get; set; }
}
```

We'll then bind to it in XAML using a static resource, much as we have in other examples. Instead of individual controls, we'll use the entire object as our data source for the new DataForm control, as shown in listing 12.6.

Listing 12.6 Binding the DataForm to a single Person object

```
<UserControl.Resources>
  <local:Person x:Key="me" />                        Person as
</UserControl.Resources>                             resource

<Grid x:Name="LayoutRoot" Margin="30">                        Binding to
  <toolkit:DataForm CurrentItem="{StaticResource me}" />       person
</Grid>
```

The property that's used to generate the form is the CurrentItem property, in this sample case bound to a single object sitting in the Resources section of this control. The resulting DataForm, as seen in figure 12.1, is impressive in the breadth of controls it has auto-generated for you. Not only did we not have to write any code specific to the DataForm, but we also didn't have to place any edit controls in the markup.

Note that the DataForm displayed a CheckBox for the bool property, a ComboBox for the enum (populated with all the possible values defined in the enumeration, of course), and a DatePicker for the DateTime property. Not bad for a default form, and certainly workable for a simple utility application.

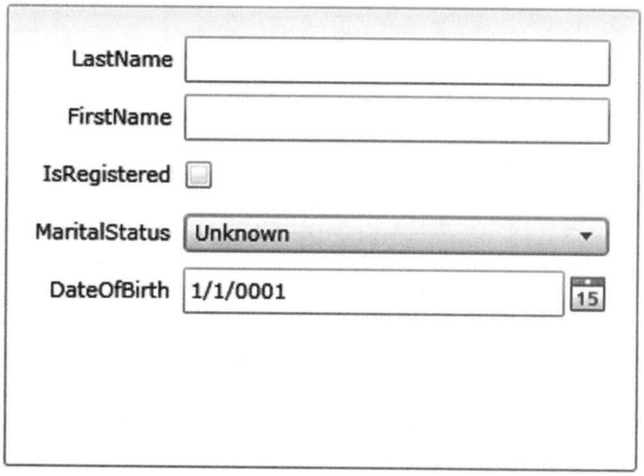

Figure 12.1 DataForm showing generated edit controls bound to a single object without a backing collection. Note that there's no toolbar or set of navigation buttons. Not all fields are shown, so your form will look slightly different.

So far we've been binding one discrete object to the DataForm. To harness the true power of the DataForm, you'll want to bind it to a list of objects much as you would a DataGrid.

12.2.2 Binding to lists of data

If you want to support the ability to add new records, you'll need to provide a place to put them. For this example, we'll create a simple class that holds some dummy data. Of course, you could wire this up to a service to load a collection of Person objects, should you desire.

Listing 12.7 shows a class named PeopleRepository that will hold our Person objects. Note that this doesn't follow the formal Repository pattern; it's closer to a View-Model (covered in chapter 16).

Listing 12.7   The `PeopleRepository` class

```
public class PeopleRepository
{
  private ObservableCollection<Person> _people =          ◁── Observable collection
    new ObservableCollection<Person>();                         of Person

  public ObservableCollection<Person> People
  {
    get { return _people; }
  }
  public PeopleRepository()                                ◁── Load dummy
  {                                                            data
    _people.Add(new Person()
    {
      FirstName = "Captain", LastName = "Avatar",
      IsRegistered = true,
      MaritalStatus = MaritalStatus.Unknown,
      DateOfBirth = DateTime.Parse("1912-01-01")
    });
    _people.Add(new Person()
    {
      FirstName = "Derek", LastName = "Wildstar",
      IsRegistered = true,
      MaritalStatus = MaritalStatus.Single,
      DateOfBirth = DateTime.Parse("1954-11-15")
    });
  }
}
```

Once you have a suitable repository for the data (whether it's a view-model or something else), one of the easiest things to do is to supply an ObservableCollection<T> to the ItemsSource property, as shown in listing 12.8.

Listing 12.8   Binding the `DataForm` to the `PeopleRepository` class

```
<UserControl.Resources>
  <local:PeopleRepository x:Key="repository" />          ◁── Repository as resource
</UserControl.Resources>
```

```
<Grid x:Name="LayoutRoot" Margin="30">
  <toolkit:DataForm
          DataContext="{StaticResource repository}"
          ItemsSource="{Binding People}"
          CurrentIndex="0">

  </toolkit:DataForm>
</Grid>
```

Repository reference

Observable collection

In the example, I use the `PeopleRepository` class from listing 12.7 with a collection of `Person` objects exposed through a property named `People`. In XAML, I create a resource to hold a reference to that repository and set the `DataContext` of the `Data-Form` to that `StaticResource`. (You could, of course, also create the repository and set the `DataContext` from code.) I then bound the `ItemsSource` to the collection of `Person` objects. The resulting `DataForm` looks like figure 12.2.

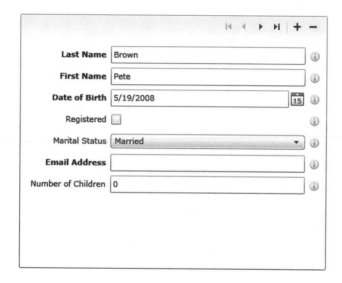

Figure 12.2 A `DataForm` **bound to a collection of objects. Note the presence of the toolbar including the add/remove and navigation buttons, sometimes called the VCR control. (Display annotations, covered in 12.3.1, were used in this example.)**

Note the new toolbar at the top of the `DataForm`. This provides navigation as well as Add (the plus sign) and Delete (the minus sign) capabilities. For each of the operations (Add, Delete, Validate, and so on) appropriate events are raised with the capability to cancel operations based on criteria you set in your code.

VCR control?

Ack! Was that the dreaded VCR binding control I just saw in that screenshot?

Yes—but since this is Silverlight, you have control over what that toolbar looks like, where it's displayed (if at all), and how a user navigates through the records. You also get good event support when you move from record to record, as well as the ability to properly validate the data.

(continued)

So, yes, it looks like the same old VCR control we grew up with in old VB, but it bears about as much technical resemblance to the old VB data binding controls as Blu-ray does to VHS.

The toolbar can be customized both by templating and via the `CommandButtonsVisibility` property, whose possible values are shown in table 12.4.

Table 12.4 `DataForm CommandButtonsVisibility` **values**

Template property	Description
`All`	Show all buttons.
`Add`	Show the add new item button.
`Cancel`	Show the cancel edit button. If the underlying item implements `IEditableObject`, this calls the `CancelEdit` function.
`Commit`	Show the commit edit button. If the underlying item implements `IEditableObject`, this calls the `EndEdit` function.
`Delete`	Show the delete button
`Edit`	Show the edit button. This button is typically not necessary if `AutoEdit` is set to true.
`Navigation`	Show the VCR control navigation buttons.
`None`	Don't show any command buttons.

Figure 12.3 shows what the toolbar looks like with all of the command buttons visible. The OK and Cancel buttons at the bottom are the commit and cancel buttons. The

**Figure 12.3 The `DataForm`
with all command buttons
displayed. The OK and Cancel
buttons are the commit and
cancel buttons, respectively.**

pencil in the upper right (currently disabled) is the edit button. The other buttons are as described earlier.

To alter the appearance of the OK and Cancel buttons without retemplating the DataForm, you can use CommitButtonContent and CancelButtonContent to set the contents of the buttons and CommitButtonStyle and CancelButtonStyle to restyle the buttons.

As with just about everything else in Silverlight, you can completely style the way the DataForm looks. You may want to change not only the style but also the field label display and the data type controls.

12.2.3 Customizing display

The DataForm provides multiple levels of UI customization, ranging from how to display field labels and descriptions all the way to providing your own complete DataTemplate for each of the various modes of the control.

CUSTOMIZING FIELD LABELS

In addition to the ability to change the text of the field labels, the DataForm provides the ability to change the position of the labels relative to the edit control. This capability is exposed through the LabelPosition property, the values of which are shown in table 12.5.

Table 12.5   Possible values for LabelPosition and the resulting display

Value	Result
Left	Marital Status [Married ▼] **Email Address** [ ] Number of Children [0]
Top	Marital Status [Married ▼] **Email Address** [ ] Number of Children [0]
Auto	When there is a parent DataForm, the label position will be inherited. When there's no additional parent DataForm, this value is treated as Left.

The field label provides the primary way you should indicate the expected contents of a field. Should the user require additional information, it may be provided via the field description.

CUSTOMIZING FIELD DESCRIPTIONS

Field description elements are the small icons and related tooltips that typically appear to the right of any control bound to a property that has an associated display description. Later in this chapter, we'll discuss how to set the description text for individual fields on the form using the `DisplayAttribute`.

The `DataForm` provides the property `DescriptionViewerPosition`, which enables you to set the relative location of the description viewer icon. The possible values are described in table 12.6.

Table 12.6 Possible values for `DescriptionViewerPosition` and the resulting display

Value	Result
`BesideContent`	Marital Status [Married ▼] ⓘ **Email Address** [ ] ⓘ Number of Children [0] ⓘ
`BesideLabel`	Marital Status ⓘ [Married ▼] **Email Address** ⓘ [ ] Number of Children ⓘ [0]
`BesideLabel` (with `LabelPosition` set to `Top`)	Marital Status ⓘ [Married ▼] **Email Address** ⓘ [ ] Number of Children ⓘ [0]
`Auto`	When there is a parent `DataForm`, the position will be inherited. When there's no additional parent `DataForm`, this value is treated as `BesideContent`.

With the label and description covered, we can turn our attention to the field controls and edit them using the three available template properties.

12.2.4 *Customizing edit, add, and display templates*

The no-code/no-markup out-of-the-box experience is good, but those types of solutions only get us so far before they break down. The `DataForm` gets us further than most controls but, if you couldn't completely customize the `DataForm`, we all know it would be a nonstarter for production-ready real-world applications. Luckily, the `DataForm` supports customization of the associated data templates for the three values of the `Mode` property: `AddNew`, `Edit`, and `ReadOnly`.

In chapter 11, we covered how to use data templates. The `DataForm` control provides three places where we can insert our own data templates: the `EditTemplate`, `NewItemTemplate`, and `ReadOnlyTemplate`, all described in table 12.7.

Table 12.7 `DataForm` templates corresponding to the `DataForm` mode

Template property	Description
`EditTemplate`	Corresponds to the `Edit` value of the `Mode` property. This template is used when the user or application code puts the form in edit mode or when `AutoEdit` is `true`.
`NewItemTemplate`	Corresponds to the `AddNew` value of the `Mode` property. This template is used when the user or application code adds a new item.
`ReadOnlyTemplate`	Corresponds to the `ReadOnly` value of the `Mode` property. This template is used when the current item is read only.

The mechanics of defining the data templates for the three different modes are the same, so we'll concentrate on just the `EditTemplate` in the following examples.

CREATING THE DATATEMPLATE

Most of us will create our data forms ourselves, with our own aesthetics accounted for. Supplying your own data templates enable you to do a few primary things:

- You have complete control over the layout of the form and can, therefore, make it look as the designer intended.
- You can customize the individual field edit control types.
- You can change the binding characteristics to include your own value converters.

What you give up, of course, is the magic. Unlike the case when you started manually adding fields to the `DataGrid`, the `DataForm` provides a nice assortment of capabilities when adding fields. You'll still need to add a field in markup for each field you want on the form but, in reality, this is no more work than we would've had to do if we created the forms without the help of the `DataGrid`, with some significant savings in application plumbing code.

In a departure from its `DataGrid` cousin, the `DataForm` takes a more flexible approach to specifying the individual fields. Rather than have some built-in field types you must choose from or use a template for the remaining, you simply need to wrap edit controls within a `DataField` content control, as shown in listing 12.9.

Listing 12.9 Wrapping the controls in an edit template

```
<toolkit:DataForm.EditTemplate>        ◁──  EditTemplate
  <DataTemplate>                             property
    <StackPanel>
                                                        DataField
      <toolkit:DataField>                       ◁──┐  definition
        <TextBox Text="{Binding LastName, Mode=TwoWay}" />
      </toolkit:DataField>

      <toolkit:DataField>
        <TextBox Text="{Binding FirstName, Mode=TwoWay}" />
      </toolkit:DataField>
```

```
      <toolkit:DataField LabelVisibility="Collapsed">
        <CheckBox IsChecked="{Binding IsRegistered, Mode=TwoWay}"
                  Content="Is Registered" />
      </toolkit:DataField>

    </StackPanel>
  </DataTemplate>
</toolkit:DataForm.EditTemplate>
```

The resulting `DataForm` edit controls look like figure 12.4. Note that I hard-coded the `CheckBox` content property to `IsRegistered` and hid the associated `DataField` label so that I could demonstrate how to use the built-in `CheckBox` content property.

Last Name	Brown	ⓘ
First Name	Pete	ⓘ
	☐ Is Registered	ⓘ

Figure 12.4   Customized `EditTemplate` showing the `CheckBox` label to the right of the `CheckBox`

The `DataField` content control has a number of properties that mirror those on the `DataForm` itself. These are used for controlling where or if the description displays, where to put the field label, and so on. Those may all be set on a field-by-field basis in order to override the `DataForm`-level settings.

Finally, if you don't want the additional support provided by the `DataField` control, you can simply omit it and add the `TextBlocks` and `TextBoxes` (and other controls) directly to the template and bind them to the appropriate fields, without wrapping in `DataField` controls.

That's how you control the editing experience at a field and form level. Now let's look at how to control the overall editing and commit experience from a workflow standpoint.

12.2.5   *Finer control over editing and committing data*

The `DataForm` and similar controls provide several other settings and hooks that may be used to customize the overall editing workflow. These range from altering the object state based on whether it's about to go into the edit mode or not, how to commit changes, and finally how to manually check if the form includes only valid data.

IEDITABLEOBJECT

`System.ComponentModel.IEditableObject` is an interface that allows controls such as the `DataForm` to make method calls into an object when it's about to be edited. Specifically, the interface defines the three methods listed in table 12.8.

Those three functions allow you to control exactly what happens to the object's data when it's put in the edit mode, the edit mode is cancelled, and the edits are committed. Though the sky's the limit with what you might do in these functions, common approaches include versioning, single or multiple-level undo, storing a history of changes, and lazy-loading data required for the edit process.

Table 12.8 `IEditableObject` **interface**

Template property	Description
`BeginEdit`	Called when the object is put into the edit mode
	This is where you may want to cache undo information. If the `DataForm`'s `AutoEdit` property is set to true, this is called as soon as an edit field receives focus. Otherwise, it's called as a result of the user clicking the edit button on the toolbar.
`CancelEdit`	Called when the object was previously in the edit mode but now is to be put back into the read-only mode, reverting any changes
	On the `DataForm`, this is called when the user clicks the Cancel button.
`EndEdit`	Called when the edit is complete and the changes should be committed
	If the `DataForm`'s `AutoCommit` property is set to true, this will happen when the user navigates off the item and the item is both dirty and valid.

The Silverlight `DataForm` control respects these methods and calls them at the appropriate times if your class implements the `IEditableObject` interface. Another place where the `DataForm` allows customization in the object workflow is in checking the item state.

CHECKING FOR DIRTY STATE AND VALIDITY

The `DataForm` also provides a way to check the object's changed state, often called its *dirty state*, from within the `DataForm` itself. This doesn't require any dirty tracking infrastructure in place within the entity being edited; the `DataForm` takes care of all of that. To check whether the current item has been changed, simply refer to the `IsItemChanged` property as follows:

```
if (dataForm.IsItemChanged) {…}
```

If the item has changed, you'll probably be interested in knowing if it's valid. Luckily, the `DataForm` provides a property for that as well: the `IsItemValid` property. This property returns true if the currently edited item, the item visible on the `DataForm`, has met all associated validation rules (covered in chapter 13). The syntax for the read-only `IsItemValid` property is as shown here:

```
if (dataForm.IsItemValid) {…}
```

The `DataForm` by itself is a nice way to handle data entry in your applications. Without sacrificing the capabilities it offers, you have a great deal of control over how the content is rendered and how navigation is handled. The `DataForm` will help do for forms what the `DataGrid` did for tabular data.

The `DataGrid` and `DataForm` are two powerful controls for displaying and editing data. If you're writing a line-of-business application or something that's otherwise very data heavy, I strongly recommend you consider using these controls. Both provide commonly understood UI metaphors in an easy-to-use package. You can do pretty much anything you'd need to do with them more efficiently than writing analogous controls from scratch, especially when you consider the annotations we'll cover in the next section.

Now that we've seen how to edit data in the `DataGrid` and `DataForm`, we'll want to impose some parameters around how the data is displayed. We can do this in code, but it's typically more efficient to use data annotations.

12.3   *Annotating for display*

The `DataForm` and `DataGrid` both offer the ability to set the properties of columns and labels, including things such as the display caption and tooltips. But, if you share the data between many instances of the controls, instances which may vary in their display properties in other ways, it can be both tedious and a maintenance burden to have to repeat this configuration in multiple places.

Autogeneration of columns and labels often leaves us with even uglier results. Sadly, many internal applications go into production with programmer-friendly but user-unfriendly display properties because it was too much effort to keep the UI updated and in sync with the data model.

The `System.ComponentModel.DataAnnotations` assembly and namespace found in the Silverlight SDK provide a number of attributes designed to make data validation and display hinting easier for controls such as the `DataForm`, `DataGrid`, and some third-party controls. The approach taken by these attributes is to mark up the properties in your entities using attributes in code rather than require code within the properties or external to your entities.

The two main attributes that we'll cover here are `Display` and `Editable`. In chapter 13, we'll take a look at the validation attributes and how they can further enhance the `DataGrid` and `DataForm`.

12.3.1   *The Display attribute*

Both the `DataGrid` and the `DataForm` provide the capability to automatically generate display and edit controls, and associated labels or column headers, at runtime. Though the controls themselves provide a number of ways to customize the field information, there are times when you'd be better served by a centralized definition of that metadata.

One way to centralize that metadata is to annotate the properties on the entities themselves. The assembly `System.ComponentModel.DataAnnotations` provides a number of attributes designed specifically for this purpose (see listing 12.10).

> **Listing 12.10   The `Person` class with `Display` attributes attached**

```
public class Person
{
...
  [Display(Name = "Registered",
    Description = "Check if this person has registered with us.")]
  public bool IsRegistered { get; set; }
```

```
[Display(Name = "Marital Status",
    Description = "Optional marital status information.")]
  public MaritalStatus MaritalStatus { get; set; }
...
}
```

The result of including the Display attribute with the name and description can be seen in figure 12.5. Note that the MaritalStatus field has its correctly formatted display name shown in the label, and the Registered field shows the information icon with the associated tooltip containing the description property.

Figure 12.5 Portion of a DataForm showing the tooltips with the Description property of the Display attribute and the field captions pulled from the Name property of the same attribute.

The DisplayAttribute enables us to control a number of different aspects of the onscreen representation of the control, above and beyond just the field label and the tooltip. It can control whether the field is automatically generated as a column in the DataGrid or field in the DataForm. It can also control the order the fields are displayed in or information on the string to use when localizing. Table 12.9 has the complete list of the different properties available.

Table 12.9 DisplayAttribute properties and their uses

Property	Description
AutoGenerateField	Set this value to false if you don't want controls like the DataForm to automatically generate a control for this property.
AutoGenerateFilter	Set to true if you want the filtering UI automatically displayed for this field. It is currently unused by the DataGrid and DataForm controls.
Description	A resource name or regular text that will be displayed by the rendering control. In the case of the DataForm, this shows up in a tooltip over the information icon.
GroupName	A resource name or regular text to display as the heading for a group of related fields. Currently unused by the DataGrid and DataForm controls.
Name	A resource name or regular text to display as the name of this field. This is typically used in field labels.
Order	Relative order for this field in display. By default, fields are displayed in the order they're defined in the class. This property allows you to override that behavior.
Prompt	Specifies a prompt, such as a watermark, to use when displaying this field. Currently unused by the DataGrid and DataForm controls.

Table 12.9 `DisplayAttribute` **properties and their uses** *(continued)*

Property	Description
ResourceType	If you intend to use localized resources, specify the type container for those resources here.
ShortName	A resource name or regular text to display as the name of this field. This is typically used in column headers.

In several instances in table 12.9, I wrote that a property is "typically used as" something or other. The `DisplayAttribute` simply contains data; it doesn't provide behavior or any enforcement of proper use. It's up to the consuming control—typically a `DataGrid`, `DataForm` or a third-party control—to decide how that data will be used.

In addition to the `DisplayAttribute` and its properties, one final important attribute-based setting you have as a developer is the ability to mark individual properties as editable or read only.

12.3.2 *The Editable attribute*

On occasion, you may want to designate certain properties as read only from a UI point of view but still allow them to be manipulated via code. One way to handle that is to provide an accessor (property get) with no corresponding property set and then provide an explicit mutator method. Unfortunately, that makes the programming interface more cumbersome.

Another approach is to provide a normal property getter and setter but mark the property as read only at the UI level. Like the `Display` attribute discussed in the previous section, you could certainly do this on a form-by-form basis. But you may want to instead centralize this information on the entity itself, as shown in listing 12.11.

Listing 12.11 Controlling editability using the `Editable` **attribute**

```
public class Person
{
...
   [Display(Name = "Marital Status",
       Description = "Optional marital status information.")]
   [Editable(false)]                                              ◁── Editable
   public MaritalStatus MaritalStatus { get; set; }                   attribute
...
}
```

In this example, we've marked the Marital Status field as read only by applying an `EditableAttribute` with the editable flag set to false. The result will be an onscreen field that's disabled, as shown in figure 12.6.

Figure 12.6 shows the Marital Status field disabled. Note also that its information icon isn't displayed, even though we've included a display description. The display of the field control itself will depend upon the disabled state for the control in use. This

Figure 12.6   The Marital Status field has been disabled because its underlying property is marked as read only.

is something that may be easily changed by editing the control template as shown in chapter 23.

There is a number of other attributes in the `DataAnnotations` namespace, including some specifically geared toward object-relational mapping (ORM). Take a look around in there and you may find other attributes that can help with specific challenges you're facing in your applications.

Annotations are a powerful way to provide metadata for your entities. When combined with annotation-aware controls like the `DataForm` and `DataGrid`, you can provide UI information such as field labels and help text, and control whether fields are editable on forms and in grids. WCF RIA Services, covered in chapter 17, provides other options for surfacing this metadata.

12.4 Summary

For business and forms-over-data applications, the `DataGrid` and `DataForm` often form the heart of the UI. Even nontraditional applications sometimes use heavily styled `DataGrids` due to their rich programming model. Though the controls are complex, they're equally powerful and worth the time it takes to master them.

The `DataGrid` is great for tabular data, whether it's flat grid-style or contains images or richer content. There are lots of options for the types of content it contains as well as how you style both the content and the columns and rows that contain it. When you need to display and edit data in a tabular form, look first to the `DataGrid`.

The `DataForm` is the 90-degrees-off equivalent of the `DataGrid`, with columns shown as fields rather than columns. Like the `DataGrid`, it can work on multiple rows of data but, unlike the `DataGrid`, it shows only one at a time. Though certainly useful on its own, the `DataForm` is often combined with the `DataGrid` for master-detail layouts.

The `DataGrid` and `DataForm` both understand the display annotations such as the `Display` and `Editable` attributes. These allow you to mark up your classes or buddy partial classes to control the rendering of the controls in the grid and the form.

Now that we've covered binding (chapter 11) and the `DataGrid` and `DataForm`, we'll move on to validation. When you combine the grid, form, binding, and validation, you'll be well on your way to having a set of tools that cover the majority of the data manipulation needs of a business application UI.

13

In chapter 11, we covered binding. In chapter 12, I mentioned that I believe binding to be one of the single most important topics for Silverlight developers. Another reason for that is because all the validation approaches covered in this chapter build directly on the binding system.

Validation is something almost every nontrivial application with a `TextBox` will need to do at some point. Often, we punt and do simple checking in the code-behind. But, if you want to truly leverage binding, take advantage of patterns such as the ViewModel pattern, and just have better structure to your code, you'll want to use one of the established validation mechanisms provided by Silverlight.

Silverlight provides several ways to validate data. The simplest and oldest approach is to use exception-based validation. In that approach, property setters simply throw exceptions when the validation doesn't pass. This is the code equivalent of my toddler's spitting out the food she doesn't like and, like that, anything more complex than a couple of peas is going to get pretty messy.

It wasn't well-known, but Silverlight 2 included basic exception-based validation capabilities. With the releases of Silverlight 3 and 4, these capabilities became more advanced and the exception-based approach was looked at as more of a stopgap, useful in only the simplest of validation scenarios. For those reasons, we'll concentrate the majority of this chapter on the more modern approaches to validation, such as IDataErrorInfo and INotifyDataErrorInfo.

The IDataErrorInfo and INotifyDataErrorInfo interfaces are the newer approach for validating data in Silverlight 4. They're a bit more complex to implement. (when working with them, start out by creating some helper classes to handle all the goo. You'll thank me for it; and, if you do want to thank me, donations and chocolate are always welcome.)

One main difference with these interfaces, as opposed to an exception-based approach, is how far you allow invalid data to get. With exception-based validation, the accepted approach was to not complete the set operation if the validation fails. Using the new interfaces, invalid data will often make it into the class, and will need to be removed or otherwise handled during the final validation or save processes.

Due to the more flexible nature as well as decoupling from the property setters, these interfaces also allow for cross-field validation, where changing the value of one field can invalidate the value of another field.

The final approach to validation is geared to work with the DataGrid and Data-Form covered in chapter 12—data annotations. In chapter 12, we saw that data annotations may be used to control various aspects of display and even editability. In this chapter, we'll investigate the use of data annotations specifically for validation.

To keep the examples consistent, we need to do a little setup work and establish a baseline class to use as our binding source: the Employee class. Once we have that set, we'll briefly look at exception-based validation and the shared validation presentation, then tackle synchronous and asynchronous validation with IDataErrorInfo and INotifyDataErrorInfo, and finally end on attribute-based validation as used by the DataForm and DataGrid covered in chapter 12.

13.1   *The validation example source and UI*

Throughout this chapter, we'll refer back to the Employee class defined here, which will be used as our binding data source. This class represents a fictional employee in a human resources management system.

The Employee class contains the public properties shown in table 13.1.

The class source code is shown in listing 13.1. Note that the Employee class implements the INotifyPropertyChanged interface to support binding change notification, discussed in chapter 11.

Table 13.1   Employee class properties

Property	Description
Last Name	The employee's last (or family) name
First Name	The employee's first (or given) name
Level	The employee's salary level This puts the employee into specific salary "buckets."
Salary	The salary, in USD, for this employee

Listing 13.1   Employee class to be used in the validation examples

```
public class Employee : INotifyPropertyChanged
{
  private string _lastName;
  public string LastName
  {
    get { return _lastName; }
    set
    {
      _lastName = value;
      NotifyPropertyChanged("LastName");
    }
  }

  private string _firstName;
  public string FirstName
  {
    get { return _firstName; }
    set
    {
      _firstName = value;
      NotifyPropertyChanged("FirstName");
    }
  }

  private int _level;
  public int Level
  {
    get { return _level; }
    set
    {
      _level = value;
      NotifyPropertyChanged("Level");
    }
  }

  private decimal _salary;
  public decimal Salary
  {
    get { return _salary; }
    set
    {
```

```
        _salary = value;
        NotifyPropertyChanged("Salary");
    }
}
```

PropertyChanged event

```
#region INotifyPropertyChanged Members

public event PropertyChangedEventHandler PropertyChanged;
```

◁

```
protected void NotifyPropertyChanged(string propertyName)
{
    if (PropertyChanged != null)
        PropertyChanged(this,
                    new PropertyChangedEventArgs(propertyName));
}

#endregion
}
```

Property Changed helper code

◁

You won't see validation in action unless you wire up some UI, so we'll build a basic user interface that works against a single instance of the Employee class. We'll keep it simple and use code-behind, but I refer you to chapter 16 for best practices on structuring your application using the ViewModel pattern. The XAML and C# for the UI are shown in listing 13.2.

Listing 13.2   User interface XAML and code-behind to use for validation examples

XAML:

```
<UserControl x:Class="ValidationExample.MainPage"
     xmlns="http://schemas.microsoft.com/winfx/2006/xaml/presentation"
  xmlns:x="http://schemas.microsoft.com/winfx/2006/xaml"
  xmlns:d="http://schemas.microsoft.com/expression/blend/2008"
  xmlns:mc="http://schemas.openxmlformats.org/markup-compatibility/2006"
  mc:Ignorable="d"
  d:DesignHeight="190"
  d:DesignWidth="350">
  <UserControl.Resources>
    <Style TargetType="TextBlock">
      <Setter Property="VerticalAlignment" Value="Center" />
      <Setter Property="HorizontalAlignment" Value="Right" />
      <Setter Property="Margin" Value="4" />
    </Style>
    <Style TargetType="TextBox">
      <Setter Property="VerticalAlignment" Value="Center" />
      <Setter Property="HorizontalAlignment" Value="Left" />
      <Setter Property="Margin" Value="4" />
      <Setter Property="Height" Value="22" />
      <Setter Property="Width" Value="200" />
    </Style>
  </UserControl.Resources>

  <Grid x:Name="LayoutRoot" Background="White" Margin="20">
    <Grid.ColumnDefinitions>
        <ColumnDefinition Width="*" />
        <ColumnDefinition Width="2*" />
    </Grid.ColumnDefinitions>
```

Styles—see chapter 23

◁

```xml
        <Grid.RowDefinitions>
            <RowDefinition Height="Auto" />
            <RowDefinition Height="Auto" />
            <RowDefinition Height="Auto" />
            <RowDefinition Height="Auto" />
            <RowDefinition Height="Auto" />
        </Grid.RowDefinitions>

        <TextBlock Grid.Row="0" Grid.Column="0"
                Text="Last Name" />
        <TextBox Grid.Row="0" Grid.Column="1"
                Text="{Binding LastName, Mode=TwoWay}" />          ◁

        <TextBlock Grid.Row="1" Grid.Column="0"
                Text="First Name" />
        <TextBox Grid.Row="1" Grid.Column="1"
                Text="{Binding FirstName, Mode=TwoWay}" />         ◁

        <TextBlock Grid.Row="2" Grid.Column="0"
                Text="Level" />
        <TextBox Grid.Row="2" Grid.Column="1"
                Text="{Binding Level, Mode=TwoWay}" />             ◁

        <TextBlock Grid.Row="3" Grid.Column="0"
                Text="Salary" />
        <TextBox Grid.Row="3" Grid.Column="1"
                Text="{Binding Salary, Mode=TwoWay}" />            ◁

        <Button x:Name="SubmitButton" Grid.Row="4" Grid.Column="1"
                Content="Submit"
                Margin="4"
                HorizontalAlignment="Left"
                Width="100"/>
    </Grid>
</UserControl>
```

**Binding statements—
see chapter II**

C#:

```csharp
public partial class MainPage : UserControl
{
  private Employee _employee = new Employee();

  public MainPage()
  {
    InitializeComponent();
    Loaded += new RoutedEventHandler(MainPage_Loaded);
  }

  void MainPage_Loaded(object sender, RoutedEventArgs e)
  {
    this.DataContext = _employee;
  }
}
```

The user interface includes four text boxes, each with a label. There's also a Submit button, but it's there just for aesthetic purposes; all of our validation will happen on lost focus (*blur* for you web folks). The resulting form should look like figure 13.1. Note that the Level and Salary both show 0; this shows that binding is working for those fields.

That sets up a basic single-entity data entry form we can use for the validation examples included in this chapter minus the ones specific to the `DataForm` and `DataGrid`. Throughout this chapter we'll modify various aspects of the `Employee` class, as well as the binding statements in the form XAML. As we move through the examples, it may be helpful to refer back to these listings.

Last Name	
First Name	
Level	0
Salary	0
	Submit

Figure 13.1   Runtime view of the validation form

The first type of validation we'll look at is also the simplest and the one with the most history: exception-based validation.

13.2   *Exception-based property validation*

It wasn't well-known, but Silverlight 2 included basic validation capabilities. With the release of Silverlight 3, these capabilities became more advanced, so we now have the ability to validate bound data and display appropriate error messages using the built-in controls in a standardized and easy to template way. The binding syntax continues to use the `ValidatesOnExceptions` parameter to enable the display of validation messages when a property setter raises an exception, but the built-in control templates have been updated to provide appropriate display of error state.

Though no longer widely used, it's worth covering exception-based validation for those times when it really is the most appropriate approach. It's also necessary to understand so you can respond to the built-in type validation exceptions.

In this section, we'll look at the basics of using exception-based validation both for your own errors and built-in system errors and then move on to custom validation code and combining multiple validation messages. We'll wrap up this section with a look at the built-in Validation UI in Silverlight, something that applies to all forms of validation.

13.2.1   *Handling exception validation errors*

Even if you don't plan to have your own exception-based validation errors, it's worth handling them in order to get the benefits of automatic type checking. Binding with exception-based validation enabled, in its simplest form, looks like this:

```
<TextBox Grid.Row="0" Grid.Column="1"
        Text="{Binding LastName, Mode=TwoWay,
                              ValidatesOnExceptions=True}" />
```

The example binds the `TextBox` to the `LastName` property of the object that's the current data context. The `ValidatesOnExceptions` parameter informs the binding system to report any binding exceptions to the `TextBox`.

One nice side effect of this is that you get data type validation for free. For example, if you try to enter letters into a `decimal` property such as the `Salary` field, you'll get a type mismatch validation error.

In addition to simple data type validation, you can perform virtually any type of validation you want by writing a little code inside the property setter.

13.2.2 *Custom validation code*

Referring back to the `Employee` class from listing 13.1, let's modify the `LastName` property to perform some basic validation. We'll make the last name a required field and then make sure it has a length of at least two characters:

```
public string LastName
{
  get { return _lastName; }
  set
  {
    if (string.IsNullOrEmpty(value))
      throw new Exception("Last Name is a required field.");

    if (value.Trim().Length < 2)
      throw new Exception("Name must be at least 2 letters long.");

    _lastName = value;
    NotifyPropertyChanged("LastName");
  }
}
```

For brevity, I used the base `Exception` class for our validation errors. In practice, you'll want to be less generic with your exception types, just as you would when throwing exceptions for hard errors in code. In order for this code to work, you'll need to run without debugging (or ensure the appropriate IDE debugging break options are set, now a default in Visual Studio 2010); otherwise, you'll hit a break in the property setter.

COMBINING VALIDATION MESSAGES

In our setter, we have two guard conditions that throw exceptions when unmet. Since these are real exceptions, the first one hit will pop out of the setter. If you want to have more than one validation rule checked simultaneously, you'll need to combine your checks and throw only a single exception, perhaps like this:

```
private string _lastName;
public string LastName
{
    get { return _lastName; }
    set
    {
        string message = string.Empty;
        bool isOk = true;

        if (string.IsNullOrEmpty(value))
        {
            message += "Last Name is a required field. ";
            isOk = false;
        }

        if (value.Trim().Length < 5)
        {
            message += "Last Name must be at least 2 letters long. ";
```

```
        isOk = false;
    }

    if (isOk)
    {
        _lastName = value;
        NotifyPropertyChanged("LastName");
    }
    else
    {
        throw new Exception (message.Trim());
    }
  }
}
```

Admittedly, that's a hack, especially once you have more than a couple of rules associated with a single field. If you want to stick with exception-based validation, you're forced to live with the limitations imposed by an exception-based system, including both single checks and the debugging hassles.

13.2.3 *Validation error display*

When you bind the TextBox to the instance of the Employee class with the simple (one message) exception-based validation code in-place, change the binding statement to validate on exceptions as shown earlier, and try to enter data that violates the rules, you'll get an experience like that shown in figure 13.2 when you tab off the field.

Like almost everything else in Silverlight, the display of the validation error tooltip and the error state of the TextBox are both completely customizable by editing the control template. We'll discuss styling and control templates in chapter 23.

Validation using exception code inside properties can be convenient, but it certainly doesn't look clean. It makes debugging sometimes difficult because there are exceptions on the stack. Another issue is that validation errors can only be raised when a setter is called, not in response to another action such as the changing of a value in a related field. And, truthfully, many of us just have an aversion to using exceptions for business or validation rules.

Silverlight 4 introduced the IDataErrorInfo and INotifyDataErrorInfo interfaces. IDataErrorInfo, covered in the next section, was previously available in WPF, but INotifyDataErrorInfo, covered in section 13.4, is a completely new interface. These interfaces help eliminate some of the issues present with exception-based validation because they have a completely different exception-free implementation. But the same styling guidelines and error display features still apply. In addition, they offer some features, such as asynchronous validation, that would be cumbersome or impossible to implement in an exception-based model.

Figure 13.2   Default binding validation error display for the Last Name TextBox, illustrating a custom error message

13.3   *Synchronous validation with IDataErrorInfo*

IDataErrorInfo was introduced in order to address some of the concerns raised by exception-based validation. Unlike exception-based validation, there are no exceptions on the call stack when validation fails. This approach is also more flexible when it comes to setting validation errors for individual fields, regardless of whether their setters are called.

We'll start the discussion of IDataErrorInfo by taking a look at the interface members and the binding statement. We'll then work on handling simple validation errors. Once we have the right approach for handling simple validation errors, we can look at something that IDataErrorInfo can do that was difficult with exception-based validation: cross-field validation errors. Finally, since you'll want to combine the built-in type checking with your custom validation errors, we'll look at what it takes to combine IDataErrorInfo validation with exception-based validation.

13.3.1 *The IDataErrorInfo interface*

Located in the System.ComponentModel namespace, the IDataErrorInfo interface is meant to be implemented by any class you want to use as a binding source and also want to have surface validation errors.

The IDataErrorInfo interface contains two properties: Error and Item. These properties are described in table 13.2.

Table 13.2 **IDataErrorInfo** members

Property	Description
Error	Set this to have a single error message that applies to the entire object.
Item	A collection of errors, indexed by property name. Set these to have errors specific to individual fields.

You can already see how this is going to provide more options than the exception-based approach. With a simple collection of messages, we can add and remove them using code in any place in our class. In addition, the class-scoped error message lets us provide errors that are difficult to attach to any single property.

BINDING WITH VALIDATESONDATAERRORS

In return for this flexibility, you'll need to write a bit more code. Before we do that, though, we need to modify the form XAML so that it responds to the IDataErrorInfo errors rather than the exception-based errors. The binding statement for each TextBox should look like this:

```
Text="{Binding LastName, Mode=TwoWay, ValidatesOnDataErrors=True}"
```

Note the ValidatesOnDataErrors property versus the ValidatesOnExceptions property. As the name suggests, setting ValidatesOnDataErrors to true tells the binding system to watch the IDataErrorInfo interface on your class and respond to any errors reported.

Now that the binding is set up for each of the TextBox instances on the form, we can get to the actual validation code. We'll put the validation code inline in the Employee class. Once you have some experience with it, you may want to pull the common validation helper code out into a separate class, called from your entities.

13.3.2 *Simple validation with IDataErrorInfo*

The first thing to do is to implement IDataErrorInfo in the class. The modifications to the Employee class to do this look like listing 13.3.

Listing 13.3 Implementing IDataErrorInfo in the Employee class

```
public class Employee : INotifyPropertyChanged, IDataErrorInfo
{
  ...

  #region IDataErrorInfo Members

  private string _dataError = string.Empty;              ⟵  Class-level
  string IDataErrorInfo.Error                                error property
  {
    get { return _dataError; }
  }

  private Dictionary<string, string> _dataErrors =
                  new Dictionary<string,string>();
  string IDataErrorInfo.this[string columnName]         ⟵  Field-level
  {                                                          error property
    get
    {
      if (_dataErrors.ContainsKey(columnName))
        return _dataErrors[columnName];
      else
        return null;
    }
  }
  #endregion
}
```

The Dictionary of strings holds the field-level error messages, whereas the single string property holds the class-level error message. To try out the interface, we'll implement the same validation we did in the simple exception-based validation example and check the length of the LastName field:

```
public string LastName
{
  get { return _lastName; }
  set
  {
    if (string.IsNullOrEmpty(value))
      _dataErrors["LastName"] = "Last Name is required";
    else if (value.Trim().Length < 2)
      _dataErrors["LastName"] =
              "Last Name must be at least 2 letters long.";
```

```
    else
      if (_dataErrors.ContainsKey("LastName"))
        _dataErrors.Remove("LastName");

    _lastName = value;
    NotifyPropertyChanged("LastName");
  }
}
```

There are two primary differences in the structure of this rule-checking code as opposed to the exception-based code. First, we needed to include a branch that clears the error when valid, and second, the rules as written let potentially bad data into the class. The second difference is a matter of preference and business rules; you may easily change it so the data is only set when valid. The former check is required because the only thing the binding system uses to check for the presence of an error is whether employee["FieldName"] returns a string or null.

Running the application produces the same results as the exception-based version, as it should. We changed only our implementation of validation at the business object level, not the user interface elements that display the results.

13.3.3 *Cross-field validation with IDataErrorInfo*

What about cases when you want to validate more than one field? For example, let's say that we need to ensure that an employee's salary is in range when related to his or her level. The valid salary ranges for each level are listed in table 13.3.

You could put this in the setter for one of the fields, but unless you include the check in both, you're making the mistake of assuming the field data will be input in a specific order. In cases like this, it's better to pull the validation code out into a common function and call it from both setters, as shown in listing 13.4.

Level	Allowable salary range
100	50,000–64,999
101	65,000–79,999
102	80,000–104,999

Table 13.3   Validation rules for salary and level

Listing 13.4   Cross-field validation code using `IDataErrorInfo`

```
private int _level;
public int Level
{
    get { return _level; }
    set
    {
        if (ValidateSalaryAndLevel(value, Salary))        ◁─┐ Call to validation
        {                                                     function
            _level = value;
            NotifyPropertyChanged("Level");
        }
    }
```

```
}
private decimal _salary;
public decimal Salary
{
    get { return _salary; }
    set
    {
        if (ValidateSalaryAndLevel(Level, value))       Call to validation
        {                                                function
            _salary = value;
            NotifyPropertyChanged("Salary");
        }
    }
}

private bool ValidateSalaryAndLevel(int level, decimal salary)
{
    if (level < 100 || level > 102)
    {
        _dataErrors["Level"] = "Level must be between 100 and 102";
        return false;
    }

    bool isValid = false;            Check for
                                     valid salary
    switch (level)
    {
        case 100:
            isValid = (salary >= 50000 && salary < 65000);
            break;

        case 101:
            isValid = (salary >= 65000 && salary < 80000);
            break;

        case 102:
            isValid = (salary >= 80000 && salary < 105000);
            break;
    }

    if (isValid)
    {
        if (_dataErrors.ContainsKey("Level"))
            _dataErrors.Remove("Level");
                                                          Clear existing
        if (_dataErrors.ContainsKey("Salary"))            errors
            _dataErrors.Remove("Salary");
    }
    else                                  Set new errors
    {
        _dataErrors["Level"] = "Level does not match salary range";
        _dataErrors["Salary"] = "Salary does not match level";
    }

    return isValid;
}
```

Figure 13.3　**Cross-field validation showing errors for both salary and level**

In this example, I decided not to allow invalid values into the class. Validation using this interface makes that a simple choice to make. The code that makes that decision is inside the properties themselves.

The ValidateSalaryAndLevel function is the meat of the validation for these two properties. It takes in both the salary and the level (one of which will always be the current value and the other an entered but not set value) and first validates the level, then validates that the salary falls within the correct range for the level. If so, it clears any previous errors. If not, it sets new errors.

One thing you may have noticed is the proliferation of magic strings (the property names). When implementing this in your own code, you'll want to either use constants for the string names, or use reflection to dynamically pull property names from the classes. The former is quicker both to develop and at runtime; the latter is more robust but slower.

When run, the cross-field validation looks like this figure 13.3. If not, you may have forgotten to add the ValidatesOnDataErrors property to your binding statement. IDataErrorInfo is great, but one thing we lost in the process was the automatic errors when validating the data types. To continue to support that, we'll need to return to exception-based validation.

13.3.4　*Combining exceptions and IDataErrorInfo*

When we turned on ValidatesOnDataErrors, we removed the ValidatesOnExceptions parameter. That's used not just by our own code but also by the built-in type checking. For example, when you try to assign a string like "dfdf" to an int, you'll get an exception. That exception bubbles up and, if not handled by the binding system, it just disappears.

Luckily, this is easy to fix. Simply modify the binding statement to include both parameters:

```
Text="{Binding Level, Mode=TwoWay,
            ValidatesOnDataErrors=True,
            ValidatesOnExceptions=True}"
```

When run, the result will look like figure 13.4. Note that, since the exception will be thrown before your property setter code executes, this exception takes precedence over your own validation code.

Figure 13.4　**Built-in exception-based checking takes precedence over your code.**

Using both modes gives you the best of both worlds: you don't need to handle basic type checking, and you get more robust validation support for your own custom code.

IDataErrorInfo is a powerful interface for surfacing your own validation errors. It provides a way to surface errors for the entire class or for individual fields. It also makes it possible to perform cross-field validation or multifield validation without invoking all involved property setters through the binding system.

It's not without its faults, though. String-based property access can get you into trouble when you refactor (or have a typo), and the validation code is all synchronous, run on the client. There are tricks for working around the string-based problem (constants, reflection), but what do you do when you want to validate through a service or do some other long-running validation call? For those instances, we have INotifyDataErrorInfo.

13.4 Asynchronous validation with INotifyDataErrorInfo

IDataErrorInfo is a synchronous operation validation approach. Though you can bend it to surface errors in an asynchronous way, it's not really optimized for that. In addition, IDataErrorInfo doesn't support having multiple errors for a single property.

INotifyDataErrorInfo solves both of these issues. Though similar in concept to IDataErrorInfo, its design specifically supports asynchronous validation and the method for returning validation errors supports multiple errors for a single field.

We'll start our coverage of INotifyDataErrorInfo with the interface members and how to implement them in your own class. Then we'll move on to the modifications required in the binding statement. Next, because we'll need to show asynchronous validation, we'll implement a simple WCF-based web service. Finally, we'll implement an asynchronous validation function to call the service and call that from our class.

13.4.1 The INotifyDataErrorInfo interface

Like the IDataErrorInfo interface, the INotifyDataErrorInfo interface is located in the System.ComponentModel namespace. The interface has only three members, as shown in table 13.4, and is conceptually similar to IDataErrorInfo but optimized for asynchronous operation.

Table 13.4 INotifyDataErrorInfo **members**

Member	Description
GetErrors	This is a method that returns all of the validation errors for a specific field. If the propertyName parameter is null or string.Empty, the method returns errors for the entire object.
HasErrors	This is a property that returns true if the object has errors; false otherwise.
ErrorsChanged	This is an event similar to the PropertyChanged event in binding. Whenever you add, remove, or change errors, you must raise this event to notify the binding system.

One difference from IDataErrorInfo you'll immediately notice is the addition of the event ErrorsChanged. Since INotifyDataErrorInfo is meant to be used in asynchronous validation scenarios, it uses an event-based mechanism for notifying listeners of new validation errors.

GetErrors will require the most setup because you need a backing store with a collection of validation error messages for each field you'll validate.

> **NOTE**   Silverlight will call GetErrors on each public member of your class, even if you don't explicitly support listening to INotifyDataErrorInfo in every given binding statement. Be sure to handle this situation in your own code.

13.4.2 *Implementing the interface*

As was the case with IDataErrorInfo, the increase in flexibility means an increase in code. The interface itself is simple enough but, behind that, you must maintain several collections in order to surface the errors. The code to implement INotifyDataErrorInfo is shown in listing 13.5.

Listing 13.5 INotifyDataErrorInfo implementation

```
public class Employee : INotifyPropertyChanged, INotifyDataErrorInfo
{
...
  #region INotifyDataErrorInfo Members

  private Dictionary<string, ObservableCollection<string>>        Field
            _validationErrors;                                    errors
  private ObservableCollection<string>            Class
            _classValidationErrors;               errors

  public event EventHandler<DataErrorsChangedEventArgs> ErrorsChanged;

  public Employee()              Create errors
  {                              collections
    _validationErrors =
      new Dictionary<string, ObservableCollection<string>>();

    _classValidationErrors =
      new ObservableCollection<string>();

    CreateErrorsCollection("Level");
    CreateErrorsCollection("Salary");
  }

  private void CreateErrorsCollection(string propertyName)
  {
    if (!_validationErrors.ContainsKey(propertyName))
    {
      _validationErrors.Add(propertyName,
        new ObservableCollection<string>());
    }
  }

  IEnumerable INotifyDataErrorInfo.GetErrors(string propertyName)
  {
```

```
     if (!string.IsNullOrEmpty(propertyName))
     {
       if (_validationErrors.ContainsKey(propertyName))        Return errors
         return _validationErrors[propertyName];               for field
       else
         return null;
     }
     else
     {
       return _classValidationErrors;
     }
   }

   bool INotifyDataErrorInfo.HasErrors
   {                                          Check for
     get                                      existing errors
     {
       if (_classValidationErrors.Count > 0)
         return true;

       foreach (string key in _validationErrors.Keys)
       {
         if (_validationErrors[key].Count > 0)
           return true;
       }

       return false;
     }
   }

   #endregion
}
```

That's what's needed for the interface. I included the code for it but rarely—if ever—bother with class-level errors, preferring instead to light up specific fields. Your mileage may vary.

13.4.3 Binding support

In addition to implementing the interface, the binding on the fields will need to be modified to support listening to the INotifyDataErrorInfo interface, just as we did with the other validation approaches:

```
Text="{Binding LastName, Mode=TwoWay,
➡        ValidatesOnNotifyDataErrors=True}"
```

The next step is to create some code to do the actual validation. Let's assume for a moment that the salary and level validation requires a web service call rather than a simple in-code lookup table. The web service may call out to a rules engine or may simply look up values in the database.

13.4.4 Building the WCF web service

In the web project associated with this Silverlight project, add a folder called Services and into it add a new Silverlight-Enabled WCF Service called ValidationService. The template is essentially a SOAP web service served up using WCF. You'll find it easier to use than full-blown WCF and more functional than an .asmx service.

Inside the service code, create a `ValidateSalaryAndLevel` method that looks like listing 13.6; we'll cover web services in more detail in chapter 14.

Listing 13.6   WCF service code for `ValidateSalaryAndLevel`

```
[OperationContract]
public bool ValidateSalaryAndLevel(int level, decimal salary)                          WCF
{                                                                              operation contract
  bool isValid = false;

  switch (level)
  {
    case 100:
      isValid = (salary >= 50000 && salary < 65000);
      break;

    case 101:
      isValid = (salary >= 65000 && salary < 80000);
      break;

    case 102:
      isValid = (salary >= 80000 && salary < 105000);
      break;
  }
  return isValid;
}
```

For simplicity, I chose the simple route of returning a Boolean and left it up to the client to assign the appropriate messages to the controls. You may decide instead to return a class that has a Boolean indicating whether validation passed and then a collection of error messages with field names or a couple of strongly-typed properties with the error messages for each field.

13.4.5 *Adding the client service code*

The next step is to add a service reference in your Silverlight project to the WCF web service in the web project. Right-click the Silverlight project, select Add Service Reference, click Discover, and name the reference `ValidationServices`.

Once the reference is added, add the client code from listing 13.7 into the `Employee` class.

Listing 13.7   `ValidateSalaryAndLevelAsync` in the `Employee` class

```
private void ValidateSalaryAndLevelAsync(int level, decimal salary)
{
  var client = new ValidationServices.ValidationServiceClient();

  client.ValidateSalaryAndLevelCompleted += (o, e) =>
    {                                                              Clear existing
                                                                   errors
      _validationErrors["Level"].Clear();
```

```
    _validationErrors["Salary"].Clear();          ◁──┐ Clear existing
                                                      │ errors
    if (e.Result)               ◁──┐ Only set
    {                               │ fields if valid
      _level = level;
      _salary = salary;
      NotifyPropertyChanged("Level");
      NotifyPropertyChanged("Salary");
    }
    else
    {
      if (level < 100 || level > 102)
      {
        _validationErrors["Level"]
          .Add("Level must be between 100 and 102.");
      }                                              ┌ Set error
                                                     │ messages
      _validationErrors["Level"]           ◁─────────┘
        .Add("Level does not match salary range.");
      _validationErrors["Salary"]
        .Add("Salary does not match level.");
    }                                          ┌ Error change
                                               │ notification
    if (ErrorsChanged != null)       ◁─────────┘
    {
      ErrorsChanged(this, new DataErrorsChangedEventArgs("Level"));
      ErrorsChanged(this, new DataErrorsChangedEventArgs("Salary"));
    }
  };
  client.ValidateSalaryAndLevelAsync(level, salary);     ◁──── Call service
}
```

The `ValidateSalaryAndLevelAsync` class calls out to the web service and validates the salary and the level. If the web service says the values are valid, the underlying fields are updated. If it says the values are invalid, it sets up error messages for the fields. For grins, on an invalid return, it also validates the level number itself.

There are other ways to handle this type of validation, of course. You could have a separate local client method that evaluates the level and call that either asynchronously or synchronously from the client. You could also have the web service return error messages.

Also, for simplicity, the web service client code is in the `Employee` entity class. In a real application, I strongly encourage you to separate this code out into a separate service client layer that is, at most, loosely coupled to the `Employee` entity. See chapter 16 on the ViewModel pattern for guidance on this and other topics.

13.4.6 *Property modifications*

The last step is to add the calls to `ValidateSalaryAndLevelAsync`. In my code, I handle the property setting and the change notification inside the async method so the setters are significantly simplified:

```
private int _tempLevel;
private int _level;
public int Level
```

```
{
  get { return _level; }
  set
  {
    _tempLevel = value;
    ValidateSalaryAndLevelAsync(value, Salary);
  }
}
private decimal _tempSalary;
private decimal _salary;
public decimal Salary
{
  get { return _salary; }
  set
  {
    _tempSalary = value;
    ValidateSalaryAndLevelAsync(Level, value);
  }
}
```

Note the _tempSalary and _tempLevel variables. Due to the asynchronous nature of the validation, I needed some place to store the possibly invalid values; otherwise, you could never jump out of the validation error condition (one of the properties would always be the default value during validation) and correct the data. These properties are where I choose to store the temporary values. Consider them "draft" or "unverified" values.

Some caveats to the code I presented here. I don't propose that these are best practices or even stable for production code. The code has been simplified to show the core concepts and stay within the reasonable bounds of a chapter. For example, in the preceding code, you may run into race conditions for multiple property changes that happen during a slow-running web service call. If they happen to get queued out of order, you can end up with skewed validation and entry.

The INotifyDataErrorInfo class implementation is more complex than the other methods presented here. For that reason, you may prefer to implement it only on some fields and use either exception-based or IDataErrorInfo on the remaining fields. The choice is up to you; all of the methods coexist nicely in the same class. The binding system will know which ones to use based on the properties of the binding statement.

INotifyDataErrorInfo fills in the missing gap left by the other methods by enabling you to provide asynchronous validation error reporting and supply multiple validation messages for a single field.

IDataErrorInfo and INotifyDataErrorInfo are the premier ways of handling validation in Silverlight but they require a fair bit of code to implement. What if you want to do something more lightweight? Do you need to turn to exceptions? No, if you're using the DataForm or DataGrid, you can annotate your data using validation attributes.

13.5 Annotating for validation

There are innumerable ways to validate data and an equally diverse number of ways in which to store that validation information including the rules logic and the messages. In section 13.2, we saw how you can use exceptions in property setters to expose validation information to the user interface. In sections 13.3 and 13.4, we saw how to use specialized interfaces to support additional forms of validation.

Though you can continue to code validation directly into properties setters or use interfaces, the `System.ComponentModel.DataAnnotations` assembly and namespace found in the Silverlight SDK provide a number of attributes designed to make data validation and display hinting easier for controls such as the `DataForm`, `DataGrid`, and some third-party controls. The approach taken by these attributes is to mark up the properties in your entities using attributes in code rather than require code within the properties or external to your entities.

If your scenario supports their use, validation attributes are simple to implement and easy to use. In our discussion of these attributes, we'll first go over the available set of attributes and how to implement a select set of them in your own classes. Then, we'll extend the reach of the attributes to call out to external validation functions in your code. Finally, we'll create our own custom validators to handle situations not easily handled by the built-in set. All of these techniques help us create validation code that's cleaner and easier to read than many of the other methods.

13.5.1 Validation attributes

Previously we saw how to provide property-level validation using exceptions and synchronous and asynchronous interfaces. Though those work in almost any situation, they're not a very clean approach and lead to a significant amount of branch/check code inside the property setters in your entities. They also require significant code modification to your entities—a luxury we don't always have. One better way to tackle basic validation is to use attributes tied to the properties in the class.

To support attribute or annotation-based validation, the `DataAnnotations` namespace includes the validation attributes shown in table 13.5.

Table 13.5 Validation attributes in `System.ComponentModel.DataAnnotations`

Validation attribute class	Validation capabilities
`EnumDataTypeAttribute`	It specifies that the value must be parsable as one of the members of a specified `enum`.
`RangeAttribute`	It specifies that the value must be between two other values. The type can be any type that implements `IComparable`.
`RegularExpressionAttribute`	It enables you to associate a regular expression to validate a value. This is useful for things such as phone numbers and email addresses, as well as any other data that must adhere to one or more specific formats.

Table 13.5 Validation attributes in `System.ComponentModel.DataAnnotations` (continued)

Validation attribute class	Validation capabilities
`RequiredAttribute`	It specifies that the value for this property must be nonnull and not empty.
`StringLengthAttribute`	It enables you to check the length of the value—must be between the specified minimum and maximum length.
`CustomValidationAttribute`	A catch-all validator that allows you to call custom code to perform the validation.
`ValidationAttribute`	The abstract base class for all other validators. You can create your own validation attributes by deriving from this class.

Note that this namespace also defines the `ValidationException` type. You'll recall that in our earlier example we simply used `System.Exception`. With the introduction of this DLL, you can now use the `ValidationException` rather than the base `System.Exception`. But since this DLL provides so many other ways to handle validation, I'd encourage you to try packaging your validation code in either a function used from a `CustomValidationAttribute`, or as a class derived from `ValidationAttribute`.

We'll only cover a handful of these attributes because the pattern is the same across the set. In addition, only the `DataGrid` and `DataForm` (and a handful of third-party controls) support these annotations, so these attributes aren't necessarily a solution for all applications.

13.5.2 Annotating your entity

If we take the same `Person` class we used for the `DataForm` examples in chapter 12, we can now mark that up to include some basic validation capabilities. To show off validation, we'll also add two new properties: `EmailAddress` and `NumberOfChildren`. The final class, with appropriate validation attributes in place, looks like listing 13.8.

Listing 13.8 The `Person` class with validation attributes in place

```
public class Person
{
  [Required]
  [StringLength(25)]
  public string LastName { get; set; }

  [Required]
  [StringLength(25)]
  public string FirstName { get; set; }

  [Required]
  public DateTime DateOfBirth { get; set; }

  public bool IsRegistered { get; set; }

  public MaritalStatus MaritalStatus { get; set; }
```

```
    [Required]
    [StringLength(320)]
    [RegularExpression(@"^[a-zA-Z][\w\.&-]*[a-zA-Z0-9]@[a-zA-Z0-9]
      [\w\.-]*[a-zA-Z0-9]\.[a-zA-Z\.]*[a-zA-Z]$")]
    public string EmailAddress { get; set; }

    [Range(0, 20)]
    public int NumberOfChildren { get; set; }
}
```

Note that email address validation is complicated, and I don't present the regular expression used here as a fully correct version of an email validation expression, just as an example.

If we then load up the DataForm we used in the earlier examples and let it autogenerate the fields based on the updates to the Person class, we get the result shown in figure 13.5.

The validation attributes may be used both with the DataGrid and with the Data-Form and with some third-party controls. Without altering the controls themselves, there are workarounds to use some of the attributes in your own code, but they're neither robust nor fully implemented, so I won't include them here.

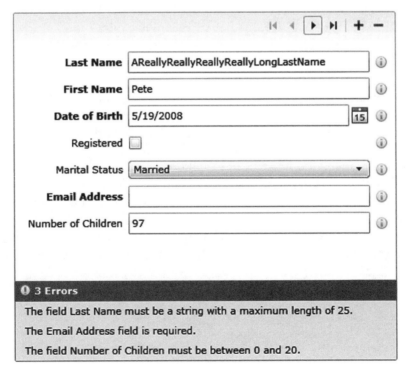

Figure 13.5 The DataForm with validation rules in place, showing the Validation Summary and default validation messages

13.5.3 *Calling external validation functions*

One of the validation attributes that could be used in your entities is the CustomVali-dationAttribute. This attribute takes as parameters a .NET type and the string name of a method to call on that type.

If we wanted to extend our Person class to only allow names that begin with B, we could create a simple validation method and class like listing 13.9.

Listing 13.9 A simple custom validation function

```
public class CustomValidationMethods
{
  public static ValidationResult NameBeginsWithB(string name)
  {
    if (name.StartsWith("B"))
      return ValidationResult.Success;
    else
      return new ValidationResult("Name does not begin with 'B'");
  }
}
```

The static method simply needs to take in the appropriate type and return a Valida-tionResult indicating whether the value passed validation. We then wire it up to our Person class using the CustomValidationAttribute like this:

```
[CustomValidation(typeof(CustomValidationMethods),
    "NameBeginsWithB"]
public string LastName { get; set; }
```

When validation is performed on the field, your custom function will be called and you'll get a validation error message that contains the text supplied in the Valida-tionResult or, if provided, the custom error message tied to that instance of the Cus-tomValidationAttribute. An example may be seen in figure 13.6.

The custom validation function has an alternate signature that's worth consideration. In addition to taking in the value to be validated, it can also take as a parameter a value of type ValidationContext. ValidationContext provides some additional information that the validation function may wish to use either in building the error message or in performing the actual validation. Taking the previous example and adding the context property results in the validation function shown in listing 13.10.

Listing 13.10 A custom validation function with ValidationContext

```
public static ValidationResult NameBeginsWithB(
    string name, ValidationContext context)
{
    if (name.StartsWith("B"))
        return ValidationResult.Success;
    else
        return new ValidationResult(
            string.Format("{0} does not begin with 'B'",
            context.DisplayName));
}
```

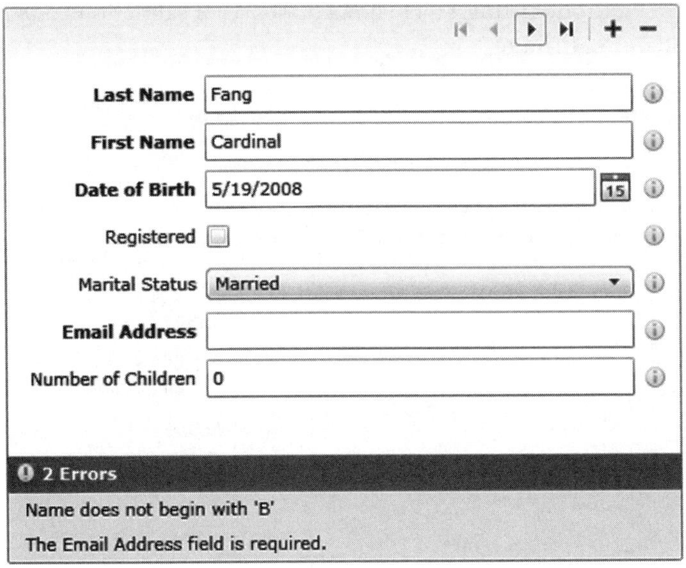

Figure 13.6
The Last Name field failed our custom validation check, as indicated in the error message at the bottom. Note that the field name isn't included in the error message.

Note how we used the `DisplayName` from the context to make the error message a little more meaningful. The resulting error on the `DataForm` looks like figure 13.7.

Because `ValidationContext` also supplies you with the parent object to which the member being validated belongs, you can use custom validation functions to effectively extend the validation system to support cross-field validation checks. Of course, you'll need to be careful so that you don't find yourself in the circular dependency hole that many cross-field checks ultimately end in.

Custom validation functions are one nice way to extend the validation system. They're simple to use and simple to create. Their main downside is they have external dependencies and, therefore, are not entirely self-contained. In addition, the method name is a string, and can be prone to typos or errors resulting from refactoring. To create more robust validation code, you'll want to create a custom validator.

13.5.4 Creating custom validators

Similar in concept to custom validation functions, custom validators are classes you write that inherit from `ValidationAttribute` in the `System.ComponentModel.DataAnnotations` namespace. The code itself is almost identical to what you'd write in

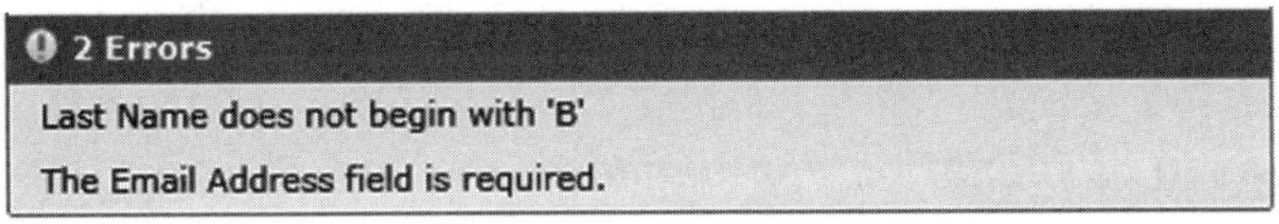

Figure 13.7 The enhanced error message with field name courtesy of the `ValidationContext`

a custom validation method. Listing 13.11 shows our custom validation code packaged into a custom validation attribute.

Listing 13.11   Custom validation attribute

```
public class NameBeginsWithBAttribute : ValidationAttribute
{
  protected override ValidationResult IsValid(
    object value, ValidationContext validationContext)
  {
    if (!(value is string))
      return new ValidationResult(
        "Incorrect data type. Expected string");

    if (string.IsNullOrEmpty((string)value))
      return ValidationResult.Success;

    if (((string)value).StartsWith("B"))
      return ValidationResult.Success;
    else
      return new ValidationResult(
        string.Format("{0} does not begin with 'B'",
        validationContext.DisplayName));
  }
}
```

Guard condition due to object typing

Allow empty/null

Actual validation code

The only thing we're required to do is override the `IsValid` function and return an appropriate `ValidationResult`. Once we do that, we can use the validator just like we would any other:

```
[NameBeginsWithB()]
public string LastName { get; set; }
```

The end result is the same error message display we saw with the custom validation function approach. But our validator is both simpler to use and less prone to breaking because it's self-contained inside a custom validator attribute class.

   That's attribute-based validation in a nutshell. If you can use the `DataGrid` and `DataForm` as your primary controls, attribute-based validation is, by far, the easiest approach to getting validation into your classes. Not only does the markup avoid code in your class, but you can also add buddy classes (partial classes) to mark up existing entities from your ORM.

   We'll cover the enhanced cross-tier validation features brought by WCF RIA Services in chapter 17. Until then, keep in mind that binding and validation are core Silverlight features and work without the addition of a framework such as WCF RIA Services or a pattern such as ViewModel (see chapter 16).

13.6   *Comparison of validation approaches*

Let's wrap up our discussion of validation by summarizing what I consider to be the pros and cons of each validation method, shown in table 13.6.

Table 13.6 Validation approach summary

Method	Pros	Cons
Exceptions `ValidatesOnExceptions=True`	Free type validation Simple inline code; no interfaces	Only invoked when property set; cross-field validation difficult or impossible Only one error per field
`IDataErrorInfo` `ValidatesOnDataErrors=True`	Cross-field validation No exceptions on the stack	Doesn't handle type validation Only one error per field Slightly more complex implementation than exceptions
`INotifyDataErrorInfo` `ValidatesOnNotifyDataErrors=True`	Cross-field validation No exceptions on the stack Asynchronous validation Multiple errors per field (note: current Silverlight UI templates only support showing the first error)	Doesn't handle type validation More complex implementation than exceptions
Validation attributes	No exceptions on the stack Multiple validators per field Simple No code other than attribute	Only works with `DataForm`, `DataGrid`, and some third-party annotation-aware controls

These three main approaches to validation are universally supported in Silverlight, requiring no special client-side control code or styles. Most third-party controls will also respect these forms of validation.

My recommendation is:

- Always support exceptions, so you get type checking.
- Use attributes if you're doing everything in a `DataForm` or `DataGrid`.
- Use `IDataErrorInfo` if you're doing all your validation on the client.
- Use `INotifyDataErrorInfo` if you need to call out to services to perform the validation.

Of course, your specific situation may dictate a different solution, but the guidelines here will apply to most applications.

13.7 Summary

Input validation is a core requirement of almost every application with a `TextBox`. Though Silverlight contains a number of different approaches, evolved over the versions, these are at least structured ways to handle validation.

For general Silverlight applications, exception-based validation is one of the easiest approaches to use. It's also very limited but, if your validation requirements aren't heavy, it can often handle the job.

For more robust implementations, turn to `IDataErrorInfo` and `INotifyDataErrorInfo`. The two can be complex to implement, especially the latter, but you're provided with pretty much everything you'd need to implement your own validation framework on top of the base interfaces.

When combined with the `DataGrid` and `DataForm`, attribute-based validation, along with the UI hinting covered in chapter 12, provides an incredibly simple and powerful way to create capable user interfaces with little plumbing code required.

Now that we've covered binding in chapter 11 and validation in this chapter and introduced the concept of a web service, it's time we dove right into the communications and networking stack that drives most Silverlight applications. Chapter 14 will cover how to use web and REST services as well as how to implement other forms of communication in your applications.

Networking
and communications

This chapter covers

- Working with web requests
- Performing duplex communication
- Consuming RESTful APIs and SOAP web services
- Working with JSON data
- Working with point to point and multicast sockets

Chapter 11 introduced you to the convenient data-binding mechanisms available within Silverlight. Although binding isn't restricted to just what we'd commonly think of as data, the truth of the matter is that's what it's usually used for. Working with data is essential to most applications, but you have to get the data into your application somehow. This is where networking and communications come in.

Silverlight provides numerous methods to get to data hosted on other systems, from complex web services to a simple XML document. The networking and communications features of Silverlight enable you to send and receive data with a variety of technologies including SOAP services, XML, JSON, RSS, Atom, and even sockets.

We'll start this chapter with the basics of Silverlight networking and the limitations of the browser stack. From there, we'll look at how to connect to SOAP services and RESTful services using the browser networking stack.

With the basics under your belt, it's then time to examine the client networking stack, introduced for out-of-browser applications but available even to applications running in-browser. This stack works around many of the limitations inherent in straight browser-based networking.

Then, because you'll need to do something with the data returned from these networking calls, we'll look at the deserialization support in Silverlight for things such as XML and JSON.

Our next stop will be to look at the WCF service enhancements available to Silverlight; then, we'll dive into WCF duplex services, or *polling duplex* as it's often called. Polling duplex enables push communications between the server and client, much like sockets, but without as much code.

Speaking of sockets, regular point-to-point sockets and UDP multicast sockets will be our last IP networking topics for the chapter. Multicast sockets are new to Silverlight 4 and enable a number of scenarios previously difficult or impossible in Silverlight.

We'll wrap up with a local non-IP networking feature that enables communication between two or more Silverlight applications, in-browser or out, running on the same machine.

14.1 *Trust, security, and browser limitations*

You must consider several basic concepts when using the communication APIs in Silverlight. These concepts—trust, security, and the limitations of the browser—apply to all methods of communication discussed in this chapter, with a partial exception granted to the Silverlight cross-application communication we wrap up with.

Silverlight executes within the confines of the client browser. Even the standard out-of-browser mode discussed in chapter 5 lives in this sandbox. Because of this, you have to retrieve data differently than the way you may be used to with a server-side technology such as ASP.NET. For example, you can't directly connect to a database without using something as a proxy, most commonly a web service. Although this method of communicating resembles that used by Ajax, there are significant differences.

Imagine you're building a Silverlight application that allows users to add items to a shopping cart. As soon as users add an item to their cart, you want to reserve it for them. Because Silverlight executes in the browser, you can't just call the database and mark the item as reserved. You need something acting as a proxy to the database. Throughout this chapter, we'll discuss methods of connecting to remote services to accomplish tasks like this. For now, let's move to the first basic concept: trust.

14.1.1 *Cross-domain network access*

The concept of trust applies to cross-domain access. If your application is hosted at http://10rem.net and you're attempting to access a web service hosted at http://silverlight.net, the request is made cross-domain. In the case of cross-domain access, it isn't a matter of whom your application trusts, but of who trusts your application. In the vein of increased security, Silverlight, like Flash before it, has restricted client applications to connecting only to the same domain that hosts the application itself. For those familiar with web services, this seems counterproductive, so the Silverlight team also worked in an exemption that requires the involvement of the server hosting the web service. Administrators of web servers can create policy files to give access to only the resources they want exposed to the requesting domains they trust. A simple XML file is added that tells the Silverlight application what it has access to on the foreign server.

> **NOTE** Cross-domain policy files aren't required for elevated trust (trusted) out-of-browser applications, described in chapter 5. Normal trust out-of-browser applications and in-browser applications still require them. Cross-domain policy files typically aren't required for images and media.

The clientaccesspolicy.xml file defines these policies; it needs to be placed at the root of the domain hosting any web service that's allowed to be accessed from a different domain. Even if there's a valid policy file, if it's located anywhere other than the root of the hosting domain, your application won't find it, and the request will fail. If the file is in place and has the proper attributes, your application is considered trusted, and the call will return as expected. So, what does a properly formatted policy file look like? Take a look at this example:

```
<?xml version="1.0" encoding="utf-8"?>
<access-policy>
    <cross-domain-access>
        <policy>
            <allow-from http-request-headers="*">
                <domain uri="*"/>
            </allow-from>
            <grant-to>
                <resource path="/" include-subpaths="true"/>
            </grant-to>
        </policy>
    </cross-domain-access>
</access-policy>
```

This shows the minimum needed in a clientaccesspolicy.xml file to allow HTTP access to all web services hosted on the current domain. If you want to have different rights for different services or to allow for socket access to the server, you can make additions to that file. Sockets are described in section 14.5. The example here is as open as possible-requests from any domain can access any resource in the host domain, and host headers are allowed. Table 14.1 shows the elements and attributes that make up a clientaccesspolicy.xml file. Attributes are shown after the element they apply to.

I know that you're anxious to see how to connect to data from within your application, but you need to create a solid foundation on which to build service access. You can make the policy file as open or as restrictive as you desire. By changing the domain element, you can limit access to a single domain. You can also add multiple policy

Table 14.1   Elements and attributes allowed in clientaccesspolicy.xml

Element/attribute	Required	Description
access-policy	Yes	Root element for the policy file.
cross-domain-policy	Yes	Container for one or more policy elements.
policy	Yes	Defines rules for a single domain or a group of domains.
allow-from	Yes	Container for permitted domains. If it contains no domain elements, no cross-domain access is granted.
http-request-headers	No	Defines which headers are allowed to be sent to the web services hosted at the current domain. If absent, no headers are allowed.
domain	Yes	Defines domains affected by the policy element in which the domain is a child.
uri	Yes	Specifies the exact domain allowed for the current policy.
grant-to	Yes	Container for one or more resource elements.
resource	Yes	Required for WebClient or HttpWebRequest classes. Defines server resources affected by the current policy.
Path	Yes	Required for WebClient or HttpWebRequest classes. Identifies individual files or services allowed or denied by the current policy. Format is a URI relative to the root of the domain.
include-subpaths	No	Optional for WebClient or HttpWebRequest classes. If absent, subfolder access is denied.
socket-resource	Yes	Required for socket access. Defines socket resources affected by the current policy.
Port	Yes	Required for socket access. Defines a port or range of ports, which must fall between 4502 and 4534, affected by the current policy.
Protocol	Yes	Required for socket access. Defines what protocols are allowed under the current policy. The only protocol currently allowed is TCP.

elements to apply different rules to requests from different domains, as shown in the next example.

Two separate policies are defined in this example. The first allows any request coming from a Silverlight application hosted at sometrusteddomain.com to have unrestricted access to the entire application; the second forces requests from any other domain to be restricted to the API folder and to have HTTP headers denied:

```
<?xml version="1.0" encoding="utf-8"?>
<access-policy>
  <cross-domain-access>
    <policy>
      <allow-from http-request-headers="*">
        <domain uri="http://sometrusteddomain.com"/>
      </allow-from>
      <grant-to>
        <resource path="/" include-subpaths="true"/>
      </grant-to>
    </policy>
    <policy>
      <allow-from>
        <domain uri="*"/>
      </allow-from>
      <grant-to>
        <resource path="/api"/>
      </grant-to>
    </policy>
  </cross-domain-access>
</access-policy>
```

The elements and attributes shown apply for connecting to any HTTP-based resource. Modifications are needed if you're using TCP sockets, which are described in section 14.5.

Even if this file isn't in place, you may still be in luck. Silverlight will also use policy files created for use with Adobe Flash, known as crossdomain.xml files, for cross-domain access. There are two restrictions when using a crossdomain.xml file:

- It may only be used for `WebClient`, `HttpWebRequest`, or service reference proxy access. Socket access isn't permitted.
- The entire domain must be allowed access for Silverlight to use a crossdomain.xml file. Silverlight doesn't parse the advanced properties of crossdomain.xml.

If the domain hosting the web service you're calling has either a clientaccesspolicy.xml or a crossdomain.xml file with the correct attributes in place, it's considered trusted and will return a result.

It's necessary to have an outside source trust your application, but should you trust everyone else? Let's look at a few ways to ensure that your application is as safe and secure as possible.

Why have cross-domain policies at all?

Any old native client or server application can access any service it wants to, so you may wonder why you have to jump through hoops when contacting network services through Silverlight.

Let's say for example that some services in your company include sensitive data. Maybe you work at a bank, an insurance company, or a government institution. The services are open to anyone authenticated on the LAN.

(continued)

You then browse to a site that has a cool Silverlight (or Flash) game you want to try out, and you run that and start enjoying a fine game of malware-tris, firewall-poker, or steal-your-data-bobble. While you're playing, the application sniffs for services in your local network (or uses a known lookup table from a disgruntled employee, or perhaps even something standard like UDDI) and starts downloading data from one of those services and uploading it to its own server.

Because you're executing the application and you're already authenticated locally, this malware has no problem grabbing data from any service you're authorized to and that it has the technology to access (SOAP, REST, and so forth). That is, unless you have a client that respects cross-domain policies. In that case, the Silverlight client can't connect to your local services because those servers presumably don't have a cross-domain policy file that will open the sensitive data to the world.

That's one of the main reasons cross-domain policy files are required by Flash and Silverlight, and why you need to carefully consider when and where you place cross-domain policy files on your own properties.

14.1.2 *Making your application secure*

Just as you put a valid policy file in place for security reasons, you can take other steps to make your application more secure. In this section, we'll briefly discuss data integrity, using HTTPS, and attaching HTTP headers to your request.

DATA INTEGRITY

Never trust that your data source will return pure, clean data every time. It's possible that, either purposefully or as a result of an error on the part of the service creator, harmful data may be returned to your application. You should always take steps to validate that the data you receive is compatible with the use you intend.

HTTPS

Any time you're passing sensitive data, you should use Hypertext Transfer Protocol over Secure Sockets Layer (HTTPS), which encrypts the message to prevent eavesdropping. In order to access cross-scheme services and data (HTTP to HTTPS or HTTPS to HTTP), the cross-domain policy file must permit that access.

COOKIES

Because Silverlight typically uses the browser's networking stack, cookies for the current domain also get added to requests from your Silverlight application. This is good if you're hosting your Silverlight component in an authenticated application that uses tokens stored in a cookie. In this case, the token also authenticates the requests originating from your Silverlight application, ensuring that you can access the resources you're authorized for.

One potential problem using this method is that when a user has a cookie-based token for a given domain, any Silverlight request to that domain contains the auth cookie, even if the request is from a different Silverlight application than the one you intend. Another issue is that this method of authentication relies on the client browser having session cookies enabled—which isn't always true.

Trust and security are important for any application; before we move on to the meat of accessing data, let's make sure the browser itself is capable of doing everything you're asking of it. This question brings us to the next basic concept: limitations of the browser.

14.1.3 Limitations of the browser

A few limitations apply to Silverlight due to its use of the networking API of the host browser. These limitations have affected browsers for years, and now they carry over into Silverlight as well when using the browser networking stack. We've already discussed the client-side nature of Silverlight and how that affects data access, so now we're going to talk about two similar limitations: connection limits and asynchronous calls.

CONNECTION COUNT LIMIT

The number of concurrent connections to a single subdomain (for example, http://10rem.net and http://images.10rem.net are two different subdomains) is limited in most browsers to two. This limit has been increased in Internet Explorer 8 to six concurrent connections; but because Silverlight runs in multiple browsers, you should still be aware of it. Because Silverlight uses the browser's networking stack for its communications by default, it's bound by the same limits. You may need a combination of resources or other approaches to ensure that this doesn't create unnecessary delays in your application. Keep in mind that the browser may be loading objects outside the scope of the Silverlight application as well, such as stylesheets, images, and JavaScript files. All these objects count toward the limit of two concurrent connections. You should keep this fact in mind, particularly when performing duplex communication as described in section 14.4.

Increasing effective connections

A common trick to increase the throughput for your application, especially now that clients often have significant bandwidth at their disposal, is to spread the application network requests across separate subdomains. Take these, for example:

- api.10rem.net hosts the web services and the cross-domain file.
- images.10rem.net has the image resources.
- www.10rem.net serves up the web pages.

Each subdomain has at least two simultaneous connections available per browser. In that way, calls to the API won't cause image downloads to stall and vice versa, assuming the client and server both have sufficient bandwidth. Providing for a separate subdomain for the API as well provides a better way to segment out the API and therefore be sure that you aren't running into issues with granting cross-domain access to areas that host user interfaces.

(continued)

You can play with those as best suits your application or follow completely different approaches that round-robin (from the client) to a pool of identical servers. You'll have more options for redirecting to different servers, as well as increase your effective connection limit.

Of course, this assumes you want people to have six open connections to your network. If you don't want that, another approach is to package requests into chunky calls: reduce chattiness in service calls, and package assets such as images into zip files rather than individual image URIs. We'll discuss more about this approach when we get to the `WebClient`.

ASYNCHRONOUS ONLY

All communication from within the Silverlight application is done asynchronously because of the Silverlight development team's decision to use the browser's networking API, and to keep the APIs tight with only one way to accomplish any given task. The most common way of making asynchronous calls requires a few simple steps, which we'll detail in the following section. Typically, all you need to do is create an event handler to be executed when the call returns.

If you want to create a more synchronous experience for your application, you can enable some kind of blocking element, such as a download-progress animation, when the call begins and then remove it once the request has returned its data. We'll discuss how to create animations in chapter 22.

Note that the asynchronous behavior can occur on multiple threads, a fact that can cause trouble when you aren't aware of it. In section 14.2.2, we'll point out where you need to be careful with which thread you're on, and show you a technique to avoid trouble. Now that we have the basics out of the way, let's get to the point of this chapter: connecting to data sources.

14.2 Connecting to data sources

Nearly every application built today, even using Silverlight, needs data to accomplish its goal. In chapter 11, you saw how to take data and bind it to properties on controls, but where does that data come from? Because Silverlight executes on the client, often on the other side of a firewall, it doesn't have direct access to a database as do server-based technologies such as ASP.NET. To get access to the data from within Silverlight, you need to use a proxy of some sort, typically a web service. A *web service* is a resource made available to clients using a defined protocol. Most web services fall into two categories: SOAP and REST. We'll explain these popular formats, and how to use them, in this section.

14.2.1 Using SOAP services

When you think of a classic web service, you're thinking about SOAP. SOAP services follow a strict protocol that defines the format in which messages are passed back and forth. Silverlight has great support for SOAP Services, supporting the WS-I Basic Profile 1.0 (SOAP 1.1 over HTTP), SOAP 1.2, and WS-Addressing 1.0, as well as a small subset of WS-Security. Using SOAP services in Silverlight allows for both the simplest implementation and most powerful data-transfer mechanism of any service type through the use of the service reference. Over the next few pages, you'll create a proxy object for the service, call a method on it, and download the results. After you've created and used a proxy to connect to a SOAP service, you'll be amazed at how simple yet powerful this capability is.

> **NOTE** SOAP originally stood for *Simple Object Access Protocol*, but that definition fell into disuse and was officially dropped with version 1.2 of the W3C SOAP standard.

SERVICE REFERENCES

The easiest way to connect to a service is through a service reference proxy. If the web service you're connecting to supports Web Services Description Language (WSDL), Visual Studio can read that information and create a proxy in your application for you. Creating a service reference in your Silverlight application takes three simple steps:

1 In Visual Studio 2010, right-click your Silverlight project and choose Add Service Reference.

2 This brings up the Add Service Reference dialog box. On this form, you can either type in the URI of the service you wish to connect to and click the Go button or, if the services are part of the same solution, click the Discover button. Either option tells Visual Studio to poll the chosen location for available services and analyze their signatures. When the services have been displayed, you can open them and look at what methods are available on each service. You can then enter in the text box a namespace by which you want to refer to the service and click OK to create the proxy.

3 You can modify more advanced settings either by clicking the Advanced button in the previous dialog or by right-clicking the service reference and selecting Configure Service Reference. One particularly useful capability of this form is the ability to change the collection types returned by the service. The default collection type can vary depending on the service you're connecting to, but you can also change it to use other collection types, even generics.

When the service reference is created, Visual Studio also adds references to the `System.Runtime.Serialization` and `System.ServiceModel` assemblies. These are used by Silverlight in connecting to web services and in serializing and deserializing the SOAP message.

When you've created your service reference, it's easy to use for both sending and receiving data. First, let's talk about calling SOAP services using the service reference you just created.

RECEIVING DATA WITH THE PROXY

Connecting to and downloading data from a simple SOAP service is easy. You need to add two Using statements to your page, one for System.ServiceModel and another for System.ServiceModel.Channels. Next, you need to create a proxy to the service using the service reference as created in the previous section. Name the service reference namespace SilverService for this example. Then, you add an event handler to catch the return of the asynchronous call to the exposed method on the service. These steps are demonstrated in listing 14.1.

Listing 14.1 Calling a SOAP service

Result:

3:44:12 AM   Get Time

XAML:

```
<Grid x:Name="LayoutRoot">
  <Grid.ColumnDefinitions>
    <ColumnDefinition Width="*" />
    <ColumnDefinition Width="Auto" />
  </Grid.ColumnDefinitions>
  <TextBlock x:Name="Results"
    Grid.Column="0" Margin="5"/>
  <StackPanel Grid.Column="1">
    <Button x:Name="GetTime" Click="GetTime_Click"
      Content="Get Time" Height="33" Width="90"/>
  </StackPanel>
</Grid>
```

C#-Silverlight:

```
private void GetTime_Click(object sender, RoutedEventArgs e)
{
  Binding myBinding = new BasicHttpBinding();          ◁─── Binding
  EndpointAddress myEndpoint = new
    EndpointAddress(
      "http://localhost:55905/SampleAsmx.asmx");       ◁─┐ Port number
                                                          │ will be different
  SilverService.SampleAsmxSoapClient proxy = new     ❶
    SilverService.SampleAsmxSoapClient
      (myBinding, myEndpoint);

  proxy.GetTimeCompleted += new                        ❷
    EventHandler<SilverService.GetTimeCompletedEventArgs>
    (proxy_GetTimeCompleted);

  proxy.GetTimeAsync();            ❸
}

void proxy_GetTimeCompleted(object sender,
  SilverService.GetTimeCompletedEventArgs e)
{
  Results.Text = e.Result.ToLongTimeString();      ❹
```

```
      (sender as SilverService.SampleAsmxSoapClient).CloseAsync();
}
```

C#-SampleAsmx.asmx service in web project:

```
[WebService(Namespace = "http://services.10rem.net/")]
[WebServiceBinding(ConformsTo = WsiProfiles.BasicProfile1_1)]
[System.ComponentModel.ToolboxItem(false)]
public class SampleAsmx : System.Web.Services.WebService
{
    [WebMethod]
    public DateTime GetTime()
    {
        return DateTime.Now;
    }
}
```

This shows the entire process of creating the proxy ❶, adding an event handler ❷, calling an asynchronous method ❸, and handling the results ❹. In this example, the SOAP service you're connecting to exposes a method called GetTime, which accepts no input properties and outputs a DateTime of the current time. You first create a Binding of type BasicHttpBinding. This tells the proxy that the service you're connecting to uses SOAP 1.1. The default constructor for BasicHttpBinding creates a Binding with no security. An optional parameter on the constructor accepts a BasicHttpSecurityMode, which allows you to tell the binding how to secure itself; for example, you can tell the binding to use SSL when transmitting the SOAP message. You also create an EndpointAddress that points to the URI of the service you're about to call. Finally, you create the proxy using the service reference created earlier and pass into it the binding BasicHttpBinding and the initialized EndpointAddress objects.

> **NOTE** The port number for your development-mode web service may change from time to time, breaking any service references. To force the port number to stick, right-click the web project, select Properties, and click the Web tab. Then, select the option to always use the specified port number.

Next, you need to add an event handler to be called when your asynchronous method call returns. You can do this by using the Visual Studio shortcut of pressing the + key, then the = key, and then pressing Tab twice after selecting the GetTimeCompleted event on your proxy. Using this shortcut automatically finishes the event handler declaration for you and creates a stubbed method as the event handler. Finally, you call the GetTimeAsync() method on the proxy to begin the asynchronous call to the service. IntelliSense will show you a [webmethod]Completed event and a [webmethod]Async() method for each method exposed by the SOAP service. When you created the service reference in the previous step, Visual Studio queried the service to see what methods were available and made proxy methods for each of them.

After the service returns, the method declared as the event handler-proxy_GetTimeCompleted-gets called with the results. Because the method is outputting the results as a Datetime object, you can convert it to a string using standard .NET conversion methods, which you can then assign to the Text property of a TextBlock. The only other task to perform in the return method is to close out the connection using the `CloseAsync()` method on the proxy. Garbage collection will technically come through and close any old connections, but it's good programming practice to close any connection when you're done using it.

And that's all there is to it—you've now connected to a SOAP service, called a method on it, and displayed the results. Sending data to a SOAP service is just as easy.

SENDING DATA USING THE PROXY

If you're thinking that all you need to do to send data to a SOAP service using a service reference is to include a parameter in the method call, you're right. Let's look at listing 14.2 for an example.

Listing 14.2 Sending data to a SOAP service

Result:

one   **Get Time**

           Get String

XAML:

```
<Grid x:Name="LayoutRoot">
  <Grid.ColumnDefinitions>
    <ColumnDefinition Width="*" />
    <ColumnDefinition Width="Auto" />
  </Grid.ColumnDefinitions>

  <TextBlock x:Name="Results"
    Grid.Column="0" Margin="5"/>

  <StackPanel Grid.Column="1">
    <Button x:Name="GetTime" Click="GetTime_Click"
      Content="Get Time" Height="33" Width="90"/>
    <Button x:Name="GetString" Click="GetString_Click"
      Content="Get String" Height="33" Width="90"/>
  </StackPanel>
</Grid>
```

C#-Silverlight client:

```
private void GetString_Click(object sender, RoutedEventArgs e)
{
  Binding myBinding = new BasicHttpBinding();
  EndpointAddress myEndpoint = new
    EndpointAddress("http://localhost:55905/SampleAsmx.asmx");
  SilverService.SampleAsmxSoapClient proxy = new
    SilverService.SampleAsmxSoapClient(myBinding, myEndpoint);
  proxy.GetCoolTextCompleted +=
    new EventHandler<SilverService.GetCoolTextCompletedEventArgs>(
      proxy_GetCoolTextCompleted);            Service call with
                                              parameter |
  proxy.GetCoolTextAsync(1);
```

```
}
void proxy_GetCoolTextCompleted(object sender,
  SilverService.GetCoolTextCompletedEventArgs e)
{
  Results.Text = e.Result;
(sender as SilverService.SampleAsmxSoapClient).CloseAsync();
}
```

C#-web service:

```
[WebMethod]
public string GetCoolText(int number)
{
  switch (number)
  {
    case 1: return "one";
    case 2: return "two";
    case 3: return "three";
    ...
  }
}
```

Listing 14.2 builds on the code from listing 14.1. This is an example of sending of a single int as a parameter to the GetCoolText method on the web service. This approach is fine for sending a simple data value, but what about complex data types? Still no problem.

USING COMPLEX DATA TYPES

Sending and receiving complex data types over a SOAP service is also a simple matter. When you created the service reference, the signatures for objects used in the SOAP message were automatically analyzed and a client-side proxy made for those as well. With this proxy, you can instantiate objects of that type in your application (see listing 14.3).

Listing 14.3   Using complex data types with a SOAP service

Service:

```
[WebMethod]
public void SetSomething(int count, WsUser myObject)
{
  //Perform database operations here
}

...
public class WsUser
{
  public int Id { get; set; }
  public string Name { get; set; }
  public bool IsValid { get; set; }
}
```

C#:

```
private void UploadUser()
{
  Binding myBinding = new BasicHttpBinding();
```

```
EndpointAddress myEndpoint =
  new EndpointAddress("http://localhost:55905/SampleAsmx.asmx");
SilverService.SampleAsmxSoapClient proxy = new
  SilverService.SampleAsmxSoapClient(myBinding, myEndpoint);

SilverService.WsUser myData = new
  SilverService.WsUser()
  { Id = 3, Name = "John", IsValid = true };

proxy.SetSomethingCompleted += new
  EventHandler<System.ComponentModel.AsyncCompletedEventArgs>
  (proxy_SetSomethingCompleted);

proxy.SetSomethingAsync(1, myData);
}
void proxy_SetSomethingCompleted(object sender,
  System.ComponentModel.AsyncCompletedEventArgs e)
{
  (sender as SilverService.SampleAsmxSoapClient).CloseAsync();
}
```

This listing shows how you can use complex data types on SOAP services from within your Silverlight application. The service itself is left as an exercise for you, and the example is illustrative only. As you can see in the web method declaration, the method SetSomething expects two parameters: an int and a WsUser. WsUser is made up of three properties. Note that both the web method and the WsUser class are part of the ASMX web service, not the Silverlight application.

Now, let's use WsUser in the example application. Because WsUser is a return type on a method, a copy of its type exists on the proxy for you to use. In this example, you create an instance of the WsUser class and fill its properties. Then, you add the instance of the object as a parameter on the asynchronous method call, SetSomethingAsync.

USING THE CONFIGURATION FILE

So far, we've shown the slightly more verbose way of calling a service, where all the endpoint information is handled in code. Silverlight provides another option: you can use the information in the ServiceReferences.ClientConfig file.

> **NOTE** ServiceReferences.ClientConfig is an XML file created automatically when you add a service reference. It's packaged into the .xap file (see chapter 3 for more on .xap files) and is deployed with your application. You may update this configuration file at any time by unzipping the .xap, changing the file, and rezipping it. Some clever developers have even come up with tools to handle this automatically; Bing them (www.bing.com) to find out more.

An example configuration file is shown in listing 14.4. The configuration file specifies, among other things, the type of encoding, the maximum receive message and buffer sizes, the binding contract, and endpoint information.

Listing 14.4 The ServiceReferences.ClientConfig file

```
<configuration>
  <system.serviceModel>
    <bindings>
```

```
    <customBinding>
      <binding name="CustomBinding_HelloWorldService">        Binary
        <binaryMessageEncoding />                      ◄──┘   encoding
        <httpTransport maxReceivedMessageSize="2147483647"            ◄─┐
                       maxBufferSize="2147483647">
        </httpTransport>                                       Buffer/message
      </binding>                                               size limits
    </customBinding>
    </bindings>
    <client>                                                   Endpoint
      <endpoint                                          ◄──┘  definition
➡   address="http://localhost:23867/Services/HelloWorldService.svc"
        binding="customBinding"
        bindingConfiguration="CustomBinding_HelloWorldService"
        contract="Services.HelloWorldService"
        name="CustomBinding_HelloWorldService" />
    </client>
  </system.serviceModel>
</configuration>
```

Although certainly not a requirement, this example uses the new WCF binary encoding with a WCF SOAP service on the server-a new feature enabled by default in Silverlight when using the Silverlight Enabled WCF Service template mentioned in section 14.5.1. This reduces the message size considerably in situations where the server and client aren't using GZIP compression on the content and the server is running .NET 3.5 SP1 or above.

In addition, the server side is able to handle more requests due to the binary nature of the messages. The downside is that the service clients are restricted to those aware of the proprietary format, unless you add a second endpoint.

What about NetTcp?

Another protocol option, which like binary SOAP is specific to WCF, is the NetTcp protocol. Silverlight 4 added support for that protocol using the net.tcp:// scheme. This is a lighter-weight protocol that eliminates the overhead of HTTP in the transaction.

Although I won't go into detail here, because it's not commonly used and requires no real changes to your code, I do want to mention that even when using NetTcp, you need to have a policy file on a regular port 80 HTTP server at the same IP address as your NetTcp service. The protocol to include in the Client Access Policy is `tcp`:

```
<grant-to>
  <socket-resource port="4502-4534" protocol="tcp" />
</grant-to>
```

If you leave the policy file out or don't have the server mapped correctly, you'll receive a rather long-winded `CommunicationException` that tells you the socket connection was forbidden.

To test, open your browser and browse to

```
http://<IpAddressOfYourNetTcpService>:80/clientaccesspolicy.xml
```

(continued)

and verify that the file downloads. If it does, you're good. If not, then you need to check your IP address and domain names.

Other than that, you use NetTcp just as you would SOAP or SOAP with binary encoding. From a proxy usage standpoint, there are no important differences.

When using the information from the .ClientConfig file and eliminating all the setup code, your client-side code becomes considerably simpler, as shown in listing 14.5.

Listing 14.5   Client-side code using ServiceReferences.ClientConfig file

XAML:
```
<StackPanel Margin="30" Width="100">
  <TextBlock x:Name="Results" />
  <Button x:Name="CallService"
          Click="CallService_Click"
          Content="Call Service" />
</StackPanel>
```

C#:
```
private void CallService_Click(
            object sender, RoutedEventArgs e)
{
  var client = new HelloWorldServiceClient();        ⊲—— Proxy

  client.HelloWorldCompleted +=                      ⊲—┐ Event handler
    new EventHandler<HelloWorldCompletedEventArgs>      │ wire-up
    (client_HelloWorldCompleted);
  client.HelloWorldAsync();

}                                                      ┐ Event
                                                       │ handler
void client_HelloWorldCompleted(                    ⊲—┘
    object sender, HelloWorldCompletedEventArgs e)
{
    Results.Text = e.Result;
}
```

The code has been simplified considerably because you externalize the settings. This time around, you don't need to create bindings or endpoints and pass them in to the proxy. Whether this is appropriate for your situations comes down to whether you want to handle the bindings in code or in configuration files.

In code, you can get the address of the current server and base your service call on that, if appropriate. But if you want to change that algorithm and, say, move from www.mydomain.com/services to api.mydomain.com, you'll need to change code and recompile/redeploy the client.

In configuration, you can set the URL to be anything you wish, but you must remember to change it when moving between servers (such as from development to test to staging to production). Given that this doesn't require a recompile and the format is XML inside a standard zip, there's little risk to this approach.

Simplifying async method calls

If you want an even tighter format for your service-call processing, regardless of whether you're using SOAP, REST, or something else, you can use a lambda expression to build a delegate to handle the service call return. In that case, you get the entire service call neatly wrapped up into one visible function:

```
private void CallService_Click(
            object sender, RoutedEventArgs e)
{
  var client = new HelloWorldServiceClient();
  client.HelloWorldCompleted += (s, ea) =>
  {
      Results.Text = ea.Result;
  };
  client.HelloWorldAsync();
}
```

In this example, the separate event handler is replaced with one defined inline. The handler takes s for the sender and ea for the event arguments. This doesn't turn the call into a synchronous call-it's still async. You simply compact the event wire-up step.

When used inside a function like this, there is no downside to this approach, so I use it constantly due to its compactness and readability. Don't use this approach for class-level handlers, because you may end up with multiple handlers without any way to remove them.

That's all it takes to use SOAP services in Silverlight. Silverlight isn't limited to SOAP services. Next, we'll discuss consuming REST services through Silverlight, a topic that opens up a whole new arena of data providers.

14.2.2 *RESTful services*

Representational State Transfer, or *REST*, means several things; in this case, it refers to the approach of making services accessible through a set of simple URIs and HTTP verbs. Before the days of web services and stateful web applications, everything on the web was RESTful, meaning that all traffic over HTTP used one of the HTTP verbs to define its purpose, and all calls were complete without requiring server-side state. Over the years, the use of these verbs dwindled down to nearly all traffic using only the GET and POST verbs for requesting a page and submitting form data, respectively. Recently there's been a trend toward moving simple web services to a simpler framework.

Many web service providers incorrectly use the term REST to mean any service that isn't SOAP. The main thing to realize is that the URI, and possibly the HTTP verb, may change depending on the action being performed. Typically, a creator of RESTful services will try to follow an intuitive structure where the URI first contains a type followed by an instance. For example, a URI with the structure http:// www.arestfuldomain.com/Users might return an array of user records, whereas the

URI http://www.arestfuldomain.com/Users/JohnSmith might return a single user record for John Smith. This isn't a rule of REST services; it's more of a guideline.

Silverlight currently supports only the GET and POST verbs when using the default networking stack (see the end of this chapter for more options). This is another limitation of using the browser's networking stack. Luckily, because this is a common browser limitation, most service creators are aware of it and try to use those two verbs for all actions.

In the previous section, you saw how to use service references to create proxies to SOAP services. Consuming a REST service takes a little more work on the side of the Silverlight developer. Silverlight nicely handles calling RESTful services through the HttpWebRequest object that you're already familiar with. In this section, we'll show you how to use this class to read data from and send data to a RESTful service. The asynchronous nature of these calls can cause problems accessing the UI, so let's solve that first.

> **NOTE** You can also use the simpler WebClient class for accessing RESTful services. Because HttpWebRequest is both more complex and more powerful, and therefore requires an example, we'll cover that here.

BYPASSING THREADING PROBLEMS

The asynchronous nature of Silverlight web service calls can create threading problems for the developer. When you're dealing with service reference-generated proxies, threading isn't an issue; when you're creating the connection yourself, you have to deal with this part as well. When you attempt to access UI elements directly within callback methods, you get a threading exception. You deal with this by creating a class-level variable of type SynchronizationContext, which gives you a handle back to the correct thread to do UI updates:

```
private SynchronizationContext UIThread;
private void btnSingleXml_Click(object sender, RoutedEventArgs e)
{
  UIThread = SynchronizationContext.Current;
  ...
  request.BeginGetResponse(SingleXmlCallBack, request);
}
private void SingleXmlCallBack(IAsyncResult result)
{
  ...
  UIThread.Post(UpdateUiText, responseStream);
}
private void UpdateUiText(object stream)
{
  ...
}
```

The first thing you do in this example is create a class variable of type SynchronizationContext. Scoping it at the class level means you'll have access to it no matter where you are in the process. Next, in the method that starts the request (we'll detail the request in the next section), you assign a reference to the current thread to the variable previously created. Then, in the callback method, you call the Post method on the SynchronizationContext variable, which has two parameters. The first parameter accepts a method to do the UI update with, and the second accepts an object. In this case, it's simplest to send the entire response stream as the second parameter. Finally, in the method called by the Post method, you can cast the received object into a Stream and perform whatever UI updates you need. You don't need to pass the entire response stream to the method that updates the UI—you can send any object. It's my personal preference to let the update method also do any deserialization; by using this technique, you ensure that your UI updates will succeed.

As you can see, as long as you know how to get back to the UI thread, there isn't a problem here. Now, let's GET to the meat of REST services.

GETTING FROM REST SERVICES

In relation to Silverlight, although REST may dictate the method in which a resource is accessed, it doesn't dictate the format of the data received. The most common ways to return data from a RESTful web service are Plain Old XML (POX) and JSON. We'll discuss how to consume both POX and JSON in section 14.3.

The basics of calling a REST-based web service from Silverlight involve creating an HttpWebRequest object, setting its destination URI, and calling it asynchronously (see listing 14.6).

Listing 14.6 Getting data from a REST service

C#:
```
private void GetSingleXml_Click(object sender, RoutedEventArgs e)
{
  UIThread = SynchronizationContext.Current;
  string rawPath
    = "http://www.silverlightinaction.com/Authors.svc/SingleXml/{0}";
  Uri path = new Uri(string.Format(rawPath, Input.Text),
    UriKind.Absolute);

  HttpWebRequest request = (HttpWebRequest)WebRequest.Create(path);
  request.BeginGetResponse(SingleXmlCallBack, request);
}
private void SingleXmlCallBack(IAsyncResult result)
{
  HttpWebRequest request = (HttpWebRequest)result.AsyncState;
  HttpWebResponse response
    = (HttpWebResponse)request.EndGetResponse(result);
  Stream responseStream = response.GetResponseStream();
  UIThread.Post(UpdateUiText, responseStream);
}
```

In this example, you make a simple request to a RESTful web service. Three steps are necessary when making a GET request, all of which are demonstrated here:

1 Create a Uri object and initialize it with the path and, optionally, the UriKind.
2 Create an HttpWebRequest object for the Uri.
3 Call BeginGetResponse on your HttpWebRequest object and pass it the name of a callback method, as well as the HttpWebRequest itself.

The BeginGetResponse method initiates the call to the service and registers the passed-in method as a callback method. When the response returns, that method will be called with the current HttpWebRequest being passed to it as type IAsyncResult.

In the callback method, the first thing is to cast the AsyncState of the IAsyncResult into an HttpWebRequest object. In the next statement, you call the EndGetResponse method on the request object to both end the connection and return an HttpWebResponse object. Finally, you call the GetResponseStream method of the HttpWebResponse object to get the Stream, the response to your web service call. We'll cover deserializing the Stream into useful data in section 14.3.

POSTING TO REST SERVICES

Most RESTful services use GET to retrieve data and POST to send it. Because the default HTTP verb used when using HttpWebRequest is GET, you need to do a few things differently when you want to perform a POST. Listing 14.7 shows the process of sending data to a REST service.

Listing 14.7   POSTing data to a REST service

C#:
```csharp
private void Test_Click(object sender, RoutedEventArgs e)
{
  UIThread = SynchronizationContext.Current;
  Uri path = new
    Uri("http://www.silverlightinaction.com/Authors.svc/Update/Brown",
    UriKind.Absolute);
  HttpWebRequest request = (HttpWebRequest)WebRequest.Create(path);
  request.Method = "POST";
  request.ContentType = "application/xml";
  request.BeginGetRequestStream(AddPayload, request);
}

private void AddPayload(IAsyncResult result)
{
  HttpWebRequest request = (HttpWebRequest) result.AsyncState;
  StreamWriter dataWriter =
    new StreamWriter(request.EndGetRequestStream(result));
  dataWriter.Write("<?xml version=\"1.0\"?><Author><FirstName>Bob" +
    "</FirstName><LastName>Smith</LastName></Author>");
  dataWriter.Close();
  request.BeginGetResponse(SingleJsonCallBack, request);
}

private void SingleJsonCallBack(IAsyncResult result)
{
  HttpWebRequest request = (HttpWebRequest)result.AsyncState;
  HttpWebResponse response =
    (HttpWebResponse)request.EndGetResponse(result);
  Stream responseStream = response.GetResponseStream();
  UIThread.Post(UpdateUiText, responseStream);
}
```

Because REST services don't have methods, and instead deal with entities, you need to add any data to be sent to the service to the message being sent. In listing 14.7, instead of calling `BeginGetResponse` from the initial call, you call `BeginGetRequestStream`. This event handler allows you to add information to the stream after it's created but before it's sent to the service. After that's been done, you register the `BeginGetResponse` event handler as is done during GET operations.

Knowing how to do GETs and POSTs is only half of the battle; you need to be able to use what gets returned as well. REST services normally return either XML- or JSON-formatted data. In section 14.4, we'll talk about ways to take the response stream containing these common data formats and convert it into useful objects.

The browser stack only allows POST and GET, not DELETE or PUT. Those limitations, and the need for out-of-browser networking support, prompted the team to create a second separate networking stack: the client HTTP Stack.

14.3 The client HTTP stack

Silverlight 3 introduced a second networking stack, meant primarily for use when running out-of-browser, but accessible in in-browser scenarios as well. This stack eliminates some of the restrictions of the browser-based HTTP stack.

The two stacks included in Silverlight are known as the *browser HTTP stack* and the *client HTTP stack*. As their names indicate, the browser HTTP stack goes directly through the browser for all networking calls, whereas the client HTTP stack doesn't. This opens up a plethora of new capabilities, such as additional verbs like PUT and DELETE, as well as getting around the limitations on simultaneous connections. There are some caveats, though. We'll discuss those after we go through the mechanics of using the stack.

In this section, we'll first look at how to manually create the client stack. Then, because manually creating the stack every time can be a real chore, and impossible with generated code, you'll see how to automatically select the stack at runtime. Finally, we'll look at one important difference from the browser stack: cookie management.

14.3.1 Manually creating the client stack

One way to create an instance of the `ClientHttp` network stack is to use the `System.Net.Browser.WebRequestCreator` object. That object serves as a kind of a factory and includes two static properties: `BrowserHttp` and `ClientHttp`. Call the `Create` method on the `ClientHttp` property as shown:

```
private void CallNetwork_Click(object sender, RoutedEventArgs e)
{
  HttpWebRequest request =
    (HttpWebRequest)WebRequestCreator.ClientHttp.Create(
    new Uri("http://api.10rem.net/Authors"));

  request.Method = "PUT";

  . . .

}
```

This approach to creating the stack is usable only when you're using the low-level `HttpWebRequest` class. That's helpful, but what if you want it to automatically be used by any `WebRequest`-derived classes?

14.3.2 *Automatically using the client stack*

A second way to use the client stack is to have it automatically selected based on specific URLs or schemes. That way, any call to the specified URL or scheme will use the stack you specify. The FTP, FILE, HTTP, and HTTPS schemes are already assigned to the browser stack, but you can override them or go a more specific route and specify that the client stack should be used for any HTTP* calls to a specific web site, or a specific service at a known URL. For example, if you want all calls to 10rem.net, both regular and SSL, to use the client stack, you'd put the following early in your code:

```
WebRequest.RegisterPrefix(
    "http://10rem.net", WebRequestCreator.ClientHttp);

WebRequest.RegisterPrefix(
    "https://10rem.net", WebRequestCreator.ClientHttp);
```

After this is done, any classes that use `WebRequest` or a class which derives from it will automatically use the client HTTP stack you have specified.

The client stack brings along a number of enhancements, including the ability to automatically and manually set some HTTP header values previously unavailable to you.

14.3.3 *Automatically setting the HTTP Referer and other headers*

When a HTTP request is sent across the wire, it includes a number of headers that we typically don't see. For example, if I open up Yahoo! in my browser, the request contains the following info:

```
GET http://www.yahoo.com/ HTTP/1.1
Accept: */*
Accept-Language: en-us
User-Agent: Mozilla/4.0 (compatible; MSIE 7.0; Windows NT 6.1;
    Trident/4.0; SLCC2; .NET CLR 2.0.50727; .NET CLR 3.5.30729;
    .NET CLR 3.0.30729; Media Center PC 6.0; Tablet PC 2.0;
    .NET CLR 3.0.30618; .NET CLR 3.5.21022; InfoPath.2;
    Media Center PC 5.0; MS-RTC LM 8; SLCC1; WWTClient2; Zune 4.0;
    .NET4.0C; .NET4.0E; MS-RTC LM 8)
Accept-Encoding: gzip, deflate
Connection: Keep-Alive
Host: www.yahoo.com
Cookie: [lots of cookie stuff]
```

The first line is the verb and the target. In this case, we're GETting the Yahoo! home page. Most of the stuff after that is pretty standard. IE8 is sending some information about the browser in use, what formats it'll accept, the cookies, and so on. Collectively, those are called *HTTP headers*. New to Silverlight 4, and unique to the client networking stack, is the ability to send the HTTP Referer (sic) header with all requests, including out-of-browser network requests.

REFERRING SITE HEADER

The HTTP Referer header is a web standard used to indicate the origin of a request. Often, this is used to figure out what other pages are linked to your page, or what other pages are attempting to post to your form.

> **NOTE** Don't use the HTTP Referer header to implement any type of important security check. Some browsers include utilities that allow users to eliminate the referer or replace it with one they manually input.

When using the client stack, Silverlight automatically sets the HTTP Referer to the base URL of the .xap file where the out-of-browser application originated. This is useful, because an out-of-browser application doesn't really have a URL and certainly doesn't have a hosting web page.

For example, if I access my web site from a trusted out-of-browser application (remember, in trusted applications, there's no check for a client access policy), the request headers look like this:

```
GET http://10rem.net/ HTTP/1.1
Accept: */*
Accept-Language: en-US
Referer: http://localhost:21597/ClientBin/RefererTest.xap
Accept-Encoding: identity
User-Agent: ...
Host: 10rem.net
Connection: Keep-Alive
```

I removed the user-agent for brevity; it's the same as the previous example. But note the value of the HTTP Referer header. I ran this example from Visual Studio, so the host is localhost:21597. The full path of the .xap is included as the Referer automatically.

> **NOTE** Currently, Firefox doesn't set the HTTP Referer header for any HTTP GET requests from plug-ins running in-browser. If you must have a HTTP Referer set for GET requests, you'll need to use the client stack as shown here. POST requests are handled properly.

You can't manually set the HTTP Referer header; it's one of a number of restricted headers. In addition to the Referer, Silverlight also sets headers such as the Content-Length, User-Agent, and others. Some of those, such as Content-Length, Content-Type, and Authentication, have dedicated request properties that map to the appropriate headers. It's unusual to change Content-Length and Content-Type, but setting authentication credentials is a must for any serious web application.

14.3.4 Authentication credentials

Many endpoints on the Web, and even more on internal networks, are protected by some sort of authentication scheme. In order to access those endpoints, you must be able to provide authentication information along with the request.

The client networking stack supports NTLM, basic, and digest authorization, allowing you to pass credentials to the endpoint of a request via the `Credentials` property. Listing 14.8 shows how to use credentials with the client networking stack.

> ### Listing 14.8 Passing credentials along with a request, using the client stack

C#:

```
private void SendRequest()
{
  HttpWebRequest.RegisterPrefix(                      Use client
    "http://", WebRequestCreator.ClientHttp);    ◁──┘ stack

  HttpWebRequest req = (HttpWebRequest)HttpWebRequest.Create(
    new Uri("http://10rem.net"));

  req.UseDefaultCredentials = false;                  New
  req.Credentials =                              ◁──┘ credentials
    new NetworkCredential("Pete", "password");

  req.BeginGetResponse(OnRequestCompleted, req);
}

private void OnRequestCompleted(IAsyncResult asyncResult)
{
  HttpWebRequest request =
    (HttpWebRequest)asyncResult.AsyncState;

  HttpWebResponse response =
    (HttpWebResponse)request.EndGetResponse(asyncResult);

  ...

}
```

Optionally, you can pass a third parameter to the `NetworkCredential` constructor: the domain name. Passing a domain name is required for some forms of authentication, including NTLM. To modify listing 14.8 to work with those forms, change the `NetworkCredential` constructor call to include the domain, like this:

```
... new NetworkCredential("Pete", "password", "domain");
```

Of course, you'd use a real username, password, and domain name in the call. It's also important to note that you have no client-side control over what type of authentication is used. If the server challenges with basic authentication, the credentials will be sent across in plain text. Unlike the full desktop API, there's no `CredentialCache` class that can be used to hold credentials by challenge type.

With the additional capabilities offered by this stack, such as security and the avoidance of cross-domain checks for trusted applications, it may seem like a no-brainer to use it in place of the browser stack. But there are some important differences to keep in mind. For example, the location of the download cache may be different depending on the operating system and whether you were using the default OS browser to begin with. It's not common to concern yourself with that level of detail. But one of the biggest and most important differences is the way in which cookies are handled.

14.3.5 *Managing cookies with the CookieContainer*

In the browser stack, the browser handles all cookie management. The browser automatically sends up, with each request, the cookies appropriate to that domain and page.

When using the client stack, you need to manually manage the cookies that are sent up with each request. The HttpWebRequest class contains a CookieContainer property that's used for managing the cookies for that specific request.

Listing 14.9 shows how to use the CookieContainer with the HttpWebRequest class, combined with the Register prefix function described in the previous section.

Listing 14.9 Using the `CookieContainer` with a request and response

C#:
```
private void SendRequest()
{
  WebRequest.RegisterPrefix(
    "http://", WebRequestCreator.ClientHttp);            ◄─┐
  WebRequest.RegisterPrefix(                                 │  RegisterPrefix
    "https://", WebRequestCreator.ClientHttp);           ◄─┘

  HttpWebRequest req = (HttpWebRequest)HttpWebRequest.Create(
    new Uri("http://api.10rem.net"));

  CookieCollection cookies = new CookieCollection();
  cookies.Add(new Cookie("firstName", "Pete"));
  cookies.Add(new Cookie("lastName", "Brown"));
  cookies.Add(new Cookie("lastAccess", DateTime.Now.ToString()));

  req.CookieContainer = new CookieContainer();            Cookies in
  req.CookieContainer.Add(                                request
    new Uri("http://api.10rem.net"), cookies);       ◄─┘

  req.BeginGetResponse(OnRequestCompleted, req);
}

private void OnRequestCompleted(IAsyncResult asyncResult)
{
  HttpWebRequest req =
    (HttpWebRequest)asyncResult.AsyncState;

  HttpWebResponse response =
    (HttpWebResponse)req.EndGetResponse(asyncResult);

  ...                                                      Cookies in
                                                           response
  foreach (Cookie cookie in response.Cookies)          ◄─┘
  {
    Debug.WriteLine(cookie.Name + ":" + cookie.Value);
  }

}
```

Managing cookies manually is pretty easy, as you saw in this example. But keep in mind that the cookies won't be shared between the two stacks. Take, for example, an application in which the user is authenticated using ASP.NET forms-based authentication.

The web pages handle the authentication before the Silverlight application is displayed. Many web applications, and even larger platforms such as SharePoint, can use this model.

After the user is authenticated via the browser, the Silverlight application is displayed. If the Silverlight application then makes a network request, using the client stack, to the hosting server, the request will fail. Why? Because the ASP.NET authentication cookie, which is automatically sent up with all browser stack requests, isn't set up by the client stack request.

We've looked at two different ways to instantiate the client stack. You have the option of setting the stack preferences globally in your application or handling it on a request-by-request basis. We also looked at how to manage cookies for each request. When you're working with the client stack for all but the most basic requests, this is essential.

The client stack was originally designed for use in out-of-browser situations; but despite its limitations, it's found use in in-browser Silverlight applications as well. The stack definitely has advantages, but only if you understand the limitations.

When you get the data, regardless of form or networking stack used, you need to process it and do something useful with it. In the next section, we'll cover working with XML and JSON data in Silverlight.

14.4   *Making the data usable*

We've now discussed ways to request data from both SOAP and REST services. What we haven't talked about is how to do anything with what you've received. In the case of a SOAP service using a service reference, you have strongly typed objects to deal with. In the case of a REST service, you typically receive raw XML or JSON. Luckily, Silverlight gives you several ways to take the incoming data and make it usable in your application.

In the following sections, we'll show you how to deserialize a stream containing either POX or JSON. In addition, we'll talk about a specialized way to work with feeds following either the RSS or the Atom standard.

Several examples in this section use a publicly available service hosted by www.geonames.org. This service returns geographic and demographic data in various formats including XML and JSON. Connecting to free services like this is a great way to test methods for connecting to remote systems.

14.4.1 *Reading POX*

Plain Old XML (POX) has been the data format of choice on the Internet for nearly a decade. The fact that it's human-readable, customizable, and platform-independent virtually guaranteed its acceptance. Due to its long life and universal acceptance, the Silverlight team built in several ways to use POX after it's available in the application.

In this section, we'll describe the three major ways to use POX content. The three built-in methods to use XML content are LINQ to XML, also known as XLINQ, `Xml-Reader`, and `XmlSerializer`. In the following examples, we'll demonstrate each of these ways to read the same data using different methods.

SETTING UP

Each example that follows uses the same Silverlight application and the same web service call. First, we'll show you what you're getting and then how to deal with it. Listing 14.10 shows how to use a latitude/longitude service to get the name for a location.

Listing 14.10 Getting the XML from a latitude/longitude geo service

---

Result:

Lat: `40.78343`   Long: `-73.96625`   [Get XML]

City: New York City-Manhattan

Name: Central Park

Raw Results:
```
<neighbourhood>
<countryCode>US</countryCode>
<countryName>United States</countryName>
<adminCode1>NY</adminCode1>
<adminName1>New York</adminName1>
<adminCode2>061</adminCode2>
<adminName2>Manhattan</adminName2>
<city>New York City-Manhattan</city>
<name>Central Park</name>
</neighbourhood>
```

XAML:
```xml
<Grid x:Name="LayoutRoot" Background="#FF959595">
  <Grid.RowDefinitions>
    <RowDefinition Height="25" />
    <RowDefinition Height="25" />
    <RowDefinition Height="25" />
    <RowDefinition Height="*" />
  </Grid.RowDefinitions>
  <StackPanel Grid.Row="0" Orientation="Horizontal" Margin="5,5,0,0">
    <TextBlock Text="Lat:"/>
    <TextBox x:Name="Lat" Height="22" Width="85" Text="40.78343"/>
    <TextBlock Text="Long:"/>
    <TextBox x:Name="Long" Height="22" Width="85" Text="-73.96625"/>
    <Button x:Name="GetXML" Content="Get XML" Click="LoadXML"/>
  </StackPanel>
  <StackPanel Grid.Row="1" Orientation="Horizontal" Margin="5,5,0,0">
    <TextBlock Text="City:"/>
    <TextBlock x:Name="City" FontSize="12" FontFamily="Courier New"
      VerticalAlignment="Center" />
  </StackPanel>
  <StackPanel Grid.Row="2" Orientation="Horizontal" Margin="5,5,0,0">
    <TextBlock Text="Name:" />
    <TextBlock x:Name="Name" FontSize="12" FontFamily="Courier New"
      VerticalAlignment="Center"/>
  </StackPanel>
  <StackPanel Grid.Row="3" Margin="5,5,0,0">
    <TextBlock Text="Raw Results:" />
    <TextBlock x:Name="Results" TextWrapping="Wrap"
      FontFamily="Courier New" FontSize="11"/>
```

```
    </StackPanel>
</Grid>
```

C#:

```
SynchronizationContext UIThread;

private void LoadXML(object sender, RoutedEventArgs e)
{
  UIThread = SynchronizationContext.Current;
  string uriPath =
    "http://ws.geonames.org/neighbourhood?lat={0}&lng={1}&style=ful";
  Uri uri = new Uri(string.Format(uriPath, Lat.Text, Long.Text),
    UriKind.Absolute);
  HttpWebRequest request = (HttpWebRequest)WebRequest.Create(uri);
  request.BeginGetResponse(GetResults, request);
}
public void GetResults(IAsyncResult e)
{
  HttpWebRequest request = (HttpWebRequest)e.AsyncState;
  HttpWebResponse response =
    (HttpWebResponse)request.EndGetResponse(e);
  Stream responseStream = response.GetResponseStream();
  UIThread.Post(UpdateUiText, responseStream);
}
```

In listing 14.10, you use the `HttpWebRequest` object to retrieve the response stream from a web service that returns POX. The following examples show different versions of the `UpdateUiText` method, one for each way of parsing POX.

XLINQ

XLINQ is a flavor of LINQ used to navigate and parse XML content. It facilitates both property and query syntax to access the nodes and attributes in a chunk of XML. Add a reference to `System.Xml.Linq`, and then add the following to the code-behind:

```
public void UpdateUiText(object stream)
{
  XmlReader responseReader = XmlReader.Create((Stream)stream);
  XElement xmlResponse = XElement.Load(responseReader);
  XElement root = xmlResponse.Element("neighbourhood");
  Results.Text = root.ToString();
  City.Text = (string)root.Element("city");
  Name.Text = (string)root.Element("name");
}
```

This example shows the LINQ to XML version of `UpdateUiText`. It shows how using XLINQ to access the data contained within individual XML elements is incredibly simple. The first step is to create an `XmlReader` from the response stream. You can load that into an `XElement`, which represents the root element. You can then access any element or attribute by name to get its value.

This is a simple example of LINQ to XML, but it can be even more powerful when used to parse larger XML structures using the query syntax. Next, let's look at using the `XmlReader` directly.

XMLREADER

It's possible to use the `XmlReader` itself, without using a higher-level object to parse the XML for you:

```
public void UpdateUiText(object stream)
{
  XmlReader responseReader = XmlReader.Create((Stream)stream);
  responseReader.Read();
  responseReader.ReadToFollowing("city");
  string city = responseReader.ReadElementContentAsString();
  responseReader.ReadToFollowing("name");
  string name = responseReader.ReadElementContentAsString();
  responseReader.ReadEndElement();
  responseReader.ReadEndElement();
  City.Text = city;
  Name.Text = name;
}
```

This example uses the plain `XmlReader` to step through the returned XML to find the values you want. The approach is rather clunky but does work. Because the `XmlReader` is forward-only, you have to be careful to get everything you need from the information the first time through-a potentially cumbersome task on complex documents.

In the next example, you can also see the same results using the `XmlSerializer` from the `System.Xml.Serialization` namespace, which is included in the SDK, so you need to add a reference to use it in your application.

XMLSERIALIZER

The `XmlSerializer` provides a way to convert an `XmlReader` into strongly typed objects. This approach takes a little more setup but is incredibly useful in many business applications. Listing 14.11 shows how to use the `XmlSerializer` to parse an XML document.

Listing 14.11 Using the `XmlSerializer` to parse an XML document

C#:
```
public void UpdateUiText(Object stream)
{
  XmlReader responseReader = XmlReader.Create((Stream)stream);   ← Navigate to
  responseReader.ReadToFollowing("neighbourhood");                  correct position

  XmlSerializer serializer =                              ┐ Target
    new XmlSerializer(typeof(neighbourhood));           ←┘ type
  neighbourhood nh =
    (neighbourhood)serializer.Deserialize(responseReader);   ←— Deserialize

  City.Text = nh.city;
  Name.Text = nh.name;
}
...
public class neighbourhood
{
  public string countryCode { get; set; }
  public string countryName { get; set; }
```

```
    public string adminCode1 { get; set; }
    public string adminName1 { get; set; }
    public string adminCode2 { get; set; }
    public string adminName2 { get; set; }
    public string city { get; set; }
    public string name { get; set; }
}
```

You can see in listing 14.11 that using an XmlSerializer allows you to create a strongly typed object from the incoming XML data. To use this approach, you need to define a class that matches the format of the incoming XML. This class can be defined in your application, in a referenced class library, or in a service reference proxy. The first step is to move your XmlReader to the correct location. You also need to create a new XmlSerializer and initialize it with the target type you want the XML deserialized into. The final step is to use the Deserialize method on the XmlSerializer instance you just created and pass in the XmlReader. The Deserialize method returns an object of the type it's defined as or, if the deserialization failed, null.

Now that you've seen how to use POX, let's look at another common data format. In the next section, you'll learn how to use JSON-formatted data. JSON can be returned from a RESTful service just as easily as XML can, so let's dig into that format now.

14.4.2 *Converting JSON*

If you've worked with Ajax, it's likely that you're already familiar with JSON. JSON provides a relatively simple way to create data objects using JavaScript. Because JSON is already prevalent in client-side programming and is used as the return type from my public services, Microsoft has made a simple way to convert managed objects into and out of JSON objects.

The next example shows a sample of what a JSON object looks like. You can accomplish this conversion in a couple ways, such as using a DataContractJsonSerializer or even using LINQ syntax against a JsonObject. For the example, let's use the same method to load the data as was used in listing 14.10, but change the URI to

```
ws.geonames.org/neighbourhoodJSON?lat={0}&lng={1}
```

The resulting JSON response looks like this:

```
{
  "neighbourhood": {
    "adminName2": "New York County",
    "adminCode2": "061",
    "adminCode1": "NY",
    "countryName": "United States",
    "name": "Central Park",
    "countryCode": "US",
    "city": "New York City-Manhattan",
    "adminName1": "New York"
  }
}
```

This example shows a simple but typical JSON object. As you can see, the returned JSON represents the same object as the XML returned in listing 14.10, but in a more compact form. Luckily, the methods for converting the JSON object into a useful format are similar as well. Let's start by taking a look at using the JsonObject syntax.

JSONOBJECT

As with XML, there's more than one way to use JSON-formatted data returned from a web service. The JSON being deserialized in these examples is shown in the previous example. The ways of working with JSON data differ greatly, as the following examples will show:

```
public void UpdateUiText(Object stream)
{
  JsonObject nh = (JsonObject)JsonObject.Load((Stream)stream);
  City.Text = nh["neighbourhood"]["city"];
  Name.Text = nh["neighbourhood"]["name"];
  Results.Text = nh.ToString();
}
```

One way to read JSON data is by using JsonObject.Load to convert the stream into an object based on the structure found within the stream. To get access to the JsonObject, you need to add a reference to the System.Json assembly and add a Using statement for the same namespace to the page. After the JsonObject has been created, it's a matter of using the name of the property you want as the key. If the property is nested, you add more keys, as when accessing the city property inside the Neighbourhood class.

DATACONTRACTJSONSERIALIZER

Another way to access returned JSON involves using the DataContractJsonSerializer to deserialize the stream into objects of predefined types. This new object to serialize and deserialize JSON is included in the System.Runtime.Serialization.Json namespace and in the System.ServiceModel.Web assembly. The two methods of the DataContractJsonSerializer are ReadObject and WriteObject, which deserialize and serialize JSON objects respectively.

The following example again uses the Neighbourhood class defined earlier:

```
public class MyResults
{
  public Neighbourhood neighbourhood { get; set; }
}
...
public void UpdateUiText(Object stream)
{
  DataContractJsonSerializer ser =
    new DataContractJsonSerializer(typeof(MyResults));
  MyResults nh = (MyResults)ser.ReadObject((Stream)stream);
  City.Text = nh.neighbourhood.city;
  Name.Text = nh.neighbourhood.name;
}
```

This example shows the classes that hold the data after it's deserialized, as well as the method that does the work. This approach is simple. First, you instantiate the

`DataContractJsonSerializer` with the type of object you want filled. All that's left is to pass the response stream into the `ReadObject` method of the `DataContractJsonSerializer` you just created. You access the data as you would with any other strongly typed .NET object. In the case of two well-known schemas, RSS and Atom, there's no need to deserialize the stream yourself. We'll look at these specialized classes, which make consuming published feeds easy and straightforward.

14.5   *Using advanced services*

You've seen how to download data and various ways to parse the returned data streams into usable pieces. Let's now talk about a few special networking cases. Some SOAP services can be crafted in such a way as to provide additional functionality beyond basic SOAP. Windows Communication Foundation (WCF) is part of the .NET Framework 3.0 and provides a framework for creating SOAP web services. Although this technology is fairly new, it's growing in usage.

Another special case is that of *two-way services*, also known as *push services*. Silverlight supports two kinds of push technology in the form of WCF duplex services and TCP sockets. Although the topics in this section are more complex, the abilities to add push communications and advanced error handling on service calls make this all good to know.

14.5.1   *WCF service enhancements*

Connecting to a WCF service is accomplished in the same way as connecting to any other SOAP service, as described in section 14.2.1. Creating a service reference allows the use of a client proxy, which exposes all referenced types and methods to the Silverlight application. WCF can expose features not allowed in Silverlight; so, when you're creating a WCF service for Silverlight consumption, there are a few restrictions. We've already stated that Silverlight supports the 1.1 version of the SOAP protocol with the addition of optional binary encoding. Another limitation is that Silverlight doesn't support the WS-* series of protocols made available through WCF.

Due to Silverlight's service limitations, Visual Studio has a special template for creating a WCF service to be consumed by Silverlight called Silverlight-Enabled WCF Service. Describing how to create a WCF service is beyond the scope of this book, but the template should help ensure that the service is consumable by Silverlight. If you create your own WCF service, you have the ability to enhance the error-handling capability of calls to it from Silverlight.

ERROR HANDLING

One of the nice things about WCF is the ability to throw exceptions on a service call. Unfortunately, Silverlight doesn't support this. Any exception thrown by the service gets translated by the browser into a 404 File Not Found error. The creator of the WCF service can still add error messages by adding them as an OUT parameter.

When the signature of the WCF service contains an OUT parameter, you can access it directly through the `EventArgs` on the event handler for the completed call, as shown in listing 14.12.

> **Listing 14.12 Reading an out parameter from a WCF service**

WCF C#:

```
[OperationContract]
string GetSomeData(int Id, out MyErrorObject myError);
```

Silverlight C#:

```
void serviceProxy_GetSomeDataCompleted(object sender,
  GetSomeDataCompletedEventArgs e)
{
  if (e.Error != null)
  {
    Message.Text = e.Error.Message;
  }
  if (e.myError != null)
  {
    Message.Text = e.myError.Message;
  }
  else
  {
    Message.Text = e.Result.ToString();
  }
}
```

In this example, you see a standard `[ServiceMethod]Completed` method like those shown throughout this chapter. This example also demonstrates error trapping and a custom out parameter.

Now that you've seen standard WCF services, let's dig deeper and look at how WCF duplex services can enable you to push data from a server to Silverlight.

14.5.2 *WCF duplex services*

So far, we've talked about ways to send and receive data that requires the Silverlight application to initiate each individual request. A couple of options allow the server to push data directly to your application. Duplex WCF services and sockets each provide a channel that allows properly configured server resources to send data without an explicit client request each time.

Duplex services give the server the ability to send, or *push*, data directly to the client as it becomes available. Ajax applications have to send a request for updates to the server that execute on a loop with a timer. This approach, known as *polling*, creates overhead, both in your application and on the network, that can be avoided by using these techniques.

Duplex communication is possible in Silverlight using properly configured WCF services. This is useful if you're building an application that needs to receive notifications of changed properties on the server, such as when scores change in a sporting event, or an open record changes in a database. To enable duplex communication within Silverlight, a pair of new assemblies, both named `System.ServiceModel.PollingDuplex.dll`, need to be referenced-one by the server application hosting the duplex service and the other by your Silverlight application. They're identifiable by their location within the Silverlight SDK, because one is in the Libraries\Server path and the other is in the Libraries\Client path.

CONNECTING TO THE SERVICE

See the source code at Manning.com for everything required to set up a polling duplex service in a web project. When you have a functioning WCF service set up to enable duplex communication, let's attach it to a Silverlight application. In the test application, a `Button` initiates the duplex communication and a `TextBlock` displays the results, so the XAML is simple. Here, you're building a simple application that registers with the service to get updates on scores from a game (see listing 14.13).

Listing 14.13   Sample application to get score updates

Result:

XAML:

```xml
<Grid x:Name="LayoutRoot" Background="#FF6F93C3" Width="300">
  <Button Height="41" HorizontalAlignment="Stretch"
    VerticalAlignment="Top" Content="Get Scores!"
    Margin="199,8,0,0" x:Name="GetScores"
    Click="GetScores_Click"/>
  <TextBlock Height="41" Margin="8,8,0,0" VerticalAlignment="Top"
    Text="Get scores for your team!" TextWrapping="Wrap" Width="187"
    HorizontalAlignment="Left" FontFamily="Arial" FontSize="20"/>
  <TextBlock Margin="8,70,8,8" Text="" TextWrapping="Wrap"
    x:Name="Scores" FontFamily="Courier New" FontSize="10"/>
</Grid>
```

The only thing of note in the XAML is that the `Click` attribute of the button points to the `GetScores_Click` method, which we'll discuss in listing 14.14. In this example, you grab a link to the current `SynchronizationContext` before beginning your asynchronous operations. This ensures that you always have a way to update the user interface.

Listing 14.14   Creating the polling duplex client

C#:

```csharp
SynchronizationContext _uiThread;                          // SynchronizationContext

private void GetScores_Click(object sender, RoutedEventArgs e)
{
  _uiThread = SynchronizationContext.Current;              // Polling
                                                           // client
  var poll = new PollingDuplexHttpBinding();

  poll.InactivityTimeout = TimeSpan.FromMinutes(1);

  IChannelFactory<IDuplexSessionChannel> channelFactory =
```

```
    poll.BuildChannelFactory<IDuplexSessionChannel>(new
      BindingParameterCollection());

  IAsyncResult factoryOpenResult =
    channelFactory.BeginOpen(new
      AsyncCallback(OnOpenFactoryComplete), channelFactory);

  if (factoryOpenResult.CompletedSynchronously)
  {
    OpenTheChannel(factoryOpenResult);
  }
}
```

In this example, you start the process of binding to a duplex web service. You begin by creating a `PollingDuplexHttpBinding` object, on which you set the timeout properties. You then use that polling object to create an `IChannelFactory` of type `IDuplexSessionChannel`. The next step is to begin the asynchronous call using the `BeginOpen` method of the factory you just created.

The `PollingDuplexHttpBinding` constructor accepts an optional parameter that allows you to specify either single messages per poll or multiple messages per poll. If you want to support HTTP *message chunking*-multiple messages per poll-you can pass the parameter in to the constructor like this:

```
var poll = PollingDuplexHttpBinding(
          PollingDuplexMode.MultipleMessagesPerPoll);
```

Using the multiple messages option can significantly reduce the round trips for services that typically have more than one message waiting in response to a poll, allowing the service to scale better.

One thing you'll see throughout these samples is the calling of `CompletedSynchronously` immediately after the asynchronous call. You do this in case the response is immediate, as can occur for some small asynchronous operations. With this in mind, note that all the asynchronous calls are to methods that also check the `CompletedSynchronously` property and then either return or call the proper next method. Here's an example of one such method:

```
void OnOpenFactoryComplete(IAsyncResult result)
{
  if (result.CompletedSynchronously)
    return;
  else
    OpenTheChannel(result);
}
```

For the rest of this sample, we won't show the `On[action]Completed` methods, because they all follow the pattern of this example. The next step is to open the channel with the WCF service and to begin polling it for queued messages, as in listing 14.15.

> **Listing 14.15 Opening the duplex channel and establishing polling**

C#:
```
void OpenTheChannel(IAsyncResult result)
{
```

```
IChannelFactory<IDuplexSessionChannel> channelFactory =
  (IChannelFactory<IDuplexSessionChannel>)result.AsyncState;

channelFactory.EndOpen(result);

IDuplexSessionChannel channel = channelFactory.CreateChannel(new
  EndpointAddress("http://localhost:51236/ScoreService.svc"));

IAsyncResult channelOpenResult = channel.BeginOpen(new
  AsyncCallback(OnOpenChannelComplete), channel);

if (channelOpenResult.CompletedSynchronously)
{
  StartPolling(channelOpenResult);
}
}

void StartPolling(IAsyncResult result)
{
  IDuplexSessionChannel channel =
    (IDuplexSessionChannel)result.AsyncState;
  channel.EndOpen(result);

  Message message =
    Message.CreateMessage(channel.GetProperty<MessageVersion>(),
    "Silverlight/IScoreService/Register","Baseball");

  IAsyncResult resultChannel = channel.BeginSend(message,
    new AsyncCallback(OnSendComplete), channel);

  if (resultChannel.CompletedSynchronously)
  {
    CompleteOnSend(resultChannel);
  }
  PollingLoop(channel);
}
```

The method `OpenTheChannel` in this code shows where you define the service you're attempting to connect to. It's assigned as an endpoint on the duplex channel. The `StartPolling` method creates the SOAP message for the initial call and sends it to the service.

Listing 14.16 shows that `CompleteOnSend` receives the response from the initial call. This is also the first use of the `uiThread` `SynchronizationContext` to update text in the XAML.

> **Listing 14.16 Looking for messages**

C#:
```
void CompleteOnSend(IAsyncResult result)
{
  IDuplexSessionChannel channel =
    (IDuplexSessionChannel)result.AsyncState;
  channel.EndSend(result);
  _uiThread.Post(UpdateScore, "Registered!" + Environment.NewLine);
}

void UpdateScore(object text)
```

```
{
  Scores.Text += (string)text;
}

void PollingLoop(IDuplexSessionChannel channel)
{
  IAsyncResult result =
    channel.BeginReceive(new AsyncCallback(OnReceiveComplete),
    channel);
  if (result.CompletedSynchronously)
    CompleteReceive(result);
}
```

The PollingLoop method assigns CompleteReceive (see listing 14.17) as the method
to handle messages received from the duplex service and then closes the channel
when the game is over.

> **Listing 14.17   Reading the message**

C#:
```
void CompleteReceive(IAsyncResult result)
{
  IDuplexSessionChannel channel =
    (IDuplexSessionChannel)result.AsyncState;
  try
  {
    Message receivedMessage = channel.EndReceive(result);
    if (receivedMessage == null)
    {
      _uiThread.Post(UpdateScore, "Channel Closed");
    }
    else
    {
      string text = receivedMessage.GetBody<string>();
      _uiThread.Post(UpdateScore, "Score Received: " +
        text + Environment.NewLine);

      if (text == "Game Over")
      {
        IAsyncResult resultFactory =
            channel.BeginClose(new AsyncCallback(OnCloseChannelComplete),
            channel);
        if (resultFactory.CompletedSynchronously)
        {
          CompleteCloseChannel(result);
        }
      }
      else
      {
        PollingLoop(channel);
      }
    }
  }
  catch (CommunicationObjectFaultedException)
  {
```

```
      _uiThread.Post(UpdateScore, "Channel Timed Out");
  }
}

void CompleteCloseChannel(IAsyncResult result)
{
  IDuplexSessionChannel channel =
    (IDuplexSessionChannel)result.AsyncState;
  channel.EndClose(result);
}
```

Creating and consuming a duplex-enabled WCF service take more effort than a standard SOAP service, but there are definitely benefits. The ability to open a channel to the server to get requests as they're available is powerful. Another approach you can take to accomplish this uses sockets, which we'll discuss next.

14.5.3 Connecting to sockets

We've already discussed using a specially configured WCF service to enable push communications, so now let's talk about using sockets for the same purpose. A *socket* is a communications endpoint that enables a connection to be established. After it's established, information can flow in either direction along the open channel. The only socket protocol supported by Silverlight is TCP, and the ports are restricted to the range of 4502–4534 using IPv4 or IPv6 addresses.

SERVING THE POLICY FILE

Sockets require a clientaccesspolicy.xml file with a few changes. The resource element isn't used and is replaced with the socket-resource element. Both element types may exist in the file and apply the style to the specific type or request. The following is an example of a simple client access policy giving access to sockets using TCP over port 4502:

```xml
<?xml version="1.0" encoding="utf-8"?>
<access-policy>
  <cross-domain-access>
    <policy>
      <allow-from>
        <domain uri="*"/>
      </allow-from>
      <grant-to>
        <socket-resource port="4502" protocol="tcp"/>
      </grant-to>
    </policy>
  </cross-domain-access>
</access-policy>
```

Your Silverlight application will typically be served up from port 80, a web server. Sockets, on the other hand, don't require a web server to be present and are on ports other than 80. For those reasons, you must serve up a sockets policy file, because every call is considered cross-domain (or at least cross-port).

You have two options for serving up the policy file. You may either host it on a web server on port 80 on the same IP address as the sockets server, or on a sockets server on port 943. Typically, you'll set up a separate thread or a separate socket server that listens for a connection on 943, sends the socket policy file, and closes the connection.

Before we move on to opening the connection, refer to this book's page on Manning.com for the source code for a simple sockets server.

OPENING THE CONNECTION

Opening a socket connection with a socket server can be done in a few simple steps that are similar to the other forms of communicating you've already seen. The first step is to open the socket. Listing 14.18 shows how to open the socket on the client.

Listing 14.18   Opening the socket connection on the client

C#:

```csharp
public void OpenTheSocket()
{
  DnsEndPoint tcpEndpoint =
    new DnsEndPoint(Application.Current.Host.Source.DnsSafeHost, 4502);
  Socket tcpSocket = new Socket(AddressFamily.InterNetwork,
    SocketType.Stream, ProtocolType.Tcp);
  SocketAsyncEventArgs socketArgs = new SocketAsyncEventArgs();
  socketArgs.UserToken = tcpSocket;
  socketArgs.RemoteEndPoint = tcpEndpoint;
  socketArgs.Completed +=
    new EventHandler<SocketAsyncEventArgs>(socketArgs_Completed);
  tcpSocket.ConnectAsync(socketArgs);
}
```

The example creates an endpoint and a socket and then using them to asynchronously request a connection to the remote socket server. You use `Application.Current.Host.Source.DnsSafeHost` to get the IP address of the host of the Silverlight application in a form usable for creating a socket endpoint. Using this technique to create the endpoint is only useful when the socket and the Silverlight application are hosted in the same location.

HANDLING THE RESPONSE

Sockets are bidirectional in nature. After you've requested the connection, you need to handle the response. Listing 14.19 shows how to handle the incoming response on the client.

Listing 14.19   Handling the socket response

C#:

```csharp
public void socketArgs_Completed(object sender,
  SocketAsyncEventArgs receivedArgs)
{
  switch (receivedArgs.LastOperation)
  {
    case SocketAsyncOperation.Connect:
      if (receivedArgs.SocketError == SocketError.Success)
```

```
      {
        byte[] response = new byte[1024];
        receivedArgs.SetBuffer(response, 0, response.Length);
        Socket socket = (Socket)receivedArgs.UserToken;
        socket.ReceiveAsync(receivedArgs);
      }
      else
        throw new SocketException((int)receivedArgs.SocketError);
      break;

    case SocketAsyncOperation.Receive:
      ReceiveMessageOverSocket(receivedArgs);
      break;
  }
}
```

You can determine the type of response by evaluating the value of the LastOperation property of SocketAsyncEventArgs, as shown in table 14.2.

Value	Description
None	Connection not yet established
Connect	Connection established
Receive	Packets received
Send	Packets sent

Table 14.2 `SocketAsyncEventArgs` `LastOperation` values

Now you need to set up the connection to receive data, as shown here:

```
public void ReceiveMessageOverSocket(SocketAsyncEventArgs receivedArgs)
{
  string message = Encoding.UTF8.GetString(receivedArgs.Buffer,
    receivedArgs.Offset, receivedArgs.BytesTransferred);
  UIThread.Post(UpdateUIControls, message);
  Socket socket = (Socket)receivedArgs.UserToken;
  socket.ReceiveAsync(receivedArgs);
}
```

When the message comes in, it needs to be converted into the correct format (a string, in this case); it can then be deserialized using any of the methods described in previous sections, depending on the format of the incoming data.

In additional to the traditional point-to-point connection offered by the Socket class, Silverlight supports multicast sockets where there may be many broadcasting servers or a single broadcasting server, sending to multiple clients.

14.5.4 *Multicast sockets*

The System.Net.Sockets namespace includes another type of socket implementation: UDP multicast sockets. IP multicast is a component of the core IP protocols, supporting one-to-many communication over IP, most often using UDP. Multicast is an efficient way for forwarding the IP datagrams to many receivers, enabling the service to scale out to more connected clients.

IP multicast has a dependency on the routers and other equipment in use between the service and the connected clients. That equipment must all support IP multicast in order for the service to function. Luckily, most modern hardware and firmware implementations support IP multicast.

A common scenario for IP multicast is the virtual classroom. In those cases, you may have hundreds or even thousands of clients connected, watching a single streaming video and receiving updates from virtual whiteboards, teacher notes, and public discussion streams.

Silverlight supports two types of multicast protocols, described in table 14.3.

Table 14.3 Multicast support in Silverlight

Client	Protocol and description
UdpAnySourceMulticastClient	Internet Standard Multicast (ISM) or Any Source Multicast (ASM).
	This client can receive multicast traffic from any source in a multicast group.
UdpSingleSourceMulticastClient	Source Specific Multicast (SSM).
	This client can receive multicast traffic from a single source.

ANY SOURCE MULTICAST/INTERNET STANDARD MULTICAST

The Any Source Multicast (ASM) approach enables a single client to receive traffic from any source in a single multicast group. An example of this might be a virtual meeting with multiple broadcasters or an event with several cameras and commentary, all set up as individual servers in the same group.

When Silverlight first attempts to join a multicast group, it sends out an announcement message in the form of a UDP packet to port 9430. In the any-source model, this goes to the group, and any responder in the group can send the ok back to port 9430.

Listing 14.20 shows the basics of connecting to a multicast group in preparation for receiving data.

Listing 14.20 Opening a connection using ASM

C#:
```
private void OpenMulticastConnection()
{
  IPAddress groupAddress = IPAddress.Parse("224.156.5.5");
  int localPort = 1212;

  var client = new UdpAnySourceMulticastClient(
                             groupAddress, localPort);

  client.BeginJoinGroup(OnBeginJoinGroup, client);
```

```
}

private void OnBeginJoinGroup(IAsyncResult asyncResult)
{
  UdpAnySourceMulticastClient client =
    (UdpAnySourceMulticastClient)asyncResult.AsyncState;

  client.EndJoinGroup(asyncResult);

  ...
}
```

In addition to the any-source approach, you can also designate that you want to listen only to a single server using the Source Specific Multicast (SSM) model.

SOURCE SPECIFIC MULTICAST

The SSM approach is more common than the any-source model. Of course, at the time of this writing, neither is particularly common. The source-specific model has been used for broadcasting video and even software images on large campuses and in some organizations. The benefit is the massive savings in bandwidth as compared to more traditional means.

When Silverlight first attempts to join a multicast group, it sends out an announcement message in the form of a UDP packet to port 9430; but unlike the any-source model, this packet goes directly to the single source IP.

Opening the connection and joining the multicast group is similar to the any-source approach, but the constructor takes in the IP address of the single source in addition to the group information.

Listing 14.21 shows how to connect to a multicast group and target a single source address as the address to be listened to.

Listing 14.21 Opening a connection to a single source

C#:
```
private void OpenMulticastConnection()
{
  IPAddress sourceAddress = IPAddress.Parse("192.168.1.1");
  IPAddress groupAddress = IPAddress.Parse("224.156.5.5");
  int localPort = 1212;

  var client = new UdpSingleSourceMulticastClient(
                    sourceAddress, groupAddress, localPort);

  client.BeginJoinGroup(OnBeginJoinGroup, client);
}

private void OnBeginJoinGroup(IAsyncResult asyncResult)
{
  UdpAnySourceMulticastClient client =
    (UdpAnySourceMulticastClient)asyncResult.AsyncState;

  client.EndJoinGroup(asyncResult);

  ...
}
```

The differences between listing 14.20 and 14.21 are minimal, coming down to the inclusion of the additional IP address in the constructor.

> **NOTE** MSDN Code Gallery includes examples of both a multicast server and a multicast client. The full examples are impractical to place in a book due to their length. You can download the SilverChat examples from http://code.msdn.microsoft.com/silverlightsdk.

Multicast is just starting to take off in the media, education, and large business sectors. If you're looking at streaming media to a large number of clients, streaming stock-ticker quotes, or building your own webcasting software, you'll definitely want to learn more about multicast socket development. Fortunately, Silverlight will be able to support you as a good client in those scenarios.

Sockets in general are a great choice when you want to have complete control over the messaging, such as you might when creating a game and you want to have the tightest possible real-time messaging protocol. WCF duplex is a good choice when you're willing to trade wire-level control for the ability to use all the great features, such as automatic serialization, that WCF provides. Different problems call for different solutions, sometimes within the same physical application. It's great to see Silverlight offer such a spectrum of capabilities you can use when connecting applications to the outside world.

Sockets and WCF duplex are great for bidirectional communication between a Silverlight client and a server, or via two machines using the server as a proxy. Straight SOAP and REST are useful when consuming public or application-specific APIs. Silverlight has another mechanism, similar to sockets, that you can use to connect two Silverlight applications running on the same client machine.

14.6 Connecting to other Silverlight applications

The new local connection API in `System.Windows.Messaging`, introduced in Silverlight 3, allows communication between two or more instances of the Silverlight plug-in, whether they're on the same page in the same browser instance, on different pages in different browsers, or even some in browsers and others running out-of-browser.

In this example, you'll set up a pair of applications, the second of which echoes the text entered into a `TextBox` on the first. Much like socket programming, you'll need to designate one application or piece of code as a sender and another as a receiver. You'll start with the receiver.

14.6.1 Creating the receiver

Each receiver has a unique name. Think of it as the address of an endpoint. You define the name when creating the `LocalMessageReceiver` object as shown:

```
private LocalMessageReceiver _receiver =
        new LocalMessageReceiver("InAction");
```

The overload for the constructor enables you to indicate whether you want to listen only to specific domains or to all domains (what's called the *namescope*, not to be confused with XAML namescope), and to provide a list of acceptable domains. Additionally, it provides the same ability to supply a receiver name.

In this case, the receiver is named InAction. Remember, this name needs to be unique within the namescope. If it isn't, you'll get a ListenFailedException when executing the next step, listening for senders:

```
public void Listen()
{
    _receiver.MessageReceived +=
            new EventHandler<MessageReceivedEventArgs>
            (_receiver_MessageReceived);

    _receiver.Listen();
}

void _receiver_MessageReceived(object sender, MessageReceivedEventArgs e)
{
    MessageText.Text = e.Message;
}
```

Much like the other communications APIs, you first wire up an event handler, call a method, and then wait for a response within the handler. As is often the case, the event args class specific to this process—MessageReceivedEventArgs—includes a number of additional properties, shown in table 14.4.

Table 14.4 MessageReceivedEventArgs properties

Property	Description
Message	The message from the sender.
NameScope	A value of either Domain or Global. Domain indicates the receiver is configured only to listen to applications from the same domain. Global indicates the receiver may listen to all Silverlight applications. This property is also available directly on the LocalMessageReceiver object. The default is Domain, but it may be set in the constructor.
ReceiverName	The name of the LocalMessageReceiver tied to this event.
Response	A response provided by the receiver. This makes it easy to immediately respond to a message, perhaps with something as simple as an ACK (acknowledge).
SenderDomain	The domain of the Silverlight application that sent this message.

After you've created the listener, the next step is to create something to send the messages: the sender.

14.6.2 Creating the sender

The sender is extremely simple to create. All it needs to do is create a LocalMessageSender object specifying a particular listener and optionally the listener's domain, and then start sending messages:

```
private LocalMessageSender _sender =
        new LocalMessageSender("InAction");

public MainPage()
{
    ...
    MessageText.TextChanged +=
        new TextChangedEventHandler(OnTextChanged);
}

void OnTextChanged(object sender, TextChangedEventArgs e)
{
    _sender.SendAsync(MessageText.Text);
}
```

In the example, whenever the text changes in the TextBox, you send the entire Text-Box contents across the pipe and to the listener.

14.6.3 Putting it all together

The next step is to place both Silverlight control into the same HTML page, using separate object tags. When run, the application will look something like figure 14.1.

Of course, if you want, you can host the two instances in separate browser windows and still allow them to communicate, as shown in figure 14.2. Create a page for the sender and one for the receiver. The two browsers don't need to be the same brand, as long as they're both supported by Silverlight.

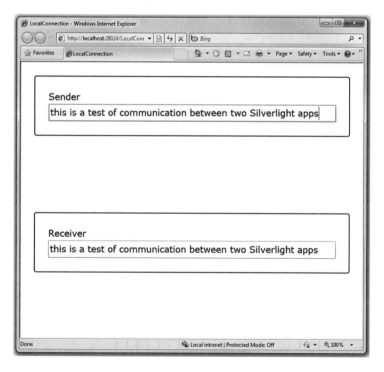

Figure 14.1 Two Silverlight control instances on the same page, communicating with each other

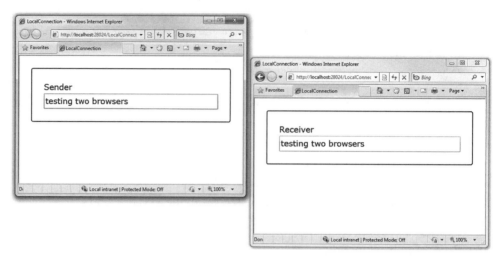

Figure 14.2   Sender and receiver in separate browser windows, communicating across processes

You can also have one or both of the applications running out of the browser, as shown in figure 14.3.

The new local connection API provides a great way to let two or more Silverlight applications communicate. Unlike the old methods of using the DOM to send application messages, this doesn't rely on the applications being in the same DOM tree or even in the same browser instance. This new API enables scenarios such as disconnected but coordinating web parts on a SharePoint page, composite applications, and many more.

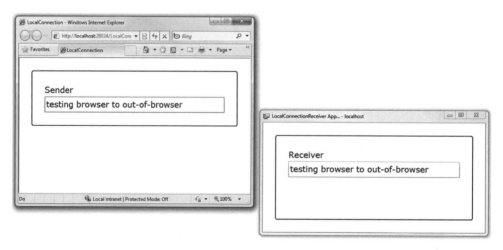

Figure 14.3   Sender in a browser window, and receiver running out-of-browser

14.7 *Summary*

Most Silverlight applications don't live in a vacuum, self-contained and apart from the rest of the world. In most cases, applications need to either gather data from or send data to services on the Internet or intranet. The various networking approaches we discussed here will help you connect your applications to the outside world and even to other Silverlight applications.

As a web technology, Silverlight as a platform must be able to connect to services and consume various types of data as a top-tier feature. Silverlight doesn't disappoint in this area. From low-level HTTP access through to SOAP, REST, sockets, multicast sockets, and duplex communications, Silverlight provides a full spectrum of capabilities for accessing information on other machines.

Of course, if you had to manually parse all that data, it wouldn't be a great platform feature. Luckily, Silverlight has us covered here as well. Silverlight supports multiple ways to access XML data-one of the most popular data formats on the web today. In addition, Silverlight supports the lightweight and nimble JSON format introduced with Ajax applications.

Silverlight also supports a pseudonetworking mechanism for connecting two Silverlight applications running on the same machine, even in different browsers or out-of-browser instances.

Silverlight provides numerous ways to connect to, download, and use a variety of types of data. With support for technologies ranging from the decade old POX to WCF Data Services and WCF RIA Services, there's sure to be something to fit any application framework.

In the next chapter, we'll combine the information on networking, binding, and other topics and learn how to handle navigation.

Navigation and dialogs

15

This chapter covers

- Browser navigation
- The Navigation Application template
- Using navigation with out-of-browser applications
- Working with common dialogs
- Creating custom dialogs and pop-ups

When you first created a Silverlight 2 application, you ended up with a project that contained a single white main page, probably sized at 300 x 400, depending on the template you used. There was no guidance for structuring your application or how to move from page to page. Unlike HTML pages or WPF/Windows Forms, the navigation structure wasn't something intuitive, building on a decade or more of knowledge and established patterns. Instead, most new Silverlight developers were left staring that that blank page, wondering what to do next.

Silverlight 3 introduced not only a complete navigation framework, but also an application template built on this framework. The navigation framework takes a modern browser-oriented approach to navigation, supporting concepts such as journal histories, back-and-forward navigation, and uniquely addressable pages. This framework addressed the needs of both application structure and end-user navigation.

Silverlight also supports dialog content. In addition to the standard open and save dialogs provided by the operating system, you can create your own simulated dialogs using controls such as `Popup` and `ChildWindow`.

In this chapter, we'll dive deep into Silverlight navigation, followed up with a look at how to handle pop-ups and dialogs. We'll look to history to inform us about how navigation is handled in the browser and how hashtags or URI fragments work. From there, you'll start building an application using the navigation template. The navigation template will then be used to explore navigation to individual pages and customization of navigation.

After we complete the tour of navigation, we'll turn our eye to dialogs and child windows, including the operating system–provided file dialogs and the Silverlight `Popup` and `ChildWindow` classes.

Before diving into Silverlight navigation, let's take a look at a well-established navigation paradigm as used by the web browser.

15.1 *Browser navigation background*

The introduction of GUI web browsers hailed a new approach to navigation. Prior to Mosaic, the typical modes for navigation were either keyboard commands or drop-down menus. Most applications had multiple windows and were wizard-driven or dialog-driven. Browsers introduced two key things:

- Navigation to previously visited pages using Back and Forward buttons, with retained history on both
- Navigation to new pages using hyperlinks

This may seem pretty unexciting now, but it wasn't a mainstream approach at the time. Applications didn't contain a single frame that was swapped in and out with different bits of content.

With the ubiquity of web browsers came new demands for how applications worked. It was expected that your applications, especially if hosted in a browser, would use a forward/backward and link paradigm. This worked fine for the period of time when browser applications were all server-processed and static client. Think ASP, CGI, and similar application types.

Outlook Web Access (OWA), released in 2000, had bits of functionality that other application developers realized could make the web a better place. OWA was making network calls back to the server to get new content, but did it without any sort of postback or even an `iframe`. Developers looked to see how this application (and others such as Gmail in 2004) were written, and began to adopt the approach themselves. Around 2003 (give or take a year or two), Ajax applications based on JavaScript, asynchronous network calls, and client-side HTML DOM manipulation began to rise in popularity. Ajax applications are and were a web approach designed to provide interactive client-side desktop application–like functionality to the web pages.

Unfortunately, as Ajax applications became more and more complex, they made browser back/forward navigation unreliable. Newsgroups at the time were full of

"How do we disable the Back button?" questions. Clicking the Back button navigated off the page, completely destroying the application state. Java applets and, later, Flash applications ran into the same problem.

Eventually, both browser makers and the application framework developers were able to work together to provide an approach for interacting with the browser journal, the structure in the browser that keeps track of your navigation history. The rest is, well, history.[1]

In this section, we'll briefly cover how the browser journal works and how it interacts with anchor tags on a typical web page. With that grounding, we'll then be able to look at Silverlight navigation in the subsequent sections.

15.1.1 *Browser journals*

The *browser journal* keeps track of your navigation history for a session. It's what allows you to click the Back button to open the previous page and then click the Forward button to return to where you were.

Browsers each implement their history journal and its API in subtly different ways. For example, Internet Explorer 7 required the use of an HTML `iframe` in order to generate an actual history entry when you navigate to a hashtag. Other browsers didn't update their JavaScript API objects, such as `location.hash`, to reflect changes to the hashtag. Some other browsers were just plain buggy and didn't consistently keep the correct state. There were other smaller differences in addition to gross API differences.

> **NOTE** Ever wonder why you need that `iframe` in the HTML page in a Silverlight project? It's there for navigation support in older browsers, including IE7. IE7 wouldn't generate a history entry when you navigated to a hashtag unless you also navigated a frame at the same time. Some pretty clever scripting avoids a server round-trip in there, all happily wrapped inside the navigation API. IE8 doesn't require this hack.

Back around 2007-2008, Ajax libraries started to include functionality to wrap all this journal ugliness. Happily, Silverlight, with Silverlight 3 in 2009, was able to build on this body of work to provide the same functionality.

The entire navigation structure for rich, client-side browser applications is built around hash tags.

15.1.2 *Anchor hashtags*

Hashtags, more properly known as *fragments* when part of a larger URI, were originally designed to enable navigation within the same page without requiring a round trip to the server. They were for top-level tables of contents on really long pages. Here's an example in HTML:

---

[1] You didn't think I'd get past this section without cracking that joke, did you?

```
<ul>
<li><a href="#first">First</a></li>
<li><a href="#second">Second</a></li>
</ul>

<p><a style="height:600px" name="first"/>
This is the first content paragraph</p>

<p><a style="height:600px" name="second"/>
This is the second content paragraph. Put me below the fold.</p>
```

If you paste this into a file with an .html extension and view it in your browser, you'll see how clicking the links at the top brings the bottom content into view and updates the address at the top of the browser. If the content is already in view, you won't see any on-page changes, but you'll still see the hashtag change in the URL. Figure 15.1 illustrates this.

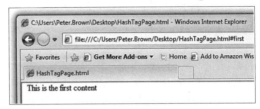

Figure 15.1   I just clicked the First link at the top of the page. The browser scrolled to bring the content into view and updated the URL with the hashtag #first.

You can achieve a similar effect using JavaScript. Rather than having to click a link, you can use this one line of JavaScript code:

```
window.location.hash = "#first";
```

As you learned back in chapter 4, Silverlight can manipulate the browser DOM for any page it's on. Silverlight uses this and the plug-in model to handle the journal manipulation for you, saving you the aggravation of coming up with a cross-platform, cross-browser, custom solution or hand-crafting JavaScript.

The hashtag approach provides a way to uniquely address content. It's common to see, for example, blog engines using this to uniquely address comments on a page. In Ajax applications and in-browser RIAs, you can use it the same way: to uniquely identify content that's on the same browser page, but nested within your application.

Assuming you're already on the browser page specified in the URL, all of this is done without a page refresh, which is the key to making it work with your applications.

15.1.3 *Back and forth*

Browsers have a long history[2] with their current navigation paradigm. When running an application in the browser, and increasingly when running desktop applications, users have come to expect that the approach of Back buttons, Forward buttons, and hyperlinks will be, if not the primary navigation mechanism, at least one form that's available to them. It has even reached a level mainstream enough to be incorporated into the Windows shell, as shown in figure 15.2.

The Back and Forward buttons have their own settled UI convention (left and right arrows). As expected, Back navigates the browser history backward, toward the

---

[2] I did it again! I kill me.

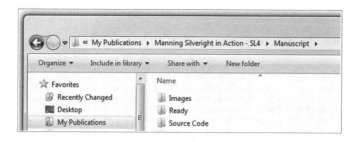

Figure 15.2
The Back and Forward buttons have even made it into the Windows shell, in the file explorer windows.

first page in the navigation chain, and Forward navigates forward as far as you've gone in this chain. Of course, Forward only works if you've used the Back button already. When you click another hyperlink, the forward chain is rebuilt starting at the current point.

With the background in browser navigation, journals, and hashtags, we can now look at the Silverlight implementation and make more sense of the design choices made, as well as the knobs provided for tweaking the approach. The easiest and most obvious way to explore the navigation framework is to start with the Silverlight Navigation Application template.

15.2   *The Navigation Application template*

When creating a new Silverlight project, you can choose from several stock templates. For most of the projects in this book, we've used the generic Silverlight Application template. That template is great if you want a blank slate to start with.

The Silverlight Navigation Application template is another good one. This template provides the fundamental structure and plumbing required to allow your application to work using a familiar web page navigation model. In addition, the template provides for easy theming of your application.

The Silverlight Navigation Application template isn't required when you want to incorporate navigation in your application. But you'll find the template provides a good starting point.

In this section, you'll create a new navigation project and use it to explore the Navigation Application template, including modifying the navigation to include an additional page and the link to that page. We'll wrap up with an example showing you how to use the free online themes to customize the UI of the navigation application.

15.2.1   *Creating a navigation application*

As the name suggests, the Silverlight Navigation Application template structures the application around the navigation API first introduced with Silverlight 3. This API makes it easy to move between pages. The template provides a best-practices structure for using the capabilities provided, as well as a good starting point for your own applications.

The first step is to create the new project using the navigation template. Figure 15.3 shows the correct template selected in the Visual Studio 2010 New Project dialog. I named the application NavigationExample.

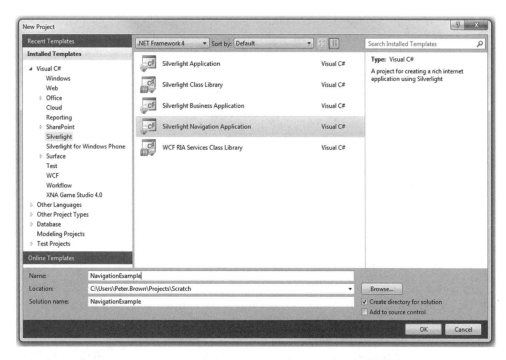

Figure 15.3 Picking the Navigation Application template in Visual Studio 2010

After the project has been created, you end up with a structure that includes an Assets folder with application styles (see chapter 23 for more on styling) and a Views folder that includes two pages and an error window dialog. You'll also see the usual Main-Page.xaml and App.xaml files in the project root.

When you run the unmodified application, using the default application style, you'll end up with something that looks like figure 15.4.

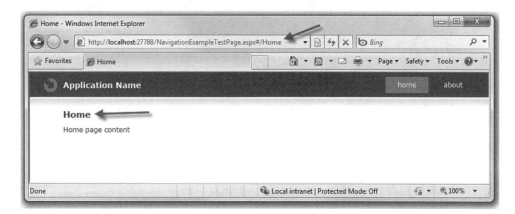

Figure 15.4 The Navigation Application default project. Note how the URL corresponds to the current page visible in the application, and how the navigation menu on the right is synchronized with the two.

The application template includes all the wiring required to synchronize the menu (the Home button at upper right in the screen shot) with the page in view, and synchronizes both with the hashtag in the URL. If you click the About navigation button, you'll see that the URL changes. Even better, you can use the browser's Back button to get back to the home page of the application.

Although this is a great structure, an application with only home and about pages would probably not be particularly engaging. To grow beyond this, you need to add a new page and modify the navigation menu.

15.2.2 Adding a new page

Much like regular web pages, the functionality and content for a navigation application are in the pages. Adding a new page to a navigation application involves three steps:

1 Add the new view to the Views folder.
2 Add a link to the top menu.
3 Add functionality to the page.

The first step is as simple as dropping a new file into a folder. The second step involves some modification to MainPage.xaml; and the third step is what you'd normally do in any application, so we'll skip it here.

ADDING THE NEW VIEW

Views are instances of the Silverlight Navigation `Page` class defined in the `System. Windows.Controls.Navigation` namespace. The Silverlight tools include a template for a blank page deriving from the `navigation:Page` class, a class which is essentially a `UserControl` that has been beefed up to support navigation.

Right-click the Views folder, and select Add New Item. In the Add New Item dialog, select the Silverlight Page template, and name the file CustomerDetail.xaml. Figure 15.5 shows the Add New Item dialog with the correct selections.

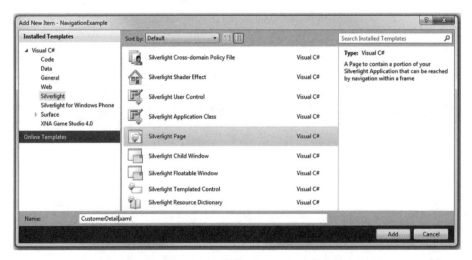

Figure 15.5   The Add New Item dialog with the Silverlight Page template selected. This is the template to be used for views in a Silverlight navigation application. I may have more templates than you; I've installed some add-ins.

After you've added the new page, you need to provide a way for the end user to find it. In a regular desktop application, this may be a menu or toolbar. For this navigation application, you'll use a HyperlinkButton.

ADDING THE LINK TO THE TOP MENU

In this template, navigation to individual pages is accomplished by HyperlinkButton instances on MainPage.xaml. The pages themselves are loaded in the navigation: Frame element named ContentFrame.

On MainPage.xaml is a Border named LinksBorder. This is the navigation menu that appears at upper right. The default XAML for this area is shown in listing 15.1.

Listing 15.1 LinksBorder showing navigation menu

Result:

XAML:

```
<Border x:Name="LinksBorder"
        Style="{StaticResource LinksBorderStyle}">
  <StackPanel x:Name="LinksStackPanel"
              Style="{StaticResource LinksStackPanelStyle}">        Page
    <HyperlinkButton x:Name="HomeLink"                             link
                     Style="{StaticResource LinkStyle}"
                     NavigateUri="/Home"
                     TargetName="ContentFrame"
                     Content="home"/>
                                                                   Your link
                                                                   goes here

    <Rectangle Style="{StaticResource DividerStyle}"/>

    <HyperlinkButton x:Name="AboutLink"
                     Style="{StaticResource LinkStyle}"
                     NavigateUri="/About"
                     TargetName="ContentFrame"
                     Content="about"/>
  </StackPanel>
</Border>
```

This Border contains the top menu navigation structure for the application. It's a simple StackPanel of elements: HyperlinkButton instances separated by vertical lines (narrow rectangles).

Note that I removed the x:Name from the divider rectangle, because it's not needed. The names in the HyperlinkButton instances also aren't needed, but I gave them meaningful names to help with the discussion here, and in case you decide to do something with them in code. In your own project, you can remove the names if you'd like.

To add your own page to the navigation structure, you need to follow this pattern and add a divider rectangle (optional, but recommended) and a HyperlinkButton pointing to your page. Place this markup in the XAML in the spot indicated in the previous listing:

```
<Rectangle Style="{StaticResource DividerStyle}" />

<HyperlinkButton x:Name="CustomerDetailLink"
                 Style="{StaticResource LinkStyle}"
                 NavigateUri="/CustomerDetail"
                 TargetName="ContentFrame"
                 Content="customer" />
```

When copying and pasting from the other links, I left the divider alone but changed a couple properties of the HyperlinkButton. The first is the x:Name property, which is optional because it's not used in any code, binding, or animation in the default template. The second is the Content. This is what will be displayed on the menu bar. You could easily use images rather than text if you'd like. You're also free to change the LinkStyle resource to modify the appearance. The final property is the NavigateUri. That needed to be changed to point to the newly added page.

You may have noticed that the URI for the page is set to /CustomerDetail, when the actual page is stored in /Views/CustomerDetail.xaml. This is handled by the URI mapper, which we'll cover later in this chapter.

Although it isn't unique to the navigation API, one other nice feature of the navigation application is its ability to be easily styled or themed.

15.2.3 *Changing the application theme*

When the Silverlight team created the navigation template, they enlisted the help of an in-house designer to both ensure that the template could be themed and to create themes for use with it. Long after the release, the design team has continued to put out new themes, each more impressive than the last.

You can get the set of templates that's current as of this writing by visiting http://bit.ly/sltemplates and clicking the big download link at the top. Be sure to grab the VisualStudio2010 zip file, which contains the .vsix (Visual Studio Install Package) files for the themes. This will install a number of new project templates, one for each theme you install.

Because you've already started your project, you'll need to steal some theme files from another project. In another instance of Visual Studio, create a new Silverlight Navigation Application - Cosmopolitan Theme (or a different theme if you prefer) application. Save that. Then, find the folder where you stored that project, open it in Explorer, and drag all the contents *except the SDKStyles.xaml and ToolkitStyles.xaml files* from the Assets folder in the temp project into the Assets folder of your chapter project. Be sure to overwrite (or first rename) the old Styles.xaml file so you pick up the new one.

> **IMPORTANT**   Make sure each of the theme XAML styles is compiled with a build action of Page and a Custom Tool of MSBuild:Compile. You'll find both settings in the property panel for the file. The build action provides compile-time errors. The custom tool tells Visual Studio what to do with the file and how to include it in the assembly.

If you include SDKStyles.xaml or ToolkitStyles.xaml, you'll get compile errors unless you also have the required SDK and Toolkit assembles (respectively) referenced in the application.

Finally, open App.xaml in the project you've been working in, and merge in the new resource dictionaries:

```
<Application.Resources>
  <ResourceDictionary>
    <ResourceDictionary.MergedDictionaries>
      <ResourceDictionary Source="Assets/Styles.xaml" />
      <ResourceDictionary Source="Assets/CoreStyles.xaml" />
    </ResourceDictionary.MergedDictionaries>
  </ResourceDictionary>
</Application.Resources>
```

After you have all the DLLs referenced, rebuild your application and run. I picked the Cosmopolitan theme, so my application looks like figure 15.6. I didn't change a single line of page XAML, just the applied styles. Note how the sizes, colors, fonts used, and locations of the elements have all changed-pretty awesome. You'll learn more about styling and resource dictionaries in chapter 23.

Most of the rest of what you'll do inside the pages is straight Silverlight code and design. You'll write code either in the code-behind or using something like the MVVM pattern described in chapter 16.

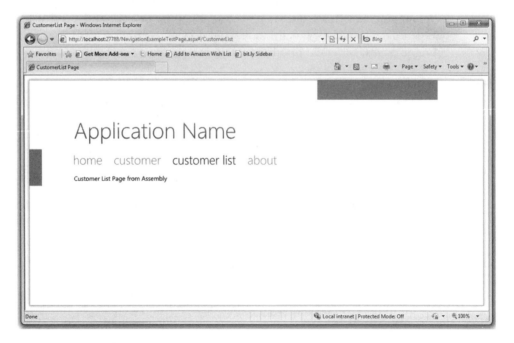

Figure 15.6   The Silverlight navigation application with a new style. The Cosmopolitan style is similar to the Metro theme used by Zune software.

As we continue to explore the navigation framework, you'll use this application in the examples. Now that you've seen how straightforward it is to create a Silverlight navigation-enabled application using the template, it's time to dig into the classes and methods that make the template possible.

15.3   *Navigating to pages*

In the previous section, you saw what it takes to add a new page into the navigation structure. In a nutshell, all you need to do is add the page to the Views folder and then to the navigation links on the top.

Pages are the most frequently used part of the navigation framework. They're the primarily location for your content. In addition to pages, there are several other important parts. First, the `NavigationService` class provides the underlying property and event information required to make navigation work. Then you have the `Frame` element, which loads pages using URIs and supports features such as URI mapping. Both the pages and frames also support forms of caching to minimize the reload time for any given information. Also, much like HTML, frames can be nested and have multiple levels of navigation, or even navigation to pages in other assemblies.

All of these classes collectively fall under the Navigation framework, and all of them are involved in navigating to pages in your Silverlight application.

In this section, we'll dig deeper into what makes navigation possible, looking at the core `Page` class and its properties. From there, we'll uncover how the `Frame` class and URI mapping work to load those pages, and how to pass and receive parameters between page instances. Finally, we'll wrap up with caching pages for reuse and navigating to pages contained in other assemblies.

15.3.1   *The Page class*

The `Page` class, in the `System.Windows.Controls` namespace, provides the behavior expected of content to be loaded into a navigation `Frame`. The `Page` itself is analogous to an HTML page or to a regular Silverlight `UserControl`, but with the addition of navigation events, members, and a navigation service. The page also provides caching capabilities in concert with the `Frame` class; we'll cover that and other features later in this chapter.

In addition to the standard `Title` property, which provides a unique friendly title to the page, and some navigation objects that we'll discuss shortly, the `Page` class includes several virtual functions used to provide information about the current navigation state.

NAVIGATION VIRTUAL FUNCTIONS

The `Page` class includes four navigation-related virtual functions. Override these when you want to perform an action on a specific navigation step. Table 15.1 lists the functions of each.

These four events were implemented as virtual functions to eliminate the requirement of hooking up event handlers, potentially keeping pages around longer than intended.

Table 15.1 `Page navigation members`

Navigation event	Description
`OnFragmentNavigation`	Called when a fragment inside the Silverlight application is navigated to. For example, /Views/CustomerDetail.xaml#Item1234. This is different from the top-level hash or fragment used to support Silverlight navigation. Equivalent to the `FragmentNavigation` event on the `NavigationService` class.
`OnNavigatedFrom`	Called when this page is no longer the active page in the frame. Use this for any final cleanup code. Equivalent to the `Navigated` event of the `NavigationService` class.
`OnNavigatingFrom`	Called just before this page is swapped out for another page. The event args allow for canceling the navigation. You can use this to prompt the user to save data, for example. Equivalent to the `Navigating` event of the `NavigationService` class.
`OnNavigatedTo`	Called when the page becomes the active page in the frame. In most cases, you'll use this where you'd use the `Loaded` event in nonnavigation scenarios.

You'll use the `OnFragmentNavigation` when you want to respond to subnavigation within the current page. This is a powerful but seldom-used capability similar in intent to hashtag or fragment navigation on HTML pages.

A good place for page cleanup code, or persisting to a backup cache, is the `OnNavigatedFrom` method. This is fired when the page is no longer the active page, so it's too late to use to prompt the user for saving. Use the `OnNavigatingFrom` method when you need to prompt the user.

The `OnNavigatingFrom` method provides a facility for informing the user that the page is about to be navigated away from. The method signature allows for canceling the navigation, typically in response to a prompt to the user.

Finally, the `OnNavigatedTo` method is the one most commonly used in navigation pages. This is typically used for any data loading or data-cache retrieval, as well as any page setup. Because pages can themselves be cached, this is the place to check the state of that page cache and perform any operations necessary to make the page available to the user.

The source of the event information is the `NavigationService` class, which also has several other useful properties and methods.

15.3.2 *The NavigationService class*

The navigation `Page` class exposes a `NavigationService` class with a property of the same name. This service is useful as a means to hook into the navigation system for the hosting frame from within page code.

The `NavigationService` class provides five methods used for navigating away from this page, reloading the current page, and stopping asynchronous navigation actions. Table 15.2 provides detail on each function.

Table 15.2   The `NavigationService` class functions

Member	Description
GoBack	Navigates to the previous entry in the history. Throws an exception if no previous entry exists in the history.
GoForward	Navigates to the next entry in the history. Throws an exception if no next entry exists in the history.
Navigate	Navigates to an arbitrary URI.
Refresh	Reloads the current page. Note that this is useful only when you provide a custom `INavigationContentLoader` for the `Frame`'s `ContentLoader` property.
StopLoading	Cancels any asynchronous navigation actions that haven't yet been processed.

`GoBack` and `GoForward` use the currently active journal to move backward and forward through the journal history. These methods are provided both here and at the `Frame` level to allow you to create your own navigation UI, typically for use when running out-of-browser applications where there's no browser UI. You can certainly use these in-browser, though-something which may be useful for full-screen applications in particular.

The `Navigate` method takes a URI and starts the process of loading the new content and replacing the current content. We'll cover the `Navigate` method in more detail when we discuss the `Frame` class.

In all cases, when using these navigation functions, the events listed in table 15.3 will be fired at their appropriate times.

In addition to the navigation functions, two other methods are available. The first, `Refresh`, is similar in functionality to the browser's Refresh button. Typically this is used only when you have custom content loaders and are performing some sort of authentication step that must happen before the content appears. This method reloads the page but doesn't force it to be regenerated: if the page is cached, it'll be read from the cache. The second, `StopLoading`, is similar to the browser's Stop or Cancel button. It stops an asynchronous or long-running page-load process. Given the structure of most navigation applications, with local compiled pages, `StopLoading` is rarely used.

Highly related to those functions are four properties that provide information on the navigation history as well as the current and planned page. Table 15.3 shows these properties.

These properties are typically used in concert with functions from table 15.1 For example, you'll check the `CanGoBack` property before calling the `GoBack` function. Listing 15.2 shows several of these in use in a hypothetical page.

Table 15.3   The `NavigationService` class properties

Member	Description
CanGoBack	Returns true if there's at least one previous entry in the history.
CanGoForward	Returns true if there's at least one next entry in the history.
CurrentSource	Returns the URI of the currently displayed page. This value changes when navigation has completed.
Source	Gets or sets the page to be displayed. If set, when navigation completes, `Source` and `CurrentSource` will be the same. In the interim, they may be different.

Listing 15.2   Using the `NavigationService` class to navigate forward or backward

XAML:

```
<Grid x:Name="LayoutRoot">
  <StackPanel Orientation="Horizontal" Height="30">
    <Button x:Name="NavigateBack"
            Click="NavigateBack_Click"
            Content="Back"
            Width="100" />
    <Button x:Name="NavigateForward"
            Click="NavigateForward_Click"
            Content="Forward"
            Width="100" />
  </StackPanel>
</Grid>
```

C# code-behind:

```
private void NavigateBack_Click(object sender, RoutedEventArgs e)
{
  if (NavigationService.CanGoBack)            ◁─┐ Always check or
    NavigationService.GoBack();                 │ risk exception
}

private void NavigateForward_Click(object sender, RoutedEventArgs e)
{
  if (NavigationService.CanGoForward) #1
    NavigationService.GoForward();
}
```

These functions and properties are useful for those odd times when you need to perform navigation directly from the page. The more typical approach, shown later in section 15.4, is to call them from the UI that hosts the navigation `Frame` control.

The final bit of functionality provided by the `NavigationService` class is surfaced through a set of five events that provide information about the current state of navigation. Table 15.4 shows the events exposed by this class.

Several of the events on the `NavigationService` class are equivalent to the virtual functions exposed by the page class, discussed earlier. Two of them, the `NavigationFailed` and `NavigationStopped` events, have no equivalent and so bear more investigation.

Table 15.4 The `NavigationService` class events

Member	Description
FragmentNavigation	Raised when the system navigates to a hashtag (fragment) on the current page. Equivalent to the `Page.OnFragmentNavigation` method.
Navigated	Raised when the system has navigated away from the page. Equivalent to the `Page.OnNavigatedFrom` method.
Navigating	Raised when the system is planning to navigate away from the page. This is a cancellable event. Equivalent to the `Page.OnNavigatingFrom` method.
NavigationFailed	Raised when the frame is unable to navigate to the requested page. Provides the exception information.
NavigationStopped	Raised when navigation has been stopped.

The `NavigationService` class provides much of the core functionality of the navigation system in Silverlight. Although accessing it from within a page is a fine way to use those capabilities, it's more common to access the equivalent properties and methods directly exposed by the `Frame` class to navigate using URIs or the history journal.

15.3.3 *Frames and URIs*

In Silverlight, `Pages` are loaded into `Frames` and are uniquely addressable via URIs. These two types-the `Frame` and the URI-are conceptually similar to their HTML counterparts in that the frame is both a container and a bit of a walled garden, used to host content.

The `Frame` class is a `ContentControl`, so it can have only one item as its content. In most cases, that's another XAML page, but that's controllable using the `Content-Loader` property of the `Frame` class.

The `Frame` class exposes many of the same properties and methods that the `NavigationService` exposes. One benefit at the `Frame` level is that most of these are exposed as dependency properties and can therefore be used to control the `IsEnabled` state of navigation controls via binding.

You can load content into a frame in a few different ways: using the `GoBack` and `GoForward` methods seen in the previous section, or via URI using the `Navigate` method, which we'll cover here. Frames also support URI mapping to change ugly URLs into more user-friendly versions. This mapping also helps better support page parameters.

LOADING CONTENT WITH THE NAVIGATE METHOD

Silverlight navigation applications load content pages into frames. In our walkthrough of the Navigation Application template in section 15.2, you saw that the `HyperlinkButton` in the MainPage.xaml file invokes navigation for you. Although using a `HyperlinkButton` is an easy way to get content into a frame, it's not the only way. Take for example

```
ContentFrame.Navigate(new Uri("/CustomerDetail", UriKind.Relative));
```

If the page /CustomerDetail maps to a valid page via the in-force URI mapping, this example will navigate to that page. You could put this type of code in a button or any sort of other handler in the application. The ability to navigate using code means you're not stuck with using HyperlinkControls for your application navigation: you can use traditional menus, ListBoxes, Buttons, or pretty much anything you'd like.

When working with navigation pages, you typically don't navigate to pages using a full filename such as CustomerDetail.xaml. Instead, you map friendly URIs to these absolute URIs. This is done through a property on the Frame class.

URI MAPPING

The Frame class exposes a property named UriMapper of type UriMapperBase. This is responsible for translating real application URIs into something more user-friendly. The default implementation is a class containing a collection of UriMapping objects. Table 15.5 shows the members of the UriMapper class.

Table 15.5　The members of the `UriMapper` class

Member	Description
UriMappings	Collection of UriMapping objects representing a single pair of URIs to be mapped. Each UriMapping object contains a Uri property and a MappedUri property as well as a MapUri function.
MapUri	Inherited from UriMapperBase and overridden in the default UriMapper class. Function accepts a regular URI and returns the URI that it maps to. In the default UriMapper implementation, calls the MapUri function of the UriMapping that matches the input URI.

The UriMapper property of the frame class is read/write. Should you desire, you can create your own UriMapper implementation, using your own scheme for mapping URIs. To do so, inherit from UriMapperBase and provide the required functionality in the MapUri function.

In the example at the beginning of this chapter, you saw how the mapper automatically translated /CustomerDetail into /Views/CustomerDetail.xaml. The default UriMapper class exposes the UriMappings collection. Here's the full XAML for the mapping:

```
<navigation:Frame.UriMapper>
  <uriMapper:UriMapper>
    <uriMapper:UriMapping Uri=""
                          MappedUri="/Views/Home.xaml"/>
    <uriMapper:UriMapping Uri="/{pageName}"
                          MappedUri="/Views/{pageName}.xaml"/>
  </uriMapper:UriMapper>
</navigation:Frame.UriMapper>
```

Given this mapping, and assuming an application URI of http://myapp.com/app.aspx, when the user visits http://myapp.com/app.aspx#/CustomerDetail, the second mapping will come into play and map to http://myapp.com/app.aspx#/Views/CustomerDetail.xaml. Also note the hashtag in both cases; the mapping only comes into play with that fragment.

This mapping XAML fragment sits inside the `navigation:Frame` element and provides the two mappings required for the URLs you'd normally use: no page and a specific page. Maps are read top-down and complete when the first match is hit. If you want to pass parameters to your page, you can get more complex and include support for query string values.

PASSING AND RECEIVING PAGE PARAMETERS

A common pattern in web applications is to pass parameters to a page using the query string. The *query string* is the set of delimited name/value pairs after the question mark in a URL. For example:

```
http://myapp.com/app.aspx?customer=1234
```

In this case, the query string would produce two name/value pairs: `customer` with a value of `27` and `invoice` with a value of `2506`.

That works well for passing parameters to an actual HTML page, but how does it fit in with the hashtag approach used with Silverlight navigation? How do you pass parameters to internal Silverlight pages? In a Silverlight application, much as we've gotten used to elsewhere on the Web, you may want something a little friendlier:

```
http://myapp.com/app.aspx#/CustomerDetail/1234
```

In this case, when you have mapping set up, Silverlight will load the `CustomerDetail` page and pass in a parameter of `1234`. How is that parameter passed in? It's entirely up to you and how you do the mapping. For example, let's say you want 1234 to map to a `CustomerID` query string variable. You provide a map that looks like this:

```
<uriMapper:UriMapping Uri="/CustomerDetail/{CustomerID}"
        MappedUri="/Views/CustomerDetail.xaml?CustomerID={CustomerID}" />
```

That map needs to appear near the top, preferably after the `Home` mapping, in order to be hit. Remember, the maps are evaluated top-down, and the first match is the only one that will be executed.

Retrieving the parameter from within the `Page` is super simple. The `Navigation-Context` object on the property of the same name in the `Page` class includes a `QueryString` property that may be used to retrieve the parameters passed into the page. It's an `IDictionary` of strings, so no parsing is required; use the name/value pairs as they're provided:

```
protected override void OnNavigatedTo(NavigationEventArgs e)
{
  if (NavigationContext.QueryString.ContainsKey("CustomerID"))
  {
    string id = NavigationContext.QueryString["CustomerID"];

    if (!string.IsNullOrWhiteSpace(id))
      LoadCustomerDetails(id);
  }
}
```

This example shows how easy it is to grab the ID from the query string passed into the page. Although I left them out for brevity here, you'll want to have all your query string key names in constants or an enum.

This approach enables you to provide meaningful deep links into data-oriented Silverlight applications, pulling up the appropriate records or other state. Back when I worked primarily with Windows Forms in the .NET 1 and 1.1 days, this was a feature many customers asked for: "How can I email a link to a specific page in the application?" We had all sorts of strange solutions involving custom URI schemes and more. I'm glad to see it's much simpler now.

When you have a data-oriented application, that typically means individual pages cause some sort of database transaction and web service call to run when you load them. The query string parameter may contain a record ID used to load some data. When the user is bouncing back and forth between pages in the application, you don't necessarily want to take a service or database hit on each page; that's where caching comes into play.

15.3.4 Caching pages

There are all sorts of ways to cache information in a Silverlight application: you can cache data at the service level on a web server or using a server-side caching product. You can cache locally on the client using cookies and isolated storage. With elevated trust applications, you can even cache to files in the My Documents folder. Of course, because Silverlight applications are stateful, you could cache everything you need in memory on the Silverlight client. The Page cache is a specialized form of this in-memory approach.

PAGE CACHE SETTINGS

Normally, when you navigate to a page using the navigation framework, you'll get a new instance of that page. This includes times when you click the Back button to get to that page. In order for Silverlight to cache that page, you need to enable caching at the page level using the NavigationCacheMode property. Table 15.6 shows the three possible values for page caching.

Table 15.6 The values for NavigationCacheMode for a Page

Value	Description
Disabled	The default value. The page is never cached.
Required	The page is cached, and the cached version is used for every request. Pages marked as required don't count against the Frame's cache limit and won't be discarded.
Enabled	The page is cached but is discarded when the Frame's cache limit is reached.

The cache mode is specific to the URI in use. When using parameters, each unique URI, including the query string, results in a new cached page if caching is turned on.

Given the way parameters usually affect the data on the page, this is a desirable effect. If you want to avoid this, you can cancel the navigation using code in the `Navigating` event or by overriding the `OnNavigatingFrom` function on the `Page`.

Typically, you'll set the page's cache mode in the constructor. Cached pages will still receive the navigation events, so you may do any page-loading work inside the `OnNavigatedTo` override.

The page cache is handled at the `Frame` level, so it makes sense for that to be the location of the cache settings.

FRAME CACHE SETTINGS

The `Frame` instance is responsible for any caching of pages it loads. It uses a simple in-memory structure keyed by the URI of the page to be cached. By default, the size of this cache is set to 10 pages, but you can change that by setting the `Frame.CacheSize` property in either markup or code. Recall that this limit doesn't include pages that require cache, only pages that enable it.

Logically, the cache is a queue: new pages are added to one end, and old pages fall off the other. The cache itself is opaque; you don't have direct access to it and can't manually manipulate the pages contained within. If you need that level of cache control, you can consider creating your own custom `INavigationContentLoader` and bypassing the built-in cache.

Caching is a powerful way to improve the performance of your application. Using the built-in page cache takes the guesswork out of dealing with individual page instances in a navigation application.

So far, you've seen a number of pages being loaded (and cached) using straightforward URIs. Those pages all existed in the currently executing assembly. It's rare for an application of any complexity to have all of its user interface contained within the main assembly.

For the last topic of this section, we'll cover how to navigate to pages contained in other assemblies.

15.3.5 *Navigating to pages in other assemblies*

Nontrivial applications almost always contain multiple assemblies. In many cases, those assemblies may contain user interface pages that must be integrated with the rest of the application. The Silverlight navigation framework supports navigating to pages included in other assemblies.

There are multiple ways to get the assembly down to the local machine. First, it can of course be packaged in the same .xap file with the initial application download. This doesn't help download time, but it does help keep the application modular. The assembly can be a shared assembly sitting on the server, resolved by the Silverlight assembly caching resolver. It can be an assembly dynamically downloaded using the Managed Extensibility Framework (MEF) or via an `HttpWebRequest` as seen in chapter 14.

URI SYNTAX

Regardless of the download mechanism, the navigation approach remains the same when you have the assembly available to Silverlight. Silverlight uses a specialized form of URI to reference the page. You may have seen this when loading resource files. For example, to get to CustomerList.xaml in a Views folder in the assembly `CustomerModule`, the URI looks like this:

```
/CustomerModule;component/Views/CustomerList.xaml
```

That says to load the `CustomerModule` component and look in the Views folder for a file named CustomerList.xaml. You could use this syntax as is, but it's much nicer to integrate it with the URI mapper. First, let's modify the project to include a new assembly with the CustomerList page so you can try this out.

ADDING THE ASSEMBLY

To the existing solution, add a new Silverlight Class Library project named Customer-Module. In that project, create a new Views folder. In the Views folder, add a new Silverlight page named CustomerList.xaml. Feel free to remove the default Class1.cs class that came along for the ride.

The XAML for the CustomerList file is short:

```
<Grid x:Name="LayoutRoot">
    <TextBlock Text="Customer List Page from Assembly" />
</Grid>
```

The next step is to reference this assembly from the main Silverlight application. First, build the solution. Then, right-click the Silverlight app and choose Add Reference. From the Projects tab, select the newly added CustomerModule assembly.

At this point, you have everything needed for a page in a separate assembly, included in the main .xap file. The next step is to build the URI mapping rule.

MAPPING THE URI

Unless you have a specific pattern to the URIs in your external assemblies, you'll need to create individual mapping rules for them. This alone can be a good reason to group pages by a common name prefix (such as Customer) and partition them into assemblies based on those names.

In this case, you'll add a specific URI mapping as the first rule in the URI mapper in MainPage.xaml. The rule looks like this:

```
<uriMapper:UriMapping Uri="/CustomerList"
        MappedUri="/CustomerModule;component/Views/CustomerList.xaml" />
```

When the mapping is in place, all you have to do is add some navigation controls on-page.

ADDING THE NAVIGATION MENU ITEM

Still in MainPage.xaml, locate the `LinksBorder` where you previously added the Customer menu item. Right under the `CustomerDetailLink`, add the following XAML:

```
<Rectangle Style="{StaticResource DividerStyle}" />

<HyperlinkButton x:Name="CustomerListLink"
                Style="{StaticResource LinkStyle}"
```

```
NavigateUri="/CustomerList"
TargetName="ContentFrame"
Content="customer list" />
```

When you run the application and click the Customer List menu option, you'll see something like figure 15.7. With the mapped URI, the fact that the page isn't in the main assembly is completely transparent to the user. Not only is this generally a good practice, but it'll make any further refactoring easier, as you can keep the URIs the same regardless of which assembly the pages live in.

Navigation in Silverlight is based primarily around Pages, Frames, and URIs. Individual pages have unique URIs and are loaded by those URIs into frames in the application. Frames provide a location to host pages, as well as a common interface to the navigation facilities offered by the NavigationService class and services such as the URI mapper. Both frames and pages participate in caching to help improve application performance. Finally, pages can be loaded from resources inside the executing assembly, or from external assemblies resolved at compile time or runtime.

So far, everything you've done has been for in-browser applications, where you have the browser's navigation UI and history journal to rely on. Out-of-browser applications obviously can't take advantage of these things. Luckily, the Silverlight navigation framework has taken this scenario into consideration and provided everything you need to have proper out-of-browser navigation.

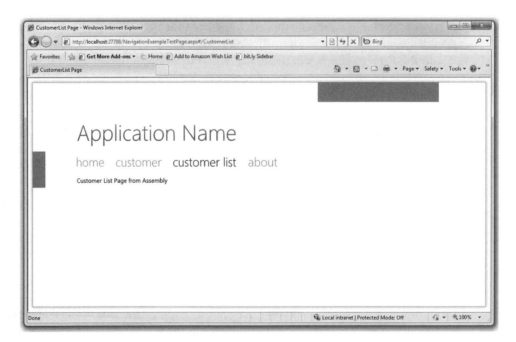

Figure 15.7   The navigation application with a customer list page loaded from an external assembly

15.4   Navigation out of the browser

Out-of-browser applications don't have the benefit of the browser-based navigation UI. From a user experience standpoint, this is excellent, because you'll want to provide your own in-theme navigation controls anyway. Consider the Microsoft Zune software client (see figure 15.8): it uses familiar navigation metaphors but looks different from a web browser.

The Zune client uses some of the traditional controls and navigation concepts (primarily links and the Back button) but provides a custom look and feel. The Zune client also eschews the use, in this case, of a Forward button.

A user interface along the lines of the Zune client is well within the capabilities of a Silverlight out-of-browser application with custom chrome and navigation. In this section, we'll look at what it takes to create custom navigation controls, hook up to an appropriate journal, and support navigation out of the browser.

15.4.1   Providing custom navigation controls

In the previous sections, you've seen how the `Frame` class provides various properties, methods, and events you can use to control and respond navigation. You've also created

Figure 15.8   The Zune software client. Note the small arrow Back button at upper left. Also note the two-level navigation using links such as Quickplay, Collection, Marketplace, and Social. (I get my *Doctor Who* fix using Zune. It's cheaper than cable.)

a shell of a navigation application that integrated with the browser to provide standard URI and back and forward navigation.

The next step is to take this application out-of-browser and provide your own custom navigation user interface.

CREATING THE NAVIGATION CONTROLS

The application needs, at a minimum, a Back button and a Forward button. For this, you'll use the metro theme (Windows Phone 7 and Zune) icons from http://metro.windowswiki.info/. From that set, drag both the back.png and next.png black icons into the project's Assets folder. When they're in place, modify MainPage.xaml to add the XAML in listing 15.3 right before the closing `Grid` tag at the bottom of the file.

Listing 15.3   The Back and Forward buttons on MainPage.xaml

```
<Grid x:Name="OutOfBrowserNavigationControls"
      VerticalAlignment="Top" HorizontalAlignment="Left"
      Margin="15">
  <Grid.Resources>
    <Style TargetType="Button">
      <Setter Property="Cursor" Value="Hand" />
      <Setter Property="Margin" Value="2" />
      <Setter Property="Opacity" Value="0.5" />
      <Setter Property="VerticalAlignment" Value="Top" />
      <Setter Property="Template">
        <Setter.Value>                                      ◁──┤ Button
          <ControlTemplate>                                     template
            <Grid>
              <VisualStateManager.VisualStateGroups>
                <VisualStateGroup x:Name="CommonStates">
                  <VisualState x:Name="Normal" />
                  <VisualState x:Name="Disabled">
                    <Storyboard>
                      <DoubleAnimation Duration="0"
                        Storyboard.TargetName="Content"
                        Storyboard.TargetProperty="Opacity"
                        To=".2" />
                    </Storyboard>
                  </VisualState>
                </VisualStateGroup>
              </VisualStateManager.VisualStateGroups>
              <ContentPresenter x:Name="Content" />
            </Grid>
          </ControlTemplate>
        </Setter.Value>
      </Setter>
    </Style>
  </Grid.Resources>                                          ◁──┤ Navigation
  <StackPanel Orientation="Horizontal">                         button
    <Button x:Name="BackButton"
            Click="BackButton_Click"
            Width="40" Height="40">
      <Image Source="Assets/back.png" />
    </Button>
```

```
        <Button x:Name="ForwardButton"
                Click="ForwardButton_Click"
                Width="25"
                Height="30">
            <Image Source="Assets/next.png" />
        </Button>
    </StackPanel>
</Grid>
```

← Navigation button

The XAML in listing 15.3 adds two buttons: a Back button and a Forward button. The style resource (resources are covered in chapter 23) creates a button that has no real appearance other than its content. When you run the application, the UI displays the two new buttons at upper left on the main page, as shown in figure 15.9.

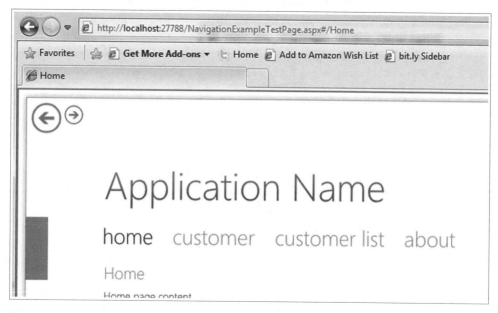

Figure 15.9 The new navigation buttons appear at upper left in the user interface.

The new UI looks pretty good. With the buttons in place, you'll need to wire them up to the content frame to make navigation happen.

WIRING UP THE BUTTONS

In the button-click event handlers for the two new navigation buttons, you'll place some code similar to what you wrote in listing 15.2 earlier in this chapter. This time, though, you'll use the `Frame` class directly rather than the `NavigationService` class. Listing 15.4 shows the code-behind for the MainPage.xaml page.

Listing 15.4 Navigation code in MainPage.xaml.cs

```
private void BackButton_Click(object sender, RoutedEventArgs e)
{
    if (ContentFrame.CanGoBack)
```

```
      ContentFrame.GoBack();
}

private void ForwardButton_Click(object sender, RoutedEventArgs e)
{
  if (ContentFrame.CanGoForward)
    ContentFrame.GoForward();
}
```

With this code in place, you can use either the browser buttons or the custom navigation buttons to move backward and forward through the journal. There's currently no visual cue indicating whether either navigation option is available, though. You can do this using binding, because the `CanGoBack` and `CanGoForward` properties of the `Frame` class are implemented as dependency properties. As you learned in chapter 11, you can use element binding to get to the properties on `ContentFrame`, as shown here:

```
<Button x:Name="BackButton"
        IsEnabled="{Binding CanGoBack, ElementName=ContentFrame}"
...
</Button>
<Button x:Name="ForwardButton"
        IsEnabled="{Binding CanGoForward, ElementName=ContentFrame}"
...
</Button>
```

With that in place, you'll see the Forward and Back buttons ghost out when the function isn't available. Note how the buttons are in sync with the browser navigation buttons. Now, let's try it without the browser.

OUT OF BROWSER

The next step is to turn the application into an out-of-browser application. Chapter 5 covered out-of-browser applications in detail; if you haven't yet read that, you may wish to take a brief detour over there now.

Right-click the main application project, select Properties, and select the Enable Running Application Out of the Browser check box on the Silverlight tab. Next, on the Debug tab, select Out-of-browser Application as the start action. Finally, set the NavigationExample project as the startup project by right-clicking the project and selecting Set as Start-up Project.

With those steps complete, run the application. The result will look something like figure 15.10.

One other important option relates to custom navigation: controlling who owns the journal.

CONTROLLING THE JOURNAL

The `Frame` class includes a property named `JournalOwnership`. This property lets you decide who should own the history journal. In a top-level navigation frame in an in-browser application, the default is to let the browser own the journal. In an out-of-browser application, the default is to let the frame own the journal. Table 15.7 shows the three possible values of the `JournalOwnership` property.

Figure 15.10   The navigation application running out-of-browser, with custom navigation controls

Given the defaults, leaving journal ownership at the default value will be sufficient for most cases, including your out-of-browser application. For out-of-browser applications, it wouldn't hurt to set the journal ownership to OwnsJournal, but other than a short decision tree, you're not really saving any code.

There was a time when a series of dialogs could be considered the main user interface for a number of applications. Not any more. Pages are the main way you present content to users. But dialogs still have their place for presenting important information to the user, such as error messages or details, or for gathering discrete bits of information such as filenames.

Table 15.7   Values for the JournalOwnership property of the Frame class

Value	Description
Automatic	If the frame control is a top-level frame and is running in-browser, the browser's journal is used. Otherwise, the frame maintains its own journal.
OwnsJournal	The frame maintains its own journal.
UsesParentJournal	Uses the browser's journal. This may only be used with a top-level (not nested) frame.

In addition to the page-navigation approach you've seen so far, Silverlight has support for two discrete types of dialogs: in-application floating windows with simulated modality, and system dialogs.

15.5 *Showing dialogs and pop-ups*

There are certain times when you need to grab the user's attention and display something that overlays other page content. Maybe you need to display details about a critical error. You could do this with the message box, but that can be limiting. For more intricate dialogs, you may want to consider the other two alternatives available in Silverlight.

Throughout this section, you'll learn about the four types of visual prompts available in Silverlight. We'll briefly cover the Popup control first, followed by the ChildWindow control-a control that provides the capability to display in-Silverlight dialogs. Then, we'll dive into the two system dialogs made available in Silverlight: the OpenFileDialog, which is useful for getting a file from the user's local file system, and the SaveFileDialog, which helps specify a location for saving a file on the local file system.

15.5.1 *The Popup control*

In Silverlight 2, if you wanted to create a dialog-like experience, you likely used the Popup control from the System.Windows.Controls.Primitives namespace. The Popup control provided a way to guarantee that your content would show up at the top of the z-order, regardless of which control created it. But it wasn't really a dialog substitute.

The Popup control has no visuals of its own. Typically, you'll enclose a UserControl or a number of elements within the Popup to give it the behavior you want. Because sizing and positioning can be tricky otherwise, it's recommended that you apply a fixed size to the content in the Popup and then perform any centering or other position calculations.

Assuming that the XAML namespace xmlns:primitives points to System.Windows.Controls.Primitives, the syntax for the popup is simple:

```
<primitives:Popup x:Name="MyPopup"> content </primitives:Popup>
```

To display the pop-up in the example, you'd then use the IsOpen property:

```
MyPopup.IsOpen = true;
```

In Silverlight 3 and 4, the use of the Popup control is more for floating nondialog items to the top of the stack, but not really for simulating dialog boxes, so we won't spend much time on it. The Popup control is used by Silverlight to support other elements such as tooltips, the drop-down in the ComboBox, and, of course, the ChildWindow control introduced with Silverlight 3.

15.5.2 *Displaying a dialog box with the ChildWindow control*

Silverlight 3 introduced a new class, ChildWindow, which provides a window-like experience over the base Popup control. Where the Popup control provided only z-order management, the ChildWindow adds window overlays, dialog results, OK/Cancel buttons, and window title functionality.

Figure 15.11 The Silverlight `ChildWindow` is a first-class element like `UserControl` and `Page`.

Unlike `Popup`, `ChildWindow` is considered a first-class element, like `Page` and `UserControl`, and has a template in the project items template list, as shown in figure 15.11.

That said, `ChildWindow` isn't located in the core Silverlight runtime; it's located in the `System.Windows.Controls` assembly in the SDK. The primary reason for keeping it out of the runtime is that it's not an essential or enabling technology; you could live with `Popup` if you absolutely needed to.

After you create a new `ChildWindow`, you're presented with its default template, as shown in listing 15.5.

Listing 15.5 The default `ChildWindow` template

Result:

XAML:

```
<controls:ChildWindow x:Class="SilverlightApplication20.ChildWindow1"
    xmlns="http://schemas.microsoft.com/winfx/2006/xaml/presentation"
    xmlns:x="http://schemas.microsoft.com/winfx/2006/xaml"
    xmlns:controls="clr-namespace:System.Windows.Controls;
```

```
⇒   assembly=System.Windows.Controls"
    Width="400"
    Height="300"
    Title="ChildWindow1">
 <Grid x:Name="LayoutRoot" Margin="2">
   <Grid.RowDefinitions>
     <RowDefinition />
     <RowDefinition Height="Auto" />
   </Grid.RowDefinitions>
```

  Window content goes

```
   <Button x:Name="CancelButton" Content="Cancel"
     Click="CancelButton_Click"
     Width="75" Height="23" HorizontalAlignment="Right"
     Margin="0,12,0,0" Grid.Row="1" />

   <Button x:Name="OKButton" Content="OK"
     Click="OKButton_Click"
     Width="75" Height="23" HorizontalAlignment="Right"
     Margin="0,12,79,0" Grid.Row="1" />
 </Grid>
</controls:ChildWindow>
```

Listing 15.5 shows the default look and feel of the `ChildWindow` control. Before we get into how to customize that, we'll cover the mechanics of showing and hiding the window.

SHOWING THE CHILDWINDOW

A `ChildWindow` is typically displayed from code rather than included as an inline element in XAML. To facilitate this, the control has several members that handle showing, closing, reporting results, and allowing cancellation. Table 15.8 lists those members and their related functions.

Table 15.8   Properties, methods, and events related to showing and closing the `ChildWindow`

Member	Description
`DialogResult` property	A nullable boolean that indicates whether the dialog was accepted or cancelled. This is typically set to `true` in the handler for an OK button and `false` in the handler for a Cancel button.
`Show` method	Displays the child window and immediately returns. Whereas the behavior of a `ChildWindow` is logically modal, from a programmatic standpoint, `Show` is a nonblocking and therefore nonmodal method.
`Close` method	Closes the window. Typically, this is called from a button on the child window itself.
`Closing` event	Raised when the child window is closing. The handler for this event has the opportunity to cancel the close operation and force the window to stay open.
`Closed` event	Raised after the child window has been closed. Note that due to animations, the window may still be visible on the screen for a moment longer, but it's be in the process of closing for good. Use this event to inspect the `DialogResult` property.

The typical way to use a `ChildWindow` is to call the `Open` method from code and then to take some action based on the dialog result available during the `Closed` event. Listing 15.6 shows this process in more detail.

Listing 15.6 Displaying a `ChildWindow` and capturing the `DialogResult`

C#:
```
void MainPage_Loaded(object sender, RoutedEventArgs e)
{
  ChildWindow dialog = new MyDialog();

  dialog.Closed += (s, ea) =>
    {
      if (dialog.DialogResult == true)        ◁──┘  User
      { ... }                                        clicked OK
      else if (dialog.DialogResult == false)  ◁──┐  User clicked
      { ... }                                     │  Cancel
      else
      { ... }
    };

  dialog.Show();
}
```

The example shows how to display a `ChildWindow` and handle the three possible `DialogResult` values set when the user closes the window. Note that this example also uses a lambda expression to create the event handler. This is a shortcut way to create a delegate inline in your code rather than create a separate event handler function. In this example, s is the variable that contains the sender, and ea is the variable that contains the event arguments. The code to display the window could also have been written like this:

```
ChildWindow dialog = new MyDialog();
dialog.Closed += new EventHandler(dialog_Closed);
dialog.Show();
```

Of course, in that instance, you'd need to create a separate function named `dialog_Closed` that had the event handler logic in it. Either way is valid.

Note also that you do a true/false/else check on the `DialogResult` value. This is because the `DialogResult` is a nullable boolean type, and it's not usually sufficient to check for true or false. Nullable booleans also don't allow you to write code like this:

```
if (dialog.DialogResult)     { ... }
```

You'll get a compile-time error unless you cast the value to a regular `bool`. For that reason, you check explicitly against true, false, and the null (default) value.

When you ran the code in listing 15.6, you probably noticed that the content behind the window was overlaid with a gray rectangle. The color and opacity of the overlay are a couple of the knobs you can tweak to customize the way the `ChildWindow` looks.

CUSTOMIZING THE CHILDWINDOW

Like almost everything else in Silverlight, you can do some basic customization of a ChildWindow to change things such as background and overlay colors without messing around with the control template. Some of those properties specific to ChildWindow are listed in table 15.9.

Table 15.9   Properties of the ChildWindow control

Property	Description
HasCloseButton	Set this value to determine whether the close button, typically at upper right, is visible or collapsed. If you set this to false, make sure you provide another way to close the window.
OverlayBrush	When the ChildWindow is displayed, it includes an overlay that covers all other content in the current Silverlight application. This gives the illusion of a modal dialog. Use OverlayBrush to set the brush to be used for that overlay.
OverlayOpacity	Sets the opacity of the overlay. A higher opacity means less background content shines through.
Title	Displays content in the window title bar. Although typically text, this can be any element.

The ChildWindow provides the capability to create any in-application dialog that you need. Two other types of dialogs are more operating system–specific in their display and use: the OpenFileDialog and the SaveFileDialog.

15.5.3 *Prompting for a file*

The OpenFileDialog class enables you to ask users for one or more files from their filesystems. From there, you can load the data from the selected files into memory, giving you the flexibility to do any number of things. For instance, you can send the contents of a file to a server or load the contents into your Silverlight application. The SaveFileDialog performs a similar function but provides a mechanism to save a single file to the filesystem. Either way, before you can do any of these items, you must understand how to interact with the OpenFileDialog and SaveFileDialog classes.

Throughout this section, you'll learn the three steps involved in interacting with an OpenFileDialog. The first step involves launching and configuring an instance of the OpenFileDialog class. Next, you must wait for and retrieve the results of a user's interaction with an OpenFileDialog. Finally, you'll parse the results if a user has selected at least one file.

LAUNCHING THE DIALOG BOX

To give your users the opportunity to select a file or multiple files, you must instantiate an instance of the OpenFileDialog class from procedural code; you can't create an OpenFileDialog from XAML. After it's created, you can use several properties to customize the selection experience. These properties and their descriptions are provided in table 15.10.

Table 15.10   The configuration properties available on the `OpenFileDialog` and `SaveFileDialog`

Property	Description
`Filter`	Represents the type of files that are displayed in the dialog.
`FilterIndex`	Determines which filter is specified by default if the filter specifies multiple file types.
`Multiselect`	`OpenFileDialog`-only. Specifies whether users may select multiple files. By default, users may select only one file.
`DefaultExt`	`SaveFileDialog`-only. Specifies the default extension to use if the user types in a filename without an extension.

As this table shows, you have flexibility in customizing the selection experience, but you don't have complete control over the dialog box. For instance, you can't dictate the appearance of the dialogs. Instead, the dialogs use the user's OS to determine the general look of the dialog box. By using the values in table 15.10, you can guide the selection experience, as shown in figure 15.12.

The following is the code to achieve this:

```
OpenFileDialog openFileDialog = new OpenFileDialog();
openFileDialog.Filter =
  "Text files (*.txt)|*.txt|Xml Files (*.xml)|*.xml";
bool? fileWasSelected = openFileDialog.ShowDialog();
```

This example shows an `OpenFileDialog` box that enables a user to select a text or XML file. You can accomplish this by appropriately setting the `Filter` property of the `Open-FileDialog` object. The dialog is then launched by calling the `ShowDialog` method. The code for a `SaveFileDialog` is similar. Unlike the `ChildWindow`-type dialog shown in the previous section, this method is a blocking call that prevents the execution of any

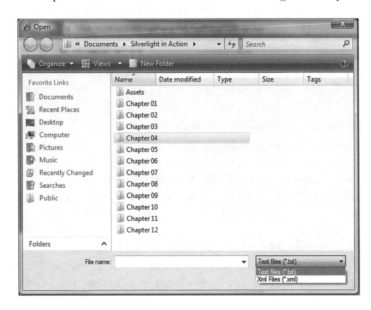

Figure 15.12   Guiding the selection using filter properties

additional code until the user exits the dialog. After the user exits the dialog, the Show-Dialog method returns a nullable bool that signals the end of a user's interaction with the dialog. The code then continues executing, giving you the opportunity to retrieve and analyze the results.

RETRIEVING THE RESULTS

When a user exits the dialog, the ShowDialog method returns a nullable bool value. This value will be false if the user chose to close out of or cancel the dialog. If the user clicked the OK button, a true value will be returned. After the value is returned, you can access the file(s) that the user selected.

The file(s) selected within an OpenFileDialog are available through the File and Files properties. The SaveFileDialog, because it only supports a single file, has only the File property. These properties will be null if a user left the OpenFileDialog without clicking the OK button, so you should check the value returned from the ShowDialog method before attempting to retrieve the selected file(s). Here's an example:

```
bool? fileWasSelected = openFileDialog.ShowDialog();
if (fileWasSelected == true)
{
  FileInfo fileInfo = openFileDialog.File;
  StreamReader reader = fileInfo.OpenText();
}
```

From this example, you can see that after a user opens the dialog box, you can get the selected file through the File property. If the Multiselect property had been set to true, the Files property would have been more applicable. Either way, if a user hadn't selected a file, both those property values would have been null. If a file or multiple files had been selected, you could have retrieved the details of each file through the FileInfo object.

The SaveFileDialog, because it only supports a single file, has a helper method to use for opening the file. The code for a SaveFileDialog looks like this:

```
bool? fileWasSelected = saveFileDialog.ShowDialog();
if (fileWasSelected == true)
{
  Stream stream = saveFileDialog.OpenFile();
}
```

If you wish to retrieve the name of the file entered or selected by the user, use the SaveFieldDialog.SafeFileName string property.

READING THE RESULTS

The FileInfo class provides a special bridge from the local filesystem to the security sandbox in which Silverlight runs. This class is specifically designed for use with the OpenFileDialog and SaveFileDialog. This object provides two methods that allow you to read the contents of a file—OpenRead and OpenText-and one method that may be used in the case of the SaveFileDialog to write to the file-OpenWrite.

The OpenRead method is designed to handle binary file scenarios. This method returns a read-only System.IO.Stream object, which is well-suited for handling bytes of information. Similarly, the `OpenWrite` method returns a write-only stream, but only if called on a `FileInfo` object returned from the `SaveFileDialog`. Alternatively, the `OpenText` method is better suited for reading text-related files. This method returns a basic `System.IO.StreamReader`, as shown here:

```
FileInfo fileInfo = openFileDialog.File;
StreamReader reader = fileInfo.OpenText();
myTextBlock.Text = reader.ReadToEnd();
```

As this example shows, working with a text file in Silverlight is incredibly trivial. It's just as easy to work with a binary file. The key to either approach is to understand working with streams of data. This topic is a general concept in .NET development that's beyond the scope of this book.

The `OpenFileDialog` provides a way to ask a user for a file to open. The `SaveFile-Dialog` provides a way to ask for a filename for saving a file. The `Popup` element and `ChildWindow` control provide another way to prompt your users. These options help Silverlight deliver a richer experience than you can easily get with HTML. In addition, other controls that haven't been covered also help provide a rich experience.

15.6 *Summary*

In the old days, we had chisels and stone, manual typewriters, and the MDI and dialog application navigation styles. At some point in the late 1990s, developers started taking cues from web browsers and decided that their navigation approach-using Back and Forward buttons and uniquely addressable pages-made sense for many applications. It certainly made more sense than MDI in nondocument applications.

Silverlight builds on this history and application navigation trends to nicely support the back/forward and URI navigation paradigm. Silverlight pages can be uniquely addressed via URIs (including parameters for deep links directly into specific bits of data) using hashtags as pioneered by Ajax. The navigation API even includes support for caching and for customizing the navigation UI.

Setting up a project to use the navigation API can be tricky, so the Silverlight tools include a Navigation Application template that includes all the plumbing necessary to get you well on your way to building the application. The template even includes excellent support for skinning and theming.

Dialogs, of course, are still useful in discrete scenarios. Silverlight provides support for custom dialogs using the `ChildWindow` and `Popup` classes, as well as access to system-level file dialogs for opening and saving files.

Navigation is but one of many important pieces when structuring an application. In the next chapter, we'll tackle one of the most important architectural patterns for Silverlight developers: the Model-View-ViewModel pattern.

16

Structuring and testing with the MVVM/ViewModel pattern

This chapter covers

- The ViewModel or MVVM pattern
- Creating services for use with MVVM
- Using commands and the `CallMethodAction` behavior
- Testing using the Silverlight Unit Testing Framework

When the community stops worrying about how to do basic things in a particular technology and starts working out how to do complex things well, you know the technology has reached a point of maturity. The emergence of architectural patterns and testing capabilities for a platform are a good indicator that the technology is ready for real-world use in nontrivial applications.

One of the main patterns to be applied to Silverlight is the *Model-View-ViewModel (MVVM) pattern*, also known as the *ViewModel pattern*.

NOTE MVVM or ViewModel Pattern? Different groups like to call it different things. I'll use both interchangeably until the community settles on one over the other. There are some influential folks on both sides of this debate.

As part of my job at Microsoft and my life as an MVP before that, I give a fair number of presentations, almost all of which include code demos. For timing and retention reasons, I'll often implement the code directly in the code-behind. At least 75 percent of audience members don't know anything about patterns such as MVVM, and the few times I've tried to include bits of that pattern in my demos, the audience was lost and completely missed the main thing I was teaching. So, I've taken to explaining MVVM at a high level before the talk and apologizing for not using it in the demo. Basically, I say "I'm doing this just to show *X*. Never write real code this way."

It sounds amusing, but in a way, it's a bit depressing. Many folks aren't exposed to the pattern, but many more are exposed and pass on it because they're presented the full pattern without any background or helpful ladder rungs to get to the full implementation. That's a real problem. In math class, I was always told to show my work, and I think the same applies here.

Rather than describe the pattern and take it chunk by chunk in this chapter, we'll look at the default technique—using the code-behind approach in order to get a baseline—and then start with an overview of MVVM and a simple implementation of the pattern. Next, you'll refactor it to take advantage of other best practices typically associated with the pattern such as using services, commands, and behaviors. I'll even throw in a bit of information on using interfaces, view model locators, and Inversion of Control. Finally, we'll follow that up with some testing approaches.

My point in this chapter isn't to provide one official implementation of the MVVM pattern or tell you how you need to build your applications. Instead, I'm providing you with the groundwork so you can see how the spectrum of implementations of MVVM/ViewModel fits into your application development and make informed choices about how to use (or not use) the pattern in your next project.

In addition, I'm not going to use a particular MVVM toolkit in this chapter. Those toolkits are great, but much like that expensive calculator in math class, they do a lot of the work for you, so you don't learn much.

In the end, you'll have a spectrum of implementations to choose from, any of which may be used on your projects as your own requirements dictate. You'll also gain a better understanding of what each additional bit of complexity provides you in return.

16.1 Project setup and traditional code-behind approach

You may wonder why I'd start a chapter on MVVM with a bunch of code-behind code. To understand where you can go, you need to start with where you are. The code-behind approach is by far the way most applications on the Microsoft stack are built these days. Acceptance of patterns such as MVVM and MVC is changing that, but slowly.

Starting with the code-behind approach will serve two purposes. First, it'll give us a working application baseline for refactoring. Second, it'll allow us to easily compare the approaches as we move through the chapter.

In this section, you'll create a project that'll serve you for the rest of the chapter. It'll be a Silverlight navigation application, much like the one covered in chapter 15. You'll then take that project and add in some service calls to get data from a SQL Server database, using WCF as the intermediary. Finally, you'll add a list form and a pop-up details form to round out the project.

16.1.1 *Project and service setup*

This solution will be based on the Silverlight Navigation Application template covered in chapter 15. Create a new solution named MvvmApplication using that template. Figure 16.1 shows the New Project dialog with the appropriate selections. When prompted, be sure to host the application in a new web site (the default setting).

After you have the overall solution structure in place, follow the instructions in appendix A to set up the database connection and entity data model. When complete, you should have a solution with an untouched Silverlight Navigation Application template–based client and a web project with access to the AdventureWorks database via the entity data model.

The next step is to set up a web service to allow the Silverlight client to access that data.

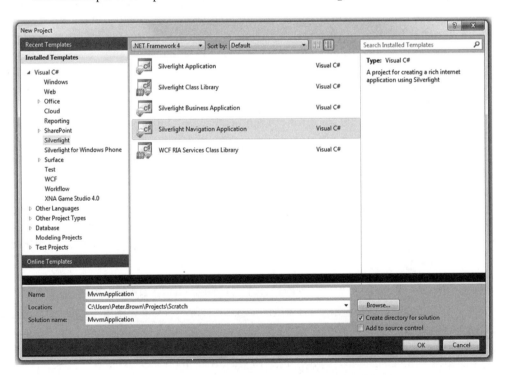

Figure 16.1   For this solution, you'll use the Navigation Application template introduced in chapter 15.

WEB SERVICES

Silverlight applications run on the client and can talk to server-side databases only via a service of some sort. You can choose multiple types of services. For example, you could go with a REST-based solution (chapter 14) or something using WCF RIA Services (chapter 17). For this, you'll use a regular Silverlight-enabled WCF service: a SOAP web service built using WCF. Create a folder named Services in the web project, and add into it a new Silverlight Enabled WCF Service named EmployeeService.svc. Listing 16.1 shows the code for that service.

Listing 16.1   WCF service to expose data to the Silverlight application

```
using MvvmApplication.Web;

[ServiceContract(Namespace = "services.web.mvvmapplication")]
[AspNetCompatibilityRequirements(RequirementsMode =
                AspNetCompatibilityRequirementsMode.Allowed)]
public class EmployeeService
{
  [OperationContract]
  public IList<Employee> GetEmployees()
  {
    var context = new AdventureWorksEntities();

    return context.Employees.ToList();
  }
}
```
Return all employees, unsorted

The service is a basic Silverlight-enabled web service. It uses the entity data model to return the list of all employees in the database. You could also use a LINQ expression to be more selective about the list, narrow down the number of columns returned (which would also require a new return type), or sort the data. The function could also return an IQueryable<Employee> to enable better client-side LINQ integration.

When the service has been created, add a web reference from the Silverlight application to the newly created service. Be sure to do a build first, or the service reference will typically fail. Name the service reference namespace Services. Be sure to refer to chapter 14 as needed for more information on services and service references.

EMPLOYEE LIST VIEW

Next, in the Views folder, add a new view (Silverlight Page) named EmployeeList.xaml. For information on adding pages to Silverlight navigation applications, please see chapter 15. The EmployeeList.xaml markup should look like listing 16.2. (Note: Drag the DataGrid onto the design surface from the toolbox in order to get all the references and namespaces automatically set up.)

Listing 16.2   EmployeeList.xaml markup

```
<Grid x:Name="LayoutRoot">
  <sdk:DataGrid AutoGenerateColumns="True"
            Margin="12,55,119,12"
            x:Name="EmployeesGrid" />
```

```
<Button Content="More Vacation!"
        Height="23" Width="101" Margin="0,55,12,0"
        HorizontalAlignment="Right" VerticalAlignment="Top"
        x:Name="AddMoreVacation" />
<Button Content="Edit"
        Height="23" Width="101" Margin="0,110,12,0"
        HorizontalAlignment="Right" VerticalAlignment="Top"
        x:Name="EditEmployee" />

<Grid x:Name="LoadingProgress"
      Background="#CCFFFFFF"
      Visibility="Collapsed">
  <ProgressBar Height="25" Width="200"
               IsIndeterminate="True" />
</Grid>
</Grid>
```

Listing 16.2 includes a DataGrid that contains all the employees, as well as two buttons for manipulating the data. Finally, a semitransparent white overlay named Loading-Progress is displayed when the data is being fetched.

Next, add the new employee list page to the navigation menu. The process to do this was covered in chapter 15; but for reference, you'll need to add a new hyperlink button and divider to the LinksStackPanel in MainPage.xaml:

```
<HyperlinkButton x:Name="EmployeeListLink"
                 Style="{StaticResource LinkStyle}"
                 NavigateUri="/EmployeeList" TargetName="ContentFrame"
                 Content="employees" />

<Rectangle Style="{StaticResource DividerStyle}" />
```

After the employee list view is set up, you'll add an employee detail view.

EMPLOYEE DETAIL VIEW

In the Views folder, add a new ChildWindow named EmployeeDetail.xaml. This will be a pop-up window used to edit a subset of the fields of the Employee object. This window, in the designer, looks like figure 16.2.

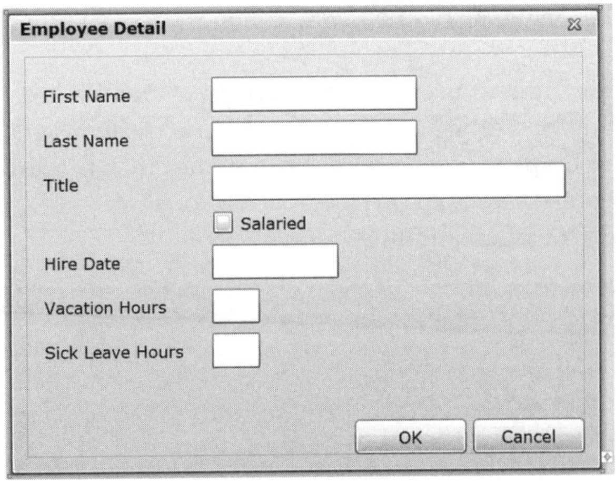

Figure 16.2   Designer view of the ChildWindow used to edit employee details

After the button definitions in the `EmployeeDetail ChildWindow` XAML, add the XAML from listing 16.3.

Listing 16.3 Employee detail `ChildWindow` controls additional XAML

```
<TextBlock Height="23" Margin="12,18,0,0"
        HorizontalAlignment="Left" VerticalAlignment="Top"
        Text="First Name"/>
<TextBox Height="23" Width="140" Margin="127,14,0,0"
        HorizontalAlignment="Left" VerticalAlignment="Top"
        x:Name="FirstName"
        Text="{Binding Contact.FirstName, Mode=TwoWay}" />

<TextBlock Height="23" Margin="12,47,0,0"
        HorizontalAlignment="Left" VerticalAlignment="Top"
        Text="Last Name" />
<TextBox Height="23" Width="140" Margin="127,43,0,0"
        HorizontalAlignment="Left" VerticalAlignment="Top"
        x:Name="LastName"
        Text="{Binding Contact.LastName, Mode=TwoWay}" />

<TextBlock Height="23" Margin="12,76,0,0"
        HorizontalAlignment="Left" VerticalAlignment="Top"
        Text="Title"/>
<TextBox Height="23" Width="239" Margin="127,72,0,0"
        HorizontalAlignment="Left" VerticalAlignment="Top"
        x:Name="TitleField"
        Text="{Binding Title, Mode=TwoWay}" />

<CheckBox x:Name="Salaried" Height="16" Margin="127,101,0,0"
        HorizontalAlignment="Left" VerticalAlignment="Top"
        Content="Salaried"
        IsChecked="{Binding SalariedFlag, Mode=TwoWay}" />

<TextBlock Height="23" Margin="12,127,0,0"
        HorizontalAlignment="Left" VerticalAlignment="Top"
        Text="Hire Date"/>

<TextBox Height="23" Width="87" Margin="127,123,0,0"
        HorizontalAlignment="Left" VerticalAlignment="Top"
        x:Name="HireDate"
        Text="{Binding HireDate, Mode=TwoWay}" />

<TextBlock Height="23" Margin="12,156,0,0"
        HorizontalAlignment="Left" VerticalAlignment="Top"
        Text="Vacation Hours"/>
<TextBox Height="23" Width="33" Margin="127,152,0,0"
        HorizontalAlignment="Left" VerticalAlignment="Top"
        x:Name="VacationHours"
        Text="{Binding VacationHours, Mode=TwoWay}"/>

<TextBlock Height="23" Margin="12,185,0,0"
        HorizontalAlignment="Left" VerticalAlignment="Top"
        Text="Sick Leave Hours"/>
<TextBox Height="23" Width="33" Margin="127,181,0,0"
        HorizontalAlignment="Left" VerticalAlignment="Top"
        x:Name="SickLeaveHours"
        Text="{Binding SickLeaveHours, Mode=TwoWay}"/>
```

> TwoWay binding for all fields

You'll use this project for the remainder of the chapter. You may change a few binding statements later, but for the most part, the XAML will stay the same.

With the UI in place, it's time to turn our attention to the code. As promised, we'll first look at a typical code-behind approach.

16.1.2 *A typical code-behind solution*

The first stop along the way to structuring your applications with the ViewModel pattern is to look at what, for most applications of any complexity, can be considered an antipattern: the heavy code-behind approach. Unfortunately, the tooling and information all help you fall into writing code this way. That's because it's easy for beginners to grasp, and it's perfectly acceptable for smaller applications.

So far, you have XAML for two views and a service you can use to populate them. The next step is to put in some code to call the service and populate the DataGrid. Listing 16.4 shows the code-behind for the Employee List page.

> **Listing 16.4   Employee list code-behind**

```
public partial class EmployeeList : Page
{
  public EmployeeList()
  {
    InitializeComponent();                                     | Cache
                                                               | this Page
    NavigationCacheMode = NavigationCacheMode.Enabled;    <----|
  }

  protected override void OnNavigatedTo(NavigationEventArgs e)
  {
    if (EmployeesGrid.ItemsSource == null)                          ❶
    {
      LoadingProgress.Visibility = Visibility.Visible;              ❷

      var client = new EmployeeServiceClient();

      client.GetEmployeesCompleted += (s, ea) =>
        {
          LoadingProgress.Visibility = Visibility.Collapsed;

          EmployeesGrid.ItemsSource = ea.Result;                    ❸
        };

      client.GetEmployeesAsync();
    }
  }
}
```

Listing 16.4 includes enough code to load the DataGrid. When the page is navigated to, you first check to see whether the DataGrid already has data ❶. If it doesn't, you show the LoadingProgress overlay ❷ and then call the service, loading the result into the DataGrid ❸. This check is done because the pages are cached (per the setting in the constructor), and you'd rather not make extra service calls. When you run the application, it should look like figure 16.3.

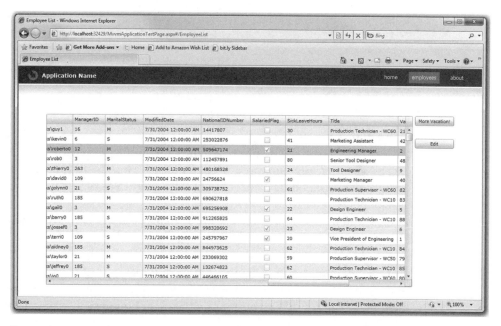

Figure 16.3   The Employee List page shown with an item selected in the grid. Note that the scrollbar is scrolled to the right to get past the columns you don't need.

As you can see by the grid results, you haven't done anything to reduce the number of columns showing up nor to display the values from the nested class. This could be easily accomplished by manually defining columns in the `DataGrid` or by using a specialized purpose-built class as the return value from the service. Although you'll fix that when we talk about MVVM, it's not a deficiency with the code-behind pattern itself.

Next, you need to add the code-behind for the Employee Detail window and then come back to this list page to fill out the rest of the code.

The Employee Detail `ChildWindow` needs code to take in an `Employee` object and bind the UI. Listing 16.5 shows this code.

Listing 16.5   Employee detail code-behind for `ChildWindow`

```
public partial class EmployeeDetail : ChildWindow
{
  public EmployeeDetail()
  {
    InitializeComponent();
  }

  private Employee _employee;
  public Employee Employee
  {
    get { return _employee; }                                    ❶ Employee
    set { _employee = value; DataContext = _employee; }             property
  }

  private void OKButton_Click(object sender, RoutedEventArgs e)
```

```
    {
      this.DialogResult = true;
    }
    private void CancelButton_Click(object sender, RoutedEventArgs e)
    {
      this.DialogResult = false;
    }
  }
```

Listing 16.5 shows the additions to the `ChildWindow` code-behind. Specifically, the additions are the `Employee` member variable and property, and the setting of the `DataContext` ❶ when the employee property is set. This last bit, the setting of the `DataContext`, allows the binding system to use the _employee object as the base for all binding statements in XAML.

One issue you'll see in the code-behind is that you don't clone the `Employee` or something to allow for undo/cancel. That's certainly doable in this instance, but I've left it out for this example. As was the case with the column definitions in the list view, this isn't a limitation of the code-behind approach itself.

With the `ChildWindow` code in place, we'll turn our attention to the last two bits of code: the functionality of the two buttons on the main Employee List view. Listing 16.6 shows this code.

Listing 16.6   Employee list code-behind for functions

```
public EmployeeList()
{
  InitializeComponent();

  NavigationCacheMode = NavigationCacheMode.Enabled;

  AddMoreVacation.Click += new RoutedEventHandler(AddMoreVacation_Click);
  EditEmployee.Click += new RoutedEventHandler(EditEmployee_Click);
}
...
private EmployeeDetail _employeeDetail = new EmployeeDetail();
void EditEmployee_Click(object sender, RoutedEventArgs e)
{
  _employeeDetail.Employee = EmployeesGrid.SelectedItem as Employee;
  _employeeDetail.Show();                                               ◁─┐ Display
}                                                                         │ child
void AddMoreVacation_Click(object sender, RoutedEventArgs e)              ┘ window
{
  var selectedEmployee = EmployeesGrid.SelectedItem as Employee;

  if (selectedEmployee != null)
  {
    selectedEmployee.VacationHours += 10;
  }
}
```

Note that in listing 16.6, you go back and modify the `EmployeeList` constructor to add the two event handlers. This could be done in XAML, but we'll look at alternatives to event handlers when we discuss the MVVM version of this code.

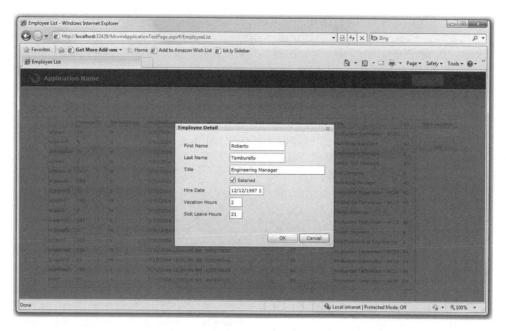

Figure 16.4   The employee detail pop-up view, showing the information from the selected employee

The code in this listing enables the pop-up `EmployeeDetail ChildWindow` as well as a simple function to add 10 vacation hours to the selected employee. Run the application, select a row in the grid, and click the Edit button. You should see a pop-up that looks like figure 16.4.

That's it for the code-behind version of the application. For space reasons, and because it doesn't change your approach, I've left out deleting and saving changes. For a solid way to handle those, look at WCF RIA Services in the next chapter.

The main things I needed to demonstrate here are filling a list from a service call and passing information from one view to another. Now that the basic application is set up and covers both of these scenarios, we'll look at an MVVM version.

16.2   *Model-View-ViewModel basics*

Originally conceived for WPF around 2005, and first presented in a blog posting by John Gossman,[1] the MVVM pattern has become the most popular architectural pattern for Silverlight and WPF applications.

The MVVM pattern is a specialization of the PresentationModel pattern by Martin Fowler. Whereas Fowler's pattern was platform independent, Grossman's specialization was created to take advantage of the capabilities of WPF and Silverlight. Otherwise, they're conceptually identical.

---

[1] John Gossman, *Introduction to the Model/View/ViewModel pattern for building WPF apps*, http://blogs.msdn.com/ johngossman/archive/2005/10/08/478683.aspx (October 8, 2005).

If you're familiar with the Model View Controller (MVC) pattern, you'll find similarities. But the MVVM pattern is optimized more for modern UI models whereas the UI markup is completely separated from the logic, using messages and binding to pass information back and forth, assuming the UI and ViewModel can both be stateful.

By default, you build applications with a good bit of your code in the code-behind, just as you saw in the previous section. You may use external services or entities and even reusable logic, but at the end of the day, the vast majority of programs still end up with critical logic buried in the code-behind.

A typical code-behind approach looks like figure 16.5.

This comes in degrees, of course. Some code-behind applications are better architected than others. You'll find, though, that those that are architected well tend to have less logic in the code-behind. Instead, they have UI support code, or maybe binding wire-up. Critical calculations and similar functionality take place outside of the code-behind.

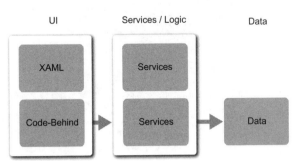

Figure 16.5   In the usual code-behind approach, a fair bit of logic is tightly coupled to the UI and to other layers. Services in this case mean both web services and logical services (utility functions, reusable business logic, and so on).

Why is that important? Why take the extra step to move this code out from the code-behind?

Testing is certainly one reason. After you decouple the logic from the user interface, you're then able to test the logic. Ease of UI design is another. With a well-architected application with a strong separation of concerns between the logic and the UI, a designer can create the user interface and drop it into the project. As a developer, you can even provide the designer with mock interfaces or dummy classes to use to design against, as long as those classes adhere to the same interface or contract as your own support classes.

One reason I think the MVVM pattern works well for developers is because it eliminates many of the binding problems you run into when coding in code-behind. Often, developers find they have to work some convoluted code to get the XAML to bind to a `DependencyProperty` defined in the code-behind, messing with overriding `DataContext` at different layers or otherwise making a horrible mess of the code and XAML. It happens to the best of us. It's a pit that you can easily fall into when you don't follow a pattern such as MVVM.

What does a MVVM application look like in contrast to a code-behind application? Figure 16.6 shows the architecture of a basic MVVM implementation.

As figure 16.6 shows, when using the MVVM pattern, the application is made up of three main parts: the Model, the View, and the ViewModel. Table 16.1 describes their function.

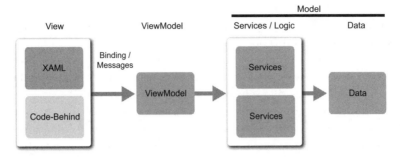

Figure 16.6 **In the MVVM pattern, the View contains minimal code-behind and uses binding and messages (actions or commands) to communicate with the ViewModel. The ViewModel provides a single façade into the rest of the system, optimized for that specific view. Keep in mind that** *services* **doesn't always mean web services; they're anything that provide a service to the application.**

Table 16.1   The three main parts of the MVVM pattern

Part	Description
Model	The model of the business or the model of the data, sometimes also called the model of the application. This can contain entities and services (web services, business services, logic services, and so on), data access, and more.
View	The XAML file and its code-behind. Its sole responsibility is interaction with the user. The only code here should be code that's logically part of the View itself (managing interactions between view elements or animations, for example).
	The View typically has enough knowledge of the structure of the ViewModel to bind to it but knows nothing of the rest of the system.
ViewModel	The interface between the View and the Model. This is part entity, part façade, and part controller, but it contains minimal logic of its own. Use binding to let the View pull/push data, and commands or behaviors (messages) to call methods.
	The ViewModel has no knowledge of the structure of the view.[a]

a. One of the tech reviewers suggested I put this in a blink tag or marquee or something to make sure the point is driven home. The ViewModel has no knowledge of the view. Perhaps if you break the rule, you should have to put a big red label on the code: "Warning! Lark's Vomit!" (thank you, Mr Cleese).

Taken to logical ends, the structure of an MVVM application would include interfaces at all the key points, allowing you to easily swap out individual layers or objects for equivalents either manually or via dependency injection. We'll investigate those scenarios later in this chapter.

In this section, you'll take your code-behind solution from the first section and refactor it into a basic MVVM application. You'll pull the code-behind apart, put much of the functionality into a ViewModel class, and ready it for additional refactoring and application of patterns later in this chapter.

16.2.1   *Keep it simple: a basic ViewModel implementation*

So far, you have a simple and tight code-behind application running. It's small. In fact, it's small enough that showing you the MVVM version will make you wonder why you're adding so much code. Like many examples, we have to start small both to get the concepts across and to fit in a publication like this. (I'm pretty sure bookshelves everywhere would protest if this book hit 1,000 pages.)

That said, if you stick with me throughout this section, I think you'll see how the structure set up by the MVVM pattern makes it possible to add functionality to the application without shoehorning it into some dank corner of code.

In this section, you'll make basic changes to factor some of the code out of the code-behind and into a ViewModel. Although this isn't a "full" ViewModel/MVVM implementation, it provides many of the benefits and is a good, understandable place to start. Most of my early experiments with the pattern looked much like what we'll cover in this section.

Who owns the ViewModel?

Sure, let's jump right into controversy on your very first foray into this pattern!

I'm writing this book, so I could put my opinion forth as the definitive approach, but I'd rather not have coders with pitchforks and burning torches marching down my driveway in a few months. Instead, let's look at the three main opinions in this space.

The code owns the ViewModel.

In this case, the code-behind for the view instantiates the ViewModel in a constructor or loaded event, setting it as the `DataContext` for the view. This is convenient and provides a clean way to create the ViewModel. But it doesn't allow the View to be reused in situations where the ViewModel may be provided externally, as is the case in a Detail edit View.

The markup owns the ViewModel.

This is, in a real sense, the same as the first option. From an implementation standpoint, though, it looks very different. In this case, the ViewModel is instantiated right in the markup either as a static resource or directly in the `<navigation:Page.Data-Context>` property. From a coupling standpoint, there's no difference. What you usually gain is the ability to have even less code in the code-behind.

Both of these approaches involve the View owning the ViewModel. They're simple to implement and are often appropriate for early forays into the ViewModel pattern. You may even find that they work well for the majority (or all) of the applications you create. But one more approach is worth investigating.

The ViewModel is provided externally.

Most MVVM toolkits of merit provide some sort of functionality for locating the appropriate ViewModel for a View. In some cases, the ViewModels are created in a separate holding class that provides the ViewModel when requested. This provides significant flexibility in terms of sourcing the ViewModel.

(continued)

Note also that dependency injection can come into play here. An Inversion of Control (IoC) container can provide the ViewModel to the views based on types, convention, or configuration. Some MVVM toolkits use IoCs or IoC-like functionality to supply the ViewModel.

In this case, the ViewModel isn't owned by the View; it's used by the View. As you progress further in your understanding of MVVM, I encourage you to investigate this approach.

The first step in working with the pattern is to create a short base class from which all ViewModel classes will derive.

BASE VIEWMODEL

The base `ViewModel` class provides the common `INotifyPropertyChanged` implementation. As you may recall from chapter 11 on binding, `INotifyPropertyChanged` is required whenever other classes may be bound to your class, except when using dependency properties—which don't really belong in a ViewModel.

In a larger implementation, the base `ViewModel` class may contain other useful functionality or may be factored into several classes to support specialized types of ViewModel implementations. Regardless, this is the class you'll use as the base class for the other ViewModels created in this project, starting with the list page ViewModel.

In the Silverlight project, add a new folder named ViewModels. In the ViewModels folder, add a class named `ViewModel`. Listing 16.7 shows the code that makes up this class.

Listing 16.7 The base `ViewModel` class

```
using System.ComponentModel;

namespace MvvmApplication.ViewModels
{
  public abstract class ViewModel : INotifyPropertyChanged
  {
    public event PropertyChangedEventHandler PropertyChanged;

    protected void NotifyPropertyChanged(string propertyName)
    {
      if (PropertyChanged != null)
        PropertyChanged(this, new PropertyChangedEventArgs(propertyName));
    }
  }
}
```

Raise PropertyChanged event

In my own implementations, I often have a base class named `Observable` that includes the functionality shown in this `ViewModel` class. I then derive a `ViewModel` base class from `Observable`. This enables me to support `INotifyPropertyChanged` with entities and other non-ViewModel classes and still have a base `ViewModel` that can be used for other shared functionality.

LIST PAGE VIEWMODEL

Typically, each view in the ViewModel pattern has its own dedicated ViewModel. This isn't written in stone, but it's how most applications end up being designed. A 1:1 relationship between View and ViewModel eliminates the need to shoehorn in the inevitable compromises, because Views that share the ViewModels diverge in functionality when many Views share the same ViewModel. It's also acceptable, when using smaller ViewModels or nested `UserControls`, to have a 1:*n* relationship between the View and the ViewModel. The situation to avoid in most cases is *n*:1 between View and ViewModel.

> **TIP** When naming your ViewModel, pick a consistent convention. I typically name mine with the view name plus *ViewModel*, so the `EmployeeList` view has an `EmployeeListViewModel` class. Some MVVM toolkits expect you to follow a convention so their locator services can find the correct ViewModel for a View.

In the ViewModels folder, create a new class named `EmployeeListViewModel`. This ViewModel will include the functionality required for the `EmployeeList` page, including calling the web service and providing the functionality currently located in the button click code.

Listing 16.8 includes the code for the `EmployeeListViewModel` implementation.

Listing 16.8 `EmployeeListViewModel` implementation

```
using System.Collections.ObjectModel;
using System.ComponentModel;
using MvvmApplication.Services;

namespace MvvmApplication.ViewModels
{
  public class EmployeeListViewModel : ViewModel
  {
    private Employee _selectedEmployee;            Selected
    public Employee SelectedEmployee          <──┘ employee
    {
      get { return _selectedEmployee; }
      set
      {
        _selectedEmployee = value;
        NotifyPropertyChanged("SelectedEmployee");
      }
    }

    private ObservableCollection<Employee> _employees;      Full set of
    public ObservableCollection<Employee> Employees    <──┘ employees
    {
      get { return _employees; }
      private set
      {
        _employees = value;
        NotifyPropertyChanged("Employees");
      }
```

```
    }
    public event EventHandler EmployeesLoaded;
    public void LoadEmployees()
    {
      var client = new EmployeeServiceClient();

      client.GetEmployeesCompleted += (s, ea) =>
        {
          Employees = ea.Result;
          OnEmployeesLoaded();
        };

      client.GetEmployeesAsync();
    }

    public void AddVacationBonusToSelectedEmployee()
    {
      if (SelectedEmployee != null)
        SelectedEmployee.VacationHours += 10;
    }

    protected void OnEmployeesLoaded()
    {
      if (EmployeesLoaded != null)
        EmployeesLoaded(this, EventArgs.Empty);
    }
  }
}
```

In this listing, you have the full implementation of a basic ViewModel class. This includes all the functionality required to load the list of employees and make it available to the DataGrid on the view.

The Employees property contains the collection with all the employees returned from the service call. This is used to populate the DataGrid but, because it's available here, it could also be manipulated in ViewModel code to sort, filter, or perform other operations.

The SelectedEmployee property is used to keep track of which employee is selected in the grid. Exposing it in your ViewModel keeps the responsibility for maintaining this information away from the UI control. This makes it easier to use different types of controls in the UI. In addition, you can manipulate this property from within the ViewModel (for example, to highlight something based on a search or hotkey), and the UI will automatically respond.

UPDATED LIST VIEW XAML

The following code includes the updates to the view to bind the DataGrid to the Employees collection and the SelectedEmployee property:

```
<sdk:DataGrid AutoGenerateColumns="True"
      ItemsSource="{Binding Employees}"
      SelectedItem="{Binding SelectedEmployee, Mode=TwoWay}"
      Margin="12,55,119,12"
      x:Name="EmployeesGrid" />
```

The updates to the DataGrid element involved first setting the ItemsSource to the Employees collection on the ViewModel and then binding the SelectedItem to the SelectedEmployee property of the ViewModel. Note that the binding on SelectedEmployee is TwoWay, so both the DataGrid and code may update this value.

UPDATED LIST VIEW CODE-BEHIND

With the addition of the ViewModel and the changes to the XAML, you need to make some changes to the code-behind for the EmployeeList page. Listing 16.19 includes the new code-behind with those changes included.

Listing 16.9   EmployeeList view code-behind

```
public partial class EmployeeList : Page
{
  public EmployeeList()
  {
    InitializeComponent();

    NavigationCacheMode = NavigationCacheMode.Enabled;          Cache
                                                                this Page
    AddMoreVacation.Click +=
              new RoutedEventHandler(AddMoreVacation_Click);
    EditEmployee.Click +=
              new RoutedEventHandler(EditEmployee_Click);
  }

  private EmployeeListViewModel _viewModel = null;

  protected override void OnNavigatedTo(NavigationEventArgs e)      ❶
  {
    if (_viewModel == null)
    {
      _viewModel = new EmployeeListViewModel();          ❷
      _viewModel.EmployeesLoaded += (s, ea) =>
        {
          LoadingProgress.Visibility = Visibility.Collapsed;
        };

      DataContext = _viewModel;

      LoadingProgress.Visibility = Visibility.Visible;

      _viewModel.LoadEmployees();                          ❸
    }
  }

  private EmployeeDetail _employeeDetail = new EmployeeDetail();
  void EditEmployee_Click(object sender, RoutedEventArgs e)
  {
    _employeeDetail.Employee = _viewModel.SelectedEmployee;
    _employeeDetail.Show();
  }

  void AddMoreVacation_Click(object sender, RoutedEventArgs e)
  {
    _viewModel.AddVacationBonusToSelectedEmployee();          ❹
  }
}
```

The `OnNavigatedTo` function ❶ now includes code to create the ViewModel ❷ if it's not already present, and to call the `LoadEmployees` method ❸ on the ViewModel. In addition, the event handler for the Add More Vacation! button now calls directly into the ViewModel to execute the code ❹.

Now you have the same functionality as the code-behind solution, but with quite a bit more code. In fact, you have just as much code-behind as you did in the code-behind-only solution! Keep in mind, this is just the first layer of the onion, so you haven't received all the benefits of MVVM yet. What you have gained is subtle:

- The `DataGrid` is now divorced from the code-behind, using solely binding to get its items and synchronize the selected item. A designer could now change the `DataGrid` to be a `ListBox` or some other type of control if desired, and the code wouldn't need to change.

- The data access (service call) is now removed from the page, giving you the potential to substitute a different type of service call without making any changes to the page code. You'll find an even better spot for it later in this chapter.

- The business logic to add the vacation bonus to the selected employee is now pulled out of the page. Like the service call, you can do better, and you will later in this chapter.

- The code-behind is no longer manipulating the `Employee` type directly. This makes it easier to replace the `Employee` type later, should you want to do so.

At this point, you have a ViewModel that's essentially the code-behind for the View. You've taken your first steps into the MVVM pattern and away from packing all your code in the code-behind. To build on this, it'd be nice if you could refactor to take advantage of some best practices associated with the ViewModel pattern and with coding in general. In the next section, we'll dive deeper into the pattern and show how to factor out common code such as service access and business rules.

16.3 *Factoring out reusable code*

The *Single Responsibility Principle (SRP)* states (surprisingly enough) that every object should have a single responsibility,[2] and that every object should have one and only one reason to change. I don't try to adhere to this as though it were dogma but rather make informed decisions based on this principle representing the perfect state.

SRP can sometimes be difficult to apply to something as façade-like as a ViewModel class, but it's obvious we didn't even try here. The ViewModel class for the list page is responsible for tracking page state, calling the web service to load data, and applying a vacation bonus to selected employees. If the vacation bonus changes, this class must also change. If the service access changes, this class must change. You need to do something about that.

---

[2] Robert C. Martin, *Principles of OOD*, http://www.butunclebob.com/ArticleS.UncleBob.PrinciplesOfOod (May 11, 2005).

In this section, you'll do a little refactoring to make the ViewModel class a bit lighter and allow reuse of code, starting with the business logic to add the vacation bonus.

16.3.1 Business rules and logic

The easiest thing to pull out of the `EmployeeListViewModel` is the code that adds the vacation bonus. You can deal with this several ways—I prefer using a service approach. That is, rather than bake the bonus into a special employee class, you have a service you can call that deals with bonuses using a simple function call. This is distinct from the idea of a web service.

Create a new folder named Services in the Silverlight client. In that folder, add a class named `EmployeeVacationBonusService`. Listing 16.10 shows the code for this class.

Listing 16.10 The `EmployeeVacationBonusService` class

```
public class EmployeeVacationBonusService
{                                                          Dependency
  public static void AddVacationBonus(Employee employee)   ◁── on Employee
  {
    int vacationBonus;
    DateTime dateOfHire = employee.HireDate;

    DateTime today = DateTime.Today;

    int yearsInService = today.Year - dateOfHire.Year;

    if (dateOfHire.AddYears(yearsInService) > today)
      yearsInService--;

    if (yearsInService < 5)
      vacationBonus = 10;
    else if (yearsInService < 10)
      vacationBonus = 20;
    else if (yearsInService < 20)
      vacationBonus = 30;
    else
      vacationBonus = 40;

    employee.VacationHours += vacationBonus;
  }
}
```

The vacation bonus algorithm has been beefed up. Rather than a blanket 10 hours, you use some of the data to reward those with the longest time at the company. You also implement the functionality using static methods here. Some developers prefer to use instance methods. Either way is fine as long as you understand why you're doing it and what flexibility you lose when going with static methods (such as the ability to mock), and you have some consistency to your decisions.

There are also multiple ways you can model this class. For example, it could modify the class directly as shown here or it could return a bonus amount based on a set of parameters such as current vacation hours, date of hire, some sort of level information, and so on. Taking in individual parameters like that, rather than passing in an Employee object, helps reinforce the SRP and decouple from the rest of the system because the class no longer needs to be changed if the Employee class changes.

Listing 16.11 shows the final version of this service, taking individual parameters rather than the Employee object.

Listing 16.11   A better version of the `EmployeeVacationBonusService` class

```
public class EmployeeVacationBonusService
{
  public static int GetVacationBonus(DateTime dateOfHire)
  {
    int vacationBonus;

    DateTime today = DateTime.Today;

    int yearsInService = today.Year - dateOfHire.Year;

    if (dateOfHire.AddYears(yearsInService) > today)
      yearsInService--;

    if (yearsInService < 5)
      vacationBonus = 10;
    else if (yearsInService < 10)
      vacationBonus = 20;
    else if (yearsInService < 20)
      vacationBonus = 30;
    else
      vacationBonus = 40;

    return vacationBonus;
  }
}
```

In this version, it's the responsibility of the calling code to add the bonus to whatever employee class it happens to be working with. That removes the dependency from this class and makes it reusable in places where you may have different employee entities or perhaps just a few key fields.

With that change made, the EmployeeListViewModel code to add the employee vacation bonus now looks like this:

```
public void AddVacationBonusToSelectedEmployee()
{
  if (SelectedEmployee != null)
  {
    SelectedEmployee.VacationHours +=
            (short)EmployeeVacationBonusService.GetVacationBonus(
                    SelectedEmployee.HireDate);
  }
}
```

The EmployeeListViewModel class is no longer responsible for calculating the vacation bonus. That's one extra responsibility down. Now, let's look at that web service logic.

16.3.2 *Data access and service calls*

In Silverlight, it's a given that data will come from a web service. Or will it? Who says the data can't come from reading a local file in elevated trust mode, or from isolated storage? Perhaps with the new Elevated Trust mode, one of the pure-.NET SQL databases will be an option. Plus, for all you know, a future version of Silverlight may have local database access built in.

If every ViewModel class in the project is making a web service call to get the data, that means you have to change each and every one of them if anything about the service call changes—obviously, not great design. In a small project like this, it's not a huge problem; but when you get into an application with dozens of pages and ViewModels, it gets pretty ugly.

I've seen lots of great examples of how to abstract service or data access calls away from the rest of the application. Some use singleton classes with names like `Application-Data` to host a number of collections and load functions, with built-in caching. Others use individual classes, each responsible for a specific type of data. Others use combinations of the two ideas, but with no singleton involved so dependency injection works better. I'm not going to weigh in on the merits of the various approaches; I don't think there's a one-size-fits-all solution. Instead, you'll create a simple example to solve just the problem at hand. The version I'm showing doesn't support cross-view data caching, because you'd need to keep an instance of the data service alive in a locator class or an IoC container.

In the Services folder, add a new class named `EmployeeDataService`. The code for this class is shown in listing 16.12

Listing 16.12   The `EmployeeDataService` class used for loading `Employee` data

```
using System;
using System.Collections.ObjectModel;

namespace MvvmApplication.Services
{                                                           Employees
    public class EmployeeDataService                        collection
    {
        private static ObservableCollection<Employee> _employees;
        public static ObservableCollection<Employee> Employees  ◁──┘
        {
            get { return _employees; }
            private set { _employees = value; }
        }

        private static bool _areEmployeesLoaded;
        public static bool AreEmployeesLoaded
        {
            get { return _areEmployeesLoaded; }
            private set { _areEmployeesLoaded = value; }
        }

        public static void LoadEmployees()
        {
```

```
        var client = new EmployeeServiceClient();
        AreEmployeesLoaded = false;

        client.GetEmployeesCompleted += (s, ea) =>
        {
            Employees = ea.Result;
            AreEmployeesLoaded = true;
            OnEmployeesLoaded();
        };

        client.GetEmployeesAsync();
    }

    public static event EventHandler EmployeesLoaded;      ◁──┐ Employees
    protected static void OnEmployeesLoaded()                  │ loaded event
    {
        if (EmployeesLoaded != null)
            EmployeesLoaded(null, EventArgs.Empty);
    }
  }
}
```

The sole purpose of this class is to provide an interface to the employee data. In this
case, that's performed using a service call. In a larger system with more moving parts,
you may want to factor this class into two pieces: one that provides connection information for the web service and this class, which makes the service call. You may also
consider caching this class on the client (via a locator or similar collection of classes)
so the data can be shared across multiple ViewModels. The `AreEmployeesLoaded`
property has been defined with that in mind.

Listing 16.13 shows the changes needed in the `EmployeeListViewModel` class to
support the user of the new `EmployeeDataService` class.

Listing 16.13 Updates to the `EmployeeListViewModel` class

```
private EmployeeDataService _dataService = new EmployeeDataService();
public event EventHandler EmployeesLoaded;
public void LoadEmployees()
{
    if (_dataService.AreEmployeesLoaded)
    {
        Employees = _dataService.Employees;
        OnEmployeesLoaded();
    }
    else
    {
        _dataService.EmployeesLoaded += (s, e) =>          ◁──┐ Employees in
            {                                                  │ data service
                Employees = _dataService.Employees;
                OnEmployeesLoaded();
            };

        _dataService.LoadEmployees();
    }
}
```

With this example, you now have a ViewModel class that's responsible only for passing through information and functionality specific to the related View. This makes the code more easily reused, as well as more easily testable. You still have a fair bit of code in the code-behind, though, including some event handlers that could be handled differently. In the next section, you'll work to remove this extra layer and provide better View-to-ViewModel communication without so much event-handler code.

16.4   *Better separation from the UI*

"Good fences make good neighbors." As it turns out, good fences (or perhaps, good chasms)—strong separation between otherwise independent classes—make for better code. You've already seen how pulling code out of the code-behind and into the View-Model, and then out of the ViewModel and into services, has made the code less brittle and more reusable. At the end of this chapter, you'll also see that it has made the code more testable.

One of a few places where you're still tightly coupled is via the use of events and event handlers to intercept clicks from the UI and call functions on the ViewModel. This isn't horrible; it just limits the things that can listen for and respond to the UI actions, and it makes testing a little harder because there's code in the code-behind that must be duplicated in the test.

In this section, we'll look at two ways you can have elements in XAML invoke methods in the ViewModel. The first approach, ICommand, is the traditional way initially introduced in WPF and supported in most MVVM toolkits. The second, the CallMethodAction behavior, is a new approach introduced with Expression Blend 4.

Structured method invocation isn't the only way to separate the UI from the rest of the system. Some slightly more insidious couplings have made it through right under our noses; we'll need to address them. The first is the use of entities coming from your database model. You can do this if you really want, but for a number of reasons to be explained, I don't like to. The second coupling is through the use of concrete types referenced from your various classes. In section 16.4.4, we'll take a conceptual look at what's involved in reducing this coupling.

16.4.1   *Using commands*

The commanding system in WPF and Silverlight isn't tied directly to the ViewModel pattern. Instead, it's a generic approach to wiring functionality directly to buttons in XAML UI. In the commanding system, rather than respond to something in a button click event, you bind the command to the button and allow the button to execute it directly.

In WPF, this approach was first used for application-wide commands and to allow menu options, keystrokes, and toolbars to all execute the same functionality and keep their UI state in sync.

When the MVVM pattern was introduced, the commanding system was incorporated into it to wire the XAML UI to the ViewModel class. But because the ViewModel held the functionality, different types of commands were created to allow forwarding or relaying the call to the ViewModel.

The `ICommand` interface is the core of the commanding system in Silverlight. The button-derived controls (and menus) that support binding to commands do so through the `ICommand` interface. Similarly, the custom commands created for the MVVM pattern also implement this interface. Table 16.2 shows the three members of `ICommand`.

Table 16.2 The `ICommand` interface members

Member	Description
CanExecute	Property that returns true if this command is allowed to execute. For example, if the command is an undo command, this returns `false` if the undo stack is empty.
Execute	Method that executes the function the command represents.
CanExecuteChanged	Event raised when the value of `CanExecute` changes. This is typically used to update UI state to show the action is now available.

A commonly used implementation of `ICommand` for the MVVM pattern is a command that accepts delegates for both the `Execute` and `CanExecute` members. This allows you to reuse the same command implementation rather than create unique commands for every logical command.

In the Silverlight project, in the ViewModels folder, add a new class named `ViewModelCommand`. The code for the generic command is shown in listing 16.14.

Listing 16.14   Silverlight MVVM-friendly implementation of `ICommand`

```
public class ViewModelCommand : ICommand
{
  public ViewModelCommand(Action<object> executeAction,        ❶
                     Predicate<object> canExecute)
  {
    if (executeAction == null)
      throw new ArgumentNullException("executeAction");

    _executeAction = executeAction;
    _canExecute = canExecute;
  }

  private readonly Predicate<object> _canExecute;
  public bool CanExecute(object parameter)          ⊲─── ICommand.CanExecute
  {
    if (_canExecute == null) return true;

    return _canExecute(parameter);
  }

  public event EventHandler CanExecuteChanged;      ⊲─── ICommand.CanExecuteChanged
  public void OnCanExecuteChanged()                 ❷
```

```
{
  if (CanExecuteChanged != null)
    CanExecuteChanged(this, EventArgs.Empty);
}

private readonly Action<object> _executeAction;
public void Execute(object parameter)                    ◁── ICommand.Execute
{
  _executeAction(parameter);
}
}
```

This command implementation takes in delegates ❶ for `CanExecute` and `Execute` and exposes a public method `OnCanExecuteChanged` ❷ to force raising the `CanExecuteChanged` event. In the ViewModel, any code that affects the `CanExecute` function should call this method to raise the event.

There are lots of implementations of this type of command. If you pick an MVVM toolkit to work with, you're almost guaranteed to have a command similar to this one included in the library. It may be called something similar to `DelegateCommand` or `RelayCommand`.

To surface the command to the page, hang it off the ViewModel as a public property. Listing 16.15 shows how to do this for the vacation bonus functionality on the `EmployeeListViewModel` class.

Listing 16.15   Surfacing the vacation bonus functionality as an `ICommand`

```
private Employee _selectedEmployee;
public Employee SelectedEmployee
{
    get { return _selectedEmployee; }
    set
    {
        _selectedEmployee = value;
        NotifyPropertyChanged("SelectedEmployee");
        AddVacationBonusCommand.OnCanExecuteChanged();          ❶
    }
}

...
public bool CanAddVacationBonus
{
    get { return SelectedEmployee != null; }
}

private ViewModelCommand _addVacationBonusCommand = null;
public ViewModelCommand AddVacationBonusCommand                  ◁── ICommand
{
    get
    {
        if (_addVacationBonusCommand == null)                   ❷
        {
            _addVacationBonusCommand = new ViewModelCommand
            (
```

```
            p => AddVacationBonusToSelectedEmployee(),
            p => CanAddVacationBonus
        );
    }

    return _addVacationBonusCommand;
    }
}
...
```

These changes to the ViewModel show both the call to OnCanExecuteChanged ❶ and the exposing of the AddVacationBonusCommand. This command is created as needed ❷ the first time it's referenced. I've also seen implementations where these commands were created as static members in the class.

   The command is then wired up to the UI directly in the XAML. Because the View-Model has already been set as the data context, a simple binding statement on the button is all you need:

```
<Button Height="23" Width="101" Margin="0,55,12,0"
      HorizontalAlignment="Right" VerticalAlignment="Top"
      Content="More Vacation!"
      x:Name="AddMoreVacation"
      Command="{Binding AddVacationBonusCommand}" />
```

The last line of XAML is the new line, binding the Command property to the new command you added to the ViewModel. Don't forget to remove the event handler wireup from the code-behind. This button no longer needs that.

   You'll notice now that the More Vacation! button is disabled by default and enabled only when you select a row in the DataGrid. That's a function of the CanExecute property and the CanExecuteChanged event working together and being updated from within the SelectedEmployee property setter. The Button class has built-in code to change its enabled state based on the command's CanExecute property.

Wait, what about the Edit button?

Most MVVM toolkits include their own good command implementations based on ICommand. Some MVVM toolkits also include a robust messaging structure that may be used in place of events, and in some cases in place of commands and behaviors. Many even include specialized messages used to requesting that the View display the dialog UI. That messaging system for invoking a dialog is something missing in this implementation. Rather than show you an approach that will likely never be used by anyone, I recommend you use the approach recommended by the toolkit you're using.

Okay, if you're really curious, here's how I would've done it. The command would call an EditSelectedEmployee method on the ViewModel. That method would check to see whether SelectedEmployee was null. If not, it would raise an event named ShowEmployeeEditDialog with a custom EventArgs class that included the selected employee as a property. That event would be caught in the code-behind, and the code-behind would show the dialog.

(continued)
Why not do that all from the ViewModel? The ViewModel shouldn't be in the business of showing dialogs or message boxes of any type. Instead, it should message the UI layer saying it needs some UI to be displayed. In this way, not only is the ViewModel potentially agnostic of Silverlight/WPF/other technology, it remains testable because the event handler in the test code could directly manipulate the values rather than show the dialog. This also allows the code-behind to keep its affinity with the View, being presentation-layer code rather than other logic.

Commands are the traditional and still most common way of performing this functionality. They have deep support in WPF and decent support in Silverlight. A new approach to accomplishing this has recently been introduced by the Expression Blend team. This approach eschews commands and instead uses designer-friendly behaviors.

16.4.2 *Using the CallMethodAction behavior*

Introduced with Expression Blend 4, the `CallMethodAction` behavior provides an easy and designer-friendly way to wire any event from any control to a method. In some ways, it's an alternative to using `ICommand` and may even seem redundant. But many applications will use both approaches due to the usefulness of `ICommand` with buttons and menus and `CallMethodAction`'s support for other controls, and events other than `Click`.

You can either install Expression Blend 4 or download the Blend 4 SDK. In either case, add a project reference to the Blend SDK assembly from your main MvvmApplication project. The main assembly you want is Microsoft.Expression.Interactions.dll. You'll also need System.Windows.Interactivity.dll to support that.

The behavior approach doesn't give you everything the command approach does—specifically, it lacks the ability to enable or disable the button—but it provides support for controls other than buttons—a key limitation of the command approach.

Listing 16.16 shows how to use the `CallMethodAction` behavior to create the link between the More Vacation! button and the ViewModel method that implements that behavior.

Listing 16.16 Using the `CallMethodAction` behavior instead of the command

```
<Button Height="23" Width="101" Margin="0,55,12,0"
        Content="More Vacation!"
        HorizontalAlignment="Right" VerticalAlignment="Top"
        x:Name="AddMoreVacation">
    <i:Interaction.Triggers>
        <i:EventTrigger EventName="Click">            ❶
            <ei:CallMethodAction                              ⟵— Behavior
                MethodName="AddVacationBonusToSelectedEmployee"
                TargetObject="{Binding}" />
        </i:EventTrigger>
    </i:Interaction.Triggers>

</Button>
```

The `EventTrigger` ❶ responds to the firing of the click event. The action taken is the `CallMethodAction`, which is responsible for calling the method on the current object in the data context: in this case, the ViewModel. It's a simple and elegant solution that works with just about any event and any parameterless function.

In support of this, the following two namespaces were added to the top of the XAML file:

```
xmlns:i="http://schemas.microsoft.com/expression/2010/interactivity"
xmlns:ei="http://schemas.microsoft.com/expression/2010/interactions"
```

Those namespaces are required for the `EventTrigger` and `CallMethodAction` to be visible to XAML. Both are implemented inside the Blend SDK DLL you added as a reference.

Despite the limitations (a potential performance hit due to use of reflection, and the inability to set the `IsEnabled` property automatically), the `CallMethodAction` behavior is a good low-code-overhead approach to wiring up method calls. And remember, unlike `ICommand`, the `CallMethodAction` is supported on just about any event on any control.

Commands and behaviors are a great way to help separate the View from the View-Model, keeping the contract at just a binding statement or name of a method. But they've done nothing to fix the tight coupling problem you have between the database, the ViewModel, and the UI. For that, you'll turn to creating View-specific entities or ViewModels.

16.4.3 *View-specific entities and ViewModels*

So far, you've been passing the data entities straight through to the user interface. Although this is common, it's often not a great idea; you've introduced coupling from your UI all the way back to the database. A change to the database entity now means changes throughout the application. Take, for example, the columns you see in the grid. There's a fair bit of information that's not helpful at the UI level but that's required to maintain data integrity. One way to handle that would be to ignore it at the UI layer by defining columns directly in the `DataGrid`. Another way would be to have the web service return a purpose-built entity with only the columns you want.

Neither of those solutions is helpful from a reuse standpoint. In many systems, different screens show different aspects of what could be the same entity. Others, such as this example, have to compose two data entities into a single displayable result. Working with entities shaped like that can be a pain. Returning only a subset of the information back from the web service may help, but only if no other information is required for a successful update and no other areas of the system need the remaining information.

One way to deal with situations like this is to create per-View entities. The View-Model surfaces a collection of these View-specific entities, doing the shaping behind the scenes. This way, the designer of the View need not be concerned with composing entities, combining fields such as first and last name, and more.

In the MVVM pattern, those entities are frequently promoted up as ViewModels themselves. If you consider that the definition of a ViewModel includes both the data and the functionality required for a View, this makes sense. Consider that these View-Models can provide the functionality for calling the vacation bonus service and can then be reused in the detail pop-up, and you can quickly see how these entity-like ViewModel classes can be helpful.

For this example, you'll update the application to use new `EmployeeViewModel` classes in all the client-side places that once used the `Employee` data entity. First, listing 16.17 shows the new `EmployeeViewModel` class. Add it as a new class in your View-Model folder.

Listing 16.17   `EmployeeViewModel` class

```
using System;
using System.ComponentModel.DataAnnotations;
namespace MvvmApplication.ViewModels
{
  public class EmployeeViewModel : ViewModel
  {
    private string _firstName;
    [Display(Name="First Name")]
    public string FirstName
    {
      get { return _firstName; }
      set
      {
        _firstName = value;
        NotifyPropertyChanged("FirstName");
        NotifyPropertyChanged("FullName");
      }
    }

    private string _lastName;
    [Display(Name = "Last Name")]
    public string LastName
    {
      get { return _lastName; }
      set
      {
        _lastName = value;
        NotifyPropertyChanged("LastName");
        NotifyPropertyChanged("FullName");
      }
    }

    [Display(Name = "Full Name")]
    public string FullName
    {                                                              ◁─┐ Calculated
      get { return LastName + ", " + FirstName; }                    │ field
    }

    private string _title;
    public string Title
```

```
  {
    get { return _title; }
    set { _title = value; NotifyPropertyChanged("Title"); }
  }

  private DateTime _hireDate;                            Friendly
  [Display(Name = "Hire Date")]                          field name
  public DateTime HireDate
  {
    get { return _hireDate; }
    set { _hireDate = value; NotifyPropertyChanged("HireDate"); }
  }

  private short _vacationHours;
  [Display(Name = "Vacation Hours")]
  public short VacationHours
  {
    get { return _vacationHours; }
    set
    {
      _vacationHours = value;
      NotifyPropertyChanged("VacationHours");
    }
  }

  private short _sickLeaveHours;
  [Display(Name = "Sick Leave Hours")]
  public short SickLeaveHours
  {
    get { return _sickLeaveHours; }
    set
    {
      _sickLeaveHours = value;
      NotifyPropertyChanged("SickLeaveHours");
    }
  }

  private bool _salaried;
  public bool Salaried
  {
    get { return _salaried; }
    set { _salaried = value; NotifyPropertyChanged("Salaried"); }
  }
  }
}
```

Note that this class looks like most entity classes. There's a calculated field for the FullName, as well as direct exposure of each of the other properties of interest in the employee data class. You use Display annotations from System.Component-Model.DataAnnotations to make the DataGrid show friendly column names for these properties. Annotating for display was discussed in chapter 12. You could also include validation annotations from chapter 13, but that's unnecessary for this example.

Whether you consider this class to be a ViewModel depends on how you'll use it. If you add functionality to call services, for example, it becomes more clear-cut in most people's eyes that this is a real ViewModel. For me, ViewModel or entity isn't a huge issue, as long as you follow the separation of concerns you've been working toward throughout this chapter.

The `EmployeeListViewModel` class also needs to change to support the new `EmployeeViewModel` class. Listing 16.18 shows the changed properties and methods of the `EmployeeListViewModel` class. Note that the other properties and methods, including the `AddVacationBonusToSelectedEmployee` method, the `OnEmployee-sLoaded` method, the `CanAddVacationBonus` property, and the `AddVacationBonus` command property, all stay the same.

Listing 16.18   Changes to `EmployeeListViewModel` class

```
private EmployeeViewModel _selectedEmployee;
public EmployeeViewModel SelectedEmployee
{  ...  }

private ObservableCollection<EmployeeViewModel> _employees;
public ObservableCollection<EmployeeViewModel> Employees
{  ...  }

...

public void LoadEmployees()
{
  if (_dataService.AreEmployeesLoaded)
  {
    ShapeAndLoadEmployees(_dataService.Employees);
  }
  else
  {
    _dataService.EmployeesLoaded += (s, e) =>
      {
        ShapeAndLoadEmployees(_dataService.Employees);
      };

    _dataService.LoadEmployees();
  }
}

private void ShapeAndLoadEmployees(IList<Employee> employees)       ❶
{
  var shapedEmployees = new ObservableCollection<EmployeeViewModel>();

  foreach (Employee emp in employees)
  {
    EmployeeViewModel vm = new EmployeeViewModel
    {
      FirstName = emp.Contact.FirstName,          Flatten
      LastName = emp.Contact.LastName,            structure
      Title = emp.Title,
      Salaried = emp.SalariedFlag,
      SickLeaveHours = emp.SickLeaveHours,
      VacationHours = emp.VacationHours,
      HireDate = emp.HireDate
    };
```

```
      shapedEmployees.Add(vm);
    }

    Employees = shapedEmployees;
    OnEmployeesLoaded();
}
```

The largest change in this class is the LoadEmployees method. You add a bit of data shaping and flatten the two-class Employee/Contact combination into a single EmployeeViewModel class with only a few properties. The majority of this work is done in the ShapeAndLoadEmployees method ❶. It iterates through the employees in the data service and builds out the ViewModel classes, assigns the collection to the Employees property, and then raises the data-loaded event.

The last place affected by this change is the EmployeeDetail ChildWindow. Listing 16.19 shows the changes to the two TextBox instances and one CheckBox instance in the EmployeeDetail pop-up XAML.

Listing 16.19   Changes to EmployeeDetail.xaml

```xml
<TextBox Height="23" Width="140" Margin="127,14,0,0"
        HorizontalAlignment="Left" VerticalAlignment="Top"
        x:Name="FirstName"
        Text="{Binding FirstName, Mode=TwoWay}" />
...
<TextBox Height="23" Width="140" Margin="127,43,0,0"
        HorizontalAlignment="Left" VerticalAlignment="Top"
        x:Name="LastName"
        Text="{Binding LastName, Mode=TwoWay}" />

...
<CheckBox x:Name="Salaried" Height="16" Margin="127,101,0,0"
        HorizontalAlignment="Left" VerticalAlignment="Top"
        Content="Salaried"
        IsChecked="{Binding Salaried, Mode=TwoWay}" />
```

The only changes required here are the binding statements, due to the different property names and property paths for the new simplified class. Contact.FirstName becomes FirstName, Contact.LastName becomes LastName, and SalariedFlag becomes Salaried. The code-behind requires even fewer changes—just the Employee property, in this case:

```
private EmployeeViewModel _employee;
public EmployeeViewModel Employee
{
  get { return _employee; }
  set { _employee = value; DataContext = _employee; }
}
```

The EmployeeList.xaml and related code-behind require no changes. With all the other changes in place, run the application. The first thing you'll notice is the reduced column count in the DataGrid, as well as the friendly column headers. Figure 16.7 shows the newly refactored application. There's also the calculated Full Name field, which was unavailable in the entity data model.

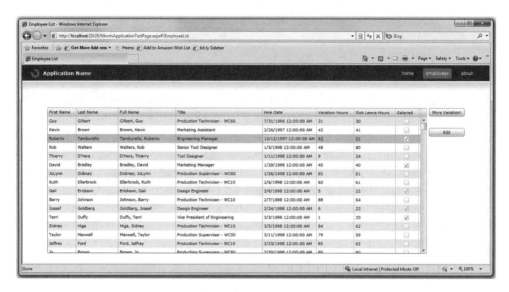

Figure 16.7   View of the application using the newly-minted `EmployeeViewModel` entity ViewModel class. Note the reduced column count as well as the nice column headers. Note also the Full Name calculated field.

16.4.4 Interfaces, IoC, and ViewModel locators

So far, all the changes you've made have improved the separation of concerns in the application and have helped its overall structure. But although you may have eliminated onerous coupling, such as that between the UI and the database, each of the classes are still tightly coupled to each other. For example, the View is tightly coupled to a ViewModel, using a `new` statement in the code-behind to create it. Similarly, that `EmployeeListViewModel` is tightly coupled to the `EmployeeDataService` and the `EmployeeVacationBonusService`.

At first glance, you may think "So?" and I wouldn't blame you. This is definitely one area where the benefits are highly proportional to the size of the system and the amount of code churn. If you have a highly active development project or a really large system, you'll want to pay extra attention.

INTERFACES AND IOC

By implementing ViewModels and services as interfaces, you can allow them to be swapped in and out with alternative implementations. This can be useful when you're developing and don't yet have the real data store, when you're designing the UI and don't want the designer to have to have the full development environment, and when you're testing where you may want to substitute scenario-driven classes and data that will return specific results each time.

Inversion of Control (IoC) enables developers to design the system in such a way that they don't *new up* (directly create) any objects of consequence in their code. Instead, they ask an IoC container to resolve for an object of a given type. The IoC container can make a number of decisions based on the request—returning a test version or a production version, for example. The IoC container can also serve up a single shared class instance, effectively a singleton without the singleton plumbing.

Some developers use interface-based development and IoC for everything because they've mastered its use and have found it to speed up their work. I'm not one of those developers, but I can certainly appreciate where mastery of this pattern can allow effective use across projects regardless of size or complexity.

Another interesting concept is that of the ViewModel locator. Often, ViewModel locators are themselves implemented using IoC.

VIEWMODEL LOCATOR

Closely related to IoC is the idea of a *ViewModel locator*. A ViewModel locator is a service that can supply a ViewModel instance to a View. That instance may be internally cached, hard-coded, or delivered via IoC. I've even seen some interesting implementations that use the Managed Extensibility Framework (MEF).

An extremely simple ViewModel locator that keys off the view name may look something like listing 16.20. Create the `ViewModelLocator` class in the ViewModels folder.

Listing 16.20 A simple `ViewModel` locator using hard-coded ViewModel instances

```
using System.Collections.Generic;

namespace MvvmApplication.ViewModels
{
  public class ViewModelLocator
  {
    private Dictionary<string, ViewModel> _viewModels =
        new Dictionary<string, ViewModel>();

    public ViewModelLocator()
    {
      _viewModels.Add("EmployeeList", new EmployeeListViewModel());
      _viewModels.Add("EmployeeDetail", new EmployeeViewModel());
    }

    public ViewModel this[string viewName]          ◁──┐ Indexer for
    {                                                   │ binding
      get { return _viewModels[viewName]; }
    }
  }
}
```

In practice, a real locator would have a much more robust mechanism for discovering and adding ViewModel instances to its internal list. In this example, they're all hard-coded, and you don't allow for more than one instance of any specific type. Additionally, the only usable one is the `EmployeeListViewModel`, because the `EmployeeDetail` would need instancing.

The ViewModel locator is surfaced as a resource to be used in binding. The resource itself would be defined in a resource dictionary merged into App.xaml in order to have applicationwide scope. Listing 16.21 shows an updated App.xaml with this resource included and a new Resources.xaml file in the Assets folder.

Listing 16.21 The `ViewModel` locator in XAML

App.xaml:

```
<Application x:Class="MvvmApplication.App"
  xmlns="http://schemas.microsoft.com/winfx/2006/xaml/presentation"
  xmlns:x="http://schemas.microsoft.com/winfx/2006/xaml">

  <Application.Resources>
    <ResourceDictionary>
      <ResourceDictionary.MergedDictionaries>
        <ResourceDictionary Source="Assets/Styles.xaml" />
        <ResourceDictionary Source="Assets/Resources.xaml" />      ◁─┐ Merged
      </ResourceDictionary.MergedDictionaries>                        │ dictionary
    </ResourceDictionary>
  </Application.Resources>
</Application>
```

Assets/Resources.xaml:

```
<ResourceDictionary
    xmlns="http://schemas.microsoft.com/winfx/2006/xaml/presentation"
    xmlns:vm="clr-namespace:MvvmApplication.ViewModels"
    xmlns:x="http://schemas.microsoft.com/winfx/2006/xaml">

  <vm:ViewModelLocator x:Key="ViewModelLocator" />          ◁─── **ViewModelLocator**

</ResourceDictionary>
```

To use this locator, you eliminate the ViewModel creation from the code-behind and bind to this resource. In the EmployeeList.xaml file, this is as easy as adding the following line to the `navigation:Page` element.

```
DataContext="{Binding [EmployeeList],
➥    Source={StaticResource ViewModelLocator}}"
```

That bit sets the `DataContext` of the page to the value returned from the calling the `ViewModelLocator`'s indexer function, passing in the string `EmployeeList`.

You then change the `EmployeeList` code-behind so the `OnNavigatedTo` event uses the ViewModel provided by the locator rather than one created in the code-behind. Listing 16.22 shows the updated `OnNavigatedTo` method.

Listing 16.22 Updated `OnNavigatedTo` method in `EmployeeList` code-behind

```
private EmployeeListViewModel _viewModel = null;

protected override void OnNavigatedTo(NavigationEventArgs e)
{
  _viewModel = DataContext as EmployeeListViewModel;
  _viewModel.EmployeesLoaded += (s, ea) =>
    {
      LoadingProgress.Visibility = Visibility.Collapsed;
    };

  LoadingProgress.Visibility = Visibility.Visible;

  _viewModel.LoadEmployees();
}
```

Note that this is one place where an interface makes good sense: have the locator return a class that implements the interface, and have the code in the code-behind aware only of that interface, not of the concrete class itself. After all, if you're going to go through the effort to dynamically resolve the ViewModel, it makes little sense to work with concrete types that could be instantiated.

A larger discussion around these topics, especially interface-based development and IoC, would take more room that I have in this chapter, but I did want to make you aware of them because they're often used with the ViewModel pattern. Many MVVM toolkits include support for interface-based design as well as various types of locators. When evaluating those toolkits, you'll now know how they're used.

Commands and behaviors help decouple the user interface from the code that supports it. Rather than having concrete compile-time hooks into various other classes in the system, the hooks are more dynamic and resolved via binding or even string lookup at runtime. One of the more egregious couplings in the system was the entity data-model types permeating all layers, effectively tying the entire application to the database schema. Fixing that by introducing the entity-type ViewModel goes a long way toward freeing the front end from the back end. Finally, the use of interfaces, ViewModel locators, and patterns such as Inversion of Control take the decoupling to a higher level, making the application as a whole more resilient to change and easier to maintain. In addition, this loose coupling makes it easier to break these pieces apart, especially for testing.

In the next section, we'll cover how to test Silverlight applications, specifically those that have been designed with the principles in this chapter taken to heart.

16.5 *Testing*

Testing is a heavily overloaded word. For some people, it's a way to spec out a system, using tests as the drivers and documentation. For others, it means running through a few verification steps as part of a build process. For still others, it's a project manager banging away at a keyboard and "trying to break the system."

Each of those definitions has tools that best support it. Many great unit-testing, test-driven development, and keyboard-jockey testing tools are available out there, both free and open source as well as commercial.

For this section, I'll focus on unit testing of Silverlight functionality, using the free Silverlight Unit Testing Framework. You'll first try a few tests that have nothing to do with your application. Then, because it must be broken apart to support testing, you'll refactor the application into two projects. When the refactoring is complete, you'll try three simple tests to exercise synchronous logic through the ViewModel class. The final test will be an asynchronous data-loading test, used to verify that the employees are being correctly downloaded from the server.

16.5.1 *Introduction to the Silverlight Unit Testing Framework*

The Silverlight Unit Testing Framework consists of a test runner and test metadata developed as part of the Silverlight toolkit. To use the Silverlight Unit Testing Framework,

Figure 16.8   Adding a new Silverlight Unit Test Application to the solution. I named the project MvvmApplication.Tests, but the name isn't important.

you'll need to install the Silverlight Toolkit. If you don't already have it installed, you can grab the latest version from http://silverlight.codeplex.com.

When you have the bits installed, you'll get a new template in Visual Studio. Continuing with the same solution you've been working with for this chapter, add a new Silverlight Unit Test Application project. I named mine MvvmApplication.Tests. Figure 16.8 shows the Add New Project dialog with the correct options selected.

The project template automatically includes a single default test. You'll replace that with three simple tests that show how to use the `Assert` object and its functions. Listing 16.23 shows the three tests in place in the default `Tests` class.

Listing 16.23   Simple tests

```
namespace MvvmApplication.Tests
{
  [TestClass]
  public class Tests
  {
    [TestMethod]
    public void TestToMakeSureTrueIsActuallyTrue()
    {
      Assert.IsTrue(true);
    }

    [TestMethod]
```

```
    public void TestToMakeSureTheListObjectIsNotNull()
    {
      List<int> l = new List<int>();
      Assert.IsNotNull(l);
    }

    [TestMethod]
    public void ThisTestShouldFail()
    {
      Assert.IsTrue(false);
    }
  }
}
```

The tests include two that should pass without any issue and one that should fail 100% of the time. Set the automatically added test .aspx file in the web project to the start page, and run (run; don't start in debug mode unless you want to break on the exception). When you do, it'll look something like figure 16.9.

Simple tests are… simple. They help you understand how the test system works, but they're not doing anything useful for you yet. You want to test functionality in the application itself. To do that, you'll need to put all the testable stuff into one or more class libraries. To keep things simple, you'll move everything but the views into a single core project.

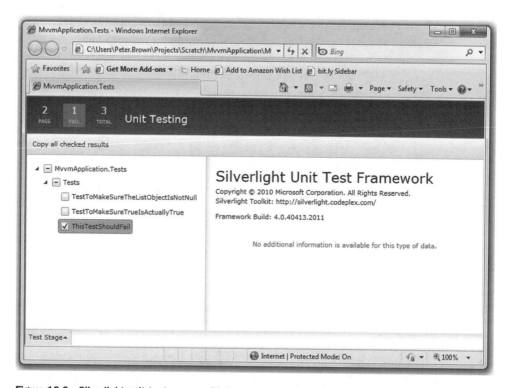

Figure 16.9   Silverlight unit test runner with two passed tests and one failed test

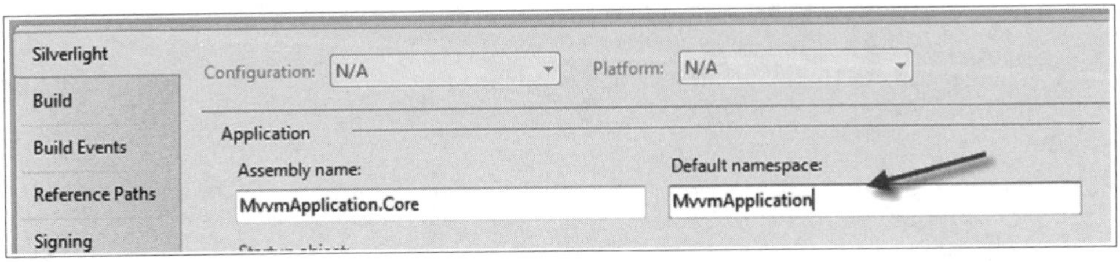

Figure 16.10   Setting the default namespace on a class library project

Create a Silverlight Class Library named MvvmApplication.Core. Then, go into its project properties and set the default namespace to be MvvmApplication, as shown in figure 16.10.

Setting the namespace will allow you to keep everything the same as it was in the main Silverlight application.

Next, create a Services folder and a ViewModels folder in the new class library project. Drag the contents of those folders from the old project to the new, and then remove the folders and their contents from the old project.

The next step is to swap the service reference over to the new project. In the MvvmApplication.Core project, right-click, and choose Add Service Reference. Pick the web service in the web project, and set the namespace to Services as you did in the original project. Then, delete the service reference from the original Silverlight project.

Before you do any in-code/markup cleanup, you need to add a project reference from the main application to the core application. Right-click the MvvmApplication project, choose Add Reference, and select the MvvmApplication.Core project.

Do a build, and clean up the errors. You'll need to add a reference to System.ComponentModel.DataAnnotations in the core project. When that's done, you'll need to crack open the Resources.xaml file and change the vm prefix to point to

```
xmlns:vm="clr-namespace:MvvmApplication.ViewModels;
    assembly=MvvmApplication.Core"
```

The last step is to delete the old ServiceReferences.ClientConfig from the MvvmApplication Silverlight project and then add the one from core as a reference. When you've deleted the old file, right-click the MvvmApplication project and choose Add > Existing Item. Navigate to the core project, and select the ServiceReferences.ClientConfig file. Click the drop-down arrow on the Add button, and select the option to add as a link, as shown in figure 16.11.

If you do this correctly, you'll now see the ServiceReferences.ClientConfig file in the main MvvmApplication project. Its icon will have the standard shortcut arrow overlay, which indicates it's a link. The build action should be automatically set to Content.

The last step is to add a project reference from the MvvmApplication.Tests project to the MvvmApplication.Core project. Right-click the MvvmApplication.Tests project, select Add Reference, and select the MvvmApplication.Core project.

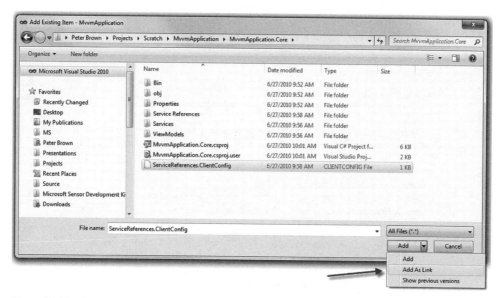

Figure 16.11 Add the ServiceReferences.ClientConfig file from the core project to the main project using the Add As Link option.

When you've completed all these steps, set the application test page in the web project as the start page, and run the solution. Make sure the Silverlight app is running and working as it did before. If everything is good, you're ready to move on to doing some real testing.

16.5.2 *Testing the ViewModel*

In a well-architected MVVM application, testing the ViewModel covers the majority of the scenarios you'd normally test through UI automation. The more value converters or UI magic in use, the less meaningful the ViewModel test becomes. I don't want to scare you away from using awesome things such as value converters or validation annotations, but it's something you need to keep in mind when you're testing.

Caveats aside, testing the ViewModel will give you a pretty high level of confidence that the majority of the system is working as designed, so let's start there. In the test project, remove the test class you created earlier. Add a new Silverlight Test Class file to the MvvmApplication.Tests project, and name it `EmployeeListViewModelTests`. Listing 16.24 shows your first two tests.

Listing 16.24 The first ViewModel tests

```
[TestClass]
public class EmployeeListViewModelTests
{
  [TestMethod]
  public void SelectedEmployeeCanBeSetAndRetrieved()          <—— SelectedEmployee
  {
    EmployeeViewModel employee = new EmployeeViewModel();
```

```
      EmployeeListViewModel vm = new EmployeeListViewModel();

      vm.SelectedEmployee = employee;

      Assert.ReferenceEquals(employee, vm.SelectedEmployee);
    }

    [TestMethod]
    public void EmployeeVacationBonusIsProperlyApplied()
    {
      EmployeeViewModel employee = new EmployeeViewModel();
      EmployeeListViewModel vm = new EmployeeListViewModel();

      vm.SelectedEmployee = employee;

      employee.VacationHours = 0;
      employee.HireDate = DateTime.Today.AddYears(-4);
      vm.AddVacationBonusToSelectedEmployee();
      Assert.AreEqual(employee.VacationHours, 10);

      employee.VacationHours = 0;
      employee.HireDate = DateTime.Today.AddYears(-8);
      vm.AddVacationBonusToSelectedEmployee();
      Assert.AreEqual(employee.VacationHours, 20);

      employee.VacationHours = 0;
      employee.HireDate = DateTime.Today.AddYears(-15);
      vm.AddVacationBonusToSelectedEmployee();
      Assert.AreEqual(employee.VacationHours, 30);

      employee.VacationHours = 0;
      employee.HireDate = DateTime.Today.AddYears(-25);
      vm.AddVacationBonusToSelectedEmployee();
      Assert.AreEqual(employee.VacationHours, 40);
    }
}
```

Bonus test ←

The first test tests the utility of the SelectedEmployee property. It checks to see that when you assign an object to the property, the object can be retrieved. The second test exercises the vacation bonus logic. Note that this test doesn't have 100 percent coverage for the full domain of hire dates and vacation hours; to do that, every value from zero through some reasonable upper bound would need to be tested.

Both of these tests cover synchronous functionality only—you do something and hang around until the result comes back. If you want to test anything network-related in Silverlight, you need to use an asynchronous test.

16.5.3   *Testing asynchronous operations*

Testing asynchronous operations takes a little extra work. You'll need a different test base class and the asynchronous methods it exposes. Listing 16.25 shows an asynchronous call test against the EmployeeDataService class.

Listing 16.25   Asynchronous call test

```
[TestClass]
public class EmployeeDataServiceTests : SilverlightTest
{
```

```
[TestMethod]
[Asynchronous]
public void TestEmployeeServiceCallReturnsData()
{
  var service = new EmployeeDataService();

  service.EmployeesLoaded += (s, e) =>
    {
      Assert.IsNotNull(service.Employees);
      Assert.IsTrue(service.Employees.Count > 0);          Mark as
                                                           complete
      EnqueueTestComplete();
    };

  service.LoadEmployees();
}
}
```

This example shows the test class inherited from the SilverlightTest base class. This immediately makes your class fall outside of code compatibility with the full Visual Studio testing framework. That's a concern only if you want to share your tests with full .NET projects, or if you have plans to migrate them to another testing platform in the future.

The SilverlightTest base class supplies the critical EnqueueTestComplete method. That method tells the test framework that the method is complete, and the framework can release it from the holding pattern created by the [Asynchronous] attribute.

Before running the test, there's one more step. Just as you did when breaking the original Silverlight project in two, you need to add the ServiceReferences.ClientConfig file to the MvvmApplication.Tests project, as a link. That file is generated by the project that has the service reference, but it must be located by the project that is the main entry point of execution.

The Silverlight Unit Testing Framework is a capable test framework for Silverlight. When it first came out, there were no other supported Silverlight testing frameworks. Now you have several choices.

The Silverlight Unit Testing Framework has some trade-offs, such as not being integrated with any build processes and requiring a run to see the results rather than keeping an open window or a docked pane in the IDE. You'll need to evaluate those for your own projects and stack up the framework against other robust unit-testing frameworks.

When you structure your application using MVVM principles and good coding and architecture practices, it makes your applications much easier to test. It's important to test. It's important to unit-test functionality and to keep those tests up to date. It's beneficial to use tests to drive functionality using a TDD-derived approach. If there were no way to test Silverlight code, you definitely wouldn't be in your happy place. I hope the simplicity of the Silverlight Unit Testing Framework will help you integrate testing into your own application development cycle.

16.6 *Summary*

When you get into developing applications of complexity beyond basic samples, your code can get pretty ugly quickly if you don't follow a good architectural pattern such as MVVM. In this chapter, we've moved from a basic-but-common code-behind solution to a decent MVVM implementation. To take it to the next level, you'll want to incorporate an MVVM toolkit and use the facilities built into that.

MVVM, or the ViewModel pattern, isn't scary when you peel the onion back layer by layer, refactoring between each and incorporating features as you understand them. Silverlight includes support for behaviors and commands to help separate the UI from the functions the UI calls. The patterns you follow will help you reuse code between different ViewModels or between different parts of the system.

When you have an application with decent separation of concerns between components and layers, you open up the ability to easily test the components. The Silverlight Unit Testing Framework is a nice in-box (well, in-toolkit) solution for unit-testing Silverlight applications. It's not the only game in town, but it's certainly a decent player.

While we're looking at what it takes to build real systems, we'll turn to WCF RIA Services in the next chapter.

WCF RIA Services

This chapter covers

- Using the Business Application project template
- Exposing data from a domain service
- Filtering, sorting, grouping, paging, and updating data
- Using the presentation model for loose coupling
- Sharing logic between the client and server
- Securing the application

Data-oriented Silverlight applications are multitier by nature—they have a client, a server with services, and a data store. As you learned in chapter 14, the way Silverlight handles network calls requires setting up asynchronous proxies (or performing raw asynchronous network operations). Sometimes, sharing entities between the client and server is a simple task; sometimes it's not. In general, the amount of code that goes into what could be considered plumbing and standard CRUD methods ends up being a significant portion of the overall source code for the application.

In many organizations, the code that makes up those plumbing and standard operations, despite best efforts, ends up being duplicated in project after project. Reuse is rarely seen, and when it is, it's in relatively trivial things such as logging services or caching. When reuse is enforced, it can be overly cumbersome to use across the suite of applications and difficult to update.

459

When developing WCF RIA Services (also called just *RIA Services* for short), Microsoft realized that most applications built (again, despite best efforts) are actually mini silos from the client through to the database interface, and often through to the database tables themselves. I know from personal experience at many clients around the country that this is true—it's our industry's dirty little secret, despite all the talk about OOP reuse, SOA, and more. Applications have a silo of functionality they use and some minor integration points with other systems using web services. I bring this up to point out that a nongoal of RIA Services is the creation of robust service-oriented architecture (SOA) solutions, in the true sense of SOA, not the "we used a service" sense.

WCF RIA Services is a framework and set of tools that attempts to make building modern multitier applications as simple as building classic two-tier client/server applications. WCF RIA Services doesn't tie you to the single application model, but it's optimized to support it as the most prevalent application model. We're talking about building real, scalable, efficient, and easily coded multitier applications that work cleanly from front to back using a minimum amount of ceremonial code. This is accomplished through a framework and set of tools that provide the following benefits:

- Automatic creation of common Create Read Update Delete (CRUD) methods for entities
- Automatic generation and synchronization of service methods and their client-side proxies
- Validation rules and arbitrary business logic methods that are shared between the client and server without duplication of effort
- High-level client-side data source controls that make data manipulation simple
- Integration with ASP.NET security
- Through the project template, an overall application structure you can build on

In addition, when combined with the `DataGrid` and `DataForm` covered in chapter 12, you get automatic user-interface generation for entities, as well as simple UI wire-up for CRUD operations and validation.

This is all done in a way that allows you to maintain the level of control you want. There are enough extension points to let you hook into processes as well as manage client operations from code rather than the controls if you desire. Although optimized for the full application front-to-back scenario, it's flexible enough to incorporate other services and even other RIA Services servers into the overall solution. You can even expose your RIA Services service calls and data in a number of ways to allow interoperating with other systems.

Although RIA Services does support other clients such as ASP.NET, the functionality is at its strongest when used with Silverlight. Throughout its development, RIA Services was almost exclusively a Silverlight technology, giving back to the framework as techniques and code were developed. Almost 100 percent of the users of RIA Services, at the time of this writing, are building Silverlight applications. The reason is simple. RIA Services helps solve a problem that is strongest in Silverlight: how to build multitier data-oriented applications with different but mostly compatible frameworks on the client and server, without native database or ORM access from the client, and perform all requests asynchronously while keeping the footprint down.

Our tour of RIA Services will start with a look at the tooling and templates that make it easy to use in Visual Studio. You'll create a project that'll be used in the examples through the rest of the chapter. After that, we'll look at what it takes to expose data to external clients and to Silverlight, as well as how to filter, sort, group, and page that data. Of course, there's more to application development than read-only data, so we'll go through the update process to make sure the data can make a full round trip. Then, because I spent the last chapter telling you how important it is to decouple your layers, we'll look at how to support loose coupling in an otherwise tightly coupled system. We'll wrap up the chapter with a look at where to put business logic, followed by securing your applications.

I'm excited about the efficiency that RIA Services brings to the table, so let's get building.

17.1 *WCF RIA Services architecture, tooling, and template*

WCF RIA Services applications are similar to traditional Silverlight applications in that there's both a client application and a home server. The server serves up the Silverlight application and also contains the services the application is to use. RIA Services works with multiple-server and multiple-client scenarios; but as mentioned in the introduction, the typical scenario is one server per application domain. Figure 17.1 captures this typical architecture at a high level.

At first glance, the architecture looks like any other Silverlight application, except for that odd shared bit. That's one of the many things that make RIA Services worth the effort to learn.

RIA Services includes strong support for creating client-side proxies and entities that preserve, with high fidelity, the validation rules and logic written on the server. As

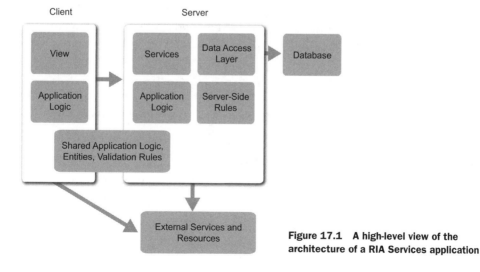

Figure 17.1 A high-level view of the architecture of a RIA Services application

a developer, you only need to write the code once, and RIA Services will take care of the rest. We'll cover this in depth later in the chapter.

In this section, we'll look at the tooling that makes RIA Services work. Then, we'll dive right in to creating a new project using the Silverlight Business Application template, a WCF RIA Services version of the navigation template we covered in chapter 15. You'll build on this project throughout the rest of the chapter.

17.1.1 RIA Services tooling support

Much of what makes WCF RIA Services tick is the magic that happens as part of the build process. When you first create a Silverlight application and select the option to Enable WCF RIA Services, you've set up a client-to-server project link. That option puts a single line in the Silverlight .csproj project file:

```
<LinkedServerProject>..\Chapter17.Web\Chapter17.Web.csproj
    </LinkedServerProject>
```

That one line of XML makes possible the auto-generation of the client proxies, types, and more. That also means a Silverlight application can be directly attached to at most one RIA Services server. To get around this limitation, you can create Silverlight class library projects and allow them to link to different servers, and then use the class libraries in your own project.

If you're curious, check out the obj/Debug folder in your Silverlight project. In it, you'll find a number of files generated by the RIA Services tooling, to keep track of server references, source files, and more. It's mostly unicorn and rainbow[1] magic, but it's fun for the curious and perhaps helpful during an odd debugging session.

The main body of code that is generated falls under the Generated_Code folder on the Silverlight application. This includes a single .g.cs file with all the context and proxy classes, and one or more subfolders with the additional model classes. Because this code is autogenerated, you won't want to change it. But having the source code available is useful when you're trying to understand exactly what RIA Services is doing in the client application, or when you're involved in complex debugging.

Throughout the remainder of the chapter, feel free to inspect the .g.cs file and the rest of the code in the Generated_Code folder as you add methods to various server-side classes.

Now that you understand the relationship between the web project and the client project, you can create the start of an application using the Silverlight Business Application template.

17.1.2 Creating a project with the template

The Silverlight tools for Visual Studio 2010 include a WCF RIA Services solution template, based on the navigation template discussed in chapter 15. This template is

---

[1] If you're really and truly bored and need a break from reading, check out http://cornify.com/ to add unicorns and rainbows to any web site or photo. Warning: 5th grade girls' Trapper Keeper graphics overload.

Figure 17.2 Creating a new WCF RIA Services application using the Silverlight Business Application template

called the Silverlight Business Application template. Although you don't need to use this template to create a RIA Services project (you need to select the Enable WCF RIA Services check box when creating a new Silverlight project as mentioned in the previous section), it does provide a good project structure to start with.

Figure 17.2 shows the New Project dialog with this template selected. You'll use this project, Chapter17, throughout the rest of the chapter.

Note that when you create a new WCF RIA Services project, you're not prompted with the usual second New Project dialog, asking whether to create a web site or enable WCF RIA Services. In a RIA Services project, both are required.

Despite the fact that they're based on the same original template, the styling steps described in chapter 15 won't work exactly with this template. Instead, you'll need to install the Silverlight Business Application templates (they're just zip files) included in the download and use them as the basis for your new project. At the time of this writing, no .vsix installers exist for the templates, so you have to manually install them. In addition, the trick of copying the styles over wasn't working when I wrote this. The team is investigating, so the experience may be better by the time you try it.

When you run the application, you'll get something that looks similar to the chapter 15 template, but with a few additions. Figure 17.3 shows the bare application at runtime.

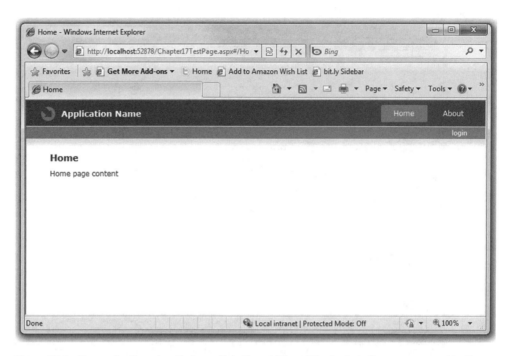

Figure 17.3   The application when first run. Note the addition of the Login button as compared to the navigation template shown in chapter 15.

At runtime, the main difference you'll notice is the addition of the Login button. If you click that, you'll get a `ChildWindow` login prompt. We'll discuss authentication later in this chapter.

The other changes, compared to the navigation application, require a little more digging.

APPLICATION RESOURCES

The Silverlight Business Application template has good support for customization and localization of the strings presented to the user. If you crack open the Assets\Resources\ ApplicationStrings.resx file, you'll see that you can change key prompts, window titles, and more without altering the XAML.

Although not strictly required, when adding your own pages or prompts, a best practice is to place the text in one of the three resource files (ApplicationStrings, ErrorResources, or SecurityQuestions) rather than directly into XAML or code. Of course, you can create your own resource files if the text doesn't logically fit in one of these three.

To test the application resources approach, change the `ApplicationName` property to something different. I chose "Chapter 17 Example". Run it, and you'll see the changed name. It doesn't change in the designer right away; but after a build (or build and run), you'll see the title update in the designer as well. In this way, the resource files don't block your design-time experience.

How and why does this work? Open MainPage.xaml, and find the `TextBlock` named `ApplicationNameTextBlock`. Its definition looks like this:

```
<TextBlock x:Name="ApplicationNameTextBlock"
        Style="{StaticResource ApplicationNameStyle}"
        Text="{Binding ApplicationStrings.ApplicationName,
                    Source={StaticResource ResourceWrapper}}"/>
```

The displayed `Text` value is bound to a property of the generated resource file class `ApplicationStrings`. The `ResourceWrapper` class provides a single location from which you can access all the resource classes. The resource property name is the same as that defined in the resource file. I've used traditional resource files before, and it was never this easy to get values into the UI. The power of binding in Silverlight makes using traditional resource files a no-brainer.

OTHER DIFFERENCES

The client project file has a number of other differences compared to the straight navigation template. As you explore the project structure, you'll see a number of additional controls (such as the `BusyIndicator`), helper classes, additional views, and more. You'll run across many of them as you create your RIA Services application in the upcoming sections.

WCF RIA Services, especially through the use of the application template, makes it easy to structure a full business application, following best practices. The tooling in Visual Studio helps automatically synchronize the client and server, avoiding a cumbersome manual step.

The architecture of WCF RIA Services, although geared toward Silverlight applications, is usable by other application types as well through the server-side services. We'll leave the client project alone for a moment while we concentrate on the server (web) project in order to learn how to expose data to the application.

17.2 *Exposing data with the domain service*

WCF RIA Services applications are typically used with a database back-end. It's possible to use something other than a database; RIA Services itself doesn't care what type of backing store you use, as long as a base domain service class exists for it.

Traditional Silverlight applications use a WCF, SOAP, or REST service server-side to access data. Those services, in the case of SOAP and WCF, expose methods for retrieving and updating data. They may expose domain methods to perform other functions or calculations as well. REST-based services typically expose a domain model in an entity-centric way.

In a RIA Services application, the service to use is a *domain service*. A domain service, which is built on WCF, provides LINQ-based access to domain objects or data, as well as traditional service access to additional domain functions. It sits between the database and your client code, combining many of the advantages of the other services with the added bonus that the wire-up with the client happens automatically. The domain services are the heart of a WCF RIA Services application.

In this section, you'll first create a domain service in the web project. We'll then look at what's required to expose the data and functionality in that service in a number of different ways, including OData, JSON, and SOAP. With the interoperability question out of the way, we'll dive into the primary scenario the service was built for: integration with the Silverlight client. We'll wrap up this section with an in-depth look at the common domain service methods and what it takes to add your own methods to the service.

17.2.1 Creating the domain service

For this project, you'll use the Entity Framework and the Adventure Works database. Follow the instructions in appendix A and set up the database, connection, and Entity Framework Model in the existing web project.

Build the project before adding the domain service. This will ensure that the appropriate metadata is available from the Entity Framework Model. When that's done, right-click the Services folder in the web project, and choose Add New Item. The item you want to add is the Domain Service Class, included in the top-level Visual C# template list in the New Item dialog. Figure 17.4 shows the correct template in use.

Name your domain service EmployeeService.cs, and click Add. You'll then be presented with the RIA Services-specific Add New Domain Service Class dialog shown in figure 17.5.

This dialog requires careful attention. First, you want to make sure the Enable Client Access option is checked. When checked, it allows the domain service to be used by clients such as Silverlight. If unchecked, the service will only be available server-side.

Figure 17.4 Creating the EmployeeService domain service. You can find the Domain Service Class template in the top-level Visual C# template list.

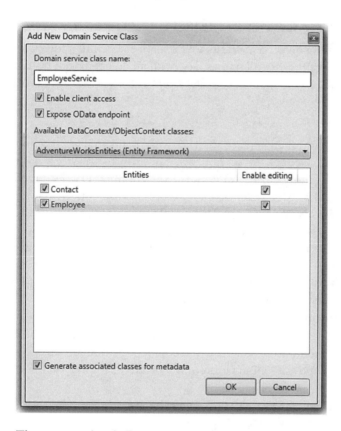

Figure 17.5 The Domain Service setup dialog. If your dialog entity list is empty, cancel out and build the project.

The next option is Expose OData Endpoint. OData is an XML-based data format. For most projects, this is entirely optional, but because we'll be discussing OData in a bit, it needs to be checked.

The middle of the dialog includes a list of entities from the Entity Framework Model. If this list is empty, you need to cancel the dialog and build the project. Select each entity that will be handled from this domain service; typically this is only one entity, or a small number of highly related entities, such as you have in this case. By default, the service handles retrieve operations only; if you want to allow create, update, and delete, ensure that the checkbox under Enable Editing is selected.

Finally, Generate Associated Classes for Metadata is an important option. When selected, this creates a class you can use to provide attribute-based validation and metadata for each of the entities. This class is named `<domainservice>.metadata.cs`.

If all the correct options are selected, when you click OK, the two classes (service and metadata) will be created in the Services folder on the web project. The `Employ-eeService` class automatically includes all the appropriate domain service methods to perform CRUD operations on both the selected `Contact` and the `Employee` types.

Silverlight applications rarely exist in a vacuum. Before we get in depth into using the domain service in the Silverlight application, it's important to discuss how you can use the domain service with other types of clients.

17.2.2 *Exposing the domain service to other clients*

Every client-exposed domain service is also a WCF service. The full address of the WCF service is the web server plus the full namespace, with all dots replaced by dashes, plus svc. For example, for `EmployeeService`, in the `Chapter17.Web.Services` namespace, the full URL is

```
http://localhost:<port>/Chapter17-Web-Services-EmployeeService.svc
```

If you start the project and then replace the URL with that, you'll get the normal WCF service page. Unlike an .asmx SOAP service, you can't run the service from this page (which is good for preventing curious end users from running services directly).

You can use the Add Service Reference menu option from any WCF-aware project type (WPF, Windows Forms, ASP.NET, or even console) and use the service directly. You won't get the rich metadata and client-side validation provided by a native RIA Services client, but you'll be able to access the data and queries, as well as any defined domain methods in the service.

In addition to this approach, which should be your first option if supported in your client, several other possible endpoints are supported.

EXPOSING AN ODATA ENDPOINT

RIA Services can expose a read-only OData endpoint for use by any application that can speak the OData/AtomPub protocol. When creating the domain service, you were offered the option to expose an OData endpoint. For this example, you did that. That did two things:

- Added a system.serviceModel\domainServices\endpoints name of OData to the web.config file
- Added `IsDefaultQuery` to the retrieve methods in the domain service class

Because the name added is OData, the service name has /OData appended to it. In this case, the service name is

```
http://localhost:<port>/Chapter17-Web-Services-EmployeeService.svc/OData
```

If you want to see metadata about the service (the OData rough equivalent of SOAP WSDL), you can append /$metadata to the endpoint name. For this service, it's as follows:

```
http://.../Chapter17-Web-Services-EmployeeService.svc/OData/$metadata
```

To access the root entities sets exposed by the domain service, you append `Set` to the name of the entity so `Employee` becomes `EmployeeSet`. Then, append that to the OData endpoint URL, as shown here:

```
http://.../Chapter17-Web-Services-EmployeeService.svc/OData/ContactSet
http://.../Chapter17-Web-Services-EmployeeService.svc/OData/EmployeeSet
```

Currently, accessing a single entity by ID isn't supported in the OData endpoint. With a full OData endpoint, you'd be able to do something like this:

```
http://.../Chapter17-Web-Services-EmployeeService.svc/OData/EmployeeSet(1)
(NOTE: this is not supported)
```

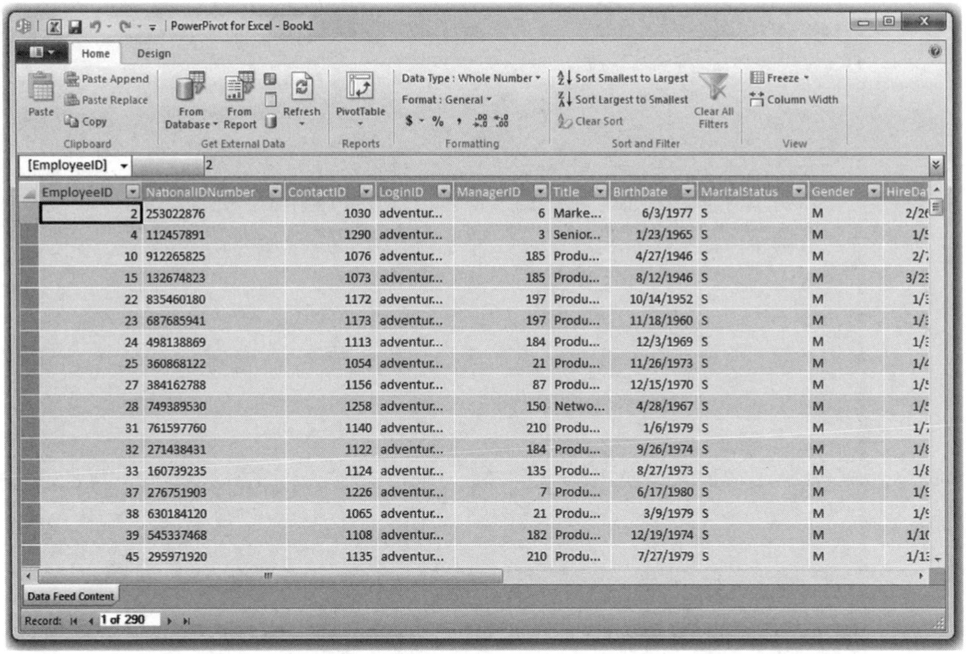

Figure 17.6 Data from the WCF RIA Services OData endpoint, loaded into PowerPivot for Excel 2010. PowerPivot is a C# .NET Office add-in application, by the way.

You can easily test the OData endpoint in Microsoft PowerPivot[2] for Excel 2010 by selecting the From Data Feeds option while the application is running, and providing the full `EmployeeSet` or `ContactSet` URL. When executed, the `EmployeeSet` query returns the results directly into PowerPivot, as seen in figure 17.6.

OData endpoints are good for querying data on the web or using tools such as PowerPivot. Although OData could be used for Ajax applications, you'll be better served using the native JSON endpoint.

EXPOSING A JSON ENDPOINT

Both the JSON and SOAP endpoints require the use of assemblies in the RIA Services Toolkit, which can be installed, like all other Silverlight tools, using the Microsoft Web Platform Installer.[3] If you performed a default Silverlight 4 tools installation with RIA Services, you have the toolkit installed. If you don't have a toolkit folder under the Program Files\Microsoft SDKs\RIA Services 1.0\ folder, you can manually install the toolkit from http://silverlight.net/getstarted/riaservices/.

From the web project, you'll need to add an assembly reference to the `Micro-soft.ServiceModel.DomainServices.Hosting` assembly in the RIA Services toolkit. Figure 17.7 shows the Add Reference dialog with the correct assembly selected.

---

[2] You can download Microsoft PowerPivot for Excel 2010 from http://powerpivot.com.
[3] You can download the Web Platform Installer from http://bit.ly/WebPI.

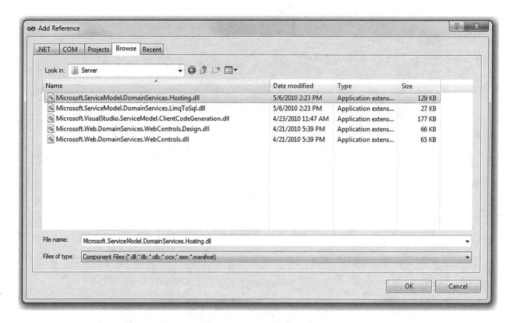

Figure 17.7   The Add Reference dialog with the correct assembly selected to allow exposing JSON and SOAP endpoints

When the project reference is set, you'll need to modify the web.config file to add the new JSON endpoint. In the domainServices\endpoints section, where the OData endpoint also lives, add the following XML:

```
<add name="JSON"
    type="Microsoft.ServiceModel.DomainServices.Hosting.JsonEndpointFactory,
        Microsoft.ServiceModel.DomainServices.Hosting, Version=4.0.0.0,
        Culture=neutral, PublicKeyToken=31bf3856ad364e35" />
```

That configuration entry sets up a WCF endpoint using the factory included in the RIA Services toolkit DLL. When it's configured, the root URL will be, as it was in the OData case, the service name with /<endpoint>:

```
http://localhost:<port>/Chapter17-Web-Services-EmployeeService.svc/JSON
```

You can call the endpoint anything you want, as long as you use the same endpoint name in the configuration file and in the URL. By convention, you use the return type—JSON. To perform a query, use Get<EntityName>s as the format. For example:

```
http://.../Chapter17-Web-Services-EmployeeService.svc/Json/GetEmployees
```

Note that if you call that URL using Internet Explorer 8, you'll get a download error. If you use Google Chrome, or another browser or JSON tool, you'll be able to see the text of the JSON content. If you have nothing handy, create this simple HTML file (see listing 17.1) in the web the project and select View in Browser. I called mine Test-JsonEndpoint.html and used a little jQuery to handle the Ajax call.

Listing 17.1 Testing the JSON endpoint from JavaScript using jQuery

```html
<html>
<head>
<title>Awesome JSON Endpoint Test</title>

<script src="http://ajax.microsoft.com/ajax/jQuery/jquery-1.4.2.min.js"
        type="text/javascript">
</script>

</head>
<body>
<button type="button" onclick="query()">Query</button>

<div id="results">
</div>

<script type="text/javascript">
  function query() {
    $.ajax({
      type: "GET",
      url: "Chapter17-Web-Services-EmployeeService.svc/JSON/GetEmployees",
      success: function (data) {
        $("#results").append("<ul>");
        var employees = data.GetEmployeesResult.RootResults;    ◁── Note
                                                                      path
        $.each(employees, function (i, entity) {
          $("#results").append("<li>" + entity.EmployeeID +
➥             " " + entity.Title + "</li>");
        });

        $("#results").append("</ul>");
        alert("Data received");
      }
    });
  }
</script>

</body>
</html>
```

This example HTML page shows how to test the retrieve method of the JSON endpoint
for your RIA Services domain service class. Using the `EmployeeID` and `Title`, it creates
a single list item for each employee returned in the query and then displays an alert
when the query returns. Note the path used to get to the root of the results: it's the
name of the query with `Result` appended, plus the name `.RootResults`. This is consistent for any RIA Services JSON `get` call.

jQuery[4] makes the service call and processing simple. If you haven't yet been
exposed to jQuery, definitely check it out. jQuery has been the one thing that makes
JavaScript and DOM manipulation tolerable for me. It's a great library for handling
on-page work, and it interacts nicely with Silverlight.

---

[4] I put this in as jQuery just so Rey Bango will stop picking on me about the ugly cabinets in my home office via
the back channel chat in every team meeting. You can see them in the background in the webcam shots in
chapter 20. If you want to pick on me yourself, I'll try not to cry, really. :)

The JSON endpoint also supports updating data. For space and relevance reasons, I won't create a full update UI here, but the code is similar to any other JSON Ajax call using a POST.

JSON is great for Ajax applications, but the format itself can be limiting. Although not as rich as the WCF native formats, another widely understood format is SOAP.

EXPOSING A SOAP ENDPOINT

Like JSON endpoints, SOAP endpoints are updatable services exposed using a service endpoint definition in the web.config. The entry to add for SOAP is

```
<add name="Soap"
type="Microsoft.ServiceModel.DomainServices.Hosting.SoapXmlEndpointFactory,
➥   Microsoft.ServiceModel.DomainServices.Hosting, Version=4.0.0.0,
➥   Culture=neutral, PublicKeyToken=31bf3856ad364e35" />
```

This requires the same assembly reference the JSON example required. Note that the public key token and other assembly information are identical as well.

Unlike the JSON approach, the SOAP endpoint ends up working right at the root service level. For example, to get the Web Services Description Language (WSDL) for the SOAP service in your solution, hit this URL with the browser:

```
http://.../Services/Chapter17-Web-Services-EmployeeService.svc?wsdl
```

You don't need to add /Soap to the URL.

To fully utilize the SOAP client, you'll need to add a service reference from another project and generate the client. As was the case in the JSON version, the service is read/write but doesn't expose the entity metadata to the client. To take advantage of WCF RIA Services, you'll want a full Silverlight application, aware of WCF RIA Services and aware of the metadata it uses.

17.2.3 *Domain service method types*

The methods in the domain service have names starting with Get, Insert, Update, and Delete. This naming convention allows for automatic wire-up of the operations with the client. This convention-over-configuration approach is common outside the Microsoft developer ecosystem and is just starting to make its way into Microsoft products.

Conventions don't always work for everyone or in every situation, though. For instances where you'd rather not go with convention, you can use a series of attributes to make your choices explicit. Table 17.1 shows the attributes, conventions, and their descriptions.

Table 17.1   Naming conventions, equivalent attributes, and their purposes

Name prefix	Attribute	Purpose
(Any)	[Query()]	A method that returns data without any side effects. The usual approach is to prefix with Get, but any prefix is fine as long as the function returns an instance of an entity T, an IEnumerable<T>, or an IQueryable<T>.
Insert, Add, Create	[Insert()]	An operation that inserts a single entity into the data store. The method takes the entity as a parameter.

Table 17.1 Naming conventions, equivalent attributes, and their purposes *(continued)*

Name prefix	Attribute	Purpose
Update, Change, Modify	[Update()]	An operation that updates a single entity in the data store. The method takes the entity as a parameter.
Delete, Remove	[Delete()]	An operation that deletes an entity in the data store. The method takes the entity as a parameter.
(Any)	[Invoke()]	A business method that must be executed without tracking or deferred execution. It may or may not have side effects. Use only when one of the other method types can't be used.
(Any)	[Update()]	A named update with UsingCustomMethod=true set in the attribute. This is a purpose-built function that performs a specific type of update. An example may be a product discount or firing an employee.

In the remainder of this section, we'll go through each of the types of operations on the domain service.

QUERY METHODS

Query methods are methods that return a single entity or a set of entities. The default query method generated by the template returns all instances of the entity in the data store. This allows you to further compose the query on the client with additional criteria to limit the result set.

Query methods may be indicated by convention or attribute, as shown previously. When using the attribute, you have a few options to set. These are shown in table 17.2.

Table 17.2 QueryAttribute members

Member	Description
HasSideEffects	Queries shouldn't typically have side effects that would alter data. If they do, set this property to true so clients can make decisions as to how to use the method. For example, an HTTP client may send a POST instead of a GET.
IsComposable	Set this to true if the query allows composing to add additional criteria.
IsDefault	Set this to true if this query is the default query for the entity type.
ResultLimit	This is the maximum number of results the method should return. Defaults to 0, which indicated unlimited results.

Creating a query method on the service is pretty simple if you follow the naming and method signature conventions. Here's an example of one that returns only salaried employees:

```
public IEnumerable<Employee> GetSalariedEmployees()
{
    return from Employee emp in ObjectContext.Employees
           where emp.SalariedFlag == true
           select emp;
}
```

When the solution is compiled, the method is turned into a client-side method named GetSalariedEmployeesQuery on the generated EmployeeContext domain context object.

TYPES OF QUERY METHODS

Query methods fall into three primary buckets:

- Methods returning a single concrete instance of an entity
- Methods returning a collection or enumerable of zero or more entities
- Methods returning an IQueryable of the entity

The first two are easily understood, falling squarely into patterns you've used since functions were first conceptualized in computer science. The third option is a little different and provides real flexibility.

A function with an IQueryable return type returns an expression tree. This is a LINQ concept for a generic query that's to be executed by a query provider. The IQueryable interface inherits from IEnumerable, so it also represents the results of that expression tree. Even when you build the LINQ query on the client, the query itself is executed server-side, typically all the way back at the database for a provider such as the Entity Framework.

In effect, this means you can have this query method on the server

```
public IQueryable<Employee> GetEmployeesSorted()
{
    return from Employee emp in ObjectContext.Employees
           orderby emp.Title, emp.HireDate
           select emp;
}
```

and use it like this on the client:

```
EmployeeContext context = new EmployeeContext();

EntityQuery<Employee> query =
    from emp in context.GetEmployeesSortedQuery()
    where emp.SalariedFlag == true
    select emp;
```

Note that the query is composed—the server-side query and the client-side query are combined to return a set of results. That's a powerful way to provide prefiltered or presorted data to the client. For example, the query could've taken a parameter to use in the filter or used security to decide which records could be returned to the client. The query execution itself is deferred; it's not executed until the client code first accesses the result data.

We'll cover more about using the domain service query methods from the client later in this chapter. Another class of methods the service provides is for data manipulation: insert, update, and delete operations.

INSERT, UPDATE, AND DELETE METHODS

The generated code for the insert, update, and delete methods takes in a single entity and uses the backing data store to perform the appropriate operation. For example, the update code looks like this:

```
public void UpdateEmployee(Employee currentEmployee)
{
  this.ObjectContext.Employees.AttachAsModified(currentEmployee,
                   this.ChangeSet.GetOriginal(currentEmployee));
}
```

That tells the server-side object context to add this employee and mark it in the modified state, using the passed-in employee object as the current state and the original object as the last-known state from the data store. The `Attach` and `AttachAsModified` functions are all provided by the Entity Framework. The specific function used for your data provider may vary.

For a given entity, it's unusual to create alternate general insert, update, and delete methods. Doing so would confuse RIA services, not to mention your fellow programmers. There's one exception—the *named update method.*

NAMED UPDATE METHODS

Normally, the update methods are handled automatically based on the state of the data. But you may have situations where you need to provide a custom update method that you'll call directly rather than let Silverlight infer the update operation for a particular entity during the `SubmitChanges` call on the domain context.

To mark an update operation as a named update operation, it needs to have the usual update operation signature and the `Update` attribute with `UsingCustomMethod = true`. Here's an example:

```
[Update(UsingCustomMethod = true)]
public void SpecialCascadedUpdate(Employee emp)
{
   ...
}
```

This approach exists to allow you to handle special cases related to business logic or database complexities. It's still called as part of the batched `SubmitChanges` call. If you want to immediately execute a function, another approach is available.

INVOKE METHODS

CRUD methods are called as part of a batch—the entities have the CRUD operations performed on them but aren't sent to the server for the actual action until the call to `SubmitChanges` is made on the client.

Invoke methods are normal methods you can use to perform some sort of calculation or return a piece of data. They're operations that need to be executed without change tracking or deferred execution. Invoke methods shouldn't be used to load data; that's what query methods are intended for. Returning an entity from an `Invoke` method bypasses the pattern and won't cause the appropriate change tracking and entity generation to occur on the client.

Although the `Invoke` attribute is optional, to be considered an invoke method, a method shouldn't take entities as a parameter or return an entity, `IEnumerable`, or `IQueryable` of entities as a result.

A typical invoke method, if there could be such a thing, might look like this (example shamelessly stolen from chapter 16 on MVVM):

```
[Invoke()]
public int CalculateVacationBonus(DateTime hireDate)
{
  int vacationBonus;
  DateTime today = DateTime.Today;

  int yearsInService = today.Year - hireDate.Year;

  if (hireDate.AddYears(yearsInService) > today)
    yearsInService--;

  if (yearsInService < 5)
    vacationBonus = 10;
  else
    vacationBonus = 20;

  return vacationBonus;
}
```

It's a regular business method. Given that it's on the server, you probably have a reason—it may call another web service, or it may hit a database to do a lookup. In this case, it's on the server to illustrate the invoke type.

As mentioned, the `Invoke` attribute is optional. When in doubt, add the attribute to make your intentions clear. For normal CRUD methods where the name is sufficiently patterned using the naming conventions, this is usually unnecessary. But I find that `Invoke` methods can be ambiguous at first glance. Speaking of naming conventions, what happens when you want to avoid having them kick in?

IGNORING METHODS DESPITE THE NAME

Some of these operations require the use of attributes, but many are autogenerated via the naming conventions. If you don't want RIA Services to generate a domain method for your service method, apply the `Ignore` attribute to that method, as shown here:

```
[Ignore()]
public void UpdateEmployeeButNotReally(Employee emp)
{
...
}
```

With that attribute in place, despite the fact that the method uses the Update naming convention and method signature, it won't be generated as an update call on the client.

The domain service provides a number of standard method types, many of which are autogenerated from the tooling but may be modified or replaced. Domain services provide CRUD operations in the form of insert, update, delete, and query methods. In addition, arbitrary functionality may be included in invoke methods.

When discussing the `IQueryable` type, I sneaked an `EmployeeContext` object into the example. What's that, and what does it provide? That's the subject of the next section.

17.2.4 *Using a domain service from Silverlight*

Domain services execute on the server, running under the full .NET 4 framework. The client-side equivalent of the domain service is the domain context object. Domain context objects provide a proxy for the service methods, as well as change tracking, operation batching, and more.

For each domain service on the server, RIA Services will generate one domain context object on the client. In the case of the `EmployeeService` domain service, the client domain context is named `EmployeeContext`.

The domain service may be wired up to Silverlight via RIA Services controls in the UI that go through the context object, or via explicit use of the context object in code. Both have advantages and disadvantages and will impact the overall architecture of your application. I'll cover both here, starting with the most involved approach: creating the connection from code.

CONNECTING VIA CODE

One way to use the domain service is to reference the client context object from code and execute queries directly against it. Because this is the most traditional way when compared to the usual pattern of working with services and WCF service proxies, I'll start with it.

In the Home.xaml.cs file, replace the `OnNavigatedTo` method with the following short bit of code:

```
protected override void OnNavigatedTo(NavigationEventArgs e)
{
    EmployeeContext context = new EmployeeContext();

    EntityQuery<Employee> query = context.GetEmployeesQuery();

    context.Load<Employee>(query);
    EmployeeGrid.ItemsSource = context.Employees;
}
```

When the page is navigated to, this code automatically loads all the employees and assigns that collection to the `ItemsSource` of a `DataGrid`. The `EmployeeContext` object, in this instance, serves as the proxy for the domain service. Note that though you don't bother to hook up a method to the `Load` method asynchronous return, it's still executed asynchronously, and the results appear through binding.

The query system is flexible: you could change the query to add some criteria and a sort if you wanted to. (Be sure to add `using System.Linq;` to the top of the code before you try to compile.)

```
EntityQuery<Employee> query =
    from emp in context.GetEmployeesQuery()
    where emp.SalariedFlag == true
    orderby emp.HireDate
    select emp;
```

This example selects all the employees that are salaried and sorts them by hire date. The query itself is executed on the server, as you learned in the previous section. When using the Entity Framework with SQL Server as you are here, the query is executed all the way back at SQL Server, and only the items matching the query are returned.

You can't test the connection without having something to bind it to. So, time for a trusty `DataGrid`. Replace everything else in the `LayoutRoot`, starting with the `Scroll-Viewer`, with this XAML:

```
<Grid Margin="10">
  <Grid.ColumnDefinitions>
    <ColumnDefinition Width="*" />
    <ColumnDefinition Width="350" />
  </Grid.ColumnDefinitions>

  <my:DataGrid x:Name="EmployeeGrid"
               Grid.Column="0" Margin="5" />
</Grid>
```

It'll be easiest if you first drag the `DataGrid` onto the design surface in order to set up the correct namespaces and project references. Besides, "it's not a real demo unless someone drags a `DataGrid`."[5]

When you run the application, you'll get something that looks like figure 17.8.

Connecting via code allows you to better take advantage of advanced patterns such as MVVM and have complete control over the execution path. As you get more into advanced patterns, that can be a significant benefit.

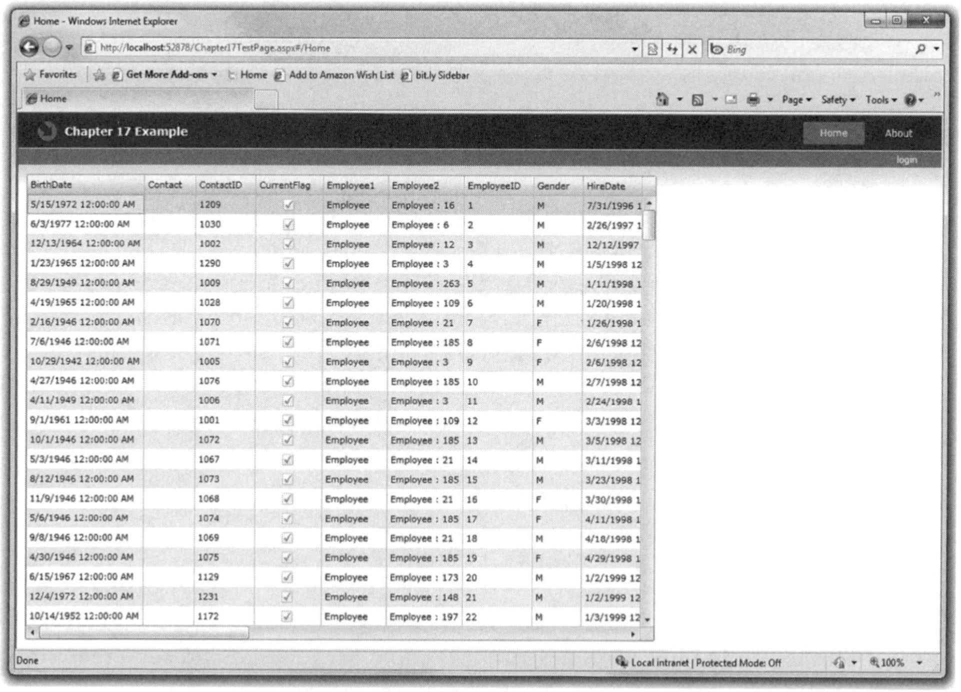

Figure 17.8 The `DataGrid` populated using the `DomainDataSource` control in XAML

---

[5] Scott Hanselman talking about a 2010 keynote demo for WCF RIA Services.

> **TIP** I set the `DataGrid ItemsSource` property via code. There's no reason you couldn't set up a ViewModel (chapter 16) and bind the `ItemsSource` to an exposed `Employees` property. If you go with using the domain context object from code, follow the ViewModel/MVVM pattern when you do it; you'll thank yourself later.

I'll cover the domain context class in more detail in various parts of this chapter, primarily in section 17.3 when I discuss update functionality.

There's another approach that's easier to use and includes a ton of built-in functionality. Before making up your mind which approach you want to use, look at the `DomainDataSource` control.

USING THE DOMAINDATASOURCE CONTROL

The `DomainDataSource` control provides an all-XAML way to interface with the domain service. I've heard this described as a bad thing, akin to wiring your UI directly to your database. I strongly disagree with that assessment, but I do agree that despite the utter simplicity of using the control, there are some drawbacks when it comes to testing, mocking, and application structure.

Before making up your mind that the control is a Bad Thing, let's look at what it can do. After all, some applications may benefit from this approach. Despite how it looks, it's not like you're binding VB3 UI controls directly to tables in an access database;[6] there are a few layers of abstraction in between.

To use the `DomainDataSource` control, you'll need to add a Silverlight assembly reference to the RIA Services SDK assembly `System.Windows.Controls.DomainServices`. When that's done, inside the `LayoutRoot Grid` of /Views/Home.xaml, add the following markup:

```
<riaControls:DomainDataSource x:Name="DataSource"
                              AutoLoad="True"
                              QueryName="GetEmployees">
    <riaControls:DomainDataSource.DomainContext>
        <domain:EmployeeContext />
    </riaControls:DomainDataSource.DomainContext>
</riaControls:DomainDataSource>
```

This markup sets up a new `DomainDataSource` control, tells it to automatically call the query when loaded, and sets the query name to the one that loads the employee information from the domain service. For this to work, you'll also need to set up the `ria-Controls` and domain namespaces in the same XAML file. They are as follows:

```
xmlns:riaControls="clr-namespace:System.Windows.Controls;
➥        assembly=System.Windows.Controls.DomainServices"
xmlns:domain="clr-namespace:Chapter17.Web.Services"
```

The first namespace, `riaControls`, defines the location for the `DomainDataSource` control. The second defines the location for the generated domain context class: the client-side proxy for the domain service on the server.

---

[6] I see the old VB3/4/5/6 VCR data-binding control in my nightmares from time to time. It's up there with the one about having a physics final today but having skipped the class all semester to spend time MUDding.

TIP If you're curious about where the client-side proxy is defined and what it looks like, select the Silverlight project and, from the Project menu, select Show All Files. Scroll down, and you'll see a Generated_Code folder. In that folder, you'll find a number of interesting files, but the one that contains the proxies and entity definitions is Chapter17.Web.g.cs.

The `DataGrid` then needs to be bound to the new data source. Because the data source has an assigned context object, the data itself is located in the `Data` property:

```
<my:DataGrid Grid.Column="0" Margin="5"
            ItemsSource="{Binding Data, ElementName=DataSource}" />
```

What you've changed on the grid is the `ItemsSource`. The markup here binds the `DataGrid` to the data property of the `DomainDataSource`. Because the `DataGrid` instance is set up by default to autogenerate columns and show all data, you'll end up with an application that looks like the previous example in figure 17.8 when run; the UI hasn't changed, just the way you get data on the client. Be sure to comment out or remove the code you previously added.

The `DomainDataSource` is easy to use. Although "Look ma, no code!" isn't the most important reason to pick one approach over another (and in some cases can be a reason not to pick an approach), the domain data source is powerful and flexible enough to make it a real contender for how you connect to your domain service.

One other reason I like the `DomainDataSource` control is because both the team and the community are working to come up with better approaches that allow using that control with a ViewModel directly. Yep, using your ViewModel while still taking advantage of most of the coolness of the `DomainDataSource` is on everyone's radar.

The `DomainDataSource` and the underlying domain context objects support updating as well as querying, of course. But before we look at that, it's worth exploring one of the more compelling reasons to use the `DomainDataSource` control: filtering, sorting, grouping, and paging.

17.3 *Filtering, sorting, grouping, and paging*

User interfaces used to be simple to design because user expectations were so low. Character-mode terminals, difficult-to-memorize commands, and complex keystrokes that required keyboard function key overlays[7] were the norm at one point, with some approaches persisting even into the GUI era.

As applications gained more chrome functionality, things such as sorting and grouping became expected functionality. In the mid-'90s, I remember developing applications in Visual Basic, and the users assuming they could do things like sort grids using column headers, drag to rearrange, and so forth. Unfortunately, these assumptions didn't come out until user-acceptance testing.

---

[7] During the '80s and '90s, there was a robust market for keyboard overlays for WordPerfect, WordStar, Lotus 123, and others. Most used the function keys in normal, shift, alt, and control modes, all for different commands.

These days, anything that helps meet the bar for base application functionality (for business applications, this is typically defined by what Microsoft Windows or Microsoft Office does in similar situations) is something I appreciate.

One reason I appreciate the DomainDataSource control is how well it integrates with other client-side controls to allow for filtering, sorting, grouping, and paging of the data. Any of those features, done right and done well, can amount to a fair bit of code and a testing burden.

Consider that you want to ensure they execute server-side for the best performance. You also have to handle the always-troublesome paging algorithms. What happens when users add a new item to a paged set? What happens when they sort? Fortunately, the RIA Services team has made intelligent decisions about behavior in each of these scenarios and implemented them into the code base.

You'll progressively add each of these capabilities—filtering, sorting, grouping, and paging—to the DomainDataSource-based version of your code, starting with filtering.

17.3.1 Filtering

Microsoft Excel and Microsoft SharePoint have brought filtering of table- or grid-based data up to the level of basic functionality for most applications. Proper filtering that performs efficiently isn't a huge effort, but it's a chunk of code that has to be maintained and tested. Having filtering support built in, so that all you need to provide is a filtering UI, is a huge benefit to most applications.

The first step is to create a basic single-field filter UI. Modify the controls in the home page XAML so you have these three controls where the DataGrid alone used to be:

```
<TextBlock Height="23" Width="84" Margin="6,10,0,0"
        HorizontalAlignment="Left" VerticalAlignment="Top"
        Text="Title Contains"
<TextBox x:Name="FilterText" Height="23" Margin="96,6,5,0"
        HorizontalAlignment="Stretch" VerticalAlignment="Top" />
<my:DataGrid x:Name="EmployeeGrid" Grid.Column="0" Margin="0 40 5 5"
            ItemsSource="{Binding Data, ElementName=DataSource}" />
```

This markup creates some space (via the margins on the DataGrid) and fills it with a TextBlock and TextBox that you'll use to gather filter information from the user. Although the DomainDataSource controls are smart enough to be able to filter on any column using a number of different operators, you'll go with a straight contains filter on a single field to keep things simple.

The next step is to wire the filter TextBox, named FilterText, to the data source and specify what field it'll operate on. Before you do that, let's look at how filtering is implemented on the DomainDataSource class.

FILTER DESCRIPTORS EXPLAINED

Filtering is implemented via two properties on the DomainDataSource. The first is the FilterOperator, which can be And or Or and controls how the filter descriptors are combined. The second is the collection of FilterDescriptor objects named, appropriately, FilterDescriptors.

Filter descriptors are discrete filter instructions that may be combined to produce an effective filter for a query. Conceptually, they're applied like a where clause in SQL, although the actual implementation is ultimately up to how the provider implements the composed where functionality in a LINQ query. Table 17.3 shows the properties of the FilterDescriptor class.

Table 17.3 Properties of the `FilterDescriptor` class

Property	Description
IgnoredValue	The value to be used for something like (all), where you don't want any value appended to the filter.
IsCaseSensitive	If true, the filter is case-sensitive for string values. How this works depends on settings in the data store used by the domain service.
Operator	A FilterOperator that explains the relationship between PropertyPath and Value. Supported values are shown in table 17.4.
PropertyPath	The path to the data item to be evaluated against the Value property. This is the property of your entity.
Value	The value to use for the filter condition.

Of these properties, the relationship Property Operator Value is the most interesting and the most relevant to filtering. A number of operators are supported, each of which is described in table 17.4.

Table 17.4 Values for the `Operator` property of the `FilterDescriptor`

Value	Description
IsLessThan	The data value must be smaller than the filter value.
IsLessThanOrEqualTo	The data value must be smaller than or equal to the filter value.
IsEqualTo	The data value must be equal to the filter value.
IsNotEqualTo	The data value must be different from the filter value.
IsGreaterThanOrEqualTo	The data value must be larger than or equal to the filter value.
IsGreaterThan	The data value must be larger than the filter value.
StartsWidth	The data value must start with the filter value (strings only).
EndsWidth	The data value must end with the filter value (strings only).
Contains	The data value must contain the filter value (strings only).
IsContainedIn	The data value must be contained in the filter value (strings only).

It may seem somewhat redundant to list the descriptions for each of these values given their names, but there are three important bits of information to get from this table:

- A pretty comprehensive set of filter operators is available.
- The order of the statement, read left to right, is `Property Operator Value`.
- Some of the operators make sense only on strings, because they perform substring operations.

The reason for the lengthy member names is twofold: you can't have operators like `>=` in XAML without ugly and unreadable escaping like `&gt;=`, and you need an enumeration to set the property in XAML or from code. Primarily, the list is optimized for using from XAML.

Because it's optimized for XAML, you'd think the properties would all support binding—and you'd be right. It's possible to build a complete filter expression using filters created using binding, meaning you can provide the user with a drop-down list of fields, a drop-down list of operators, and a `TextBox` for the value. All six properties of the `FilterDescriptor` class are dependency properties that support binding.

USING FILTER DESCRIPTORS WITH THE DOMAINDATASOURCE

Despite the binding flexibility, you'll implement a simple filter where only the filter value itself is bound. You already have the `TextBox` for the value in place, so the next step is to add the associated `FilterDescriptor` to the `DomainDataSource`. This markup shows the updated filter including the descriptor and `FilterOperator`:

```
<riaControls:DomainDataSource x:Name="DataSource"
                              AutoLoad="True" FilterOperator="And"
                              QueryName="GetEmployees">
    <riaControls:DomainDataSource.DomainContext>
        <domain:EmployeeContext />
    </riaControls:DomainDataSource.DomainContext>
    <riaControls:DomainDataSource.FilterDescriptors>
        <riaControls:FilterDescriptor PropertyPath="Title"
                Operator="Contains"
                Value="{Binding Text, ElementName=FilterText}" />
    </riaControls:DomainDataSource.FilterDescriptors>
</riaControls:DomainDataSource>
```

This markup augments the `DomainDataSource` to add a `FilterDescriptor`. That `FilterDescriptor` targets the `Title` property of the `Employee` entity and checks to see that it contains (using the `Contains` operator) the current value in the `Text` property of the `FilterText` field on the same page.

When run, you'll have an experience like that shown in figure 17.9.

Type in the Title Contains field, and pause for a second or two. The pause will kick in the filter, executing the query on the server and displaying the results in the grid.

By adding just a few lines of XAML, you were able to add property-value filtering (which also works with sorting, grouping, and paging, as you'll see in the next sections) without having to wire up anything at the database level or even the service level. This makes sense. Like all the other features in this section, filtering should be a given for an application; there's little point in each of us implementing the same tired old filtering code again and again. The same goes for sorting, the next topic.

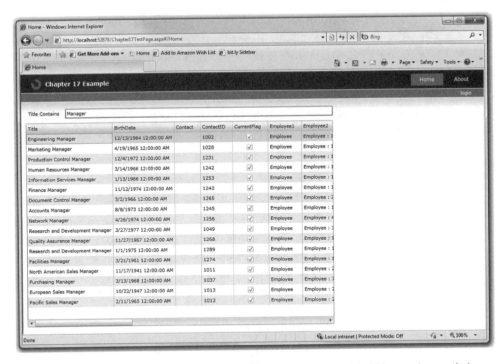

Figure 17.9 Filtering the results to those that contain *Manager* in the title. This was done entirely with the DomainDataSource and a little in-XAML binding.

17.3.2 *Sorting*

You may have already noticed that the DataGrid, when wired to the DomainData-Source (or any other ICollectionView or even IList), provides automatic sorting capabilities when you click column headers. The DomainDataSource also provides a way to perform a default sort on the data using SortDescriptor objects. For instance, to have the data sorted by Title and HireDate by default, you can add the following markup to the inside of the DomainDataSource markup:

```
<riaControls:DomainDataSource.SortDescriptors>
    <riaControls:SortDescriptor Direction="Ascending"
                                PropertyPath="Title" />
    <riaControls:SortDescriptor Direction="Ascending"
                                PropertyPath="HireDate" />
</riaControls:DomainDataSource.SortDescriptors>
```

When you run the application, you'll see that the DataGrid isn't ignorant of the sort. In most applications, when you sort queries in the database, the client has no idea the data was sorted. With the DomainDataSource, the DataGrid is aware. See figure 17.10 for the proof in the column headers.

Of course, you can also sort server-side as part of the query code, as you've seen earlier in this chapter. In either case, sorting is recommended for grouping and required for paging.

Title ▲	HireDate ▲	BirthDate	Contact	ContactID	CurrentFlag
Accountant	3/22/1999 12:00:00 AM	2/4/1966 12:00:00 AM		1246	✓
Accountant	4/9/1999 12:00:00 AM	8/1/1969 12:00:00 AM		1247	✓
Accounts Manager	3/3/1999 12:00:00 AM	8/8/1973 12:00:00 AM		1245	✓

Figure 17.10 Data sorted with the `DomainDataSource`**. Note the column headers.**

17.3.3 Grouping

Supporting grouping is as easy as sorting. Following the trend we've shown so far, grouping is also accomplished through a collection of descriptors. In this case, the descriptors are `GroupDescriptor` objects. For example, if you want to group on `Title`, you add the following XAML to the `DomainDataSource` markup:

```
<riaControls:DomainDataSource.GroupDescriptors>
    <riaControls:GroupDescriptor PropertyPath="Title" />
</riaControls:DomainDataSource.GroupDescriptors>
```

This relies on the previous sort for the grouping to make any sense. As expected, this integrates nicely with the `DataGrid`. Figure 17.11 shows the `DataGrid` control with the new grouping in place.

With the grouping in place, you can still sort using the column headers, but the sort happens within the defined grouping.

The final and perhaps most interesting of the features is the support for paging.

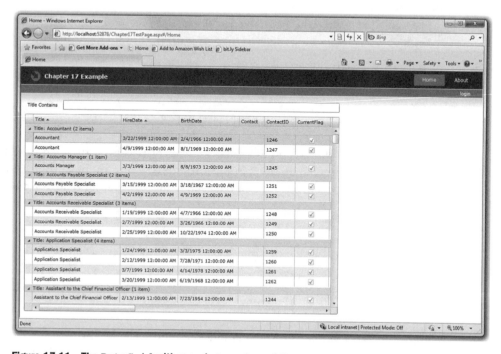

Figure 17.11 The `DataGrid` **with grouping, courtesy of the** `DomainDataSource` **control**

17.3.4 Paging

There currently exist three main UI paradigms for dealing with a large number of records. You can preload everything and allow scrolling, you can implement an *infinite scroll* that performs lazy fetching of additional data (a good example is the Bing image search), or you can use data paging. When the web started to define how we built applications, data paging became the most common way to deal with large volumes of data. After all, if it's good enough for Google, it must be good enough for your application, right?

I've never been a fan of paging, but it certainly has some advantages when it comes to getting a lot of information in front of a user while reducing network traffic and database load.

When you're building RIA Services applications, paging is accomplished with a combination of two items:

- The `PageSize` and `LoadSize` in the `DomainDataSource`
- A `DataPager` control

The `PageSize` property of the `DomainDataSource` controls how many items appear on a single page. The `LoadSize` controls how many items the `DomainDataSource` loads into memory at one time. For example, if you have a `PageSize` of 15 and a `LoadSize` of 30, every other page will cause a network hit to the server to get the next 30 items. Because RIA Services doesn't know the usage pattern of your application, these two knobs are left entirely up to you.

For this example, you'll set the `PageSize` to 15 and the `LoadSize` to 30. The `DomainDataSource` opening tag with these two properties set looks like this:

```
<riaControls:DomainDataSource x:Name="DataSource"
                              PageSize="15"
                              LoadSize="30"
                              AutoLoad="True"
                              FilterOperator="And"
                              QueryName="GetEmployees">
```

The next thing to do is to add a `DataPager` control (easiest if dragged onto the surface or markup) and change the margins on the `DataGrid` to make room at the bottom. The updated `DataGrid` and new `DataPager` markup should read as follows:

```
<my:DataGrid x:Name="EmployeeGrid"
             Grid.Column="0"
             Margin="0 40 5 40"
             ItemsSource="{Binding Data, ElementName=DataSource}" />

<my:DataPager Grid.ColumnSpan="2"
              Source="{Binding Data, ElementName=DataSource}"
              HorizontalAlignment="Stretch"
              VerticalAlignment="Bottom" />
```

With this markup in place, run the application and navigate through the pages. The application, still with sorting and grouping in place, should look like figure 17.12.

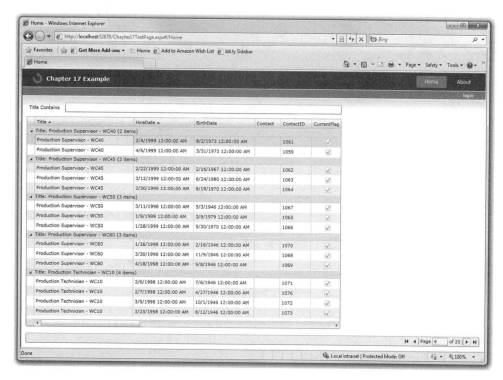

Figure 17.12　The `DataPager` in use with a page size of 15 and a load size of 30

In order to make the most of the `DataPager`, its source must be set to an `IEnumerable` that implements the `IPagedCollectionView` interface, an example of which is the `DomainDataSource` control. The data must also be sorted, either via the query on the server or via sorting specified in the `DomainDataSource`. If the data isn't presorted, you'll get an exception at runtime.

DATAPAGER PROPERTIES

The `DataPager` is a fully templatable control, supporting the lookless model Silverlight and WPF are famous for. In addition, the `DataPager` has a number of properties that control its behavior and appearance.

In addition to helpful utility properties such as `CanMoveToFirstPage` and `Can-MoveToNextPage`, the `DataPager` includes a `DisplayMode` property that is used to control which buttons and boxes are shown in the UI. Table 17.5 shows the different values this property can be set to.

As you can see, the control provides a number of different paging interfaces, covering the gamut typically seen in applications and on the Web. For the ones that show page numbers, you can use the `NumericButtonCount` property to control how many numbers are displayed. In addition, you can use the `AutoEllipsis` property to display an ellipsis, rather than a number, to indicate more pages.

Table 17.5 `DisplayMode` **property values and their associated UI**

Property	Runtime appearance
`FirstLastNumeric`	|◄| 1 2 3 4 5 |►|
`FirstLastPreviousNext`	|◄ ◄	Page 1 of 20	► ►|
`FirstLastPreviousNextNumeric`	|◄ ◄	1 2 3 4 5	► ►|
`Numeric`	1 2 3 4 5
`PreviousNext`	◄	Page 0	►
`PreviousNextNumeric`	◄	1 2 3 4 5	►

The `DomainDataSource` control makes it easy to add common data-browsing capabilities—filtering, sorting, grouping, and paging—to your applications. Combined, these are high-value, high-effort development tasks in most applications. Having the functionality built in saves you from having to reinvent the wheel or tell your customer "no" when the feature is requested (or worse, assumed).

So far, everything you've done has been with read-only data. Real applications typically need to update data as well.

17.4 *Updating data*

Most data-oriented applications have to do more than read data; they need to perform inserts, updates, and deletes as well. In the discussion about the domain service methods, I touched on the three data modification methods that begin with the prefixes `Insert`, `Update`, and `Delete`.

WCF RIA Services makes updating data as easy as retrieval. The domain service methods are trim, and autogenerated for the usual cases. The client-side domain context methods (which we'll cover in 17.4.2) that provide access to those services are also autogenerated.

In this section, you'll start with creating a user interface using the `DataForm` that allows you to update the data in the domain service. We'll then look at the client-side counterpart of the domain service: the domain context. Finally, we'll go through how the entity class and its buddy class with validation and display metadata work together to make it easier to have a robust and feature-rich data container on the client.

17.4.1 Using the DataForm UI

The DataForm, like the DataGrid, is extremely powerful when matched up with WCF RIA Services and the DomainDataSource control. The DataForm, in fact, was originally part of WCF RIA Services before it was pulled out and made part of the Silverlight Toolkit. The DataForm is covered in full in chapter 12, so I won't repeat that content here. But you'll use it to provide the update UI for the entities in this application.

The right side of the page has been empty so far. You've been leaving room for the DataForm in that space. This bit of XAML, to be placed right after the DataGrid element and before the DataPager element, will get you set up for a detail view of the selected item in the grid:

```
<toolkit:DataForm Grid.Column="1"
                  Margin="5 40 0 40"
                  ItemsSource="{Binding Data, ElementName=DataSource}"
                  CurrentItem="{Binding SelectedItem,
                      ElementName=EmployeeGrid, Mode=TwoWay}"/>
```

This sets up a DataForm that uses the same ItemsSource as the DataGrid, so it's also bound to the DomainDataSource control. The CurrentItem property is bound to the DataGrid's selected item, keeping the form in sync with what's shown in the DataGrid. Note that the binding is two-way, so the DataForm navigation controls can be used. Figure 17.13 shows the application with the new addition.

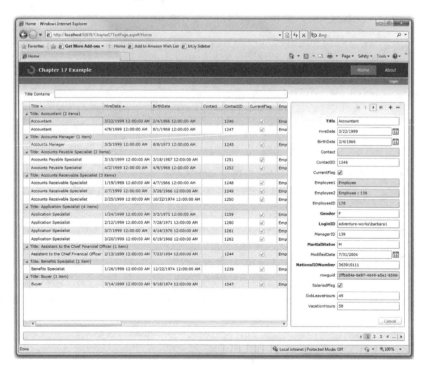

Figure 17.13 The application with the details DataForm on the right, populated from the selected grid item. Row navigation works from both the grid and the DataForm.

Navigate around using the grid and using the navigation buttons at upper right. When you're sure it's all working, you'll wire up the save functionality.

SAVING CHANGES

To submit the changes to the server, you need to have a button wired up to the `SubmitChangesCommand` of the `DomainDataSource`. That command does the equivalent of calling `SubmitChanges` on the domain context from code. Place this right below the `DataForm` markup:

```
<Button x:Name="SubmitChanges"
        Grid.Column="1" Margin="5"
        HorizontalAlignment="Right" VerticalAlignment="Top"
        Height="25" Width="120"
        Command="{Binding SubmitChangesCommand, ElementName=DataSource}"
        Content="Submit Changes" />
```

This adds a Submit Changes button at upper right on the screen. In theory, you have a fully working application at this point; you can perform CRUD[8] operations using the UI. Use the + button to add a new record and the - button to delete the current record. When you're finished, click the new Submit Changes button to call the `SubmitChanges` function behind the scenes. This function, like most everything else in the `DomainDataSource` control, relies on the generated domain context object. In this case, it's the `EmployeeContext`.

17.4.2 *The domain context*

One of the types of classes that's generated based on the domain service is a client-side domain context. The domain context is 1:1 with the domain service. In your solution, for example, you have an `EmployeeService` domain service and an `EmployeeContext` domain context.

In addition to the previously seen query methods, the domain context has a number of properties and methods. The most commonly useful are shown in table 17.6, using `Employee` as the example.

Table 17.6   The properties and methods of the generated domain context class

Member	Description
`CalculateVacationBonus` method	The method generated from your server-side `Invoke` operation
`EntityContainer` property	Internal, but important for holding the actual entities and tracking insert and delete operations
`HasChanges` property	True if the domain context is tracking any entities with changes (updates, inserts, deletes)
`IsLoading` property	True if the domain context is loading data

---

[8] Note that due to the relationship with the `Contact` object and other relationships, deletes and inserts currently fail. Updates work fine. We'll take care of that later in this chapter.

Table 17.6 The properties and methods of the generated domain context class *(continued)*

Member	Description
IsSubmitting property	True if the domain context is submitting changes
RejectChanges method	Rejects all pending changes and reverts objects back to their unedited state
SubmitChanges method	Sends all pending change operations to the domain service for processing

INVOKE OPERATIONS

In this example, a client-side invoke operation was created for the CalculateVacationBonus function you added to the domain service. Because all network calls in Silverlight are asynchronous, you can't call the function and get the result. Instead, you need to set up a callback. For example, listing 17.2 includes the client-side code to call the CalculateVacationBonus function and do something useful with the results.

Listing 17.2 Calling an `invoke` operation from the client

```
private void CalculateBonus()
{
  var context = DataSource.DataContext as EmployeeContext;

  var emp = EmployeeGrid.SelectedItem as Employee;

  if (emp != null)
  {
    DateTime hireDate = new DateTime(2002, 05, 16);          Execute invoke
                                                             operation
    var invokeOp = context.CalculateVacationBonus(   ◁───┘
                     hireDate, OnInvokeCompleted, emp);
  }
}

private void OnInvokeCompleted(InvokeOperation<int> invokeOp)
{
  if (invokeOp.HasError)
  {
    MessageBox.Show(invokeOp.Error.Message);
    invokeOp.MarkErrorAsHandled();
  }
  else
  {
    Employee emp = invokeOp.UserState as Employee;

    if (emp != null)
    {
      emp.VacationHours += (short)invokeOp.Value;
    }
  }
}
```

This code, from the code-behind for Home.xaml, shows how to call an invoke method. Note the parameters to the CalculateVacationBonus client-side method.

On the server, the method took only a single parameter. On the client, it takes that same parameter, plus a callback and a data item. In this case, the data item is the Employee you're working with. You use that because you need access to the Employee inside the callback method.

The callback method executes when the asynchronous call has completed. The single parameter for the callback is an InvokeOperation object with a number of properties, including the UserState and error information.

In this method, you check for an error. If there's no error, you cast the UserState back to an Employee object, check it for null, and then use the function return value (the calculated bonus) and add that to the existing vacation hours. That object is then marked as HasChanges = true on the entity. The entity is then eligible for the Submit-Changes call.

SUBMITCHANGES

Referring back to table 17.6, you'll notice that no Insert, Update, or Delete methods were generated. Instead, those are called via SubmitChanges.

SubmitChanges is an asynchronous batching operation. It handles sending all method calls to the server, with the exception of Invoke and Query operations.

When you insert new items or delete existing items, those operations occur only on the client. When you call SubmitChanges, it loops through the entities on the client and sends to the server those entities that require a persistence operation, calling the appropriate operation for each entity.

To cancel all pending changes for the domain context, call the RejectChanges method. It reverts entities back to their previous state, removes any newly inserted items, and reinstates any deleted items.

The domain context is the client-side proxy for the domain service, as well as the container within which all instances of a given entity reside. It provides an interface for invoke operations and query operations, as well as an implicit interface to the insert, update, and delete operations through the SubmitChanges method.

The entity classes Employee and Contact both inherit from a common client-side base class that provides much of the required change-tracking and other plumbing functionality. This class is named, appropriately enough, Entity.

17.4.3 *The Entity class*

Each client-side entity you work with, Employee and Contact in this example, derives from the Entity base class. This class provides a number of important change-tracking properties and methods.

Table 17.7 shows the most important public members of the Entity base class

Your derivations of the Entity class (the Contact class and the Employee class) also include all the individual properties that correspond to the fields coming from the database. Because this code was generated by the tools and not shared with the server, the properties have INotifyPropertyChanged and several other events injected into them. In this way, your otherwise-plain classes on the server can support binding and

Table 17.7 Important public members of the `Entity` class

Member	Description
EntityState	The data state of this entity: `Detached`, `Unmodified`, `Modified`, `New`, or `Deleted`
HasChanges	Indicates that this entity has changed since the last time it was saved
HasValidationErrors	Indicates that this entity has failed validation
ValidationErrors	Returns a collection of validation errors
GetOriginal	Returns an instance of the unchanged entity from cache

events on the client. To give you an idea of the robustness of the properties set up, listing 17.3 shows the `Gender` property for the `Employee`.

Listing 17.3 The generated client-side `Employee` `Entity` property `Gender`

```
[DataMember()]
[Required()]                          Validation
[StringLength(1)]                     attributes
public string Gender
{
    get
    {
        return this._gender;
    }
    set
    {
        if ((this._gender != value))
        {
            this.OnGenderChanging(value);
            this.RaiseDataMemberChanging("Gender");
            this.ValidateProperty("Gender", value);
            this._gender = value;
            this.RaiseDataMemberChanged("Gender");
            this.OnGenderChanged();
        }
    }
}
```

The setter for the property includes a number of calls to generated methods. Those methods perform validation and take care of `INotifyPropertyChanged` notification as well as raise information events, such as `DataMemberChanging` and `DataMemberChanged`.

In this example, the `OnGenderChanging` and `OnGenderChanged` methods are partial methods that you can implement in a buddy class on the client, should you wish. A *buddy class* is a partial class you create to augment an existing partial class. In this way, you can modify the behavior of the class without introducing an inherited class.

Note the use of attributes to tell the UI that this is a required field with a maximum length of 1. This information was automatically inferred from the entity model on the server at code-generation time. For that reason, changes to the database will require updates to the .edmx model and then automatic downstream updates here.

In addition to the validation and display attributes described in chapters 12 and 13 and shown in this example, a number of other attributes are used in the entity. Although we'll get to how to use the special validation and display metadata attributes in the next section, table 17.8 shows some of the helper attributes you'll likely run across.

Table 17.8   Interesting attributes on the `Employee` Entity

Attribute	Description
DataMember	Indicates that this property should be serialized by WCF and is part of the data contract.
Association	Specifies that the property is part of a relationship, such as a foreign key. You'll find this on the nested entities such as `Contact`.
XmlIgnore	Indicates that this property shouldn't be serialized. Useful on nested entities.
RoundtripOriginal	Sends the object back to the server with its original value when the object is updated, even though this property hasn't changed.
Key	Indicates that this field is part of the primary key.

Seeing the attributes in place provides a little insight into how Silverlight keeps track of various properties. For example, you now know how the client knows that a certain field is the primary key for the entity.

Although the `Entity` class provides extensibility points on the client, it's rare for an application to use them for validation or anything remotely like a business function. Extensions provided on the client can't be used back at the server and so can become a disconnect between the two models. In order to keep the two in sync, the RIA Services team provided a server-side model for extending the entity: metadata.

17.4.4   *Using validation and display metadata*

When you first created the domain service on the server, the wizard offered an option to generate the associated metadata class. This metadata class is a partial class that exists on the server and relates to a single entity. If you open the EmployeeService.metadata.cs file in the server project, you'll see both the `Contact` and `Employee` partial classes.

These partial classes include nested classes with the same public properties that are also defined in the entity classes. Those are just placeholders, providing a location on which you can define metadata to control the display and validation of the fields.

But wait—why am I covering metadata in this section? Because this metadata is useful only if the client understands it. Silverlight and parts of ASP.NET are currently the only clients that can make sense of attribute-based annotation metadata for validation and display.

CONTROLLING DISPLAY

The `DataForm` labels and the `DataGrid` column headers have that ugly PascalCase text formatting. It'd be nicer to introduce actual spaces to make the fields more human-readable. You may even want to provide some tooltip descriptive information for certain fields.

In the EmployeeService.metadata.cs class on the server, scroll down to the `Employee` partial class and the nested `EmployeeMetadata` class within it. Find the `BirthDate` field, and add this attribute:

```
[Display(Name="Birth Date",
         Description="The date this person was born.")]
public DateTime BirthDate { get; set; }
```

That says to use the string "Birth Date" for column headers and field labels; and if a tooltip or other description approach is available, use this description. Figure 17.14 shows how this looks at runtime.

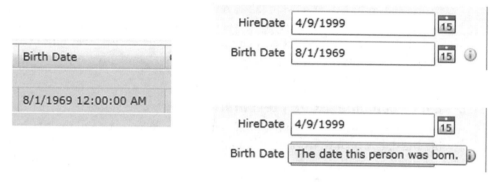

Figure 17.14 The `Display` annotation in use on the `DataGrid` on the left and the `DataForm` on the right. At lower right is the `Description` property in a tooltip.

As you learned in chapter 13, annotations can be used for more than display. One of the more powerful uses is for validation.

ADDING VALIDATION

You get data type validation and the inferred validation (string length, required, and so forth) from the database for free. But you'll typically want to add your own validation to make the UI more bulletproof.

In the EmployeeService.metadata.cs class, scroll down to the `Employee` partial class and the nested `EmployeeMetadata` class within it. Find the `Gender` field, and add this attribute:

```
[RegularExpression("[MmFf]",
                   ErrorMessage="Specify (M)ale or (F)emale, please")]
public string Gender { get; set; }
```

Run the application, and attempt to type something else into the `Gender` field. The regular expression restricts the valid input choices to M, m, F, and f. The metadata entered on the server was automatically carried over to the client. If you open the Chapter17.Web.g.cs file on the client and navigate to the generated `Gender` property, you'll see the addition of the new attribute:

```
[DataMember()]
[RegularExpression("[MFmf]",
                  ErrorMessage="Specify (M)ale or (F)emale, please")]
[Required()]
[StringLength(1)]
public string Gender
...
```

The `StringLength`, `Required`, and `DataMember` attributes were previously there as part of the inferred metadata coming from the data model.[9]

Annotation for display and validation is a nice, easy way to add significant robustness to your classes. Because the information goes into metadata buddy classes, you don't have to worry about the autogeneration process stepping on them.

What you've seen so far is a model where the entity generated by the data access layer, typically based directly on tables or views on the database, makes its way from the database through the service to the client and into the UI. That's okay sometimes, especially when you have good mapping at the data access layer, but an additional layer of abstraction could help protect the UI from changes in the database. That layer is called a *presentation model*.

17.5 *Loose coupling: using presentation models*

So far, you've created a tight coupling between your database and the UI due to bringing the data structure through from back to front. RIA Services enables you to create entities that combine data from multiple entities in the data access layer—for example, combining the `Contact` and `Employee` classes into a single logical entity.

When using a presentation model, you can respond to changes in the database or database model by changing only how the presentation model aggregates that data. Also, you can simplify the client code by designing a model that aggregates only those fields that are relevant to users of the client.

Although conceptually similar, the presentation model here shouldn't be confused with the Presentation Model pattern. The pattern shares some similar goals and approaches, but the RIA Services approach is more server-centric.

I consider the presentation model to be one of the most important additions to WCF RIA Services in terms of making it work with best practices and patterns such as MVVM. As great as RIA Services is without it, it always bothered me that the data model was logically coupling the UI to the services to the data access layer to the database. Change one, and they all have to change—not a good situation to be in.

Ideally, you'd have a good object-persistence mapper that would flatten objects and relationships and handle all this for you, along with the knowledge to use it. That alone would eliminate most uses of the presentation model approach, including the

---

[9] For more information on annotating your classes, look at chapters 12 and 13.

example I'll include in this chapter. In many cases, developers don't have this available to them, or don't have the knowledge required to set up an existing one, or perhaps are further constrained by other business or environmental factors.

The presentation model approach is also good for combining data from multiple sources. You can create a single entity that's composed of fields from multiple databases.

In all of these cases, the presentation model approach can be a huge help.

In this section, you'll take the employee service and model you've been working with and convert (more correctly, rewrite) it to introduce a presentation model. I'll show you how to query data, update data, and insert data using this new model.

17.5.1 *Creating the employee presentation model*

You've been unable to perform insert and update operations on the `Employee` class so far because it's tied to the `Contact` class. This relationship is purely a database thing. It makes little or no sense from an end-user perspective; they're logically part of the same entity. This is a common scenario, because we tend to factor out things such as contact information, address information, and more in the database, and it always causes no end of annoyances at the UI level.

You have two goals in creating an employee presentation model:

- Expose the contact information as first-class fields of a logical employee entity.
- Limit the other fields that are returned to the client.

The first step in creating a presentation model is to create a class named `EmployeePresentationModel` on the server project. Create this class in the server-side Models folder. Listing 17.4 shows the code to use.

Listing 17.4 The `EmployeePresentationModel` class

```
public class EmployeePresentationModel
{
  [Key]
  [Display(AutoGenerateField = false)]
  public int EmployeeID { get; set; }
  [Required]
  public string NationalIDNumber { get; set; }
  [Required]
  public string FirstName { get; set; }
  [Required]
  public string LastName { get; set; }
  [Required]
  public bool NameStyle { get; set; }
  [Display(AutoGenerateField=false)]
  public int ContactID { get; set; }
  [Display(Name="Email Address")]
  public string EmailAddress { get; set; }
  [Required]
  public int EmailPromotion { get; set; }
  public string Phone { get; set; }
  [Required]
  public string Title { get; set; }
```

```
    [Display(Name="Birth Date")]
    public DateTime BirthDate { get; set; }
    [Required]
    [Display(Name = "Hire Date")]
    public DateTime HireDate { get; set; }
    [Required]
    public string LoginID { get; set; }
    [Required]
    public string MaritalStatus { get; set; }
    [Required]
    [StringLength(1)]
    [RegularExpression("[MFmf]",
                ErrorMessage = "Specify (M)ale or (F)emale, please")]
    public string Gender { get; set; }
    [Required]
    public bool SalariedFlag { get; set; }
    [Required]
    public int VacationHours { get; set; }
    [Required]
    public int SickLeaveHours { get; set; }
    [Required]
    public bool CurrentFlag { get; set; }
}
```

In this listing, you create an aggregate `Employee` class that includes fields from both the `Employee` and `Contact` classes you've been using so far. Also, because the metadata is no longer inferred from the database or read using the metadata buddy class you previously created, you add a minimum amount of metadata to ensure that required fields are marked as such and to make a few of the names easier to read.

In your own classes, you'll need to make sure you account for required fields. If you can't infer them when performing an insert or update operation, you'll need to include them in the class so the user can input their values.

This new class now abstracts you from the database. If the structure of the database changes, you can change the query and update operations—the UI won't be affected (assuming it's a structural change, not a change in what defines an employee).

The next step is getting this information down to the client. To do that, you'll need to create at least one query operation and wire it through all the way to the `Domain-DataSource` you've been using.

17.5.2 *Supporting query operations*

The presentation model approach requires a completely new domain service and new query and update operations. The new domain service class will no longer be directly based on the `LinqToEntitiesDomainService` base class, but will instead be based directly on the `DomainService` base class.

For lack of a better name, I called the domain service `EmployeeContactService`, because it aggregates both the `Employee` and `Contact` entities. Create a new class file with this name, and place it in the Services folder on the server project. Listing 17.5 contains the code for this service.

Listing 17.5   The `EmployeeContactService`

```
[EnableClientAccess]
public class EmployeeContactService : DomainService
{
  private AdventureWorksEntities _context = new AdventureWorksEntities();

  public IQueryable<EmployeePresentationModel> GetEmployees()
  {
    return from e in _context.Employees
           orderby e.Title, e.HireDate
           select new EmployeePresentationModel()
           {
             BirthDate = e.BirthDate,
               ContactID = e.ContactID,
             CurrentFlag = e.CurrentFlag,
             EmailAddress = e.Contact.EmailAddress,
             EmailPromotion = e.Contact.EmailPromotion,
             EmployeeID = e.EmployeeID,
             FirstName = e.Contact.FirstName,
             LastName = e.Contact.LastName,
             NameStyle = e.Contact.NameStyle,
             NationalIDNumber = e.NationalIDNumber,
             Phone = e.Contact.Phone,
             SalariedFlag = e.SalariedFlag,
             SickLeaveHours = (int)e.SickLeaveHours,
             Title = e.Title,
             HireDate = e.HireDate,
             Gender = e.Gender,
             VacationHours = (int)e.VacationHours
           };
  }
}
```

The main code in this function performs a standard mapping of properties from two entities to one other. Note that even with the custom methods, you're still able to return `IQueryable` and to allow composition on the client.

WIRING UP TO THE UI

Because you have the same query name as you used in the `EmployeeService` domain service, to use the new service from the UI, you need to make only one change—change the `DomainContext` property of the `DomainDataSource` to point to the `EmployeeContactContext`:

```
<riaControls:DomainDataSource.DomainContext>
    <!--<domain:EmployeeContext />-->
    <domain:EmployeeContactContext />
</riaControls:DomainDataSource.DomainContext>
```

Be sure to build before making this change; otherwise, the `EmployeeContactContext` class won't exist on the client. Note that you didn't have to update any service references or add a new service reference—the WCF RIA Services tooling took care of that for you. That alone is worth the price of admission.

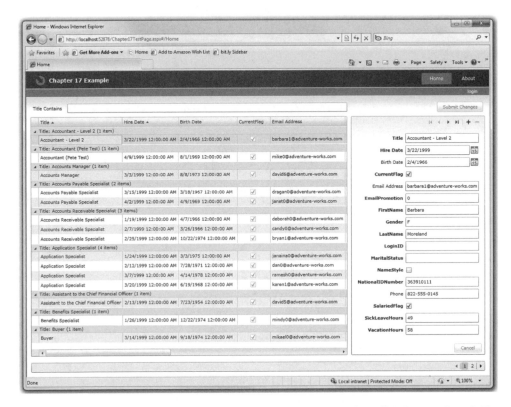

Figure 17.15 The UI using the new `EmployeePresentationModel` class. Note how you have fields from the contact object now available to the UI.

When you run the application, you'll see something like figure 17.15. The new UI has fewer fields and looks a lot better than what you had before.

You have a lot fewer fields in the UI now. Some, like Birth Date, which have had the `Display` attribute applied, have better labels and column headers. You could set the display name for the remaining ones, and the display order, as well using the same attribute. For space reasons, I didn't include the attributes in the listings here.

The presentation model approach certainly works in this situation. It's not meant just for flattening objects, although you can use it for that. It also shines in situations where you need to do joins in LINQ and combine the results into a single logical object.

Retrieval is fine for a demo, but the real test comes when you need to use this information in an update operation.

17.5.3 *Supporting update operations*

To perform an update using the presentation model approach, you'll need to map from the presentation model class to the back to the entities used in the backing store. Essentially, you're doing the reverse of what you did in the query operation.

Listing 17.6 shows how to map from the presentation model back to the database entities.

Listing 17.6 The `UpdateEmployee` method

```
private void MapEmployee(Employee emp, EmployeePresentationModel
            employeePM)
{
    emp.BirthDate = employeePM.BirthDate;
    emp.CurrentFlag = employeePM.CurrentFlag;
    emp.Contact.EmailAddress = employeePM.EmailAddress;
    emp.Contact.EmailPromotion = employeePM.EmailPromotion;
    emp.Contact.FirstName = employeePM.FirstName;
    emp.Contact.LastName = employeePM.LastName;
    emp.Contact.NameStyle = employeePM.NameStyle;
    emp.Contact.Phone = employeePM.Phone;
    emp.NationalIDNumber = employeePM.NationalIDNumber;
    emp.SalariedFlag = employeePM.SalariedFlag;
    emp.SickLeaveHours = (short)employeePM.SickLeaveHours;
    emp.Title = employeePM.Title;
    emp.HireDate = employeePM.HireDate;
    emp.Gender = employeePM.Gender;
    emp.VacationHours = (short)employeePM.VacationHours;
    emp.MaritalStatus = employeePM.MaritalStatus;
    emp.LoginID = employeePM.LoginID;
}                                                        Get current
                                                         persisted entity
[Update]
public void UpdateEmployee(EmployeePresentationModel employeePM)
{
    Employee emp = _context.Employees.
                Where(e => e.EmployeeID == employeePM.EmployeeID)
                .FirstOrDefault();

    MapEmployee(emp, employeePM);

    EmployeePresentationModel original =
                this.ChangeSet
                .GetOriginal<EmployeePresentationModel>(employeePM);

    if (original.CurrentFlag != employeePM.CurrentFlag ||
        original.EmailAddress != employeePM.EmailAddress ||
        original.EmailPromotion != employeePM.EmailPromotion ||
        original.FirstName != employeePM.FirstName ||
        original.LastName != employeePM.LastName ||
        original.NameStyle != employeePM.NameStyle ||
        original.Phone != employeePM.Phone)
    {
        emp.Contact.ModifiedDate = DateTime.Now;
    }                                               Save to
    _context.SaveChanges();                         database
}
```

You're definitely in manual-plumbing land at this point. Of course, if you want to have separation between two layers, you'll have some mapping. Here, the mapping is in a reusable function so the Insert method can use it. Note how you check the original employee to see if there were any changes before setting the modified date for the Contact object. You'll want to do the same for the Employee object; I left that out for space considerations.

The code you write in this function will be pretty dependent on your choice of data access layer. The code here works well with the Entity Framework objects.

The next type of operation you'll need to support is the insertion of new objects. This one can get tricky due to the creation of dependent entities and the generation of keys.

17.5.4 *Supporting insert operations*

Update operations are easy, because you often don't have to worry much about entity relationships or foreign keys. Insert operations usually have a few extra steps to perform in addition to the mapping.

Listing 17.7 shows the InsertEmployee function. This function makes use of the MapEmployee function from the previous listing.

Listing 17.7 The `InsertEmployee` function

```
[Insert]
public void InsertEmployee(EmployeePresentationModel employeePM)
{
    Contact contact = _context.Contacts.CreateObject();
    Employee emp = _context.Employees.CreateObject();
    emp.Contact = contact;

    MapEmployee(emp, employeePM);

    contact.ModifiedDate = DateTime.Now;
    contact.rowguid = Guid.NewGuid();
    contact.PasswordHash = "Adventure";
    contact.PasswordSalt = "xyzzy";

    emp.ModifiedDate = DateTime.Now;
    emp.rowguid = Guid.NewGuid();

    _context.Contacts.AddObject(contact);
    _context.Employees.AddObject(emp);

    _context.SaveChanges();
}
```

This function creates the Contact and Employee data entities and sets the contact to be the contact for the Employee. It then calls the MapEmployee function from the previous listing to map the presentation model properties to the data entity properties. The next step is to set a few fields; the password-related fields here are dummies, but the modified date fields are correct. The last step before saving changes is to add the Contact and Employee to the entity sets. Finally, with a call to SaveChanges, the information all goes in the database.

I've included the query, update, and insert methods. For space reasons, I left out delete. This is a pretty simple function to build following the pattern established by the code included here.

The presentation model approach allows you to continue to benefit from WCF RIA Services while also benefitting from the increased decoupling of the layers. Although the database-through-UI coupling won't be a problem for many applications, for anything expected to survive into a maintenance mode, it can be a real pain.

The presentation model approach isn't without its issues. First, you have to write more CRUD operation code, including mapping. This code has a habit of getting out of sync; it's also a great place to find typos and copy-paste errors. When using this approach, I highly recommend building tests around your mapping functions and keeping them up to date.

So far, you've seen normal CRUD operations and simple validation. I threw in one business function for calculating a vacation bonus, but otherwise you haven't seen any real business logic. The next section covers how to include this critical code in a RIA Services application.

17.6 *Business logic*

A business application without business logic is just a forms-over-data maintenance application. Although apps like that are easy to build using WCF RIA Services, they're not the usual case.

Business logic usually consists of discrete functions that implement discrete rules. Some may come in the form of validation, others may look like calculated fields, and still others may be helper methods that return a current piece of data from an external system.

There are several places where you can put logic in your code. I've tried to capture some general guidelines in table 17.9.

Table 17.9 Where to put your business logic

Type	Location
Data validation	Attributes on metadata or entities.
Field validation rule	Noncritical: custom validators.
	Critical: code in domain methods on the domain service. Prevent persistence if criteria aren't met.
External data access	Domain methods on the server calling out to web services.
	Services classes on the client, if the result won't be required for server-side validation.
	Shared code services proxy or shared binary.
Calculated field	If self-contained within the entity, as an additional property of the entity.
	If requires integration with other data or services, as a method on the domain service or shared code or a binary file.

Table 17.9   Where to put your business logic *(continued)*

Type	Location
General calculation or business logic	As a method on the domain service if a server round-trip is okay or required. As a method in shared code or a binary file if needed on the client and server with local calculation for speed.
On insert/update logic	In the Insert/Update method in the domain service.
Reusable logic shared between projects	Domain service. Shared code or binary file.
Anything else	Shared code or binary file.

You've already seen how to write methods on the domain service. In the previous chapter, we also looked at how to write business services on the client. In this section, we'll look at how to place logic in entities as well as how to share logic or code between the client and server.

17.6.1 *Business logic in entities*

When a calculated field is part of the business logic for your application, one place you can place it is directly on the entity. This makes sense if the data required for the calculation exists on the entity itself. If the data is external, consider making the calculation a service that you call to get the results.

A reasonable type of calculation might be, for example, one to take into account your start date and how many vacation hours you have when deciding if you can go in the hole to take a longer vacation than you would've been allowed to take if going strictly by the book.

Going back to the original generated classes, add the function in listing 17.8 to the `Employee` class using a new file named Employee.shared.cs stored in the \Shared folder on the web project.

Listing 17.8   An example business method on the `Entity` class

```
using System;

namespace Chapter17.Web
{
  public partial class Employee
  {
    public int AllowedOverdraftVacationHours
    {
      get
      {
        DateTime today = DateTime.Today;

        int yearsInService = today.Year - HireDate.Year;

        if (HireDate.AddYears(yearsInService) > today)
          yearsInService--;
```

```
        if (yearsInService < 1)
          return 0;
        else if (yearsInService < 5)
          return 20;
        else
          return 40;
      }
    }
  }
}
```

The example in listing 17.8 performs a simple calculation. The key thing to note is that it's using information already available as part of the parent class. I don't recommend this approach if external information is required.

17.6.2 *Sharing code*

So far, you've put all the business logic into methods of the domain service or used it as a property of the entity. The domain service is a great place to put logic you want accessible to the client or server but executed on the server. For methods that match, including them on the entity class is a great idea. Sharing code and controlling where it executes is important.

SHARED SOURCE FILES

In the previous example, you saw how the code went into a file with the .shared.cs extension. That naming is a convention understood by RIA Services. Anything with a .shared.cs name is copied to the client on build as part of the code-generation process. As long as you keep the namespaces clean, this provides an easy way to share classes between the tiers.

LINKED SOURCE FILES

Visual Studio has long had the capability to link source files from one project to another. As long as the contained source code (including namespace-using statements) is compatible across both projects, it'll work fine.

This is source-level sharing. I've used it with WCF applications and also when dual-targeting Silverlight and WPF. Just consider one project the master, and add the file to it. Then, choose Add Existing Item in the other project, navigate to the source, and click the Add drop-down button so you can add a link. As my favorite black-helmeted villain would say, "All too easy."

SHARED BINARIES

Silverlight 4 along with .NET 4 introduced another option for sharing: .NET 4 applications can add references to a Silverlight class library, as long as that class library uses only certain namespaces. The allowable references and namespaces are strict but are likely to expand over time.

I've never been a big fan of this approach, because it feels a little dirty to me. But for this type of use, it should be perfectly acceptable.

Conceptually, one of the most important pieces of business logic for any given application is often its security model. Business applications must be able to secure data and functions in a way that integrates with existing web sites and systems without requiring yet another mechanism for maintaining security for the application.

17.7   *Authentication and authorization*

Authentication is the process of identifying a user. *Authorization* is the process of granting the user access to parts of the system. Business applications almost always require some form or authentication and typically lock down critical functions using an authorization scheme. It's a rare system indeed where every user has complete access to every function. But until RIA Services came along to help with this, implementing security in Silverlight applications was a difficult process at best.

WCF RIA Services authentication is built on ASP.NET authentication and membership. I won't go into great detail on how to configure ASP.NET, but any tutorial on ASP.NET membership and authentication configuration will apply here.

The Silverlight Business Application template includes much of the authentication infrastructure built in. Normally, you'd have to add in the authentication domain service and the appropriate entity classes. Fortunately, those are all there, just waiting to be activated.

In this section, we'll look through the authentication and authorization capabilities of ASP.NET, surfaced through WCF RIA Services. We'll examine the UI and services that the template provides and that build on the RIA Services libraries. Throughout, we'll look at both forms-based authentication and Windows authentication.

17.7.1 *Authentication*

Authenticating users usually involves getting their user name and some sort of secret password (or PIN or biometric data), and comparing the pair against data stored in the database. Figure 17.16 shows the built-in Login dialog that comes with the Silverlight Business Application template.

The dialog is wired up to the `AuthenticationService` on the web site, which in turn uses ASP. NET membership. It also includes an appropriate validation display for incorrect username and password combinations. Figure 17.17 shows this view.

Figure 17.16   The Login dialog in the Silverlight Business Application template. Note the registration link on the left.

Figure 17.17   The Login dialog when an incorrect password was entered

There are two ways of validating this information in a RIA Services application: forms-based authentication and Windows authentication.

FORMS-BASED AUTHENTICATION

Forms-based authentication (FBA) is cookie-based authentication in ASP.NET. Almost any ASP.NET web site with an on-page login form is using a form of forms-based authentication. Rather than relying on system tokens and security credentials provided by the operating system, each site or application can store user information in a database. For the vast majority of applications running outside the firewall, this is the way security is handled.

To configure the users and roles for an application using FBA, you'll use the ASP.NET application configuration site. This site writes to the aspnetdb database (or other database if so configured) where the membership data is stored. More often than not, this database is located in the App_Data folder on the ASP.NET site.

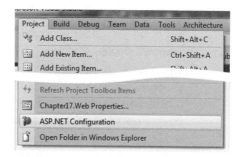

To configure this application, select the web project and choose the ASP.NET Configuration option from the Project menu. Figure 17.18 shows the menu you'll see.

You can create new users through the administration site. In addition, the Silverlight Business Application template includes a self-service registration UI (which you can disable if you desire) for allowing self-registration of users. This form, shown in figure 17.19, is wired up through the UserRegistrationService on the server.

Figure 17.18 The Project menu showing the ASP.NET Configuration option selected. This is the option used to configure the authentication database. If you don't see it, make sure the right project is selected.

Figure 17.19 The Register dialog in the Silverlight Business Application template. For most business applications, you'll secure or eliminate this dialog.

Configuring the site and application to use FBA is a two-step process. The first step is to open the web.config file and ensure that the authentication mode is set to Forms:

```
<authentication mode="Forms">
  <forms name=".Chapter17_ASPXAUTH" />
</authentication>
```

The second step is to open App.xaml.cs and check the constructor to ensure the Authentication property of the web context is set to FormsAuthentication:

```
webContext.Authentication = new FormsAuthentication();
```

With those two options set and a user created, you're ready to try out the application. Try logging in via the link on the main page. You'll see the UI change to indicate your login name, and the credential information itself will be available throughout the application.

Although FBA is the most common form of authentication, we can't forget good old Windows authentication.

WINDOWS AUTHENTICATION

Windows authentication relies on the Windows operating system and security infrastructure to provide the appropriate authentication scheme and tokens. For behind-the-firewall systems, Windows authentication is usually the better approach because there's no separate login process. Instead, the Silverlight application participates in single sign-on (SSO) along with other applications on the client.

To configure the application to use Windows authentication, first set the authentication mode in web.config:

```
<authentication mode="Windows" />
```

Then, in the App.xaml.cs file, modify the constructor to set the authentication to Windows:

```
webContext.Authentication = new WindowsAuthentication();
```

The business application template has startup logic that attempts to automatically resolve the credentials of the signed-in user. You'll find with WindowsAuthentication that a second or two after the application launches, you're greeted with your credentials in the upper-right corner. No Login dialog required!

REQUIRING AUTHENTICATION

Regardless of which approach you use (forms or Windows), you can require authentication from code or via attributes. On a domain service, it's easy to mark a single method as requiring a valid user account by applying the RequiresAuthentication attribute:

```
[Insert]
[RequiresAuthentication]
public void InsertEmployee(EmployeePresentationModel employeePM)
```

Technically, this falls under authorization because you're granting access based on security. But the authorization system is even more powerful than this.

17.7.2 *Authorization*

When you authorize users, you're granting them permission to perform an action. Authorization comes in many forms: client-side code can check to see whether users are authenticated, as well as whether they're members of a specific role; and server-side code or attributes can grant access to individual service methods.

The usual approach when working with authorization in ASP.NET and in RIA Services is to use role-based authorization. This is especially useful with forms-based authentication, because the roles can be configured using the same ASP.NET administration application.

ROLE-BASED AUTHORIZATION

Although you could enable access to individual features on a user-by-user basis, role-based authorization is by far the most common way to grant access. In this model, users belong to roles, such as Manager, Administrator, or HR, and individual permissions are granted to the roles.

To enable roles in the RIA Services application, ensure that the `roleManager` entry in web.config is set to true:

```
<roleManager enabled="true" />
```

When that setting is confirmed and you've created some users and added them to appropriate roles, you can start to modify the application to look for those roles. The easiest and most powerful check you can make is on the service methods on the domain service. This is done via the `RequiresRole` attribute:

```
[Insert]
[RequiresRole("Manager")]
public void InsertEmployee(EmployeePresentationModel employeePM)
```

The `RequiresRole` attribute takes in one or more role names as strings. When the client attempts to access the service method, the server consults the security tokens provided and checks to see whether the user has the correct role. If the user isn't a member of that role, the service call results in an exception, which you must trap on the client.

You must handle this exception and gracefully inform the user that access isn't allowed. When using the `DomainDataSource` control, you do this in the `LoadedData` event:

```
private void DataSource_LoadedData(object sender, LoadedDataEventArgs e)
{
  if (e.HasError)
  {
    if (e.Error is DomainOperationException &&
        e.Error.Message.Contains("denied"))
    {
      MessageBox.Show("Insufficient permissions for operation. Nyah!");
      e.MarkErrorAsHandled();
    }
  }
}
```

In the case of the `EmployeeContactService`, you require the Manager role for both the `Insert` and `Update` methods and `RequiresAuthentication` for the query method. For methods tagged with `RequiresRole`, you don't need to also add `RequiresAuthentication`; it's assumed in the role check.

The second way to check for authorization is to use the client-side `WebContext` object. This is useful to enable/disable menu options and buttons, as well as to perform client-side checks. Don't rely on this as your only security check, though, because you always want the server to be secured.

Here's a simple security check in the code-behind:

```
if (WebContext.Current.User.IsInRole("Manager"))
    SubmitChanges.Visibility = Visibility.Visible;
else
    SubmitChanges.Visibility = Visibility.Collapsed;
```

I put this in the `OnNavigatedTo` handler, but that's not the best place. Instead, you want to reevaluate any UI changes like this whenever the user logs in or logs out.

WCF RIA Services makes it easy to integrate authentication and authorization into your own application. Because it builds on ASP.NET membership and security, you know it's using a well-known and time-tested approach, which is already supported by the community.

17.8   Summary

I hope I've given you a taste of what WCF RIA Services can help you accomplish. Despite the depth of this chapter, we've just scratched the surface. RIA Services supports transactions and concurrency schemes with conflict resolution; and it supports composed entities where master-detail relationships can be saved in one chunk. There are many more attributes that can be used, and variations on the domain services.

RIA Services is big. Although associated with Silverlight, it's a product in and of itself. In this chapter we've looked at the business application template and used it as the basis for developing a RIA Services application. We then dove right into the WCF-based domain services both to expose the data via OData, JSON, and SOAP, as well as via the native approach with Silverlight. The domain service included all the usual CRUD (Create, Read, Update, Delete) operations, plus the ability to support arbitrary functions.

We also looked at the sometimes controversial `DomainDataSource` control, and its amazing support for filtering, sorting, grouping, and paging. This control saves a ton of time and a large amount of code.

The `DomainDataSource` and the domain service combined to help us update data. The natural UI counterpart to all this was the `DataForm` control. In fact, using the `DataForm`, the `DomainDataSource`, and the generated domain service, you had a complete CRUD UI with no code at all.

One unfortunate side effect of all that was a tight coupling of the entities from the database all the way through to the UI. Although it requires some extra effort, WCF

RIA Services has an answer for this coupling in the presentation model approach. In that, you have to create entities and the domain service from scratch, but once done, everything else "just works."

What about business logic? You can put your business logic inside invoke methods on a domain service, as methods added to the partial class for the entity, and as shared code that can be downloaded to the client as part of the build process. Not to mention that you can use the standard Silverlight-supported approaches of shared source or shared binaries.

Finally, I've yet to see a serious business application that didn't include authentication and authorization of some sort. No one wants to leave data-oriented applications open for anyone to mess around with. Silverlight and WCF RIA Services can take advantage of the security models in ASP.NET, building on proven technologies and knowledge you may already possess.

All this combines to be an intense and robust platform for building business applications—and it's only at version 1!

These last few chapters have been interesting and hopefully useful, but pretty heads-down on the business side of things. In the next chapter, we'll take a break from virtual number crunching and dive into the vector graphics system and pixel shaders.

Part 3

Completing the experience

In Silverlight, developers are often exposed to tasks that used to be delegated solely to design staff. Graphics, animation, behaviors, styles, and templates are all the domain of the designer and integrator but are crucial for the developer to understand in order to work effectively with them. We'll even take a look at creating your own controls that build upon the templating system.

Additionally, media features are often an additional component of larger applications. In these chapters you'll learn how to integrate the various types of video and audio media as well as work directly with bitmap-based images.

We'll wrap up this part, and the book as a whole, with a discussion about an often overlooked part of our projects: the plug-in and application installation experiences. You'll learn how to handle situations where the user doesn't have Silverlight installed as well as how to create application preloaders.

Graphics and effects 18

This chapter covers

- Creating basic shapes and geometries
- Painting with brushes
- Working with effects
- Creating pixel shader effects

In previous chapters, you've seen interesting controls that include text, rectangles, and sometimes even more complex shapes. Even the lowly button, for example, has text, a couple of rectangles, and a gradient background. Controls such as the pop-up `ChildWindow` control have drop shadows to enhance their appearance and help them stand out in the eyes of the user. Those buttons and other controls use vector graphics, brushes, and effects.

Graphics within Silverlight are vector-based; they're mathematically based objects. They're ideal for Internet distribution because vector-based graphics can be condensed to a smaller file size than their raster counterparts for images larger than a thumbnail.

Vector-based graphics are more than eye candy—they're an extension to accessibility. In traditional application environments, users with diminished eyesight generally have to squint to absorb visual content such as text and icons. Through scalability, these same users can fully enjoy your application with ease. Vector graphics retain full fidelity when scaled up, something you can't say about bitmap images. Vectors actually *improve* in quality when scaled up.

Silverlight also includes rich support for effects to help make your elements and graphics stand out. The built-in drop shadow and blur effects have endless uses throughout the application. When you want to do something more than a shadow or a blur, there's also the ability to create your own pixel shader effects, just as you can in WPF and DirectX/XNA.

Throughout this chapter, you'll see the expanse of graphical capabilities within Silverlight. We'll start by discussing the most primitive shapes such as lines, rectangles, and ellipses. After discussing the concept of geometries, we'll lead you down a new path and show you how to paint shapes and alter the way in which they're rendered. From there, you'll add a little effect to your elements before venturing into the sometimes arcane world of custom pixel shaders.

18.1   *Shapes*

Shapes are probably the most regularly used elements when creating an illustration because a Shape is the common basis for the Line, Rectangle, and other Shape elements, which you'll see shortly. Each Shape is painted by two fundamental Brush elements. (Brushes are discussed later.) The first Brush, called Stroke, defines the outline of a Shape. The second Brush, called Fill, describes how everything inside the boundary of the Shape should be painted. It's possible to create a Shape without specifying the Stroke and Fill properties, but if you don't specify the Stroke or Fill, you'll basically paint an invisible shape.

Throughout this section, we'll build on the concept of an abstract Shape to create concrete visual elements. A lot of these visual elements will resemble shapes you learned on *Sesame Street*, and some of these shapes will be a bit more complex. Table 18.1 provides a list of the shapes we'll discuss.

Table 18.1   The Shape objects available within Silverlight

Element	Description
Line	A thin, continuous mark that connects two points
Ellipse	In layman's terms, a circle that can be stretched vertically or horizontally
Path	A collection of connected curves and lines
Polygon	A series of connected lines that make a closed shape
Polyline	A series of connected straight lines
Rectangle	A four-sided plane with four corners

The following sections describe each Shape listed in the table in greater detail. The shapes are described in order of relative complexity. The Path element is part of a more general category that'll be covered later in this chapter. First, you'll learn about the most rudimentary shape, the Line.

18.1.1 *Lines*

A Line is, obviously, a continuous line that connects two end points. Listing 18.1 shows a basic line between two points and the XAML used to define it.

> **Listing 18.1   A basic Line in black**

Result:

XAML:

```
<Canvas x:Name="myCanvas" Height="20" Width="50">
  <Line Stroke="Black" X1="10" Y1="10" X2="30" Y2="30" />
</Canvas>
```

Four double-precision floating-point properties (X1, Y1, X2, Y2) specify the x and y coordinate pairs that define the beginning and ending points of the Line. Without these properties, your Line will be little more than a figment of your imagination.

Interestingly, these coordinates don't represent an absolute position. They specify a *relative position* within the coordinate space of the containing layout panel. Note that, although Silverlight won't automatically define the endpoints of a Line, the coordinate space of the containing layout panel may be automatically created. Regardless, the values of the coordinates represent pixel values, whether absolute or relative positioning is used.

The Canvas used in listing 18.1 has a specific area. But, as described in chapter 7, some layout panels provide a more dynamic layout environment. For instance, if this Line were the second element defined within a StackPanel, it could end up in a potentially undesirable location because the coordinates within a Line element specify a relative position.

18.1.2 *Rectangle*

A Rectangle does exactly what its name implies—it defines a rectangle. The Rectangle in Silverlight provides one interesting tidbit that we'll discuss after listing 18.2, which shows the basic syntax of a Rectangle.

> **Listing 18.2   A basic Rectangle in black with no fill**

Result:

XAML:

```
<Rectangle Stroke="Black" Width="104" Height="64"
  Canvas.Left="8"  Canvas.Top="8"/>
```

This example shows an archetypal `Rectangle`. The key properties involved in the definition of the element are `Width` and `Height`. Collectively, these `double` properties assist in creating the boundary of the `Rectangle`. You can determine the area of the `Shape` by multiplying these two property values. (This nostalgic mathematical fact isn't the interesting tidbit alluded to earlier.)

The `Rectangle` element exposes two properties, `RadiusX` and `RadiusY`, which empower you to easily round off the corners of any `Rectangle`. Before you see an example of this, consider how difficult this task would be in traditional HTML. Although there are several options, the most straightforward involves importing an image. Examine the XAML in listing 18.3, and note how simple it is to implement this elegant feature.

Listing 18.3   A `Rectangle` with rounded corners

Result:

XAML:

```
<Rectangle Stroke="Black" Width="104" Height="64"
  Canvas.Left="8" Canvas.Top="8" RadiusX="10" RadiusY="10"/>
```

The `RadiusX` and `RadiusY` double-precision floating-point properties allow you to set the radius of the ellipse used to round off the corners of the `Rectangle`. (You'll see the `Ellipse` element in two shakes of a pup's tail.) By lopsidedly setting the `RadiusX` and `RadiusY` properties, you can give a `Rectangle` a bulging look, as shown in listing 18.4.

Listing 18.4   A bulging `Rectangle`

Result:

XAML:

```
<Rectangle Stroke="Black" Width="104" Height="64"
  Canvas.Left="8"  Canvas.Top="8" RadiusX="15" RadiusY="50"/>
```

The bulging `Rectangle` is a fun little option. But occasionally, you may need a fully rounded shape. This is where the `Ellipse` comes into play.

18.1.3 *Ellipse*

An `Ellipse` defines a basic circular shape. Listing 18.5 shows a basic `Ellipse` and the XAML used to define it.

Listing 18.5   The syntax and look of a basic `Ellipse`

Result:

XAML:

```
<Ellipse Stroke="Black" Width="104" Height="64"
  Canvas.Left="8" Canvas.Top="8"/>
```

The `Ellipse` doesn't provide any properties that distinguish it from the `Rectangle`. The difference lies in how the two `Shape` elements are rendered. It's important to recognize that Silverlight provides this type of `Shape` for your graphical needs—if for nothing else than to know that you can draw a circle. Now, let's move on to something a little more interesting: the `Polyline`.

18.1.4   Polyline

What if you need to create an application that represents an EKG (or ECG) monitor? How do you go about displaying the electrical impulses projected by a heart? Or, perhaps you need to create a line chart that represents sales or financial trends. These types of scenarios can entail large amounts of data that may be best illustrated through intricate line-art drawings.

You could use several `Line` elements, but this could prove to be cumbersome. The `Polyline` provides a nice alternative that allows you to create a series of connected line pieces using a single element. Listing 18.6 shows a `Polyline` in action.

Listing 18.6   A `Polyline`

Result:

XAML:

```
<Polyline Stroke="Black"
  Points="10,50 20,40 23,44 25,49 40,12 46,50 51,42 55,50" />
```

The `Polyline` uses a space-delimited list of coordinate pairs to define the line drawn. Although each coordinate pair in this example contains integer values, each value represents a `Point`. A `Point` is represented in the form of *[X-Coordinate],[Y-Coordinate]*. Collectively, all these `Point` elements are stored in the `Points` property. In being consistent with the `Line`, each `Point` within the list is relative to the containing layout panel.

18.1.5   Polygon

The `Polygon` goes one step beyond the `Polyline` by ensuring that the `Shape` is always closed. A `Polyline` creates an open `Shape`, whereas a `Polygon` always draws a closed `Shape`. Listing 18.7 shows a basic trapezoid created with a `Polygon`.

Listing 18.7   A Polygon

Result:

XAML:

```
<Polygon Stroke="Black" Points="10,40 20,10 60,10 70,40 10,40" />
```

Like the sibling `Polyline`, the `Polygon` also utilizes the `Points` property. This property works in a manner similar to the `Points` property of the `Polyline`; but regardless of your selected coordinates, the `Polygon` always draws a closed shape.

Listing 18.8 shows a `Polyline` and a `Polygon` using the same coordinates to illustrate how Silverlight renders them.

Listing 18.8   An open shape (Polyline) compared to a closed shape (Polygon)

Result:

XAML:
```
<Polyline                              <Polygon
   Stroke="Black"                         Stroke="Black"
   Fill="White"                            Fill="White"
   Points="10,40 20,10 60,10 70,40"     Points="10,40 20,10 60,10 70,40"
/>                                      />
```

The available shapes provide a lot of flexibility to give your users valuable graphical experiences. Occasionally, your requirements may exhaust the abilities of the various shapes. A `Geometry` is a much more versatile option that can address the inadequacies of a `Shape`.

18.2   *Geometry*

At first, a `Geometry` seems similar to a `Shape` because they both describe 2D shapes. Unlike `Shape` elements, `Geometry` objects aren't `UIElement` entities. `UIElement` objects have an intrinsic ability to render themselves and expose graphical properties, such as `Opacity`, that `Geometry` objects don't have. Why, then, would you consider using a `Geometry`? Well, a `Geometry` allows you to do the following:

- Define a geometric shape. For example, imagine creating a user-based rating system. In this scenario, you may want to use a set of five-pointed stars to rate an item. Although a star isn't a predefined shape, you could create this element using a `Geometry`.
- Define a region for clipping. Clipping is used to limit the visible area of another object.
- Define a region that can be used for hit-testing.

These compelling reasons make examining the Geometry object a worthwhile endeavor. A Geometry is an abstract concept. In fact, you can't deliberately create just a Geometry. Instead, you must rely on the geometrical concepts spread across three basic categories: simple, path, and composite geometries.

18.2.1 Simple geometries

A *simple geometry* reflects some of the primitive geometrical shapes that you've already seen. Simple geometries—such as LineGeometry, RectangleGeometry, and Ellipse-Geometry—are provided to help you illustrate lines, rectangles, and circles.

A LineGeometry illustrates the geometry of a basic line. Listing 18.9 shows how to draw a line using a LineGeometry element. The example also shows what the same markup would look like if you used the basic Line Shape described earlier.

Listing 18.9   Comparison between Line and LineGeometry

Result:

Path XAML:
```
<Path Stroke="Black" StrokeThickness="1" >
  <Path.Data>
    <LineGeometry StartPoint="8,8" EndPoint="72,72" />
  </Path.Data>
</Path>
```

Line XAML:
```
<Line X1="8" Y1="8" X2="72" Y2="72"
  StrokeThickness="1" Stroke="Black" />
```

From this example, you can see that using the Line Shape XAML is much more compact. But you can use also Geometry objects for clipping and hit-testing.

In addition to the LineGeometry, a RectangleGeometry is also provided. The RectangleGeometry defines the geometry of a rectangle. Listing 18.10 shows how to create a rectangle using a RectangleGeometry and also provides the corresponding definition with the Rectangle Shape.

Listing 18.10   A RectangleGeometry compared to a Rectangle

Result:

Path XAML:
```
<Path Fill="Navy" Stroke="Black" StrokeThickness="1">
  <Path.Data>
    <RectangleGeometry Rect="8,8,64,64" />
```

```
    </Path.Data>
</Path>
```

Rectangle XAML:

```
<Rectangle Stroke="Black" StrokeThickness="1" Height="64"
  Width="64" Canvas.Top="8" Canvas.Left="8" Fill="Navy">
</Rectangle>
```

Like the `Rectangle Shape`, the `RectangleGeometry` also supports corner-rounding via the `RadiusX` and `RadiusY` properties. Finally, we'll review the `EllipseGeometry` for the sake of completeness (see listing 18.11).

Listing 18.11   An `EllipseGeometry` compared to an `Ellipse`

Result:

Path XAML:

```
<Path Fill="Navy" Stroke="Black" StrokeThickness="1">
  <Path.Data>
    <EllipseGeometry Center="40,40" RadiusX="36" RadiusY="36" />
  </Path.Data>
</Path>
```

Elipse XAML:

```
<Ellipse Canvas.Left="4" Canvas.Top="4" Height="72" Width="72"
  Fill="Navy" StrokeThickness="1" Stroke="Black" />
```

As useful as lines, rectangles, and circles are, occasionally, you need to create a more dynamic shape. To create more complex shapes, Silverlight supports the use of the `PathGeometry`.

18.2.2 *Path geometries*

A `PathGeometry` enables you to construct complex, detailed illustrations composed of a variety of arcs, curves, and lines. These intricate depictions consist of a collection of `PathFigure` objects, with each `PathFigure` representing a small section of the overall illustration. In turn, each `PathFigure` is made up of a series of `PathSegment` objects. Each `PathSegment` object describes a small piece of the overall figure. Before we get too far ahead of ourselves, let's review a basic example that shows a variety of meaningless squiggly lines for the sake of illustration (see listing 18.12).

Listing 18.12   A `PathGeometry`

Result:

XAML:

```
<Canvas
    Width="100" Height="100" Background="Gray">
    <Path Stroke="Red" StrokeThickness="2">
        <Path.Data>
            <PathGeometry>
                <PathGeometry.Figures>
                    <PathFigure StartPoint="5,5">
                        <PathFigure.Segments>
                            <ArcSegment Size="10,10" RotationAngle="30"
                                        Point="20,10" IsLargeArc="False"
                                        SweepDirection="Clockwise" />
                            <BezierSegment Point1="40,0" Point2="60,60" Point3="75,90"/>
                            <LineSegment Point="80,15" />
                            <PolyLineSegment Points="50,90 3,7" />
                            <QuadraticBezierSegment Point1="90,90" Point2="70,60"/>
                        </PathFigure.Segments>
                    </PathFigure>
                </PathGeometry.Figures>
            </PathGeometry>
        </Path.Data>
    </Path>
</Canvas>
```

This example uses five different segment types to create random squiggles. Each individual segment sequentially connects to the previous one, much like cars in a freight train. Table 18.2 shows all the available segment types.

From the options presented, it's clear to see that you have tons of flexibility when it comes to creating a geometrical shape. Sometimes you may need to explicitly use other geometry objects. In these scenarios, you can use a composite geometry.

Table 18.2   Available segment types

Segment type	Usage
LineSegment	A straight line connecting two points
PolyLineSegment	A series of lines
ArcSegment	An elliptical arch between two points
BezierSegment	A cubic Bézier curve between two points
PolyBezierSegment	A series of cubic Bézier curves
QuadraticBezierSegment	A quadratic Bézier curve
PolyQuadraticBezierSegment	A series of quadratic Bézier curves

18.2.3   *Composite geometries*

You may need to create a complex shape that consists of disconnected entities. Or, maybe you need to use Geometry entities, and you want to combine their area. The

GeometryGroup adequately addresses these scenarios. A GeometryGroup is a collection of Geometry entities. Listing 18.13 illustrates how to orchestrate a composite geometry.

Listing 18.13   A composite geometry to make a key

Result:

XAML:
```
<Path Stroke="Navy" StrokeThickness="8" Fill="Navy">
  <Path.Data>
    <GeometryGroup FillRule="Evenodd">
      <EllipseGeometry Center="20,40" RadiusX="15" RadiusY="15" />
      <LineGeometry StartPoint="20,40" EndPoint="70,40" />
      <LineGeometry StartPoint="66,38" EndPoint="66,55" />
      <LineGeometry StartPoint="55,38" EndPoint="55,55" />
      <EllipseGeometry Center="14,40" RadiusX="8" RadiusY="8" />
    </GeometryGroup>
  </Path.Data>
</Path>
```

This listing illustrates how to create a key using a complex geometry via the GeometryGroup. It also introduces a property called FillRule, which determines how conflicting areas should be filled. There are two acceptable values: EvenOdd and Nonzero.

EvenOdd, the default used in the previous example, is pretty simple. It begins at a point and goes outside of the overall shape, counting each line that it intersects along the way. If the count is odd, the point is inside the shape. If the count is even, the point is outside the shape. This rule determines how to fill the area.

Alternatively, if the previous example had used the Nonzero option, the hole to place the key on a key ring would've been filled because Nonzero counts the number of lines it intersects along the way. But it also considers the direction of the line. Based on the direction, the count is either incremented or decremented. At the end of counting, if the total is zero, it's assumed that the point is inside the overall shape.

To take control of how an element is filled, you can use one of Silverlight's many brushes.

18.3   Brushes

Up to this point, you've seen how to define the boundaries of the various Shape elements. It's equally important to understand how to fill the area within a Shape. To paint the interior of a Shape or a variety of other visual elements, you must choose from myriad Brush options including SolidColorBrush, LinearGradientBrush, RadialGradientBrush, ImageBrush, and VideoBrush.

18.3.1 *SolidColorBrush*

The SolidColorBrush is without a doubt the most rudimentary of the Brush options. A SolidColorBrush uses a single, solid color to paint an area. Listing 18.14 shows a basic circle using a SolidColorBrush.

Listing 18.14 A basic SolidColorBrush with the color Navy Blue

Result:

XAML:
```
<Ellipse Stroke="Black" StrokeThickness="3"
  Width="64" Height="64" Canvas.Left="8" Canvas.Top="8">
  <Ellipse.Fill>
    <SolidColorBrush Color="Navy" />
  </Ellipse.Fill>
</Ellipse>
```

This SolidColorBrush uses a System.Windows.Media.Color property named Color to specify which color fills the area. Properties of this type can accept values represented in one of the following ways:

- *A predefined named color, such as Navy, that matches one of the names supported in Internet Explorer, .NET Framework, and Windows Forms.* Importantly, the Color class in Silverlight belongs to the System.Windows.Media namespace. In Windows Forms, it belongs to the System.Drawing namespace.
- *A Red, Green, Blue (RGB) hexadecimal string in the format of #RxGyBz.* For instance, in listing 18.14, you could replace Navy with its hexadecimal representation, #000080.
- *An RGB hexadecimal string with an alpha channel in the format of #aRGB.* This format gives you a greater range than the typical RGB hexadecimal string because it has built-in support for the opacity channel. As an example, you could convert Navy to #AA000080 to give the color a washed-out appearance.

These color options give you a lot of flexibility when you're defining a SolidColorBrush. If you're using XAML, it's much more convenient to explicitly set the Fill property of a Shape, or any property that's a Brush, and let Silverlight automatically convert the value to a SolidColorBrush for you. Because of this, you could condense the previous markup to this:

```
<Ellipse Stroke="Black" StrokeThickness="3" Fill="Navy"
  Width="64" Height="64" Canvas.Left="8" Canvas.Top="8">
</Ellipse>
```

Although this explicit approach is convenient, it's still important to remember the SolidColorBrush, because if you're trying to use solid colors through managed code, you'll need to use the System.Windows.Media.SolidColorBrush class.

Occasionally, you may want something richer and more vibrant than a solid color. Thankfully, Silverlight provides several alternatives such as the LinearGradientBrush.

18.3.2 *LinearGradientBrush*

The LinearGradientBrush paints an area with a gradual, soothing shift between colors along a theoretical line. This Brush can shift between one or more colors through the use of a series of predefined locations represented as GradientStop elements. Each GradientStop element specifies where one color should shift to another. Listing 18.15 shows a basic LinearGradientBrush that uses two GradientStop elements to shift from one Color to another.

> **Listing 18.15   A LinearGradientBrush rendered on a diagonal**

Result:

XAML:
```
<Ellipse Stroke="Black" StrokeThickness="3"
  Width="64" Height="64" Canvas.Left="8" Canvas.Top="8">
  <Ellipse.Fill>
    <LinearGradientBrush>
      <GradientStop Color="Navy" Offset="0" />
      <GradientStop Color="White" Offset="1" />
    </LinearGradientBrush>
  </Ellipse.Fill>
</Ellipse>
```

This Ellipse illustrates how the LinearGradientBrush can be used to shift from Navy in the upper-left corner to White in the lower-right corner. Each GradientStop in the LinearGradientBrush specifies an Offset property that determines where the color, specified in the Color property, should be reached within the Brush coordinate space. But how does the Offset property know that 0 means the upper-left corner and 1 means the lower-right corner?

The Offset property relies on two other properties, which are defined within the LinearGradientBrush definition itself. These two System.Windows.Point-based properties are Start-Point and EndPoint and ultimately determine the beginning and ending of a gradient. Collectively, these two properties define a rectangular boundary in which the Offset property works. This coordinate space can best be visualized as shown in figure 18.1, where each corner displays a Point value.

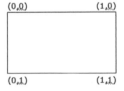

Figure 18.1   The Brush coordinate space

By default, the StartPoint property is set to represent the upper-left corner (0, 0) of this coordinate space. Conversely, the EndPoint defaults to represent the lower-right corner (1, 1) of the coordinate space. You can manipulate both property values to take full control of the range in which the gradient occurs, as well as the direction.

Imagine taking the previous example and making the gradient run horizontally instead of diagonally. This can be accomplished by altering the StartPoint and End-Point property values, as shown in listing 18.16.

Listing 18.16 A `LinearGradientBrush` rendered horizontally

Result:

XAML:
```
<Ellipse Stroke="Black" StrokeThickness="3"
  Width="64" Height="64" Canvas.Left="8" Canvas.Top="8">
  <Ellipse.Fill>
    <LinearGradientBrush StartPoint="0,0" EndPoint="1,0">
      <GradientStop Color="Navy" Offset="0" />
      <GradientStop Color="White" Offset="1" />
    </LinearGradientBrush>
  </Ellipse.Fill>
</Ellipse>
```

Although you could've rotated the imaginary gradient line by altering the Offset property values of each of the GradientStop elements, the StartPoint and EndPoint properties give you control over the entire range of the gradient. This fact becomes particularly important when you begin to consider using multiple color transitions.

Both the LinearGradientBrush and the RadialGradientBrush, which you'll see shortly, allow you to define as many GradientStop elements as you want. The more GradientStop elements that are added, the more important it is to understand the relationship between the Offset property and the StartPoint and EndPoint properties. Listing 18.17 shows how to use multiple GradientStop elements by adjusting the Offset property.

Listing 18.17 A horizontal `LinearGradientBrush` with multiple transitions

Result:

XAML:
```
<Rectangle StrokeThickness="0" Width="200"
  Height="64" Canvas.Left="8" Canvas.Top="8">
  <Rectangle.Fill>
    <LinearGradientBrush StartPoint="0,0" EndPoint="1,0">
```

```
        <GradientStop Color="Yellow" Offset="0" />
        <GradientStop Color="Orange" Offset=".45" />
        <GradientStop Color="Blue" Offset=".55" />
        <GradientStop Color="Green" Offset="1" />
      </LinearGradientBrush>
    </Rectangle.Fill>
  </Rectangle>
```

As the previous examples have shown, the LinearGradientBrush provides you with a lot of opportunity to add richness to your applications. Occasionally, you may want to add a sense of depth to your graphics. Although Silverlight supports only 2D graphics, you can still deliver the illusion of depth by using a RadialGradientBrush.

18.3.3 *RadialGradientBrush*

The RadialGradientBrush is similar to the LinearGradientBrush except that the color transitions begin from an originating Point. As the Brush radiates from the center, it gradually paints elliptical transitions until a GradientStop is encountered. This process continues from one GradientStop to the next until each one has been rendered. Listing 18.18 illuminates a basic RadialGradientBrush.

> **Listing 18.18   A RadialGradientBrush**

Result:

XAML:
```
<Ellipse Width="75" Height="75" Stroke="Black">
  <Ellipse.Fill>
    <RadialGradientBrush>
      <GradientStop Color="Black" Offset="0"/>
      <GradientStop Color="Black" Offset="1"/>
      <GradientStop Color="Gray" Offset="0.5"/>
    </RadialGradientBrush>
  </Ellipse.Fill>
</Ellipse>
```

As this example shows, the brush begins at the center of the Ellipse by default. This originating Point can be customized in one of two ways. The first approach involves specifying a Point value within the Center property. The Center Point represents the focal point of the outermost ellipse of the gradient. Alternatively, or in conjunction with the Center, you can use the GradientOrigin property to specify the Point that defines where the radial gradient emanates from.

As a radial gradient is rendered, it grows from the GradientOrigin in a circular fashion. Sometimes it's necessary to use a more elliptical gradient instead of a pure circular effect. To define an elliptical gradient, you need to utilize the RadiusX and RadiusY properties, which are consistent with the properties of the same name from the `Ellipse` element. Listing 18.19 compares several ellipses using different `RadiusX` and `RadiusY` properties, which both default to `.5`.

Listing 18.19   Comparing uses of the `RadiusX` and `RadiusY` properties

Result:

XAML:

```
<Canvas Width="245" Height="75" Background="White">
  <Ellipse Width="75" Height="75" Stroke="Black">
    <Ellipse.Fill>
      <RadialGradientBrush>
        <GradientStop Color="Black" Offset="0"/>
        <GradientStop Color="Black" Offset="1"/>
        <GradientStop Color="Gray" Offset="0.5"/>
      </RadialGradientBrush>
    </Ellipse.Fill>
  </Ellipse>
  <Ellipse Width="75" Height="75" Canvas.Left="85"
    Stroke="Black">
    <Ellipse.Fill>
      <RadialGradientBrush RadiusX=".25">
        <GradientStop Color="Black" Offset="0"/>
        <GradientStop Color="Black" Offset="1"/>
        <GradientStop Color="Gray" Offset="0.5"/>
      </RadialGradientBrush>
    </Ellipse.Fill>
  </Ellipse>
  <Ellipse Width="75" Height="75" Canvas.Left="170"
    Stroke="Black">
    <Ellipse.Fill>
      <RadialGradientBrush RadiusY=".25">
        <GradientStop Color="Black" Offset="0"/>
        <GradientStop Color="Black" Offset="1"/>
        <GradientStop Color="Gray" Offset="0.5"/>
      </RadialGradientBrush>
    </Ellipse.Fill>
  </Ellipse>
</Canvas>
```

As the previous examples show, you can use a `RadialGradientBrush` to provide basic linear and radial effects. Although these `Brush` elements are appropriate in certain situations, occasionally you need to deliver a richer, more textured effect. Textures are often delivered via images, which can be painted on visual elements using an `ImageBrush`.

18.3.4 *ImageBrush*

The `ImageBrush` allows you to fill an area with an image instead of a solid or shifting color. The `ImageBrush` utilizes a picture specified within the `ImageSource` property to paint a raster graphic. This `Brush` supports both .jpg and .png formats to deliver a textured effect to your visual elements. Listing 18.20 shows a basic `ImageBrush` using an image named man.png.

Listing 18.20   An example of an `ImageBrush`

Result:

XAML:

```
<Ellipse Width="60" Height="60" Stroke="Black">
  <Ellipse.Fill>
    <ImageBrush ImageSource="http://www.silverlightinaction.com/man.png" />
  </Ellipse.Fill>
</Ellipse>
```

As you can imagine, an `ImageBrush` can easily add a rich, vibrant touch to your painting surface. Sometimes, you may want your painting surface to be more dynamic and livelier. With the same type of simplicity as the `ImageBrush`, you can paint a surface with a video, using the `VideoBrush`.

18.3.5 *VideoBrush*

Imagine watching a shooting star speed across the night sky through the elliptical eyepiece of a telescope. With the `VideoBrush` in action, you can deliver this type of scene by drawing an `Ellipse` and filling it with a `MediaElement`. Listing 18.21 shows exactly how to use the `VideoBrush`.

Listing 18.21   An example of a `VideoBrush`

Result:

XAML:

```
<MediaElement x:Name="myMediaElement" Opacity="0"
  Source="http://www.silverlightinaction.com/video2.wmv" />
<Ellipse Width="100" Height="100" Stroke="Black">
  <Ellipse.Fill>
    <VideoBrush SourceName="myMediaElement" />
  </Ellipse.Fill>
</Ellipse>
```

As this example shows, the `VideoBrush` references a `MediaElement` through the `SourceName` property. This fact allows you to manipulate the playback functionality of a VideoBrush by altering the playback of the MediaElement as defined in chapter 7. If you want to pause or stop the video displayed within a VideoBrush, you call the Pause() or Stop() method of the MediaElement that the VideoBrush references.

Up to this point, the Brush elements have been used in relation to a basic Ellipse. An Ellipse was chosen for the sake of illustration; you can use all the Brush elements that we've covered in any number of visual elements, including but not limited to a Canvas, a TextBox, or even a TextBlock, as listing 18.22 shows.

Listing 18.22   An example of a videoBrush within a TextBlock

Result:

XAML:

```
<MediaElement x:Name="myMediaElement" Opacity="0"
  Source="http://www.silverlightinaction.com/video2.wmv" />
<TextBlock Text="HELLO" FontFamily="Verdana"
  FontSize="80" FontWeight="Bold">
  <TextBlock.Foreground>
    <VideoBrush SourceName="myMediaElement" />
  </TextBlock.Foreground>
</TextBlock>
```

This sample only begins to show the potential allotted by the different Brush elements. All the Brush options are usable in any property that has a Brush type. You can have a video paint text, or an image paint shapes or even controls. The sky's the limit.

In addition to these rich Brush options, Silverlight supports an interesting set of features that can further alter the appearance of your shapes. Collectively, these are called *effects*.

18.4   *Effects*

Much as is the case with animation, the subtle and appropriate use of effects can make the difference between a UI that just sits there and one that really pops, drawing your eye to information that's important to you.

Effects in Silverlight come in two primary forms: *built-in effects*, implemented in the native Silverlight hardware-accelerated runtime code; and *pixel shaders*, implemented by folks like us using a combination of managed code and High Level Shader Language (HLSL) and run in software. The former allows for maximum performance for common effects such as blur and shadows. The latter provides a lot of flexibility to allow us to provide our own effects, while not breaking out of the sandbox.

In this section, we'll cover both types of effects. We'll start with how to use the built-in effects and follow that up with a primer on creating your own pixel shader effects.

18.4.1 *Using built-in effects*

Silverlight has two built-in effects: blur and drop shadow. The effects may be used on any element or group of elements in the visual tree.

Elements that have effects applied remain as interactive as they did prior to the effect. Although it may be hard to read the text in a blurred-out TextBox, the TextBox is still fully functional.

BLUR EFFECT

The *blur effect* in Silverlight, implemented through the BlurEffect class, provides a way to shift an element or group of elements out of focus, as though you were looking at it through frosted glass or a bad lens.

Blur has only one property of interest: Radius. The Radius property controls how large an area is sampled when the blur is run: the larger the radius, the blurrier the result. Note that the larger the radius, the more computations required to achieve the blur—a potential performance consideration, especially if a large area or animation is involved.

Listing 18.23 shows how to use the BlurEffect on a group of UI elements in a StackPanel.

Listing 18.23   A blur with a 4-pixel radius

Result:

Hello World

This is a textbox

Button

XAML:
```
<StackPanel x:Name="Elements" Margin="10">
  <TextBlock Text="Hello World" Margin="10" />
  <TextBox Text="This is a textbox" Margin="10" />
  <Button x:Name="Button" Content="Button" Margin="10"/>     Effect on
                                                              StackPanel
  <StackPanel.Effect>
    <BlurEffect Radius="4" />
  </StackPanel.Effect>

</StackPanel>
```

In listing 18.23, the blur effect is applied to the entire StackPanel containing all the UI elements. The net result is to blur everything inside that container. You can also apply a blur to individual elements, of course. The effect is attached to the Stack-Panel using the Effect property. The Effect property can have only one effect at any point in time. If you want multiple effects on a single element, you need to use nested panels or borders and apply the effects one per panel/border.

The blur effect is useful when combined with things such as a pop-up modal window (see chapter 15). In that case, a slight blur of the page contents helps drive home the fact that the pop-up is modal and demands all of your attention.

The second built-in effect is the drop shadow.

DROP SHADOW EFFECT

The *drop shadow effect* is one of those effects that's best used in moderation, and used subtly when used at all. Not only is there a performance and rendering quality concern, but aesthetically, those of us who aren't designers tend to use bold shadows more often than looks good in an application.

The `DropShadowEffect` class has several knobs you can use to fine-tune the effect. Table 18.3 shows the five properties that alter the appearance of the effect.

Table 18.3   Important `DropShadowEffect` properties

Property	Description
Color	Specifies the color of the shadow. Default is `Black`.
ShadowDepth	Distance in pixels to displace the shadow relative to the element the effect is applied to. Default is 5 pixels.
Direction	An angle in degrees from 0 to 360 (counterclockwise), indicating where the shadow lies relative to the element the effect is applied to. The default is 315, which places the shadow in the lower-right corner.
BlurRadius	Controls the blurriness of the shadow. A double value between 0 and 1, with 1 being the softest. Default is 0.5.
Opacity	Specifies how opaque the shadow is. A double value between 0 and 1, with 1 being fully opaque. Default is 1.

When playing with shadows, I've found it more aesthetically pleasing to have the `ShadowDepth` be 0 or close to 0, the `Opacity` set to some value around 0.5 or so, and the `BlurRadius` set to a value that spreads out the effect—10 usually works well. That gives you a light shadow that bleeds around all the edges. Listing 18.24 shows these settings in use in the effect.

Listing 18.24   A subtle drop shadow

Result:

XAML:

```xml
<Grid x:Name="LayoutRoot" Background="White">
  <Grid Background="White" Width="180" Margin="25">      ❶
    <StackPanel x:Name="Elements" Margin="10">
      <TextBlock Text="Hello World"
                 Margin="10" />
      <TextBox Text="This is a textbox"
               Margin="10" />
      <Button x:Name="Button" Content="Button"
              Margin="10"/>
    </StackPanel>

    <Grid.Effect>
      <DropShadowEffect BlurRadius="10"
                        Opacity="0.5"
                        ShadowDepth="1" />
    </Grid.Effect>
  </Grid>
</Grid>
```

In listing 18.24, note that the effect is applied to a grid with an opaque background ❶. If the grid had a transparent background, the effect would be applied individually to each of the items inside the grid.

As described before the listing, this example uses a large blur radius, 50 percent opacity, and a shadow depth of only 1 pixel. This provides a more pleasing and subtle effect than the default shadow appearance. Compare that to figure 18.2, with the properties all left at their default values.

Most people would find the default appearance a bit jarring, or at least a little outdated. Fortunately, the Silverlight team gave us all the tweaks we need to be able to make the shadow look better.

In addition to these designer-type recommendations, you should keep a few other things in mind when using effects.

Figure 18.2   The default appearance of the `DropShadowEffect`

TRICKS AND CONSIDERATIONS

The built-in effects perform well, but they'll tax your system resources if you apply them to a really large area and/or animate any of the values on the effect. For example, one thing I did early on was animate the background blur from 0 to 5 when displaying a new dialog. It worked, but it was a processing hog.

In addition to processing time, another consideration is the quality drop in the result. Any elements with an effect applied to them are rendered out to a bitmap. That means you automatically lose ClearType font rendering and fall back to grayscale rendering. One way to get around this is to apply the effect to a shape of the same size that sits behind the elements. Listing 18.25 shows how to use a rectangle behind the grid to ensure that the grid contents stay at top rendering quality.

Listing 18.25 Applying the drop shadow to a background `Rectangle`

```
<Grid x:Name="LayoutRoot" Background="White">
  <Grid Width="180" Margin="25">
    <Rectangle Fill="White">                              ◁─┐  Background
      <Rectangle.Effect>                                     │  Rectangle
        <DropShadowEffect BlurRadius="10"
                          Opacity="0.5"
                          ShadowDepth="1" />
      </Rectangle.Effect>
    </Rectangle>

    <StackPanel x:Name="Elements" Margin="10">
      <TextBlock Text="Hello World" Margin="10" />
      <TextBox Text="This is a textbox" Margin="10" />
      <Button x:Name="Button" Content="Button"
                Margin="10"/>
    </StackPanel>
  </Grid>
</Grid>
```

This example removes the effect from the grid and places it on a background rectangle sitting behind the elements. Because the rectangle isn't a parent of the elements, the effect isn't applied to them. The only thing that's rasterized in this example is the `Rectangle`. The text retains ClearType font rendering.

The Silverlight team may add more effects over time. Requests include true multi-pass effects such as glow. In the meantime, it's possible to create your own single-pass effects using a little Silverlight code and the shader language.

18.4.2 *Creating custom pixel shaders*

Most people who know about pixel shaders have run across them in game development. Games and various types of shaders have gone hand in hand because video cards became powerful enough to offload most or all of the shader calculation and logic. Most work done with pixel shaders is performed using the DirectX SDK and optionally XNA.

WPF also supports pixel shaders. Entire libraries of transitions and effects are available on CodePlex, all built using hardware-accelerated shaders.

Pixel shaders in Silverlight are a simplified form of the full pixel shaders used in games or in WPF. For security reasons, the shaders are all run in software and currently support only Pixel Shader level 2. By not running them in hardware, Silverlight can sandbox the code and avoid someone running malicious code on your video card. But as technology progresses, the Silverlight team will likely consider allowing the shaders to run on hardware in selected scenarios.

HOW PIXEL SHADERS WORK

Pixel shaders perform per-pixel processing on input. That input can be anything you see in the visual tree in Silverlight, including images, video, and controls. Pixel shaders in Silverlight are created using two main files. The first is a .NET class that's used to wrap the shader functionality and expose it to the rest of Silverlight. The second is the pixel shader itself, written in HLSL as an .fx file and compiled into a .ps file as a resource in the Silverlight project.

Pixel shaders are written in HLSL, a C-like language optimized for pixel processing. The language is geared toward running on video card hardware, so you have to deal with things such as registers, fixed numbers of variables, and limitations on overall complexity. In some of those ways, it's like working in assembly language. You can find a reference on HLSL syntax on MSDN at http://bit.ly/HLSLReference.

Pixel shaders in Silverlight are software-rendered, but are parallelized. Although they don't take specific advantage of capabilities of video hardware, they're executed using the CPU's fast SSE instruction set.

Silverlight supports the `ps_2_0` profile of the Shader Model 2 specification. A *shader profile* is the target for compiling a shader, whereas a *shader model* is a specification for capabilities of the shader. You'll need to understand this when looking at existing shader implementations to port to Silverlight or learning about HLSL syntax. In the case of Shader Model 2, the limitation you're likely to hit is the 96-instruction limit. That limit is broken down into 64 arithmetic instructions and 32 texture-sample instructions. The 64 arithmetic instruction limit will almost certainly be a bounding limit for shaders of any complexity. In addition, if you manually compile the shaders using the DirectX SDK, you'll need to know what profile to use.

ENVIRONMENT SETUP

The most difficult part of writing a pixel shader is setting up the environment to allow them to compile. There are three main options:

1 Download the DirectX SDK, and use the compiler there to build the shader.
2 Repurpose the WPF pixel shader build step.
3 Use a tool such as Shazzam to create and compile the shader.

You can download the DirectX SDK and use its command-line tools to compile the shader. The SDK is roughly 500 MB and may be a bit much just to compile a shader.

Option 2 is to repurpose the WPF pixel shader build step. Tim Heuer put together a great blog post covering the steps required to set up your environment for developing pixel shaders. It'd be too much to include in this book, so I refer you to his post here: http://bit.ly/SLPixelShaderCompile. I chose option 2, using a build task. It involves some configuration as well as a template for the shader development.

Another option is to use a tool such as Shazzam (http://shazzam-tool.com) to compile the shader and manually add that into your project. Most Silverlight and WPF developers doing serious work with pixel shaders use this tool. It also includes a number of training videos to help you get started with pixel shader development. Finally, Shazzam includes a bunch of existing shaders in source form that you can learn from.

Despite its hackish nature, if you want everything to happen inside Visual Studio, I think you're better off starting with Tim's approach for the project structure. If you don't need everything integrated into Visual Studio and can add the files manually, you'll find that Shazzam is the best long-term solution. In either case, you'll likely have Shazzam open while you explore pixel shader development.

When your environment is set up and you can compile pixel shaders, you're ready to develop one of your own. Go ahead and set up your environment now. I'll wait.

SHADER CODE

Pixel shaders are typically fairly complex; they do things such as alter the visual location of pixels based on a complex algorithm. Learning how to write shaders is like learning any other programming language, but with a heavy focus on performance and optimization.

A good place to learn is the WPF Pixel Shader Effects library on CodePlex: http://wpffx.codeplex.com. Although originally intended for WPF use, Silverlight effects were added once Silverlight supported HLSL-based pixel shaders.

Listing 18.26 shows the HLSL source code for a pixel shader that takes a color and multiplies every pixel by that color. The result is an image that appears to have been photographed through a tinted lens.

Listing 18.26　A simple pixel shader that applies a color filter

```
//-------------------------------------------------------------------
//
// Silverlight ShaderEffect HLSL -- ShaderEffect1
//
//-------------------------------------------------------------------

//-------------------------------------------------------------------
// Constant register mappings (float,double,Point,Color,Point3D...)
//-------------------------------------------------------------------

float4 colorFilter : register(C0);                              ◀─┐

//-------------------------------------------------------------------
// Sampler Inputs (Brushes, including ImplicitInput)               ❶
//-------------------------------------------------------------------

sampler2D implicitInputSampler : register(S0);                  ◀─┘

//-------------------------------------------------------------------
// Pixel Shader
//-------------------------------------------------------------------

float4 main(float2 uv : TEXCOORD) : COLOR              ◀─  Standard main
{                                                            function
  float4 color = tex2D(implicitInputSampler, uv);
  return color * colorFilter;                        ❷
}
```

The shader first maps values into registers ❶ supported by the shader model. Each input and constant must be mapped to a register. A *register* is a well-known place in hardware (virtual hardware in the Silverlight case) that can be used to store a value. Registers are much faster than regular RAM when it comes to accessing values. If you've ever done any x86 assembly language programming, or even any old DOS interrupt programming, you know well the concept of registers.

The section comments aren't required, but you'll find them in almost every pixel shader implementation. Usually I'd leave them out of a code listing in this book, but the shader is completely naked without them.

The actual code starts under the Pixel Shader section. Like all pixel shaders in Silverlight, this has a main function that takes in a *UV coordinate* (a standard way of referring to an x and y position on a texture or image, but normalized into the range of 0 to 1 rather than absolute pixels) and returns a `float4` color ❷.

When you have the HLSL source for your shader, you'll need to write a .NET class to expose it in your project.

WRAPPER CLASS

To use a pixel shader, you need to provide a way for the rest of .NET to interact with it. The wrapper class (often called just the *pixel shader class*) is responsible for loading the compiled shader code and for exposing properties used to tweak the shader. The Pixel Shader file template includes a wrapper class. In addition, Shazzam will generate the wrapper class for you. The wrapper class for this example is shown in listing 18.27.

Listing 18.27   A pixel shader wrapper class

```
public class ShaderEffect1 : ShaderEffect
{
  private static PixelShader _pixelShader = new PixelShader();

  static ShaderEffect1()                      ❶
  {
    _pixelShader.UriSource = new
        Uri("/SilverlightApplication61;component/ShaderEffect1.ps",
        UriKind.Relative);
  }
  public ShaderEffect1()                      ◁──┐ Public instance
  {                                              │ constructor
    this.PixelShader = _pixelShader;

    UpdateShaderValue(InputProperty);
    UpdateShaderValue(ColorFilterProperty);
  }
}

public Brush Input
{
    get { return (Brush)GetValue(InputProperty); }
    set { SetValue(InputProperty, value); }
}

public static readonly DependencyProperty InputProperty =
    ShaderEffect.RegisterPixelShaderSamplerProperty("Input",
                typeof(ShaderEffect1), 0);                       ❷

public Color ColorFilter
{
    get { return (Color)GetValue(ColorFilterProperty); }
    set { SetValue(ColorFilterProperty, value); }
}

public static readonly DependencyProperty ColorFilterProperty =
    DependencyProperty.Register("ColorFilter", typeof(Color),
    typeof(ShaderEffect1), new PropertyMetadata(Colors.Yellow,
                PixelShaderConstantCallback(0)));               ❸
}
```

The static constructor ❶ loads the pixel shader resource into a static `PixelShader` typed property. Note the .ps extension: it's loading the compiled resource. The `PixelShader` is static because only one copy of the compiled code is needed within an application.

Each of the dependency properties maps to a register in the shader. One of the properties, of type `Brush`, is mapped implicitly ❷. Any additional properties must be mapped directly to registers. In this source, you can see that the `ColorFilterProp-erty` maps to constant register zero ❸ in the pixel shader. The `PixelShaderConstantCallback` takes the register number as a parameter. In the HLSL source, constant register zero is mapped to the variable `colorFilter`.

But how did a `Color` property become a `float4`, and what's a `float4` anyway? Those are built-in vector types in the language. Table 18.4 has the mapping.

Table 18.4   Mapping from .NET types to HLSL types

Shader type	Description	.NET type
float	A single floating-point number	double, single
float2	A vector with two floating-point numbers	Point, Size, Vector
float3	A vector with three floating-point numbers	(Unused in Silverlight)
float4	A vector with four floating-point numbers	Color

The member names for the individual floats depend on their usage. For example, a color has the properties r, g, b, and a.

HLSL is interesting in that it can perform multiplication and other operations on whole structures. In that way, the number of instructions is reduced, but it can be hard to understand when you first look at it. For example, the exmple multiplies together two `float4` values.

USING THE SHADER

With the shader compiled and the wrapper class in place, it's time to try the shader in your own application. Like any other element used in XAML, you must either include an implicit namespace in your application settings or map a namespace in the XAML file. In this case, because the shader is in the project with the XAML, you'll use an explicit map in the XAML.

Listing 18.28 shows the effect of using the shader with a red tint. It'll look gray in print, but you can tell there's a tint over the whole image.

Listing 18.28   Using the pixel shader effect in XAML

Result:

Code:

```
<UserControl x:Class="SilverlightApplication61.MainPage"
    xmlns="http://schemas.microsoft.com/winfx/2006/xaml/presentation"
    xmlns:x="http://schemas.microsoft.com/winfx/2006/xaml"
    xmlns:d="http://schemas.microsoft.com/expression/blend/2008"
    xmlns:mc="http://schemas.openxmlformats.org/markup-compatibility/2006"
        xmlns:local="clr-namespace:SilverlightApplication61"
    mc:Ignorable="d"
    d:DesignHeight="300" d:DesignWidth="400">

    <Grid x:Name="LayoutRoot">
        <Grid Background="White" Width="180" Margin="25">
            <StackPanel x:Name="Elements" Margin="10">
                <TextBlock Text="Hello World" Margin="10" />
                <TextBox Text="This is a textbox" Margin="10" />
                <Button x:Name="Button" Content="Button"
                        Margin="10" />
            </StackPanel>

            <Grid.Effect>
                <local:ShaderEffect1 ColorFilter="Red" />        ❶
            </Grid.Effect>
        </Grid>
    </Grid>

</UserControl>
```

This is the same example used in previous sections, but instead of a drop-shadow, it uses the pixel shader with a parameter of Red for the ColorFilter property ❶. The end result is an angry red form. As was the case in the other examples, the use of a pixel shader has reverted the text back to grayscale font smoothing.

Pixel shaders are a great way to provide your own custom effects or to use effects developed by others. Learning HLSL can be difficult at times, but the payoff is worth it: you can use pixel shaders in Silverlight, in WPF, and, of course, in DirectX and XNA. Pixel shaders, even the software-rendered ones in Silverlight, are extremely efficient as well. When considering pixel-manipulation strategies in an application, the creation of a pixel shader should be high on your list of options.

18.5   Summary

Silverlight's inherent graphical capabilities go far beyond cartoons and visual fireworks. By shaping these elements into illustrations, graphics can provide a bridge to your users to help them connect with difficult concepts. These valuable illustrations can be composed of a series of shapes compiled from arcs, curves, and lines. These shapes can then be filled with gradient colors or textured visuals such as images and videos.

Effects augment both graphics and controls. The use of a subtle drop shadow or a blur can help users focus their attention on a specific part of the screen. If those effects aren't sufficient, you also have the option to create your own effects in the form of pixel shaders.

Vector graphics and effects are definitely some of the strong points in Silverlight. Previous technologies had no equivalents; you had to write everything from scratch or use primitive drawing options. Silverlight also has rich support for images and media, another of its strong points. We'll discuss that in chapters 20 and 21. Before we get there, let's put our newfound vector graphics skills to use on that oldest of modern media: paper.

19

Printing

This chapter covers

- An overview of the printing API
- How to print onscreen content
- How to scale content for print
- Getting data from a service for a report
- Creating headers, footers, and more

Silverlight 4 is the first release that can be considered truly "ready for business." The support for binding and validation, WCF RIA Services, and out-of-browser trusted applications are all major factors in this. One equally important reason is the added support for printing.

Many business applications need to print paper forms and reports as a standard part of their process. Very large-scale applications typically farm that functionality out to a server somewhere with centralized print systems. Most other applications use printers directly mapped and available on the client workstation. For those applications, platform support for printing is essential.

Printing support opens up other nonbusiness scenarios as well. Now you can make that coloring-book creator or recipe application you've had in your "cool app ideas" folder. I joke about printing, but I used to print directions before I had a GPS, and flight information before it was synchronized to my phone via exchange. There are still many interesting and legitimate uses of printing inside and outside of business.

In our tour of printing, we'll take a look under the hood to understand how printing works in Silverlight, then handle the use case of printing onscreen content. From there, we'll look at considerations that come into play when building multipage documents. Wrapping up, we'll look at an example of a simple report writer with headers, footers, and items rows.

19.1 How Silverlight printing works

When designing the printing system, the Silverlight team wanted something that would work with all current onscreen visuals, while not adding a large feature payload to the overall runtime. Team members also wanted something that would work cross-platform and be available in all modes of operation: in-browser, out-of-browser trusted applications, and out-of-browser sandboxed applications.

For those reasons, the printing process resembles the overall screen layout process (see chapter 6), with additional printing-specific steps tagged on. Figure 19.1 shows the printing process at a high level.

The printing process starts by creating a `PrintDocument` object and calling its `Print` method. The `PrintDocument` then raises the `BeginPrint` event if there are any listeners. Your own startup code can run inside that event handler. Then, for each page to be printed, the `PrintDocument` raises the `PrintPage` event. Inside the handler for that event, you'll set the page visual and tell Silverlight if there are any more pages. The printing system then lays out the content and rasterizes it into a bitmap to send to the printer driver. Once that page is sent to the printer driver, Silverlight raises the `PrintPage` event if you've indicated that there are more pages, or raises the `EndPrint` event if not. During this process, the primary object you're interacting with, the object raising the three mentioned events, is the `PrintDocument` class.

In this section, we'll start with the `PrintDocument` class, covering its properties, methods, and events. In detail, we'll cover the `PrintPage` event and the actions you

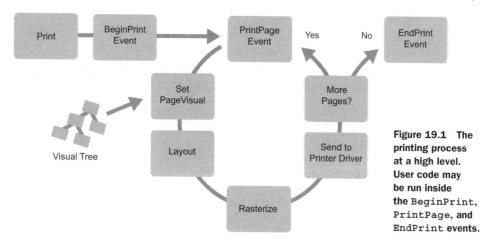

Figure 19.1 The printing process at a high level. User code may be run inside the `BeginPrint`, `PrintPage`, and `EndPrint` events.

take within it. After that, we'll take a deeper look at the rasterization step and how that affects the process.

19.1.1 *The PrintDocument class*

The heart of printing in Silverlight is the `PrintDocument` class, located in the `System.Windows.Printing` namespace. The `PrintDocument` class includes the single `Print` method required to kick off the process, a helper property to provide access to the page count, and three important events raised at different points in the process. Table 19.1 describes each of these members.

Table 19.1 `PrintDocument` **members**

Member	Description
`Print` method	Displays the Printer dialog and, if accepted, raises the `BeginPrint` event followed by the `PrintPage` event to begin the printing process.
`PrintedPageCount` property	A dependency property containing the total number of pages printed.
`BeginPrint` and `EndPrint` events	Events fired at the beginning and ending of the print job, respectively.
`PrintPage` event	The most important event. This is the event that enables you to build and print a single page.

In the remainder of this section, we'll look at these properties, methods, and events in more detail, starting with the `Print` method.

PRINT METHOD

The first step after instantiating the `PrintDocument` class is to call the `Print` method. The `Print` method takes in a parameter specifying the name of your document. This document name is what shows up in the operating system print spooler. The name should be descriptive, containing the title of your report or document. If your application plans to print many of these, you may want to add an identifier such as the patient's name in the case of a medical report, or perhaps some criteria used to generate the report. Listing 19.1 shows how to use the `Print` method.

Listing 19.1   Using the `Print` method and specifying a document name

XAML:

```
<Grid x:Name="LayoutRoot" Background="White">

  <Button x:Name="Print" Content="Print"
          Width="100" Height="30"
          Click="Print_Click"/>

</Grid>
```

TextBlock will go here

C#:

```
private PrintDocument _document;

public MainPage()
{
  InitializeComponent();

  Loaded += new RoutedEventHandler(MainPage_Loaded);
}

void MainPage_Loaded(object sender, RoutedEventArgs e)
{                                                          ⟵  Create
  _document = new PrintDocument();                            PrintDocument
}

private void Print_Click(object sender, RoutedEventArgs e)
{
  PrintForm("Brown, Pete");
}

private void PrintForm(string patientName)
{                                                          ⟵  Event wire-up
                                                              will go here
  doc.Print("Admittance form for " + patientName);
}
```

This example doesn't do anything meaningful yet—it doesn't print anything. We'll use this as the base for the rest of the examples centered around `PrintDocument`. Specifically, the placeholders for the `TextBlock` and the event wire-up will be filled out in later examples.

As written, the code is fairly simple. It sets up the required `PrintDocument` class instance and calls the `Print` method. The `Print` method is asynchronous: it immediately returns once you call it. But it raises all of its events back on the calling thread, so the UI thread can still be blocked.

Note that in untrusted applications, the `Print` method must be called from a user-initiated event, such as a button click event. Trusted out-of-browser applications (see chapter 5) eliminate this restriction. Once you wire up the `PrintPage` event (coming up shortly), you'll see that the print spool entry document name will contain the value passed into the `Print` method. Figure 19.2 shows the Windows 7 print spooler with a Silverlight print document spooled.

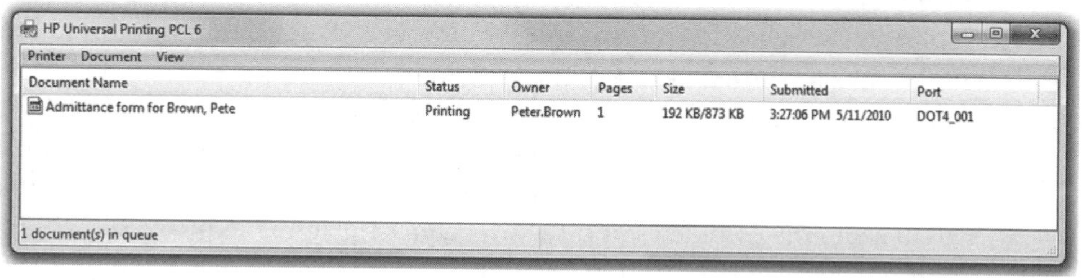

Figure 19.2   The Windows 7 print spooler showing the Silverlight document titled "Admittance form for Brown, Pete," created in listing 19.1.

The PrintDocument supports multipage printing. While printing, you'll find it useful to get the current number of pages that have been printed, in order to report the print status to your user. The PrintedPageCount property provides us with this information.

PRINTEDPAGECOUNT PROPERTY

The PrintedPageCount property contains the number of pages sent to the print driver. This doesn't necessarily correspond to the number of pages physically printed, as printers are typically much slower than the PC they're attached to. But it's useful as a general way of reporting status to the user.

PrintedPageCount is a read-only dependency property, so you can bind to that in XAML. Continuing from our example in listing 19.1, we can modify the code and XAML as shown in listing 19.2 to support this. Add the TextBlock in the XAML to the spot reserved with the comment.

> **Listing 19.2 Showing the number of pages printed**

XAML:
```
<TextBlock x:Name="PrintStatus"
           HorizontalAlignment="Center"
           VerticalAlignment="Bottom"         Binding
           Text="{Binding PrintedPageCount}"  statement
           FontSize="40" />
```

C#:
```
void MainPage_Loaded(object sender, RoutedEventArgs e)
{
  _document = new PrintDocument();          TextBlock
  PrintStatus.DataContext = _document;      DataContext
}
```

Now, when you print a multipage document, the status text will display the number of pages that have been printed so far. This is similar to what you see when you print a document in Microsoft Word, where a status dialog appears with a number showing the progress.

> **TIP** The PrintedPageCount property is incremented after the PrintPage event returns. Any check you do after setting the PageVisual will need to take into account that the PrintedPageCount hasn't yet been incremented.

In addition to the PrintedPageCount property, two other events can be used for status reporting, as well as for startup and shutdown code: BeginPrint and EndPrint.

THE BEGINPRINT AND ENDPRINT EVENTS

The BeginPrint and EndPrint events are raised at the beginning and end of the print job, respectively. Specifically, BeginPrint is raised before the first call to the Print-Page event, but after the printer dialog is shown, and EndPrint is raised after the last call to EndPrint completes or if the user cancels printing in-progress.

If the user cancels printing from the printer selection dialog, neither BeginPrint nor EndPrint will be raised. Similarly, if Silverlight can't print due to issues with paper format or memory allocation, BeginPrint may not be called.

Continuing our example, the following code shows how to wire up the two events. We won't do anything with `BeginPrint` in this example, but we'll show a message box when completed using the `EndPrint` event handler. The event handlers should be inserted into the listing 19.1 code, in the `PrintForm` method, where the event wire-up comment is located:

```
_document.BeginPrint += (s, e) =>
    {
    };
_document.EndPrint += (s, e) =>
  {
    MessageBox.Show("Print job completed.");
  };
```

The `BeginPrint` and `EndPrint` methods may be used for status reporting or for doing document build-up and tear-down. Unlike the `PrintPage` event, their event arguments don't contain any actionable information. It's not essential to wire them up, but you'll find that a complete printing solution typically requires one or both of them.

One event that's not optional is the `PrintPage` event.

19.1.2 The PrintPage Event

The `PrintPage` event is the heart of the user-code side of the printing system in Silverlight. This is where you'll obtain key layout information from the system and use it to create or otherwise lay out the visuals you use to represent the page. It's also the event where the assignment of the printer page root visual occurs, and the event where the decision is made as to how many pages the print document will contain.

For each page that will be printed, the `PrintDocument` class raises the `PrintPage` event. The `PrintPage` event passes in an instance of the `PrintPageEventArgs` class, specific to that page. Table 19.2 shows the properties of the class.

Table 19.2 `PrintPageEventArgs` **members**

Member	Description
`PageMargins` property	Gets the margins of the page as set by the printer driver settings. Represented at 96dpi.
`PrintableArea` property	The size (width and height) of the printable area inside the margins of the page. This is represented at 96dpi.
`HasMorePages` property	Set to true if there are additional pages after this one.
`PageVisual` property	Set this to the root element (typically a panel) that makes up the page content.

We'll cover each of the properties next, starting with the properties that report the size of the area you can use for content: `PageMargins` and `PrintableArea`.

PAGEMARGINS AND PRINTABLEAREA PROPERTIES

The PageMargins property is a standard Thickness property like those used for margins throughout the rest of Silverlight. It reports the size of the margins set in the printer configuration dialogs in your system.

The PrintableArea property is a Size property that indicates the width and height of the area within the margins. This is the area in which you can lay out your content.

It's important to note that the PageMargins and PrintableArea measurements are all provided at 96 dpi, consistent with screen layout. My printer handles resolutions up to 1200 dpi (normally set to 600 dpi). Despite that, the printable page area comes through at 784 x 1024 and the margins come through at 16,16,16,16. Add 32 (right and left margin) to 784 and divide by 96, and you get 8 1/2 inches. Do the same for the height and you get 11 inches. 8 1/2 x 11 inches is, in the US, the size of a standard sheet of letter-sized paper. The print quality itself is better than that, but still not as good as what you may be used to.

> **NOTE** Silverlight is currently limited to printing documents sized at A3 or smaller. Large-format pages may work in certain situations, but aren't supported. For reasons why, see the section on rasterization.

Similarly, if you print using the Microsoft XPS Document print driver (a great test driver), you'll see that it has no enforced margins, and therefore provides a size of 816 x 1056.

If the content you have won't fit on a single page, Silverlight will clip it to the dimensions specified in PrintableArea. In those cases, you may want to handle manually clipping and saving the remaining elements for the next page. To indicate additional pages, use the HasMorePages property.

HASMOREPAGES PROPERTY

Printed documents may consist of more than one page. But without precalculating all the page content (not a bad idea, but not required), you won't know the number of pages until you're done printing. Similarly, you don't necessarily know if a page is the last page until you try to fit all the content into the printable area and see what fits.

For those reasons, the PrintPage event includes the boolean HasMorePages property. Simply assign true to this property to indicate that the current page isn't the last page to be printed. This will cause Silverlight to raise another PrintPage event upon the completion of the current one. When you have no more pages to print, set HasMorePages to false (the default value) to end printing. The following code expands upon listing 19.1 to do a simple check against a hard-coded number of pages. The -1 is because the PrintedPageCount is incremented after the PrintPage event returns:

```
int numberOfPages = 5;

_document.PrintPage += (s, e) =>
  {
    Debug.WriteLine("Printing page");
```

```
       e.PageVisual = LayoutRoot;
       e.HasMorePages =
          _document.PrintedPageCount < numberOfPages - 1;
   };
```

Note also that we're effectively doing a print-screen in this example, by passing the `LayoutRoot` in as the `PageVisual` to be printed. We'll discuss `PageVisual` in detail in a moment.

You can also allow the user to cancel printing by setting `HasMorePages` to `false` when he hits a cancel button. Doing so will terminate printing after the current page. To do that, you'll need to set a flag in your class and have your code in the print method check for this flag. Additionally, if you know the user has hit cancel before you set the `PageVisual`, you can both skip setting the `PageVisual` and set `HasMoreP-ages` to `false` to avoid printing the current page and any subsequent pages.

PAGEVISUAL PROPERTY

The `PageVisual` property is the property you use to assign the root element of your page. Think of your root element like `LayoutRoot` on a typical Silverlight page. This will usually be a panel of some sort, but any `UIElement` will work.

Before assigning the element to the `PageVisual` property, you need to ensure that it has all of its children in place. When `PageVisual` is set, it's then measured and laid out. Since it's not part of the proper Silverlight visual tree, adding elements to the visual doesn't cause an automatic measure and layout pass (see chapter 6 for more information on measuring and layout). You can either manually force a measure and layout, or simply populate the visual completely prior to assigning it to the `PageVisual` property.

Figure 19.3 shows the result of adding child elements after assigning the `PageVisual`.

When assigning the `PageVisual`, keep in mind that any content outside the rectangle defined by the `PrintableArea` will be clipped. If you

Pete's Awesome Silverlight Report

Figure 19.3 The result of assigning the page visual prior to adding child elements to a part of the visual. Layout doesn't happen automatically, so all the elements are stacked on top of each other.

need to fit more content on the page, you can apply a scale transform (see chapter 6) to shrink the content down by a ratio that will fit it all on-page.

We'll cover more on setting the `PageVisual` when we look at some specific printing use cases in sections 19.2 and 19.3.

Once the `PageVisual` is set and the `PrintPage` event returns, Silverlight prepares the page for printing by first calling `Measure` and `Arrange` (the layout pass described in chapter 6), and rasterizing it to a single bitmap representing the page.

19.1.3 Rasterization

In chapter 6, we discussed the rendering process for onscreen elements. One step of that process was the rasterization of vector and text elements, and the included blitting of raster (bitmap) elements. Printing follows the same general process, down to the rasterization step.

When you print a tree of elements by assigning it as the page visual, those elements are all rasterized into a page-sized bitmap (or larger if you overrun the size of the page), clipped to the page dimensions, and sent to the printer.

If you're familiar with how printing normally works when using printer languages such as PCL or PostScript, you may find the rasterization approach a little odd. In typical document printing, the print driver sends a list of commands to the printer; those commands contain information such as drawing commands, raster images, font and style specifications, and text commands. The end result is a smaller payload, and the printer is free to optimize the printing for its own capabilities and resolution.

The bitmap-based approach in Silverlight is flexible, is functional across platforms, and supports anything Silverlight can render onscreen. But it's fairly time- and memory-intensive. A Microsoft Word document with text and images prints fairly quickly on my HP LaserJet 1320, taking just a few seconds between my hitting the Print button and seeing output on the printer. A similar document printed through Silverlight takes considerably longer because it's treated as one (approximately) 8 1/2 x 11 inches bitmap.

For those reasons, I don't consider the printing API in Silverlight to be a good choice for large reporting solutions. You'll be waiting quite a long time for a 50-page report to come off the printer. The actual speed is as much a function of the printer hardware as anything, so your own mileage may vary.

Caveats aside, we'll now turn to a few common printing use cases and walk through how to implement them using the Silverlight printing system, starting with printing content as it appears onscreen.

19.2 *Printing onscreen Information*

If a user wants to print the entire web page, she can do so using the browser's Print button. This will also print the contents of any Silverlight control, but only what's visible onscreen. If you have content in a `ListBox`, for example, and want to have it expand to show its entire contents, you won't be able to do that. If your Silverlight application extends below the fold on the browser (if it's taller than the visible portion of the browser page), you're also out of luck.

Additionally, if you want to print only the contents of your Silverlight page and not the surrounding web page, that's not something most browsers will support. For that scenario, you'll want to use the printing API.

In this section we'll explore three ways of printing onscreen content: printing it as is, providing a new root so it can perform layout specific to the printer page, and a combination of providing a new root and using a `ScaleTransform` to ensure the content fits on the printed page.

19.2.1 *Printing the content as is*

The easiest way to print content is to simply hand off the root of your UI and print it as is. This simple approach works for things that fit onscreen, or to provide the equivalent of a print-screen function for your application. Figure 19.4 shows an example

Figure 19.4 The example
application from listing 19.3.
The application has a fixed
height and width.

application with a fixed height and width. We'll want to perform the equivalent of a
print-screen on this application.

Figure 19.4 shows the results of listing 19.3. Note that the application doesn't automatically scale to the size of the page, as it has a hard-coded height and width. Not
also that not all the content fits onscreen due to the hard-coded size.

Listing 19.3 shows the markup for a little application that lists several images from
my web site. We'll use this application markup throughout the rest of the examples in
this section.

Listing 19.3   UI XAML for the content printing example

```
<UserControl x:Class="SilverlightPrintTest.MainPage"
  xmlns="http://schemas.microsoft.com/winfx/2006/xaml/presentation"
  xmlns:x="http://schemas.microsoft.com/winfx/2006/xaml"
  Height="400" Width="500">                                        ⟵┐ Hard-coded
                                                                    │ application
  <Grid x:Name="LayoutRoot" Background="White" Margin="5">   ⟵     │ size
    <Grid.RowDefinitions>                                           │
      <RowDefinition Height="Auto" />            Root visual ┘
      <RowDefinition Height="*" />
      <RowDefinition Height="Auto" />
    </Grid.RowDefinitions>

    <TextBlock Text="Images from Pete's Site"
               FontSize="30"
               TextAlignment="Center" />          ┌ ScrollViewer
    <ScrollViewer Grid.Row="1">              ⟵────┘ with images
      <StackPanel>
        <Image
          Source="http://10rem.net/media/507/
    pete-brown-silverlight-in-action.png"
          Stretch="None"/>
        <Image
```

```
                Source="http://10rem.net/media/33418/wpfdisciples.png"
                Stretch="None" />
            <Image
                Source="http://10rem.net/media/17094/commodorelogo_100x100.png"
                Stretch="None" />

        </StackPanel>
    </ScrollViewer>

    <Button x:Name="Print" Content="Print"
            Grid.Row="2"
            Width="100" Height="30"
            Click="Print_Click"/>

  </Grid>
</UserControl>
```

If you use the browser to print that same content, all you'll see is what's visible on the browser page. To get the same effect from Silverlight, you'll simply assign the User-Control or LayoutRoot to PageVisual in the printing code. Listing 19.4 shows how to do that in the code-behind, using the XAML from listing 19.3.

Listing 19.4   Printing the entire `UserControl` and retaining visual size

```
public partial class MainPage : UserControl
{
  public MainPage()
  {
    InitializeComponent();
  }

  private PrintDocument _document = new PrintDocument();

  private void Print_Click(object sender, RoutedEventArgs e)
  {
    _document.PrintPage += (s, ea) =>
      {
        Debug.WriteLine("Printing page");          Print entire
                                                   user control
        ea.PageVisual = this;            ◁───┘
        ea.HasMorePages = false;
      };

    _document.Print("Silverlight screen print");
  }
}
```

When you hit the Print button, the result is exactly what you see onscreen, but on a printed page. Note that you could also assign the LayoutRoot as the element you wanted to print. As the LayoutRoot already belongs to another visual tree, it won't be resized or anything when assigned to the PageVisual. One way around this is to reroot the root element.

19.2.2   *Rerooting the elements to fit*

One way around the issue with fixed-size content is to take the LayoutRoot (or another element) and *reroot* (or *reparent*) it in a printer-specific root element. That new root element is sized to fit the printer page. Listing 19.5 shows how to reroot the element using the `BeginPrint` and `EndPrint` events for setup and repair.

Listing 19.5 Rerooting an element into a printer-specific root

```
public partial class MainPage : UserControl
{
  public MainPage()
  {
    InitializeComponent();
  }

  private PrintDocument _document = new PrintDocument();

  private void Print_Click(object sender, RoutedEventArgs e)
  {                                                          New printer-
    Grid printRoot = new Grid();                             specific root

    _document.BeginPrint += (s, ea) =>
      {
        this.Content = null;                        ❶
        printRoot.Children.Add(LayoutRoot);
      };

    _document.EndPrint += (s, ea) =>
      {
        printRoot.Children.Remove(LayoutRoot);
        this.Content = LayoutRoot;                  ❷

        MessageBox.Show("Print job complete.");
      };

    _document.PrintPage += (s, ea) =>
      {
        printRoot.Height = ea.PrintableArea.Height;   Size print root
        printRoot.Width = ea.PrintableArea.Width;     to printer page

        ea.PageVisual = printRoot;        ◁── Print it
        ea.HasMorePages = false;
      };

    _document.Print("Silverlight screen print");
  }
}
```

The process is picky, but relatively straightforward. Before you can move an element to be a child of another element, you must first remove it from its current parent ❶. In `BeginPrint`, we remove `LayoutRoot` from the page (its current parent) and add it to the children of the new printer root. In `EndPrint`, we reverse the process ❷. When printing, we simply size the new printer root to the dimensions provided by the printing system, then assign to the `PageVisual` the new printer root element as opposed to the user control itself.

This whole swapping process exists only to allow us to provide layout dimensions that differ from the onscreen dimensions. If you could resize the elements onscreen, that would also work, but may be jarring to the user watching the process.

Depending upon the complexity of what you're trying to do, this could be tricky. For example, there may be unintended consequences associated with additional layout passes for controls you're using, or you may have binding information or resources that are no longer accessible once rerooted. It's not an approach I recommend without first testing for your specific scenario. That being said, it gets around the issue with having fixed-size page content and wanting to print the content in full.

Another option is to scale the content to fit. Similar to this approach, you'll need to make a decision whether to do it live onscreen or scale using an offscreen visual tree.

19.2.3 *Scaling content to fit*

Scaling the content to fit on a single page is another way to print onscreen elements. As was the case with the previous approaches, you can scale the content onscreen, in the live visual tree, or you can reroot and scale the print-specific visual tree.

In most cases, it'd be pretty jarring to scale the onscreen content, so for this example, we'll use the print-specific visual tree.

In this example, I duplicated the content inside the ScrollViewer five times, in order to provide sufficient content to illustrate the example. Simply copy and paste the three Image elements in the XAML so they each appear five times.

Next, modify the code from example 19.5 so it does an automatic scale using a ScaleTransform (see chapter 6 for information on render transforms). Listing 19.6 shows the changed code in the two affected event handlers.

Listing 19.6   Transforming the content to fit on the printed page

```
_document.EndPrint += (s, ea) =>
  {
    LayoutRoot.RenderTransform = null;          ⟵⎯ Clear out render
    printRoot.Children.Remove(LayoutRoot);            transform
    this.Content = LayoutRoot;

    MessageBox.Show("Print job complete.");
  };

_document.PrintPage += (s, ea) =>
  {
    printRoot.Measure(                          ⟵⎯ Measure for max
         new Size(double.PositiveInfinity,           desired size
                  double.PositiveInfinity));
      printRoot.Width = printRoot.DesiredSize.Width;
      printRoot.Height = printRoot.DesiredSize.Height;

    ScaleTransform transform = new ScaleTransform();

    if (printRoot.Height > printRoot.Width)
    {                                           ⟵⎯ Calculate
      transform.ScaleX = transform.ScaleY =          scaling factor
            ea.PrintableArea.Height / printRoot.Height;
    }
    else
    {
```

```
    transform.ScaleX = transform.ScaleY =
          ea.PrintableArea.Width / printRoot.Width;     ◁──┐ Calculate
  }                                                         │ scaling factor

  LayoutRoot.RenderTransform = transform;        ❶

  ea.PageVisual = printRoot;
  ea.HasMorePages = false;
};
```

Clipped

Figure 19.5 The content on the left had the transform applied directly to the PageVisual. It was clipped prior to transforming. The content on the right had the transform applied one level below the Page-Visual, at the Layout-Root. The LayoutRoot was transformed, and the PageVisual was clipped, providing the result we were looking for.

If you look closely, you can see that in listing 19.6 I did something strange: I assigned the render transform to LayoutRoot ❶ instead of printRoot. Why did I do that?

It turns out that the print clipping is applied directly to the PageVisual you supply. If you also have a transform attached to that visual, it'll transform the clipping rectangle as well. The effect is having something that's sized to fit the page, but is clipped in exactly the same spot it would be if it were at 100% scale—not what we want.

There are a couple ways you could solve this. You could put yet another visual between the PageVisual and the LayoutRoot, or if it suits you, attach the transform to the element one level below the PageVisual: the LayoutRoot in this case. Figure 19.5 illustrates how this clipping and transforms interact.

The figure shows what happens when you put the transform on the same level as the clip (left image) or one level down, as shown on the right-side image.

If you apply a transform to resize content and you attach it to an onscreen visual, make sure you remove it when complete. If the content already has a transform applied to it, you'll need to either create a transform group, or—my recommendation—inject a second visual between your element and the PageVisual.

Printing the onscreen content is certainly useful, and often a desirable feature in applications. More common is printing information specifically created for the printer. Such content often spans more than one page, so we'll look at printing purpose-built trees and supporting multipage documents in the next section.

> **Whatever happened to the paperless office?**
>
> I often lament the fact that the paperless office promised in the 1990s never really came to fruition. We make baby steps every year, but paper printouts are still essential to the world of business. Most important forms are still passed around in paper format. Many computer systems are linked only by a manual paper and human data entry process sitting between them.
>
> Recently, I heard a story on NPR about a school system that's going to save millions of dollars in printer toner by changing the default email font to one that uses less toner—yes, employees print email that much! Oddly enough, no one suggested "please don't print email" as a potential cost-saving measure.
>
> It's great to support printing in your application, and essential in many cases, but consider other ways to service the use case when possible. For example, do they need to print that appointment information your application is storing, or would it be equally or perhaps more useful to provide them with an iCal file that they can import into their own scheduling software and synchronize with their phone?

19.3 *Multipage printing dedicated trees*

Multipage printing comes in many flavors. You could be printing documents or letters, perhaps with mail-merge fields. You may be printing a long tabular report, or you may have to print a complex multipage form. All three have two things in common: they may span more than one page and they contain information formatted specifically for the printer.

Before we continue, let me reiterate: Silverlight printing isn't currently optimized for large multipage documents. Each page is a large bitmap, and takes some time to print—how much depends on the printer and driver. If your application needs to do a lot of printing, consider sending it through a server printer or another approach, such as using COM automation to generate a report using Microsoft Word or Excel.

That out of the way, I'll show you how and let you figure out whether it works in your situation. In the remainder of this section, we're going to build a simple report with a page header and footer, and a number of lines in-between. This isn't a full report writer, although I do have something akin to that on http://silverlightreporting. codeplex.com. We'll start with building a little infrastructure, then print out pages with just the line items. From there, we'll add simple headers and footers to each page. First, let's set up our report data.

19.3.1 *Prerequisites*

For this example, we'll use the same AdventureWorks database and entity model used in other chapters. Please refer to appendix A for instructions on setting up the database, connection, and entity model in your web project.

Once you have the database connection information and model set up, we can turn our attention to creating a WCF service to surface the data to the Silverlight client.

CREATING THE SERVICE

Continuing in the web project, it's time to create the service. The first step is to create a folder named Services and into it add a new Silverlight Enabled WCF Service. Figure 19.6 shows the Add New Item dialog with the correct template selected and named.

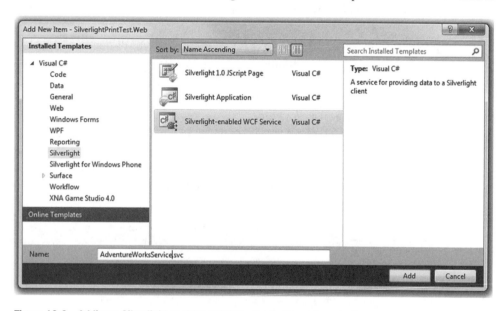

Figure 19.6   Adding a Silverlight-enabled WCF Service to the web project

For this demo, we're only interested in read-only data, so we're going to create a basic service method that returns data from the Adventure Works entity model. We won't support create, update, or delete options. If you're interested in options for that functionality, read chapter 17 on WCF RIA Services.

We'll implement the service methods soon. Before we can do that, we need to create the `EmployeeReportItem` class.

CREATING THE EMPLOYEEREPORTITEM CLASS

The `EmployeeReportItem` class represents a single row of data for our report. We could simply send down the complete entities from the model, but that would be wasteful and perhaps even confusing. Instead, we'll create a denormalized entity that contains properties from both the `Employee` and the `Contact` classes.

In the `Services` folder of the web project, create a new class named `EmployeeRe-portItem`. Listing 19.7 shows the implementation of this class.

Listing 19.7   The `EmployeeReportItem` class

```csharp
public class EmployeeReportItem
{
    public int EmployeeID { get; set; }
    public string FirstName { get; set; }
    public string LastName { get; set; }
    public string Title { get; set; }
    public string EmailAddress { get; set; }
    public string Phone { get; set; }
    public DateTime HireDate { get; set; }
}
```

Note that since we're using .NET 4 on the server, we don't need to include `DataCon-tract` and `DataMember` attributes in the class. WCF will serialize all public members by default.

Once the `EmployeeReportItem` class is in place, we can use it from our service.

ADDING THE SERVICE IMPLEMENTATION

The last step on the server-side of the project is to add the implementation of the `GetEm-ployeeReportData` method of the service. This implementation will join the two entities and pull out fields from them to create `EmployeeReportItem` instances. Those instances will then be returned to the caller, our Silverlight client in this case. Listing 19.8 lists the code required in the service.

Listing 19.8   The `GetEmployees` method of the `AdventureWorksService` class

```csharp
[OperationContract]
public List<EmployeeReportItem> GetEmployeeReportData()
{
  using (AdventureWorksEntities context =
     new AdventureWorksEntities())    {
    var items =
      (from emp in context.Employees
        select new EmployeeReportItem()          ◁─── Shape into
        {                                              EmployeeReportItem
          EmployeeID = emp.EmployeeID,
          FirstName = emp.Contact.FirstName,
          LastName = emp.Contact.LastName,
          Title = emp.Title,
          EmailAddress = emp.Contact.EmailAddress,
          Phone = emp.Contact.Phone,
          HireDate = emp.HireDate               ◁─── Limit return
        }).Take (100)                                  count
          .ToList ();

    return items;
  }
}
```

The service pulls information from the AdventureWorks database, using LINQ to both limit the number of items returned to a reasonable number (100) as well as merge the entities to create a single `EmployeeReportItem` for each row of data.

ADDING A REFERENCE TO THE SERVICE

The final required step before we get into the report itself is to add a reference to the WCF service. First build the solution and ensure that there are no errors. Then, right-click the Silverlight project and choose Add Service Reference.

In the dialog, click Discover to find the services in your solution. If successful, you'll see something like figure 19.7.

In the namespace area, enter the name `Services`. On the Silverlight client, that will be the namespace (under our root namespace) into which the service client proxy and the `EmployeeReportItem` class will be generated.

TEST THE SERVICE

Before we move into printing, let's add one last step: testing. This is optional, but I recommend doing it to ensure that all the other bits are working correctly.

In the code-behind for the main page of your project, add the code shown in listing 19.9. Be sure to right-click `AdventureWorksServiceClient` and choose Resolve (or hit Alt-Shift-F10) to automatically add the correct `using` statement to the code file.

```
public MainPage()
```

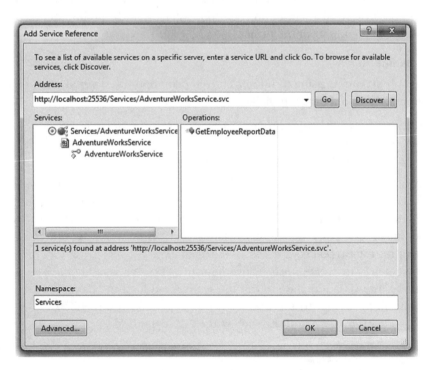

Figure 19.7   Adding a service reference from our Silverlight project to the WCF Service in the web project

Listing 19.9 Code to test the service reference from Silverlight

```
{
  InitializeComponent();

  Loaded += new RoutedEventHandler(MainPage_Loaded);
}

void MainPage_Loaded(object sender, RoutedEventArgs e)
{
  var client = new AdventureWorksServiceClient();

  client.GetEmployeeReportDataCompleted += (s, ea) =>
    {
      if (ea.Result != null)
      {
        foreach (EmployeeReportItem item in ea.Result)
        {
          Debug.WriteLine(item.LastName + ", " + item.FirstName);
        }
      }
    };
  client.GetEmployeeReportDataAsync();
}
```

When you run the project, take a look at your Output window and see if it displays 100 names. If it does, you're good. If not, debug any error you receive and try again. Once it's working, you're ready to build the report, starting with the line items. Be sure to remove the test code from the project.

19.3.2 *Printing line items*

For the report, we're going to build a custom print-optimized visual tree using a combination of code and data templates.

> **NOTE** This report is optimized for learning the concepts and fitting into a book. It's not meant to be a reusable report class, but rather a starter to provide insight into how you might create your own reports in Silverlight.

In this and the following sections, we'll first get the data from the WCF service into the report class. Then we'll print a single-page version of the report using just the line items and a data template. The next step is modifying the report to support page breaks. From there, we'll add a header and footer before wrapping up.

CREATING THE EMPLOYEEREPORT CLASS AND LOADING DATA

The first step is to create, in the Silverlight project, a class named EmployeeReport. Into that class, we'll add code to call the service and load the data. The code to load the data will be similar to the test code in listing 19.9. Listing 19.10 shows the class with a LoadData method and the shell of the Print method.

Listing 19.10 The EmployeeReport class

```
public class EmployeeReport : FrameworkElement
{
  public EmployeeReport() { }
```

```
    public event EventHandler DataLoaded;                          Line items
                                                                   for report
    private IEnumerable<EmployeeReportItem> _items;          ⟵┘

    public void LoadData ()
    {
      var client = new AdventureWorksServiceClient();

      client.GetEmployeeReportDataCompleted += (s, e) =>
      {
        _items = e.Result;

        if (DataLoaded != null)
          DataLoaded(this, EventArgs.Empty);
      };

      client.GetEmployeeReportDataAsync();
    }                                                         Handles actual
    private void InternalPrintReport()                ⟵┘     report printing
    {
    }
}
```

I chose to derive from `FrameworkElement` for two reasons:

1 I need to derive from some `DependencyObject`-derived class in order to support the dependency properties that will be used for the templates.
2 I want the element to be on-page and accessible in XAML.

For more on `FrameworkElement`, see chapter 6.

Listing 19.10 forms the shell of our new report class. Because we'll use it in XAML, in addition to deriving from `FrameworkElement`, I needed to include a default constructor. It's an empty constructor, but its presence means that it can be instantiated in XAML. Additionally, as we need to support a user-initiated print process, I raise a `DataLoaded` event when the data is loaded. The UI can then capture that and allow the user to click a button to perform the printing.

Now that the class has been created, we'll add support for the first template: the item template.

ADDING THE ITEMTEMPLATE

The next step is to add a dependency property for the item template used to format items on the report. The `DependencyProperty` will hold a `DataTemplate` containing visuals and binding statements for the items rows. Listing 19.11 shows the code you'll need to add to the `EmployeeReport` class.

> **Listing 19.11 The `ItemTemplate` on the `EmployeeReport` class**

```
public DataTemplate ItemTemplate
{
  get { return (DataTemplate)GetValue(ItemTemplateProperty); }
  set { SetValue(ItemTemplateProperty, value); }
}

public static readonly DependencyProperty ItemTemplateProperty =
```

```
DependencyProperty.Register("ItemTemplate",
typeof(DataTemplate), typeof(EmployeeReport),
new PropertyMetadata(null));
```

We'll have a few more dependency properties to add before we're through. Before we do that, let's crack open the MainPage XAML and add a reference to the EmployeeReport type and flesh out the data template for the item rows.

Listing 19.12 shows the MainPage XAML file with a reference to the local namespace, and an instance of the report with an appropriate yet simple data template. I've also added a Print button (with a click handler in the code-behind) to provide a way to print the report.

Listing 19.12 `MainPage` **markup with an instance of our report and template**

```
<local:EmployeeReport x:Name="Report">
  <local:EmployeeReport.ItemTemplate>
    <DataTemplate>
      <Grid>
        <Grid.ColumnDefinitions>
          <ColumnDefinition Width="40" />
          <ColumnDefinition Width="180" />
          <ColumnDefinition Width="180" />
          <ColumnDefinition Width="210" />
          <ColumnDefinition Width="100" />
          <ColumnDefinition Width="70" />
        </Grid.ColumnDefinitions>

        <TextBlock Grid.Column="0"
                Text="{Binding EmployeeID}" />

        <StackPanel Grid.Column="1" Orientation="Horizontal">
          <TextBlock Text="{Binding LastName}" />
          <TextBlock Text=", " />
          <TextBlock Text="{Binding FirstName}" />
        </StackPanel>

        <TextBlock Grid.Column="2"
                Text="{Binding Title}" />

        <TextBlock Grid.Column="3"
                Text="{Binding EmailAddress}" />

        <TextBlock Grid.Column="4"
                Text="{Binding Phone}" />

        <TextBlock Grid.Column="5"
              Text="{Binding HireDate, StringFormat='{}{0:d}'}" />
      </Grid>
    </DataTemplate>
  </local:EmployeeReport.ItemTemplate>
</local:EmployeeReport>
```

The local namespace is mapped to the project the code and markup reside within. The ItemTemplate contains a DataTemplate that has a grid column for each column displayed on the report. Each column contains one or more fields bound to the properties of the `EmployeeReportItem` class. The `EmployeeReport` element itself resides in the `LayoutRoot` grid, left out of the listing for space considerations. Also in the `LayoutRoot` grid is the button previously mentioned:

```
<Button x:Name="Print" Content="Print" Width="100" Height="30"
        IsEnabled="False"
        Click="Print_Click"/>
```

Note that the button isn't enabled by default. We'll enable it once the data is loaded from the service. The code to run the report can't be included in the service return event handler, because (in normal trust applications) it must be run from a user-initiated event.

Listing 19.13 shows the code-behind with the code to load the report data and handle the print report button click.

Listing 19.13 Code-behind for `MainPage`

```
public MainPage()
{
  InitializeComponent();

  Loaded += new RoutedEventHandler(MainPage_Loaded);
}

void MainPage_Loaded(object sender, RoutedEventArgs e)
{
  Report.DataLoaded += (s,ea) =>
    {                                          ◁──┐ Enable button
      Print.IsEnabled = true;               ◁──┘ when loaded
    };

  Report.LoadData();              ◁──── Load data
}

private void Print_Click(object sender, RoutedEventArgs e)
{
  Report.Print();
}
```

With the item template in place, and our print button wired up, we'll turn our eyes back to the `PrintDocument` class and the `PrintPage` event.

THE PRINT METHOD

The `EmployeeReport` class currently has a `Print` method that does nothing. We'll flesh that out a little more to include the usual trifecta of print event handlers, as shown in listing 19.14.

Listing 19.14 The three printing event handlers, wired and ready to go

```
private void Print()
{
  PrintDocument doc = new PrintDocument();

  IEnumerator<EmployeeReportItem> itemsEnumerator =      ◁──┐ Enumerator
    _items.GetEnumerator();                           ◁──┘ explained shortly

  doc.BeginPrint += (s, e) =>
```

```
    {
        itemsEnumerator.Reset();      ⟵──┐ Enumerator
    };                                     explained shortly

  doc.EndPrint += (s, e) =>
    {
        MessageBox.Show("Report complete.");
    };                                 ┌── PrintPage event
  doc.PrintPage += (s, e) =>       ⟵──┘ handler
    {
    };

  doc.Print("Employee Report");
}
```

From this point forward, the majority of the code will go into the PrintPage method. For space considerations, I won't show the other event handlers or the Internal-PrintReport function itself.

ENUMERATING ROWS

When I was in college, they made me learn COBOL. Not just any old COBOL, but COBOL on an unforgiving editor on a VAX/VMS computer. If you've never written in COBOL, give it a try—it'll make you appreciate how little typing you need to get things done in C#. Perhaps my interest in curly-brace languages like C# is actually the result of the trauma I sustained in that class.

Anyway, I digress. One thing that the COBOL class did teach was how to build reports from code. That's one skill that I've been able to use in most technologies since. Up until now, though, I hadn't been able to use that in Silverlight. Luckily, that's about to change.

Normally when you process a bunch of rows of data, you'd use a LINQ statement or a for each loop. Neither approach will work particularly well here, as we need to keep a pointer to our position in the data while allowing Silverlight to raise separate events for each page. Though we could use a simple for next loop and an index that we keep track of externally, this is the type of scenario just built for IEnumerator<T>.

In listing 19.16, you can see the enumerator declared inside the Print method. This will be used to keep track of our current position in the report data. In the BeginPrint event handler, I reset the enumerator. Doing so allows Print to be called multiple times on the same data, without running into an enumerator problem.

The enumerator approach is similar to what you might use in COBOL or in record-set/rowset processing in another language, where there's the concept of a "current" record as opposed to an external loop index.

In listing 19.15, I first create a StackPanel that will be used to hold the rows of data. I then move through each row of data, instantiate the template, and add the resulting element to the panel. Finally, the panel is set as the page visual, ready for Silverlight to print.

Listing 19.15 Enumerating and printing each row of data

```
doc.PrintPage += (s, e) =>
{
  StackPanel itemsPanel = new StackPanel();        ❶

  while (itemsEnumerator.MoveNext())                          Create from
  {                                                          template
    FrameworkElement row =
      ItemTemplate.LoadContent() as FrameworkElement;

    row.DataContext = itemsEnumerator.Current;       ❷
    row.Measure(e.PrintableArea);                    ❸

    itemsPanel.Children.Add(row);                        Add to
  }                                                       panel
  e.PageVisual = itemsPanel;
  e.HasMorePages = false;
};
```

The code in listing 19.15 includes the majority of the important logic required to print a report. It first creates a `StackPanel` ❶ used to hold the content. It then loops through the line items, creating a template-based element to be the row's contents, and then setting the data context ❷ of that element to be the row data itself. It then measures ❸ the element, providing it the bounds of the page, and finally adds it to the stack panel. Once all elements have been created, the page visual is set to the stack panel and the "more pages" flag is set to false.

In setting `HasMorePages` to false and not dealing with page breaks, the code in listing 19.15 blindly prints, ignoring the end of the page. If this were old traditional printing, green-bar fan-fold paper would be flying off the printer faster than we could catch it, with printing on the seams and everywhere else. Silverlight will clip this, of course, so the result will be only a single page that doesn't overrun its boundaries. Figure 19.8 shows the top of the report page for reference, as it appears when using the XPS document print driver.

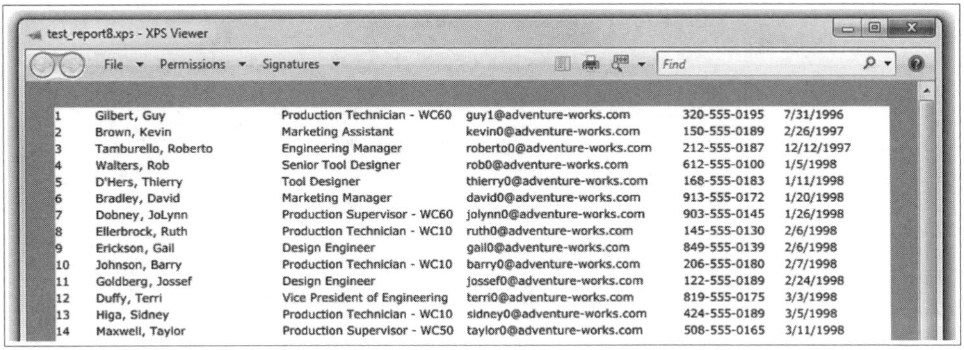

Figure 19.8 The top portion of the report, shown in the XPS viewer

A short single page is nice, but losing data off the bottom isn't. What we really want is to support multiple pages and wrap contents on to those subsequent pages.

19.3.3 *Adding multipage support*

In order to support multiple pages, we need to keep track of the size of the report at every row. You could precalculate the number of rows that will fit, but then you'd lose the flexibility to have dynamically sized rows that change height based upon their content.

Listing 19.16 shows what I did to keep track of the page size and ensure the content will fit on the page. Note the addition of the !full check in the while loop.

> **Listing 19.16   Breaking when the page is full**

```
doc.BeginPrint += (s, e) =>
{
    itemsEnumerator.Reset();
    itemsEnumerator.MoveNext();
};

doc.PrintPage += (s, e) =>
{
    StackPanel itemsPanel = new StackPanel();

    double itemsAreaHeight = e.PrintableArea.Height;
    double itemsHeight = 0.0;

    bool full = false;
    bool moreItems = true;

    while (moreItems && !full)
    {
        FrameworkElement row =
            ItemTemplate.LoadContent() as FrameworkElement;

        row.DataContext = itemsEnumerator.Current;
        row.Measure(e.PrintableArea);

        itemsHeight += row.DesiredSize.Height;

        if (itemsHeight > itemsAreaHeight)
        {                                              ⟵  Row
            full = true;                                   doesn't fit
        }
        else
        {                                              ⟵  Row fits.
            itemsPanel.Children.Add(row);                  Add it
            moreItems = itemsEnumerator.MoveNext();
        }
    }

    e.PageVisual = itemsPanel;                         ⟵  More items means
    e.HasMorePages = moreItems;                            more pages
};

doc.Print("Employee Report");
}
```

The approach I used here to move things to the next page is a little hokey. For one thing, that MoveNext in BeginPrint assumes the report will always have at least one row of data. For another, there's a wasted measure call when you reach the point of moving to a new page.

To really do multipage support correctly, you need to precalculate your pages. This is the approach I took in the version I put up on CodePlex. But for the simple example here, I decided to reserve a bit of buffer space at the bottom of the page, equal to the size of one row. Of course, this assumes fixed-height rows. To support dynamically sized rows, you'll need to measure and then move the item to the next page if it doesn't fit—something much easier to do in a precalculation routine.

Whatever approach you use, once you have some measuring infrastructure in place, it becomes fairly easy to add a header and footer.

19.3.4 Adding a header and footer

The approach we'll use to add a header and footer is similar to the items approach. The header and footer will each have an associated DataTemplate property that will be populated in XAML with the appropriate content. Listing 19.17 shows the property declarations in the EmployeeReport class.

Listing 19.17 Dependency properties for templates

```
public DataTemplate PageHeaderTemplate          ◁── Page header
{
    get { return (DataTemplate)GetValue(PageHeaderTemplateProperty); }
    set { SetValue(PageHeaderTemplateProperty, value); }
}

public static readonly DependencyProperty PageHeaderTemplateProperty =
    DependencyProperty.Register("PageHeaderTemplate",
    typeof(DataTemplate), typeof(EmployeeReport),
    new PropertyMetadata(null));

public DataTemplate PageFooterTemplate          ◁── Page footer
{
    get { return (DataTemplate)GetValue(PageFooterTemplateProperty); }
    set { SetValue(PageFooterTemplateProperty, value); }
}

public static readonly DependencyProperty PageFooterTemplateProperty =
    DependencyProperty.Register("PageFooterTemplate",
    typeof(DataTemplate), typeof(EmployeeReport),
    new PropertyMetadata(null));                  │ Read-only
                                                  ◁─┘ page number
public int PageNumber
{
    get { return (int)GetValue(PageNumberProperty); }
    private set { SetValue(PageNumberProperty, value); }
}

public static readonly DependencyProperty PageNumberProperty =
    DependencyProperty.Register("PageNumber",
    typeof(int), typeof(EmployeeReport),
    new PropertyMetadata(0));
```

Note that I added a third dependency property to hold the page number. We'll use that inside the templates to show the current page number via a binding statement. The two other dependency property declarations are pretty straightforward. We'll have one data template for the page header and another for the page footer. The XAML data templates for listing 19.17 are shown in listing 19.18.

Listing 19.18   Header and footer data templates in MainPage XAML

```
<local:EmployeeReport.PageHeaderTemplate>                    ←── Header
  <DataTemplate>
    <Grid Margin="1 1 1 10">
      <Rectangle Stroke="Black"/>
      <TextBlock Text="Adventure Works Employee Report"
                 FontSize="25" Margin="10"
                 HorizontalAlignment="Left"
                 VerticalAlignment="Center" />
    </Grid>
  </DataTemplate>
</local:EmployeeReport.PageHeaderTemplate>

<local:EmployeeReport.PageFooterTemplate>                    ←── Footer
  <DataTemplate>
    <Grid Margin="1 10 1 1">
      <Rectangle Stroke="Black" />
        <TextBlock
          Text="{Binding PageNumber,StringFormat='Page {0}'}"
          Margin="10" HorizontalAlignment="Right"
          VerticalAlignment="Center" />
    </Grid>
  </DataTemplate>
</local:EmployeeReport.PageFooterTemplate>
```

To support the page numbering used in listing 19.18, I had to add another reset line to the BeginPrint event. This line resets PageNumber to 0, assuming we may print the report more than once. Here's the additional line of code, shown in context:

```
doc.BeginPrint += (s, e) =>
{
    itemsEnumerator.Reset();
    itemsEnumerator.MoveNext();
    PageNumber = 0;
};
```

You could leave out the PageNumber reset, and the worst that would happen would be that your page numbers would continue to increment from report to report during the same Silverlight session.

   That brings us to the real core of the multipage support: the PrintPage changes. PrintPage gains a significant number of lines of code because we now need to build a grid to contain the header, footer, and content rows. The StackPanel is still there, in the central cell in the grid, but it's now positioned between two other grid rows. Listing 19.19 shows the method, with the exception of the code right above and inside the while loop, which remains untouched.

Listing 19.19   Updated `PrintPage` code for header and footer

```
doc.PrintPage += (s, e) =>
{
  PageNumber++;                                    ❶

  Grid rootGrid = new Grid();                      ❷
  RowDefinition headerRow = new RowDefinition();   ❸
  headerRow.Height = GridLength.Auto;
  RowDefinition itemsRow = new RowDefinition();    ❹
  itemsRow.Height = new GridLength(1, GridUnitType.Star);
  RowDefinition footerRow = new RowDefinition();   ❺
  footerRow.Height = GridLength.Auto;

  rootGrid.RowDefinitions.Add(headerRow);
  rootGrid.RowDefinitions.Add(itemsRow);
  rootGrid.RowDefinitions.Add(footerRow);                Create
                                                         header
  FrameworkElement header =
    PageHeaderTemplate.LoadContent() as FrameworkElement;
  header.DataContext = this;
  header.Measure(e.PrintableArea);
  Grid.SetRow(header, 0);

  StackPanel itemsPanel = new StackPanel();
  Grid.SetRow(itemsPanel, 1);                            Create
                                                         footer
  FrameworkElement footer =
    PageFooterTemplate.LoadContent() as FrameworkElement;
  footer.DataContext = this;
  footer.Measure(e.PrintableArea);
  Grid.SetRow(footer, 2);

  rootGrid.Children.Add(header);
  rootGrid.Children.Add(itemsPanel);               ❻
  rootGrid.Children.Add(footer);

  double itemsAreaHeight = e.PrintableArea.Height -          ❼
      header.DesiredSize.Height - footer.DesiredSize.Height;

    ... itemsHeight, full, moreItems, while loop ...

  e.PageVisual = rootGrid;              ❽
  e.HasMorePages = moreItems;
};
```

The additions in listing 19.19 are long, but easily understood. I first increment the page number ❶ so we can use that in the bound header and footer. I then create a new root element ❷, this time a grid. Three rows are added to the grid: the header row ❸, the items row ❹, and the footer row ❺. The header and footer rows are auto-sized; the middle items row is set to take up the remaining available space. I then create the elements from the header and footer templates and add them to the appropriate rows in the grid along with the `StackPanel` used to hold items ❻. Their data contexts are set to the report object, so they can pick up the `PageNumber` property. The final new step before the loop is to modify the way the `itemsAreaHeight` is calculated, so it takes into account the size of the header and footer ❼. Finally, rather

54	Kharatishvili, Tengiz	Control Specialist	tengiz0@adventure-works.com	910-555-0116	1/17/1999
55	Feng, Hanying	Production Technician - WC20	hanying0@adventure-works.com	319-555-0139	1/17/1999
56	Liu, Kevin	Production Technician - WC40	kevin1@adventure-works.com	714-555-0138	1/18/1999
57	Stahl, Annik	Production Technician - WC60	annik0@adventure-works.com	499-555-0125	1/18/1999

Page 1

Adventure Works Employee Report

58	Fatima, Suroor	Production Technician - WC50	suroor0@adventure-works.com	932-555-0161	1/18/1999
59	Poe, Deborah	Accounts Receivable Specialist	deborah0@adventure-works.com	602-555-0194	1/19/1999
60	Scardelis, Jim	Production Technician - WC50	jim0@adventure-works.com	679-555-0113	1/20/1999
61	Poland, Carole	Production Technician - WC30	carole0@adventure-works.com	688-555-0192	1/20/1999

Figure 19.9   The footer from page 1 and the header from page 2. Note the page number on the first page.

than assign the items panel to the `PageVisual`, I assign the entire grid, header, items, footer, and all ❽.

Figure 19.9 shows the header and footer at the page break between page 1 and page 2.

It's relatively easy to get the page number, as you see in the example code. It's more difficult to get a total page count. One common request for reports is the ability to show the page number as "Page x of y" where *x* is the current page and *y* is the total count of pages. Should you desire to do this, you'll need to precalculate the pages prior to printing—the approach I took in the version posted to CodePlex.

Supporting multipage printing with headers and footers is easily done, given the flexibility of data templates and the "no assumptions" low-level nature of the Silverlight printing API. Though the performance of the printing system isn't quite up to par for huge multipage reports, the API does nothing to prevent you from creating those types of print jobs should they be appropriate to your project.

Combining the print API with binding and templates offers a good reuse story, and allows you to spend more time in XAML using design tools and less time in code. You could even extend the template model to include a report footer for totals, or modify it further to support nested groups. The sky's the limit.

19.4 Summary

In order for Silverlight to be taken seriously in the business world, it had to support a flexible printing API. Though you can sometimes punt and skip on printing support in consumer applications, the business world is less forgiving.

With Silverlight 4, the product team delivered a very flexible printing API. It may still be rough around the edges, especially in performance and, in some cases, raster quality of the output, but it's still a 1.0 API, and quite usable at that.

The printing API in Silverlight can be used for anything from printing simple onscreen content to complex multipage reports with headers, footers, grouping, and more. In this chapter we saw how to print content as it appears onscreen, then looked at a few ways to handle scaling that content so it better fit the printer. We also looked at content that was purpose-built specifically for the printer, whether a simple single-page list or a multipage report including headers and footers.

The information in this chapter can serve as a foundation upon which you can build your own printing and reporting systems in your applications. But, should you want to take the knowledge and simply apply it to someone else's code, David Poll and I have created a simple report writer project on CodePlex at http://silverlightreporting. codeplex.com. We plan to use that as a test bed for new ideas and provide something real that you can build upon to meet your own requirements. Take a look at it, if only to see some of the other techniques described in this chapter, such as precalculating pages.

In the next chapter, we'll look at the media capabilities of Silverlight, including the exciting webcam and microphone APIs introduced in Silverlight 4, and the media APIs introduced in Silverlight 3.

Displaying and capturing media 20

This chapter covers
- Interactive playback
- Playlist management
- Working with raw media
- Working with the webcam and microphone

If you ask most non-Silverlight developers what Silverlight is, 8 out of 10 will probably say it's Microsoft's web media player. Part of that reputation comes from Silverlight 1.0, which was only good as a media player. The other part comes from the incredible advances the Silverlight team has made in making Silverlight a first class media platform for the web.

Silverlight excels at delivering high-quality HD media. In fact, it was one of the first web technologies to support true 720p and 1080p HD media over decent but not abnormal network pipes. Silverlight has been the driving media force behind Netflix, as well as many online events such as the Olympics and March Madness. Media is what has helped Silverlight expand onto the majority of internet-connected desktops.

Allowing your users to experience digital media in a meaningful and personal manner can be challenging and exciting. Throughout this chapter, you'll learn how to use items from within the System.Windows.Controls namespace to help accomplish this. You'll first see the flexible MediaElement control. Then, you'll learn how to manage the media experience through the use of playlists and interactive playback. From there, you'll learn about accessing protected content, an essential feature for large content publishers such as Netflix. We'll also learn about creating raw video and audio using the MediaStreamSource API. We'll wrap up this chapter with an examination of the webcam and microphone API introduced with Silverlight 4.

20.1 Audio and video

Integrating media into a Silverlight application is incredibly simple. To include a rich media experience, you employ a MediaElement object. This general-purpose object empowers you to deliver rich audio and video content. For a user to enjoy this high-fidelity content, though, the media item must first be loaded and configured.

Throughout the course of this section, you'll learn how to load and configure audio and video content. This section will begin with an in-depth discussion about the MediaElement's Source property. From there, you'll see the properties that you can use to configure both audio and video items. Next, you'll see the items directly related to audio content. We'll then shift toward a focus on video content. This section will conclude with an explanation of the lifecycle of a media file within a MediaElement.

20.1.1 Media source

The Source property of the MediaElement specifies the location of the audio or video file to play. This file can be referenced by using either a relative or absolute URL. If you have a video file called video.wmv in a subdirectory called Media within your web application, you could use it by setting the Source property to Media/video.wmv. This example shows a MediaElement that uses a relative media file:

```
<Grid x:Name="LayoutRoot" Background="White">
  <MediaElement x:Name="myMediaElement" Source="Media/video.wmv" />
</Grid>
```

This shows a video that belongs to the same web application as the Silverlight application. Note the use of the forward slash (/) in the Source property. This property allows you to use forward slashes, but not backslashes (\). In addition, the Source property also has support for cross-domain URIs.

Cross-domain URIs allow you to specify an absolute path to a media file. This feature gives you the flexibility to use a media asset stored on another server. If you choose to use this approach, it's important to gain permission to use the file before doing so. You do have our permission to reference the video shown here:

```
<Grid x:Name="LayoutRoot">
  <MediaElement x:Name="myMediaElement"
          Source="http://www.silverlightinaction.com/video2.wmv" />
</Grid>
```

This example shows a video, which doesn't include sound, being accessed from a remote server. When accessing content from a remote server, you must use one of the three acceptable protocols. Silverlight supports the HTTP, HTTPS, and MMS protocols. In addition, the Source property expects certain formats.

SUPPORTED FORMATS

Have you ever wanted a snack or soda and accidently put foreign currency in your local vending machine? Or, have you ever accidently put a DVD into a CD player? What happened? Most likely, either nothing happened or some type of error was displayed. These scenarios show that devices are created with specific formats in mind. Likewise, the MediaElement expects certain formats.

The MediaElement supports a powerful array of audio and video formats that empower you to deliver high-quality media experiences over the internet. The accepted audio formats ensure a truly high-fidelity aural experience. At the same time, the supported video formats ensure a viewing experience that can scale from mobile devices all the way up to high-definition displays. Table 20.1 shows the formats supported by the MediaElement.

Table 20.1   Media containers and codecs supported by Silverlight

Container	Codec
Windows Media	Windows Media Audio 7, 8, 9 (WMA Standard) Windows Media Audio 9, 10 (WMA Professional) WMV1 (Windows Media Video 7) WMV2 (Windows Media Video 8) WMV3 (Windows Media Video 9)
MP4	H.264 (ITU-T H.264 / ISO MPEG-4 AVC), AAC-LC
MP3	ISO MPEG-1 Layer III (MP3)

By targeting these media formats, the Silverlight runtime can be a self-contained environment for media experiences. Once your users install the Silverlight runtime, they can run all the supported media formats without having to download and install additional codecs.

The format for media is important, but the delivery method is equally so. Table 20.2 lists the delivery methods Silverlight recognizes for audio and video.

Table 20.2   Supported media delivery methods

Delivery method	Supported containers
Progressive download	Windows Media, MP4, MP3, ASX
Windows Media Streaming over HTTP	Windows Media Server-Side Play List (SSPL)
Smooth Streaming	fMP4
ASX	Windows Media, MP4, ASX

Table 20.2 Supported media delivery methods *(continued)*

Delivery method	Supported containers
PlayReady DRM	MP4
Server-side playlist	Windows Media
`MediaStreamSource`	Any container, as long as you write a parser for it

In addition to the progressive download formats, table 20.2 shows two different streaming methods: Smooth Streaming and Windows Media Streaming over HTTP.

SMOOTH STREAMING WITH IIS

Smooth Streaming is an HTTP-based multiple bit rate (MBR) adaptive media streaming service implemented on Internet Information Server (IIS) on Windows servers. Smooth Streaming dynamically detects client bandwidth and CPU usage and adapts to conditions in close to real-time. Smooth Streaming provides:

- Automatic adaptation to CPU constraints
- Automatic adaptation to bandwidth constraints
- Simplified caching and support for content delivery networks (CDN)

For example, if you're watching an HD video on your client and suddenly you start a CPU-intensive process such as a large compile, rather than drop frames, Smooth Streaming detects the condition and lowers the quality of the video (lowers the bit rate, which typically means a lower resolution) so your viewing sessions continues uninterrupted.

Similarly, if you're watching an HD video and someone in your house starts a large download, effectively taking up a large portion of your internet bandwidth, Smooth Streaming will adapt to that as well, lowering the bit rate to fit into the available bandwidth.

Finally, Smooth Streaming supports simplified caching of content, as the individual chunks are individual files, easily cached using standard HTTP file caching mechanisms. The caches need not know anything about media formats; the bits are just files. For the same reasons, proxies work just as well, requiring no special open ports or knowledge of the formats.

Smooth Streaming delivers small content fragments (about two to four seconds worth of video) to the client, and verifies (with the help of Silverlight) that the content all arrived on time and played at the expected quality level. If a fragment doesn't meet these requirements due to bandwidth or processor restrictions, the next fragment will be delivered at a lower quality level. If the conditions were favorable, the next fragment will be delivered at the same or higher quality level.

Similarly, if the video is available in 1080p HD, but the user is watching it on a display at 720p resolution, Smooth Streaming will send down only the 720p size chunks, saving bandwidth and processing time.

On the server, this requires that the videos be encoded to several different formats. IIS Smooth Streaming keeps all the chunks for a given format in a single MP4 file, but

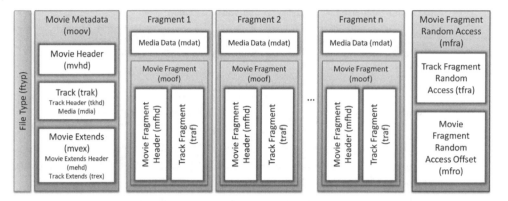

Figure 20.1   The Smooth Streaming server-side file format

delivers the chunks as individual logical files. This makes server file management (and file access) easier, while still providing for caching of chunks by local proxies and downstream servers. Smooth Streaming files have the extension .ismv for video plus audio, and .isma for audio-only. Figure 20.1 shows the structure of the Smooth Streaming file on the server.

The file includes a file type header to let us know this is the smooth streaming file. Next, it includes Movie Metadata (moov) that describes what the file contains. Following that are the individual two-second fragments for the entire movie. Each fragment contains header information for the fragment, as well as the fragment bits themselves. The file closes with an "mfra" index that allows for easy and accurate seeking within the file.[1]

In addition to the media file described here, Smooth Streaming also uses a .ism manifest file for the server, which describes the relationships between the different server files, and a .ismc client manifest file, describing the available streams, codecs, bit rates, markets, and so on. This .ismc file is what's first delivered to the client when the video is requested.

An online example of Smooth Streaming with IIS and Silverlight may be seen on the IIS Smooth Streaming site here: http://www.iis.net/media/experiencesmooth-streaming. Other examples of Smooth Streaming through a CDN may be seen at http://www.smoothhd.com.

To encode video for use with Smooth Streaming, you use Microsoft Expression Encoder. Once the videos are encoded, you can use the Expression Encoder Smooth Streaming template to serve as the start of your video player, or you can use the Silverlight Media Framework, covered in section 20.5.

The Silverlight Media Framework (SMF) is the easiest way to incorporate Smooth Streaming into your application. Before we cover that, let's look at other forms of streaming and downloading available to us.

---

[1]   IIS Smooth Streaming Technical Overview, Alex Zambelli, Microsoft, March 2009. http://bit.ly/Smooth-StreamingTech

WINDOWS MEDIA STREAMING

Though now generally out of favor due to the introduction of Smooth Streaming, Silverlight still supports streaming media content over HTTP through server-side play lists and the MMS protocol. The MMS protocol was built for sending many short messages to a client, and uses a URI that begins with mms:// instead of http:// or https://. When a media file is streamed through this protocol, your Silverlight application maintains an open connection with the hosting server. This has two advantages. It enables you to jump to any point in time within a media file, and streaming usually provides a more cost-effective approach for delivering audio and video content because only the requested content is downloaded, plus a little extra. This content is configurable through the BufferingTime property.

> **TIP** When evaluating media streaming options for HD content, lean toward IIS Smooth Streaming over Windows Media Streaming. IIS Smooth Streaming is better optimized to provide a great user experience with high bit rate content, such as HD video.

The BufferingTime property enables you to view or specify how much of a buffer should be downloaded. By default, this TimeSpan value is set to buffer 5 seconds worth of content. If you're streaming a 1-minute video, the video won't begin playing until at least 5 seconds of it has been retrieved. While this retrieval is occurring, the Current-State property of the MediaElement (which we'll discuss shortly) will be set to Buffering. While the MediaElement is in a Buffering state, it'll halt playback. You can check to see what percentage of the buffering is completed by checking the BufferingProgress property.

The BufferingProgress property gives you access to the percentage of the completed buffering. Because this property value is always between 0.0 and 1.0, you need to multiply it by 100 to get the percentage. When this property changes by a value greater than 5 percent, the BufferingProgressChanged event will be fired. This event gives you the flexibility to keep your users informed through a progress bar or some other UI construct. As you can imagine, this type of component can be valuable when you're streaming content.

Often, streamed content can be quite lengthy. Because of this, it can be advantageous to use MBR) files. MBR files enable you to provide the highest quality experience based on the available bandwidth. The really cool part is that the MediaElement will automatically choose which bit rate to use based on the available bandwidth. In addition, the MediaElement will automatically attempt to progressively download the content if it can't be streamed. That's thinking progressively.

PROGRESSIVE DOWNLOAD

Progressive downloading involves requesting a media file over the HTTP or HTTPS protocol. When this occurs, the requested content is temporarily downloaded to a user's computer, enabling the user to quickly access any part of the media that has been downloaded. In addition to fast access, using a progressive download generally provides a higher-quality media experience. Progressive downloading usually requires a longer initial wait time than streaming, so you may want to keep your users informed of how much wait time is left.

Keeping your users informed is made possible through two key items within the Media-Element. The first item is a property called DownloadProgress. It gives you access to the percentage of the content that has been downloaded. The other item is an event called DownloadProgressChanged. This event gives you the ability to do something such as update a progress bar whenever the DownloadProgress property changes. In listing 20.1, both these items are used to show the percentage of requested content that's available.

Listing 20.1 The percentage of content ready for use within a MediaElement

XAML:

```
<UserControl x:Class="Chapter20.Page"
  xmlns="http://schemas.microsoft.com/winfx/2006/xaml/presentation"
  xmlns:x="http://schemas.microsoft.com/winfx/2006/xaml"
  Width="400" Height="300">
  <Canvas x:Name="LayoutRoot" Background="White">
    <TextBlock x:Name="tb" Canvas.Top="0" />
    <MediaElement x:Name="me" Canvas.Top="20"                    ⟵— MediaElement
      Source="http://www.silverlightinaction.com/video3.wmv"

DownloadProgressChanged="me_DownloadProgressChanged" />          ❶
  </Canvas>
</UserControl>
```

C#:

```
using System;
using System.Windows;
using System.Windows.Controls;
namespace Chapter20
{
  public partial class Page : UserControl
  {
    public Page()
    { InitializeComponent(); }
    void me_DownloadProgressChanged(object sender, RoutedEventArgs e)
    {
      double percentage = me.DownloadProgress * 100.0;           ❷
      string text = String.Format("{0:f}", percentage) + "%";
      tb.Text = text;
    }
  }
}
```

This example shows a large video file (~13MB) being progressively downloaded ❶. As this download progresses, the completion percentage is calculated ❷. This percentage is then formatted and presented to the user as the video is downloaded.

Whether you stream content or progressively download it, the MediaElement expects certain formats. These file formats are then retrieved over one of the accepted protocols (HTTP, HTTPS, or MMS). The Source property simplifies this retrieval process, and it works with both audio and video files. Once the media source is loaded, the MediaElement can be used to configure the playback of a media item or obtain status information. These items are available through a set of commonly used properties.

20.1.2 Common properties

The MediaElement provides a number of properties that are common to both audio and video files. Interestingly, you've already seen several—the Source, BufferingTime, BufferingProgress, and DownloadProgress properties. There are five other properties so fundamental to the MediaElement that we should discuss them now. These properties are AutoPlay, CanPause, CurrentState, NaturalDuration, and Position.

AUTOPLAY

The AutoPlay property specifies whether the MediaElement will automatically begin playing. By default, a MediaElement will begin playing as soon as the content referenced in the Source property is loaded. You can disable this default behavior by changing the AutoPlay bool property to false. As you can imagine, once a media file has begun playing, there may be times when you want to be able to pause it.

CANPAUSE

Sometimes you may want to allow a user to halt the playback of a MediaElement. By default, the MediaElement will allow you to do this. But, by setting the CanPause property of the MediaElement to false, you can prevent your users from pausing the playback. If you allow the pausing function and a user decides to halt the playback, it'll change the value of the CurrentState property.

CURRENTSTATE

The CurrentState property represents the mode the MediaElement is in. This mode is exposed as a value of the System.Windows.Media.MediaElementState enumeration. This enumeration provides all the possible states a MediaElement can be in. These states are listed and described in table 20.3.

Table 20.3 The options available within the MediaElementState enumeration

Option	Description
AcquiringLicense	Occurs while a protected file is obtaining a license key (see section 20.4.3).
Buffering	This signals that the MediaElement is in the process of loading a media file.
Closed	The media has been unloaded from the MediaElement.
Individualizing	Occurs while Silverlight is obtaining PlayReady components (see section 20.4.2).
Opening	The MediaElement is trying to open the media item referenced through the Source property.
Paused	This represents that the MediaElement has halted playback.
Playing	This signals that the MediaElement is moving forward and the media is being enjoyed.
Stopped	The MediaElement has media loaded. It isn't currently playing, and the Position is located at the start of the file.

Table 20.3 shows the options available within the MediaElementState enumeration. This enumeration is used by the read-only CurrentState property. Considering that this property is read-only, how does it get set? This property is altered through a variety of methods you'll learn about later in this chapter. Anytime the Current-State property value is changed, an event called CurrentStateChanged is fired. The state of the media item is a natural part of working with the MediaElement, as is the duration.

NATURALDURATION

The NaturalDuration property gives you access to the natural duration of a media item. This duration is available once the MediaElement has successfully opened a media stream, so you shouldn't use the NaturalDuration property until the MediaOpened event has fired. Once the MediaOpened event has fired, you can access the total length of a media item, as shown here:

```
void me_MediaOpened(object sender, RoutedEventArgs e)
{
  tb.Text = "Your video is " + me.NaturalDuration + " long.";
}
```

This example displays the total length of a media item in an assumed TextBlock. This task takes place when the MediaOpened event of a MediaElement has triggered, so you can assume that the media stream has been successfully accessed. Then, you use the NaturalDuration property to show the length of the media stream. This length is stored as a TimeSpan within the NaturalDuration property.

The NaturalDuration property is a System.Windows.Duration entity. This type of entity is a core element of the .NET Framework, and it exposes a property called Has-TimeSpan that signals whether a TimeSpan is available. In the case of a MediaElement, this property value will always be true, enabling you to access highly detailed information about the length of a media stream through the TimeSpan property. This property is demonstrated in this example:

```
void me_MediaOpened(object sender, RoutedEventArgs e)
{
  StringBuilder sb = new StringBuilder();
  sb.Append("Your video is ");
  sb.Append(me.NaturalDuration.TimeSpan.Minutes);
  sb.Append(" minutes, ");
  sb.Append(me.NaturalDuration.TimeSpan.Seconds);
  sb.Append(" seconds, and ");
  sb.Append(me.NaturalDuration.TimeSpan.Milliseconds);
  sb.Append("milliseconds.");
  tb.Text = sb.ToString();
}
```

This shows how to access detailed information about the length of a media item. As you probably know, this information, as well as the position of the playback, is part of almost any online media player.

POSITION

The Position property represents a point, or location, within a MediaElement. This value can be read regardless of the CurrentState of the MediaElement, and it can be set if the MediaElement object's CanSeek property is true.

The CanSeek property determines whether the Position can be programmatically changed. This read-only property is set when a media item is loaded into a MediaElement. If the referenced media item is being streamed, this property will be set to false. If the referenced media item is being downloaded progressively, the CanSeek property will be set to true.

When the CanSeek property is set to true, you can set the Position property to any TimeSpan value. It's recommended that you use a TimeSpan within the NaturalDuration of a MediaElement. If you use a TimeSpan beyond the NaturalDuration, the MediaElement will jump to the end of the media item.

The Position is an important part of any media item—and so are the other common properties shared across audio and video files. These properties include NaturalDuration, CurrentState, CanPause, and AutoPlay. Additional properties are specific to the audio part of a media stream.

20.1.3 *Audio specific properties*

The MediaElement exposes several properties directly linked to audio features. These features can be used to give users greater control over their listening experiences and to engulf your users in your Silverlight application. These features can be delivered through the AudioStreamCount, AudioStreamIndex, Balance, IsMuted, and Volume properties.

AUDIOSTREAMCOUNT/AUDIOSTREAMINDEX

Occasionally, audio or video files will contain more than one audio track. As an example, a song may have one track for the guitar, one for the drums, and one for the vocals. Usually, you won't work with these kinds of audio files. Instead, you may come across multilingual videos where each language has its own track. In both these situations, you can access the track-related information through the AudioStreamCount and AudioStreamIndex properties.

The AudioStreamCount and AudioStreamIndex properties give you access to the individual audio tracks of a media file. The read-only AudioStreamCount property stores the number of tracks available. The AudioStreamIndex property specifies which of the available tracks to play (or is playing). Neither of these properties means anything until the MediaOpened event has fired.

When the MediaOpened event is fired, the AudioStreamCount and AudioStreamIndex properties get set on the client's machine. When this occurs, the audio tracks in the media file are read. While these tracks are being read, a collection is being created in the background. When this collection is fully created, the AudioStreamCount property is set to match the number of tracks in the collection. Then, the AudioStreamIndex property is set to begin using the first track in the collection.

Alternatively, if the `AudioStreamIndex` property is set at design time, that track will be used. Either way, once an audio track is playing, it's important to make sure that the sound is balanced.

BALANCE

The `Balance` property enables you to effortlessly simulate sounds such as a wave gently lapping a sandy shoreline or a swirling wind. These types of sounds often involve sound shifting from one ear to the other; it would be startling if the sounds spastically jumped from one ear to the other. The balance of the volume across your ears makes these sounds much more natural.

With the `Balance` property, you can gracefully spread out your sounds by specifying a double-precision value between −1.0 and 1.0. If you set the property value to -1, you can project sound entirely from the left-side speakers. If you set the value to 1, the sound will leap from the right speakers. If you're seeking a balance between the left and right speakers, you set the value to 0.

This property is more than an enumerator between the left, right, and center positions. It gives you the flexibility to do things like project 70 percent of a sound from the right speaker by using a value of 0.7. The remaining 30 percent projects from the left speaker. As you can imagine, you can easily depict a lifelike audible environment. Sometimes it's nice to shut out the sounds of life—enter `IsMuted`.

ISMUTED

Anything with an audio source should expose the ability to temporarily mute the audio. Thankfully, the `MediaElement` exposes an `IsMuted` property.

This property allows you to programmatically determine whether the sound associated with a `MediaElement` is audible. If a `MediaElement` is playing and this boolean property is set to `true`, the `MediaElement` will continue to play, but it won't be audible.

As a `bool`, the `IsMuted` property is all or nothing. Usually, you'll need to find a happy medium between audible and inaudible. Silverlight also gives you this type of control through the `Volume` property.

VOLUME

The `Volume` property is a double-precision, floating-point value that specifies the audible level of a `MediaElement`. This property value can range from an inaudible (0.0) all the way up to a room-shaking 1.0. The room-shaking capabilities are ultimately restrained by the user's computer volume. By default, the `Volume` value is in the middle of this range at 0.5.

The `Volume` property is one of the five properties that address audio-related features. The other properties are the `IsMuted`, `Balance`, `AudioStreamCount`, and `AudioStreamIndex` properties. The `MediaElement` also exposes a pair of properties that are specific to the visual part of a media file.

20.1.4   *Video specific properties*

The `MediaElement` exposes four properties directly related to videos. The first two are the `DroppedFramesPerSecond` and `RenderedFramesPerSecond` properties, both of which deal with video frame rates. The other two properties, `NaturalVideoHeight` and `NaturalVideoWidth`, deal with the dimensions of a video.

The `MediaElement` exposes two read-only double-precision values related to the frame rate of a video. `RenderedFramesPerSecond` gives you the number of frames that are rendered per second. The other property, `DroppedFramesPerSecond`, lets you know how many frames are being dropped per second. You can use these two properties to monitor the smoothness of a video. If a video begins to become jerky, the `DroppedFramesPerSecond` value will increase. In this scenario, you may want to consider using a video with smaller natural dimensions.

The natural dimensions of a video are provided through two read-only properties. The `NaturalVideoHeight` property represents the height of a video, the `NaturalVideoWidth` property represents the video's width. These `int` properties are both read-only because they represent the original dimensions, in pixels, of a requested video. These values are useful when a video is the primary focus of your UI. If you're using an audio file instead of a video file, these two properties will stay at their default values of 0. For this reason, these properties are specific to video scenarios. Both video and audio files are involved in a standard lifecycle.

20.1.5 *The lifecycle of a media file*

Throughout this section, you've seen a wide variety of properties. Some of these property values are likely to change throughout the life of a media file, so it's beneficial to listen for those changes. As you might expect, the `MediaElement` provides a rich set of events that enables you to watch for those changes (see table 20.4).

Table 20.4 The events of the `MediaElement`

Event	Description
BufferingProgressChanged	Triggered anytime the BufferingProgress property changes.
CurrentStateChanged	Fired anytime the CurrentState property is altered.
DownloadProgressChanged	Occurs whenever the DownloadProgress property changes.
MarkerReached	Discussed in section 20.3.2.
MediaEnded	Fired when the MediaElement is no longer playing audio and video.
MediaFailed	Triggered if the media item referenced in the Source property can't be found. Alternatively, this event will trigger if there's a problem with the media file itself.
MediaOpened	Occurs after the information associated with the media has been read and the media stream has been validated and opened.

This table shows the events exposed by the `MediaElement`. Note that some state changes trigger multiple events. For instance, if a video file runs its route within a

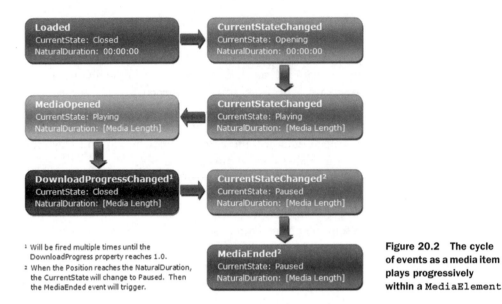

¹ Will be fired multiple times until the
DownloadProgress property reaches 1.0.
² When the Position reaches the NaturalDuration,
the CurrentState will change to Paused. Then
the MediaEnded event will trigger.

**Figure 20.2   The cycle
of events as a media item
plays progressively
within a MediaElement**

MediaElement, the CurrentStateChanged and MediaEnded events will both fire. As a result, you may need to create checks and balances within your code. To better understand the typical life of a media file, please review figure 20.2.

This figure shows the lifecycle of a media item that has played progressively through a MediaElement. The Loaded event used in the figure is of the FrameworkElement variety. This event shows when the NaturalDuration is set. As you can see, this property is set when the CurrentState is switched to Playing.

If you reference a media item that can't be found, the MediaFailed event will fire, but the CurrentStateChanged event won't be triggered. In other words, if you reference a media file that doesn't exist, only the Loaded and MediaFailed events will be triggered.

The events of the MediaElement reflect the lifecycle of a media item. This item can be impacted by a variety of audio- or video-related properties. Several properties are common to both audio and video files. One of these properties represents the Source of the media and can be referenced through a relative or remote Uri. Even more interesting is the fact that you can use the Source property to reference playlists.

20.2   *Playlists*

A playlist is a list of audio or video tracks arranged in a specific order. These lists give you a way to manage media elements that are part of a larger scheme such as a CD. Playlists are more than ordered media items, though. Playlists give you a way to generate revenue through advertising. Regardless of how you intend to use them, Silverlight has support for two playlist types.

Throughout this section, you'll learn about the two types of playlists supported in Silverlight. The first kind of playlist, a client-side playlist, enables your Silverlight application to fully control interaction with the playlist. The other kind of playlist, a server-side playlist (SSPL), gives the hosting server complete control over the media experience.

20.2.1 *Understanding client-side playlists*

A client-side playlist is an XML file that can be interpreted by a `MediaElement`. This XML file follows a special format known as *ASX*, which we'll detail in a moment. Once this file has been parsed by a `MediaElement`, the `MediaElement` will decide whether to begin playing. This decision will be based on the `AutoPlay` property. If this property is set to `true`, each of the items in the client-side playlist will begin playing one after the other. Amazingly, all this happens naturally by pointing the `Source` property to an ASX file as shown here:

```
<MediaElement x:Name="myMediaElement"
  Source="http://www.silverlightinaction.com/myPlaylist.asx" />
```

This shows how to request a client-side playlist. Note that this playlist uses the .asx file extension. This file extension is the one typically used for client-side playlists, but you can reference an ASX file with an extension of .asx, .isx, .wax, .wvx, .wmx, or .wpl. This restriction may seem odd considering that an ASX file is an XML file. Without this distinction, the `MediaElement` would be unable to quickly tell the difference between a client-side playlist and any of the other supported formats.

A client-side playlist can be an effective way to deliver multiple media tracks. To take advantage of client-side playlists, you must understand how to masterfully use ASX files. These files can have rich descriptive information, known as *metadata*, surrounding each of the tracks.

USING ASX FILES

Client-side playlists are defined as *Advanced Stream Redirector (ASX)* files—this is just a fancy name for a specific XML format. Because this format is XML, you can create a client-side playlist with your favorite text editor, Windows Media Player, or server-side application. Regardless of your choice, this file will always follow a common structure, which is shown in this example:

```
<ASX Version="3.0">
  <Title>Silverlight in Action Videos</Title>
  <Entry>
    <Title>Greetings</Title>
    <Author>Chad Campbell</Author>
    <Ref Href="http://www.silverlightinaction.com/video1.wmv" />
  </Entry>
  <Entry>
    <Title>City Scape</Title>
    <Author>Dan Herrenbruck</Author>
    <Ref Href="http://www.silverlightinaction.com/video2.wmv" />
  </Entry>
</ASX>
```

This example shows a pretty basic client-side playlist that uses a small portion of the full ASX schema. This segment isn't that far off from the full schema supported within

Silverlight. Silverlight only supports a subset of the full ASX schema, but this subset still provides plenty of elements that can be used to deliver a rich client-side playlist (see table 20.5).

Table 20.5   The ASX elements supported within Silverlight

Element	Description
Abstract	Provides a description for a client-side playlist or an entry within the playlist. This element exposes an attribute called Version. This attribute should use the value 3.0 for Silverlight applications.
Asx	The root element of a client-side playlist.
Author	Specifies the name(s) of the individual(s) that created a client-side playlist or an entry within the playlist. Only one Author element can be used per ASX or Entry element.
Base	Represents a URL that will get prepended before playing within the client.
Copyright	States the copyright information for an ASX or Entry element.
Entry	Defines an item in a client-side playlist. This element provides a boolean attribute called ClientSkip. This attribute can be used to prevent a user from skipping tracks.
MoreInfo	Enables you to specify a URL that provides more detailed information about the playlist or media item.
Param	Represents a custom parameter associated with a media item.
Ref	This element is the item that specifies which file to refer to for a media clip. The Ref element exposes a single attribute called Href that points to the URL of a media clip.
Title	Signifies the moniker of a playlist or media item. For instance, if a playlist represents a CD, the Title element in that case would represent the name of the CD. The Title can also be used to specify the name of an individual track.

This table shows the ASX elements supported within Silverlight. As you can see, an ASX file is more than a list of URLs that point to media files. The ASX file format gives you the opportunity to provide a lot of valuable metadata with a playlist. In fact, the ASX format lets you specify metadata for the media items within the playlist, so it's important to understand how to access that metadata.

ACCESSING THE METADATA

The metadata for a media item can be found within a read-only property called Attributes. This member of the MediaElement class exposes the metadata as a Dictionary<string, string>. There are two interesting characteristics about this property that deserve mentioning.

The first is in regard to what metadata is exposed. Surprisingly, the metadata embedded within a media item isn't included. Unfortunately, there isn't an elegant way to get this information. The descriptive information stored within the ASX file *is* included, so if you're using client-side playlists you should provide as much metadata as you can.

The other interesting item is related to the lifecycle of the `Attributes` property. This property stores the metadata associated with an individual media item, so the `Attributes` property is cleared and repopulated each time a different track in an ASX file is started. If you're changing your UI based on the values within the `Attributes` property, you may consider doing this in the `MediaOpened` event. Alternatively, you may decide to bypass client-side playlists altogether and use a server-side playlist.

20.2.2 *Using server-side playlists*

Server-side playlists empower content administrators to dynamically determine what content is played, and when. The server streaming the content has complete control over how the content is distributed. This approach provides several advantages over client-side playlists, including:

- Lower bandwidth costs—Generally client-side playlists serve content as separate streams for each entry. This causes your Silverlight application to reconnect to the server multiple times, wasting precious bandwidth. Because server-side playlists use a continuous stream, the Silverlight application only has to connect once.
- Dynamic playlist creation—Server-side playlists allow you to change a playlist even after a Silverlight application has connected.

To take advantage of these features, you must write a script using the Synchronized Multimedia Integration Language (SMIL). This script must be placed inside of a file with the .wsx extension. As you've probably guessed, this file extension is used for server-side playlists. Once these server-side playlists are created, you can use a `MediaElement` to reference them.

CREATING WSX FILES

Server-side playlists are defined as .wsx files. These files are XML files that follow a specific XML format, which is demonstrated in the following sample .wsx file:

```
<?wsx version="1.0"?>
<smil>
  <seq id="sq1">
    <media id="advertisement1" src="advertisement1.wmv" />
    <media id="movie" src="myMovie.wmv" />
    <media id="advertisement2" src="advertisement2.wmv" />
  <seq>
</smil>
```

This XML example shows a basic .wsx file. This playlist uses three of the elements supported by the SMIL format in Silverlight—`Media`, `Seq`, and `Smil`. Silverlight supports a total of five elements, which are listed and described table 20.6.

The elements listed in the table give a content administrator the flexibility to control how content is distributed. To distribute this content, you use a `MediaElement` to reference the .wsx file.

Table 20.6   The SMIL elements supported within Silverlight

Element	Description
Excl	"Exclusive." A container for media items. These items can be played in any order, but only one will be played at a time.
Media	References an audio or video file through an `src` attribute.
Seq	"Sequential." A container for media items. These items will be played in sequential order.
Smil	The root element for a server-side playlist.
Switch	A container for a series of items that can be interchanged if one of the items fails.

REFERENCING SERVER-SIDE PLAYLISTS

After your .wsx file has been created, you can publish it on your server. You must publish a server-side playlist before a Silverlight application can use it. Although publishing a server-side playlist is beyond the scope of this book, connecting to one isn't. You can do this from a MediaElement as shown in this example:

```
<MediaElement Source="mms://www.silverlightinaction.com:1234/myPlaylist" />
```

This line of markup shows how to reference a server-side playlist from a MediaElement. You may have noticed that the playlist doesn't include the .wsx file extension. This extension usually gets removed during the publishing process. A MediaElement must use the MMS protocol to request a server-side playlist. This playlist can be used to stream content but can't be used to serve downloadable content in Silverlight.

Server-side playlists provide a way for content administrators to control the distribution of their content. Client-side playlists turn that control over to the requesting application. Either way, both options give you a way to distribute that web-based mixtape you've always wanted to send. Of course, playlists (and media players in general) aren't very useful without providing control over the playback.

20.3   *Interactive playback*

As you've seen up to this point, Silverlight makes it easy to deploy media content with the MediaElement. This content could come in the form of an individual media item or playlist. Regardless of where that media comes from, users generally want to control their own media experiences, and Silverlight makes it easy to make each experience an interactive one.

The interactive playback features of Silverlight enable you to interact with media in a variety of ways. Over the course of this section, you'll see three key items that can enhance a media experience. For starters, you'll see how to control the play state on-the-fly. Then, you'll learn about interacting with your users throughout the course of an audio or video file. Finally, you'll see how to take advantage of Silverlight's full-screen mode to deliver a memorable media experience.

20.3.1 *Controlling the play state*

The MediaElement gives you the ability to programmatically change the play state of a media item. This can be useful for providing things such as play, pause, and stop buttons. Note that you can't change the play state directly through the read-only CurrentState property; you must rely on three basic methods to control the momentum of a media item. These methods are part of the MediaElement class and are described in table 20.7.

Table 20.7 The methods that control the progress of a MediaElement

Method	Description
Play	Begins moving the Position of the MediaElement forward from wherever it's currently located. If you're 5 seconds into a video and you pause it, this method will start playing the video 5 seconds in. Calling this method will change the CurrentState property to Playing.
Pause	Halts the playback of a media item at the current Position. This method will change the CurrentState property to Paused.
Stop	Stops the downloading, buffering, and playback of a media item. In addition, this method resets the Position to the beginning of the media item. Calling this method changes the CurrentState property to Stopped.

This table shows the three methods that can be used to control the play state. These methods are fairly straightforward and hardly worth mentioning, but this section would be incomplete without them. You probably expected the ability to play and stop a media item before seeing this list. In addition, you probably expected the ability to pause an item, but you may not have anticipated the fact that pausing a media item isn't always an option.

The Pause method will only work if the CanPause property is set to true. This read-only property will be set to true if the user's machine has the ability to halt playback of a media file. Regardless of the user's machine, a streaming media file will always set the CanPause property to false. In these situations where the CanPause property is false, you can still call the Pause method—it just won't do anything.

Providing an interactive experience often involves controlling the play state. This ability enables users to send a message to the MediaElement about what they want. Significantly, the MediaElement lets you send something back to the user when you want. That's only partially true. You'll see what I mean as you learn about interacting with your users in a timely fashion.

20.3.2 *Working with the timeline*

The MediaElement enables you to interact with your users at specific points in time. This can be a great way to provide captions or subtitles in your videos. In addition, this feature enables you to deliver advertisements, or other types of information, that are relevant to a portion of a video. Regardless of your need, time-sensitive information can be bundled with your media in the form of a *timeline marker.*

A timeline marker is metadata that's relevant to a specific point in time. This information is generally part of a media file itself and is bundled during encoding. Significantly, there are two different kinds of timeline markers. The first type is known as a *basic marker.* It's intended to be used when you need to provide fixed information. The other kind of timeline marker is a *script command;* it can be used to run a piece of code. Both kinds of markers will be represented as a `TimelineMarker` whose properties are shown in table 20.8.

Table 20.8 The properties associated with a `TimelineMarker`

Property	Description
Text	A value associated with marker. This `string` can be any value you want. You may want to think of this as the value of a parameter.
Time	The position of the marker within the media. This position is represented as a `TimeSpan`.
Type	This `string` exposes the kind of marker for a script command. If a basic marker is being used, this value will be `NAME`.

In general, these properties get populated when a `TimelineMarker` gets created. `TimelineMarker` objects are usually created when a `MediaElement` initially reads a media file. During this process, the metadata within the header of the file is used to create `TimelineMarker` objects. These objects then are added to a publicly visible collection called `Markers`.

The `Markers` collection is a collection of timeline markers associated with a media file. The items associated with this collection can't be added through XAML, unlike the majority of other collections in Silverlight, because the markers come from the media item set as the `Source` of the owning `MediaElement`. Whenever one of these timeline-marker element's `Time` has come, the `MediaElement` will fire the `Marker-Reached` event. This event provides an opportunity to recapture the data associated with a marker, which can be useful for any number of things, including showing a caption (see listing 20.2).

Listing 20.2 Using the `MarkerReached` event to show a caption on a `MediaElement`

XAML:
```
<Canvas>
  <MediaElement x:Name="me"
    Source="http://www.silverlightinaction.com/video3.wmv"
    MarkerReached="me_MarkerReached" />                              ❶
  <TextBlock x:Name="tb" Canvas.Top="330"
    Foreground="White" FontSize="20" FontWeight="Bold"  />
</Canvas>
```

C#:

```
void me_MarkerReached(object sender, TimelineMarkerRoutedEventArgs e)
{
    tb.Text = e.Marker.Text;        ◁—— Displaying marker text
}
```

This listing shows one way you can use the MarkerReached event ❶. This event provides a TimelineMarkerRoutedEventArgs parameter that gives you access to the TimelineMarker that tripped the event. Common uses for this event are captioning, displaying ads (the text contains an ID or URL), text overlays, or displaying links to videos related to that marker. Many sites such as YouTube use similar functionality to display notes you add at specific points in the video.

Markers add a whole new level of interactivity to your media player. To support basic interaction, the MediaElement provides three simple methods that let you control the play state. Regardless of how you intend to control the media experience, it must come from some server. Interestingly this server may serve up the experience as protected content.

20.4 Using protected content

The interactive playback features within Silverlight can be used to give your users an engaging media experience. Sometimes you may want to control who has access to this experience. To enable you to do this, Silverlight has built-in support for a client-access technology known as PlayReady for Silverlight.

PlayReady for Silverlight, or *PlayReady*, is a content-access technology that enables you to protect your media assets. These assets may be requested from a Silverlight application through a MediaElement instance. This control's Source property can be used to request protected content from a hosting server. Throughout this section, you'll see an overview of how Silverlight uses PlayReady technology. This overview includes requesting protected content, retrieving PlayReadycomponents, and unlocking protected content.

20.4.1 Requesting protected content

A Silverlight application can request protected content, which may be in the form of a protected stream or media file. This item can be requested through the Source property of a MediaElement, so it's safe to say that there's no difference on the client side between requesting protected and unprotected content. In fact, Silverlight doesn't know if content is protected until it's downloaded. This download happens naturally when a request is made, as shown in figure 20.3.

Figure 20.3 shows the general idea of requesting protected content from a fictional domain. After this request is made, the server

Figure 20.3 A user requests protected content from a server. This content is downloaded, in encrypted format, to the Silverlight application.

will send an encrypted version of the protected file back to the Silverlight application. This file will have a special header that tells the Silverlight runtime that it's a protected file. This header will provide the location of the licensing server to Silverlight. But before the licensing server can be reached, Silverlight must ensure that the user has the necessary PlayReady components installed.

20.4.2 *Retrieving the PlayReady components*

By default, Silverlight has the infra-structure for PlayReady, but the Play-Ready components aren't installed along with the Silverlight runtime. Instead, they're automatically down-loaded and installed when a user requests a protected item. During this one-time installation process, Silver-light goes to the Microsoft.com site and grabs the necessary components. This transparent process is shown in figure 20.4.

Figure 20.4   The process of installing the content access components. This one-time process happens the first time a user attempts to use a protected item. Future attempts to access protected content won't go through the process of downloading and installing PlayReady.

Figure 20.4 shows how the content access components are retrieved. These components may be customized for a user's machine, solely for the sake of ensuring a robust licensing experience. The user's machine is sometimes referred to as an *individualized DRM client*. This process happens automatically behind the scenes—you don't have to do a thing. Even after the PlayReady components have been installed, the content is still locked. To unlock this content, a request must be made to the licensing server.

20.4.3 *Unlocking protected content*

Once a protected item has been downloaded to your Silverlight application, it's still encrypted. This encryption can only be unlocked by a key sent from a licensing server, so if you try to play an encrypted file, Silverlight will search the encrypted file's header for the location of a licensing server. Silverlight will use this location to automatically request a key from the licensing server to decrypt the protected content.

When a licensing server retrieves a request for a key, it can either accept or deny the request. The licensing server can be used to implement some custom logic to make that decision. This custom logic must be implemented using the server-side PlayReady SDK. Unfortu-nately, this SDK is outside the scope of this book, but you can probably imag-ine how it could be used in a key request. A basic key request is shown in figure 20.5.

Figure 20.5   The media content in this figure is locked until a key is retrieved from the licensing server. This server can implement custom logic through the PlayReady SDK.

This figure shows what the request for a content-access key looks like. If this request is accepted, the licensing server will return a key. This key will unlock the protected content and begin playing it within the requesting `MediaElement`. If the request is denied, a key won't be returned. Instead, the requesting `MediaElement` will raise a `MediaFailed` event.

Silverlight has built-in support for the PlayReady content-access technology, which works behind the scenes to retrieve and unlock protected content—audio and video. One of the easiest ways to use PlayReady DRM and support HD video is to use the Silverlight Media Framework.

20.5   *Using the Silverlight Media Framework*

The Silverlight Media Framework (SMF) is Microsoft's open source scalable and customizable media player for IIS Smooth Streaming. Like IIS Smooth Streaming itself, its history dates to the Olympics video player and massive amounts of high-quality, protected video that needed to be served up in real-time during the event. It has since evolved into an excellent multipurpose media player.

If you're building an HD media player, evaluating this framework should be at the top of your task list. Key features of the framework include:

- Support for IIS Smooth Streaming with bit rate monitoring, as well as progressive download and Windows Media Streaming
- Modular, supporting plug-ins
- Support for popular ad standards
- Full styling support

The framework supports much more than that, of course, but those are the top compelling features. It has multiple points of extensibility, and if those aren't enough, full source code is provided.

In this section, we'll first look at what it takes to get the appropriate libraries for the Silverlight Media Framework, then build a simple player that supports IIS Smooth Streaming.

20.5.1   *Using the player libraries*

You can get the Silverlight Media Framework version 2 at http://smf.codeplex.com. The downloads include both the binaries and the full source code. Also, like other CodePlex projects, you can browse the full source code right on the site or download it as part of a release. Be sure to get the latest version, which at the time of this writing is version 2. Don't bother with the older version 1. Significant changes were made after the first version.

To install the player, first download and install the IIS Smooth Streaming Client player SDK using the Web Platform Installer at http://www.iis.net/download/smoothclient. If the WebPI (Web Platform Installer) doesn't work for you, there's a link right below it for downloading the MSI directly.

Next, download the Silverlight Media Framework v2 release (or the latest release available at the time you're reading this) and install that on your machine. At the time of this writing, the installer was a zip file with the DLLs. If that's the case when you use it, place them in a common location (but not a system folder such as Program Files) that you'll easily find from within Visual Studio. If copied from a zip and not an installer, be sure to unblock the files individually per this KB article so you can use them: http://go.microsoft.com/fwlink/?LinkId=179545. Figure 20.6 shows the dialog with the Unblock button.

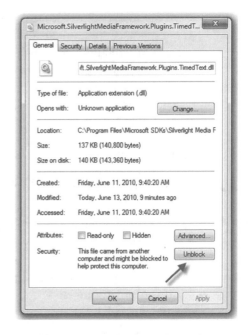

Figure 20.6   Unblocking an internet-downloaded DLL in order to be able to reference it from within a Visual Studio project

20.5.2 Creating the player

Once you have everything installed and unblocked, creating a complete media player experience is as simple as referencing the SMF DLLs and creating an instance of the player in XAML. Figure 20.7 shows the default player appearance.

Listing 20.3 shows how to instantiate the player from XAML. There are a few key namespaces to keep in mind for Smooth Streaming projects. Under the

Figure 20.7   The default SMF media player with Big Buck Bunny, an IIS Smooth Streaming video, loaded

`Microsoft.SilverlightMediaFramework` namespace, there are the `.Core`, `.Plu-gins`, and `.Utilities` namespaces and their associated assemblies. Be sure to reference them for all types of SMF projects. For regular Smooth Streaming, there's the `Microsoft.Web.Media.SmoothStreaming.dll` assembly. For progressive download projects, use the `Micosoft.SilverlightMediaFramework.Plugins.Progressive.dll` assembly instead.

Listing 20.3 Instantiating the SMF Player from XAML

```
<UserControl x:Class="SilverlightApplication57.MainPage"
  xmlns="http://schemas.microsoft.com/winfx/2006/xaml/presentation"
  xmlns:x="http://schemas.microsoft.com/winfx/2006/xaml"
  xmlns:Core="clr-namespace:Microsoft.SilverlightMediaFramework.Core;
  assembly=Microsoft.SilverlightMediaFramework.Core"                    ❶
  xmlns:Media="clr-namespace:
  Microsoft.SilverlightMediaFramework.Core.Media;
  assembly=Microsoft.SilverlightMediaFramework.Core">                   ❷

  <Grid x:Name="LayoutRoot" Background="White" Margin="15">
    <Core:SMFPlayer>                          ◁──┐ SMF player
      <Core:SMFPlayer.Playlist>                   │                     ❸
        <Media:PlaylistItem DeliveryMethod="AdaptiveStreaming"          ❹
                            MediaSource=
          "http://video3.smoothhd.com.edgesuite.net/ondemand/
          Big%20Buck%20Bunny%20Adaptive.ism/Manifest" />
      </Core:SMFPlayer.Playlist>
    </Core:SMFPlayer>
  </Grid>
</UserControl>
```

The Silverlight Media Framework player requires two namespaces to be included. The first ❶, Core, is for the player itself. The second ❷, Media, is for the playlists and features related to the media supported in the player. Due to the flexibility of the player, loading media takes a few more lines than the usual `MediaElement`. In particular, the player supports a playlist ❸ with one or more playlist items queued in it. Each playlist item includes a single piece of media with a specified delivery method ❹. The valid values for `DeliveryMethod` are shown in table 20.9.

Table 20.9 Possible values for `DeliveryMethod` for the SMF player

Value	Description
NotSpecified	The default value. This will attempt to use the first media plug-in loaded. As this can be unreliable in players that support more than one type of media delivery method, always specify one of the following below.
AdaptiveStreaming	The player will use IIS Smooth Streaming.
ProgressiveDownload	The player will use a progressive download approach for playing the media. This approach requires no server-side support.
Streaming	The player will use Windows Media Streaming to play the media.

It's important to realize that the delivery methods supported are entirely controlled by what plug-ins you package with your Silverlight application. If you leave out the Progressive Download plug-in, for example, your player won't support that delivery method.

The Silverlight Media Framework is an excellent way to get a fully functional and feature-rich player up and running in a minimum amount of time. It's perfect for traditional video and audio. But what about media that ventures further into the nontraditional? How about managed codecs or real-time-generated media? For those, collectively called *raw media*, we have the Media Stream Source API.

20.6   *Working with raw media*

Silverlight has a strong but finite set of codecs it natively supports for audio and video playback. If you want to use a format not natively supported, such as the WAV audio file format or the AVI video format, that wasn't an option until the Media Stream Source (MSS) API was added.

The MSS API was included in Silverlight 2, but that version required you to transcode into one of the WMV/WMA/MP3 formats natively supported by Silverlight. In Silverlight 3, the MSS API was augmented to support raw media formats where you send the raw pixels or audio samples directly through the rest of the pipeline. This made its use much easier, as it required knowledge only of the format you want to decode. For the same reason, it runs faster, as an extra potentially CPU-intensive encoding step is avoided.

The MediaStreamSource API supports simultaneous video and audio streams. In this section, we'll look at creating raw video as well as raw audio. In both cases, we'll use algorithmically derived data to drive the raw media pipeline.

20.6.1   *A custom MediaStreamSource class*

To implement your own custom stream source, derive a class from MediaStream-Source. As the name suggests, this class will be used as the source for a MediaElement on the page. Table 20.10 shows that MediaStreamSource has several methods that you must override in your implementation.

Table 20.10   MediaStreamSource **virtual methods**

Method	Description
SeekAsync	Sets the next position to be used in GetSampleAsync. Call ReportSeekCompleted when done.
GetDiagnosticAsync	Used to return diagnostic information. This method can be a no-op as it's not critical. If used, call ReportGetDiagnosticCompleted when done.
SwitchMediaStreamAsync	Used to change between configured media streams. This method can be a no-op as it's not critical. If used, call ReportSwitchMediaStreamCompleted when done.

Table 20.10 `MediaStreamSource` **virtual methods** *(continued)*

Method	Description
`GetSampleAsync`	Required. Get the next sample and return it using `ReportGetSampleCompleted`. If there's any delay, call `ReportGetSampleProgress` to indicate buffering.
`OpenMediaAsync`	Required. Set up the metadata for the media and call `ReportOpenMediaCompleted`.
`CloseMedia`	Any shutdown and cleanup code should go here.

One thing you'll notice about the functions is that many of them are asynchronous. The pattern followed in those methods is to perform the processing and then call a `ReportComplete` method, the name of which varies by task, when finished.

The asynchronous nature of the API helps keep performance up and keeps your code from slowing down media playback.

Listing 20.4 shows the skeleton of a `MediaStreamSource` implementation, including the methods I just described. We'll continue to build on this throughout the remaining raw media sections.

Listing 20.4 The basic `MediaStreamSource` structure

```
public class CustomSource : MediaStreamSource
{
  private long _currentTime = 0;

  protected override void SeekAsync(long seekToTime)
  {
    _currentTime = seekToTime;
    ReportSeekCompleted(seekToTime);
  }

  protected override void GetDiagnosticAsync(
      MediaStreamSourceDiagnosticKind diagnosticKind)
  {
    throw new NotImplementedException();
  }

  protected override void SwitchMediaStreamAsync(
      MediaStreamDescription mediaStreamDescription)
  {
    throw new NotImplementedException();
  }

  protected override void GetSampleAsync(                    ⟵─── GetSampleAsync
      MediaStreamType mediaStreamType)
  {
    if (mediaStreamType == MediaStreamType.Audio)
      GetAudioSample();
    else if (mediaStreamType == MediaStreamType.Video)
      GetVideoSample();
  }

  protected override void OpenMediaAsync() {    }            ❶
```

No-op methods (annotation for `GetDiagnosticAsync` and `SwitchMediaStreamAsync`)

```
    protected override void CloseMedia()        {   }

    private void GetAudioSample()    {   }
    private void GetVideoSample()    {   }
}
```
❷

The most important methods for our scenario are the `OpenMediaAsync` method ❶ and the two methods ❷ that are used to get the next sample. Those two methods are called from the `GetSampleAsync` method whenever an audio or video sample is requested.

Once we have the `CustomSource` class created, we'll need to use it as the source for a `MediaElement` on a Silverlight page. Listing 20.5 shows how to wire this up using XAML for the user interface and C# code for the actual wire-up.

> **Listing 20.5   Using a custom `MediaStreamSource` class**

XAML:
```xml
<Grid x:Name="LayoutRoot" Background="White">
  <MediaElement x:Name="MediaPlayer"                    ❶
                AutoPlay="True"
                Stretch="Uniform"
                Margin="10" />
</Grid>
```

C#:
```csharp
public partial class MainPage : UserControl
{
  public MainPage()
  {
    InitializeComponent();

    Loaded += new RoutedEventHandler(MainPage_Loaded);
  }
  CustomSource _mediaSource = new CustomSource();         // Custom MediaStreamSource

  void MainPage_Loaded(object sender, RoutedEventArgs e)
  {
    MediaPlayer.SetSource(_mediaSource);        ❷
  }
}
```

In this listing, I first create a `MediaElement` ❶ that will span the size of the page, then assign the `CustomSource` instance to the source property ❷ using the `SetSource` method of the `MediaElement`. Once that's completed, the `MediaElement` is set to play and will start requesting samples from the `CustomSource` class.

Right now, our `CustomSource` class doesn't return any samples, so running the application would show nothing. We'll modify the class to return both video and audio, starting with video.

20.6.2 *Creating raw video*

Being able to create video from raw bits is pretty exciting—it opens up all sorts of scenarios from bitmap-based animation to custom video codecs. I first played with raw video when I created my Silverlight Commodore 64 emulator (mentioned in chapter 5). I tried a few different video presentation approaches before I settled on generating the video display in real-time as a 50fps `MediaStreamSource` video at 320 x 200.

For this video example, we're going to generate white noise, much like you see on an analog TV when the signal is lost. When complete, the application will look like figure 20.8. If you lived in the US prior to cable TV, this is what you saw after the national anthem finished playing.

We'll start with the logic required to set up the video stream, and follow it up quickly with the code that returns the individual frame samples.

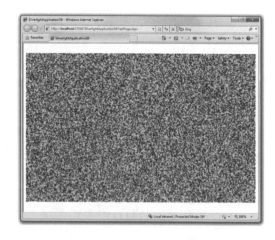

Figure 20.8   The completed white noise video generator. When I was a boy, I used to imagine I was watching an epic ant battle from high overhead. Well, until I saw *Poltergeist*, which forever changed the nature of white noise on the TV.

SETTING UP THE VIDEO STREAM

When creating raw video, the first step is to set up the video stream parameters. The parameters include things such as the height and width of the frame, the number of frames per second, and the actual video format.

Silverlight supports a number of different video formats, each identified by a *FourCC code*. FourCC is a standard four-character code that's used to uniquely identify video formats. In addition to all of the existing formats (for example, `H264` for h.264 video), two new formats were added specifically for use raw media and the `MediaStreamSource` API. Those are listed in table 20.11.

Table 20.11   Supported raw media FourCC codes in Silverlight

FourCC code	Description
RGBA	Raw, uncompressed RGB pixels with an alpha component. Silverlight currently ignores the alpha component during processing.
YV12	YUV 12. This is a common media output format used in many codecs.

In the example in this section, we'll use the RGBA format to push raw pixels without any special processing or encoding. It's the easiest format to use, requiring no algorithm other than providing a single pixel with a single color. Listing 20.6 shows the video setup code for our simple white noise generator.

Listing 20.6 Setting up the video stream

```
private int _frameTime = 0;
private const int _frameWidth = 320, _frameHeight = 200;
private const int _framePixelSize = 4;
private const int _frameBufferSize =
                    _frameHeight * _frameWidth * _framePixelSize;
private const int _frameStreamSize = _frameBufferSize * 100;

private MemoryStream _frameStream = new MemoryStream(_frameStreamSize);
private MediaStreamDescription _videoDesc;

private void PrepareVideo()
{
  _frameTime = (int)TimeSpan.FromSeconds((double)1/30).Ticks;        ◁─┐ 30 frames
                                                                         per second
  Dictionary<MediaStreamAttributeKeys, string> streamAttributes =
      new Dictionary<MediaStreamAttributeKeys, string>();

  streamAttributes[MediaStreamAttributeKeys.VideoFourCC] =         ❸
                          "RGBA";
  streamAttributes[MediaStreamAttributeKeys.Height] =              ❹
                          _frameHeight.ToString();
  streamAttributes[MediaStreamAttributeKeys.Width] =
                          _frameWidth.ToString();

  _videoDesc = new MediaStreamDescription(                         ❺
      MediaStreamType.Video, streamAttributes);
}

protected override void OpenMediaAsync()
{
  Dictionary<MediaSourceAttributesKeys, string> sourceAttributes =
      new Dictionary<MediaSourceAttributesKeys, string>();

  List<MediaStreamDescription> availableStreams =              ◁─┐
      new List<MediaStreamDescription>();                         │
                                                                  │
  PrepareVideo();                                                 ❶
                                                                  │
  availableStreams.Add(_videoDesc);                           ◁─┘

  sourceAttributes[MediaSourceAttributesKeys.Duration] =      ◁─┐ 0 is infinite
      TimeSpan.FromSeconds(0).Ticks.ToString(                      time
      CultureInfo.InvariantCulture);

  sourceAttributes[MediaSourceAttributesKeys.CanSeek] =
      false.ToString();

  ReportOpenMediaCompleted(
      sourceAttributes, availableStreams);                    ❷
}
```

Listing 20.6 shows two functions: OpenMediaAsync and PrepareVideo. They've been broken up that way because OpenMediaAsync will also need to support audio later in this section.

When the class is wired up to a MediaElement, Silverlight will first call the OpenMediaAsync function. In that function, you need to tell Silverlight what streams are available ❶, a single video stream in this case. Then you need to set up attributes for the duration of the video, infinite in our case, and whether you allow seeking. You take that information and pass it into the ReportOpenMediaCompleted method ❷ to tell Silverlight you're ready.

The PrepareVideo method sets up some variables that will be used when we generate the samples. First, we identify the amount of time per frame. This can vary over the course of the video, but it'll be easier on the developer if you pick a constant frame rate. Then we set up a dictionary of attributes that identifies the format of the video ❸ and the dimensions of each frame ❹. Finally, that's all packed into a MediaStreamDescription ❺ to be used when we start generating frames.

Once the video stream is set up, the next thing to do is to start pumping out frames to be displayed.

RETURNING THE SAMPLE

The main purpose of a MediaStreamSource implementation is to return samples. In the case of video, a sample is one complete frame, ready to be displayed. Listing 20.7 shows the GetVideoSample function, called by GetSampleAsync.

Listing 20.7 Returning the video frame sample

```
private int _frameStreamOffset = 0;
private Dictionary<MediaSampleAttributeKeys, string> _emptySampleDict =
    new Dictionary<MediaSampleAttributeKeys, string>();
private Random _random = new Random();
private byte[] _frameBuffer = new byte[_frameBufferSize];

private void GetVideoSample()
{
    if (_frameStreamOffset + _frameBufferSize > _frameStreamSize)
    {
        _frameStream.Seek(0, SeekOrigin.Begin);          Rewind
        _frameStreamOffset = 0;                          when at end
    }

    for (int i = 0; i < _frameBufferSize; i+= _framePixelSize)
    {
        if (_random.Next(0, 2) > 0)
        {
            _frameBuffer[i] = _frameBuffer[i + 1] =
                _frameBuffer[i + 2] = 0x55;
        }
        else
        {
            _frameBuffer[i] = _frameBuffer[i + 1] =
                _frameBuffer[i + 2] = 0xDD;
        }                                        Alpha value
        _frameBuffer[i + 3] = 0xFF;             OxFF = Opaque
    }

    _frameStream.Write(_frameBuffer, 0, _frameBufferSize);         ❷

    MediaStreamSample msSamp = new MediaStreamSample(             ❸
      _videoDesc, _frameStream, _frameStreamOffset,
```

❶

```
    _frameBufferSize, _currentTime, _emptySampleDict);

   _currentTime += _frameTime;

   _frameStreamOffset += _frameBufferSize;

   ReportGetSampleCompleted(msSamp);
}
```

The `GetVideoSample` function first checks to see whether we're approaching the end of the allocated video buffer. If so, it rewinds back to the beginning of the buffer. This is an important check to make, as you don't want to allocate a complete stream for every frame, but a stream can't be boundless in size.

Once that's done, I loop through the buffer, moving four bytes at a time (the size of a single pixel in the buffer) and generate a random pixel value. The pixel will either be almost white or almost black ❶. When playing with the sample, I found that pure black and white was far too harsh, and these two slightly gray values looked more natural. Though not obvious here, when setting the pixel values you need to do so in Blue, Green, Red, Alpha (BGRA) order.

The next step is to write the buffer to the stream ❷. In this simple example, I could've written the bytes directly to the stream and eliminated the buffer. But in anything more complex than this, you're likely to have at least two buffers (a read-from and a write-to buffer), and even more likely to have a queue of frame buffers used for preloading the individual frames.

Once the stream is populated, I then create the media stream sample ❸, increment our time counters, and call `ReportGetSampleCompleted` to return the sample to Silverlight.

One interesting note in this is how sample time is used rather than frame numbers. The use of a time for each frame allows Silverlight to drop frames when it starts to lag behind. This was a key reason why I chose `MediaStreamSource` over other approaches in the Silverlight C64 emulator. When the user's machine is busy, or in case it's too slow to run the emulator at full frame rate, I continue to chug along and let Silverlight skip frames it doesn't have time to show. This helps keep everything in sync time-wise, which is crucial when you're also creating audio.

20.6.3 *Creating raw audio*

In the previous section, we created a white noise video generator. Let's take that all the way and add in white noise audio. Surprisingly, audio is somewhat more complex to set up than video. This is due to the number of options available to you: audio can have different sample bit sizes, be mono or stereo, have different sample rates, and more.

All this information is stored in a class known as `WaveFormatEx`. In order to fit the listing into this book, I'm going to use a greatly simplified, but still functional, version of this class. Listing 20.8 shows the class. Create this as a separate class file in your project.

Listing 20.8 A simplified `WaveFormatEx` structure

```
public class WaveFormatEx
{
  public short FormatTag { get; set; }
  public short Channels { get; set; }
  public int SamplesPerSec { get; set; }
  public int AvgBytesPerSec { get; set; }
  public short BlockAlign { get; set; }
  public short BitsPerSample { get; set; }
  public short Size { get; set; }
  public const uint SizeOf = 18;
  public byte[] ext { get; set; }

  public const Int16 FormatPCM = 1;             Main output
                                                function
  public string ToHexString()           <-----
  {
    string s = "";

    s += ToLittleEndianString(string.Format("{0:X4}", FormatTag));
    s += ToLittleEndianString(string.Format("{0:X4}", Channels));
    s += ToLittleEndianString(string.Format("{0:X8}", SamplesPerSec));
    s += ToLittleEndianString(string.Format("{0:X8}", AvgBytesPerSec));
    s += ToLittleEndianString(string.Format("{0:X4}", BlockAlign));
    s += ToLittleEndianString(string.Format("{0:X4}", BitsPerSample));
    s += ToLittleEndianString(string.Format("{0:X4}", Size));

    return s;
  }

  public static string ToLittleEndianString(string bigEndianString)
  {
    if (bigEndianString == null) { return ""; }

    char[] be = bigEndianString.ToCharArray();

    if (be.Length % 2 != 0) { return ""; }

    int i, ai, bi, ci, di;
    char a, b, c, d;
    for (i = 0; i < be.Length / 2; i += 2)
    {
      ai = i; bi = i + 1;

      ci = be.Length - 2 - i;
      di = be.Length - 1 - i;

      a = be[ai]; b = be[bi]; c = be[ci]; d = be[di];
          be[ci] = a; be[di] = b; be[ai] = c; be[bi] = d;
    }

    return new string(be);
  }
                                                Utility
                                                functions
  public Int64 AudioDurationFromBufferSize(  <-----
                 UInt32 cbAudioDataSize)
  {
    if (AvgBytesPerSec == 0) return 0;
    return (Int64)(cbAudioDataSize * 10000000 / AvgBytesPerSec);
  }
}
```

The WaveFormatEx class is simply a way to specify the format to be used for PCM wave data in Silverlight. It's a standard structure, forming the header of the .WAV file format, which is why you get oddities such as the big-to-little-endian format conversions. The class-based version here includes a single helper utility function AudioDuration-FromBufferSize, which will be used when we output the PCM samples.

There are more complete implementations of WaveFormatEx to be found on the web, including one in my Silverlight Synthesizer project at http://10rem.net. Those implementations typically include a validation function that makes sure all the chosen options are correct.

With that class in place, we'll turn our eye to the actual stream setup.

SETTING UP THE WAV MEDIA SOURCE

The first step in setting up the sound source is to modify the OpenMediaAsync function. That function currently includes a call to PrepareVideo followed by adding the video stream description to the list of available streams. Modify that code so that it also includes the audio description information as shown here:

```
...
PrepareVideo();
PrepareAudio();

availableStreams.Add(_videoDesc);
availableStreams.Add(_audioDesc);
...
```

Once those changes are in place, we'll add the PrepareAudio function to the class. The PrepareAudio function is the logical equivalent to the PrepareVideo function; it sets up the format information for Silverlight to use when reading our samples. Listing 20.9 shows the code for that function and its required class member variables and constants.

Listing 20.9   The PrepareAudio **function**

```
private WaveFormatEx _waveFormat = new WaveFormatEx();          <— WaveFormatEx
private MediaStreamDescription _audioDesc;
private const int _audioBitsPerSample = 16;
private const int _audioChannels = 2;                           ❶
private const int _audioSampleRate = 44100;

private void PrepareAudio()
{
  int ByteRate = _audioSampleRate * _audioChannels *
        (_audioBitsPerSample / 8);                              ❷

  _waveFormat = new WaveFormatEx();
  _waveFormat.BitsPerSample = _audioBitsPerSample;
  _waveFormat.AvgBytesPerSec = (int)ByteRate;
  _waveFormat.Channels = _audioChannels;
  _waveFormat.BlockAlign =
        (short)(_audioChannels * (_audioBitsPerSample / 8));    ❸
  _waveFormat.ext = null;
  _waveFormat.FormatTag = WaveFormatEx.FormatPCM;
```

```
_waveFormat.SamplesPerSec = _audioSampleRate;        ⎤ Must be
_waveFormat.Size = 0;                          ⟵────⎦ zero

Dictionary<MediaStreamAttributeKeys, string> streamAttributes =
    new Dictionary<MediaStreamAttributeKeys, string>();
streamAttributes[MediaStreamAttributeKeys.CodecPrivateData] =
    _waveFormat.ToHexString();                                   ❹
_audioDesc = new MediaStreamDescription(
    MediaStreamType.Audio, streamAttributes);
}
```

The most important parts of this listing are the constants controlling the sample format ❶. For this example, we're generating 16-bit samples, in two channels (stereo sound), at a sample rate of 44,100 samples per second: CD-quality audio.

Once those constants are established, they're used to figure out almost everything else, including the number of bytes per second ❷ and the block alignment ❸. Once the WaveFormatEx structure is filled out with this information, I set it as the Codec Private Data ❹ using its little-endian hex string format. Finally, I create the audio description from that data, to be used when reporting samples back to Silverlight.

CREATING SOUND SAMPLES

The final step is to output the audio samples. This requires generating the individual samples and returning them in chunks of predefined size. We'll use a random number generator to generate the noise, much like we did with video. Listing 20.10 shows how to fill a buffer with audio and return those samples to Silverlight.

Listing 20.10 Outputting audio samples

```
private long _currentAudioTimeStamp = 0;
private const int _audioBufferSize = 256;                          ⟵──⎤ Internal
private const int _audioStreamSize = _audioBufferSize * 100;          ⎦ buffer size
private byte[] _audioBuffer = new byte[_audioBufferSize];
private MemoryStream _audioStream = new MemoryStream(_audioStreamSize);
private int _audioStreamOffset = 0;
private double _volume = 0.5;

private void GetAudioSample()
{
  if (_audioStreamOffset + _audioBufferSize > _audioStreamSize)     ❶
  {
    _audioStream.Seek(0, SeekOrigin.Begin);
    _audioStreamOffset = 0;
  }

  for (int i = 0; i < _audioBufferSize;
                  i += _audioBitsPerSample / 8)
  {
    short sample =                                        ⎤ Sample
      (short)(_random.Next((int)short.MinValue,     ⟵────⎦ randomizer
                      (int)short.MaxValue) * _volume);

    _audioBuffer[i] = (byte)(sample & 0xFF00);               ⎤❷
    _audioBuffer[i + 1] = (byte)(sample & 0x00FF);           ⎦
  }
```

```
_audioStream.Write(_audioBuffer, 0, _audioBufferSize);

MediaStreamSample msSamp = new MediaStreamSample(              ❸
  _audioDesc, _audioStream, _audioStreamOffset, _audioBufferSize,
  _currentAudioTimeStamp, _emptySampleDict);

_currentAudioTimeStamp +=
  _waveFormat.AudioDurationFromBufferSize((uint)_audioBufferSize);

_audioStream = new MemoryStream(_audioStreamSize);

ReportGetSampleCompleted(msSamp);              ❹
}
```

The process for generating the white noise audio sample is similar to generating the frames of video. But instead of having a fixed-width x height buffer we must fill, we can generate as long or as short a sample as we want. This is controlled by the audio buffer size set in code. In general, you want this number to be as low as possible, as larger numbers typically introduce latency as well as skipped video frames—the system is too busy generating audio to show the video frame. But set the number too low, and the audio will stutter. If you find the white noise stuttering on your machine, up the buffer to 512 or so and see how that works for you.

> **TIP** To help with latency, you can also play with the `AudioBufferLength` property of the `MediaStreamSource` class. In most cases, you won't be able to get that below 30ms or so, but that value is itself very hardware-dependent. That property is my own contribution to the class, as I was the only one insane enough to be writing a Silverlight-based audio synthesizer at the time. I ran into problem after problem with the triple-buffering (my buffer, plus Silverlight MSS buffer, plus underlying DirectX buffer), to the point where all audio was delayed by about 2-3 seconds. The team worked with me to identify where the issues were, and then added this knob into the base class to help tweak for latency-sensitive applications like mine.

Once the buffer size is established, I perform the same stream overrun check ❶ that we did for video, and for the same reasons. Then, I loop through the buffer, 2 bytes (16 bits) at a time, and generate a white noise sample. Once the sample is generated, I get the 2 bytes from it using a little bit-masking ❷, and then write those bytes into the buffer. Once the buffer is filled, it's copied into the stream and the sample response built ❸. After incrementing the time counters, the last step is to report the sample to Silverlight ❹.

If you run the application at this point, you should have a short delay while the startup code is executed and the Silverlight internal buffers are filled, followed by simultaneous audio and video white noise. On the surface, this may not seem impressive. But when you consider that the video and audio is completely computer generated, it's considerably more impressive.

Raw audio and video also allow you to display any type of media for which you can write a decoder. Much of the IIS Smooth Streaming client for Silverlight, for example, is written using a custom `MediaStreamSource` implementation. Though writing a typically hardware-implemented 1080p HD codec in managed code may not lead to good performance, there are many other popular formats which don't have native Silverlight support, but which would benefit from a custom `MediaStream-Source` implementation.

So far, we've seen a number of ways to get video and audio into Silverlight. The easiest, of course, is to use a video format Silverlight supports and just point the `MediaElement` to it. Another way is to use the `MediaStreamSource` class to implement your own managed codec. One final way to get video and audio into Silverlight is to use the webcam and microphone APIs. A segment of the API, especially the `VideoSink` and `AudioSink` classes, is conceptually similar to the `MediaStreamSource` code we've completed in this section, but thankfully much simpler.

20.7 Using the webcam

Silverlight 4 introduced the ability to capture media from video capture devices and audio capture devices. Though designed with other devices (such as TV capture cards) in mind, the current implementation handles only webcams and microphones. These devices enable the Silverlight developer to capture raw video and audio data, as well as snapshot stills. Though the first release of this isn't suitable for conferencing scenarios (there's no built-in compression or encoding), it's excellent for local capture and storage and upload scenarios.

If you've ever tried to use an arbitrary webcam (or microphone) using another technology such as WPF, you'll appreciate how simple the Silverlight team has made this. Not only do you get to avoid DirectShow and similar technologies, but the webcam and mic access works cross-platform. As far as device abstraction layers go, this is pretty sweet.

In this section, we'll first cover how to gain access to the webcam and microphone in Silverlight. Then we'll examine how to work with the default webcam and microphones for the platform, including how to capture video and still images. Then, because most machines have more than one audio capture device, and some even more than one video capture device, we'll look at what's required to allow the user to select a specific webcam or microphone.

20.7.1 Gaining access to capture devices

In sandboxed applications, the application must request access to the webcam from a user-initiated event, such as a button click. This is to ensure that a rogue application on a web site doesn't start photographing you without your consent. The request is explicit as shown here:

```
if (CaptureDeviceConfiguration.AllowedDeviceAccess ||
    CaptureDeviceConfiguration.RequestDeviceAccess())
{ ... }
```

The first check is to see whether the application has already been granted access; this is true if it's running under elevated trust or the user has already allowed access.

Figure 20.9 Webcam and microphone access confirmation dialog

The second check runs only if the first check is false; it causes the webcam and microphone device access confirmation dialog to be displayed, as shown in figure 20.9.

Once the user has confirmed access, you can begin to capture using a specific device or the default devices. Typically, you'll use the default device.

CHANGING THE DEFAULT CAPTURE DEVICE

Silverlight allows the user to set the default webcam and default microphone. This is done by right-clicking on any Silverlight application and selecting the Silverlight menu option. Alternatively, the user can open Microsoft Silverlight from his program shortcuts. Once there, select the Webcam/Mic tab and pick from the list of available options. You'll see a preview of the webcam to the left and an audio level meter for the microphone on the right. Figure 20.10 shows the configuration dialog.

The settings start out using default capture devices on your machine. You can change it from there. The changes will globally affect all Silverlight applications that use the webcam or microphone.

With the default device set in Silverlight, it's time to write a little code to capture information from the default webcam.

Figure 20.10 Silverlight default webcam and microphone tab in the Silverlight settings dialog. Either that image is horizontally stretched in an unflattering way, or I need to lay off the chips.

20.7.2 *Working with video*

To get the default webcam, you need only call the `GetDefaultVideoCaptureDevice` method of the `CaptureDeviceConfiguration` class. If this method returns null, there's no recognized webcam on the machine.

Once you have a capture device, capturing video requires wiring up a capture source and using it as the input source for a `VideoBrush`. The `VideoBrush` is then used to fill a shape, typically a rectangle, on the Silverlight surface.

Listing 20.11 shows how to create a simple webcam viewer using the default webcam at a default capture resolution.

> ### Listing 20.11 Capturing video using the default capture device

Result:

XAML:
```
<Grid x:Name="LayoutRoot" Background="White">
  <Button x:Name="Capture" Content="Capture"
          Width="75" Height="23"
          HorizontalAlignment="Left" VerticalAlignment="Top"
          Margin="232,12,0,0" Click="Capture_Click" />         ❶
  <Rectangle x:Name="PresentationSurface"                      ❷
          Width="376" Height="247"
          HorizontalAlignment="Left"
          VerticalAlignment="Top"
          Margin="12,41,0,0"
          />
</Grid>
```

C#:
```
private void Capture_Click(object sender, RoutedEventArgs e)
{
  if (CaptureDeviceConfiguration.AllowedDeviceAccess ||       ❸
      CaptureDeviceConfiguration.RequestDeviceAccess())
  {
    var camera =
      CaptureDeviceConfiguration.GetDefaultVideoCaptureDevice();   ← Default
                                                                     video
    if (camera != null)                                             capture
    {                                                               device
      var source = new CaptureSource();

      source.VideoCaptureDevice = camera;              ❹
```

```
      VideoBrush videoBrush = new VideoBrush();
      videoBrush.Stretch = Stretch.Uniform;
      videoBrush.SetSource(source);                        ❺
      PresentationSurface.Fill = videoBrush;

      source.Start();              ◁──┐  Start
    }                                  │  capturing
  }
}
```

In listing 20.11, we first set up the button for the user-initiated video capture ❶ and the rectangle to hold the rendered output ❷, both in XAML. In the code, we perform the check to see whether we have access, or request it if not ❸. Then we get the default video capture device and assign it as the capture device for the CaptureSource ❹. The video display isn't a MediaElement. Instead, we create a VideoBrush, set its source to our CaptureSource ❺, and then paint the rectangle with the output. Finally, we start the capture itself.

This example used the default capture resolution. That's okay for an example, but in a real application, you'll likely want to pick a specific video format based on screen resolution or even the frames per second (FPS).

SETTING THE DESIRED VIDEO FORMAT

Webcams typically support a number of resolutions and video formats. I have a Microsoft LifeCam Cinema on my PC, and it handles everything from the smallest of postage stamps to 720p HD video. As the capabilities vary from model to model, you'll need a way to query the webcam to identify its supported video formats.

The VideoCaptureDevice class contains a number of properties. The one of interest to us in this case is the SupportedFormats collection. SupportedFormats is a collection of VideoFormat objects, the properties of which are displayed in table 20.12.

Table 20.12 The VideoFormat class

Member	Description
FramesPerSecond	A floating-point value indicating the number of frames per second.
PixelFormat	Currently, the only valid pixel format is 32 bits per pixel, ARGB.
PixelHeight	The height of the frames in pixels.
PixelWidth	The width of the frames in pixels.
Stride	The number of bytes in a single horizontal line of the frame. Divide this by PixelWidth to know the bytes per pixel, regardless of PixelFormat. A negative stride indicates the image is upside down.

To query the formats for my own camera, I injected this bit of code into the listing at the beginning of this section:

```
foreach (VideoFormat format in camera.SupportedFormats)
    Debug.WriteLine(
        format.PixelWidth + "x" +
```

```
format.PixelHeight + " at " +
format.FramesPerSecond + " fps " +
format.PixelFormat.ToString());
```

The resulting list included (among many others) these entries:

```
640x480 at 30.00003 fps Unknown
160x120 at 30.00003 fps Unknown
160x120 at 30.00003 fps Unknown
1280x720 at 15.00002 fps Unknown
1280x720 at 15.00002 fps Unknown
960x544 at 30.00003 fps Unknown
960x544 at 30.00003 fps Unknown
800x448 at 30.00003 fps Unknown
800x448 at 30.00003 fps Unknown
800x600 at 30.00003 fps Unknown
...
```

Oddly enough, the pixel format came across as Unknown in all cases. Try it with your own webcam and the results will likely vary. Once you see a video format that works for you, you can choose it by assigning it to the DesiredFormat property of the VideoCaptureDevice. This example uses a LINQ expression to grab the first format with the highest resolution:

```
var format = (from VideoFormat f in camera.SupportedFormats
             orderby f.PixelWidth * f.PixelHeight descending
             select f).FirstOrDefault<VideoFormat>();
if (format != null)
  camera.DesiredFormat = format;
```

That will pick the format with the highest total pixel count. You can modify the statement to pick just the largest width, or the largest size that will fit within a given box, and so forth. Figure 20.11 shows the 720p HD version of the webcam shot from the previous listing.

Figure 20.11
Webcam screen shot at 720p HD, selected using the Desired-Format **property and LINQ. I'm practicing my raised-eyebrow news anchor face. I'll try harder next time. Dig the C128 in the background!**

One reason you may want to capture at a high resolution is to support the capturing of still images. The Silverlight webcam API allows you to use the webcam as a simple still image camera, returning individual images as `WriteableBitmap` instances.

20.7.3 *Capturing still images*

Now that you have a reasonably high resolution selected, taking still photos makes much more sense. The Silverlight webcam API supports taking still photos by using an asynchronous capture method. You click a button and call a function, and a few fractions of a second later, the event fires with the image data.

In this section, we'll augment our webcam display application to include a `ListBox` filled with captured still images. Figure 20.12 shows the final application.

Figure 20.12 Capturing the largest video size, plus a series of still photos bound to a `ListBox` **on the right. Did I get the anchor look any better? Maybe I need a suit.**

Listing 20.12 shows the new XAML required to create the display shown in figure 20.12. Note the use of the `DataTemplate` for displaying the bound image information.

Listing 20.12 XAML Capturing still images

XAML:
```
<Grid x:Name="LayoutRoot" Background="White">
  <Button x:Name="Capture" Content="Capture"
          Width="75" Height="23" Margin="0,12,93,0"
          HorizontalAlignment="Right" VerticalAlignment="Top"
          Click="Capture_Click" />
  <Button x:Name="TakeSnapshot" Content="Snapshot"
          Height="23" Width="75" Margin="0,12,12,0"
          VerticalAlignment="Top" HorizontalAlignment="Right"
          Click="TakeSnapshot_Click" />
  <Rectangle x:Name="PresentationSurface" Margin="12,41,154,12" />
```
❶

```
<ListBox x:Name="Images" Width="136" Margin="0,41,12,12"         ❷
         HorizontalAlignment="Right"
         ScrollViewer.HorizontalScrollBarVisibility="Disabled">
  <ListBox.ItemTemplate>
    <DataTemplate>
      <Image Margin="10" Height="50" Width="100"
             Source="{Binding}" />                                 ❸
    </DataTemplate>
  </ListBox.ItemTemplate>
</ListBox>
</Grid>
```

The XAML in listing 20.12 creates a second button, for requesting a snapshot ❶, and adds a ListBox ❷ to hold the images. The DataTemplate for the ListBox is pretty simple; all it includes is a single image with its source set to be the item bound to it ❸.

Once you have the XAML in place, using the code in listing 20.13 to update the code-behind.

Listing 20.13   C# code for capturing the still images

```
public MainPage()
{
  InitializeComponent();
  Images.ItemsSource = _images;             ❷
}
                                                         CaptureSource
private CaptureSource _source;           ⟵――――          refactored to class-level
private ObservableCollection<ImageSource> _images =
  new ObservableCollection<ImageSource>();                ❶

private void Capture_Click(object sender, RoutedEventArgs e)
{
  if (CaptureDeviceConfiguration.AllowedDeviceAccess ||
      CaptureDeviceConfiguration.RequestDeviceAccess())
  {
    var camera =
        CaptureDeviceConfiguration.GetDefaultVideoCaptureDevice();

    if (camera != null)
    {
      _source = new CaptureSource();

      var format = (from VideoFormat f in camera.SupportedFormats
                    orderby f.PixelWidth * f.PixelHeight descending
                    select f).FirstOrDefault<VideoFormat>();
      if (format != null)
        camera.DesiredFormat = format;         ❸

      _source.VideoCaptureDevice = camera;

      VideoBrush videoBrush = new VideoBrush();
      videoBrush.Stretch = Stretch.Uniform;         Video display
      videoBrush.SetSource(_source);                remains same
      PresentationSurface.Fill = videoBrush;

      _source.CaptureImageCompleted += (s, ea) =>    ❹
        {
```

```
            _images.Add(ea.Result);
        };

        _source.Start();
    }
  }
}
private void TakeSnapshot_Click(object sender, RoutedEventArgs e)
{
    _source.CaptureImageAsync();        ❺
}
```

Listing 20.13 builds on our previous code, refactoring some things out to class-level variables, and adding in some new code. In addition to refactoring the Capture-Source out to class level, I added a new ObservableCollection of ImageSource ❶ to the class members. This will be used as the items source for the ListBox ❷ to support the binding of images using the DataTemplate.

The majority of the code inside Capture_Click is the same as what we've built so far. I included the LINQ method ❸ for obtaining the highest resolution, as we saw in previous examples. Toward the end of the method, before starting the webcam capture, I added an event handler ❹ to add the captured image to the ObservableCollection ❶. This image is a WriteableBitmap (covered in chapter 21) so we could do additional manipulation with it if we wanted. Finally, the button click handler for the snapshot button calls the CaptureImageAsync method ❺ of the capture source.

With that code in place, our webcam display app can now capture stills alongside displaying the output from the webcam. In theory, you could treat those stills like individual frames in a video, but a better way to access the frame data is to use a custom VideoSink.

20.7.4 *Getting the raw video data*

Obviously, capturing still images at random frames is no substitute for being able to get at the raw video bits. Currently, the only way to access the raw video stream is to create your own VideoSink class. This is a class that will take a video capture source and let the capture source push samples to it. It's possible then to get access to the raw bytes for the frames, but they'll be uncompressed. I have to stress that without fast compression, a video conferencing or chat application would be out of the question. Though possible to perform this compression from code inside Silverlight, it's unlikely to perform well enough to use on a real production application.

Disclaimers aside, let's see how to implement this ourselves. The first thing is to create the custom VideoSink class. Listing 20.14 shows how to do this. The class has no real implementation, as it'd completely depend on what you want to do with the bits. I've seen some examples that write out uncompressed (huge) AVI files, for example.

> **Listing 20.14 A sample VideoSink class for capturing raw webcam video**

```
public class CustomVideoSink : VideoSink
{
  private long _currentFrame = 0;
```

```
protected override void OnCaptureStarted()        ❶
{
  VideoFrameQueue.Open();
}

protected override void OnCaptureStopped()        ❷
{
  VideoFrameQueue.Close();
}

protected override void OnFormatChange(VideoFormat videoFormat)
{
  VideoFrameQueue.VideoFormat = videoFormat;        ◁──┐ Capture
}                                                       │ format

protected override void OnSample(
    long sampleTimeInHundredNanoseconds,
    long frameDurationInHundredNanoseconds,
    byte[] sampleData)
{
  _currentFrame++;
                                          │ Append frame
  VideoFrameQueue.Append(      ◁──┘ to queue
    _currentFrame,
    sampleTimeInHundredNanoseconds,
    frameDurationInHundredNanoseconds,
    sampleData);

  System.Diagnostics.Debug.WriteLine(_currentFrame);
 }
}
```

In this example, `CustomVideoSink` derives from the `VideoSink` class. That class provides four overridable members of interest. The `OnCaptureStarted` ❶ and `OnCaptureStopped` ❷ methods are used for startup and shutdown code. In those methods, I open and close a fictional `VideoFrameQueue` class. The implementation of that class would vary significantly based on what you intend to do with the raw bytes, so I've left it out of this example.

One other utility method is `OnFormatChanged`. This is executed when the video format is changed, and will always fire at least once, at the beginning of the capture. Once you know the video format, you can start doing something useful with the bytes that make up each frame. The `OnSample` method provides those bytes to us.

In the `OnSample` method, you'll almost certainly want to write the bytes and other required information to a queue to be processed. I've represented that with the `VideoFrameQueue` member. The queue would likely have a worker on a background thread that would write the frame to a larger file format, or do some simple encoding/compression as required. If you try to do that all inside this method, you'll run into timing issues.

The last step is to hook your custom video sink in to the processing pipeline. First, in the code-behind of the listing from the start of this chapter, add the following private member variable:

```
private CustomVideoSink _sink = new CustomVideoSink();
```

Then, in the same listing, modify the capture block in the button click event handler to look like listing 20.15.

Listing 20.15 Using a custom `VideoSink` to grab frames

```
var camera =
  CaptureDeviceConfiguration.GetDefaultVideoCaptureDevice();

if (camera != null)
{
    var source = new CaptureSource();

    source.VideoCaptureDevice = camera;

    VideoBrush videoBrush = new VideoBrush();
    videoBrush.Stretch = Stretch.Uniform;
    videoBrush.SetSource(source);        Wire up new
    _sink.CaptureSource = source;    ◁──  VideoSink
    PresentationSurface.Fill = videoBrush;

    source.Start();
}
```

In listing 20.15, we've wired our new `CustomVideoSink` into the existing code. The new line in the event handler assigns the capture source, so the sink is now wired up to the webcam. Note that you can have more than one video sink attached to any capture source, but the processor utilization will rise proportionally.

20.7.5 *A note about audio*

Video is seldom captured alone. More often than not, you'll want to capture audio as well. The Silverlight webcam and microphone API supports capturing audio independently, or along with video.

The Silverlight Microphone API is almost identical to the Webcam API, so we'll leave it out for space reasons. The primary difference is that instead of a `VideoCaptureDevice`, you'll have an `AudioCaptureDevice`. There's no native way to output the raw audio, so you'll need to create an `AudioSink` just like we created a `VideoSink` for grabbing video frames. Of course, just as I noted with the `VideoSink`, what you do in the `AudioSink` is going to depend upon what your plans are for encoding. The data format that comes from Silverlight is raw PCM audio.

The Silverlight Webcam API is a powerful way to integrate video capture devices into your application. Already I've seen some novel uses including stop-motion animation, image and gesture recognition, Facebook photo uploading, and more. The API is simple to use, providing us with the device capabilities and a simple way to request access. It works cross-platform and abstracts away all the little details you'd normally need to understand to work with webcam and microphone devices on various machines.

20.8 *Summary*

One of Silverlight's main strengths is in media delivery. Looking at all the options presented in this chapter, it's no wonder. Silverlight supports multiple formats of SD and HD video and audio right out of the box. There's an excellent CodePlex project called the Silverlight Media Framework that provides support for IIS Smooth Streaming for extremely high quality adaptive streaming.

If Silverlight doesn't support a media format you want to use, it has a provision for allowing you to create managed codecs, decoding your own format and sending the raw unencoded bytes to Silverlight. This API is so complete, I've even been able to use it to generate video and audio from code, without any original media source files.

Finally, not all media comes from files or algorithms. Sometimes, media comes from you, in the form of captured video, audio, and still images from a webcam and microphone. Silverlight has excellent support for all types of webcams and mics, cross-browser and cross-platform.

In the webcam still image capture demo, we used a couple image classes, including the `WriteableBitmap` returned in the snapshot callback. Images are often used hand-in-hand with video, both as still captures and as video thumbnails. Images are also prevalent throughout most applications as button icons and other design elements. In the next chapter, we'll go through all the ways you can work with images in Silverlight, including loading image files, generating images from scratch, and working with enormous images with Deep Zoom.

Working with bitmap images

Images are used on web pages all across the internet. They're used in the form of application icons, corporate logos, and photos of you and your friends. It's been quite a while since I've seen even a regular forms-over-data application that didn't have images in the UI somewhere. Obviously, bitmap-based images have become a mainstay of application design.

Naturally, Silverlight includes mechanisms for displaying this content through the `Image` element and the `MultiScaleImage` control.

In addition to displaying images, Silverlight includes the powerful ability to create images from scratch or from other elements using the `WriteableBitmap` type. You can even use the `WriteableBitmap` to provide support for formats not natively supported in Silverlight (such as .GIF).

In this chapter, we'll start with the basics of imaging with the `Image` element. From there, we'll move on to creating images on the fly using the `WriteableBitmap`. Once we have a handle on the `WriteableBitmap`, we'll turn to Silverlight's answer to enormous gigapixel-level images or collections of images-Deep Zoom with the `MultiScaleImage` control. Finally, we'll wrap up the chapter with a discussion of the different ways of stretching content to fit the space allotted.

21.1 Basic imaging

The `Image` element enables you to display images from across the internet. In addition to loading images relative to your project, the `Image` element allows you to retrieve images from another domain. Take a look at how listing 21.1 uses the `Source` property to get an image from the http://www.silverlightinaction.com web site.

> **Listing 21.1 An Image element that uses a picture from another domain**

Result:

XAML:
```
<StackPanel Height="200" Width="100">
  <Image Source="http://www.silverlightinaction.com/man.png" />
</StackPanel>
```

The `Image` in this markup retrieves an image from the silverlightinaction.com domain. This image is referenced through the `Source` property, which is set with a `Uri` through XAML. If this property needs to be set programmatically, you must use an `ImageSource` instead. Because this `abstract` class can't be used directly, you use a derivation known as `BitmapImage`. This class name is a little misleading because only the types listed in table are 21.1 supported.

Format	Extension(s)
Joint Photographic Experts Group	.jpg, .jpeg, .jpe, .jfif, .jfi, .jif
Portable Network Graphics	.png

Table 21.1 Image formats supported by the `BitmapImage` class. These formats are inherently supported formats of the `Image` element.

This table shows the image formats supported by the `BitmapImage` class. Because this is the type used by the `Source` property, these image formats also represent those supported by the `Image` element in general.

What are you to do if you want to load an image type that's unsupported by Silverlight, such as .gif or .bmp? In the previous chapter, we saw how you can use the `MediaStreamSource` API to provide a hook to use when a video or audio format is unsupported. Luckily, Silverlight includes an equivalent for still images, the `WriteableBitmap`.

21.2   *Creating images at runtime*

The WriteableBitmap (sometimes referred to as *The Bitmap API*) was introduced in Silverlight 3. It provides the ability to generate new images based on existing images, onscreen UI elements, or from scratch using pixel manipulation.

WriteableBitmap is a class in the System.Windows.Media.Imaging namespace, deriving from the common BitmapSource base class. Deriving from that class allows us to use the WriteableBitmap in almost every place you could normally use any other type of bitmap image class.

The uses for this feature are numerous, and all over the map. I've personally used it to generate Windows 7-style window thumbnails in a large Silverlight business application for a customer. I've seen others use it in games, for destructive 2D UI (think *Lemmings* where a bomb takes a chunk out of the ground). Still others have built their own paint programs using this feature.

In this section, we'll look at the three main ways to use the WriteableBitmap class: creating editable bitmaps from existing images, creating bitmaps from portions of the visual tree, and creating bitmaps from scratch.

Before we do that, we'll have the usual project setup to do. In this case, create a new Silverlight project and modify the MainPage.xaml markup to look like listing 21.2.

> **Listing 21.2   MainPage.xaml for the WriteableBitmap examples**

Result (in designer):

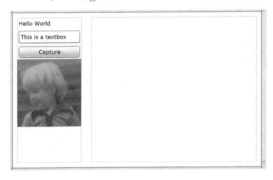

XAML:

```
<UserControl x:Class="BitmapApi.MainPage"
  xmlns="http://schemas.microsoft.com/winfx/2006/xaml/presentation"
  xmlns:x="http://schemas.microsoft.com/winfx/2006/xaml"
  xmlns:d="http://schemas.microsoft.com/expression/blend/2008"
  xmlns:mc="http://schemas.openxmlformats.org/markup-compatibility/2006"
  mc:Ignorable="d" d:DesignHeight="300" d:DesignWidth="500">

    <Grid x:Name="LayoutRoot" Background="White">
      <Grid.ColumnDefinitions>
        <ColumnDefinition Width="150" />
        <ColumnDefinition Width="*" />
      </Grid.ColumnDefinitions>
```

```
            <StackPanel x:Name="Elements"                ❶
                        Grid.Column="0"
                        Margin="10">
              <TextBlock Text="Hello World" Margin="3" />
              <TextBox Text="This is a textbox" Margin="3" />
              <Button x:Name="Capture"
                      Content="Capture" Margin="3" />
              <Image Source="Pete3YearsOld.jpg"            ⟵── Me at 3
                     Stretch="Uniform" />
            </StackPanel>

            <Image x:Name="ResultBitmap"                   ❷
                   Stretch="Uniform"
                   Margin="10"
                   Grid.Column="1" />
      </Grid>
</UserControl>
```

The markup includes a StackPanel ❶ that we'll use for our visual tree rendering example, including an image of me at three years old that we'll use to test creating from existing images, and a result bitmap ❷ that will display the writeable bitmap we create in the code-behind.

You likely don't have a picture of me at three years old hanging around (if you do, we probably need to chat), so pick any old jpeg you have on your machine and drag it into the Silverlight project as a resource, using it instead.

Our first trial of the WriteableBitmap class is going to be to create a new image from an old one.

21.2.1 Creating from existing images

If you're creating a photo-manipulation program, you'll likely want to create a WriteableBitmap from an existing image. That new bitmap will enable you to access the pixels to allow for drawing, erasing, recoloring, and pretty much anything else you can write code for.

There are some restrictions when creating images from existing images. If you download the image from another server—in other words, a cross-domain call like we discussed in chapter 14—you won't be able to access the individual pixels of the image. In our example, we'll use an image that already exists in our project. The resulting application will look like figure 21.1 once you click the Capture button.

This example shows how to use one bitmap as a source to the writeable bitmap. Once you have the image in a writeable bitmap, you can manipulate it all you'd like (within the cross-domain restrictions I mentioned). Double-click the Capture button to create an event handler, then place this code in the handler:

```
BitmapSource source = SourceImage.Source as BitmapSource;
WriteableBitmap bmp = new WriteableBitmap(source);
ResultBitmap.Source = bmp;
```

Of course, you can also load the image from a URL. This code, used in place of the previous example, shows how:

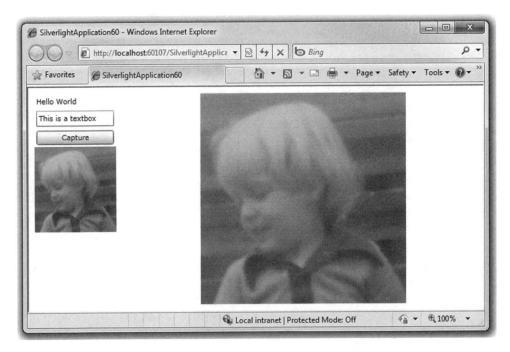

Figure 21.1 A `WriteableBitmap` (right) created from another bitmap (left)

```
Uri uri =
    new Uri("BitmapApi;component/Pete3YearsOld.jpg",
    UriKind.Relative);
StreamResourceInfo res = Application.GetResourceStream(uri);

BitmapImage image = new BitmapImage();
image.SetSource(res.Stream);
WriteableBitmap bmp = new WriteableBitmap(image);

ResultBitmap.Source = bmp;
```

This example shows how to create a `WriteableBitmap` from an existing image that hasn't necessarily been loaded into an `Image` element onscreen.

The convoluted loading scheme is required only because this file is a resource in the Silverlight project. If it's just a normal file on the server, you could've passed the URI directly to the `BitmapImage` constructor.

NOTE The image is loaded asynchronously; the data isn't available until the `BitmapImage.ImageLoaded` event has fired. This is especially important when working with images from external servers.

Another way to use the `WriteableBitmap` class is to create a rendering of a portion of the visual tree.

21.2.2 Creating from UI elements

The `WriteableBitmap` class can be used to take a snapshot of all or a portion of the visual tree. This allows you to easily create thumbnails of large forms for a Windows 7 taskbar-like effect, or capture still frames from videos playing in a `MediaElement`. Note that cross-domain pixel-access checks are enforced, so if anything in the tree fails the cross-domain check, everything will.

As it turns out, creating a snapshot of a portion of the video tree is extremely simple. You pass the root element of the branch of the tree into the constructor of `WriteableBitmap`, along with an optional render transform. For example, see figure 21.2 for a direct 1:1 representation.

To create the bitmap version of the UI as shown in figure 21.2, you only need a couple of lines of code. Place these in the click event handler in place of the other code shown so far:

```
WriteableBitmap bmp = new WriteableBitmap(Elements, null);
ResultBitmap.Source = bmp;
```

`Elements` is the name of the `StackPanel` containing the four elements. The fidelity of the capture is close, but not perfect. For example, you lose ClearType rendering for fonts, so most text will look a little different. Of course, if you pass in a render transform (to rotate, skew, resize), it'll definitely look different.

The final approach is to create an image from scratch. We'll discuss direct pixel access at the same time; it applies to all three approaches.

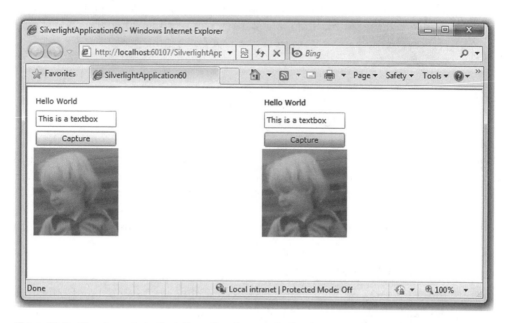

Figure 21.2 The elements to the left are live elements in the visual tree. On the right, you can see the bitmap representation of those elements, captured while the Capture button was clicked.

DIRECT PIXEL ACCESS

The third approach to using the `WriteableBitmap` is to create an image from scratch. This is useful when you want to create an image from code or allow the user to draw on an empty canvas using the mouse.

The direct pixel access techniques shown here also work for any of the previous approaches, once the base image is loaded. Keep in mind that cross-domain images don't allow direct pixel access, and you'll get an exception if you try to do so.

To create an image from scratch, you need only provide dimensions, like this:

```
WriteableBitmap bmp = new WriteableBitmap(640, 480);
```

Then you're free to start working with the image. The pixels are manipulated using the `Pixels` property, which returns an array of integers. Each 32-bit integer represents one pixel in pARGB (premultiplied alpha, red, green, blue) format. This example iterates through the array, setting completely random values for the pixels:

```
Random random = new Random();
for (int i = 0; i < bmp.Pixels.Length; i++)
    bmp.Pixels[i] = random.Next();

ResultBitmap.Source = bmp;
```

That's interesting, but not particularly helpful, as it doesn't show how to set a specific color. Setting a single pixel to a specific color is just as easy:

```
Color c = Colors.Orange;
bitmap.Pixels[i] = c.A << 24 | c.R << 16 | c.G << 8 | c.B;
```

The shifting combined with the bitwise OR operation packs the four values into their correct position within the integer. To get an existing value, the code is a little more verbose, but still amounts to the reverse of putting the pixel:

```
int pixel = bitmap.Pixels[i]
Color c = Color.FromArgb((byte)(pixel >> 24),
                         (byte)(pixel >> 16),
                         (byte)(pixel >> 8),
                         (byte)(pixel));
```

In this example, the variable c will contain the correct color code for the pixel at position i. The bitshift operators and byte masking take care of getting the correct values from the correct positions in the integer.

One interesting use of all this is to create new images using an algorithm. One of the most impressive and best-known algorithms is the Mandelbrot fractal. We'll close the section on the `WriteableBitmap` by creating our own little Mandelbrot fractal generator.

21.2.3 *A Mandelbrot fractal generator*

I love fractals. A number of the desktop wallpapers I created and offer through my personal site were generated using fractal explorer programs such as Ktaza (no longer available). In this section, we'll build a simple visualizer for the Mandelbrot set, a common fractal. The Silverlight application will be able to produce results like figure 21.3.

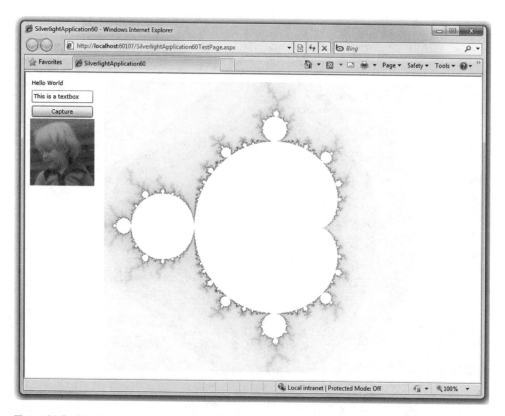

Figure 21.3 The `WriteableBitmap` sample application modified to show a Mandelbrot fractal

For efficiency, we'll simply modify the same project we've been working with throughout this section. Inside the button click handler, add the code from listing 21.3. This code generates a Mandelbrot fractal, coloring it using the escape time algorithm.

Listing 21.3 Mandelbrot fractal in `WriteableBitmap`

```
int width = 1024; int height = 768;

int[] colorTable = new int[256];

for (int i = 0; i < 256; i++)                    ❶
{
    Color c = Color.FromArgb(
        0xFF, (byte)(255 - i), (byte)(255 - i), (byte)(255));

    colorTable[i] = c.A << 24 | c.R << 16 | c.G << 8 | c.B;
}

WriteableBitmap bmp = new WriteableBitmap(width, height);

for (int x = 0; x < width; x++)
{
    for (int y = 0; y < height; y++)
```

```
    {
        double zoom = 300;
        double x0 = 0; double y0 = 0;
        double cx = (x - width / 2) / zoom;
        double cy = (y - height / 2) / zoom;

        int iteration = 0;
        int maxIterations = 1000;

        while (x0 * x0 + y0 * y0 <= 4 && iteration < maxIterations)
        {
            double xtemp = x0 * x0 - y0 * y0 + cx;
            y0 = 2 * x0 * y0 + cy;
            x0 = xtemp;

            iteration++;
        }

        if (iteration == maxIterations)
        {
            bmp.Pixels[(y * width) + x] =
                        colorTable[colorTable.GetUpperBound(0)];
        }
        else                                                     Escape time
        {                                                   ⟵─┘ coloration
            bmp.Pixels[(y * width) + x] =
                        colorTable[iteration % colorTable.Length];
        }
    }
}

ResultBitmap.Source = bmp;                    ❷
```

Listing 21.3 shows how to generate a simple Mandelbrot fractal with coloration based on the escape time algorithm. The code to make this work in Silverlight is straightforward. First, I build a color table ❶ to be used by the escape time algorithm. The colors simply fade from white to dark blue. I then create the WriteableBitmap instance.

The majority of the remaining code is an implementation of the Mandelbrot fractal algorithm. Should you want to modify the scale of the content, the zoom variable is a good place to begin.

The final step is to set the source of the bitmap onscreen to be the WriteableBitmap ❷. This is consistent with the other examples.

When I run this on my PC, the 1024 x 768 fractal generates and displays in subsecond time. I remember in the '80s I had a CBM-BASIC program that generated a Mandelbrot set, and it ran all night, just to create a 320 x 200 image. Impressive.

WriteableBitmap enables a number of important scenarios. First, you can use it to duplicate an existing image to prepare it for editing. Second, you can take a snapshot of a portion of the visual tree in order to create a thumbnail, or to snap a frame of a video. Third, you can generate images, or modify existing images, entirely from code. The scenarios for WriteableBitmap reach across all types of applications from games, to image manipulation, to forms-over-data business applications. Plus, just about anywhere you can use an Image, you can use a WriteableBitmap.

> **TIP** WriteableBitmap requires a fair bit of effort to use for generating shapes or lines. For those situations, you have to do the math to plot pixels efficiently. The WriteableBitmapEx library on CodePlex at http://writeablebitmapex. codeplex.com builds upon the WriteableBitmap to add support for these and other functions.

The Image element will support images up to 4 gigapixels (four billion pixels) in size. As you can imagine, using images this large can force your users to endure painful wait times. In addition, with advancements in digital photography and photo-stitching, what are you supposed to do with images larger than 4 gigapixels? To address these types of situations, Silverlight exposes a slick feature called Deep Zoom.

21.3 Deep Zoom

Deep Zoom is a feature of Silverlight that enables users to explore groupings of high-resolution images. Traditionally, viewing high-resolution images over the internet is associated with painful wait times because high-resolution images are generally larger in size. Silverlight's Deep Zoom feature removes the usual long wait times. In addition, Deep Zoom natively allows users to drill into an image and see its most intricate details. All this is delivered in a smooth viewing experience that runs with unprecedented performance. This kind of experience is made possible by the MultiScaleImage control.

The MultiScaleImage control, similar to the Image control, has the ability to efficiently show incredibly high-resolution images. These images can be zoomed into, giving the user a close-up view of the content. Alternatively, the user can zoom away from the image to get a bird's-eye view of the image. Either way, these zooming features are constrained to an area known as the *viewport*. This viewport can be zoomed into, zoomed out of, and moved around the surface of an image, but this image really isn't an image at all—it's a collection of images typically created by Deep Zoom Composer, a free tool from Microsoft.

21.3.1 Showing an image

Showing an image within a MultiScaleImage control is nearly identical to showing an image within an Image control. As with the Image control, the only property you need to set to display an image is Source . This property is a MultiScaleTileSource that can be used to reference a file, but this file isn't a typical image file. Instead, this file is an XML file, known as the *Deep Zoom image (DZI) file*, that describes a multiscale image. We'll share more about this file type in a moment; for now, look at how a MultiScaleImage is created in XAML:

```
<MultiScaleImage x:Name="myMultiScaleImage"
  Source="images/dzc_output.xml" />
```

This shows the XAML to load a relative multiscale image at design time. In the event that you need to load a multiscale image at runtime, you use a DeepZoomImageTileSource instance. This type derives from the abstract base class `MultiScaleTileSource`, so it can be used at runtime as shown here:

```
myMultiScaleImage.Source = new DeepZoomImageTileSource(
  new System.Uri("images/dzc_output.xml", UriKind.Relative));
```

This line of code shows how to load a multiscale image at runtime. If the referenced image can't be found, the `MultiScaleImage` object's `ImageOpenFailed` event will be fired. If the image is found, the `ImageOpenSucceeded` event will be triggered and the image will be shown. Once this happens, you may consider giving your user the ability to zoom in and out of the high-resolution image.

21.3.2   *Zooming in and out*

The `MultiScaleImage` control has the ability to show an extremely high-resolution image. This control helps remove the traditional limitations associated with screen real estate. This is accomplished by enabling your users to zoom in from a view as if they were standing on top of a mountain.

Zooming within a `MultiScaleImage` is handled by a method called `ZoomAboutLogicalPoint`. The `ZoomAboutLogicalPoint` method takes three parameters that describe the zoom attempt. The first parameter determines how much to zoom by. The second and third parameters specify from where in the image the zoom originates. These parameters and the `ZoomAboutLogicalPoint` method are shown in listing 21.4.

Listing 21.4   Implementing zoom functionality

C#:
```
public Page()
{
  InitializeComponent();
  this.KeyDown += new KeyEventHandler(Page_KeyDown);
  this.KeyUp += new KeyEventHandler(Page_KeyUp);              Input event
  myMultiScaleImage.MouseLeftButtonDown +=                   wire-up
    new MouseButtonEventHandler(myMultiScaleImage_MouseLeftButtonDown);
}
private bool shouldZoom = true;

void Page_KeyDown(object sender, KeyEventArgs e)      ◁─────┐
{                                                          │
  if (e.Key == Key.Shift)                                  ❶
    shouldZoom = false;                                    │
}                                                          │
void Page_KeyUp(object sender, KeyEventArgs e)       ◁─────┘
{
  shouldZoom = true;
}

void myMultiScaleImage_MouseLeftButtonDown(object sender,
  MouseButtonEventArgs e)                                  ❷
{
  Point point = e.GetPosition(myMultiScaleImage);
  point = myMultiScaleImage.ElementToLogicalPoint(point);
```

```
  if (shouldZoom == true)
    myMultiScaleImage.ZoomAboutLogicalPoint(1.5, point.X, point.Y);
  else
    myMultiScaleImage.ZoomAboutLogicalPoint(0.5, point.X, point.Y);
}
```

This listing looks like a lot of code. In short, this code enables the user to zoom in or out of the MultiScaleImage defined earlier. To enable this functionality, you first listen for a keypress ❶. If the keypress is made from the Shift key, the user is saying to zoom away from the image. If the Shift key hasn't been pressed, the zooming feature will default to zooming in, so you also need to listen for a user releasing a key through the KeyUp event. This event resets the zoom mode to the default after the Shift key has been pressed. The real meat of this feature is demonstrated when the user clicks the Multi-ScaleImage ❷. This action forces a call to the ZoomAboutLogicalPoint method, which zooms according to the three parameters passed to it.

The first parameter passed to the ZoomAboutLogicalPoint method determines how to zoom on the image. If this double value is less than 1, the method will zoom away from the image. If the value is greater than 1, the method will zoom into the image. Either way, you can play around with this value to also adjust the speed in which the zoom is applied. To determine where the zoom begins, you must rely on the second and third parameters.

The second parameter represents the logical x coordinate to zoom from, the third parameter represents the logical y coordinate to zoom from. Both parameters are double values that fall between 0 and 1. The fact that these values fall between 0 and 1 is what defines them as part of a logical coordinate system, but most items use a standard Cartesian coordinate system. Fortunately, the MultiScaleImage class exposes two methods that enable you to convert Point objects between the two coordinate systems. The methods are:

- ElementToLogicalPoint
- LogicalToElementPoint

ElementToLogicalPoint converts a Cartesian Point to a logical Point. This is generally used to convert the position of the mouse cursor before zooming because the ZoomAboutLogicalPoint method expects a logical point. Here's an example, assuming the user clicked the mouse at 125,200:

```
Point cartesianPoint = new Point(125, 200);
Point logicalPoint = myMultiScaleImage.ElementToLogicalPoint(cartesianPoint);
myMultiScaleImage.ZoomAboutLogicalPoint(1.5,
  logicalPoint.X, logicalPoint.Y);
```

LogicalToElementPoint converts a logical Point to a Cartesian Point. This allows you to work with a point in a more familiar interface. Here's an example of how to use this method:

```
Point logicalPoint = new Point(0.25, 0.75);
Point cartesianPoint =
myMultiScaleImage.LogicalToElementPoint(logicalPoint);
```

Together, these examples show how to convert between the two coordinate systems. The logical coordinate system is necessary because it's used for two important tasks. The first task is zooming in and out of an image—which you just saw. The other major task is selecting what part of a multiscale image to zoom in on. You'll learn how to do this in a moment. Regardless of your task, both require some knowledge of how to manage the viewport.

21.3.3 *Managing the viewport*

The viewport is a rectangular region used to view a specific area of an image. This region enables you to zoom in and focus on the details of a specific part of an image, so you may want to think of the viewport as a way to interact with an image three-dimensionally. By default, this region is the size of the entire MultiScaleImage control, but you can change the size of the viewport through the ViewportWidth property.

The ViewportWidth property sets the size of a viewport in relation to the logical coordinate space. Anytime you change the ViewportWidth property, it'll be in relation to the hosting MultiScaleImage. For instance, if you set the ViewportWidth property to 1.0, the viewport will be the same size as the hosting MultiScaleImage control. If you change the ViewportWidth property to a double greater than 1.0, you'll make the viewport larger than the MultiScaleImage. This approach would give the user a sense of zooming away from the image. Alternatively, you can focus on a smaller portion of a multiscale image by providing a value less than 1.0. Figure 21.4 illustrates this zooming-away effect.

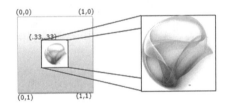

This figure shows the effects of changing the ViewportWidth property to a double less than 1.0. The figure on the left represents the original multiscale image. As you can see, the Silverlight logo in this image is only a small portion of the area shown to the user. By set-

Figure 21.4 A MultiScaleImage with a ViewportWidth of 0.33

ting the ViewportWidth property to 0.33, the Silverlight logo becomes the focus of the entire MultiScaleImage. In reality, the ViewportWidth is only part of the story. The other part involves using the ViewportOrigin property.

The ViewportOrigin specifies the position of the upper-left corner of the viewport. This position is a logical Point relative to the upper-left corner of the MultiScaleImage. Each of the coordinates within the Point will be between 0.0 and 1.0. Note that you can still define this value at design time. To do this, you have to set the ViewportOrigin property with the syntax shown here:

```
<MultiScaleImage x:Name="myMultiScaleImage"
                 Source="images/dzc_output.xml"
                 ViewportOrigin=".33,.33" />
```

This line of markup shows how to set the ViewportOrigin property value at design time. As you might expect, this value can also be set at runtime by creating an instance of the `Point` class. This explanation hardly details the real value of the `ViewportOrigin` property—that it enables you to navigate around the surface of an image once you're zoomed in. By handling a user action (see chapter 8), you can change the viewport position as necessary. The following example shows how to change the position of the viewport on a mouse click:

```
void myMultiScaleImage_MouseLeftButtonUp(object sender,
  MouseButtonEventArgs e)
{
  Point newOrigin = e.GetPosition(myMultiScaleImage);
  myMultiScaleImage.ViewportOrigin =
    myMultiScaleImage.ElementToLogicalPoint(newOrigin);
}
```

This example shows how to reposition the `ViewportOrigin` based on where a user clicked. Once it's clicked, the viewport will move to the new `Point`. This process begins with a nice smooth animation called a *spring animation*. This animation will play anytime the viewport changes size or location—anytime you zoom in or out of an image or pan the surface. This animation can be turned off by changing the `UseSprings` bool property to `false`, but you won't usually want to do this.

In general, it's recommended that you leave the `UseSprings` property set to `true` because the animation creates a rich viewing experience. In addition, it gives the `MultiScaleImage` control more time to download any necessary data. Once the viewport does change size or location, the `MotionFinished` event will be triggered, giving you an opportunity to perform any UI updates that you may want to make to the display.

The viewport is an important concept within the `MultiScaleImage` control. This item gives you the power to scan the surface of a high-resolution image. In addition, the viewport enables you to readily zoom in and out of an image. To enable this zooming functionality, you first load an image into the `MultiScaleImage` control. This image is loaded through the `Source` property, and the `Source` should reference a .xml file, which can be created by a tool. This tool is used when you're ready to deploy a multiscale image.

21.3.4 *Deploying multiscale images*

The `MultiScaleImage` control has built-in support for handling XML that details a multiscale image. This type of file can be generated programmatically or by a tool called *Deep Zoom Composer*. We won't cover this tool in detail because of its simplistic nature. Once you download and install the tool from the Microsoft Expression website, you can quickly create XML files that can be used by the `MultiScaleImage`. These files can be generated within the tool by going through a basic wizard. This wizard goes through the following steps:

1. Import—Enables you to import your own images.
2. Compose—Lets you lay out how the images should appear.
3. Export—Determines where the result will be stored.

These three steps will generate a .xml file and a file/folder structure. These two items must then be added to your web application so that the `MultiScaleImage` control can access them. Once this has been done, you can use Deep Zoom on your own images.

Deep Zoom is a powerful feature available within Silverlight. Because this technology relies on basic images and an XML file, there are no server-side requirements. In addition, the only client-side requirement is Silverlight itself. This is great news because, as you play with Deep Zoom, you'll see the rich experience it provides. This experience truly makes viewing high-resolution images over the internet enjoyable.

One of the misconceptions about Silverlight is that everything must be a vector shape. Silverlight provides a number of ways to load and display bitmap images, as well as powerful ways to manipulate them. You can load regular .png and .jpeg files from the web or a local resource; you can create images on the fly, or from other visuals; and you can quickly zoom through collections with millions or billions of pixels at play. All of this Silverlight does natively and fluidly, proving both a simple developer experience and an excellent end-user experience.

In the examples shown so far in this chapter, you may have noticed some different values for the `Stretch` property. This property is shared by video and image elements alike, and helps control how the content will fill (or not fill) the space provided.

21.4 *Dealing with dead space*

Throughout this chapter you've seen a variety of ways to deliver different kinds of media. Often, media is intended to be a secondary part of an application instead of the main attraction. For instance, a user's profile picture is part of an application but not as important as the profile information itself. As you can imagine, there's the possibility that these profile pictures may be of different sizes. This can lead to dead space, or areas that don't include content. Fortunately, there's a way to gracefully deal with these situations. Please look at figure 21.5.

The `Image`, `MediaElement`, and `Shape` (discussed chapter 18) classes expose a property called `Stretch`. This property determines how the area devoted to an element will be filled. This description will become clearer as you see the examples available in this section. This property must be set to one of the four options available in the `System.Windows.Media.Stretch` enumerator, which exposes the `None`, `Uniform`, `Fill`, and `UniformToFill` options.

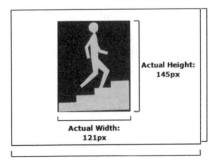

Figure 21.5 The boundary of an Image element in comparison to the actual size of the photo

21.4.1 *Filling the space*

Most of the time, photos are represented as raster-based graphics. Raster-based graphics often become pixellated and lose their detail when they're enlarged. You can prevent this from happening by using the option None for the Stretch value. This option commands an element to maintain the original size of the requested content—this option doesn't make the content stretch at all. As you probably expected, you can set this property value at design time, as shown in here:

```
<Image x:Name="myImage"
       Source="http://www.silverlightinaction.com/man.png"
       Stretch="None" />
```

The XAML in this example loads an Image and prevents it from stretching. The result from this XAML can be seen in figure 21.5, which shows the results of the None option when there's plenty of space for a piece of content. Consider the scenario where the content is larger than the hosting element. Take a look at Walker's picture (the content) in an Image element (the hosting element) smaller than the picture (see listing 21.5).

Listing 21.5   Use of the None **option on an undersized** Image **element**

Result:

XAML:
```
<Image x:Name="myImage" Width="75" Height="75"
       Source="http://www.silverlightinaction.com/man.png"
       Stretch="None" />
```

Unfortunately for Walker, his legs got cut off! (One of my slightly twisted tech reviewers suggested he should be named "Sitter" now. Thanks, Tom.) As the result in this listing shows, the original photo remains the same size, so the bottom and right edges of the photo are cropped so that the image fits within the 75px-by-75px dimension of the Image element. This illustration also erases any fears of an exception being thrown in the case of an element being smaller than its content.

At first glance, the None option may seem like the most obvious default option. It may come as a surprise to find out that another option makes even more sense as the default. When you begin to consider the fact that the Stretch option is applicable to Image, MediaElement, and Shape elements, it makes much more sense to stretch items by default, uniformly.

21.4.2 *Uniform sizing*

If you set the Stretch property to Uniform, the content of the element will symmetrically expand or contract to occupy most of the available area. While the content expands or contracts, the native aspect ratio will be preserved. This means that if you revisit Walker's picture, it'll be stretched vertically, making him stand tall and proud (see listing 21.6).

Listing 21.6   A uniformly stretched Image with a photo smaller than the element

Result:

XAML:

```
<Image x:Name="myImage" Width="300" Height="200"
       Source="http://www.silverlightinaction.com/man.png"
       Stretch="Uniform" />
```

The gray backdrop in this listing represents the area that could be filled by an image. Because the Uniform option stretches content proportionally, it must stop once either a vertical or horizontal boundary is met. But, what happens if the content is larger than the bounding element? Listing 21.7 shows how to maintain aspect ratio.

Listing 21.7   A uniformly stretched Image with a photo larger than the element

Result:

XAML:

```
<Image x:Name="myImage" Width="75" Height="75"
       Source="http://www.silverlightinaction.com/man.png"
       Stretch="Uniform" />
```

As this listing illustrates, the content remains intact. Instead of cropping the image, as was the case in listing 21.5, the content scales to a smaller size. As the content scales down, the aspect ratio stays the same. Although maintaining the aspect has its benefits, occasionally you might need to fill the entire area, no matter what. For these situations, you have the Fill option.

21.4.3   *Fill the area*

The Fill option allows you to expand or contract the content of an element to fully occupy the space allocated to it. You'll most likely use this option in backdrop scenarios where you want an Image to serve as wallpaper. Listing 21.8 shows what the Fill option does to Walker's picture.

Listing 21.8 An `Image` using the `Fill` option to stretch an image

Result:

XAML:
```
<Image x:Name="myImage" Width="300" Height="200"
       Source="http://www.silverlightinaction.com/man.png"
       Stretch="Fill" />
```

Walker looks a little bloated (it's water weight, trust me) in this listing because, although the `Fill` option will expand to ensure that every pixel allotted to an element is used, the aspect ratio of the content won't be preserved. Because of the oblong dimensions of the photo, the photo is stretched horizontally—in turn, horizontally stretching Walker.

Sometimes, you may need the flexibility to fill an element while maintaining the aspect ratio. For these circumstances, you have the `UniformToFill` option.

21.4.4 UniformToFill

As the name implies, this option is a hybrid between the `Uniform` and `Fill` options. The content within an element will maintain its aspect ratio while filling the entire bounding area. If the content has a different aspect ratio than the housing element, the overflowing content will be clipped. See listing 21.9 for a small sample using our friend Walker.

Listing 21.9 An `Image` using the `UniformToFill` `Stretch` option

Result:

XAML:
```
<Image x:Name="myImage" Width="300" Height="200"
       Source="http://www.silverlightinaction.com/man.png"
       Stretch="UniformToFill" />
```

This listing illustrates how a raster-based graphic can become pixellated when inflated. It also shows how the aspect ratio is maintained as the picture is enlarged to fill every allocated pixel. As you've probably noticed, Walker's legs are removed from this picture. This is because the bottom edge has been removed to ensure that the image fits within the allocated boundaries.

Stretching can help you address a wide variety of filling situations. Silverlight allows you to easily address any type of stretching situation through the Stretch property. This property can be used with the Image and MediaElement items discussed earlier in this chapter. Interestingly, the Stretch property isn't supported by the MultiScaleImage control. But, with those powerful deep-zooming capabilities, does it really make sense to stretch? I think not.

21.5   *Summary*

Over the course of this chapter, we explored several ways of working with bitmap (also known as *raster*) images. Silverlight natively supports .jpeg and .png images in the Image element, but provides facilities for you to be able to construct any type of image you'd like using direct pixel access with the WriteableBitmap.

The WriteableBitmap allows you to construct images from existing UI elements, from existing images, or even from individually placed pixels. This supports countless scenarios from screen thumbnails, to video stills, to games and paint programs.

For truly large images, or collections of large images, Silverlight provides the MultiScaleImage control, also known as *Deep Zoom*. Deep Zoom supports images in the millions to billions of pixels allowing for very fast enlargement of specific areas while minimizing the amount of memory, processing power, and bandwidth used.

All of the image types support various stretch options to allow them to conform to the shape of the container they're placed in. Silverlight smoothly resizes images, preserving aspect ratio if you desire.

Along with media (see chapter 20) and vector graphics (see chapter 18), bitmap images round out the graphical presentation capabilities of Silverlight, helping to put the "rich" in *rich internet application*. In the next chapter we'll learn how to use animation to move from these static shapes to a more dynamic and interactive user experience.

Animation
and behaviors

This chapter covers
- Providing interactive animations
- Using keyframes
- Using and creating easing functions
- Working with and creating behaviors

Believe it or not, there once was a time when I had to cower in my cube at a client site, trying to make sure no one saw me designing icons in a graphics program, or hand-coding subtle timer-based animation for an application UI. Working with those things was looked upon as "not real work." At the same time, the clients expected icons and application UI to magically appear as though someone just pressed the "Make it Awesome" button on an IDE.

Gladly, for most companies, those days are gone. The value of good graphics, good UX, and for the most part, good animation have become mainstream in all but the most conservative organizations. The last of those, and probably the least broadly accepted, is animation.

Animation is a relative newcomer to the world of application development. Yes, creative types have been doing it for years, but many of us haven't seen much animation in our own applications, web or otherwise. Flash, WPF, Silverlight, and jQuery, not to mention the vastly improved motion graphics on TV and in movies, have all helped to finally make animation mainstream.

Animation is a double-edged sword. Silverlight will make it simple for you to use animation as much as you want, even if that's overdoing it so much that your entire application UI appears to be suspended from a bed of Slinky springs. I won't judge, honestly. I'll just show you how to use the awesome capabilities Silverlight gives us.

We'll start by covering the basics of animation, of how animation is a change in the value of a property over time. Then we'll work with the timeline and storyboards. Once we know how to group animations in a storyboard, we'll cover how to create key frames to allow Silverlight to interpolate the values between different points in time. Of course, key frames would be pretty boring without easing functions, so that comes next. We'll even see how to create our own easing functions. Finally, we'll wrap up the chapter with some examples of using and creating behaviors.

22.1   Animation: it's about time

An animation within Silverlight boils down to changing a single visual property over a period of time. Without the concept of time, an animation would be a static graphic, and there'd be no need for this chapter. By gradually changing a visual property over the course of a time period, you can deliver dynamic effects. One such effect is shown in figure 22.1.

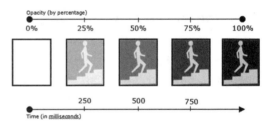

This figure shows the relationship between the Opacity property of an Image and the duration of an animation. As this animation progresses over the course of a single second, the

Figure 22.1   An image fading into view over the course of one second

Opacity value gradually increases. As the Opacity value increases, the Image gradually becomes more and more opaque. You create this dramatic animation by using the code in listing 22.1.

Listing 22.1   XAML for fading in an Image over the course of one second

XAML:

```
<Image x:Name="myImage"
  Source="http://www.silverlightinaction.com/man.png">
  <Image.Triggers>
    <EventTrigger RoutedEvent="Image.Loaded">
      <BeginStoryboard>
        <Storyboard x:Name="myStoryboard">
          <DoubleAnimation Duration="0:0:2"
                          Storyboard.TargetName="myImage"
```

```
                                    Storyboard.TargetProperty="Opacity"
                                    From="0" To="1" />
            </Storyboard>
          </BeginStoryboard>
        </EventTrigger>
      </Image.Triggers>
    </Image>
```

This example shows the XAML responsible for fading an image into view. A lot of new elements are presented within this small example; to gain an understanding of how these elements relate to one another, here's an overview of the items seen in listing 22.1:

1. The `EventTrigger` element initiates an action when the `Image` is loaded. This action is represented as the `BeginStoryboard` element. A trigger is one way to start an animation.

2. The `Storyboard` object is responsible for organizing and controlling the animations defined within it. Because of the `BeginStoryboard` action, this `Storyboard` is automatically started when the `EventTrigger` is fired.

3. The `DoubleAnimation` element specifies that you're going to animate a double-precision value. There are other animation types that we'll cover in a moment. But more importantly, the value to animate is referenced with help from the `Storyboard.TargetProperty` and `Storyboard.TargetName` properties.

As this outline demonstrates, each element serves a specific purpose. These elements work together to allow you to create lively animations. These animations ultimately revolve around time. Time is probably best represented as a line such as the one shown in figure 22.1. This timeline demonstrates how central the concept of time is to an animation.

22.2 *Mastering the timeline*

At its base, every animation represents a `Timeline` object. This object is defined within the `System.Windows.Media.Animation` namespace and is used to represent a period of time. During this period of time, you have the opportunity to change the value assigned to a visual property. To specify which property value should be changed, you answer the following simple questions:

- What type of property are you animating?
- Where are you starting from, and where are you going?
- How long should the animation run?

Although these questions sound fairly basic, there are a significant number of details surrounding each one. For this reason, we'll cover each question in detail, beginning with the first question.

22.2.1 *What type of property are you animating?*

To create an animation, you first select a single visual attribute of a single element. This item is guaranteed to have a data type associated with it. This data type will serve as the guiding light throughout the animation process. Ultimately, it's what will decide the type of animation that should be used. Imagine having a basic `Ellipse` that you want to animate. The XAML for this sample is shown in listing 22.2.

Listing 22.2   The XAML for a basic `Ellipse`

XAML:

```
<UserControl x:Class="EllipseAnimation.Page"
  xmlns="http://schemas.microsoft.com/winfx/2006/xaml/presentation"
  xmlns:x="http://schemas.microsoft.com/winfx/2006/xaml"
  Width="400" Height="400">
<Canvas x:Name="LayoutRoot" Background="White">
    <Canvas.Triggers>
        <EventTrigger RoutedEvent="Canvas.Loaded">
            <BeginStoryboard>
                <Storyboard x:Name="myStoryboard">      ⟵── Animations
                </Storyboard>                                will go here
            </BeginStoryboard>
        </EventTrigger>
    </Canvas.Triggers>

    <Path x:Name="myEllipse" Fill="Yellow" Stroke="Black"
        StrokeThickness="2" Height="400"Width="400">
        <Path.Data>
            <EllipseGeometry x:Name="EllipseGeometry"
                        Center="25,25" RadiusX="25" RadiusY="25" />
        </Path.Data>
    </Path>

</Canvas>
</UserControl>
```

This example shows an `Ellipse` named `myEllipse`. This `Ellipse` will be used in the remainder of this section to describe animating properties. Silverlight provides three types of animations to assist you in creating dramatic visual effects. These types differ in regard to the type of property being animated. Silverlight has the ability to animate `double`, `Point`, and `Color` values via the `DoubleAnimation`, `PointAnimation`, and `ColorAnimation` types. We'll begin by discussing the most useful type, the `DoubleAnimation`.

DOUBLEANIMATION

A `DoubleAnimation` enables you to animate a single property value from one double-precision floating-point value to another. This is probably the most widely used type of animation. To illustrate a `DoubleAnimation`, this example shows how you could fade out the `Ellipse` defined in listing 22.2 over one second:

```
<DoubleAnimation Storyboard.TargetName="myEllipse"
                 Storyboard.TargetProperty="Opacity"
                 From="1" To="0"
                 Duration="0:0:1" />
```

As this markup illustrates, delivering a fade effect is incredibly simple. The `DoubleAnimation` element prepares Silverlight to generate double-precision values between the

From and To values. As you can imagine, this opens the doors to tons of animation scenarios, but not every opened door should necessarily be entered.

Attempting to animate the FontSize property of a TextBlock can be a resource-consuming task. Even though this property is implemented as a double-precision value, animating it can quickly lead to poorly performing applications because the text will be smoothed on every frame—an expensive process, even when the text is using animation-optimized smoothing. For this reason, if you need to animate your text, you may want to consider converting your TextBlock into a Path and using a ScaleTransform.

Regardless, the DoubleAnimation is still applicable in a variety of scenarios: creating fades, moving elements around a Panel, and performing transformations, among other things. However useful the DoubleAnimation is, there still may be situations where you need to animate Point-related values.

POINTANIMATION

The PointAnimation type enables you to animate from one pair of x and y coordinates to another. As the name implies, this type of animation enables you to animate any property that represents a System.Windows.Point. And although this type isn't as widely used throughout the Silverlight APIs as the double type, it still has its place. For instance, you may need to animate the center of an EllipseGeometry object or dynamically change the presentation of a brush. Regardless of the need, it's nice to know that you can rely on the PointAnimation, which is illustrated here:

```
<PointAnimation Storyboard.TargetProperty="Center"
                Storyboard.TargetName="EllipseGeometry"
                Duration="0:0:2"
                From="100,100"
                To="100,300" />
```

The animation in this example changes the origin of any transforms applied to the Ellipse in listing 22.2. Generally, a PointAnimation will only be used in association with transforms and the Geometry elements mentioned in chapter 18. But, for a more subtle animation, you may consider using a ColorAnimation.

COLORANIMATION

A ColorAnimation enables you to create smooth transitions from one color to another. These transitions can be performed between any two System.Windows.Media.Color property values. For this reason, this type of animation is used primarily with a brush as shown in this example:

```
<ColorAnimation Storyboard.TargetName="myEllipse"
                Storyboard.TargetProperty="(Fill).(SolidColorBrush.Color)"
                Duration="00:00:01"
                From="Yellow" To="Red" />
```

This XAML shows an assumed Ellipse shifting from Yellow to Red over the course of one second. This animation, along with the others mentioned, shows how easy it is to animate a property. Up to this point, we've only focused on animation related to a property type. In reality you also need to know how to specify the exact property you're animating.

Each of the animation types that we've discussed exposes two attached properties that specify the target of an animation. Appropriately, these attributes are called `Storyboard.TargetProperty` and `Storyboard.TargetName`. These properties work in coordination to determine which property of a specific element will be animated. This is a simplified description of these properties; a more detailed definition will be provided in section 22.3.2. For now, let's turn our focus to the second question in our animation journey.

22.2.2 *Where are you starting from and where are you going?*

As figure 22.1 illustrated, an animation has a beginning and an end, whether inferred or explicit. The end of an animation can be specified using one of two properties. We'll discuss each of these properties in detail later in this section. Before we can discuss the end of an animation, we should first discuss the beginning.

WHERE IS THE ANIMATION COMING FROM?

There's a saying that you can't know where you're going until you know where you've been. In regard to animation, this phrase should be changed to you can't know where you're going unless you know where you're from. To identify where an animation is coming from, you rely on the aptly named `From` property.

The `From` property is accessible from all the animation types that we've discussed. This value determines where an animation will begin. The following XAML shows the `From` property in action to help jump start our discussion:

```
<DoubleAnimation Storyboard.TargetName="myImage"
                 Storyboard.TargetProperty="Opacity"
                 From="0" To="1"
                 Duration="0:0:1" />
...
<Image x:Name="myImage"
       Source=" http://www.silverlightinaction.com/man.png"
       Opacity=".25" />
```

This example is preparing to animate the `Opacity` property of an assumed `Image`. The `Opacity` property of this `Image` is initially set to 0 when the animation starts. This is determined by the value provided within the `From` property. Once the animation begins, the `Opacity` value gradually increases over the course of one second to the value of 1.

Note that this value is compatible with the animation type. The 0 may look like an integer, but at runtime, it's automatically converted into a double-precision value. If you'd attempted to set the `From` property value to `Yellow`, an exception would've been thrown because `Yellow` isn't a valid double-precision value. Alternatively, you can skip this potential problem altogether by not defining a `From` property value; the `From` property is an optional attribute.

If a `From` value isn't provided, the animation will automatically decide where to start from. To decide where to begin, the animation will examine the target specified by the `Storyboard.TargetName` and `Storyboard.TargetProperty` attributes. Once these are examined, the `From` property will be set to the current property value associated with the target, as shown in this example:

```
<DoubleAnimation Storyboard.TargetName="myImage"
                 Storyboard.TargetProperty="Opacity"
                 To="1"  Duration="0:0:1" />
...
<Image x:Name="myImage"
       Source=" http://www.silverlightinaction.com/man.png"
       Opacity=".25" />
```

When the animation in this markup begins, it automatically determines that the `Opacity` value within the animation should begin at .25. This is the current value of the `Opacity` property, which is defined as the target. This approach can help create smoother, more fluid animations. On the other hand, explicitly stating the `From` value can have unexpected effects on your animations.

Explicitly setting the `From` value can cause your animations to jump or jerk between iterations because the animation may need to reset the target property back to the value set within the `From` attribute. If you want more fluid animations, you may consider having an animation end at, or just before, the value specified within the `From` value. Alternatively, you may choose to skip setting the `From` value altogether. Either way, you need to know where the animation is going.

WHERE AM I GOING?

One way to predetermine where an animation is going is by setting the `To` property. The `To` property is exposed within the `ColorAnimation`, `DoubleAnimation`, and `PointAnimation` types. This value represents the destination of a specific animation. Like the `From` property, the value associated with the `To` property must be compatible with the type of animation. To get a better feel for this property, examine its use in this example:

```
<DoubleAnimation Storyboard.TargetProperty="Opacity"
                 Storyboard.TargetName="myEllipse"
                 Duration="0:0:1"
                 From=".75" To="0" />
```

This XAML shows the `Opacity` of the `Ellipse` changing from .75 to 0 when the animation begins. Over the course of one second, the `Opacity` of the `Ellipse` will change to 0. If you've defined a value for the `From` attribute, you don't have to set the `To` property. Instead, you can rely on the use of the `By` property.

HOW AM I GOING TO GET THERE?

The `By` property is a special shortcut that provides an alternate to the `To` property. Instead of having to know where you want to go initially, you can conveniently specify a value in the `By` attribute. When the animation is run, Silverlight adds the value defined in the `From` field to the `By` value to automatically determine the `To` value. To get a firmer understanding of how this can be used, take a look at this markup:

```
<DoubleAnimation Storyboard.TargetName="myImage"
                 Storyboard.TargetProperty="Opacity"
                 From=".25" By=".50"
                 Duration="0:0:1" />
```

This example defines the animation for an assumed Image. When the animation begins, the Opacity property of the Image is set to .25. Over the course of one second, you want this animation to increase the Opacity value by .50. When this animation has started, the To value will essentially be .75. You can also decrease the Opacity value by providing a negative value, as shown in this XAML fragment:

```
<DoubleAnimation Storyboard.TargetName="myImage"
                 Storyboard.TargetProperty="Opacity"
                 From=".25" By="-.10"
                 Duration="0:0:1" />
```

This markup shows the alternative to increasing a value. Note that the By property itself is an alternative to the To property. If both properties are defined, the To property will take precedence and the By property will be ignored.

The By and To properties enable you to provide guidance for your animations. These animations begin at the value provided within the From field. To determine how long the animation should take to get to the destination, we have one final question to address.

22.2.3 *How long should the animation run?*

As mentioned earlier, each animation is a Timeline object, so a number of valuable time-related traits are shared among all animations. The most important of these items is the Duration property.

HOW LONG?

The Duration property specifies how long it'll take for a Timeline to complete a single episode. This value can be defined using the TimeSpan syntax or it can use a predefined value, defined within the Duration struct and described in table 22.1.

Property	Description
Automatic	Means that a Timeline will automatically end when all child elements have been completed.
Forever	Signals that an animation can run forever.

Table 22.1 Options for the Duration property

Table 22.1 illustrates that you have two options when it comes to controlling the Duration of an animation. To control the playback speed of an animation, call on the SpeedRatio property.

THROTTLING THE ANIMATION

The SpeedRatio property represents the throttle for a Timeline. By default, this double-precision value is set to 1.0. This value can be set to any positive double-precision value and act as a multiplier to the Duration property value. Figure 22.2 shows the Duration, SpeedRatio, and time values for a completed Timeline.

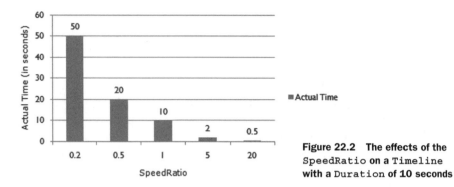

Figure 22.2 The effects of the
SpeedRatio **on a** Timeline
with a Duration **of 10 seconds**

As figure 22.2 illustrates, the SpeedRatio property can have a pretty significant impact on the Duration of a Timeline. These results show that any value less than 1 will slow down an animation. At the same time, any value greater than 1 will speed up the animation.

Besides adjusting the speed of an animation, you may need to repeat its performance. For this reason, there's a RepeatBehavior property.

PLAY IT AGAIN

The RepeatBehavior property is an interesting animal that may act differently than you're anticipating. This property enables you to specify how many times an animation should be played back-to-back. This property also enables you to specify how long the animation should run regardless of the Duration value—the animation will play back-to-back until the time specified in the RepeatBehavior property has elapsed. To get a further understanding of how this property works, examine figure 22.3.

Figure 22.3 illustrates the effects of the RepeatBehavior property in relation to an animation's Duration. The first three bars illustrate how to use the RepeatBehavior to specify the total number of times a Timeline should run. The last three bars show how to use the RepeatBehavior to specify a specific length of time for a Timeline.

As shown in the first three bars, you can append an x as the suffix to a positive, double-precision value. This suffix informs Silverlight that you want an animation to

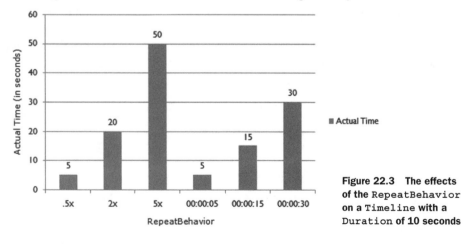

**Figure 22.3 The effects
of the** RepeatBehavior
on a Timeline **with a**
Duration **of 10 seconds**

run a specific number of times. The total number of times is represented as the value before the x. If the RepeatBehavior is set to 2.0x, the animation will run two times; if the value is set to 5.0x, it'll run five times. These types of values can have a significant impact on your animations.

If the value before the x is greater than 1.0, you may notice a jerk between the iterations of the animation because, unless your animation ends with the same value as it started, it'll need to jump to the start to be reset. If the value before the x is less than 1.0, you'll notice that the animation will stop before the animation has completed because the RepeatBehavior takes precedence over the Duration property. This can have significant implications if you specify a time value as shown in the last three bars of figure 22.3.

By specifying a specific length of time for the RepeatBehavior, you're informing the Timeline to repeat until the specified time has elapsed. This length of time can be specified using the TimeSpan format. Or, you can specify the Forever value to make the Timeline run until you programmatically force the animation to stop. Either way, at times you may want a more cyclical animation. For these situations, you may want to consider the AutoReverse property.

TURN IT AROUND

The AutoReverse property enables you to automatically play a Timeline in reverse after it has played once forward. This boolean property is, by default, set to false. Changing this property value to true can enable you to deliver a throbbing effect—among other things. Note that changing this property to true can have residual effects on the overall playback of a Timeline.

By setting the AutoReverse property to true, the overall playback time of a Timeline may be doubled. When the AutoReverse property is true, a Timeline isn't deemed finished until it plays once forward and once backward. If you're specifying a number of iterations within the RepeatBehavior property, a single iteration will take twice as long.

Once an iteration has completed, you should have the ability to decide how it should behave.

HOW WILL IT END?

When an animation reaches the end of a Timeline, it normally stays (or *holds*) at the end, but the FillBehavior property gives you the opportunity to determine what to do. When the end is reached, you can tell the playback what to do using one of the options provided by the FillBehavior enumerator. These options and their descriptions are shown in table 22.2.

Table 22.2   Available FillBehavior options

Value	Description
HoldEnd	When completed, a Timeline will stay at the end until told otherwise. This is the default value for the FillBehavior property.
Stop	Once the Timeline has completed, the playback position will automatically reset to the beginning.

You have two options: stay at the end or reset to the beginning. But the beginning of a `Timeline` isn't necessarily what it may seem. This beginning of a `Timeline` can be altered by the `BeginTime` property.

FROM THE TOP

The `BeginTime` property represents when to start playing a `Timeline`. In reality, this property sort of behaves as an offset, which can be set using the familiar `TimeSpan` format. By default, the `BeginTime` property's value is set to `null`, which translates to `0`. This setting is why animations begin playing immediately when told to do so. You can set this value to another `TimeSpan` value to provide an offset, as shown in this example:

```
<DoubleAnimation Storyboard.TargetName="myImage"
                 Storyboard.TargetProperty="Opacity"
                 From="0" To="1"
                 BeginTime="00:00:5" Duration="0:0:1" />
```

This shows an `Image` that fades in over the course of one second. Unlike the previous animations, this one won't start immediately. Instead, once the animation begins to play, it waits until the time specified within the `BeginTime` property has elapsed. Once this time period has elapsed, the image begins to fade into view. Because of this, you can assume the entire animation in this example takes six seconds to complete.

The `BeginTime` property may seem somewhat odd. It is sort of odd if you consider it only in regard to a single animation, but this property provides a significant amount of value when you have multiple animations working together. To make use of multiple animations, you must take advantage of the required `Storyboard` element.

22.3 *Storyboarding*

Every animation created within Silverlight must be defined within a `Storyboard`. A `Storyboard` enables you to organize multiple animated parts that work together simultaneously. Often, these animated parts will span different properties across different UI elements. It makes sense to have a way to collectively organize and control these animated parts. Thankfully, the `Storyboard` enables you to do just that.

22.3.1 *Understanding the storyboard*

A `Storyboard` is an umbrella under which multiple animations can be defined to address a common scenario. From a development perspective, a `Storyboard` can be considered as a collection or grouping of animations. This grouping provides you with a way to easily target and control one or more animations. The syntax is shown this example:

```
<Storyboard x:Name="myStoryboard">
  <!-- The common animations -->
</Storyboard>
```

This XAML shows the basic syntax of a `Storyboard`. This `Storyboard` element could have any number of animations placed inside it. You can place other `Storyboard` elements within it if you so desire because the `Children` property of a `Storyboard` represents a collection of `Timeline` elements. You can add any type of animation or other `Story-board` elements because they derive from the `Timeline` class. Listing 22.3 shows how you can intertwine types within a single `Storyboard`.

Listing 22.3 Syntax of `Storyboard` element with multiple animations

```
<Storyboard x:Name="myStoryboard" Storyboard.TargetName="myRectangle">
  <DoubleAnimation x:Name="myDoubleAnimation" Duration="00:00:03"
                   Storyboard.TargetProperty="Opacity"
                   From="0" To="1" />
  <ColorAnimation x:Name="myColorAnimation"
    Storyboard.TargetProperty="(Shape.Fill).(SolidColorBrush.Color)"
               Duration="00:00:03"
               From="Green" To="Blue" />
</Storyboard>
...
<Rectangle x:Name="myRectangle" Width="180" Height="60" Fill="Green"
  Opacity="0" />
```

This listing shows a `Storyboard` that changes a `Rectangle` from green to blue as it fades into view. This small sample begins to show the power allotted by the `Story-board`. Before we discuss the other powerful features of the `Storyboard`, let's look at how to define the target of your animations.

22.3.2 *Hitting the target*

As mentioned earlier, the `Storyboard` exposes two attached properties that can be used to set the target of an animation. The first is `TargetName`, and the second is `Tar-getProperty`. These two property values are codependent and both are required to create an animation. Without these values, your animations won't know what to animate. If you define these two values within a `Storyboard`, you can share their values across the child `Timeline` elements.

As shown in the previous listing, the `Storyboard` uses the `TargetName` attached property to specify the target of the animation. Each of the child animations uses the same target element. If one of these animations needs to use a different element, you can trump this value by providing a different `TargetName` value, using the approach shown in listing 22.4.

Listing 22.4 Animation overriding target of its parent `Storyboard`

```
<Storyboard x:Name="myStoryboard" Storyboard.TargetName="myRectangle">
  <ColorAnimation x:Name="myColorAnimation" Duration="00:00:03"
    Storyboard.TargetProperty="(Shape.Fill).(SolidColorBrush.Color)"
    From="Green" To="Blue" />

  <DoubleAnimation x:Name="myDoubleAnimation" Duration="00:00:03"
    Storyboard.TargetName="myRectangle2"
    Storyboard.TargetProperty="Opacity"
    From="0" To="1" />

  <DoubleAnimation x:Name="myDoubleAnimation2" Duration="00:00:05"
```

```
      Storyboard.TargetProperty="Width"
      To="180" />

</Storyboard>

...

<Rectangle x:Name="myRectangle" Width="180" Height="120" Fill="Green" />
<Rectangle x:Name="myRectangle2" Width="90" Height="30" Fill="Pink" />
```

This listing defines the primary target of the `Storyboard` as `myRectangle`. This target is used by the `myColorAnimation` and `myDoubleAnimation2` animations. `myDoubleAnimation` uses `myRectangle2` as the target instead of `myRectangle`. This is accomplished by overriding the `TargetName` value set in the storyboard itself. Note that each of the animations in this listing targets a separate property.

To target a property within an animation, you use the `TargetProperty` attached property. As you've probably guessed, this attribute allows you to specify which property of the target element should be animated. You can specify the name of this property in a couple of ways.

The first and most explicit approach involves setting the name of the property you intend to animate. This approach is used in `myDoubleAnimation` and `myDouble-Animation2`. Generally, this approach will work for most of the properties throughout the Silverlight APIs, but it won't always be enough.

Consider the situation where you want to change the color of a `Brush`. Generally, the color of a `Brush` is defined as a property within a property within a property. This is shown in the `myColorAnimation` animation of the listing. Although at first this may not seem possible within XAML, there is a way.

XAML supports a flexible property path model that enables you to access nested properties. This model allows you to access the individual properties by drilling through the hierarchy using element types. To drill down through the hierarchy, you begin at an element type. From there, you access a specific property by using a period as a delimiter. If the property represents a collection, you can access the individual items by using an indexing syntax. To gain a firmer understanding of these syntactical details, review listing 22.5.

Listing 22.5 Complex property paths in XAML `Storyboards`

```
<Storyboard x:Name="myStoryboard" Storyboard.TargetName="myRectangle">
  <ColorAnimation
    Storyboard.TargetProperty="(Shape.Fill).
    (GradientBrush.GradientStops)[1].(GradientStop.Color)"      ❶
    To="#FFBB0000" />
  <ColorAnimation
    Storyboard.TargetProperty="(Shape.Fill).
    (GradientBrush.GradientStops)[3].(GradientStop.Color)"      ❷
    To="#FFBB0000" />
</Storyboard>

...
```

```
<Rectangle x:Name="myRectangle" Width="120" Height="60" >
  <Rectangle.Fill>
    <LinearGradientBrush EndPoint="1,0.5" StartPoint="0,0.5">
      <GradientStop Color="#FFDA0000" Offset="0"/>
      <GradientStop Color="#FFA500BB" Offset="0.25"/>      ◁——— Index I
      <GradientStop Color="#FF000000" Offset="0.5"/>
      <GradientStop Color="#FFA500BB" Offset="0.75"/>      ◁——— Index 3
      <GradientStop Color="#FFDA0000" Offset="1"/>
    </LinearGradientBrush>
  </Rectangle.Fill>
</Rectangle>
```

This listing shows how to use the property path syntax to access the individual colors used within the LinearGradientBrush. An index of 1 is used within ❶ to reference the second GradientStop in the brush. At the same time, an index of 3 ❷ is used to change the color of the fourth GradientStop. In addition to the indexing syntax, it's important to recognize the use of the parentheses around each property.

Parentheses are used in the property path syntax to group a property with an element. As shown in listing 22.5, you can't begin by drilling into a property; instead, you begin with an element type. From there, you specify the name of the property you want to animate and continue by delimiting with a period. This syntax is depicted in figure 22.4.

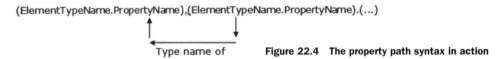

(ElementTypeName.PropertyName)ₓ(ElementTypeName.PropertyName).(...)

Type name of   **Figure 22.4   The property path syntax in action**

This figure shows the general syntax used for referencing properties using this property path syntax. This approach makes it easy to access items that haven't been explicitly named. This syntax enables you to readily take control of the properties within an element. Equally important is the way that Silverlight enables you to take control of the Storyboard itself.

22.3.3 *Controlling the Storyboard*

The Storyboard class exposes a number of valuable methods that enable you to programmatically control an animation. These methods, shown in table 22.3, reflect many of the features you've already seen within the MediaElement.

Table 22.3   Methods associated with the Storyboard object

Method	Description
Begin(...)	Turns the hourglass to start pouring the sands of time. This method starts the animations that are the Children of the Storyboard.
Pause(...)	Halts the playback of the animations associated with a Storyboard and preserves the current position.

Table 22.3 Methods associated with the `Storyboard` **object** *(continued)*

Method	Description
`Resume(...)`	Continues the animations associated with a `Storyboard` from a previous position.
`Seek(...)`	Skips to a new position within a `Storyboard`. The position is represented as a `TimeSpan` value.
`Stop(...)`	Halts the playback of the animations associated with a `Storyboard` and resets the playback position to the beginning of the `Storyboard`.

The methods described in this table enable you to programmatically interact with a `Storyboard`. In doing so, you can easily deliver a dynamic animation experience. This experience may involve leaping forward to a later part in an animation or giving the user control via interactive playback features. Either way, an important part of interacting with an animation involves knowing when it's finished. Thankfully, the `Storyboard` exposes the `Completed` event.

The `Completed` event is the only event exposed by the `Storyboard` element. In reality, this event is part of the `Timeline`. Regardless, the `Completed` event is triggered when the assigning `Storyboard` has finished. A `Storyboard` is deemed finished once all its child `Timeline` elements have completed. Listing 22.6 shows a `MediaElement` performing one complete rotation when a user clicks it. Once this animation has completed, it'll use another animation to fade the `MediaElement` out of view.

Listing 22.6 Using the `Playback` **methods and** `Completed` **event**

XAML:

```
<MediaElement x:Name="media"
              Source="http://www.silverlightinaction.com/video2.wmv"
              AutoPlay="True"
              MouseLeftButtonUp="media_MouseLeftButtonUp"
              RenderTransformOrigin="0.5,0.5">
  <MediaElement.Resources>
    <Storyboard x:Name="myStoryboard1"
                Completed="myStoryboard1_Completed">
      <DoubleAnimation Storyboard.TargetName="media"
        Storyboard.TargetProperty="(UIElement.RenderTransform).
          (TransformGroup.Children)[0].(RotateTransform.Angle)"
                       From="0" To="360"
                       Duration="00:00:02" />
    </Storyboard>
    <Storyboard x:Name="myStoryboard2">
      <DoubleAnimation Storyboard.TargetName="media"
                       Storyboard.TargetProperty="Opacity"
                       From="1" To="0"
                       Duration="00:00:02" />
    </Storyboard>
  </MediaElement.Resources>
  <MediaElement.RenderTransform>
```

```
    <TransformGroup>
      <RotateTransform Angle="0"/>
    </TransformGroup>
  </MediaElement.RenderTransform>
</MediaElement>
```

C#:
```
void media_MouseLeftButtonUp(object sender, MouseButtonEventArgs e)
{
  myStoryboard1.Begin();
}

void myStoryboard1_Completed(object sender, EventArgs e)
{
  myStoryboard2.Begin();
}
```

This listing shows how you can programmatically use the `Completed` event as well as one of the interactive playback methods. When the user clicks the `MediaElement`, the `Storyboard` defined as `myStoryboard1` will begin playing. Once this `Storyboard` has finished playing, the `Completed` event associated with it will be triggered. This event handler will then start the animation defined in `myStoryboard2`. This example also shows how you can define an animation as a resource. This is one of the two ways that you can use an animation on the road to being resourceful.

22.3.4 *Being resourceful*

`Storyboard` elements enable you to create complex and intricate animations. These animations may be used in response to an event or to something that has occurred behind the scenes. Because of this, you need multiple ways to interact with a `Storyboard`. Thankfully, Silverlight gives you two approaches for organizing `Storyboard` elements. You can define a `Storyboard` as either a resource or a trigger.

STORYBOARD AS A RESOURCE

The first approach for organizing a `Storyboard` involves defining it as a resource. A resource is an easy way to set aside a commonly used item for reuse. (We'll cover resources more in chapter 23.) This item—in our case, a `Storyboard`—can be defined as a resource by creating it within the `Resources` collection of a `UIElement`. This can be accomplished by either programmatically adding it through code, or creating it within XAML as shown in listing 22.7.

Listing 22.7 Defining a `Storyboard` as a resource

XAML:
```
<Canvas x:Name="myCanvas">
  <Canvas.Resources>
    <Storyboard x:Key="myStoryboard">
      <DoubleAnimation Duration="00:00:01"
                       Storyboard.TargetName="myImage"
                       Storyboard.TargetProperty="Opacity"
                       From="1" To="0" />
```

```
    </Storyboard>
  </Canvas.Resources>
  <Image x:Name="myImage"
         Source="http://www.silverlightinaction.com/man.png" />
</Canvas>
```

This listing shows how easy it is to define a Storyboard as a resource in XAML. The definition of the Storyboard is placed within the Resources collection of the root Canvas. The root element of a Silverlight page is generally where you'll place your resources because it makes the resources accessible to all the elements within the page. Thankfully, the Resources collection can store as many or as few resources as you need.

Once a Storyboard is defined as a resource, it's your responsibility to start it. You must first programmatically retrieve it. This step involves retrieving the storyboard by key. The following example shows the Storyboard from listing 22.7 being retrieved from the resources collection, then programmatically started via the Begin method:

```
Storyboard myStoryboard = (Storyboard)(myCanvas.Resources["myStoryboard"]);
myStoryboard.Begin();
```

This illustrates how simple it is to programmatically start a Storyboard defined as a resource.

There are times when you know that a specific action should automatically start a Storyboard. For these situations, Silverlight provides an elegant shortcut that enables you to automatically start a Storyboard when a defined event occurs.

STORYBOARD AS A TRIGGER

The second approach for defining a Storyboard involves setting it as an event handler. An EventTrigger is a special element that enables you to declaratively define a response for a specified event. When this event occurs, the EventTrigger automatically starts the defined Storyboard. To accomplish this, you follow a few simple steps.

First you decide which event you want to respond to. Currently, the only event supported within the EventTrigger is the Loaded event. To specify this event as the triggering event, you must identify the type of object responsible for the event. Once identified, you can set it, as well as the event, through the RoutedEvent property as shown in this example:

```
<EventTrigger RoutedEvent="Canvas.Loaded">
  <!-- Insert Actions here -->
</EventTrigger>
```

As this shows, the RoutedEvent property uses a syntax that resembles *elementType-Name.eventName*. The type name comes from the parent type. Generally, you'll be able to retrieve this type name from the attached property containing the trigger. This attached property is called Triggers, and it's available from all UIElement objects. If you were to expand on our previous code example, you should have something like this XAML fragment:

```
<Canvas.Triggers>
  <EventTrigger RoutedEvent="Canvas.Loaded">
    <!-- Insert Actions here -->
  </EventTrigger>
</Canvas.Triggers>
```

This example shows how the EventTrigger has been added to a Canvas. Significantly, this doesn't mean that the target of the Storyboard will be the Canvas. Instead, as discussed earlier, the target of the Storyboard is set within the Storyboard itself. To set the target of the Storyboard, you first define the Storyboard.

If you're defining a Storyboard within an EventTrigger, you must associate it with an action. Currently, Silverlight only provides one action called BeginStoryboard, which starts a Storyboard when called. You must use this action if you're creating an EventTrigger. To put all the pieces together, defining a Storyboard as a trigger would look like listing 22.8.

Listing 22.8 Defining a Storyboard as an event trigger

```
<Canvas Width="100" Height="100" Background="White">
  <Canvas.Triggers>
    <EventTrigger RoutedEvent="Canvas.Loaded">
      <BeginStoryboard>
        <Storyboard x:Name="myStoryboard">
          <DoubleAnimation Duration="00:00:01"
                           Storyboard.TargetName="myImage"
                           Storyboard.TargetProperty="Opacity"
                           From="0" To="1" />
        </Storyboard>
      </BeginStoryboard>
    </EventTrigger>
  </Canvas.Triggers>
  <Image x:Name="myImage"
         Source="http://www.silverlightinaction.com/man.png" />
</Canvas>
```

This example shows a Storyboard defined as a trigger. But the official Silverlight documentation included with the SDK recommends against using a trigger, as visual states (covered in chapter 23) and behaviors are often better ways to start the animation. Either way, the Storyboard provides a way to logically organize your animations.

These animations are all about changing a visual property over time. As you've seen, this process works in a linear fashion. To create even more dynamic visual effects, it's important to consider using a technique known as *keyframing*.

22.4 *Keyframing*

In the realm of traditional animation, animators will often present a high-level overview of a story by drawing out the main images. These images generally represent the beginning and ending points of a transition; the endpoints represent the key frames within an animation. Once the keyframes are created, the process of creating the animation in between them is fairly straightforward. Within software, this process of creating the in-between frames is known as *interpolation* or *tweening*.

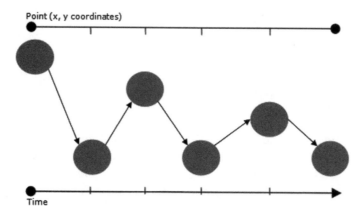

Point (x, y coordinates)

Time

Figure 22.5   A bouncing ball over some variable amount of time

To firmly grasp the concept of how keyframe animations can be used, let's consider the task of animating a bouncing ball. If you were to attempt to animate an ellipse, the ball may look like that in figure 22.5 over some period of time.

The arrows shown in this figure represent two things within the animation. They represent the direction that the ball is bouncing and the parts of the animation created via interpolation. This process of interpolation enables you to ignore having to define the To, From, and By property values you were using earlier. Instead, you must create a KeyFrame for each discrete location within an animation. Listing 22.9 shows the XAML to reproduce the animation shown in figure 22.5.

Listing 22.9   Creating a bouncing ball using keyframes

```
<Canvas x:Name="LayoutRoot" Background="White">
  <Canvas.Triggers>
    <EventTrigger RoutedEvent="Canvas.Loaded">
      <BeginStoryboard>
        <Storyboard x:Name="myStoryboard">
          <DoubleAnimationUsingKeyFrames
                    Storyboard.TargetName="myEllipse"
                    Storyboard.TargetProperty="(Canvas.Left)">
            <LinearDoubleKeyFrame KeyTime="00:00:00" Value="0" />
            <LinearDoubleKeyFrame KeyTime="00:00:01" Value="77" />
            <LinearDoubleKeyFrame KeyTime="00:00:02" Value="148" />
            <LinearDoubleKeyFrame KeyTime="00:00:03" Value="223" />
            <LinearDoubleKeyFrame KeyTime="00:00:04" Value="315" />
            <LinearDoubleKeyFrame KeyTime="00:00:05" Value="397" />
          </DoubleAnimationUsingKeyFrames>
          <DoubleAnimationUsingKeyFrames
                    Storyboard.TargetName="myEllipse"
                    Storyboard.TargetProperty="(Canvas.Top)">
            <LinearDoubleKeyFrame KeyTime="00:00:00" Value="0" />
            <LinearDoubleKeyFrame KeyTime="00:00:01" Value="132" />
            <LinearDoubleKeyFrame KeyTime="00:00:02" Value="42" />
            <LinearDoubleKeyFrame KeyTime="00:00:03" Value="132" />
            <LinearDoubleKeyFrame KeyTime="00:00:04" Value="81" />
            <LinearDoubleKeyFrame KeyTime="00:00:05" Value="132" />
```

```
            </DoubleAnimationUsingKeyFrames>
          </Storyboard>
        </BeginStoryboard>
      </EventTrigger>
    </Canvas.Triggers>

    <Ellipse Width="50" Height="50" x:Name="myEllipse"
             Fill="Maroon" Stroke="Black" />
</Canvas>
```

This example illustrates the general syntax of a KeyFrame. This example uses two key-frame animations to move an Ellipse around the Canvas. The new position of the Ellipse is interpolated between the values specified within the Value property of each KeyFrame. The KeyFrame determines how to interpolate these values by referring to the type of KeyFrame.

The type of KeyFrame always follows a naming template that mimics *[interpolation-Type]propertyTypeKeyFrame*. This syntax specifies the type of property that's the target of the animation. The syntax also specifies what type of interpolation should be used to generate the in-between values. To simultaneously address both important items, Silverlight provides the keyframe types shown in table 22.4.

Table 22.4   The keyframe types available within Silverlight

Discrete keyframe types	Linear keyframe types	Spline keyframe types
DiscreteColorKeyFrame	LinearColorKeyFrame	SplineColorKeyFrame
DiscreteDoubleKeyFrame	LinearDoubleKeyFrame	SplineDoubleKeyFrame
DiscreteObjectKeyFrame		
DiscretePointKeyFrame	LinearPointKeyFrame	SplinePointKeyFrame

Each type of keyframe helps to address specific animation scenarios. To understand when a specific type of animation is relevant, it's important to understand the various types of interpolation.

22.4.1   Interpolation: it's about acceleration

An *interpolation type* gives you control over how an animation will accelerate or decelerate as it progresses. The interpolation type signals how an animation should estimate the values in between keyframes. To estimate the values as you see fit, Silverlight provides three interpolation types: linear, spline, and discrete.

LINEAR INTERPOLATION

Linear interpolation constructs the most direct transition between two key frames. The linear descriptor is used because the change between two keyframes occurs at a constant, linear rate. Figure 22.6 shows an object moving between several points using linear interpolation.

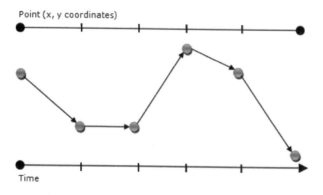

Figure 22.6 How linear interpolation is determined. Note the straight lines between points.

The idea of using an animation that occurs at a constant, predictable rate at first seems appealing. But, as this figure shows, you can easily end up with a jerky or jagged animation. This jarring can leave users feeling like they're riding an old, wooden rollercoaster. This effect occurs because the transition between two linear keyframes occurs in distinct states. These stages may be desirable, but if they aren't, there's a way to create even smoother transitions thanks to spline interpolation.

SPLINE INTERPOLATION

Splines are generally used to create smooth, seamless transitions. These transitions occur by estimating the values as if they were generated along a Bézier curve. This curve represents the values to use within a time segment. To illustrate, figure 22.7 shows a curved interpolation.

If you compare this figure to figure 22.6, you can see how using splines allows you to create a much smoother transition between keyframes. Note that the line in this figure doesn't represent the path that the ball travels along. Instead, the line gives the illusion of varying speeds. These varying speeds are controlled through the KeySpline property.

The KeySpline property enables you to control the progress of an animation through two control points, which determine the curve that the values are interpolated along. By default, this curve resembles a straight line. To generate values along something other than a line, you must understand how the KeySpline relates values to points in time. This relationship, as well as the KeySpline syntax, is shown in figure 22.8.

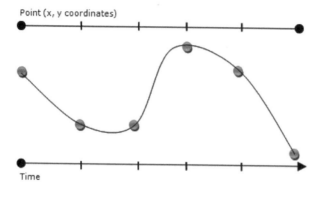

Figure 22.7 An example using spline interpolation for approximation

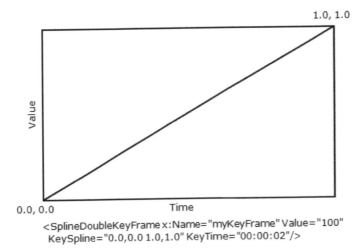

1.0, 1.0

0.0, 0.0   Time

`<SplineDoubleKeyFrame x:Name="myKeyFrame" Value="100"`
`KeySpline="0.0,0.0 1.0,1.0" KeyTime="00:00:02"/>`

Figure 22.8
The relationship between time and value as used by the `KeySpline` **property.**

This figure shows the default *curve* defined by the KeySpline property. The two control points used in this figure are specified as 0.0,0.0 1.0,1.0. These control points always follow a syntax that mimics *x1,y1 x2,y2*. In addition, each coordinate within each point is specified as a positive double-precision value between 0.0 and 1.0. Anything outside of this range will create a runtime error.

The first point defined within the KeySpline property determines how values will be generated along the first half of the curve. The second point defined within the KeySpline property determines how values will be created along the second half of the curve. Either way, if the y value is greater than the x value, the animation will run more quickly. Alternatively, if the x value is greater than the y value, the animation will run slower. Figure 22.9 shows sample curves along with their respective KeySpline values.

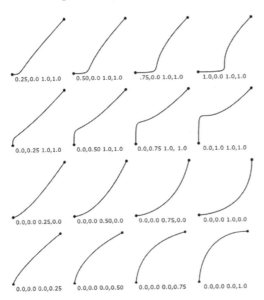

Figure 22.9   Sample time/value curves used by the `KeySpline` **property**

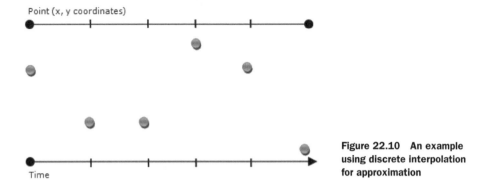

Point (x, y coordinates)

Time

Figure 22.10 An example using discrete interpolation for approximation

The curves shown in this figure represent potential curves you can use for interpolating values. In reality, you'll need to play with these values until your keyframe animation feels right. Sometimes, an animation may feel right if the transitions are more discrete.

DISCRETE INTERPOLATION

Occasionally, you may have to create an animation that jumps between values. These rifts seem counterintuitive within the realm of animation because animations are generally considered to be smooth. But, what if you were creating an animation that depicted a Whack-a-Mole game? In a Whack-a-Mole game, small critters appear at random from dark holes. This surprising effect can be effectively recreated using discrete interpolation.

When discrete interpolation is used, Silverlight generates sudden changes between two keyframes. These sudden changes make it appear as if the interpolation doesn't occur at all. That's because it doesn't! Figure 22.10 illuminates how the discrete method interpolates.

This illustration is difficult to make sense of. Everything seemingly occurs at random, just like Whack-a-Mole.

Although randomness has its place, you often need control over when a keyframe occurs. Luckily, there's is a property that allows you to do just that—KeyTime.

KEYTIME

The KeyTime property of a KeyFrame represents the time at which the value specified within a KeyFrame will be reached. In a sense, the KeyTime sort of represents a bookmark within an animation. But, the position of this bookmark is completely dependent on the TimeSpan value you use.

By providing a TimeSpan value, you can specify the exact point in time when a KeyFrame should be reached. This point in time is relative to the beginning of the animation that the KeyFrame is defined within, so the order of the keyframe elements is irrelevant. But, this value still has to be assigned to the KeyTime property, as shown in listing 22.10. In addition, the example shows an illustration of how the animation would be rendered.

Listing 22.10   Using a `TimeSpan` value to specify the `KeyTime`

Result:

XAML:

```xaml
<UserControl x:Class="CarAnimation.Page"
  xmlns="http://schemas.microsoft.com/winfx/2006/xaml/presentation"
  xmlns:x="http://schemas.microsoft.com/winfx/2006/xaml"
  Width="400" Height="400">
  <Canvas x:Name="LayoutRoot" Background="White">
    <Canvas.Triggers>
      <EventTrigger RoutedEvent="Canvas.Loaded">
        <BeginStoryboard>
          <Storyboard x:Name="myStoryboard"
            Storyboard.TargetName="myImage"
            Storyboard.TargetProperty="(Canvas.Left)">
            <DoubleAnimationUsingKeyFrames Duration="00:00:08">
              <LinearDoubleKeyFrame Value="50" KeyTime="00:00:01" />
              <LinearDoubleKeyFrame Value="250" KeyTime="00:00:03.5" />
              <LinearDoubleKeyFrame Value="325" KeyTime="00:00:06" />
              <LinearDoubleKeyFrame Value="500" KeyTime="00:00:08" />
            </DoubleAnimationUsingKeyFrames>
          </Storyboard>
        </BeginStoryboard>
      </EventTrigger>
    </Canvas.Triggers>
    <Image x:Name="myImage"
      Source="http://www.silverlightinaction.com/car.png" />
  </Canvas>
</UserControl>
```

This listing shows the typical approach for defining `KeyFrame` elements within an animation. The `KeyTime` value in each `KeyFrame` is set to a `TimeSpan` value. This approach provides a convenient and verbose way to perform an animation. This example shows how important the `KeyTime` property is in keyframe animations, which are the types of animations created by Expression Blend.

These animations have been interesting, but they've all lacked a certain amount of "pop" we've come to expect from modern applications. That's because they're not using any sort of easing functions with the keyframes. Let's fix that next.

22.5   *Easing functions*

Easing functions provide a way to liven up what would otherwise be pretty flat and boring animation. They provide acceleration/deceleration, and even bounce or spring to the approach into (or departure from) a keyframe in an animation.

If you've found animation to be a little too computer-generated so far, you'll appreciate the more organic effect that easing functions provide. Easing functions perform a function *f* over time *t*. Time is provided by the animation system; the easing function returns a value, normally between zero and one (it can over and

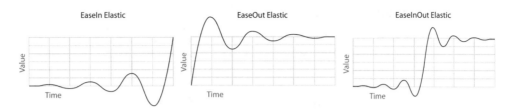

Figure 22.11 **The three modes: `EaseIn`, `EaseOut`, and `EaseInOut` for the `ElasticEase` easing function**

undershoot) that indicates progress toward the final value specified in the animation. We'll cover more of the inner workings in the second half of this section when we create our own easing function.

Easing functions have three modes of use: `EaseIn`, `EaseOut`, and `EaseInOut`. The modes affect how the easing function is applied to the animation over time. These modes are easier seen than read. Figure 22.11 illustrates what the built-in `ElasticEase` easing function looks like in all three of its modes.

From the illustration, you can see that `EaseIn` and `EaseOut` are opposites; `EaseOut` is the `EaseIn` function in reverse. `EaseInOut` is a little trickier. In that mode, the overall time remains the same, but the function used is a combination of `EaseIn` and `EaseOut`.

In this section, we'll first look at how to use the great library of built-in easing functions. Then, because customization is especially important when it comes to something as design-sensitive as how an animation functions over time, we'll look at how to build your own easing functions.

22.5.1 Using easing functions

Easing functions are used with special keyframes that start with the word `Easing`. These key frames provide a property named `EasingFunction`, which accepts an easing function to be used on that specific keyframe. Silverlight includes 11 built-in easing functions, which are listed in table 22.5.

Table 22.5 **Built-in easing functions**

Easing function	Description
`BackEase`	Retracts the motion of an animation slightly before it begins to animate in the path indicated.
`BounceEase`	Creates a bouncing effect, like a rubber ball.
`CircleEase`	Accelerates or decelerates using a circular function.
`CubicEase`	Accelerates or decelerates using a cube function (time cubed).
`ElasticEase`	An animation that resembles the oscillation of a spring. The lower the supplied `Springiness` parameter, the more elastic the bounce. You can go crazy with this and create some really fun animation.

Table 22.5 Built-in easing functions (continued)

Easing function	Description
ExponentialEase	Accelerates or decelerates using a formula based around the supplied exponent.
PowerEase	Accelerates or decelerates using a formula based on the supplied power.
QuadraticEase	Accelerates or decelerates using a squaring function.
QuarticEase	Accelerates or decelerates using a power of 4 function.
QuinticEase	Accelerates or decelerates using a power of 5 function.
SineEase	Accelerates or decelerates using the sine function.

MSDN has great documentation on the easing functions, including graphics showing each of the modes and the actual functions in use. You can find the additional information in the MSDN online library here: http://bit.ly/MSDNEasing.

To use an easing function, you need to set up an animation using storyboards and keyframes. Listing 22.11 shows an easing function attached to two animations.

Listing 22.11 Using the `ElasticEase` for some crazy animation

```
<UserControl.Resources>
  <Storyboard x:Key="AnimateTarget">
    <DoubleAnimationUsingKeyFrames Storyboard.TargetName="Transform"
                                   Storyboard.TargetProperty="ScaleX">
      <EasingDoubleKeyFrame KeyTime="0:0:0" Value="0.0" />
      <EasingDoubleKeyFrame KeyTime="0:0:3" Value="5.0">
        <EasingDoubleKeyFrame.EasingFunction>
          <ElasticEase EasingMode="EaseOut"
                       Oscillations="3" Springiness="2" />          ◁─┐
        </EasingDoubleKeyFrame.EasingFunction>                         │
      </EasingDoubleKeyFrame>                                          │
    </DoubleAnimationUsingKeyFrames>                                   │
    <DoubleAnimationUsingKeyFrames Storyboard.TargetName="Transform"   │
                                   Storyboard.TargetProperty="ScaleY"> │
      <EasingDoubleKeyFrame KeyTime="0:0:0" Value="0.0" />             │ Easing function
      <EasingDoubleKeyFrame KeyTime="0:0:3" Value="5.0">               │ parameters
        <EasingDoubleKeyFrame.EasingFunction>                         │
          <ElasticEase EasingMode="EaseOut"                           │
                       Oscillations="3" Springiness="2" />          ◁─┘
        </EasingDoubleKeyFrame.EasingFunction>
      </EasingDoubleKeyFrame>
    </DoubleAnimationUsingKeyFrames>
  </Storyboard>
</UserControl.Resources>

<Grid x:Name="LayoutRoot" Background="White">
  <Rectangle Height="20" Width="20" Fill="BlueViolet"
             RenderTransformOrigin="0.5,0.5">
    <Rectangle.RenderTransform>
```

```
        <ScaleTransform x:Name="Transform" />          ❶
      </Rectangle.RenderTransform>
    </Rectangle>

    <Button x:Name="StartAnimation" Content="Start"
        HorizontalAlignment="Center" VerticalAlignment="Bottom"
        Width="100" Height="25" Margin="5"
        Click="StartAnimation_Click"/>          ⟵── Event handler
</Grid>
```

This example shows markup that contains a single rectangle to be animated. The things we'll be animating are the ScaleX and ScaleY properties of the ScaleTransform ❶ attached to the rectangle. The result of this is a spring-type animation, which looks like you're sitting directly below a block suspended from a rubber band.

To start the animation, I used a button with the event handler wired up in markup. The code-behind code in the event handler is a single line:

```
private void StartAnimation_Click(object sender, RoutedEventArgs e)
{
    ((Storyboard)Resources["AnimateTarget"]).Begin();
}
```

The line of code in the event handler finds the resource named AnimateTarget and, assuming it's a Storyboard, calls the function to start animating. With this code in place, run the application and click the button. You'll see the rectangle bounce in and out until it comes to a quick rest. Try changing the Oscillations or Springiness parameters in the easing function for very different effects: Oscillations controls the number of bounces; Springiness controls the depth of the bounces.

The built-in easing functions will serve the vast majority of our needs; you can create just about any typical effect using them. What about atypical effects? What if you want to include physics, or a function the team didn't think of? For those situations, the Silverlight team had the foresight to open up the API to enable us to create our own easing functions.

22.5.2 Creating a custom easing function

The WPF and Silverlight teams put together a pretty comprehensive set of standard easing functions. Most folks will never need or want to write one of their own.

That said, you may come up with a specialized function and want to package that in a way that enables others to use it from XAML or code in their own animation.

To create your own easing function, you derive from EasingFunctionBase and override the EaseInCore function.

EASINGFUNCTIONBASE

EasingFunctionBase provides the structure of an easing function. It includes the EasingMode and its dependency property, as well as the Ease function, which is called by the animation system. The Ease function, in turn, calls EaseInCore, the function you provide.

EASEINCORE

This is where your easing code goes. You provide the implementation for EaseIn via the EaseInCore code, and the runtime will automatically infer EaseOut and Ease-InOut from that. EaseOut will be the reverse of EaseIn, and EaseInOut will be the two together.

EaseInCore takes a double representing normalized time, and expects you to return the progress for that point in time. If you think of time as the x axis on a graph and progress as the y axis, you're taking in x as a parameter and returning y as the result.

A standard linear ease would return the value passed in. $f(x) = x$. Instantaneous movement would be $f(x) = 1$. No movement (ever) would be $f(x) = 0$. The interesting stuff happens when the result is between those numbers.

Listing 22.12 shows a randomizing ease. This uses the built-in Random object to provide a random value that approaches the final value. The end result is a stuttering animation that eventually gets to the right place.

Listing 22.12   A custom randomizing ease

C#:

```
public class RandomEase : EasingFunctionBase
{
  private Random _random = new Random();

  protected override double EaseInCore(double normalizedTime)
  {
    return normalizedTime / 2.0 +
        _random.Next(0, 100) / 100.0 * (normalizedTime / 2.0);
  }
}
```

XAML:

```
<EasingDoubleKeyFrame.EasingFunction>
  <local:RandomEase EasingMode="EaseIn"/>
</EasingDoubleKeyFrame.EasingFunction>
```

To use this function, take the XAML from the ElasticEase demonstration and replace the two easing functions with the XAML fragment here. Be sure to map an XML namespace to the local application.

Easing functions really help liven up animation, providing a sometimes more organic but always more interesting way to move a value between two bounds. The built-in easing functions cover almost every need you'll have when animating in Silverlight. For those cases when the built-in functions aren't quite what you want, you can create your own easing functions as long as you an express the equation in code.

Easing functions were originally designed with Blend in mind. Designers love to be able to specify an easing function to use on a keyframe; they can do it right from the Blend UI. Another technology that came about due to Blend, this time from the Blend team itself, is the behavior. Behaviors are fascinating ways to add animation, code, or other reusable logic to your elements in XAML.

22.6 *Behaviors, triggers, and actions*

Behaviors, triggers, and actions are odd things. They can be virtually anything, do virtually anything. Between stock behaviors and community-created ones, I've seen everything from TextBox edit masks, to drag and drop, to physics, to effects, automatic animations, and even ICommand substitutes for calling methods on events. Because behaviors and animation are so closely tied to Expression Blend, I figured I'd pop them in here. They're reusable designer-friendly components. They interact with the UI, but aren't controls.

While lumped together, behaviors, triggers, and actions are conceptually different. Behaviors are self-contained units of functionality that act as a bit of a sidecar to an existing object. They go along for the ride and respond to the environment in which the object exists. Triggers are much like the built-in triggers we've seen in this chapter, but more flexible in their applications. Actions are simpler in concept; they're attached to an object and provide a way to invoke some functionality. The common way to refer to all three is by calling them *behaviors*, so that's what we'll do in this chapter.

One example of an action we've already seen was the CallMethodAction in chapter 16. That action allows an arbitrary event to invoke an arbitrary method on an arbitrary object. Even outside the scope of the ViewModel pattern, that's a pretty powerful component to make available to the designer.

The scope and power of behaviors are best understood by example. In order to try them out, we need to first perform a bit of project setup to pull in the right core bits.

In order to work with behaviors, you'll need to reference two Expression Blend SDK libraries. If you have Expression Blend already installed, the SDK will be under Program Files\Microsoft SDKs. If you don't have Blend installed, you can still download the SDK from http://bit.ly/Blend4SDK; it's free and doesn't require Expression Blend on the machine.

Once you have the SDK installed, reference the two Blend libraries as shown in figure 22.12.

The final step is to add the appropriate namespaces into your XAML files. We'll be working with MainPage.xaml for the remaining examples, so place the following two namespace declarations in the top element of that file:

```
xmlns:i="http://schemas.microsoft.com/expression/2010/interactivity"
xmlns:ei="http://schemas.microsoft.com/expression/2010/interactions"
```

With all the pieces in place, we're ready to start playing around with behaviors. We'll first take a look at existing out-of-box functionality and how to use it in your own applications. Then, because behaviors facilitate reuse and sharing, we'll build our own simple behavior for Silverlight.

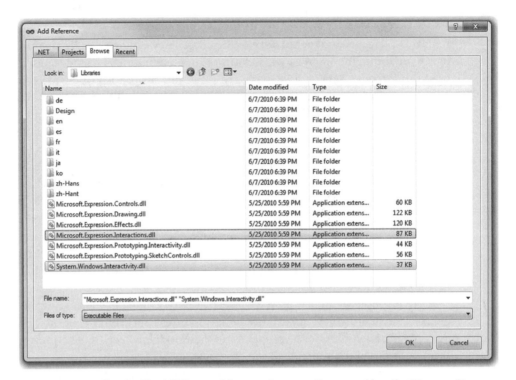

Figure 22.12   Adding the Blend SDK assemblies as references. On my machine, the `Microsoft.Expression.Interactions` library and the `System.Windows.Interactivity` library were both located in C:\Program Files\Microsoft SDKs\Expression\Blend\Silverlight\v4.0\Libraries\.

22.6.1 Using existing behaviors

In chapter 16, we saw how to use the `CallMethodAction` behavior. This is a simple but flexible action that allows you to wire up any function to any event. Another interesting behavior is the `DataTrigger`. This performs actions when the bound data meets a specified condition. One of my favorite behaviors is the `FluidMoveBehavior`. Not only does that behavior have a great visual effect at runtime, but it also builds on much of what we've learned about animation in this chapter.

USING THE FLUIDMOVEBEHAVIOR

The `FluidMoveBehavior` helps get past abrupt layout changes. It listens to the layout system, and when it finds a layout change, it smoothly animates from the old value to the new value. This is extremely useful in panels such as wrap panels where resizing may move several elements around at once.

Listing 22.13 shows how to use the `FluidMoveBehavior` on a single element in the UI. We'll use the purple square example from the last section.

> **Listing 22.13   Using the `FluidMoveBehavior` with an `Element`**

XAML:

```
<Grid x:Name="LayoutRoot" Background="White">
  <Rectangle x:Name="PurpleSquare"
             Height="20" Width="20"
```

```
                HorizontalAlignment="Left" VerticalAlignment="Top"
                Margin="20" Fill="BlueViolet">
    <i:Interaction.Behaviors>
      <ei:FluidMoveBehavior Duration="0:0:4">
        <ei:FluidMoveBehavior.EaseX>
          <ElasticEase EasingMode="EaseOut"
                    Oscillations="3" Springiness="4" />
        </ei:FluidMoveBehavior.EaseX>
        <ei:FluidMoveBehavior.EaseY>
          <ElasticEase EasingMode="EaseOut"
                    Oscillations="3" Springiness="4" />
        </ei:FluidMoveBehavior.EaseY>
      </ei:FluidMoveBehavior>
    </i:Interaction.Behaviors>
  </Rectangle>

  <Button x:Name="StartMove"
          Content="Start"
          HorizontalAlignment="Center" VerticalAlignment="Bottom"
          Width="100" Height="25" Margin="5"
          Click="StartMove_Click" />
</Grid>
```

Easing function

C#:
```
private void StartMove_Click(object sender, RoutedEventArgs e)
{
    Thickness margin = PurpleSquare.Margin;
    margin.Left += 100;
    margin.Top += 100;

    PurpleSquare.Margin = margin;
}
```

Move square

This example shows how to smoothly move an element from one location to another. What would normally have been an abrupt change in location is now a four-second animation with an elastic easing function applied. These are the same easing functions we discussed earlier in the chapter.

Behind the scenes, this behavior builds an animation whenever layout-affecting properties (margins, top, left, size, and so forth) are changed, and uses that animation to move between the original layout value and the one specified.

Other behaviors attach to objects in similar ways. The parameters may change, but the approach is generally the same. In fact, we'll see that when we create our own behavior next.

22.6.2 Creating your own behavior

The System.Windows.Interactivity library includes the base classes you'll typically want to inherit from when creating your own behavior. There are additional special-case base classes in the Blend library, including some that make it easier to work with animation from within a behavior.

For our example, we're going to use the core Interactivity DLL and inherit from Behavior<T> to provide a behavior that'll allow itself to be attached to certain types of elements.

Behavior<T> has two main methods you must override in your implementation. The first is OnAttached. OnAttached is called when the behavior is attached to an element of type T. That element is referenced by the AssociatedObject property. The second method is OnDetaching. This method allows you to perform any cleanup, such as removing event handlers.

Listing 22.14 shows our behavior attached to a button. This behavior will display a MessageBox whenever the button is clicked. We'll use the same FluidMoveBehavior XAML as the previous section and attach this behavior to the Start button.

> **Listing 22.14   A behavior that displays a MessageBox when a Button is clicked**

C#:
```csharp
public class CustomBehavior : Behavior<Button>
{
  protected override void OnAttached()
  {
    base.OnAttached();
    AssociatedObject.Click += new RoutedEventHandler(OnButtonClick);
  }

  protected override void OnDetaching()
  {
    base.OnDetaching();
    AssociatedObject.Click -= OnButtonClick;          Event handler
  }                                                   cleanup

  void OnButtonClick(object sender, RoutedEventArgs e)
  {
    MessageBox.Show("Button was Clicked!");
  }
}
```

XAML:
```xml
<Button x:Name="StartMove" Content="Start"
        HorizontalAlignment="Center" VerticalAlignment="Bottom"
        Width="100" Height="25" Margin="5"
        Click="StartMove_Click">
    <i:Interaction.Behaviors>
        <local:CustomBehavior />
    </i:Interaction.Behaviors>
</Button>
```

When you run the application and click the button, you'll first see the MessageBox from the behavior and then, because it's a blocking call, once you close the box you'll see the FluidMoveBehavior in action.

Once you've created a behavior or action that you like, be sure to share it on the Expression Gallery at http://gallery.expression.microsoft.com. There are a ton of interesting behaviors there; you may learn from some, and you may contribute others. It's a great community.

Behaviors, triggers, and actions—collectively "behaviors"—provide an excellent way to package up reusable bits of functionality without the overhead of a custom control. The Blend SDK comes with a number of important behaviors, providing a broad spectrum of capabilities. The Expression gallery includes a number of other behaviors that you can download and use in your own applications. Already, a large number of individuals and companies have developed and shared their own useful behaviors with the community. And, if the existing behaviors are insufficient for your needs, you can build your own behaviors using the same building blocks the expression team and community use.

22.7 *Summary*

Throughout this chapter, you saw the details associated with animating elements within Silverlight. When it comes down to it, it's really about manipulating a single property over a time interval. This time interval can be specified within either an animation, or higher up the tree, a `Storyboard`. The `Storyboard` enables you to organize and control multiple animations simultaneously, so you can create incredibly dramatic and engaging effects. With the help of keyframes, these effects can be developed extremely quickly and efficiently. When you add easing functions into the mix, the results are visually stunning and can provide that "pop" your application needs.

Behaviors provide reusable packages of functionality that can span a broad spectrum of capabilities. Some interact with animation and easing functions; others interact with code; still others enable you to play sounds or provide special movement to elements on a page. The community at the Expression Gallery has created a large number of reusable behaviors that you can incorporate into your own applications. If you want to create your own from scratch or contribute to that community, you already have all the tools you need with Visual Studio 2010 and the Blend SDK.

Providing an engaging user experience can be a valuable addition to any application. Providing a consistent user experience is perhaps equally, if not more, valuable. Silverlight has a variety of style and template features to help provide a consistent user experience. These features are discussed in detail in chapter 23.

Resources, styles, and control templates

This chapter covers
- Using application resources
- Control styling
- Building control templates
- The Visual State Manager

Chapter 22 described the powerful animation features available in Silverlight. These features are useful for creating entertaining illustrations and for adding a degree of richness to your application. This richness can also be applied to controls, as you'll see in this chapter.

Throughout this chapter, you'll see how to apply rich styles to your application. These styles are similar to the CSS features you may have seen in the HTML world. In general, a `Style` declaration will be part of a resource, so we'll cover resources first. From there, you'll learn how to manage resources in dictionaries before moving on to creating rich visual `Styles` themselves. We'll cover both explicit and implicit styles. Then you'll see how to expand on the definition of a `Style` to define a `ControlTemplate`, enabling you to redefine the visual structure of a `Control`.

Once we've covered that subject, you'll learn how to use the `VisualStateManager` to deliver engaging visual states and transition animations within your `Control` elements.

23.1 Being resourceful

In general, it's a good idea to create reusable items whenever possible. This practice makes your application more maintainable. In fact, creating reusable components is a common idea within object-oriented languages such as C#. But, sometimes, you may have items that represent nonexecutable pieces of data—for instance, an image, a media file, or some XAML. These types of content generally fall into one of three categories: declarative resources, loose resources, and bundled resources. We'll cover all three of these categories in this section, beginning with declarative resources, which are fairly different compared to the other two.

23.1.1 Declarative resources

Declarative resources are items intended to be shared across multiple elements in your project. They can be any `object` you want to share. For instance, a resource can be used to define a `DataTemplate` or `Storyboard`, as hinted at earlier in this book. Resources are also a vital part of the styling and templating features discussed later in this chapter. Before you see those features, let's examine the basic syntax and usage of a declarative resource (see listing 23.1).

Listing 23.1 The basic syntax and usage of a resource

Result:

DECLARATIVE
RESOURCES

XAML:

```
<StackPanel>                                          Resource
  <StackPanel.Resources>            ◄──── dictionary
    <LinearGradientBrush x:Key="myGradientBrush"          ❶
      StartPoint="0,0" EndPoint="1,1">
      <GradientStop Color="#FF575757"/>
      <GradientStop Color="#FFCDCDCD" Offset="1"/>
    </LinearGradientBrush>
  </StackPanel.Resources>

  <TextBlock Text="DECLARATIVE" FontWeight="Bold"
    FontFamily="Verdana" FontSize="40"
    Foreground="{StaticResource myGradientBrush}" />    ◄─┐
  <TextBlock Text="RESOURCES" FontWeight="Bold"            ❷
    FontFamily="Verdana" FontSize="40"
    Foreground="{StaticResource myGradientBrush}" />    ◄─┘
</StackPanel>
```

This listing shows a basic declarative resource scoped to a `StackPanel` in the form of a `LinearGradientBrush` ❶. This `GradientBrush` is used by both `TextBlock` elements defined in this listing ❷. This shared approach is possible because the resource is within the same scope as the two TextBlock elements. Within this section, you'll learn about resource scoping in further detail. In addition, you'll see how to use declarative resources at design time. This task will demonstrate to the meaning behind the x:Key attribute and StaticResource items shown in listing 23.1. Finally, this section will end with a discussion of using declarative resources at runtime.

DEFINING DECLARATIVE RESOURCES

Resources must be defined within an appropriately named collection called Resources. This collection is a ResourceDictionary, a specialized dictionary containing resources identified by implicit or explicit keys. These resources and their associated keys can be defined at both design time and runtime. Both approaches are shown in listing 23.2.

Listing 23.2   SolidColorBrush defined as a resource at design time and runtime

XAML:

```
<StackPanel x:Name="myStackPanel">
  <StackPanel.Resources>
    <SolidColorBrush x:Key="theSolidColorBrush" Color="Green" />
  </StackPanel.Resources>
</StackPanel>
```

C#:

```
SolidColorBrush brush = new SolidColorBrush();
brush.Color = Colors.Green;
myStackPanel.Resources.Add("theSolidColorBrush", brush);
```

This example shows how to define a resource at design time and runtime. Both approaches require you to specify two items. The first item is the key, which in this case is theSolidColorBrush. The other is the resource itself, which in this case is a SolidColorBrush.

The key of a resource is a string that uniquely identifies it. At runtime, this identifier is set when you add a resource to a ResourceDictionary. Because the Resource-Dictionary class implements the IDictionary interface, you can add a resource using the Add method. The first parameter of this method represents a key. The ResourceDictionary implements the IDictionary interface, so you should use the x:Key attribute to identify a resource at design time. Keys are only necessary when you want to explicitly use a resource, as shown in the examples so far. When we get into styles, you'll see how an implicit key can be useful as well. Once you've selected a key, you may move on to the details of the resource.

The resource itself is the reason for this section. This item can be virtually any object that Silverlight allows to be shared. For example, controls and visuals can't be shared. In general, you'll most likely use Storyboard, Style, and Template items as resources with the occasional low-level int or double type and maybe even instances of your own classes for data. Regardless of the type of resource, the item can only be used within its respective scope.

ALL ABOUT SCOPE

So far, we've seen resources placed into various on-page elements. That's great for nonstyle resources such as references to data objects and whatnot. When used with styles, though, it's similar to placing CSS styles directly into your HTML page—it works, but it's not really a best practice. In most cases, your resources are going to be placed in a central location, such as in App.xaml.

Resources defined in App.xaml are available to the entire application. The syntax is the same as defining resources locally. After a resource has been defined, either locally or through App.xaml, it can be referenced at design time through the StaticResource markup extension:

```
<TextBlock x:Name="myTextBlock" Text="Hello, World"
  Foreground="{StaticResource theSolidColorBrush}" />
```

The StaticResource extension expects a single value that must match a key from an in-scope ResourceDictionary. The resource must also be defined syntactically *before* it's referenced. Because of this requirement, listing 23.3 won't work.

Listing 23.3 How not to be seen

XAML:
```
<StackPanel x:Name="myStackPanel">
  <TextBlock x:Name="myTextBlock" Text="Hello, World"
    Foreground="{StaticResource theSolidColorBrush}" />
  <StackPanel.Resources>
    <SolidColorBrush x:Key="theSolidColorBrush" Color="Green" />
  </StackPanel.Resources>
</StackPanel>
```

This listing shows an invalid use of a resource; the resource is used before it's defined. If you attempt to run this example, it'll throw an XamlParseException. The order in which entries appear is especially important once you start working with independent resource dictionaries and have to merge them in the correct order.

MERGING RESOURCE DICTIONARIES

Though App.xaml may ultimately be the aggregation point for your resources, a common strategy is to place resources into individual resource dictionary files. The files are typically groups of related resources or entire application themes. Those resource dictionary files are then compiled into the application (build action of Page, Custom Tool set to MSBuild:Compile) and merged in from App.xaml or into the dictionaries of individual pages.

For example, listings 23.4 through 23.7 show how to merge two different resource files into your application using App.xaml as the aggregation point but also referencing from within the dictionaries. Listing 23.4 shows the first resource file, StandardColors.xaml.

Listing 23.4 Merging resource dictionaries—colors dictionary

StandardColors.xaml:

```
<ResourceDictionary
  xmlns="http://schemas.microsoft.com/winfx/2006/xaml/presentation"
  xmlns:x="http://schemas.microsoft.com/winfx/2006/xaml">

  <SolidColorBrush x:Key="TextColor" Color="#FF303030" />

  <SolidColorBrush x:Key="HeadlineTextColor" Color="Black" />

  <LinearGradientBrush x:Key="PageBackgroundColor"
                       StartPoint="0,0"
                       EndPoint="0,1">
    <GradientStop Offset="0" Color="#FFFFFFFF" />
    <GradientStop Offset="1" Color="#FFD0D0D0" />
  </LinearGradientBrush>
</ResourceDictionary>
```

The StandardColors.xaml resource dictionary is our base dictionary. It has no dependencies on others, but is used in several other places. This dictionary defines three Brush resources, two of which are simple SolidColorBrush instances; the third is a LinearGradientBrush.

The StandardColors.xaml resource dictionary is used by the ControlStyles.xaml resource dictionary shown in listing 23.5.

Listing 23.5 Merging resource dictionaries—control styles dictionary

---

ControlStyles.xaml:

```
<ResourceDictionary
  xmlns="http://schemas.microsoft.com/winfx/2006/xaml/presentation"
  xmlns:x="http://schemas.microsoft.com/winfx/2006/xaml">

  <ResourceDictionary.MergedDictionaries>
    <ResourceDictionary Source="StandardColors.xaml" />        ❶
  </ResourceDictionary.MergedDictionaries>

  <Style TargetType="TextBlock">
    <Setter Property="FontFamily"
        Value="Segoe UI" />
    <Setter Property="Foreground"
        Value="{StaticResource TextColor}" />
  </Style>

  <Style x:Key="HeadlineTextStyle"
        TargetType="TextBlock">
    <Setter Property="FontFamily"
        Value="Segoe UI" />
    <Setter Property="Foreground"
        Value="{StaticResource HeadlineTextColor}" />
    <Setter Property="FontSize"
        Value="20" />
    <Setter Property="Margin"
        Value="0 0 0 10" />
  </Style>
</ResourceDictionary>
```

Defined in colors dictionary

The standard colors dictionary is merged into the control styles dictionary ❶. This is required because the control styles dictionary uses resources defined in the color dictionary. As you'll see in the next listing, dependencies can't be chained; they don't ripple "upward" and must be explicitly defined in each XAML file. Listing 23.6 shows App.xaml where the dictionaries are made available to the whole application.

Listing 23.6 Merging resource dictionaries—App.xaml

App.xaml:

```
<Application
xmlns="http://schemas.microsoft.com/winfx/2006/xaml/presentation"
        xmlns:x="http://schemas.microsoft.com/winfx/2006/xaml"
        x:Class="MergeExample.App">
  <Application.Resources>
    <ResourceDictionary>
      <ResourceDictionary.MergedDictionaries>
        <ResourceDictionary Source="StandardColors.xaml" />
        <ResourceDictionary Source="ControlStyles.xaml" />
      </ResourceDictionary.MergedDictionaries>
    </ResourceDictionary>
  </Application.Resources>
</Application>
```

Merged dictionaries ❶ ❷

Listing 23.6 shows App.xaml. Both StandardColors.xaml ❶ and ControlStyles.xaml ❷ are merged into App.xaml to make their included resources available to the rest of the application. As I mentioned earlier, you can't merge resources and expect the dependencies to flow through. For example, StandardColors.xaml is merged into ControlStyles.xaml. That's not sufficient to make the resources in StandardColors.xaml available outside on the control styles; they're in a private dictionary. To expose them to the rest of the application, they're all merged into the applicationwide dictionary in the Application object (see listing 23.7).

Listing 23.7 Merging resource dictionaries—main page

MainPage.xaml:

```
<UserControl x:Class="MergeExample.MainPage"
    xmlns="http://schemas.microsoft.com/winfx/2006/xaml/presentation"
    xmlns:x="http://schemas.microsoft.com/winfx/2006/xaml"
    xmlns:d="http://schemas.microsoft.com/expression/blend/2008"
    xmlns:mc="http://schemas.openxmlformats.org/markup-compatibility/2006"
    mc:Ignorable="d"
    d:DesignHeight="300" d:DesignWidth="400">

    <Grid x:Name="LayoutRoot"
        Background="{StaticResource PageBackgroundColor}">              ❶
        <StackPanel>
            <TextBlock Text="This is a Headline"
                    Style="{StaticResource HeadlineTextStyle}" />        ❷
            <TextBlock Text="This is normal text. It is implicitly styled.
➡   We'll get to implicit styling in just a bit." />                    ❸

        </StackPanel>
    </Grid>
</UserControl>
```

Finally, we get to our main page. MainPage.xaml is using a resource ❶ defined in StandardColors.xaml. It's also using a control style ❷ defined in ControlStyles.xaml. Finally, the TextBlock ❸ is using an implicit style defined in ControlStyles.xaml.

If you're coming from a CSS background, the way the resources are nested may seem odd to you because each goes into a discrete dictionary instead of a global sheet. In the next section, we'll cover how to access those discrete dictionaries, whether they're at an element level or application level.

USING DECLARATIVE RESOURCES AT RUNTIME

Referencing resources at design time is useful for setting up the initial state of an application. As an application runs, you may need to work with those resources dynamically. To help you accomplish this feat, Silverlight enables you to search for, insert, edit, and remove resources at runtime.

Searching for a resource at runtime involves referencing the Resources property, which is a ResourceDictionary available on every FrameworkElement and Application. Because of this, you can readily search for a declarative resource by using its key. If the resource isn't found, null will be returned; if the resource is found, its object representation will be returned. Because the return value may be an object, you may need to cast the value to another type, as shown in this example:

```
var brush =
    myStackPanel.Resources["theSolidColorBrush"] as SolidColorBrush;
if (brush != null)
    brush.Color = Colors.Blue;
```

This code retrieves the SolidColorBrush defined as a resource in listing 23.2. Once it's retrieved, this Brush is changed from Green to Blue. This small but interesting change occurs at runtime. When this code is executed, the TextBlock in listing 23.2 changes to Blue without any additional code because the Silverlight system automatically listens for those changes. But, it doesn't necessarily listen for when resources are removed.

Accessing resources in elements uses the same syntax for any given element. To access resources defined in the application, it's slightly different:

```
var brush =
    Application.Current.Resources["theSolidColorBrush"] as SolidColorBrush;
if (brush != null)
    brush.Color = Colors.Blue;
```

Rather than specifying an element, you need to specify Application.Current. Once you move beyond that, the syntax is the same. This will also pick up any merged-in resources, so there's no special step required to navigate down into any other dictionaries. (Note that in XAML, the difference is abstracted away by the StaticResource extension.)

Resources may be removed at runtime through the Remove method. This method takes a string that represents the key of the resource to delete. Once it's deleted, this resource can't be used. If the resource was applied to any items in your Silverlight application, the Resources attributes will still be in use; if you remove a resource, you may want to manually update any elements using the declarative resource.

Declarative resources are those defined within your Silverlight application. These resources can be created at either design time or runtime. In addition, declarative resources can be added, edited, and removed at runtime through the readily available Resources property. In addition to declarative resources, Silverlight has another type of resource known as loose resources.

23.1.2 Accessing loose resources

In addition to using resources defined within your XAML, Silverlight enables you to access *loose resources*. A loose resource is an external entity, which may represent something such as an image hosted on some server on the Internet or some publicly visible JSON data. Regardless of the type of content, Silverlight provides the ability to access loose resources. To demonstrate accessing a loose resource, imagine an ASP.NET web application with the structure shown in figure 23.1.

Figure 23.1 shows the structure of a basic ASP.NET web application. This web application has one web page named Default.aspx. Assume that this web page hosts the Silverlight application defined within the MySilverlightApplication.xap file, which is nestled within the ClientBin directory. This will become important in a moment. Also note

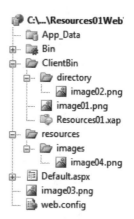

Figure 23.1 A sample web site project structure. Note the four .png files.

the four image files that are part of this web application structure: image01.png, image02.png, image03.png, and image04.png. These images represent the loose resources that we'll use throughout this section.

You'll learn two different ways to access loose resources. The first approach involves referencing loose resources whose location is relative to the Silverlight application. The second approach involves using an absolute Uri.

REFERENCING RELATIVE LOOSE RESOURCES

Silverlight allows you to access loose resources relative to the *site of origin*—the location where the requesting Silverlight application resides. In many cases, your Silverlight application will be stored within a subdirectory. For instance, in figure 23.1, the Silverlight application (MySilverlightApplication.xap) is stored within the ClientBin directory, so this directory can be considered the site of origin. If you want to access image01.png in figure 23.1, you could use the Source shown here:

```
<Image x:Name="myImage" Source="image01.png" />
```

This accesses a resource in the same directory as MySilverlightApplication.xap. This directory represents the site of origin. If you change the Source property to reference /image01.png, you'd get the same result because the site of origin represents the root directory when a relative URI is used. This syntax will still allow you to reference loose resources' in subdirectories. For instance, you could reference image02.png in figure 23.1 using the Source in this example:

```
<Image x:Name="myImage" Source="directory/image02.png" />
```

This markup shows how to reference a loose resource in a subdirectory, demonstrating that you can use subdirectories with relative references. If you reference a .xap file on a remote server, all your references will be relative to that remote reference. This is important because you can't use a relative URI to access loose resources in directories that are ancestors to the site of origin. This restriction is a security measure to help ensure that preexisting loose resources can't be used unless you explicitly allow it. To allow this use, you must expose them through the cross-domain policy file mentioned in chapter 14 and use an absolute Uri.

RETRIEVING LOOSE RESOURCES WITH AN ABSOLUTE URI

Silverlight gives you the flexibility to access loose resources via an absolute Uri. This gives you the flexibility to access resources from anywhere across the Internet as long as the target server allows it in its cross-domain policy file. This requirement is also necessary if you want to access a resource located up the directory tree from your .xap file. For instance, if the Silverlight web site structure in figure 23.1 is hosted at http://www.silverlightinaction.com, you could access image03.png by using the Source shown here:

```
<Image x:Name=
    "myImage" Source="http://www.silverlightinaction.com/image03.png" />
```

This example shows how to access a loose resource via an absolute Uri. This Uri points at the location of the resource, and this location will be loaded as a loose resource. There's also a way to bundle resources along with your Silverlight application.

23.1.3 *Bundled resources*

The third kind of resource used in Silverlight is referred to as a *bundled resource*. A bundled resource is an item included in the .xap file of a Silverlight application. The term "bundled resource" is a made-up expression used solely for the sake of communication. Bundled resources give you a way to include resources specific to a Silverlight application.

Throughout this section, you'll learn about the two types of bundled resources that can be used in Silverlight. The first is known as a *content file*—a file that's added to the .xap file and deployed alongside a Silverlight application. The other type of resource is known as an *embedded file*, which represents an item that gets embedded into a Silverlight assembly. This kind of resource can be useful for helping to hide your valuable resources.

USING CONTENT FILES

A content file is one that's added to a .xap file and deployed alongside a Silverlight application within the .xap. If you define an image as a content file, that image will be included within the resulting .xap file when the Silverlight application is built. In fact,

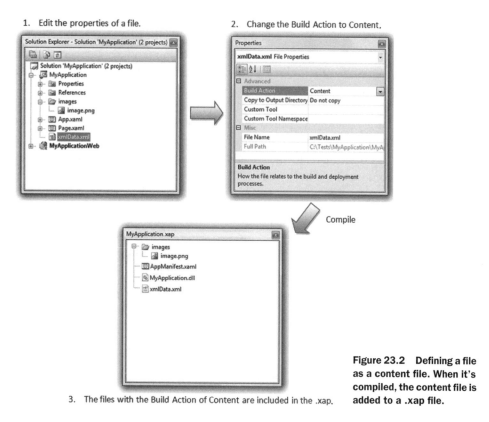

1. Edit the properties of a file.

2. Change the Build Action to Content.

3. The files with the Build Action of Content are included in the .xap.

Figure 23.2   Defining a file as a content file. When it's compiled, the content file is added to a .xap file.

any file with a build action of Content will be bundled into the resulting .xap file. Figure 23.2 shows a .png and .xml file being bundled into a .xap file as content files.

Figure 23.2 shows two files that have been added and marked as content files. The first, xmlData.xml, is a basic XML file. Once the project is built, this file ends up in the root of the .xap file structure. The second, image.png, belongs to a nested directory called images. When the project is built, this relative directory structure is carried over to the final .xap file, which can be accessed using a relative path reference. All content files can be referenced by providing a path relative to the application assembly. This approach can be used at design time, as shown in this markup:

```
<Image x:Name="myImage" Source="/images/image.png" />
```

This example shows the syntax used to reference a content file at design time. The leading forward slash (/) informs Silverlight to begin looking at the same level as the application assembly. This approach is the recommended way to include content with a Silverlight application because it makes things more easily accessible. Sometimes, you may come across somebody who does things the old-school way—the content files will be embedded within the Silverlight assembly. You'll now see how to access these embedded files.

USING EMBEDDED FILES

An embedded file is a file embedded within a Silverlight assembly, which may be either an application or a library. Either way, an embedded file becomes a part of an assembly by changing the build action to `Resource`. This file can be retrieved at design time or runtime by providing a special URL structure.

Embedded resources are accessible through a URL that has three parts. The first part names the assembly to which the resource belongs. The second piece is a special keyword called `Component` that declares a resource as being retrieved. The final part is a relative URL that maps to the location of the resource within the assembly. These three items come together to form a URL template that looks like the following:

```
[AssemblyName];component/[RelativePath]
```

This template can be used at design time or runtime. The design-time implementation relies on the element type to convert the resource. At runtime, you must manually convert the resource. First, you retrieve the embedded resource from the assembly through the `Application` class, as shown in this line of code:

```
StreamResourceInfo resource = Application.GetResourceStream(
  new Uri("SilverlightApp1;component/embedded.png", UriKind.Relative));
```

This example shows how to retrieve the resource from the assembly. This resource is represented as a `StreamResourceInfo`, which is part of the `System.Windows.Resources` namespace. This class instance must be converted to the type appropriate for your situation. As we mentioned earlier, you shouldn't come across this scenario very often. When it comes to content files, you'll probably come across a loose resource. In XAML, you'll most likely use declarative resources. This approach is especially true if you're giving your elements `Style`.

23.2 Giving your elements style

As you saw in section 23.1, resources are the nonexecutable parts of your application. These parts are useful for creating items that can be reused multiple times. In addition to being reused, resources can also be shared by multiple elements. These two characteristics make resources a natural fit for styling.

Styling is a way to consistently share the same property values across multiple elements. To see why this is a good idea, imagine needing to create a typical forms-based application. This application must use `TextBox` elements that have a bold 9 pt Verdana font for input. In addition, you want to give the `TextBox` elements a subtle gradient background to make them more appealing. Without styles, you may decide to implement these visual enhancements as shown in listing 23.8.

Listing 23.8 Brute-force approach to applying common properties

Result:

First Name: **D.P**

LastName: **Gumby**

XAML:

```
<Grid x:Name="myGrid">
  <Grid.RowDefinitions>
    <RowDefinition Height="Auto"/>
    <RowDefinition Height="Auto" />
  </Grid.RowDefinitions>
  <Grid.ColumnDefinitions>
    <ColumnDefinition Width="Auto"/>
    <ColumnDefinition Width="Auto"/>
  </Grid.ColumnDefinitions>

  <TextBlock Text="First Name: " />

  <TextBox Height="24" Width="180" Grid.Column="1"
    FontFamily="Verdana" FontSize="12" FontWeight="Bold">
    <TextBox.Background>
      <LinearGradientBrush EndPoint="0.5,1" StartPoint="0.5,0">
        <GradientStop Color="#FFFFFFFF" Offset="1"/>
        <GradientStop Color="#FFD0D0D0" Offset="0"/>
      </LinearGradientBrush>
    </TextBox.Background>
  </TextBox>

  <TextBlock Text="LastName: " Grid.Row="1" />

  <TextBox Height="24" Width="180" Grid.Row="1" Grid.Column="1"
    FontFamily="Verdana" FontSize="12" FontWeight="Bold">
    <TextBox.Background>
      <LinearGradientBrush EndPoint="0.5,1" StartPoint="0.5,0">
        <GradientStop Color="#FFFFFFFF" Offset="1"/>
        <GradientStop Color="#FFD0D0D0" Offset="0"/>
      </LinearGradientBrush>
    </TextBox.Background>
  </TextBox>
</Grid>
```

Listing 23.8 shows the brute-force approach to defining the visual properties of multiple elements. It defines two TextBox elements with the same values for the Height, Width, FontFamily, FontSize, and FontWeight properties. In addition, the same complex LinearGradientBrush definition is used for the Background of both TextBox elements. Unfortunately, this approach isn't scalable. For instance, if you need to change the font of the TextBox items, you'd have to make the change to each item, but you can overcome this minor inconvenience using a Style.

A Style is a way to share the same property values across multiple elements. Throughout this section, you'll learn how to create and use a Style. This approach will help you avoid the maintenance nightmare shown in that last listing. You'll first see how to define the visual properties of a control through a Style. From there, you'll learn how to share a Style definition across multiple elements.

23.2.1 *Defining the look*

To define the look of an element using a Style, you simply set the Style property. This instruction may sound redundant, but the property name is the same as the type name. The `Style` property is available on every `FrameworkElement`, so virtually every control in the Silverlight framework can be styled. You can do this by taking advantage of the `Style` class's `Setters` collection.

The `Setters` collection stores the entire definition of a `Style`. This definition is made up of individual property/value pairs similar to those seen in CSS within the HTML world. In Silverlight, each combination is defined within a `Setter` element, which lets you assign a value to a single visual property. Interestingly, this approach can be used to set both simple and complex property values.

SETTING SIMPLE PROPERTY VALUES

A *simple property* is a property that can be set at design time with a primitively typed value. A primitively typed value is something like an `int` or `string` value. These kinds of values can be used at design time to set the values for properties such as `FontSize` and `FontFamily`. Listing 23.9 shows how to use five simple properties as part of a `Style`.

> **Listing 23.9   A basic style definition**

Result:

> My Brain Hurts!

XAML:

```
<TextBox x:Name="myTextBox">
  <TextBox.Style>                    <―― Style property      ❶
    <Style TargetType="TextBox">
      <Setter Property="FontFamily" Value="Verdana" />
      <Setter Property="FontSize" Value="12" />
      <Setter Property="FontWeight" Value="Bold" />
      <Setter Property="Height" Value="24" />
      <Setter Property="Width" Value="180" />
    </Style>
  </TextBox.Style>
</TextBox>
```

This example shows how to define a `Style` ❶ that uses five simple properties, each of which is defined within a `Setter` element. These elements are automatically added to the `Style` object's `Setters` collection. More importantly, each of the items in this collection is defined by two publicly visible attributes.

The two attributes that define a `Setter` are called `Property` and `Value`. The `Property` attribute determines which property the `Value` will be used with. The `Property` must be a `DependencyProperty`, but the `Value` property can be set to any `object`. Because of this fact, the `Setter` element is flexible, making it a natural fit for simple properties. In addition, it's also a natural fit for complex properties.

SETTING COMPLEX PROPERTY VALUES

A *complex property* is a property whose value is a general-purpose `object`. In general, these kinds of properties have nested properties that must be set. For example, a `LinearGradientBrush` could be considered a complex property value because it has the additional stops broken out using property element syntax. Now, imagine trying to use this `LinearGradientBrush` as part of a `Style`. You must use an approach similar to that shown in listing 23.10.

Listing 23.10 A complex property in a style definition

Result:

Hullo! I'm D.P. Gumby!

XAML:

```xaml
<TextBox x:Name="myTextBox">
  <TextBox.Style>                          <⎯ Style property
    <Style TargetType="TextBox">
      <Setter Property="FontFamily" Value="Verdana"/>
      <Setter Property="FontSize" Value="12"/>
      <Setter Property="FontWeight" Value="Bold"/>
      <Setter Property="Height" Value="24"/>
      <Setter Property="Width" Value="180"/>
      <Setter Property="Background">
        <Setter.Value>                                       ❶
          <LinearGradientBrush EndPoint="0.5,1" StartPoint="0.5,0">
            <GradientStop Color="#FFFFFFFF" Offset="1"/>
            <GradientStop Color="#FFD0D0D0" Offset="0"/>
          </LinearGradientBrush>
        </Setter.Value>
      </Setter>
    </Style>
  </TextBox.Style>
</TextBox>
```

Listing 23.10 shows how to define a more complex property as part of a `Style` ❶. There aren't any new elements shown here, but it does show you how to break out the `Setter.Value` into a nested property itself. This approach gives you the flexibility to use something as complex as a `LinearGradientBrush`.

The approaches shown in both of these examples haven't solved the problem of scalability; they've just shown the syntax of a `Style` used inside of an element instead of explicit properties. To solve to problem of scalability, you must understand how to target your `Style` definitions so they may be reused.

23.2.2 *Explicitly keyed style definitions*

In CSS, one way to define styles is to include two parts. One part represents the name of the style; the other part is the name of the HTML tag the style is applicable to. An explicit `Style` in Silverlight also uses these two parts.

The first part of a `Style` uniquely identifies a `Style` definition. As shown in the previous two examples, this part is optional. It becomes a requirement only if you create a `Style` as a resource and want to refer to it explicitly. If you choose this approach, you must specify the `x:Key` attribute to uniquely identify the `Style`, and you must specify the other part—the `TargetType`.

The TargetType property signals which System.Type a Style is applicable to. This property doesn't need to be set if you define a Style within an element, as shown in the previous examples. If you define a Style as a resource, you must set this property as shown in listing 23.11.

Listing 23.11   Defining the TargetType of a Style

XAML:

```
<Grid x:Name="myGrid" Background="White">
  <Grid.Resources>
    <Style x:Key="textStyle" TargetType="TextBox">           ❶
      <Setter Property="FontWeight" Value="Bold" />
      <Setter Property="FontFamily" Value="Verdana" />
      <Setter Property="FontSize" Value="12" />
      <Setter Property="Height" Value="24" />
      <Setter Property="Width" Value="180" />
      <Setter Property="Background">
        <Setter.Value>
          <LinearGradientBrush EndPoint="0.5,1" StartPoint="0.5,0">
            <GradientStop Color="#FFFFFFFF" Offset="1"/>
            <GradientStop Color="#FFD0D0D0" Offset="0"/>
          </LinearGradientBrush>
        </Setter.Value>
      </Setter>
    </Style>
  </Grid.Resources>
  <Grid.RowDefinitions>
    <RowDefinition Height="Auto" />
    <RowDefinition Height="Auto" />
  </Grid.RowDefinitions>
  <Grid.ColumnDefinitions>
    <ColumnDefinition Width="Auto" />
    <ColumnDefinition Width="Auto" />
  </Grid.ColumnDefinitions>
  <TextBlock Text="First Name: " />
  <TextBox Grid.Column="1"
        Style="{StaticResource textStyle}" />       ⟵
  <TextBlock Text="LastName: " Grid.Row="1" />                    Style
  <TextBox Grid.Row="1" Grid.Column="1"                          in use
        Style="{StaticResource textStyle}" />       ⟵
</Grid>
```

Listing 23.11 shows a Style defined as a resource. The Style in this case is configured to be used with TextBox elements as set through the TargetType property ❶. If you were to attempt to use this Style with an element of another type, an error would occur. It can be used with any types that might derive from TextBox.

CSS supports *implicit styles*, where you simply specify the type (a DIV, for example) and CSS applies it to all DIV elements within a certain scope. Silverlight supports a similar type of implicit styling.

23.2.3 *Implicit style definitions*

In the previous example, we saw how a style may be reused by applying it to each control. In a large application with many controls, this procedure can be both tedious and error prone. Silverlight 4 introduced implicit styles.

Implicit styles look exactly like their explicit cousins, except they omit the key. That's it. If you define a style with a `TargetType` and omit the key, the `TargetType` becomes the key and the style becomes implicit.

Listing 23.12 shows the previous example but converted to an implicit style.

Listing 23.12 Defining the `TargetType` of a `Style`

XAML:
```
<Grid x:Name="myGrid" Background="White">
  <Grid.Resources>
    <Style TargetType="TextBox">                                       ❶
      <Setter Property="FontWeight" Value="Bold" />
      <Setter Property="FontFamily" Value="Verdana" />
      <Setter Property="FontSize" Value="12" />
      <Setter Property="Height" Value="24" />
      <Setter Property="Width" Value="180" />
      <Setter Property="Background">
        <Setter.Value>
          <LinearGradientBrush EndPoint="0.5,1" StartPoint="0.5,0">
            <GradientStop Color="#FFFFFFFF" Offset="1"/>
            <GradientStop Color="#FFD0D0D0" Offset="0"/>
          </LinearGradientBrush>
        </Setter.Value>
      </Setter>
    </Style>
  </Grid.Resources>
  <Grid.RowDefinitions>
    <RowDefinition Height="Auto" />
    <RowDefinition Height="Auto" />
  </Grid.RowDefinitions>
  <Grid.ColumnDefinitions>
    <ColumnDefinition Width="Auto" />
    <ColumnDefinition Width="Auto" />
  </Grid.ColumnDefinitions>
  <TextBlock Text="First Name: " />
  <TextBox Grid.Column="1" />                          ◁─┐ Style
  <TextBlock Text="LastName: " Grid.Row="1" />            │ in use
  <TextBox Grid.Row="1" Grid.Column="1" />            ◁─┘
</Grid>
```

Just as we saw in the previous example, this listing defines a style ❶ that targets the `TextBox` type. But we've omitted the `x:Key`, so this is an implicit style. Note the `TextBox` controls at the bottom of the listing: they now pick up the style without requiring any `StaticResource` setting. This is a huge timesaver for applications of any real complexity.

Styling, both explicit and implicit, is a powerful way to define the user interface standards for your application. Design professionals (or integrators, depending on how your team is set up) spend a good bit of their time defining styles, just as they would with HTML/CSS. They can work with them directly in XAML as we have here or use Expression Blend to make the process easier.

Once you've mastered styling, you're ready to take a step beyond setting simple properties and into working with the control templates themselves.

23.3 Creating templates

The styling features shown in section 23.2 are a welcome addition to the Silverlight world. These items allow you to quickly create a consistent look throughout an application. This look can be shared across the application by defining the styles as resources. But, occasionally, the styling options can be somewhat limiting. To overcome these limitations, you can use a template.

A template empowers you to redefine the entire visual representation of an element, giving you the flexibility to make any `Control` look the way you want it to look. When doing this, you don't sacrifice the behavior of the `Control`. You could create a `Button` that looks and feels like an octagon and still reacts to the `Click` event. Over the course of this section, you'll experience the full power of a template by building a control template. You'll also see how to elegantly create a reusable template.

23.3.1 Building a control template

When you build a control template, it'll ultimately be used with a `Control`. Every `Control` in Silverlight exposes a property called `Template`. This property is a `ControlTemplate` that lets you take complete control over what a `Control` looks like. In a sense, when you set this property, you're resetting the control's appearance, giving you a clean slate to work with. From there, you can make a `Control` look like whatever you want it to look like. For instance, listing 23.13 changes the look of a `Button` to make it look more like a sphere.

> **Listing 23.13   Changing the look of a Button through a Template**

Result:

XAML:
```
<Button x:Name="myButton" Content="Hello">          Template
  <Button.Template>                            ◁──┘ property
    <ControlTemplate>              ❶
      <Ellipse Height="90" Width="90" Stroke="Black" StrokeThickness="2">
        <Ellipse.Fill>
          <RadialGradientBrush GradientOrigin="0.3,0.2">
            <RadialGradientBrush.RelativeTransform>
              <TransformGroup>
                <ScaleTransform CenterX="0.5" CenterY="0.5"
                   ScaleX="1.075" ScaleY="1.141"/>
```

```
                <SkewTransform CenterX="0.5" CenterY="0.5"/>
                <RotateTransform CenterX="0.5" CenterY="0.5"/>
                <TranslateTransform X="-0.04" Y="0.07"/>
              </TransformGroup>
            </RadialGradientBrush.RelativeTransform>
            <GradientStop Color="#FFD9D9D9" Offset="0.004"/>
            <GradientStop Color="#FF2103BA" Offset="1"/>
          </RadialGradientBrush>
        </Ellipse.Fill>
      </Ellipse>
    </ControlTemplate>
  </Button.Template>
</Button>
```

This example shows a basic `ControlTemplate` ❶. This `ControlTemplate` is associated with a `Button` through its `Template` property. Notably, if you were to define a `ControlTemplate` as a resource, you'd associate the template with a specific type through the `TargetType` property. This property behaves the same way as it did with the `Style` class. Interestingly, when a template is used with a `ContentControl`, the `Content` property doesn't behave the same way.

Over the course of this section, you'll learn how to display content within a `ControlTemplate`. This content will generally be placed inside a `Panel` or `Border` because a `ControlTemplate` can have only one root element. This root element can then be used to house the contents of a `ContentControl` or an `ItemsControl`. You'll also see how to customize the way in which the `Items` of an `ItemsControl` are arranged. But first, you'll see how to use properties that are part of the target control in your templates.

CONSIDERING CONTROL PROPERTIES

Ultimately, the purpose of a `ControlTemplate` is to define the appearance of a `Control`. This `Control` may have properties set that should be used within your template. For instance, you may want to use the `Background` or `FontFamily` property values of a `Control` in your `ControlTemplate`. In these types of situations, you should use a `TemplateBinding`.

A `TemplateBinding` is a special type of data binding used within a `ControlTemplate`. This data binding uses the `Control` to which the `ControlTemplate` is applied as its data source. The data source is identified as a specific property within that `Control`. This property is referenced by name when you create a `TemplateBinding`. An example of such a reference is shown in listing 23.14.

Listing 23.14   Using a `TemplateBinding` for the target element's properties

Result:

XAML:
```
<Button x:Name="myButton" Content="Hello" Height="45" Width="45">
  <Button.Template>
```

```
        <ControlTemplate>
          <Ellipse Fill="#FF2103BA" Stroke="Black" StrokeThickness="2"
            Height="{TemplateBinding Height}"
            Width="{TemplateBinding Width}" />
        </ControlTemplate>
      </Button.Template>
    </Button>
```

Control template

This example shows the basic syntax of a `TemplateBinding` ❶. This syntax mimics the data-binding syntax explained in chapter 11. In this case, the binding causes the `Height` and `Width` property values of the `Button` to be used by the `Ellipse` in the `ControlTemplate`. These property values are simple in comparison to what the value of the `Content` property could be, though. If you're going to display the `Content` of a `ContentControl` in a `ControlTemplate`, you may want to consider using another approach.

DISPLAYING THE CONTENT

You may have noticed that the `Content` of the `Button` elements in the past two listings hasn't been shown because, when you define a `ControlTemplate`, you must tell Silverlight where to place that `Content`. To help you do this task, Silverlight provides two `FrameworkElement` instances: `ContentPresenter` and `ItemsPresenter`.

The `ContentPresenter` class empowers you to specify where the `Content` of a `ContentControl` should be shown. It may be easiest to think of this element as a placeholder for some piece of `Content`. Beyond that, the syntax of a `ContentPresenter` is the element itself, as shown in listing 23.15.

Listing 23.15   Using a `ContentPresenter` to display content

Result:

Hello

XAML:
```
<Button x:Name="myButton" Content="Hello" Height="20" Width="60">
  <Button.Template>
    <ControlTemplate>
      <Border Width="{TemplateBinding Width}" CornerRadius="8"
        BorderThickness="1" BorderBrush="Black" Background="Blue">
        <ContentPresenter HorizontalAlignment="Center" />
      </Border>
    </ControlTemplate>
  </Button.Template>
</Button>
```

This example shows the general usage of a `ContentPresenter`. As you can see, this object is a placeholder designed to be used inside a `ControlTemplate`. This element is generally limited to `ContentControl` scenarios and isn't usually used in `ItemsControl` situations. For these scenarios, you may want to consider an `ItemsPresenter` such as the one shown in listing 23.16.

Listing 23.16   Using an `ItemsPresenter` to display the `Items` of an `ItemsControl`

Result:

Item 1

Item 2

Item 3

XAML:

```
<ListBox x:Name="myListBox">
  <ListBox.Template>
    <ControlTemplate>
      <Border CornerRadius="20,7,20,7" BorderThickness="4,2,4,2"
        BorderBrush="LimeGreen"  Padding="10">
        <ItemsPresenter />
      </Border>
    </ControlTemplate>
  </ListBox.Template>
  <ListBox.Items>
    <ListBoxItem><TextBlock>Item 1</TextBlock></ListBoxItem>
    <ListBoxItem><TextBlock>Item 2</TextBlock></ListBoxItem>
    <ListBoxItem><TextBlock>Item 3</TextBlock></ListBoxItem>
  </ListBox.Items>
</ListBox>
```

Control
Template

❶

This example shows a `ListBox` with a `ControlTemplate` applied to it. The `Items` of that `ListBox` are positioned according to the `ItemsPresenter` ❶. This element is important because it determines where the `Items` will be positioned in a `ControlTem-plate`, but the `ItemsPresenter` doesn't determine how the `Items` will be arranged. That's the role of the `ItemsPanel`.

CONTROLLING ITEM ARRANGEMENT

The `Items` of an `ItemsControl` control are arranged according to the `ItemsPanel` property. This property is a special kind of template that defines the `Panel` that will be used to lay out the `Items`. By default, this property is set to use a `StackPanel` with a `Vertical Orientation`. In reality, you're free to use any of the `Panel` elements discussed in chapter 3. You could use a `Horizontal StackPanel`, as shown in listing 23.17.

Listing 23.17   Declaring the `ItemsPanel` to arrange the `Items` of an `ItemsControl`

Result:

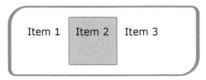

XAML:

```
<ListBox x:Name="myListBox">
  <ListBox.Template>
    <ControlTemplate>
```

```
      <Border CornerRadius="20,7,20,7" BorderThickness="4,2,4,2"
        BorderBrush="LimeGreen"  Padding="10">
        <ItemsPresenter />
      </Border>
    </ControlTemplate>
  </ListBox.Template>
  <ListBox.ItemsPanel>                  ❶
    <ItemsPanelTemplate>
      <StackPanel Orientation="Horizontal" />
    </ItemsPanelTemplate>
  </ListBox.ItemsPanel>
  <ListBox.Items>
    <ListBoxItem>
      <TextBlock Padding="5">Item 1</TextBlock>
    </ListBoxItem>
    <ListBoxItem>
      <TextBlock Padding="5">Item 2</TextBlock>
    </ListBoxItem>
    <ListBoxItem>
      <TextBlock Padding="5">Item 3</TextBlock>
    </ListBoxItem>
  </ListBox.Items>
</ListBox>
```

Horizontal
StackPanel

This example uses a Horizontal StackPanel as the ItemsPanel ❶ to arrange the Items in the ListBox horizontally. It's highly likely that you'll only use a StackPanel as an ItemsPanel. Although you can technically use another Panel element, the other options require actual code. This code will be based entirely on your particular situation, so we won't cover that topic in this section.

The ControlTemplate class enables you to redefine the way a Control looks. This new definition can use the target Control property values through a TemplateBinding. When it comes to displaying the Content of a ContentControl, you should use a ContentPresenter within a ControlTemplate. If this ControlTemplate is associated with an ItemsControl, you may need to use an ItemsPresenter to show the Items. These Items can be rendered in new ways thanks to the ItemsPanel property.

Once you've settled on a ControlTemplate, you may want to use it across multiple controls. Thankfully, Silverlight makes it easy to create reusable templates.

23.3.2   *Creating reusable templates*

Creating individual templates can be useful when you want to give individualized attention to your controls; templates can also be useful for creating a truly unique yet consistent user experience. To help make it easier to deliver a consistent user experience, Silverlight allows you to define a ControlTemplate as part of a Style (see listing 23.18).

Listing 23.18   Using a ControlTemplate within a Style

Result:

XAML:

```
<StackPanel x:Name="LayoutRoot" Background="White" Margin="10" Width="170">
  <StackPanel.Resources>
    <Style x:Key="buttonStyle" TargetType="Button">           ❶
      <Setter Property="Template">
        <Setter.Value>                    ControlTemplate
          <ControlTemplate>        ◁
            <Ellipse Fill="#FF2103BA" Stroke="Black" StrokeThickness="2"
                     Height="{TemplateBinding Height}"
                     Width="{TemplateBinding Width}" />
          </ControlTemplate>
        </Setter.Value>
      </Setter>
    </Style>
  </StackPanel.Resources>
  <Button x:Name="myButton1" Height="30" Width="30"
    Style="{StaticResource buttonStyle}" />
  <Button x:Name="myButton2" Height="70" Width="70"
    Style="{StaticResource buttonStyle}" />
</StackPanel>
```

This example shows a `ControlTemplate` defined within a `Style` ❶. Though this is a simple template, you can also define a `ControlTemplate` as complex as you need it to be. You can even go as far as defining a `ControlTemplate` that considers visual states.

23.4 Dealing with visual states

Templates give you the flexibility to completely dictate what a `Control` looks like, but the template explanation given in section 23.3 is only useful for defining the default look of a `Control`. This default look represents the `Control`'s normal state. In reality, most controls have multiple states. For instance, a `Button` can be in a pressed or disabled state. To enable you to manage what a `Control` looks like in such a state, Silverlight provides something known as the `VisualStateManager`.

The `VisualStateManager` is an element that manages the states and the transitioning between states. This element belongs to the `System.Windows` namespace. Because the `VisualStateManager` is in this namespace, it's ready to be utilized in your `Control` definitions. Before you can fully utilize the `VisualStateManager`, you must gain an understanding of components involved in state and transition management. Once you understand these components, you can leverage the power of the `VisualStateManager` itself. As you'll see in the conclusion of this section, this power can be wielded across multiple elements with the help of a `Style`.

23.4.1 Understanding the components

The `VisualStateManager` relies on a variety of components to do its job. These components make up something referred to as the *parts and states model*. This model is designed to separate a `Control` element's appearance from its behavior, ensuring that you can customize the visual pieces of a `Control` without having to change its underlying logic. To enable this feat, the parts and states model relies on three components: states, transitions, and parts.

STATES

A *state* is used to reflect a particular aspect of a control. For instance, the Button has one state that defines what it looks like by default. If a user moves the mouse over this Button, it'll enter another state. If the Button is pressed, it'll change to yet another state. These three states are shown in table 23.1.

Normal	MouseOver	Pressed
Push Me	Push Me	Push Me

Table 23.1   Several states of a Button. Each state has a slightly different visual appearance.

This figure shows three of the states exposed by the Button class. In reality, the Button class has many more states. These states are exposed to the VisualStateManager with the help of the TemplateVisualStateAttribute. This attribute can be used by a Control to identify the states a Control can be in. In addition, because a Control can simultaneously be in multiple states, the TemplateVisualStateAttribute exposes the group that a state belongs to. The states and groups available on the Button class are listed in table 23.2.

State	GroupName
Disabled	CommonStates
MouseOver	CommonStates
Normal	CommonStates
Pressed	CommonStates
Focused	FocusStates
Unfocused	FocusStates

Table 23.2   The states and groups of the Button class

Each state is identified by a Name property, which is part of the TemplateVisualState-Attribute. This property is complemented by another called GroupName, which determines the grouping for the state. The reason for this property is to logically group together visual states. This is necessary because a Control can be in multiple states at the same time. For instance, a Button can simultaneously be in a Focused state as well as a Pressed state because the Pressed state is in a different group than the Focused state. Perhaps a better example is a CheckBox being in a Checked state while also being in a Disabled state. Either way, the main thing to understand is that groups are exclusive—a Control can be in multiple states as long as those states belong to different groups. States that are part of the same group have the ability to transition between one another.

TRANSITIONS

A *transition* defines the way a Control looks as it changes from one state to another. This change is represented as a Storyboard, so you're free to implement a smooth shift between two states. You can even do this at a fine granular level because of the inclusion of parts.

PARTS

A *part* represents a specific element within a ControlTemplate. A part is generally used when some underlying logic may need to change an area of a ControlTemplate. For instance, the thumb on a Slider will change any time a user clicks the track. This event will cause some underlying logic to move the position of the thumb. Both the thumb and track are defined as parts, as shown in figure 23.3.

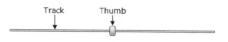

Figure 23.3 The required parts of a Slider are the thumb and the track. The actual appearance of the slider isn't important as long as it has the parts that form the UI contract.

This figure shows the two main parts of a Slider, which has more parts. These parts are defined by the TemplatePartAttribute, which enables you to specify the name and type of a UIElement that represents a part within a Control. This attribute is used to transmit data about the element that represents the part within the parts and states model. Now that this model has been explained, let's look at how to leverage it with the VisualStateManager.

23.4.2 *Leveraging the VisualStateManager*

The VisualStateManager is used by a ControlTemplate to manage the change between states. This change can be used to generate two different kinds of effects. The first is known as a *state-based effect*, which can be useful for doing something such as creating an enlarged Button if a user moves the mouse over it. The other type is known as a *transitioning effect*, which is useful for creating a fluid interface for controls that may change between states of the same group. Both kinds of effects will be covered in this section.

CREATING STATE-BASED EFFECTS

A state-based effect is a transition that occurs at the moment a Control enters a VisualState. When a Control enters this state, the Storyboard associated with the VisualState begins. This Storyboard is defined as part of a ControlTemplate. The Storyboard can be useful for creating a glowing effect or a ballooning effect (see listing 23.19).

Listing 23.19 Creating a Button that enlarges when a user hovers over it

XAML:

```
<Button x:Name="myButton" Width="75" Height="75" Content="Push Me">
  <Button.Template>
    <ControlTemplate TargetType="Button">          Template
      <Grid RenderTransformOrigin=".5,.5">
        <Grid.RenderTransform>
```

```
        <ScaleTransform x:Name="myTransform"/>
      </Grid.RenderTransform>
      <Ellipse x:Name="myEllipse" RenderTransformOrigin=".5,.5"
             Height="{TemplateBinding Height}"
             Width="{TemplateBinding Width}">
        <Ellipse.Fill>
          <RadialGradientBrush GradientOrigin="0.3,0.2">
            <RadialGradientBrush.RelativeTransform>
              <TransformGroup>
                <ScaleTransform CenterX="0.5" CenterY="0.5"
                  ScaleX="1.075" ScaleY="1.141"/>
                <SkewTransform CenterX="0.5" CenterY="0.5"/>
                <RotateTransform CenterX="0.5" CenterY="0.5"/>
                <TranslateTransform X="-0.04" Y="0.07"/>
              </TransformGroup>
            </RadialGradientBrush.RelativeTransform>
            <GradientStop Color="#FFD9D9D9" Offset="0.004" />
            <GradientStop Color="#FF2103BA" Offset="1" />
          </RadialGradientBrush>
        </Ellipse.Fill>
      </Ellipse>
      <ContentPresenter HorizontalAlignment="Center"
                        VerticalAlignment="Center" />           Visual
      <VisualStateManager.VisualStateGroups>                    states
        <VisualStateGroup x:Name="CommonStates">
          <VisualState x:Name="MouseOver">          ❶
            <Storyboard>
              <DoubleAnimation From="1.0" To="1.25"
                Storyboard.TargetName="myTransform"
                Storyboard.TargetProperty="ScaleX" />
              <DoubleAnimation From="1.0" To="1.25"
                Storyboard.TargetName="myTransform"
                Storyboard.TargetProperty="ScaleY" />
            </Storyboard>
          </VisualState>
        </VisualStateGroup>
      </VisualStateManager.VisualStateGroups>
    </Grid>
  </ControlTemplate>
  </Button.Template>
</Button>
```

This listing defines an effect that occurs when a user triggers the MouseOver Visual-State for the Button ❶. All of the items in this example have been described in the previous chapters. You should note three main things. First, the VisualStateGroups element tells the ControlTemplate that some custom Storyboard is going to be used for a state. Second, this state belongs to a predefined group, which is described by the VisualStateGroup element. Third, the VisualState items associated with this group are detailed inside the element. This approach is useful for creating effects when a Control enters a state. But the effect created in listing 23.19 would be better defined as a VisualStateTransition.

DEFINE TRANSITIONING EFFECTS

In addition to state-based transitions, the VisualStateManager enables you to define a transition between states. You can trigger this transition in code by calling the GoToState method or by using a DataStateBehavior or GoToStateAction behavior. We'll use GoToState here because it's the most useful to control authors.

To define a transition in XAML, you must use an element called VisualStateTransition, which allows you to associate a Storyboard with a change between two states. The beginning state is identified by a string property named From. The state being transitioned to is specified by a string property called To. Listing 23.20 defines a transition that changes the Button in the previous listing back to a Normal state.

> **Listing 23.20** Creating a Button that transitions when a user hovers or leaves it

XAML:
```xaml
<Button x:Name="myButton" Width="75" Height="75" Content="Push Me">
  <Button.Template>
    <ControlTemplate TargetType="Button">
      <Grid RenderTransformOrigin=".5,.5">
        <Grid.RenderTransform>
          <ScaleTransform x:Name="myTransform"/>
        </Grid.RenderTransform>
        <Ellipse x:Name="myEllipse" RenderTransformOrigin=".5,.5"
          Height="{TemplateBinding Height}"
          Width="{TemplateBinding Width}">
          <Ellipse.Fill>
            <RadialGradientBrush GradientOrigin="0.3,0.2">
              <RadialGradientBrush.RelativeTransform>
                <TransformGroup>
                  <ScaleTransform CenterX="0.5" CenterY="0.5"
                    ScaleX="1.075" ScaleY="1.141"/>
                  <SkewTransform CenterX="0.5" CenterY="0.5"/>
                  <RotateTransform CenterX="0.5" CenterY="0.5"/>
                  <TranslateTransform X="-0.04" Y="0.07"/>
                </TransformGroup>
              </RadialGradientBrush.RelativeTransform>
              <GradientStop Color="#FFD9D9D9" Offset="0.004" />
              <GradientStop Color="#FF2103BA" Offset="1" />
            </RadialGradientBrush>
          </Ellipse.Fill>
        </Ellipse>
        <ContentPresenter HorizontalAlignment="Center"
                          VerticalAlignment="Center" />
        <VisualStateManager.VisualStateGroups>              ❶
          <VisualStateGroup x:Name="CommonStates">
            <VisualState x:Name="Normal">                    ❷
              <Storyboard>
                <DoubleAnimation To="1.0"
                  Storyboard.TargetName="myTransform"
                  Storyboard.TargetProperty="ScaleX" />
                <DoubleAnimation To="1.0"
                  Storyboard.TargetName="myTransform"
                  Storyboard.TargetProperty="ScaleY" />
```

```
            </Storyboard>
          </VisualState>
          <VisualState x:Name="MouseOver">          ❷
            <Storyboard>
              <DoubleAnimation To="1.25"
                Storyboard.TargetName="myTransform"
                Storyboard.TargetProperty="ScaleX" />
              <DoubleAnimation To="1.25"
                Storyboard.TargetName="myTransform"
                Storyboard.TargetProperty="ScaleY" />
            </Storyboard>
          </VisualState>
          <VisualStateGroup.Transitions>
            <VisualTransition From="Normal" To="MouseOver">        ❸
              <Storyboard Duration="00:00:01">
                <DoubleAnimation From="1.0" To="1.25"
                  Storyboard.TargetName="myTransform"
                  Storyboard.TargetProperty="ScaleX" />
                <DoubleAnimation From="1.0" To="1.25"
                  Storyboard.TargetName="myTransform"
                  Storyboard.TargetProperty="ScaleY" />
              </Storyboard>
            </VisualTransition>
            <VisualTransition From="MouseOver" To="Normal">        ❹
              <DoubleAnimation From="1.25" To="1.0"
                Storyboard.TargetName="myTransform"
                Storyboard.TargetProperty="ScaleX" />
              <DoubleAnimation From="1.25" To="1.0"
                Storyboard.TargetName="myTransform"
                Storyboard.TargetProperty="ScaleY" />
              </Storyboard>
            </VisualTransition>
          </VisualStateGroup.Transitions>
        </VisualStateGroup>
      </VisualStateManager.VisualStateGroups>
    </Grid>
  </ControlTemplate>
 </Button.Template>
</Button>
```

This listing shows the definitions of two VisualTransition elements. The first VisualTransition scales the Button up as it changes from the Normal VisualState to the
MouseOver VisualState ❸. The second VisualTransition scales the Button down as
it goes from the MouseOver VisualState back to the Normal VisualState ❹. These
two transitions are necessary because, otherwise, the Button would be stuck looking
like it did in a MouseOver state. There are two other interesting tidbits in this example.

First, you'll also notice the addition of the two VisualState definitions ❷. These
are necessary to keep the transition animations in place. Without these definitions,
the transition animations would be lost. The other interesting piece in this example is
the use of the VisualStateGroup element ❶. You can only create transitions between
states that belong to the same group because, as we stated earlier, a Control can be in
multiple states as long as those states belong to different groups. Creating transitions

between states empowers you to create deeper and richer controls, so it's only natural to want to share these effects with multiple `Control` instances.

23.5 *Sharing your visual states*

Because the visual states you create with the `VisualTransition` and `VisualState` elements are part of a `ControlTemplate`, you can define them as part of a `Style`. For the sake of completeness, listing 23.21 shows the transitions from the previous example defined as part of a `Style`.

Listing 23.21   Creating a button that enlarges when hovered over

XAML:
```
<Grid x:Name="LayoutRoot" Background="White">
  <Grid.Resources>
    <Style x:Key="buttonStyle" TargetType="Button">
      <Setter Property="Template">
        <Setter.Value>
          <ControlTemplate TargetType="Button">        Visual state
            ...                                   <---  info goes here
          </ControlTemplate>
        </Setter.Value>
      </Setter>
    </Style>
  </Grid.Resources>
  <Button x:Name="myButton" Width="75" Height="75" Content="Push Me"
    Style="{StaticResource buttonStyle}" />
</Grid>
```

This listing shows how the previously defined `Button` `ControlTemplate` can be included in a `Style`. This `ControlTemplate` uses the `VisualState` and `VisualTransition` elements from listing 23.20. This example puts everything from this chapter together. The main thing to note is that you can leverage the `VisualStateManager` within a `Style` declaration. This is an exciting news because there can be a lot of XAML involved in creating effects for the various states and transitions of a `Control`. These states and transitions are part of something known as the parts and states model, which is supported by Microsoft Expression Blend. Because of this convenience, you're empowered to create some of the richest controls available on the Internet.

23.6 *Summary*

Resources in Silverlight come in many flavors. The ones most associated with the word *resource* are those we put in XAML, inside resource dictionaries. Those dictionaries can be parts of controls in app.xaml or in separate files merged into existing resource dictionaries. Resources defined this way can be just about anything from data source or view model classes, to styles, to brush and color definitions.

The most common uses of XAML resources are styles and control templates. Styles provide a way to factor out the common property settings for controls and store them in a location where they can be shared among many instances. Building upon styles are control templates. Control templates go a step beyond what you can do with the public properties affected with styles; they let you completely change the visual representation of a control including its visual states and transitions.

Another common type of resource is a file resource, accessed as a loose file, embedded into the compiled DLL or copied into the zipped-up .xap. You'll use these whenever you want a file to be delivered with the application itself.

Understanding resources, styles, templates, and visual states are all prerequisites to building your own controls. We've covered user controls previously. In chapter 24 we'll take on building truly lookless controls using everything we've learned so far.

This chapter covers

- Creating a custom panel
- Exploring measure and arrange layout steps
- Creating a custom control
- Supporting templating
- Implementing visual states

The power of templating in Silverlight means we rarely have to create custom panels and controls. More often than not, an existing element provides the behavior we need and a custom template will provide the appearance. But there are times when you really need something that behaves differently than any of the stock panels or controls. For those cases, Silverlight provides a way for you to create your own fully featured panels and controls, supporting all the same things that the built-in ones support.

Custom panels enable you to create your own specialized layout algorithms. For example, you may want a panel that lays out its children using concentric circles rather than a box model. Implementing custom panels also has a nice educational benefit: they help you visualize and understand the layout process. Once you've created a few panels of your own, you'll find you better understand how the built-in ones work, and can better debug issues.

Due to the power of templating and the use of UserControls, custom controls are more rare than custom panels. But there will be times when a custom control is exactly what you need to differentiate your application or support a critical bit of functionality. Silverlight supports the creation of custom controls, including full templating and visual state management, making it a cinch to create your own.

In this chapter, we'll start by creating a custom panel. As you may have guessed, it'll be a panel that lays out its children in concentric circles or orbits. We'll use that panel to learn how to manage measuring and arranging, and how to bend the layout cycle to our will. With the custom panel completed, we'll turn our attention to creating a custom control. This will be an expander control, with support for a header and content, all of which can be fully styled and templated.

24.1   Creating a custom panel

In chapter 6, I covered the layout system. In that system, the primary responsibility for positioning and sizing controls falls to the panel the controls reside in. Some panels, such as the Canvas, position using simple Left and Top coordinates. Others, such as the StackPanel, lay out children based on a series of measurements and a placement algorithm.

In this section, we're going to build a panel that doesn't currently exist in Silverlight: the OrbitPanel. This Panel will lay out elements in a circle rather than the horizontal and vertical options available with the stock StackPanel or the box layout of a Grid. The new panel in action can be seen in figure 24.1.

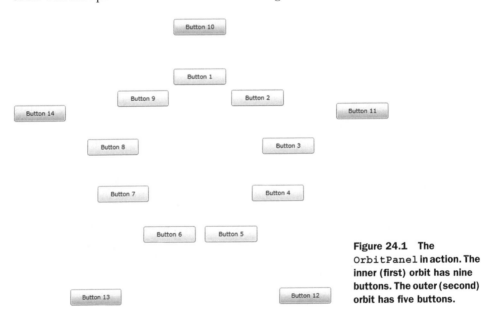

Figure 24.1   The OrbitPanel in action. The inner (first) orbit has nine buttons. The outer (second) orbit has five buttons.

The OrbitPanel control supports an arbitrary number (greater than zero) of orbits. Each orbit is a concentric circle starting at the center point. The amount of space allocated to an orbit is a function of the number of orbits and the size of the panel itself. If there are many orbits, the space will be narrower.

The layout is done starting at angle 0 and equally dividing the remaining degrees by the number of items in the specific orbit. Items added to the panel may specify an orbit via the use of an attached property.

In this section, we'll build this panel, starting with project creation, including the addition of a library project specifically made for this panel and for the custom control we'll build later in the chapter. We'll create a dependency property as well as an attached property, both because they're useful and because creating them is a necessary skill for panel and control builders. From there, we'll spend most of the time looking at how to perform the measure and arrange steps described in chapter 6 to layout the control. We'll wrap up this section with a guide for some potential enhancements should you desire to take the panel further on your own.

24.1.1 *Project setup*

For this example, create a new Silverlight project. I called mine Chapter24Controls. Once the solution is up with the Silverlight application and test website, add another project; this second project will be a Silverlight class library named ControlsLib. Though I could've put the custom panel into the same project as the Silverlight application, that's almost never done in real-world scenarios.

From the Silverlight application, add a project reference to the ControlsLib project. Do this by right-clicking the Silverlight application, selecting Add Reference, navigating to the Projects tab, and selecting the project. While you're in the project, remove the default class1.cs file that came with the template.

With the project structure in place, let's work on the OrbitPanel class.

24.1.2 *The OrbitPanel class*

The implementation of our panel will be in a single class named OrbitPanel. Inside the ControlsLib project, add a new class named OrbitPanel. This class will contain all the code for the custom panel. Derive the class from the Panel base type as shown here:

```
namespace ControlsLib
{
  public class OrbitPanel : Panel
  {
  }
}
```

Panel is the base type for all layout panels in Silverlight, including the Canvas, Grid, and StackPanel. The class itself derives directly from FrameworkElement, so it's a pretty low-level class, lacking the extras you'd find in something like Control. What it does include is important to Panels: the Children property.

The `Children` property is a `UIElementCollection`—it's a specialized collection of child elements placed inside this panel. This is the key property that makes a `Panel` a `Panel`.

In addition to the `Children` property, the `Panel` class provides a `Background` brush property and a boolean `IsItemsHost`, which is used in concert with the `ItemsControl` class. Deriving from `Panel` allows you to substitute your panel for the `StackPanel` in a `ListBox`, for example.

The `OrbitPanel` class will have two dependency properties used to control how it functions.

24.1.3 *Properties*

The `OrbitPanel` class will need to have two properties. The first, `Orbits`, will control the number of concentric circles, or orbits, available for placing items. The second is an attached property, `Orbit`, to be used on items placed into the panel; it controls which circle the item is to be placed in.

ORBITS DEPENDENCY PROPERTY

In general, controls and panels should expose properties as dependency properties. If there's any possibility that they'll be used in binding or animation, a dependency property is the way to go. In fact, when the Silverlight team exposes properties as straight CLR properties, more often than not, they get feedback that it should've been a dependency property because a customer or someone in the community tried to use it in binding or animation.

Dependency properties are specified at the class level using a static property and `DependencyProperty.Register` call. For use in code and XAML, they're also wrapped with a standard CLR property wrapper that internally uses the dependency property as the backing store. Optionally, the dependency property may specify a callback function to be used when the property changes.

Listing 24.1 shows the complete definition for the `Orbits` property, with all three of these items in place.

Listing 24.1 The `Orbits` property

```
public int Orbits                                          ◁─── CLR wrapper
{                                                               property
  get { return (int)GetValue(OrbitsProperty); }
  set { SetValue(OrbitsProperty, value); }
}

public static readonly DependencyProperty OrbitsProperty =
  DependencyProperty.Register("Orbits",
                      typeof(int),
                      typeof(OrbitPanel),
                      new PropertyMetadata(1, OnOrbitsChanged));

private static void OnOrbitsChanged(DependencyObject d,
                      DependencyPropertyChangedEventArgs e)
{
```

```
  if ((int)e.NewValue < 1)
  {
    throw new ArgumentException(
                  "Orbits must be greater than or equal to 1.");
  }
}
```

The first thing you'll notice in this code is the `Orbits` CLR property. This is a standard CLR wrapper, used for simple property access in code and required for property access in XAML. The property code uses the `GetValue` and `SetValue` methods, provided by `DependencyObject`, to access the backing dependency property. Though not required at a compiler or framework level (unless you want to use the property in XAML), providing the CLR wrapper is a standard practice when defining dependency properties.

> **TIP** Visual Studio 2010 includes a snippet for declaring dependency properties for WPF. With a slight change to rename `UIPropertyMetadata` to `PropertyMetadata` in the last parameter, this works well for Silverlight applications and saves you from remembering the exact syntax.

The next chunk of code in this listing defines and registers the dependency property. The single line both defines the property and registers it with the property system. The first parameter is the string name of the property. By convention, the name of the dependency property variable is this string plus the word *Property*. The second parameter is the type of the property itself—in this case, an `int`. The third parameter is the type you're registering the property on. The fourth and final parameter is a `PropertyMetadata` object.

The `PropertyMetadata` object can be used to specify a default value, a property changed callback, or as seen here, both. When providing the default property value, be very specific with the type. For example, a property value of `1` won't work with a double type; you must specify `1.0` or face the wrath of an obscure runtime error.

The property changed callback function enables you to hook into the process to perform actions when the dependency property changes. Note that you'd never want to do this inside the CLR wrapper, as that would only catch a few of the scenarios under which the property could change. The callback function takes in an instance of the object that owns the property, as well as an `EventArgs`-derived class that has both the new and old values available for inspection.

All three pieces—the CLR wrapper, the dependency property definition and registration, and the callback function—make up the implementation of a single dependency property in Silverlight. Though verbose, the benefits provided by dependency properties are great, as seen throughout this book. When creating your own properties for panels and controls, err on the side of implementing them as dependency properties.

A specialized type of `DependencyProperty`, the attached property is used when you want to provide a way to enhance the properties of another object. That's exactly what we need to do with the `Orbit` property.

ORBIT ATTACHED PROPERTY

Each item added to the OrbitPanel needs to be assigned to a specific circle or orbit. This is similar in concept to how a Grid needs items to specify rows and columns, or how the Canvas needs Left and Top for each element. The way those properties are specified is to use the type name (Grid or Canvas) and the property name together in the element, like this:

```
<TextBox Grid.Row="0" Grid.Column="1" />
<TextBox Canvas.Left="100" Canvas.Top="150" />
```

In these examples, the TextBox doesn't contain a Row, Column, Left, or Top property; instead it relies on another type (the Grid or Canvas) to attach them. We'll do the same with the Orbit property of the OrbitPanel. Listing 24.2 shows the implementation of the Orbit attached property in the OrbitPanel class.

> **Listing 24.2   The** Orbit **attached property in the** OrbitPanel **class**

```
public static int GetOrbit(DependencyObject obj)
{
  return (int)obj.GetValue(OrbitProperty);
}

public static void SetOrbit(DependencyObject obj, int value)
{
  obj.SetValue(OrbitProperty, value);
}

public static readonly DependencyProperty OrbitProperty =
    DependencyProperty.RegisterAttached("Orbit",
                                        typeof(int),
                                        typeof(OrbitPanel),
                                        new PropertyMetadata(0));
```

Note that attached properties don't use a CLR wrapper. Instead, you provide Get and Set methods to allow the properties to be used in code and XAML.

The RegisterAttached method is similar to the Register method seen in listing 24.1, with the parameters being identical. In this case, I didn't use a callback method, but instead provided a default value of zero.

With this property in place, we'll now be able to write markup like this:

```
<TextBox x:Name="FirstNameField" clib:OrbitPanel.Orbit="1" />
```

(The namespace declaration clib is assumed to be valid in the XAML file in which this bit of markup lives.) To inspect the value of the attached property from code, use the Get function defined in listing 24.2:

```
if (OrbitPanel.GetOrbit(FirstNameField) > 0) ...
```

In this way, we can now set and retrieve properties associated with objects, without those objects having any provision for the properties in the first place. This is a powerful way to augment types to track additional data.

Dependency properties—and the special type of dependency property, the attached property—are essential and often use parts of the property system in Silverlight. When creating your own panels and controls, you'll almost certainly rely on them as the primary means of providing "knobs" your users can use to control the behavior of your custom classes.

In the case of the `OrbitPanel`, both of these properties will come into play when performing our custom layout.

24.1.4 Custom layout

The primary responsibility of a panel is the layout of its child controls. In truth, this is what makes a panel a panel; a panel that performed no custom layout wouldn't be particularly useful.

As we learned in chapter 6, the layout pass involves two primary steps: measure and arrange. The measure step measures all the children of the panel, as well as the overall panel itself. The arrange step performs final placement of the children and sizing of the panel. As the authors of a custom panel, it's our responsibility to provide this critical functionality. Listing 24.3 shows the measure step, implemented in the `MeasureOverride` method of the `OrbitPanel` class.

Listing 24.3 The measure step

```
protected override Size MeasureOverride(Size availableSize)
{
  var sortedItems = SortElements();

  double max = 0.0;

  foreach (List<UIElement> orbitItems in sortedItems)
  {
    if (orbitItems.Count > 0)
    {
      foreach (UIElement element in orbitItems)
      {
        element.Measure(availableSize);          // Measure each child

        if (element.DesiredSize.Width > max)
          max = element.DesiredSize.Width;

        if (element.DesiredSize.Height > max)
          max = element.DesiredSize.Height;
      }
    }
  }

  Size desiredSize = new Size(max * Orbits * 2, max * Orbits * 2);

  if (double.IsInfinity(availableSize.Height) ||
      double.IsInfinity(availableSize.Width))

      return desiredSize;                        // Return panel measurements
  else
      return availableSize;
}
```

The measure pass starts by getting a list of all items, grouped by their orbit. The code for this function, SortElements, is included in listing 24.5. I loop through each orbit, then through each item in the orbit, and measure that item. I get the largest dimension (either width or height) from that element and compare it to the current max. This is admittedly a bit of a hack, as the size allotted to each item is, in theory, a pie slice, not a rectangle. In addition, due to the simplified nature of the orbit sizing, I didn't need to group the children by orbit. Nevertheless, it'll work for this example.

Once I've looped through every child item, I then calculate the desired size for this panel. That is calculated by taking the number of orbits, multiplying by two to account for the circular nature, then multiplying by the maximum item size. If the original size passed in was unlimited, I return the desired size; otherwise, I return the sized provided to the control.

The most important step in this function is the step that measures each child. That's what sets the desired size for each child in preparation for the arrange step shown in listing 24.4.

Listing 24.4   The arrange step

```
protected override Size ArrangeOverride(Size finalSize)
{
  var sortedItems = SortElements();

  double orbitSpacing = CalculateOrbitSpacing(finalSize);

  foreach (List<UIElement> orbitItems in sortedItems)
  {
    int count = orbitItems.Count;

    if (count > 0)
    {
      double circumference = 2 * Math.PI * orbitSpacing * (i + 1);
      double slotSize = Math.Min(orbitSpacing, circumference / count);
      double maxSize = Math.Min(orbitSpacing, slotSize);
      double angleIncrement = 360 / count;
      double currentAngle = 0;

      Point centerPoint =
              new Point(finalSize.Width / 2, finalSize.Height / 2);

      foreach (UIElement element in orbitItems)
      {
        double angle = Math.PI / 180 * (currentAngle - 90);

        double left = orbitSpacing * (i + 1) * Math.Cos(angle);      Place
        double top = orbitSpacing * (i + 1) * Math.Sin(angle);       child
                                                                     in final
        Rect finalRect = new Rect(                               ◁──┘ location
                centerPoint.X + left - element.DesiredSize.Width / 2,
                centerPoint.Y + top - element.DesiredSize.Height / 2,
                element.DesiredSize.Width,
                element.DesiredSize.Height);

        element.Arrange(finalRect);
```

```
        currentAngle += angleIncrement;
      }
    }
  }

  return base.ArrangeOverride(finalSize);
}
```

The arrange step is where the real layout happens. It's in this function that the individual children are placed in their final locations. This is the function that requires digging way back to 10th or 11th grade to remember that trigonometry.

This function, like the previous one, starts by sorting the children into their respective orbits. This is done via the SortElements function, the body of which is shown in listing 24.5. I then run through each orbit, calculating the size of the circle and the angular offset of each item. The angle chosen is based on the number of items in that orbit; it's 360 degrees evenly divided by the item count.

Then, I calculate the left and top position given the angle. This left and top will actually be used for the center point of the element being placed. With that calculated, I call Arrange on the element to move it to its final location.

Listings 24.3 and 24.4 relied on common functions. The code for both, CalculateOrbitSpacing and SortElements, is included in listing 24.5, wrapping up the code for the OrbitPanel class.

Listing 24.5 Supporting functions

```
private double CalculateOrbitSpacing(Size availableSize)
{
  double constrainingSize = Math.Min(
            availableSize.Width, availableSize.Height);

  double space = constrainingSize / 2;

  return space / Orbits;
}

private List<UIElement>[] SortElements()
{
  var list = new List<UIElement>[Orbits];

  for (int i = 0; i < Orbits; i++)
  {
    if (i == Orbits - 1)
      list[i] = (from UIElement child in Children
                where GetOrbit(child) >= i
                select child).ToList<UIElement>();
    else
      list[i] = (from UIElement child in Children
                where GetOrbit(child) == i
                select child).ToList<UIElement>();
  }

  return list;
}
```

CalculateOrbitSpacing uses the size of the panel to figure out the spacing of the individual concentric circles. This is done by evenly dividing up the total space. The SortElements function takes each of the children and puts it into a list by orbit.

Note that the SortElements function has special logic to group any elements in an invalid orbit into the highest orbit. It doesn't handle any cases where a negative (invalid) orbit number was specified, but that's easy enough to add.

These three listings make up the full implementation of the OrbitPanel class. With the code in place, the last thing to do is to test the panel on a page.

TEST MARKUP

To test the new panel, we'll use a simple bit of markup that creates a number of button controls and places them into two different orbits. A third orbit is defined but not used. Listing 24.6 shows the markup to be placed in MainPage.xaml. Before adding this code, build the project to get the ControlsLib namespace to resolve and the OrbitPanel IntelliSense to show.

Listing 24.6   Using the OrbitPanel from XAML

```
<Grid x:Name="LayoutRoot" Background="White">
  <Grid.Resources>
    <Style TargetType="Button">
      <Setter Property="Width" Value="100" />
      <Setter Property="Height" Value="30" />
    </Style>
  </Grid.Resources>
  <clib:OrbitPanel Orbits="3">                          ← Panel with 3 orbits
    <Button Content="Button 1" Background="Orange"
            clib:OrbitPanel.Orbit="0" />
    <Button Content="Button 2" Background="Orange"
            clib:OrbitPanel.Orbit="0" />
    <Button Content="Button 3" Background="Orange"
            clib:OrbitPanel.Orbit="0" />
    <Button Content="Button 4" Background="Orange"
            clib:OrbitPanel.Orbit="0" />
    <Button Content="Button 5" Background="Orange"
            clib:OrbitPanel.Orbit="0" />
    <Button Content="Button 6" Background="Orange"
            clib:OrbitPanel.Orbit="0" />
    <Button Content="Button 7" Background="Orange"
            clib:OrbitPanel.Orbit="0" />
    <Button Content="Button 8" Background="Orange"
            clib:OrbitPanel.Orbit="0" />
    <Button Content="Button 9" Background="Orange"
            clib:OrbitPanel.Orbit="0" />

    <Button Content="Button 10" Background="Blue"
            clib:OrbitPanel.Orbit="1" />
    <Button Content="Button 11" Background="Blue"
            clib:OrbitPanel.Orbit="1" />
    <Button Content="Button 12" Background="Blue"
            clib:OrbitPanel.Orbit="1" />
    <Button Content="Button 13" Background="Blue"
```

```
            clib:OrbitPanel.Orbit="1" />
    <Button Content="Button 14" Background="Blue"
            clib:OrbitPanel.Orbit="1" />
  </clib:OrbitPanel>
</Grid>
```

This listing produces the image from the opening of this section (figure 24.1), with two orbits of buttons. In order for this listing to work, you must define the following namespace:

```
xmlns:clib="clr-namespace:ControlsLib;assembly=ControlsLib"
```

Panels are all about measuring and arranging their children. Measuring is used to ask each child what size it wants to be, and to provide the overall size for the panel. Arranging is used to calculate the final location of each of the child elements.

This panel has been a pretty simple implementation both for space reasons and to keep to the essentials of what we need to learn. If you want to take it further, there are some enhancements I'd recommend.

24.1.5 Enhancements

The panel we created in this section is a good starting point for your own panel design. There are a number of places you could take this panel. Three enhancements I'd recommend are using start and stop angles, defining orbits using a grid-like approach, and item clipping.

START AND STOP ANGLES

Currently the panel starts calculating layout at zero degrees and completes at 360 degrees. A simple change would be to provide dependency properties for StartAngle and StopAngle, and use those in the layout calculation. This would allow arcs of controls rather than full orbits.

DEFINING ORBITS

Another potential change would be to make the orbit definitions more flexible. Rather than only providing a number of orbits, you could use orbit definitions in the same way the Grid panel uses RowDefinitions. An example of the markup might look like this:

```
<clib:OrbitPanel>
  <clib:OrbitPanel.OrbitDefinitions>
    <clib:OrbitDefinition StartAngle="25" StopAngle="40" Width="100" />
    <clib:OrbitDefinition StartAngle="340" StopAngle="270" Width="Auto" />
    <clib:OrbitDefinition StartAngle="90" StopAngle="180" Width="*" />
  </clib:OrbitPanel.OrbitDefinitions>
  ...
</clib:OrbitPanel>
```

This would enable you to support different arcs for each orbit, as well as set widths (optionally using grid units) for each orbit.

You would accomplish this by creating a custom collection type to hold the orbit definitions, then creating an OrbitDefinition class. The collection would be exposed by the panel. The measure and layout calculations would change to use the provided sizes rather than calculating sizes.

ITEM CLIPPING

The third enhancement is item clipping. I didn't implement this in the OrbitPanel because, frankly, it doesn't make a lot of sense to do so. But clipping the individual child elements is often essential to the functioning of a panel.

When an item is clipped, the portion of the element that would normally lie outside the allotted space isn't shown. This is accomplished by setting the size of the rectangle in the arrange step to be smaller than the size of the element. For example, to modify listing 24.4 to clip all elements to 30 x 30 pixel rectangles, change the final-Rect to be calculated like this:

```
double maxWidth = 30;
double maxHeight = 30;
Rect finalRect = new Rect(centerPoint.X + left - maxWidth / 2,
                          centerPoint.Y + top - maxHeight / 2,
                          maxWidth, maxHeight);
```

In a real panel, you'd calculate the maxWidth and maxHeight based upon available space in the layout slot. In addition to this calculation change, be sure to apply the same measurement to the call to the measure step, so the child has the ability to resize itself if possible.

Creating a custom panel in Silverlight is a straightforward process once you decide on a layout algorithm. The majority of the work is performed inside the measure and arrange steps. The measure step is where the panel calculates the size of each element and the size of the panel itself. The arrange step is where the panel performs the actual positioning (and optional clipping) of the child elements.

Creating a custom control is similar to creating a panel; many of the same steps apply. In the next section, we'll create a control that supports styling and visual states.

24.2 *Creating a custom control*

In the previous section, we built a custom panel. Panels differ from controls in that they typically participate in the opposite side of layout: panels are responsible for laying out controls; controls are responsible for measuring themselves.

When creating controls in Silverlight, you have two main choices: you can write a UserControl or create a custom control. User controls, covered in chapter 10, are more about composing other controls, whereas custom controls are about defining new behavior to make available to developers.

Custom controls differ from user controls in that they're lookless by default—they're expected to work with a completely different control template as long as certain contracts are adhered to. User controls bring their templates along with them in the form of the .xaml file; they support limited templating and styling capabilities.

In this section, we're going to build a custom control that can show grouped content with a header which, when clicked, shows or hides the content. There are already controls that can do this, but building it will show you how to inherit from a base class and support templating and visual states.

24.2.1 Choosing the base type

In chapter 10 we learned about the different types of controls available in Silverlight. Many of the controls had common base types. When creating your own control, the choice of base type will greatly impact how the control can be used and how other developers will expect it to work. Table 24.1 shows the common base types you can derive from.

Table 24.1   Common control base types

Type	Description
Control	This is a generic base control. If none of the specialized variants have what you need, derive from this class.
ContentControl	A control that contains a single child item for display. The Button and Label controls are examples of ContentControl.
ItemsControl	A control that contains multiple child items for display. The control supports adding individual items or binding to a list to obtain items. The items are displayed using a supplied panel.
Selector	An ItemsControl that supports selecting an item. An example of this is a ListBox.
RangeBase	A control that supports minimum, maximum, and current values. One example is the Slider control; another is the ScrollBar.
ButtonBase	A control that can be clicked to fire an event. Button and HyperlinkButton are two examples.
ToggleButton	A button-type control that supports keeping its state when clicked. Examples include the ToggleButton when used as is, the RadioButton, and the CheckBox.

When choosing a control, try to pick the richest one possible. If you're building something that naturally fits the Selector model, that's a better choice than picking ItemsControl or Control. The more you use built-in functionality, the more your control will behave like others in Silverlight without extra effort on your part.

For the control we're building, we'll start with ContentControl and build from there. In the ControlsLib project, add a new class named Expander:

```
namespace ControlsLib
{
  public class Expander : ContentControl
  {
  }
}
```

The `ContentControl` base class provides the ability to use properties such as `Content` and `ContentTemplate`. We'll definitely make use of those, but we also need to augment with our own properties for the header.

24.2.2 Properties

When supporting arbitrary content, the pattern is to have a content property of type `object` and a template property of type `DataTemplate`. That way, the developer can customize the presentation of the content without having to retemplate the entire control.

The `ContentControl` base type supplies the `Content` and `ContentTemplate` properties that perform this function for the primary content. We'll add `Header` and `HeaderTemplate` to support the same for the top header. Both properties will be defined as dependency properties, as shown in listing 24.7.

Listing 24.7   The `Header` and `HeaderTemplate` properties

```
public object Header
{
  get { return (object)GetValue(HeaderProperty); }
  set { SetValue(HeaderProperty, value); }
}

public static readonly DependencyProperty HeaderProperty =
    DependencyProperty.Register("Header",
                                typeof(object),
                                typeof(Expander),
                                new PropertyMetadata(null));

public DataTemplate HeaderTemplate
{
  get { return (DataTemplate)GetValue(HeaderTemplateProperty); }
  set { SetValue(HeaderTemplateProperty, value); }
}

public static readonly DependencyProperty HeaderTemplateProperty =
    DependencyProperty.Register("HeaderTemplate",
                                typeof(DataTemplate),
                                typeof(Expander),
                                new PropertyMetadata(null));
```

Using `object` as the type for the header enables us to use anything from a string to a `Grid` full of controls as the header. If a template is supplied, Silverlight will render using that. If no template is supplied, Silverlight will render it natively if it's a `UIElement`, or using `ToString` if it's any other type (such as an integer, string, or your custom class).

In addition to the simplicity of class inheritance, one of the main differentiators for a custom control over a user control is the control template.

24.2.3 The control template contract

When creating a custom control, it's important to define the contract with the control template. The contract consists of the things that must be in the control template in order for your control to work.

In general, you want this contract to be as small as possible. Think long and hard about what things you must have in the contract, as opposed to what could be accomplished with binding.

In our control, the contract can be kept small: just a single toggle button. We need the toggle button, in this case, because we're going to use it to expand and collapse the bottom section of the expander control. Listing 24.8 shows the class with the contract in place.

Listing 24.8 Contract with the control template

```
[TemplatePart(Name=Expander.ExpanderButtonName,          ◁─┐ Template
              Type = typeof(ToggleButton))]                 │ part
public class Expander : ContentControl
{
  private const string ExpanderButtonName = "ExpanderButton";

  private ToggleButton _expanderButton;

  public Expander()
  {
    DefaultStyleKey = typeof(Expander);
  }

  public override void OnApplyTemplate()          ◁── OnApplyTemplate
  {
    base.OnApplyTemplate();

    _expanderButton =
        GetTemplateChild(ExpanderButtonName) as ToggleButton;

    if (_expanderButton != null)
    {
      _expanderButton.Checked +=
          new RoutedEventHandler(OnExpanderButtonChecked);
      _expanderButton.Unchecked +=
          new RoutedEventHandler(OnExpanderButtonUnchecked);
    }
  }

  void OnExpanderButtonUnchecked(object sender, RoutedEventArgs e)
  { }
  void OnExpanderButtonChecked(object sender, RoutedEventArgs e)
  { }
}
```

The contract is defined both explicitly and implicitly. The explicit contract definition is the `TemplatePart` attribute on the class. Though not enforced in code, this is used by Expression Blend to enforce the contract in the tool. The attribute specifies both the name of the required element as well as its type. A best practice is to use a constant for the name, as it'll also be used elsewhere in the code.

The implicit contract is enforced by the `OnApplyTemplate` function. In this function, you're going to look for the various template parts and attempt to resolve them into variables you can use elsewhere in the class. `OnApplyTemplate` is called when the control template is loaded for this instance of the control.

In `OnApplyTemplate`, you'll typically find the control instances by name using `GetTemplateChild` (which does a `FindName` equivalent on the template) and wire up any events or other hooks.

Note also the constructor. The constructor specifies the default style key to be used. This looks a little odd because it's setting the key to the type of this class. As we'll see next, that's exactly what we want.

24.2.4 *The default template*

Custom controls are designed to support templating by the designers and developers using them. But every control should provide a default template to be used when no other template has been applied.

The default template is kept in a resource dictionary file named generic.xaml in the themes folder of the assembly containing the control. In our project, that's the `ControlsLib` assembly. Add the themes folder and the generic.xaml file. Listing 24.9 shows the style to be included inside the `ResourceDictionary` tags.

Listing 24.9   The control template

```
<Style TargetType="clib:Expander">                        ◁──┐ Note target type
  <Setter Property="Template">                                │ and no key
    <Setter.Value>
      <ControlTemplate TargetType="clib:Expander">
        <Grid>

            <Rectangle Stroke="{TemplateBinding BorderBrush}"    ◁──┐ Visual states
                    StrokeThickness="1" />                          │ will go here

            <Grid>
              <Grid.RowDefinitions>
                <RowDefinition Height="Auto" />
                <RowDefinition Height="Auto" />
              </Grid.RowDefinitions>

              <Grid x:Name="HeaderGrid" Grid.Row="0">
                <Rectangle Fill="DeepSkyBlue" />
                <ContentPresenter
                      Content="{TemplateBinding Header}"
                        ContentTemplate="{TemplateBinding HeaderTemplate}"
                      VerticalAlignment="Center"
                      Margin="5"/>

                <ToggleButton x:Name="ExpanderButton"
                          HorizontalAlignment="Right"
                          VerticalAlignment="Center"
                          Content="#" IsChecked="True"
                          Width="30" />
              </Grid>
              <Grid x:Name="ContentGrid" Grid.Row="1">
                <ContentPresenter
```

```
                        Content="{TemplateBinding Content}"
                        ContentTemplate="{TemplateBinding ContentTemplate}" />
                </Grid>
              </Grid>
          </Grid>
        </ControlTemplate>
      </Setter.Value>
    </Setter>
</Style>
```

Note that this style doesn't have a key. The key is the type it targets; that's why the constructor in listing 24.8 specifies the class type as the default style key.

This listing shows the default style and template for the `Expander` control. The template is defined just like the control templates we saw in chapter 23. In this case, I use a grid to hold both the header and the content. The header and content are both implemented using `ContentPresenter` elements. The `ContentPresenter`, when bound to appropriate content and content template properties, takes care of all the dirty work associated with presenting arbitrary content. Without it, there'd need to be some way to use a `TextBlock` when it's text, and other specialized types otherwise.

For this listing to work, the `ResourceDictionary` tag will need the following namespace added:

```
xmlns:clib="clr-namespace:ControlsLib"
```

In listing 24.9, I left room for the spot where the visual states will go. The final piece of a custom control is the support and definition of `VisualStateManager` controlled state management.

24.2.5 *Visual states*

Visual states describe the UI modes or states a control can be in. One visual state may be when the mouse is over the control; another when the mouse button is clicked. A third visual state may be when something is considered selected.

In our control, the visual states will be `Expanded` and `Collapsed`. Using visual states rather than hard-coding expand and collapse logic allows the designer or developer to completely customize what it means for the control to be expanded or collapsed. Remember, controls are *lookless*—they define behavior, not appearance.

Listing 24.10 shows the parts of the `Expander` class required for supporting visual states.

Listing 24.10 Supporting visual states

```
[TemplatePart(Name=Expander.ExpanderButtonName,
              Type = typeof(ToggleButton))]
[TemplateVisualState(Name = Expander.ExpandedStateName,     ◁──┐ Visual state
                     GroupName = "ExpanderStates")]              │ contract
[TemplateVisualState(Name = Expander.CollapsedStateName,    ◁──┘
                     GroupName = "ExpanderStates")]
public class Expander : ContentControl
{
```

```
private const string ExpanderButtonName = "ExpanderButton";
private const string ExpandedStateName = "Expanded";
private const string CollapsedStateName = "Collapsed";

void OnExpanderButtonUnchecked(object sender, RoutedEventArgs e)
{
    VisualStateManager.GoToState(this, CollapsedStateName, true);
}

void OnExpanderButtonChecked(object sender, RoutedEventArgs e)
{
    VisualStateManager.GoToState(this, ExpandedStateName, true);
}
...
}
```

Just as was the case with template parts, template visual states have both an explicit and implicit contract. The explicit contract is handled by the `TemplateVisualState` attribute. This allows Blend and other design tools to know what visual states are supported by this control.

The implicit contract is handled by calls to `VisualStateManager.GoToState`. This call works under the assumption that a particular visual state exists. If it exists, the control is put into that state. In this example, when the expander button (a template part) is checked, we enter the `Expanded` state. When it's unchecked, we enter the Collapsed state.

Using states like this allows you to define the appearance of each state completely in XAML. Of course, we'll need to provide a default implementation in the control template in generic.xaml.

24.2.6   *Visual states in template*

Visual states are designed for XAML. They're based around storyboards and references within the same XAML file. For more in-depth information on creating states, check out chapter 23.

Listing 24.11 shows the visual states definition for the Expander control. Place this markup into the spot called out in listing 24.9.

Listing 24.11   Visual states in the control template

```
<VisualStateManager.VisualStateGroups>
  <VisualStateGroup x:Name="ExpanderStates">          Expanded
    <VisualState x:Name="Expanded">                 <─┘ state
      <Storyboard>
        <ObjectAnimationUsingKeyFrames
                    Storyboard.TargetName="ContentGrid"
                    Storyboard.TargetProperty="Visibility">
          <DiscreteObjectKeyFrame KeyTime="00:00:00">
            <DiscreteObjectKeyFrame.Value>
              <Visibility>Visible</Visibility>
            </DiscreteObjectKeyFrame.Value>
          </DiscreteObjectKeyFrame>
        </ObjectAnimationUsingKeyFrames>
```

```
      </Storyboard>
    </VisualState>                              | Collapsed
    <VisualState x:Name="Collapsed">        ◄──┘ state
      <Storyboard>
        <ObjectAnimationUsingKeyFrames
                        Storyboard.TargetName="ContentGrid"
                        Storyboard.TargetProperty="Visibility">
          <DiscreteObjectKeyFrame KeyTime="00:00:00">
            <DiscreteObjectKeyFrame.Value>
              <Visibility>Collapsed</Visibility>
            </DiscreteObjectKeyFrame.Value>
          </DiscreteObjectKeyFrame>
        </ObjectAnimationUsingKeyFrames>
      </Storyboard>
    </VisualState>
  </VisualStateGroup>
</VisualStateManager.VisualStateGroups>
```

Listing 24.11 provides the markup for two different visual states: Expanded and Collapsed. Both refer by name to elements defined in listing 24.9. Using visual states like this allows us to have a control that has no real dependency on elements inside XAML. Instead, the control's behavior specifies which state to enter, and the markup (which can be changed by a developer or designer without access to the control's source) can completely define what it means to be in that state.

TESTING

The final step is to test the control. I used it to wrap the OrbitPanel we wrote in the first section, but you could use it with any type of content. Here's the MainPage.xaml markup with the new control in place:

```
<Grid x:Name="LayoutRoot" Background="White">
  ...
  <clib:Expander Header="This is an Expander Control"
                 Margin="20" BorderBrush="Black">
    <clib:OrbitPanel Orbits="3">
    ...
    </clib:OrbitPanel>
  </clib:Expander>
</Grid>
```

The result of the combination of both controls is shown in figure 24.2. The expander encloses the OrbitPanel and its contents.

Writing custom controls in Silverlight can be a rewarding experience. The templating approach means you don't have to consider every possible way someone may want to present your control; instead, you can focus on the required behavior.

Controls in Silverlight are lookless. The code you write shouldn't make assumptions, other than what's in the explicit contract, about what the UI contains or how it'll behave. The use of template binding, template parts, and template visual states helps keep this separation clean and understandable.

In general, before you create a custom control, consider whether templating an existing control will provide what you're looking for. I've seen menu systems created

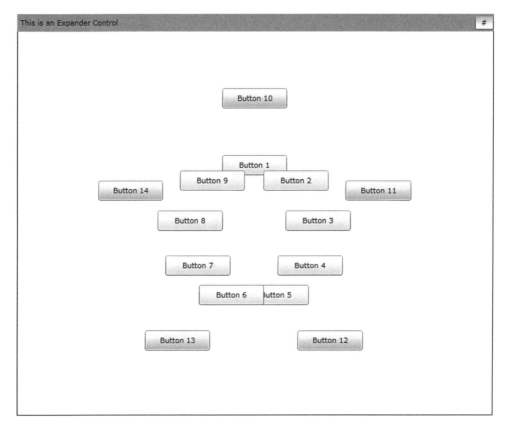

Figure 24.2   The expander control with the custom layout panel included as content

entirely from `ListBox` controls, for example (I'm even responsible for one of them). Once you're sure that the behavior of existing controls doesn't provide what you're looking for, you can embark upon creating your own control.

24.3   *Summary*

Silverlight has a highly extensible layout system. Imagine if other technologies allowed you to easily create your own elements with completely custom layout algorithms. HTML, for one, would be much more creative if you could encapsulate all that `div` manipulation into something that works as a first-class citizen on any page.

Custom panels and custom controls provide the ability to augment Silverlight with your own requirements and your own ideas of how things should work. They provide a way to extend the system, building upon the same foundations used in all of the other built-in elements. They let you do things the designers and developers of Silverlight may not have considered when building the platform.

Creating a custom panel is easy once you learn to express the layout algorithm as a pair of measure and arrange steps. Silverlight handles calling these steps when needed, so all you need to concern yourself with is the functionality directly related to your own custom layout algorithm. The sky's the limit!

Custom controls are equally powerful. If you've searched through the built-in controls, the SDK, and the toolkit, and haven't found a control with the behavior you want, you can build your own from scratch. Silverlight provides strong building blocks in the form of specialized base classes and the templating and state management patterns you leverage in the creation of your controls. You don't even need to worry about how it looks, as once you define the behavior and the contracts, a designer can make the control look any way she wants. That's the power of the lookless control model.

In the next chapter, we'll wrap up the book with a discussion around customizing the install experience for all the awesome applications you'll soon be creating.

25

The install
experience and preloaders

This chapter covers

- Handling "Silverlight not installed" scenarios
- Creating a custom preloader or splash screen

An often-overlooked aspect of putting a plug-in-based application on the Internet is the experience of a brand-new user. Truthfully, plug-in apps aren't unique in this. I've seen many Windows client applications that depended on registry entries or other files created during normal use but not present at first install. It's easy to be sloppy about testing that scenario because it's so far removed from our day-to-day lives.

Nevertheless, not everyone in the world has Silverlight installed on their machines, and not everyone has your application in their download cache. Anything that gets between your user and using your application is a barrier that will cause attrition. You need to continue to entice users to install the plug-in and wait for your application to download (if it's large) in order not to lose them.

In this chapter, we'll first look at how to customize the initial plug-in install and upgrade experience. Then, because some applications can be really large and have lots of assets, we'll look at approaches for building a custom preloader using XAML and JavaScript.

25.1 *Handling the "Silverlight not installed" scenarios*

Although Silverlight has achieved excellent market penetration since it was first introduced (it's around 60 percent at the time I'm writing this), you're still going to run into instances where the plug-in isn't installed on the user's machine. In those cases, the user will get the default Please Install Silverlight image, as shown in figure 25.1.

The default install badge is okay, but it almost certainly doesn't fit with the design of your application. More important, it offers no information about what your application will provide after Silverlight is installed.

Research has shown that in order to get users

Figure 25.1   The default image shown when users don't have Silverlight installed on their machines

to install the plug-in, they need to see what immediate benefit they'll get by doing so. The usual way to handle this is to show information about your application—perhaps an explanation, almost certainly screenshots—as part of the appearance. You then provide your own Click Now to Install button over those graphics. One of the best examples of this is the Netflix player, shown in figure 25.2.

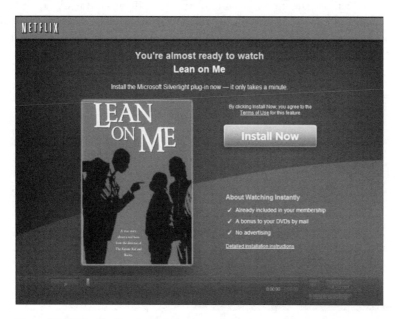

Figure 25.2   The Netflix player. This is an excellent example of a Silverlight install prompt. It includes a ghosted image of the player, information about the movie you've selected, and a clear call to action. (Image courtesy of Tim Heuer.)

This example has everything a good install prompt needs:

- *It's on-brand and consistent with the site.*   Using the default prompt would've been jarring. By using a screenshot of the existing player, you maximize consistency while also showing the purpose of the plug-in.
- *It's about the content, not the plug-in.*   The install prompt doesn't extol the virtues of Silverlight; it focuses on what you'll get (the movie *Lean on Me*) after you install it. Make the decision about the content and benefits, not the technology.
- *The call to action is simple.*   The only real action to take on this page is the install. If you look hard, there's a link with pop-up instructions, but there's no other prompting, account creation, or other cruft in the way.

In this section, you'll create a simple replacement plug-in install prompt, covering the changes to the object tag and the HTML within it. It won't be as pretty as the Netflix prompt, but it'll show how you can get there. We'll wrap up with a bit of information on how to further customize the experience.

25.1.1 *Creating your own install experience*

The experience you create to prompt for the plug-in must exist without any plug-in installed. That means it's all HTML and JavaScript. Typically, it's some static images and perhaps some text. Truly complex versions could have an application walk-through complete with a jQuery slideshow of screen shots of the application. The point is that you want something nice that entices the user to install the plug-in.

Whatever HTML you decide to provide, you can easily place it inside the object tag. Any HTML you include inside the object tag will be displayed when the plug-in isn't installed. For example, you could go with the silly text-only install prompt shown in figure 25.3.

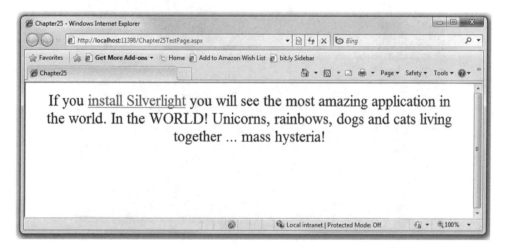

Figure 25.3   The new custom prompt to install Silverlight. I don't know about you, but I'm totally ready to install Silverlight now!

In reality, you probably want to try a little harder than that, but you get the idea. The URL I used came right from the default install experience includd with the template. Whatever design you or your web designers come up with is fair game here. Listing 25.1 shows how to insert the HTML into the object tag.

Listing 25.1   A replacement Silverlight plug-in install prompt

```
<object data="data:application/x-silverlight-2,"
        type="application/x-silverlight-2"
        width="100%" height="100%">
   <param name="source" value="ClientBin/Chapter25.xap"/>
   <param name="onError" value="onSilverlightError" />
   <param name="background" value="white" />
   <param name="minRuntimeVersion" value="4.0.50401.0" />
   <param name="autoUpgrade" value="true" />
...
  <p style="font-size:30px;margin:30px"> If you
  <a href="http://go.microsoft.com/fwlink/?LinkID=149156&v=4.0.50401.0">
      install Silverlight</a> you will see the most amazing
      application in the world. In the WORLD! Unicorns,
      rainbows, dogs and cats living together ... mass
      hysteria!</p>
</object>
```

Everything not a `param` but otherwise inside the object tag will be invisible when Silverlight is installed and displayed when it's not. The sky is pretty much the limit for what you can do here.

ALWAYS GRABBING THE LATEST PLUG-IN

By default, the tooling provides a link to the version you built against. But a better approach is to remove the version number completely, because you should always provide the latest plug-in to your users. To do that, remove everything after the link ID:

```
<a href="http://go.microsoft.com/fwlink/?LinkID=149156">
```

That will automatically grab the latest version of the plug-in when the user clicks the link. Note that the parameter `LinkID` is case-sensitive.

HANDLING THE VERSION-UPGRADE SCENARIO

In the object tag, you saw the `autoUpgrade` and `minRuntimeVersion` properties. Those two properties work together to handle scenarios where the user has Silverlight installed, but it's an old version. If the user's version isn't the latest version, but it's equal to or higher than the `minRuntimeVersion`, the user won't be prompted to upgrade. But if your application requires a newer version and you have `autoUpgrade` set to `true`, the user will receive a standard Silverlight version dialog prompting them to upgrade.

If you prefer to handle the upgrade process yourself, you can set `autoUpgrade` to false and handle the `8001 - Upgrade required` and `8002 - Browser restart required` errors in the `OnError` function. Although those errors will fire regardless of the value of `autoUpgrade`, typically you'll only do something meaningful with them when you're handling the process manually.

Silverlight.js, discussed in chapter 3, includes a number of helper functions and properties such as `getSilverlight`, `isInstalled`, `isBrowserRestartInstalled`, and

WaitForInstallCompletion that make the new install and upgrade experiences highly scriptable from JavaScript.

After you've tackled the "no plug-in installed" scenario or the upgrade scenario, and the user has the plug-in installed, you should then turn to the application-loading scenario and build a custom preloader or splash screen.

25.2   *Using a custom preloader*

Silverlight applications come in all shapes and sizes. Many of the more complex applications take a few seconds or more to load, because they have many images, large binaries, media, or more. This is one place where the Flash developers had a real leg up due to all the prior art. Every Flash application I've ever used has had a custom preloader that displays appropriate branding and, often, real creativity. Blogs and even entire sites have been created with no purpose other than to show some of the awesome preloaders that exist out there. Take a peek for yourself: www.bing.com/search?q=best+flash+pre-loaders.

Preloaders can be image-based or XAML-based and can include application-specific branding. A preloader is a chance to provide something interesting and creative to increase anticipation and excitement for the application. Some preloaders even include mini-games; but unless your application takes 20 minutes to load, that may be overkill.

Think of the preloader like the start of a movie. Although you typically want the opening cuts to finish in short order so you can watch the movie, the best ones add to the overall story, increase awareness of what's to come, and help generate some excitement.

When it comes down to it, you can have the best-looking Silverlight application out there, but if it shows several seconds of the default Silverlight loading animation, no one will consider it a complete experience. Figure 25.4 shows the default "spinning blue ball" loading experience.

The default experience is there to ensure that your users know the application is doing something while the application or the application and required assets are downloaded.

In general, you want to avoid both the default loader and the double-download situation whenever possible. It's easy to create your own custom download experience, including downloading media assets and more.

Figure 25.4   The default Silverlight "spinning blue ball" loading experience.

Throughout this section, you'll learn how to create a custom preloader. The first step in this three-step process is creating the appearance of the preloader using XAML. After it's created, you can integrate the preloader with your solution to ensure it's used while a Silverlight application is being downloaded. While this download is proceeding, you can choose to monitor its progress and update the visuals. All these steps will be shown as a basic preloader is implemented.

25.2.1   *Creating the appearance*

Preloaders, or splash screens, are shown when the loading time of your application exceeds a certain threshold, roughly half a second. The first step in creating a custom splash screen is defining its appearance. You must take three important facts into consideration:

- The preloader is used while a .xap file is being downloaded, so it doesn't make sense to create the splash screen's XAML inside of your Silverlight application. Instead, you must create the XAML within the web site that hosts your Silverlight application.
- The preloader can't use managed code, so you must use a scripting language such as JavaScript for any runtime features of a custom splash screen.
- You're not limited to the Silverlight 1.0 API. Enhancements were made to the JavaScript API post-Silverlight 1.0, such as additional panels and types of animation.

With these constraints in mind, you can move forward with creating your own preloader. Although a good preloader is a highly branded experience that seamlessly blends into the design for your application, you'll create a simple animation here for space and complexity considerations. Such an animation might be defined in an XML file on the web site called SilverlightLoader.xaml and look like the code in listing 25.2.

> **Listing 25.2   The XAML for a custom splash screen: SilverlightLoader.xaml**

Result:

XAML:

```xml
<?xml version="1.0" encoding="utf-8" ?>
<Grid xmlns="http://schemas.microsoft.com/winfx/2006/xaml/presentation"
      xmlns:x="http://schemas.microsoft.com/winfx/2006/xaml">
  <Grid.Background>
    <LinearGradientBrush>
      <GradientStop Color="#FFFFFFFF" Offset="0.25" />
      <GradientStop Color="#FFFFAF00" Offset="1.5" />
    </LinearGradientBrush>
  </Grid.Background>

  <Grid.Triggers>                                        Uses trigger to
    <EventTrigger RoutedEvent="Grid.Loaded">        ⟵   start animation
      <BeginStoryboard>
        <Storyboard Storyboard.TargetName="EllipseRotateTransform"
                    Storyboard.TargetProperty="Angle">
          <DoubleAnimation From="0" To="360"
                           BeginTime="00:00:00" Duration="00:00:01"
                           RepeatBehavior="Forever" />
        </Storyboard>
      </BeginStoryboard>
```

```
            </EventTrigger>
        </Grid.Triggers>

    <Grid HorizontalAlignment="Center" VerticalAlignment="Center"
            Height="80" Width="80" Margin="10">
        <Ellipse x:Name="myEllipse"
                Stroke="#FF000000" RenderTransformOrigin="0.5,0.5">
            <Ellipse.RenderTransform>
                <RotateTransform x:Name="EllipseRotateTransform" />
            </Ellipse.RenderTransform>
            <Ellipse.Fill>
                <RadialGradientBrush GradientOrigin="0.06,0.8">
                    <RadialGradientBrush.RelativeTransform>
                        <TranslateTransform X="-0.007" Y="0.008" />
                    </RadialGradientBrush.RelativeTransform>
                    <GradientStop Color="#FFCAFFB4" Offset="0" />
                    <GradientStop Color="#FF39AF07" Offset="0.8" />
                    <GradientStop Color="#FF7BCE09" Offset="1" />
                </RadialGradientBrush>
            </Ellipse.Fill>
        </Ellipse>

        <Ellipse Height="55" Width="55" Fill="#FFFFFFFF" Stroke="#FF000000" />

        <TextBlock x:Name="ProgressTextBlock" Width="55" Height="20"
                FontFamily="Verdana" FontSize="14" Text="0%"
                TextAlignment="Center" />
    </Grid>
</Grid>
```

This listing defines a basic set of shapes and animation within a `Grid` element. This animation rotates an `Ellipse` around a `TextBlock`, which shows the progress of the download. The progress of the download will be updated as the download progresses.

> **TIP** If you want to try this yourself on an empty project, create a new Silverlight application with a web site as usual. Then, on the Silverlight app, embed some enormous file, such as a video or big zip file, into the .xap, so it's large. As long as the download takes more than 0.5 seconds or so, you'll see your preloader screen. The more latency you have, the more you'll see of your preloader. You can even constrain your download bandwidth (time to dig out the old 9600 bps Hayes compatible) to really help it show off.

The root element of a preloader must be one of the `Panel` elements mentioned in chapter 7, so you can't use a `UserControl` element as you would if you were defining a page. This has to do with the fact that managed code can't be used with a splash screen. After you've chosen a `Panel` and created the appearance of the splash screen, you can integrate it with your web application.

25.2.2 *Integrating the custom splash screen*

The second step of using a custom splash screen is integrating it with a web application. You reference the XAML of the splash screen when you create an instance of the Silverlight plug-in. You can reference this XAML by using the `splashScreenSource` property of the object tag, as shown in listing 25.3.

Listing 25.3 Associating the preloader with the Silverlight application

```
<object data="data:application/x-silverlight-2,"
        type="application/x-silverlight-2"
        width="100%" height="100%">
  <param name="source" value="ClientBin/Chapter25.xap"/>
  <param name="onError" value="onSilverlightError" />
  <param name="splashScreenSource"
         value="SilverlightLoader.xaml" />                  ⟵— XAML URL
  <param name="onSourceDownloadProgressChanged"
         value="appDownloadProgressChanged" />
  <param name="onSourceDownloadComplete"
         value="appDownloadComplete" />
  ...
</object>
```

This listing uses the splashScreenSource property to reference the splash screen created in listing 25.2. This property isn't required by the createObjectEx function. By using this property, you can point to where a custom splash screen's XAML is stored. For security reasons, the XAML must be located on the same web site as the page with the object tag and the Silverlight .xap file. When the splash screen's XAML is loaded, you have the option of using the onSourceDownloadProgressChanged and onSourceDownloadComplete event handlers to monitor the load progress.

25.2.3 *Monitoring the load progress*

The third, but optional, step in creating a preloader is monitoring the load progress. To accomplish this, you wire up JavaScript event handlers to the onSourceDownloadProgressChanged and onSourceDownloadComplete events defined by the plug-in. These event handlers are shown in listing 25.4.

Listing 25.4 The event handlers used for monitoring the download progress

JavaScript:
```
<script type="text/javascript">
function appDownloadProgressChanged(sender, args)
{
  var progressTextBlock = sender.findName("progressTextBlock");

  progressTextBlock.Text = (Math.round(args.progress * 100)) + "%";
}

function appDownloadComplete(sender, args)
{}
</script>
```

I typically include these event handlers in the same JavaScript script block that holds the default Silverlight error handler. This listing shows the onSourceDownloadProgressChanged and onSourceDownloadComplete event handlers referenced in listing 25.3. The onSourceDownloadProgressChanged event will fire any time the progress of a download has changed by 0.5 percent or more. If this event is triggered, you may access the total progress through the second parameter of the onSourceDownloadProgressChanged event. This parameter exposes a floating-point property called `progress`. The value of this property is between 0.0 and 1.0, so you must multiply the value by 100 in order to convert the value to a percentage. When the progress has reached 1.0, the `onSource-DownloadComplete` event will fire.

The `onSourceDownloadComplete` event will fire when the requested Silverlight application has been completely downloaded. Because the Silverlight application will automatically start when it's completely downloaded, you probably won't use this event. Instead, you'll probably use the in-application `Application.Startup` event mentioned earlier in this book, because at this point, you can begin using managed code instead of relying on scripted code.

Sometimes you need to provide more than just a preloader. Sometimes you need a way to download whole portions of the application on demand, or at least in a lazy way. For these scenarios, the Managed Extensibility Framework is the way to go.

25.3 *Summary*

A custom, branded install experience for the plug-in and a custom preloader are both extremely simple to create—far less work than the overall application. If you have a designer on-team, it can often be as simple as a few graphics and some basic XAML.

But those little touches are what differentiate a great application from a good application. They're also the types of changes that keep users engaged and reduce the drop-off of new users. The return is great compared to the effort involved.

The first customization is for the plug-in install. When a new user without the Silverlight plug-in comes to your application, you have the opportunity to engage them and get them to install Silverlight. It's through solid efforts in this space that Silverlight gains market penetration and becomes easier to use in your applications.

The second customization is for the application preloader or splash screen. This is what you want to show the user while your application is loading. Most applications with a significant number of images or other media, packaged into the .xap to avoid a multitude of lazy loads later, are really big and benefit from some download progress information. Sure, you could use the generic Silverlight spinning balls animation; but to look professional, you want to use something that fits the design of your application and seamlessly sits in your site.

Combine both customizations, and you have a winning combination that will help increase eyeballs and keep visitors interested and engaged.

I hope you've enjoyed this book; I welcome your comments! If you liked it, I encourage you to write an online review on your blog or on a retailer's web site (such as Amazon.com). The official forum for this book can be found on the publisher's web site at www.manning.com/pbrown, where you can ask questions, post comments, and report any errata. You can also reach me on twitter at @Pete_Brown and on my web site at http://10rem.net. I encourage you to join me in both places to get updates and expansions to the content in this book and more. Thank you!

appendix
Database, connection,
and data model setup

This chapter covers

- Setting up a data connection
- Creating an entity data model

In several examples in this book, including those in reporting (see chapter 19), MVVM (see chapter 16), and WCF RIA Services (see chapter 17), we need to work against database data and an entity data model. For this you'll need SQL Server with the AdventureWorks database loaded.

In this appendix, we'll install the database, and create the database connection and the entity data model. The entity data model will be added to the ASP.NET web project in your Silverlight solution.

A.1   Install the AdventureWorks database

If your database installation doesn't already contain the AdventureWorks database, visit http://msftdbprodsamples.codeplex.com/ to download the latest version for your database version.

The CodePlex database sample site includes a number of database releases for the various editions of SQL Server, currently up to SQL Server 2008 R2. My own dedicated database server is running SQL Server 2008, and I have a local SQL Server Express 2008 database instance that came with Visual Studio 2010. The sample databases will install on either one.

A.1.1   Installing on a dedicated SQL Server instance

In this setup and in all of my examples, I'm using SQL Server 2008 on a dedicated server. You can install locally or use a separate server or virtual machine (VM). Though I haven't tested with older versions, this should also work on SQL Server 2005. A default installation of Visual Studio 2010 up-level versions (such as Pro and Ultimate) includes SQL Server Express 2008. If you have an MSDN subscription, you can also download the developer editions of SQL Server through your subscription program.

If you have a full SQL Server 2008 installation, you can download the full MSI and install the suite of databases. Once the database is installed, you can set up the database connection and create the entity data model.

The CodePlex site includes a walkthrough (kept current with the releases) showing how to install the sample databases. Depending on the engine you're using and the options selected when you installed your database server, some databases may not be available to you. The only database we use in this book is AdventureWorks, also called AdventureWorks OLTP. You can ignore the warehousing and reporting databases if you wish, as I don't use them in the examples in this book.

If you're not using a full dedicated installation of SQL Server, you'll want to install using SQL Server Express.

A.1.2   Installing on SQL Server Express

SQL Server Express comes with most editions of Visual Studio and installs by default. It's the default database server used for ASP.NET membership, role, and session information on a development machine. But since it doesn't install any client tools, many folks don't realize it's there.

As with the dedicated SQL Server instance install, you can download the full MSI and install the suite of databases. You can safely ignore the warehousing and reporting databases. Once the database is installed, you can set up the database connection and create the entity data model.

If you're not running a full instance of SQL Server, the databases will install locally with SQL Server Express. When using SQL Server Express, you have two options:

1 Install the databases locally, then use them like any other SQL Server installation (doesn't work in all install scenarios)
2 Install the databases locally, then drag the AdventureWorks.mdb file into your App_Data folder on the asp.net project

I prefer the second option, as it simplifies the creation of the database connection, and is supported in almost every installation scenario. But either option will typically work.

Regardless of whether you used a local SQL Server instance or a remote one, once you have the AdventureWorks database installed, you'll need to create the database connection and the entities.

A.2 Database connection and entities

First create a new Silverlight project for the example you're following. Make sure you create the associated web project (the default action), as that's where the connection information and any services will live. The new project dialog for the default Silverlight project type will look like figure A.1. The dialog for the Silverlight Business Application template will be different, and will have the options already set.

Once you have the project created, the next step is to add the database connection and create entities.

Right-click the web project in the

Figure A.1 When creating the Silverlight application, be sure to host the application in a new Web Application.

solution explorer and choose Add New Item. In the Data section of the installed templates, select ADO.NET Entity Data Model. Name that entity data model Adventure-WorksEntities.edmx. Figure A.2 shows the dialog with the correct template selected and named.

Figure A.2 Creating the AdventureWorksEntities entity data model

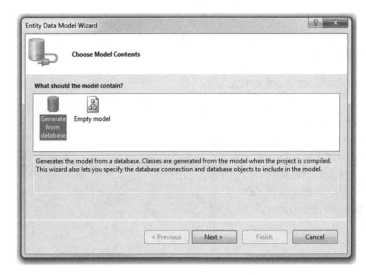

Figure A.3   The first step of the Entity Data Model Wizard. Be sure to choose Generate from Database.

Once you click Add, Visual Studio will walk you through a wizard that makes the process of generating the model pretty easy. In the first page of the wizard, choose Generate from database and hit Next. The other option, Empty model, would require you to build the entities from scratch. Figure A.3 shows the wizard dialog with the correct option selected.

You'll then be presented with the Choose Your Data Connection step, as shown in figure A.4. If the AdventureWorks database isn't located in the connection list, click the

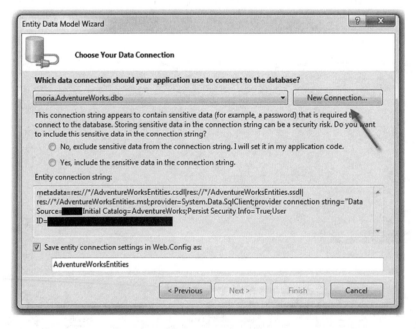

Figure A.4   The Choose Your Data Connection dialog box. If you don't already have an AdventureWorks connection created, click the New Connection button. This screenshot shows the data connection dialog with a valid data connection already selected by default.

New Connection button and create a new Microsoft SQL Server (SqlClient) connection to your database.

If you already have a connection for AdventureWorks set up, select that. The authentication method chosen will differ depending upon your SQL Server setup. Figure A.5 shows how my dialog looks, with all the interesting bits redacted.

Once the connection is created, allow the dialog to save the entity connection string as `AdventureWorksEntities`. Also, if you're using SQL Server authentication, check the option to include the sensitive data (password) in the connection string, as shown in the two radio buttons in the middle of figure A.4.

If saving the connection information makes you uncomfortable, you can either try with Windows Authentication (depends on machine/network setup) or cre-

Figure A.5   Creating a new connection to the Adventure-Works database. Be sure to test the connection.

ate a dedicated SQL Server account with limited rights just for the sample. Of the choices, I recommend the dedicated SQL Server account.

Once the connection is picked or newly set up, you'll be prompted to select the entities to be added to the model.

A.2.1   Choosing the entities to create

On the Choose Your Database Objects page, select the Employee (Human Resources) table and the Contact (Person) table. Leave the other options as is, including setting the namespace to `AdventureWorksModel`. Figure A.6 shows the correct selected tables and the correct model name.

You can of course name the model anything you'd like. But to follow the examples in the book and use the code listings, you'll want to use the names indicated in the screenshots here.

At this point, you're able to finish the wizard. The wizard will process for a few seconds, then add the connection information to your configuration file, and the model .edmx and .edmx.cs files to your web project. The created .edmx file should look something like figure A.7 when opened in the designer.

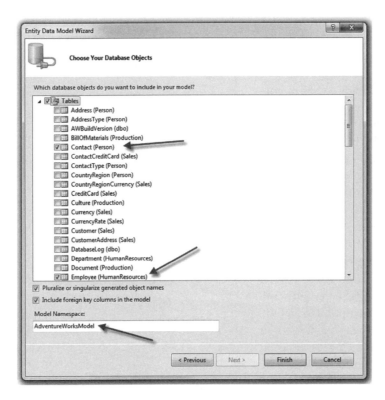

**Figure A.6
Select the Contact and
Employee tables from
the AdventureWorks
database. Leave the
model namespace
set to Adventure-
WorksModel.**

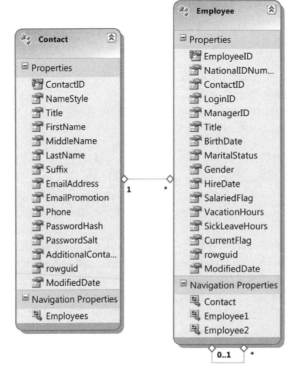

Once you have the data model in place, build the solution to get all the types loaded, and continue with the rest of the sample in the chapter.

Figure A.7 The AdventureWorks model viewed in the model designer. Double-click the .edmx file in the web project to view it on the design surface.

index

Hello! Silverlight

by Bill Reiss and Dave Campbell

ISBN: 978-1-933988-53-5
250 pages
$34.99
January 2011

jQuery in Action, Second Edition

by Bear Bibeault and Yehuda Katz

ISBN: 978-1-935182-32-0
488 pages
$44.99
June 2010

RELATED TITLES

SharePoint 2010 Web Parts in Action

by Wictor Wilén

ISBN: 978-1-935182-77-1
375 pages
$44.99
December 2010

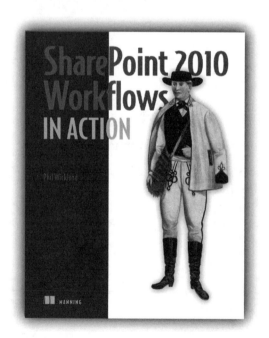

SharePoint 2010 Workflows in Action

by Phil Wicklund

ISBN: 978-1-935182-71-9
400 pages
$44.99
November 2010

For ordering information go to www.manning.com

ASP.NET MVC 2 in Action

by Jeffrey Palermo, Ben Scheirman,
  Jimmy Bogard, Eric Hexter,
  and Matthew Hinze

ISBN: 978-1-935182-79-5
432 pages
$49.99
June 2010

ASP.NET 4.0 in Practice

by Daniele Bochicchio, Stefano Mostarda,
  and Marco De Sanctis

ISBN: 978-1-935182-46-7
425 pages
$44.99
January 2011

For ordering information go to www.manning.com

C# in Depth, Second Edition

by Jon Skeet

ISBN: 978-1-935182-47-4
500 pages
$49.99
September 2010

Continuous Integration in .NET

by Marcin Kawalerowicz and Craig Berntson

ISBN: 978-1-935182-55-9
375 pages
$49.99
October 2010